The Dodals

Eva Strusková

The Dodals

Pioneers of Czech Animated Film

NFA

The author is indebted to the following institutions and individuals for providing their materials for publication and for approving their reproduction: the Czech Museum of Music; Supraphon; the National Museum; the Czech Radio Archives; the Archives of the Ministry of Foreign Affairs of the Czech Republic; the Archives of the City of Plzeň; the Association française du cinema d'animation; Filmoteka narodowa; the Fleischer Studios, Inc.; the National Archives, Prague; Nestlé Česko, s. r. o; the Museum of Applied Arts in Prague; the Military Historical Archives, Prague; Bruno Courtet-Cohl (France); Juliette Crochu (France); Lubor M. Dohnal (the Czech Republic); Marina Feodoroff (France); Caroline Hagen (the Federal Republic of Germany); Květa Krčilová (the Czech Republic); Renée Lavecká (the Czech Republic); Oscar Sandoval Martínez (Argentina); Vladimír Opěla (the Czech Republic); Márton Orosz (Hungary); Richard J. Pavlicek (USA); Hana Pinkavová (the Czech Republic); Josef Rippel (the Czech Republic); Helena Štáchová (the Czech Republic); Ricardo von Tschirnhaus (Argentina).

Czech manuscript of the book was peer-reviewed by Mgr. Martin Kaňuch

ISBN 978-80-7004-155-0
ISBN 978-80-7331-271-8

Contents

Prologue

The story which eventually became the present book began more than twenty years ago when I had the first chance of glancing into Irena Dodalová's correspondence written during the 1980s and revolving around the transfer of her personal archive from Buenos Aires to Prague. The letters pondered on the latter half of the 1930s when Dodalová and her second husband Karel Dodal headed the studio of animated film, IRE-film, and also contained many facts about her post-war professional activities in the United States and Argentina. They deeply affected me not only for their emotion and, at the same time, their matter-of-factness, but also because they featured hitherto unknown circumstances linked with animated film production prior to the Second World War. The correspondence opened an utterly new world to Czech film historians. It made me realize that the Nazi Protectorate and the ensuing developments in post-war Czechoslovakia not only definitely sealed a certain period of life and work of the Dodal couple, as well as many other members of the Czech inter-war generation, but that also much of their work disappeared without a trace. Their post-war destinies and their work from abroad remained unknown, too. Only the third member of the IRE-film team – Dodal's first wife, colleague and animator, Hermína Týrlová – stayed in Czechoslovakia, and her memories provided valuable, albeit rather taciturn, testimonies.

As I began systematically pursuing the subject of the Dodals in the National Film Archive, one of my most crucial points of departure became the personal fund of Irena Dodalová, acquired from Buenos Aires. Its basis is written, photographic and film documents about the activities of the IRE-film studio which the donor had sent to her husband to the United States in July 1939 before the Second World War, and then transported from the USA to Argentina in the late 1940s. Another important part of the fund is Dodalová's additional comments on the IRE-film activity and her lifetime journey with Karel Dodal, made after transferring the archive to Prague. All these materials served to outline the future research which initially focused on the hitherto unprocessed history of 1920s' and 1930s' Czech animation. It soon became clear that understanding the phenomenon of the Dodals would require incorporating Irena Dodalová's imprisonment in Theresienstadt and her 1942 role in making the first film about the ghetto into the research agenda, even though the fund in question did not contain any documents on this period. It was also necessary to clarify the fundamental circumstances of the Dodals' post-war exile in the United States and Argentina.

The several-year research was carried out in numerous Czech and foreign archives and museum institutions. Our work was hindered by insufficient sources on many subjects, because large part of the IRE-film archive which had remained in Czechoslovakia was destroyed during the Protectorate. The chance of studying the exile lives of the two was also limited. The Dodals remained childless and, moreover, the majority of their direct relatives and eyewitnesses had died before the research was launched. We, however, at least discovered some materials in their personal sources, such as excerpts from the post-war correspondence between Irena Dodalová and her brother Rudolf Rosner-Rohan and the family of the attorney Alfred Popp, with whom the couple had been in close contact from before the war. The correspondence between Karel Dodal and Richard J. Pavlicek from the Dodal's wartime exile in the United States also became a valuable wellspring of information.

The Theresienstadt period required much investigation in professional literature and in specialized archives dedicated to the holocaust, while confronting the written and film materials from various sources helped acquire new information about the roles of the Jewish prisoners and Irena Dodalová in filming the ghetto in 1942. The internet also played an invaluable role in the research, not just because it steered us towards more possible information sources, but mainly because e-mail enabled international collaboration with scholars from, for example, Hungary, Norway, Germany, the Netherlands, Israel, France, Austria and, last but not least, Argentina. And although the work on the present treatise began as late as in the beginning of the new millennium, a fact which substantially narrowed the circle of available eyewitnesses, only this period bore several crucial monographs about filmmakers whose careers intersected with the Dodals' (György Pál, Desider Gross, Paul N. Peroff) and numerous essays focusing on the first stages of film animation from which to start.

We now have the honour of sharing our research achievements in this book. It consists of three, chronologically lined-up parts and the conclusion. The first part, entitled "The Early Years of Czech Animation", opposes the traditional view that the history of the Czech animated film began in fact only after the Second World War. It draws attention to the foreign repertory which introduced Czech viewers to the world of animated film, explains the conditions of making the first cartoons in Prague and their aims, and illustrates from which prototypes and models these films departed. It explores the roles of Karel Dodal and Hermína Týrlová (Dodalová) in the company Elekta Journal during the 1920s and the changes in their collaboration in IRE-film following their divorce, when both the production and dramaturgy of the studio was taken up by Dodal's second wife, Irena. We furthermore track developments in the technological base for sound and colour animated film in Prague, and the strategy of the IRE-film advertising production. In connection with the promotional film *The Adventures of a Ubiquitous Fellow* (Všudybylovo dobrodružství), the book deals with the relationship of the famed puppeteer Josef Skupa to film, and with the alliance between Czech puppetry and Czech cartoons. The next chapter from this part is devoted to the subject of the Czech advertising market and explores how the Dodals' commercials enriched this field from the point of dramaturgy, film direction and film technology. Here, we had the first opportunity ever to evaluate the IRE-film authorship production of abstract pictures thanks to the film materials from Argentina. The closing chapter pursues, on individual and particular cases, the economic and political reasons which resulted in the extinction of the immensely energetic and assertive film production anchored in an ambitious authorship program and employing efficient marketing models.

Two chapters of the second part, "The Wartime Anabasis", monitor the destinies of Karel Dodal in the United States and Irena Dodalová in the Theresienstadt ghetto. The chapter "Zbraslav, Paris, Minneapolis, New York: In Search of Asylum" traces how the Czech filmmaker succeeded in making the best of his professional experience from film tricks and animation at the Minnesota University. The chapter "The Theresienstadt Years of Irena Dodalová and the Story of the Stolen Outtakes" provides yet little known information about SS filming in the ghetto in 1942, in which the imprisoned Jews also participated. The production aspect of the undertaking fell to Dodalová who had the greatest merit in hiding and rescuing the unique outtakes. The explanation also provides details of the director's theatre activities in the ghetto.

The third part of the book, "Living in Exile", encompasses the period from the mid-1940s to the late 1980s. It sums up the Dodals' efforts in producing educational and promotional animated films in the New York studio Irena Film Art, and draws on all available sources to describe the activities of the two exile filmmakers in Argentina. Dodalová's films devoted to ballet and dance, which were realized there during the 1950s and 1960s, occupied a significant place in her oeuvre. Both the written and photographic documents, as well as the testimonies provided by former members of the First Argentinian Chamber Theatre, helped the authors focus on Dodalová's teaching activities towards the end of her life.

In the Conclusion, we then attempt to discern whether the Dodals' pre-war oeuvre influenced the further developments of their profession in the Czech lands. It discusses the contradictory tendencies in animated film during the Protectorate, which was manoeuvred and financed by officials of the Third Reich but realized by Czech employees. This new generation, the majority of whom began their careers in animated film after the war, was actually unfamiliar with the Dodals' films for simply having had no chance to watch them. The vision and professional experience of the Dodal couple nonetheless remained part of the memories of their closest colleague, Hermína Týrlová, and they determined the direction of her own artistic career to a considerable extent.

A pre-war meeting between the Dodal couple and Jiří Trnka turned the puppeteer's attention to the possibilities of using puppets in film and also to folk art as a viable inspiration for this medium. The Dodals' mission and their search for new ways in European animated film embody the basic approach to animation in the Czech lands. Publishing their film oeuvre opens up the possibility of evaluating their place in the history of Czech cinematography.

The Early Years of Czech Animation / 1920s–1930s

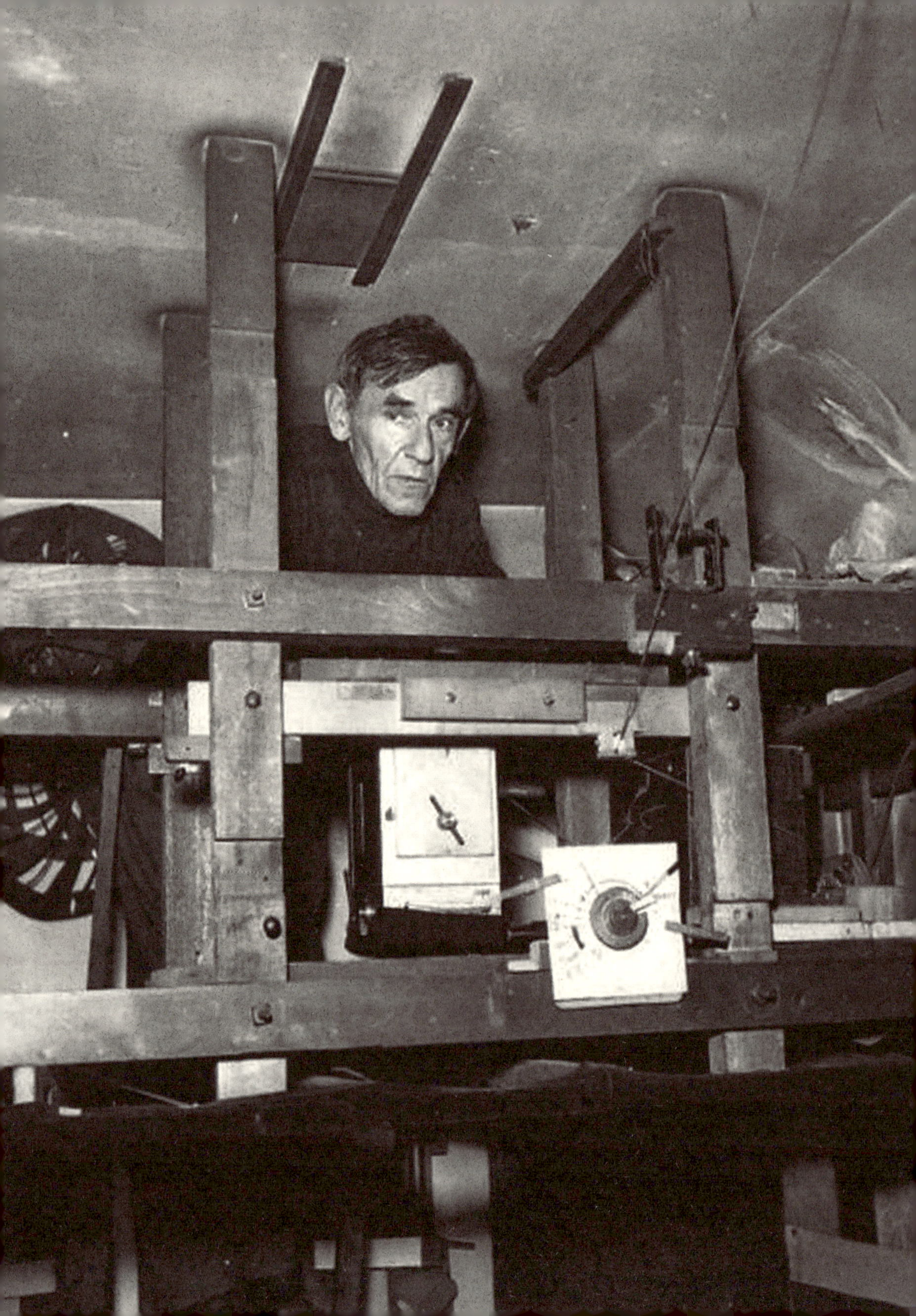

The World of Animation and the Initial Attempts of Czech Animators in Prague

Cartoon film had almost thirty years behind it in the early 1920s when Karel Dodal and his girlfriend Hermína began exploring the world of this medium. Its history greatly differed from that of feature or documentary film, mainly because it mainly developed outside the structures of the commercial film industry. The cut-out, cartoon and puppet pictures were mostly created in domestic conditions, in flats and small studios, and the only assistants and supporters were family members. Anytime the draughtsmen sought patronage from the established film studios such as Vitagraph, Pathé, Gaumont, Éclair and UFA, these merely provided temporary havens. The authors moreover usually had to pay for the possibility of using the professional technology of these studios by working on their animation commissions. The first exception in this sense was the establishment of specialized cartoon productions in the United States (e.g., Fleischer Studios and Disney Brothers Cartoon Studio) and later in Soviet Russia. If there were any private studios in the field of animation during the 1920s and 1930s in Europe at all, they were characteristic of a limited working force, insufficient production capacity and very short existence. Despite the uncertain and tricky economic conditions of the new profession, the world of animation from the 1890s attracted dozens, even hundreds, of both professional and amateur draughtsmen and draughtswomen, designers, architects and artists, convinced about the narrative and expressive possibilities of film trick technology.

Obviously, the earliest animation employed the elementary expressive and stylistic potential of the medium and its specific laws of time and space. Contrary to films with actors, which with only a few exceptions always bear a strong imprint of the time of their origination – and not only from the point of the external attributes of the captured reality, but also from the point of narration – many films made by the animation pioneers such as Winsor McCaye, Émile Cohl, Walter Ruttmann and Oskar Fischinger seem to stand outside the flow of time. McCaye's mosquito in the film *How a Mosquito Operates* (1912) today attacks the face of a sleeper with equal insistency and insolence as

Max Fleischer used pen and ink to draw Koko the Clown, inspired by his younger brother, Dave, who at that time performed as a clown at New York Coney Island. The character came to life and, having experienced many adventures also participated in by the painter, ended up back in the inkwell. The basic situation was then employed in the series of cartoon comedies entitled *Out of the Inkwell*, which the Fleischer brothers filmed between 1918 and 1929.

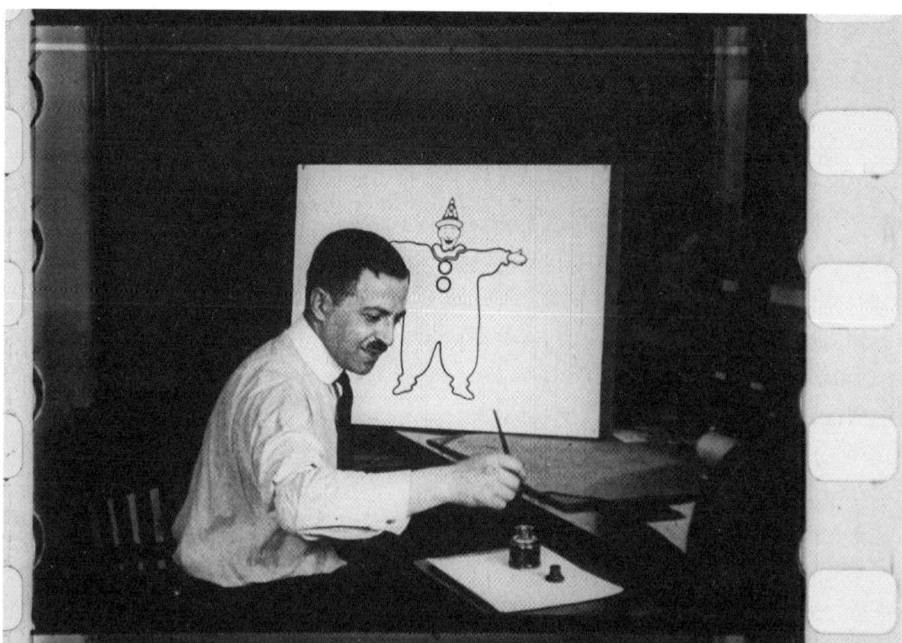

it did a century ago, and the freedom of a draughtsman who masterfully seized the projection surface to depict only parts of the annoyed male face, his still modern artistic shortcut and the used metonymy, which demonstrates a perfect understanding of the perception of the moving pictures, remains breath-taking.

Research carried out in recent decades proved that the first generation of film draughtsmen-animators and trick specialists – Émile Reynaud, Georges Méliès, James Stuart Blackton, Émile Cohl, Winsor McCaye, John Randolph Bray, Otto James Messmer as well as the arriving Walt Disney – had already laid the foundations of a new artistic tendency which later became known as animated film. All the hitherto attempts at defining it seem to be incomplete and one-sided; it is often viewed as a self-contained film genre or a fine-arts discipline, it works both in mass culture and in art, and its boundaries slowly blended with the world of audio-visual media with the arrival of digital technologies. The public has mainly associated it with productions for children for many decades and it appeared to stand on the margin of all developments in other film genres.

Deeper interest in the history of animated film dates to the late 1950s, while the authentic boom of its theoretical reflection began in the 1990s.

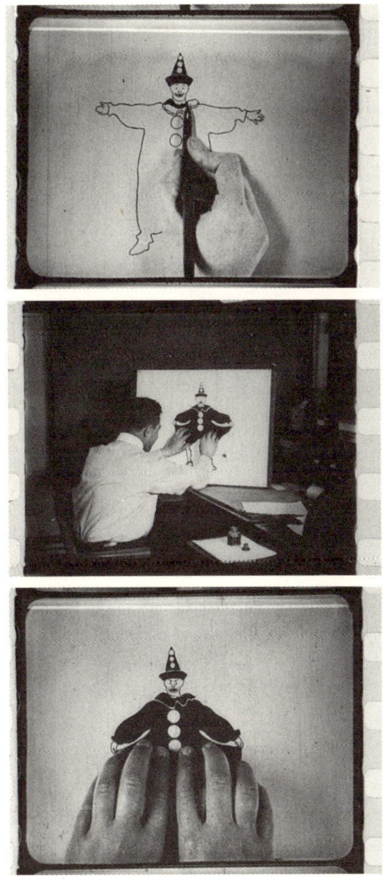

The Clown's Pups was filmed in 1919 by Max Fleischer, the American draughtsman, animator, inventor of the rotoscope, experimenter, director and producer.

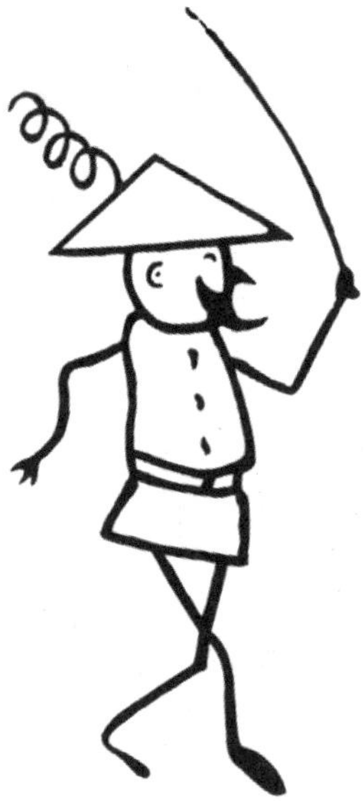

The hero of the animated films by the former Swedish sailor, reporter, draughtsman and animator, Victor Bergdåhl, became Captain Grogg boasting a very positive relationship to alcohol. Takes from the 1917 film *Captain Grogg Being Portrayed* (När kapten Grogg skulle porträtteras).

The figure of Fantôche was invented in 1908 by the French cartoonist and animator, Émile Cohl.

Giannalberto Bendazzi, author of the book *Cartoons: One Hundred Years of Cinema Animation* (1994), wrote that as soon as the centennial history of animation closed and became a matter of the past, there came a new stage of historical work which would allow for describing and analysing the real forms of animation.

The development of an animated film studio was, from historical and theoretical aspects, contributed to by the changing situation in archive keeping, whose attention gradually shifted from feature films to other types of film production. The arrival of digital technologies helped the archive workers identify and restore many films and thus also discover many yet unknown pictures which had been considered lost. It also allowed for issuing inventories of hundreds of missing cartoons previously recorded in the censorship files. Researching the early era of animation moreover resulted in the recognition that the artists had employed all contemporary methods of cartoon, puppet and cut-out filmmaking and even some forms of pixilation and that they, for instance, animated plasticine and experimented with fusing live actors and cartoon characters. Colour and the seamless blending of picture and sound soon found their way into film, too.

The prevailing opinion that the start of Czech animation came as late as with the 1945 establishment of the studio The T-Shirt Brothers (Bratři v triku) meant that the inter-war Czechoslovak cartoon production had largely escaped the attention of Czech film historiography due to the minimum interest of both the film historians and publicists. The only virtuous exception was the writing by Marie Benešová on Karel Zeman and Hermína Týrlová.

The response of the contemporary press clearly showed that one of the first trick films presented to audiences throughout the Czech lands was Méliès' magical fairies. Karel Čapek, beside others, aptly described the impression left on him and the rest of the cinema viewers by the first cartoons in his magazine article "Cinema" (Biograf) from November 1910 as follows:

"Cinema has no boundaries and nothing is impossible there! Inanimate objects being freed to move and act: a character drawn by a child's hand instantly comes to life and runs all around the world; it may be persecuted by its own destiny and may lead a tragic life and eventually die; lions smash their cages open and prowl through a city; even a bottle can come alive and turn into a human or a dog and then again perish in a square of light; or

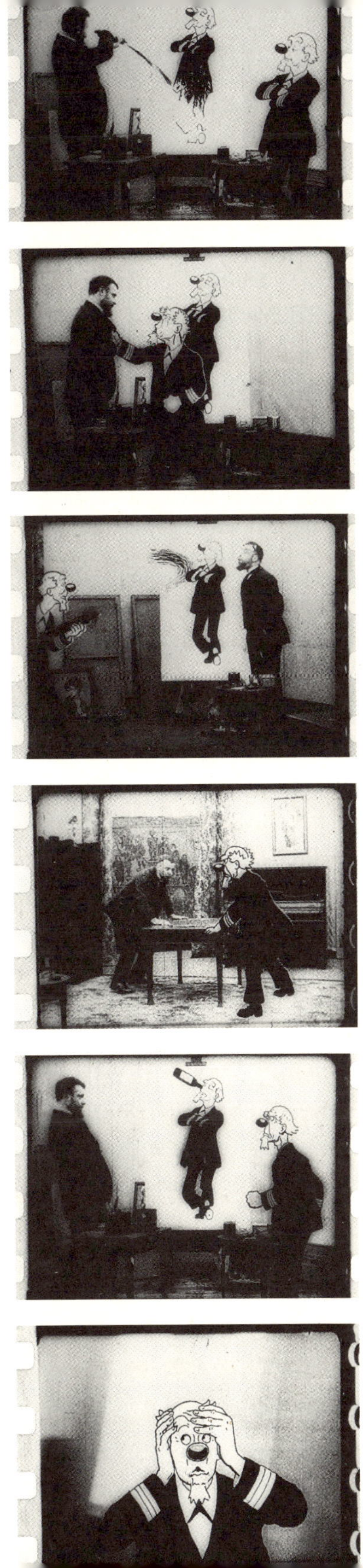

there are people acting and sinking into the most dreadful or the most bizarre fickleness of fate."[1]

Čapek's description suggests that the figure drawn by the child's hand is Cohl's *Fantôche* and the bottle metamorphoses probably refer to the animated sketches by Segundo de Chomón. We can only speculate if Čapek, at the age of twenty-two, first encountered animated film in Prague, Brno, Munich or Berlin; his brief notice nevertheless definitely testifies to the contemporary excitement and hopes laded on the new, mysterious world of animation.

At the end of 1916, the Danish cartoon *The Remarkable Journey of Captain Grog* (Kapten Groggs undrbara resa) by Victor Bergdåhl was introduced to Czech cinemas. The filmmaker at that time brought the motifs of an adventurous sailors' voyage and the images of a mermaid, a whale, a monkey, black people and hungry lions to the cartoons – i.e. characters whose many variants later re-appeared for decades in films by various authors and provenances. The next cartoon screened in Czech cinemas (in 1920) was the American promotional picture *The Sinking of the Louisiania*, which minutely reconstructed the sinking of the ship caused by the German torpedo attack. The number of cartoons presented in local cinemas then gradually increased during the 1920s. As far as German production was concerned, it was, for example, the films by Louis Seel and Lotte Reiniger as well as many German commercials, especially those created by Julius Pinschewer. The genre of puppet film was represented by Vladislav Starevich, and the animated work arriving from the new studios of Soviet Russia was also introduced. The first abstract films by Oskar Fischinger and László Moholy-Nagy, however, passed the censorship proceedings in Prague only at the end of the decade.

The most extensive collection of cartoons, nevertheless, came to Czech cinemas from the United States, and the American cartoon comedies became more than synonymous with animated film. One of the most popular were the works by the Fleischer brothers, featuring the character of Koko the Clown (renamed Bejbl or Šotek for the Czech screenings), as well as the series with Felix the Cat

In the early years of animation, the artists often employed facet, paper and silhouette film, i.e. technology which was both economically and financially advantageous. Bohuslav Šula selected it for the same reason.

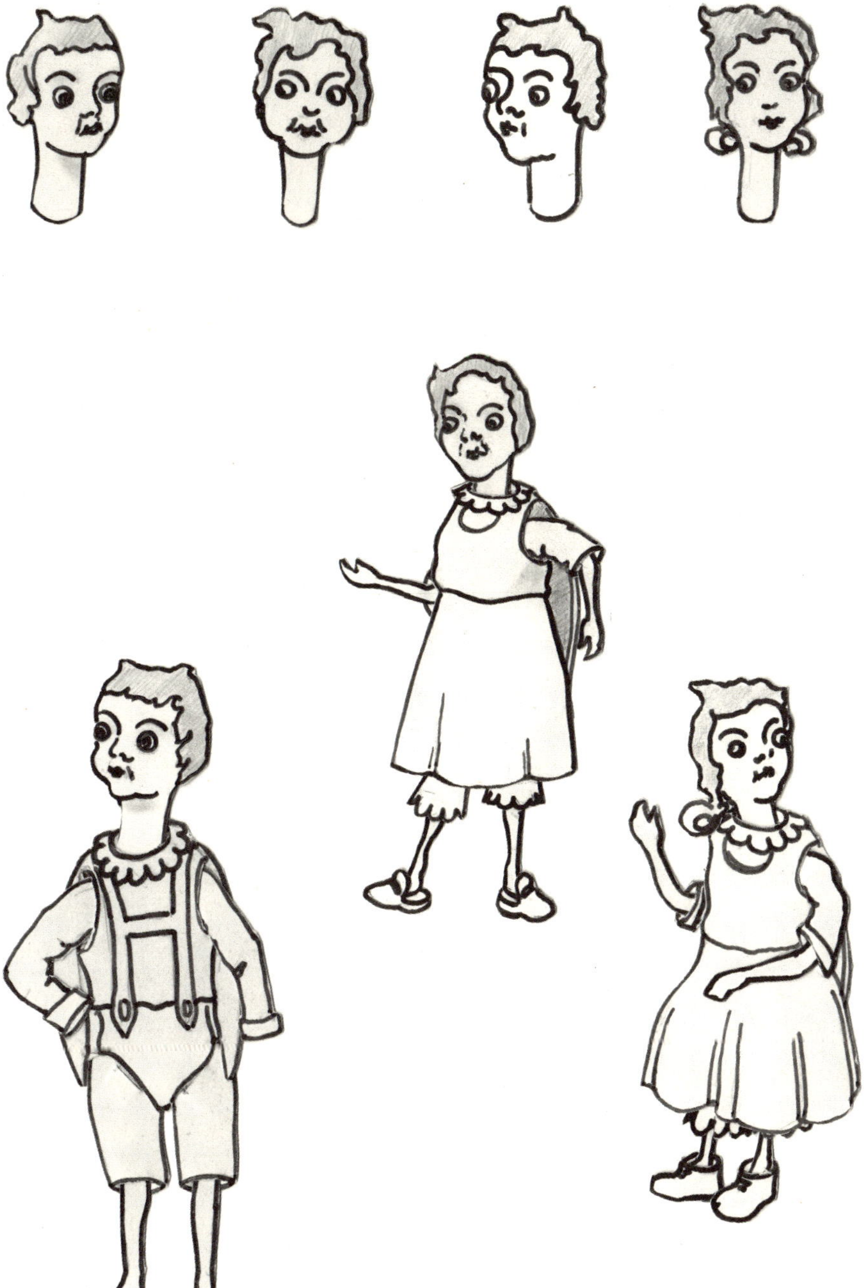

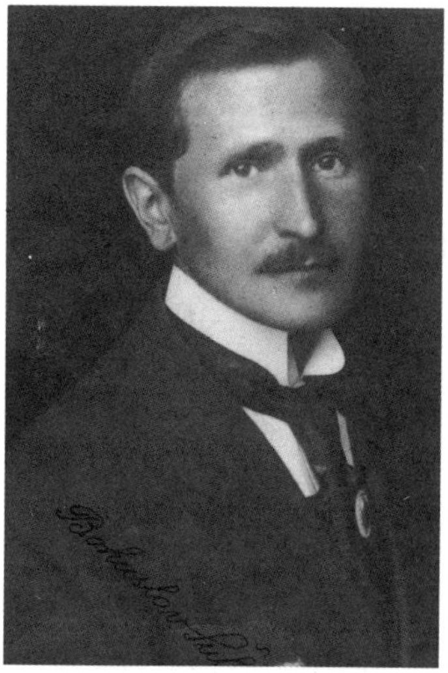

The architect Bohuslav Šula, an artist and director of the first Czech unfinished facet film, *Fireflies* (1920).

by the director Pat Sullivan and designer Otto Messmer. In 1926, these were followed by the series starring Jerry, Bobby, Pix and Flix, Ide and Mike, Mutt and Jeff, Oswald the Lucky Rabbit and many others. Mickey Mouse (initially presented as Miky or Micky in the Czech lands) arrived at local film screens in 1929 and launched a new era of American cartoon film distribution which was mainly dominated by the sound production of the Walt Disney studio from then on.

Animated films by Czech authors appeared in the cinemas from time to time already during the first half of the 1920s. Although most of the attempts from this early period are today missing, they are nevertheless worth mentioning because they tell of the difficulties which this film genre encountered in the Czech environment.

The first Czech cartoon, based on Jan Karafiát's book *Fireflies* (Broučci), was filmed in, what was then, Czechoslovakia, by the architect Bohuslav Šula in 1919 and was produced by the Praga-film company. Contrary to the United States, where the genre departed from the tradition of newspaper cartoons and comic strips and where it was rather natural that the cartoonists brought the subjects of pop and mass culture into animated film, the initial stages of Czech animation were embodied by film adaptation of a widely known literary subject.[2] Karafiát's book with its educational aspirations was a challenge for filmmaking not only due to the possibilities of presenting a humanlike world of the fireflies in the form of moving pictures but also due to the widespread popularity of the written form. It was probably his profession as architect that made Šula choose the technique of cut-out paper cartoon filming which was, moreover, less demanding from the aspect of time and realization.

Šula's "construction" of the drawn and cut-out figures, which employed pockets for inserting moving limbs and replaceable heads pasted onto

The only surviving fragment from *Fireflies* is a virage frame from the part "The Little House under the Oak Tree" (Chaloupka pod dubem).

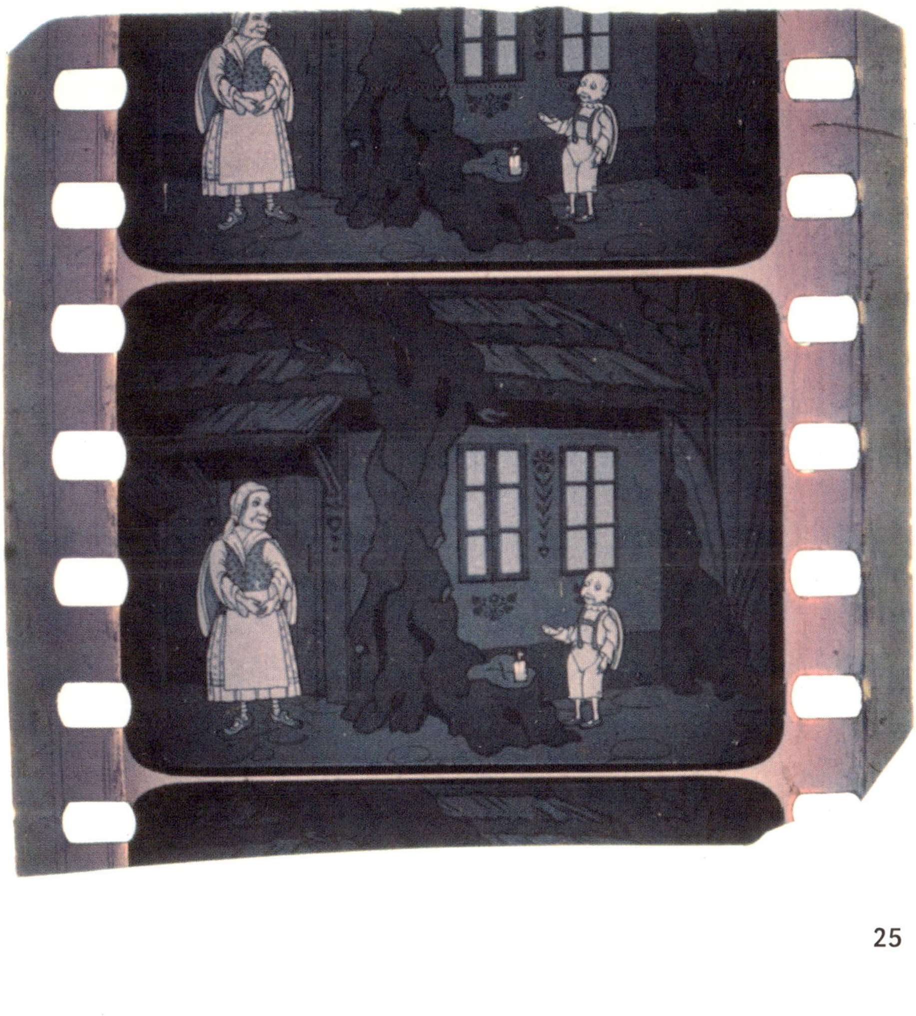

the reverse, allowed for relatively simple phasing. We can assume that the author realized his film in collaboration with its cameraman, Antonín Kopřiva. Although some memories suggest that the three short sequences presented at a working screening enjoyed extreme success, the film eventually remained unfinished. Praga-film ran into financial troubles which adumbrated the end of the production and the author, who soon became a sought-after film architect, never returned to trick film again. This early stage of animated film is today illustrated by several cut-out characters and 84 centimetres of reel, which is even colour-toned and viraged.[3]

More traces of the first animated films in Prague can be found in the reflections of the contemporary press. Some articles report that the Šula's example inspired, for instance, the architect, painter and actor Ferdinand Fiala to make three trick films in collaboration with the cameraman, actor and director Svatopluk Innemann in the Pojafilm studio. Their first cartoon, which can be viewed as the first Czech cartoon picture ever, was finished in October 1920 and was entitled

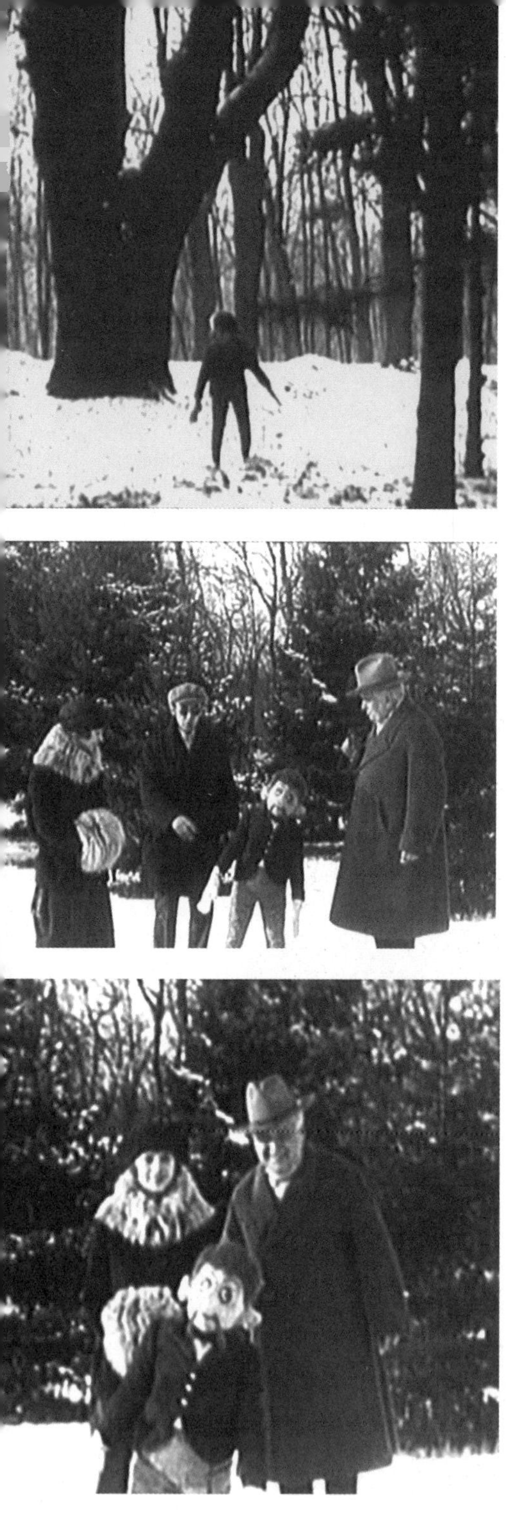

Photographs from the filming of the now missing picture *Why Don't You Laugh?*

A take of a puppet and Eman Fiala from the film *Why Don't You Laugh?*

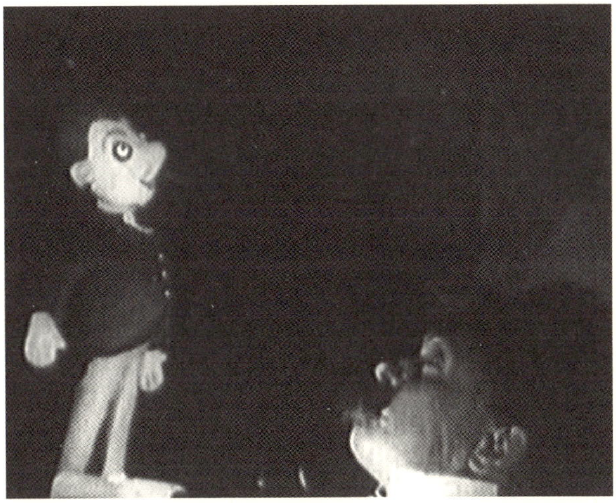

The African Adventure (Dobrodružství v Africe). In May next year, the duo Fiala–Innemann presented two more films to the invited guests in the Lucerna cinema in Prague: *The Over-There American Eccentric* (Americký výstředník Ten-Tam) and *Live Cartoons* (Živé karikatury). The film reviewer of the magazine *Cinema Public* (Kinopublikum) opined that Ferdinand Fiala had succeeded in inventing "splendid animated caricatures" armed with wit and humour which well equalled foreign models, but again suffered from the "persistent Czech disease – the footage deserving scissors".[4] The fact that none of the above-mentioned films passed the censorship proceedings seems to prove the lack of interest on the side of the film distributors.

A similar lack of interest pursued the Czech silhouette cartoons *Cinderella* (Pohádka o Popelce) and *The Stubborn Lovers* (Tvrdohlaví milenci), introduced at the film stock market in early 1923. Their author was the photographer, poster painter and subtitle draughtsman Antonín Frič, who worked for the Excelsiorfilm company. Czech cinematography during the same period, however, also saw an interesting experiment when Ferdinand Fiala animated a puppet of a forsaken figure from a toy factory, playing a role in an actors' melodrama. The combined picture – introduced in 1923 under the titles

Why Don't You Laugh? (Proč se nesměješ) and *A One-Horse Street Romance* (Románek zapadlé uličky) and, in 1926, probably in a re-edited version, *The Story of a Forgotten Man* (Román zapomenutého) – did not survive. The only proofs of its existence are the takes from the filming in the Šumava Mountains, which capture the looks of the puppet and also the fact that the rag doll was replaced by a disguised small boy in certain scenes.[5]

The first surviving cartoon film of Czech production is the commercial *See How Two Boys and a Dog Fool around These Days!* (Vizte vše, co tropí dnes kluci dva a jeden pes). Both its author and the production company are unknown.[6] The cartoon has often been attributed to Karel Dodal and it

The technology of animating cut-out silhouettes of black, non-transparent and partly transparent paper placed on a glass board under each other and lit either from the sides or below was invented by Lotte Reiniger in Germany. Takes from the 1922 picture *Cinderella* (Aschenputtel).

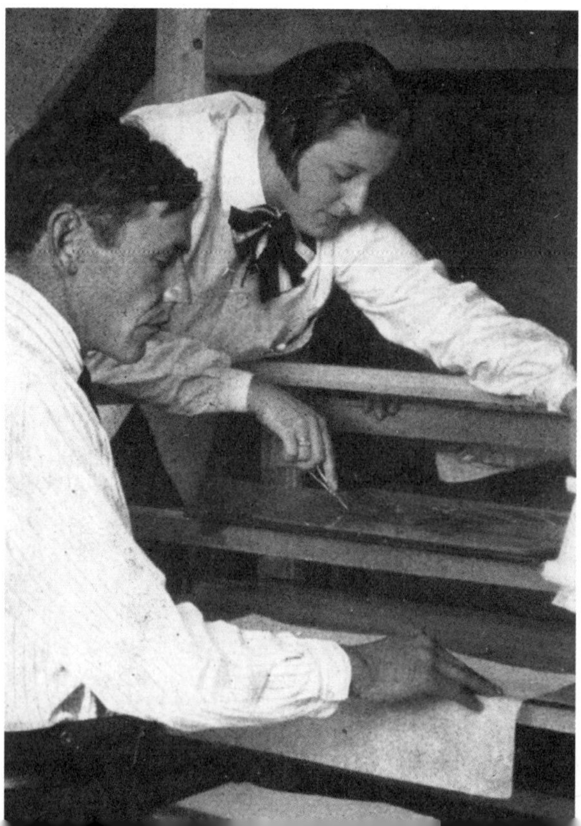

Berthold Bartosch and Lotte Reiniger, working on the film *The Adventures of Prince Achmed* in Potsdam in 1925. Bartosch in his post-war Paris period is captured in the photograph on the opening page of this chapter.

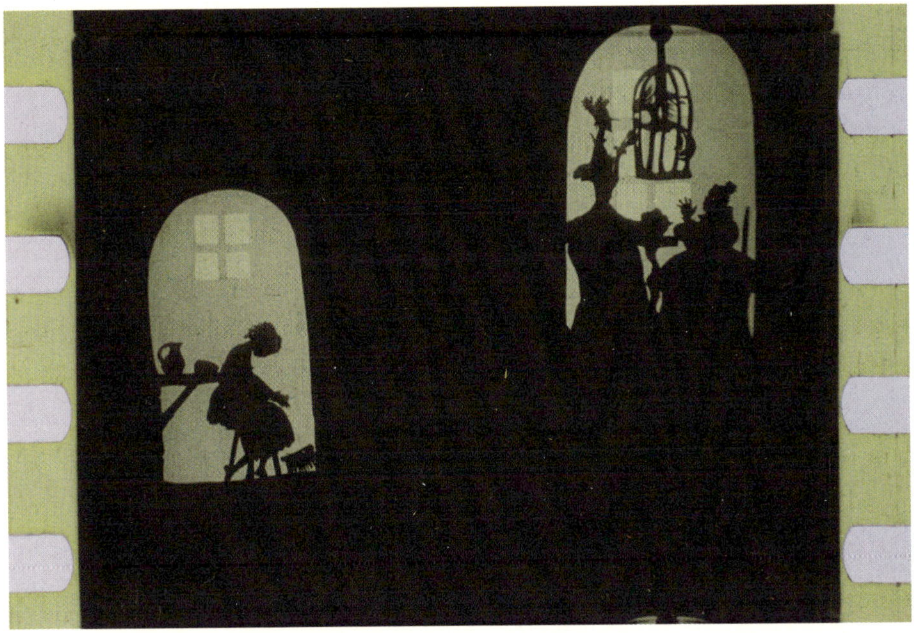

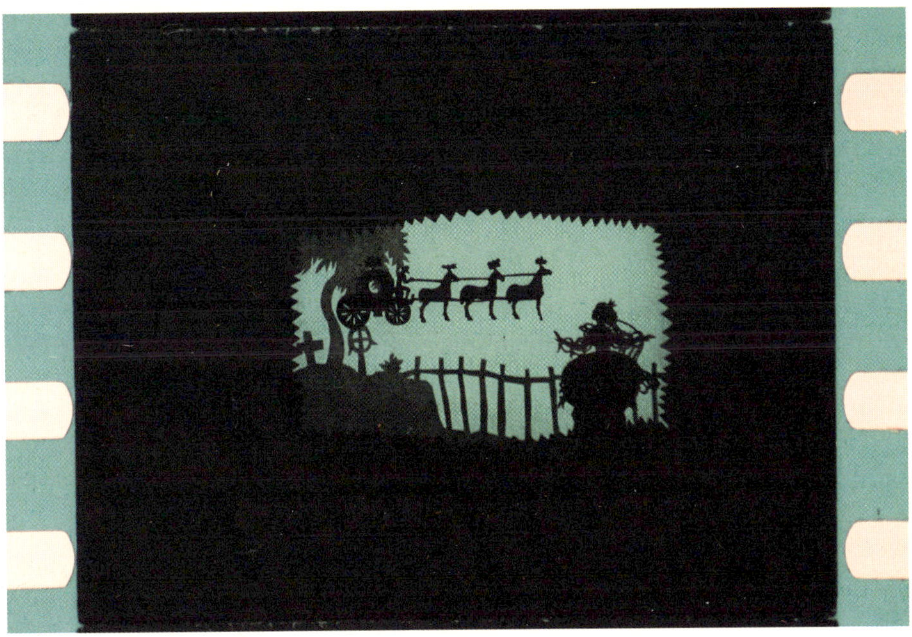

passed the censorship proceedings in 1925 when Dodal reportedly started at Elekta Journal. It employed the customary narrative means of the cartoon genre – the comic plot and pursuits (in this case, hungry boys and a wandering doggie chase a tripe sausage) which eventually served to promote Sana margarine. The Czech signpost "Hloubětín", i.e. one of the Prague suburbs where the Sana factory was located, suggests that the picture was already of Czech provenance.

We may ask at this point what actually hindered the development of animated film in the Czech lands. I do not believe in the commonplace argument that it was merely because the production of both cartoon and puppet films was time consuming, laborious and financially demanding. The above-mentioned example of the architect Šula illustrates one of the fundamental problems of this production. A film producer facilitated making a trick film only provided it was based on an attractive story and was "doing well". But as soon as a production ran into problems, it was the animated film which the producer resigned from first and dropped the easiest, even more so if the filming required additional costs. This problem naturally was not just widespread in Czech cinematography; the local situation was, however, further sharpened by weak economic support for film.

The Czech lands totally lacked institutions which would support the local development of experimental filmmaking. Post-war Germany, for example, established the Berlin Institute for Cultural Research (Institut für Kulturforschung) in 1919. A group of German enthusiasts, headed by Lotte Reiniger, could thus film seven animated pictures between 1919 and 1922. And although the facility was eventually closed due to economic reasons, it at least briefly provided a platform which, to a certain extent, allowed for the development of cut-out cartoons.[7] Lotte Reiniger subsequently found a donor, the Berlin banker

The film by Berthold Bartosch, *Idea* (L'Idée), ranks among the works whose multiple meanings can only be mediated by direct perception of the picture, because the montage of the individual film images metaphorically captures people's resistance against political and economic oppression and manipulation, while the counterpoint of the social drama is the images of outer space.

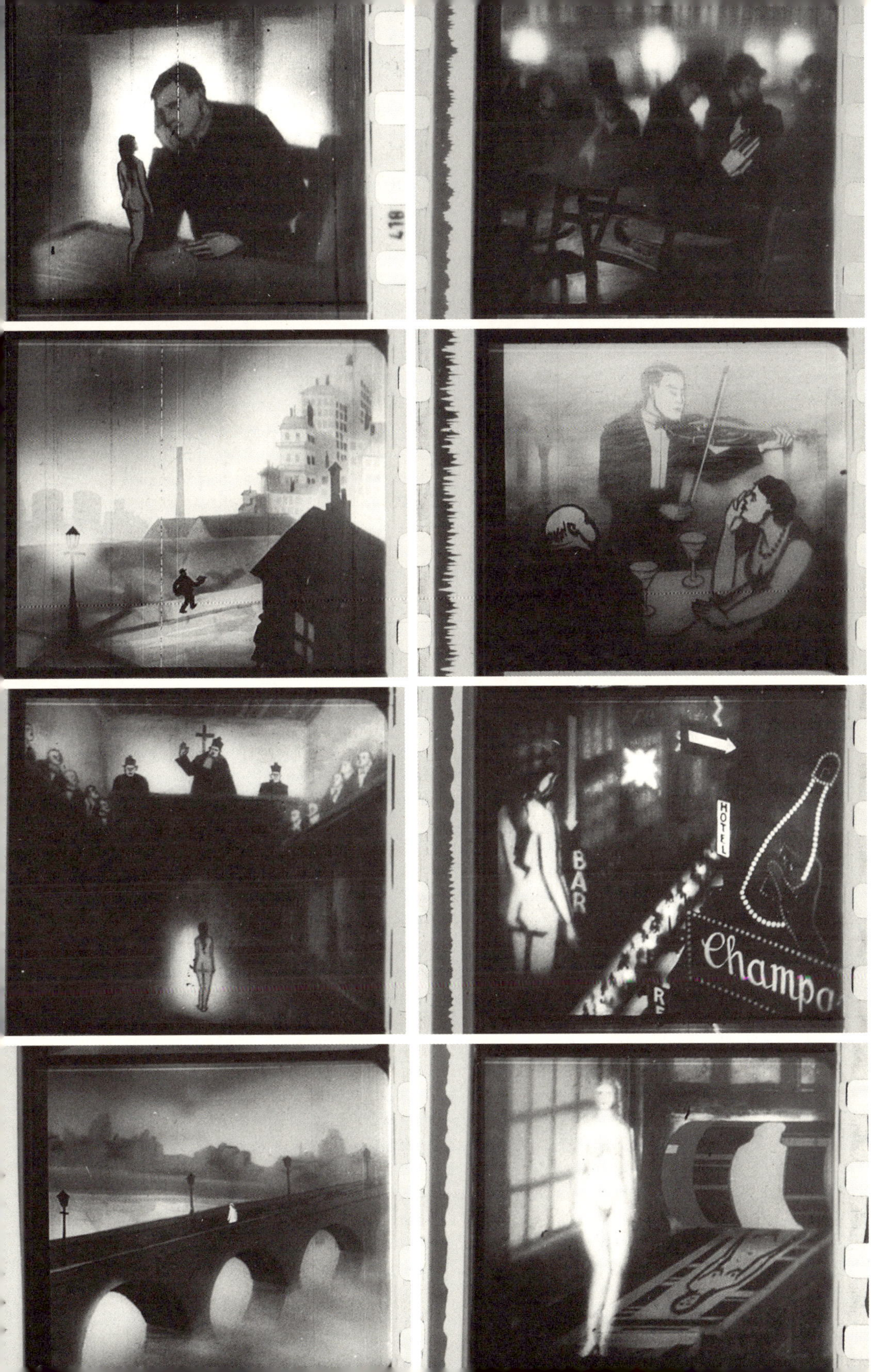
HOTEL
BAR
Champa

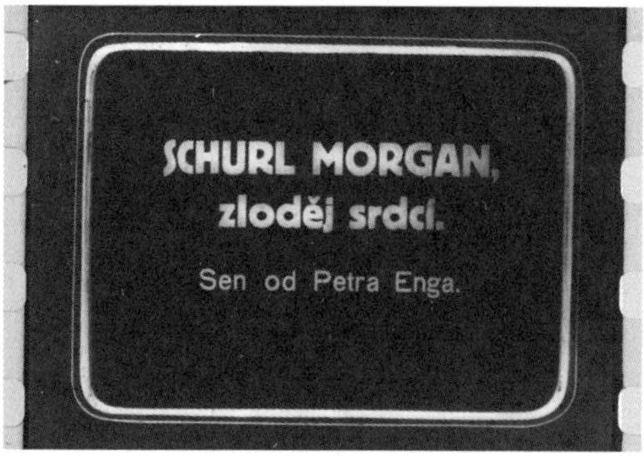

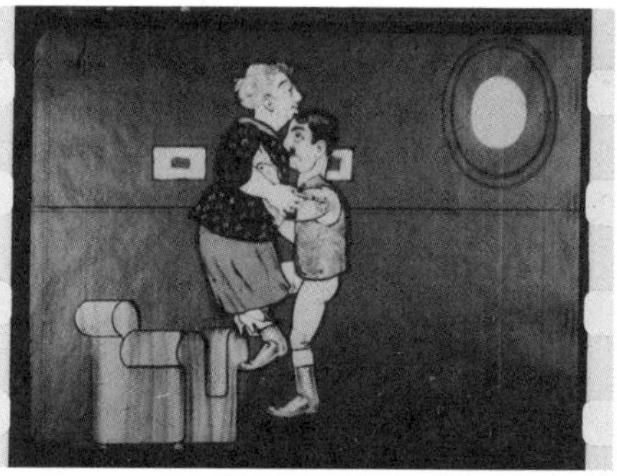

Czech subtitles to Eng's dreamy film *Schurl Morgan the Heartbreaker* (Schurl Morgan, zloděj srdcí), which the National Film Archive acquired as late as in 2003, testify that the title was screened in the inter-war Czechoslovakia. It was probably made in Vienna during the 1920s.

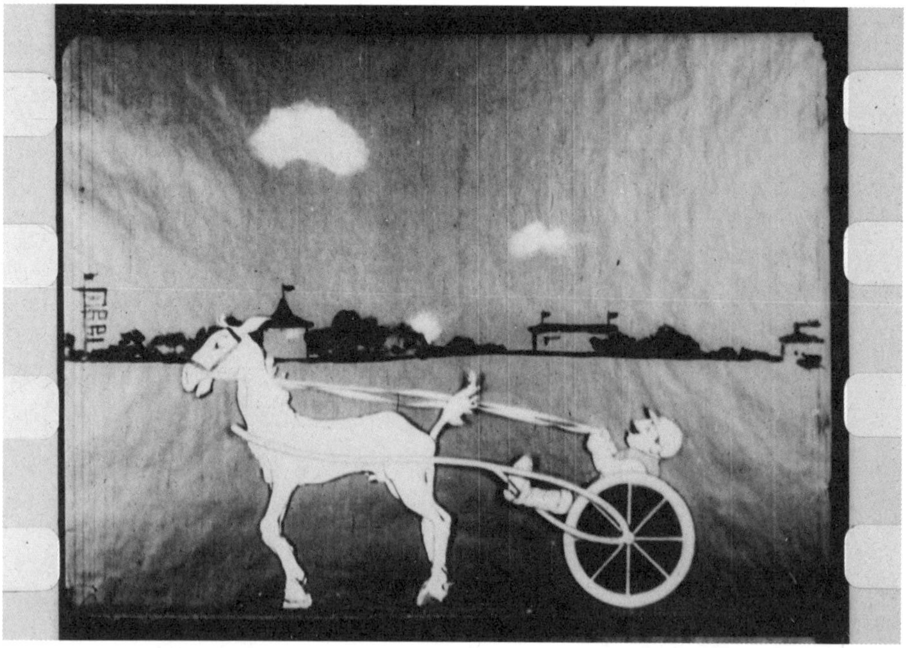

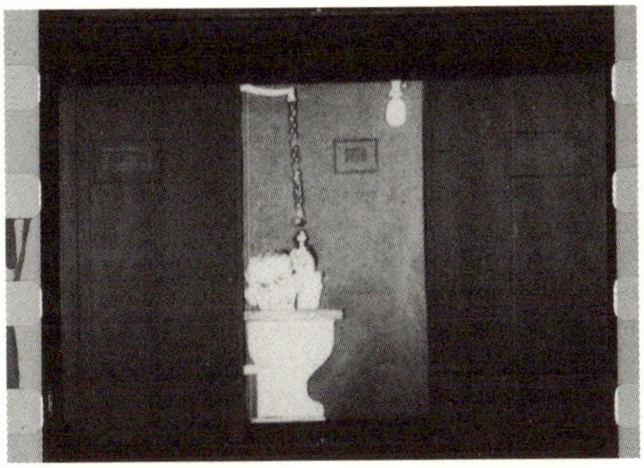 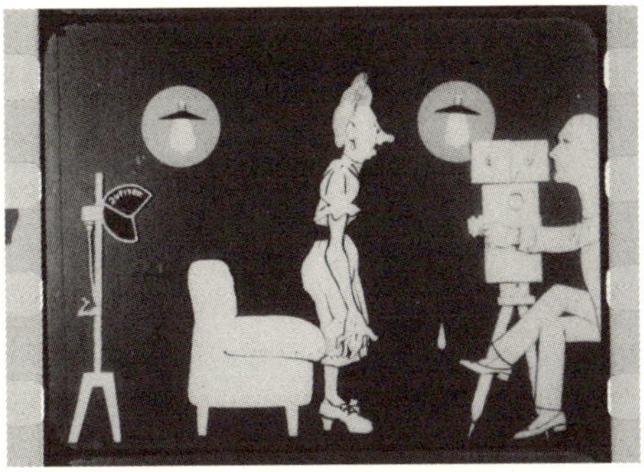

Louis Hagen, who financed the shooting of the full-length film *The Adventures of Prince Achmed* (Die Abenteuer des Prinzen Achmed; 1926) for almost three years. It must be noted, though, that the director was surrounded by reliable colleagues who served as a certain guarantee of the project. Her main support was her lifetime partner Carl Koch, a well-educated intellectual and expert in Eastern cultures and a scriptwriter and director who played the role of production manager, cameraman and, when necessary, an animator in his wife's team. Its other members were the Czech native Berthold Bartosch, an experienced experimenter who had filmed numerous pictures already during his sojourn in Vienna, and the avant-garde filmmaker Walter Ruttmann, an author of several abstract opuses.

Both Prague and Brno not only lacked a similar institution as the one established in Berlin; there was also no group of artists fully extracting the possibilities of Kinetic Art. The avant-garde artists associated in the group Butterbur (Devětsil) did evaluate film as a new medium, but their film dramas were mainly based on literary imagination. The artists had no authentic experience with film technology and production, and animated film – mainly presented by cartoon comedies to the public – lay beyond the horizon of their interest.

Three artists born in the territory of, what is today, the Czech Republic – but whose first language was German – realized their creative plans in the field of animation abroad. Berthold Bartosch (1893–1968), a native of the

North-Bohemian village of Polubný, studied architecture in Vienna and first encountered the chance of working in animated film in Berlin and later, from the end of 1930, in Paris. Peter Eng (1892–1938?), originating from the Moravian city of Olomouc, engaged in animation in Vienna after his study trips and became one of the founders of Austrian animated film. The Prague-born illustrator of children's books, Walter Trier (1890–1951), collaborated on several animated films in Berlin.[8]

The conditions for Czech animated film in the early 1920s were far from favourable – but this was to change soon with the arrival of the film company Elekta Journal.

1 Čapek, K., "Biograf", *Stopa* (Trace), 4 November 1910. In: Čapek, K., *Spisy. O umění a kultuře I.* (Writings. On Art and Culture I.). Praha: Československý spisovatel, 1984, p. 157.

2 Filming Karafiát's book, which still holds a firm position in Czech children's literature, then long remained a challenge. The Dodals incorporated the title into their dramaturgy during the 1930s, and the film producer M. Havel considered adapting *Fireflies* in the 1940s. He offered the subject to the puppeteer Trnka but the two very soon came to differ in their view of how to animate the puppets. The book was eventually adapted in the form of various programs for Czech Television many years later.

3 Anonymous typewritten manuscripts. The National Film Archive, fund Šula Bohuslav, box 1/2, Inv. Nos. 4 and 24.

4 *Kinopublikum*, 1920, No. 13, 7 May, p. 7.

5 The takes survived within the montage title *Jak se u nás kdysi filmovalo* (How We Once Made Films), compiled by the film collector B. Veselý in 1960.

6 The corresponding censorship file states the Propa company; the name was later corrected to Propaga.

7 Cürlis, H., *20 Jahre Kulturfilmschaffen. Institut für Kulturforschung e. v., und Kulturfilm-Institut G.M.B.H.* Berlin: Kulturfilm-Institut, 1939, p. 4.

8 Bartosch left his homeland for Vienna before the First World War and studied architecture and art at the local Academy of Fine Arts. He became familiar with trick film technology in the School of Applied Arts during his studies and, upon the recommendation of his Professor E. Hanslik, i.e. created two educational films illustrating the social and political ideas of T. G. Masaryk. He lived in Berlin from summer 1919, following in educational films and also participating in numerous pictures by other authors as a designer and trick expert. He was a member of the family circle of the pedagogue, writer, filmmaker and film producer C. Koch and his wife, director and artist L. Reiniger, for ten years and collaborated on their projects, one of the most significant of which was the full-length silhouette film *The Adventures of Prince Achmed.* In the late 1920s, Bartosch partook in the combined feature and animated film *Good Luck Hunting* (Die Jagd nach dem Glück; 1930) along with Koch, Reiniger and other friends, e.g. J. Renoir, C. Hessling and J. and A. Tedesco, and even took a leading part in it. The director of the now missing film (only an animated part by Bartosch and Reiniger survived), was R. Gliese. Bartosch also became close friends with B. Brecht. In 1929, he accepted an offer from the publisher K. Wolff (who, beside other writers, published Kafka) to make a film adaptation of a book of woodcuts by the Flemish painter and graphic artist F. Masereel, *The Idea* (L'Idée). The film was a metaphorical image of a world where money ruins artists' values and lives but where the idea of freedom and revolt, as represented by the character of a naked girl, survives. The final version of the film with Honegger's music premiered in the London Tivoli Palace Theatre on 16 November 1934. Between 1933 and 1939, Bartosch worked on the anti-war political picture *St Francis: Nightmare and Dreams* (Saint François ou Rêves et Cauchemars). Although the film material perished during the war, the few surviving frames testify to the artist's exceptional approach. The author destroyed the material of his anti-Hitler picture in 1940. Bartosch, with his Czechoslovak passport, survived the war side by side his wife in rather destitute conditions in the French countryside and later lived on occasional commissions. He worked on a film about outer space and its infiniteness, but his prolonged disease eventually made it impossible. He accepted French citizenship in 1950 and died in Paris in 1968. His paintings were exhibited in France only post-mortem, in the 1970s.

Eng spent his youth in Vienna and the United States. He later studied and worked in Munich, Copenhagen, Berlin and mainly back in Vienna where he, until 1934, enjoyed the company of his brother, the architect and essayist P. Engelmann, a student of Adolf Loos, a secretary of the journalist and writer K. Kraus and a friend of the philosopher L. Wittgenstein. In Vienna, Eng pursued graphic art and caricature, designed advertising posters and shot animated films, cartoon fairy-tales, industrial films and commercials. He is today perceived as one of the founders of Austrian animated film. Some information claim that he emigrated before the war and died in the United States, other sources report that he and his wife, the cartoonist and designer A. Pölz, committed suicide after the Nazis arrival to power, either in Vienna in 1938 or in Olomouc a year later.

Trier was a graphic artist, cartoonist, advertising designer and toy collector whose illustrations congenially complete the magical world of the famous children's books by E. Kästner. He lived in Germany between 1906 and 1936 where he, among other things, participated in several animated films as a designer. He held a solo exhibition in Prague in November 1934, but his plans to return to his homeland were cancelled due to the imminent danger of the German racial laws, and Trier thus left for London. Declining Disney's offer to become a designer in his US studio, Trier lived in Ontario with his wife and daughter from 1947 where he further focused on illustration and moreover gained wide attention as an author of children's books.

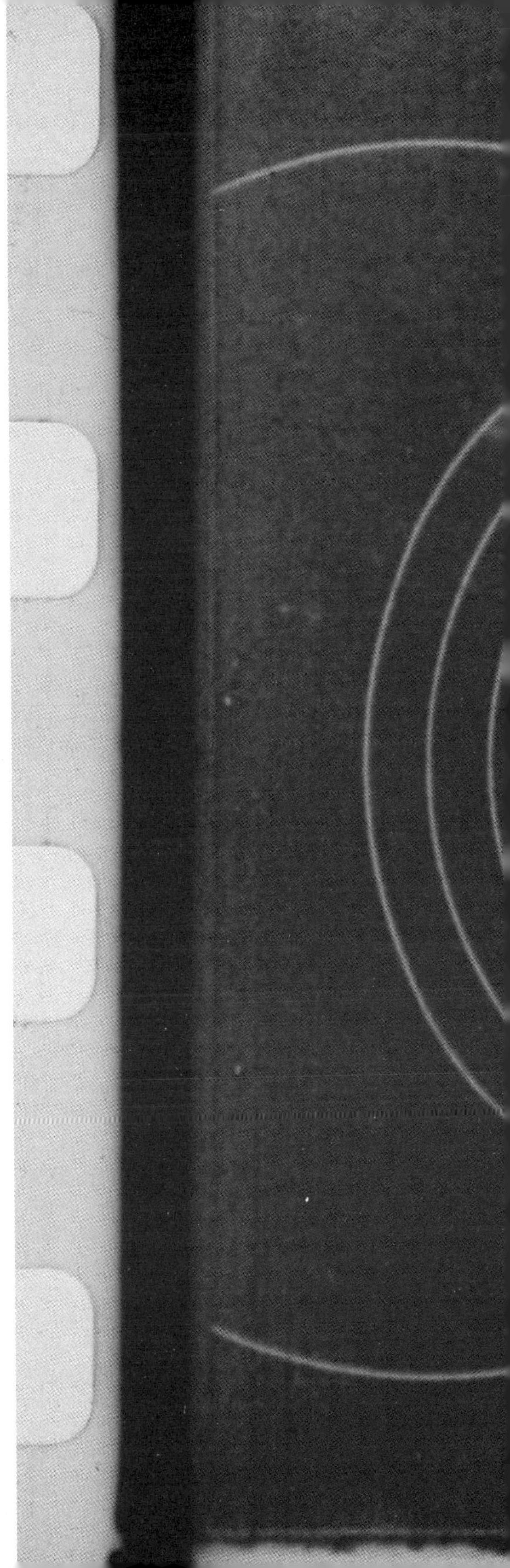

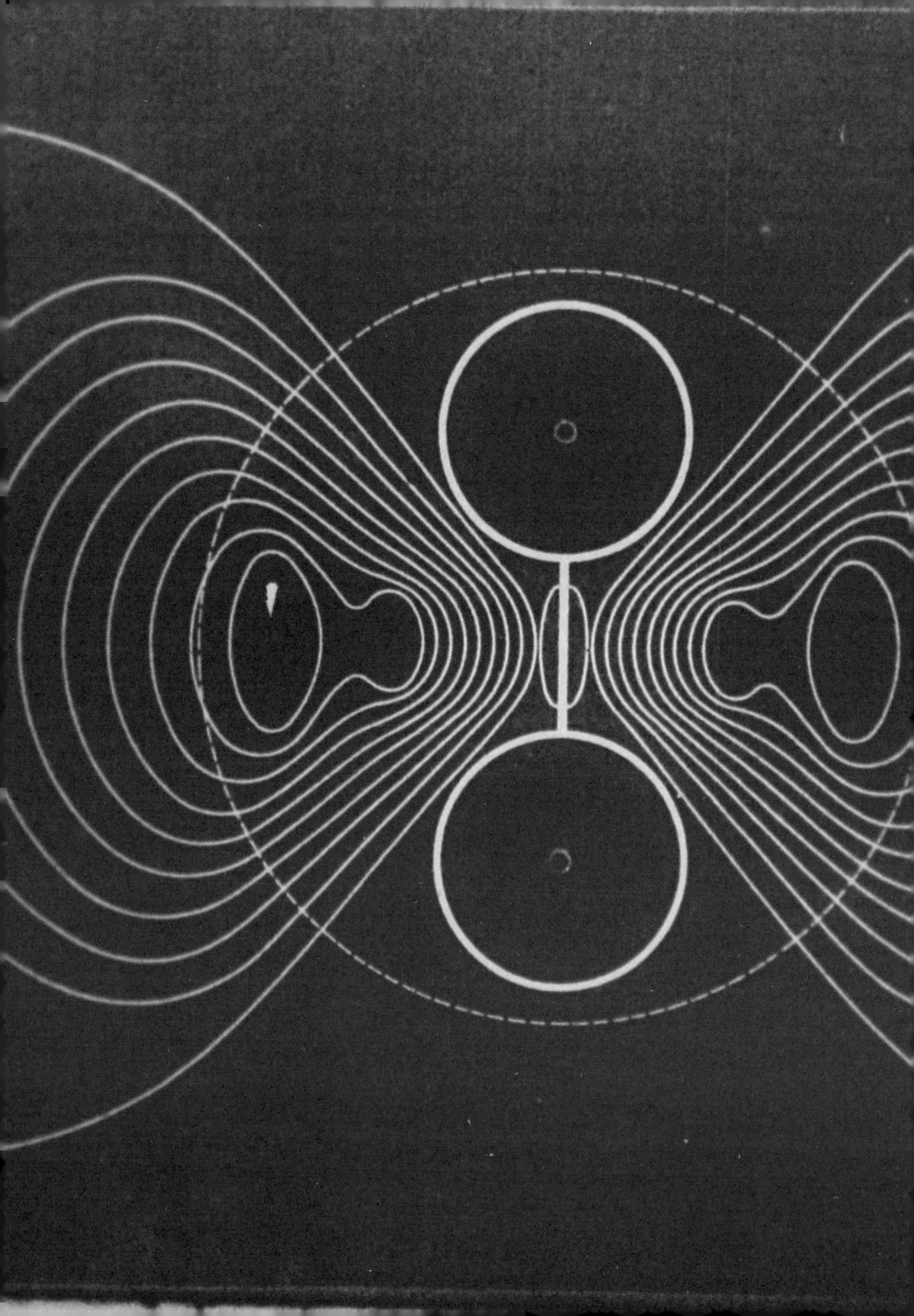

Karel and Hermína Dodal in Elekta Journal

The main credit for developing the first stage of Czech trick film undoubtedly goes to Elekta Journal – a company established in 1925 with the aim of attracting and gathering young talented filmmakers.[1] In the same year, it began publishing the very first Czech weekly newsreel and developed the production of scientific, educational and advertising pictures, as well as films focusing on nature. Its feature films translating the well-known and mainly widely popular works of Czech literature, e.g. by Vilém Mrštík, Ignát Herrmann and Popelka Biliánová, also enjoyed immense success.[2] Between 1928 and 1929, Elekta Journal briefly became the largest Prague film producer. It moreover received exclusive rights to document the Brno exhibition of contemporary culture, and especially the prestigious commission to produce the historical film *Saint Wenceslas* (Svatý Václav) made on the occasion of the millennial anniversary of the death of the Bohemian patron saint.[3] The first Czech historical epic, originating simultaneously with the arrival of sound film and under the supervision of advisors and the assistance of the press, however, did not meet the expected response and its commercial failure had an extensive impact on the company's eventual disintegration.

Nevertheless, in the latter half of the 1920s, Elekta Journal was an ambitiously managed enterprise whose activities moreover encompassed producing

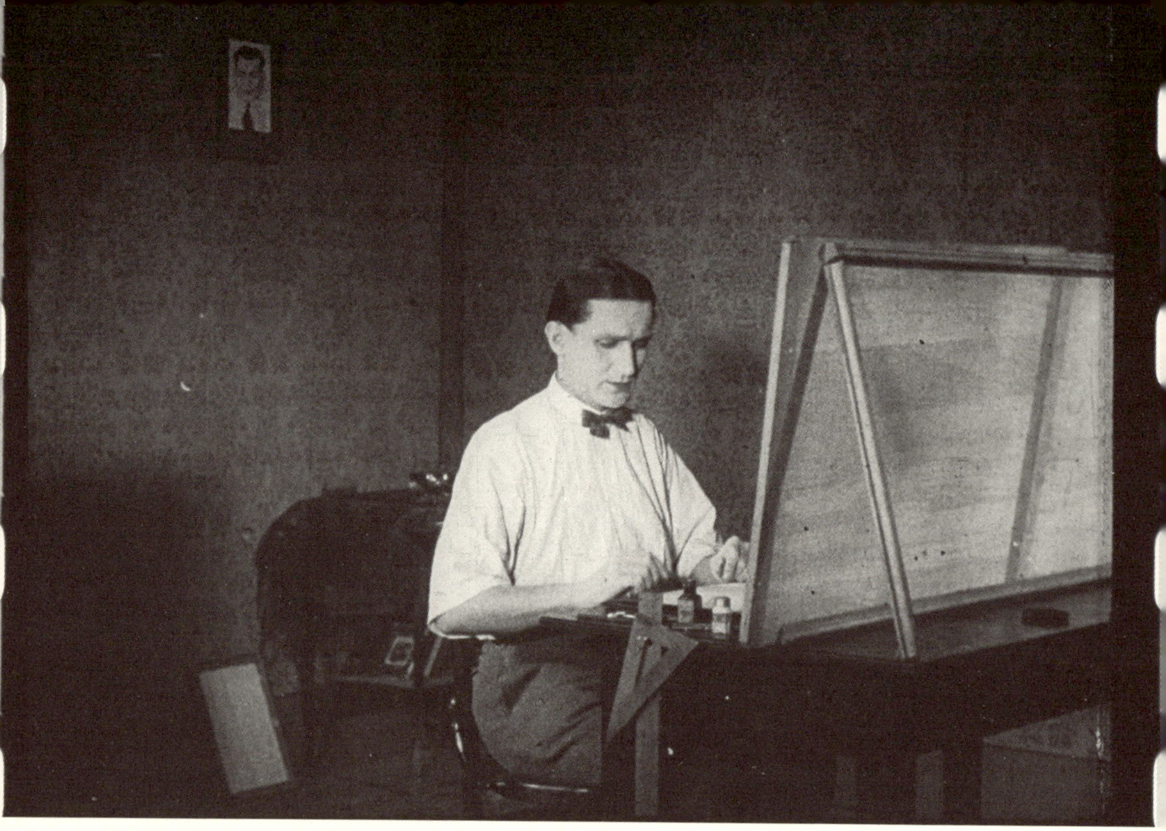

Karel Dodal in front of a drawing sheet on which Bimbo, the hero sporting a hat, was born in Prague.

trick, i.e. also cartoon, pictures. By word of mouth, this was especially thanks to the director Karel Anton, a big fan of cartoons. As far as it is known, he himself did not create any but brought Elekta Journal the young actor and draughtsman interested in animated film, Karel Dodal, who was appointed its "painter".

Information about Karel Dodal's childhood and youth is scarce. The oldest of five offspring, he was born on 27 January 1900 to a blue-collar family of a machinery locksmith. He loved to draw from his early years and was thus sent out to apprentice – as was customary in penurious families – as a varnishing painter. The young man did not accomplish his parents' expectations and did not become a civil service painter, but instead found his place in the Holešovice theatre Urania, the favourite folk scene whose auditorium could accommodate an audience of seven hundred. Some reports claim that he worked there as a set designer, but this just seems to be an additional construct and euphemistic label for his engagement in the theatre painting workshop. The information provided by the surviving Urania posters and the notes in the texts about the cast of the individual dramas read that Dodal was also an occasional actor in episodic roles in the theatre between 1923 and 1924. More information as to the duration of Dodal's Urania activity is unavailable because the building burnt down in 1946 and most of its archive was shredded in 1950. While Dodal was at Urania, he met the chorus girl Hermína Týrlová and established a long-time working and personal relationship with her. Their encounter on the local stage is, among other things, proved by the program for the performance *The Court Jester of George of Podiebrad* (Šašek Jiříka Poděbradského), written by Karel Sabina and introduced by the director Vojta Záhorčík in 1924. Karel Dodal starred as Ctibor of Cimburk and Hermína Týrlová performed the role of the "second wife".[4]

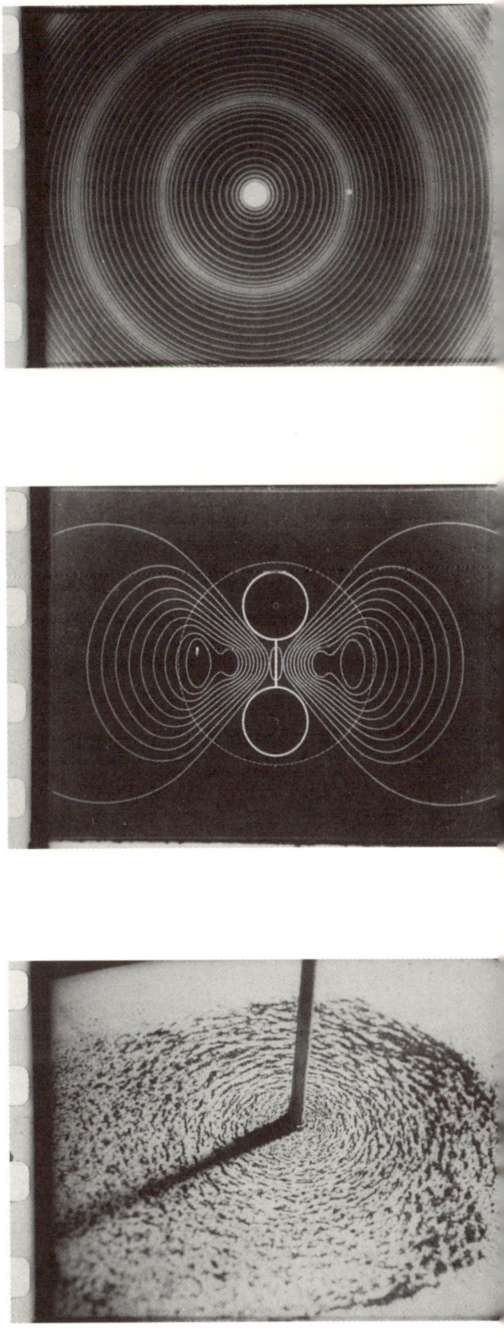

An example of employing a moving diagram which Karel Dodal created for the educational film *Electric Waves*, directed by J. Tuma. The take from the film is also on the opening page of this chapter.

Hermína Týrlová probably began in Urania earlier than Karel Dodal. Her name (she signed as Tyrlová at that time) was appearing on the theatre's boards from 1915 and the last surviving information about her in the cast comes from 1927. She was born in Březové Hory on 11 December 1900 to a family of coal miners as the youngest of five. Spending part of her childhood in an orphanage after the death of her parents, she later made it to Prague as a housemaid. Týrlová never liked to ponder over these years, and also the information she provided about her theatre beginnings were rather taciturn. According to some sources, she received her theatre training not only in Urania but also in some touring theatres.[5]

The young couple shared an interest in the world of art and the outsider's efforts to assert themselves. Karel Dodal chose cartoons while Týrlová attempted writing and drawing, but she mainly wanted to help her partner in his filmmaking career. Dodal undoubtedly had the necessary preconditions for working in the field of cinematography. An author of cartoons at that time not only had to be skilled at drawing armed with both artistic and spatial imagination but also an inventive cameraman, lighting engineer and film editor, and it was only to his advantage if he moreover mastered the film laboratory processes. In this sense, Elekta Journal offered a good background to the young adept; initially based in the Prague neighbourhood of Vinohrady, in the studios of the AB company, it was equipped with film studios,

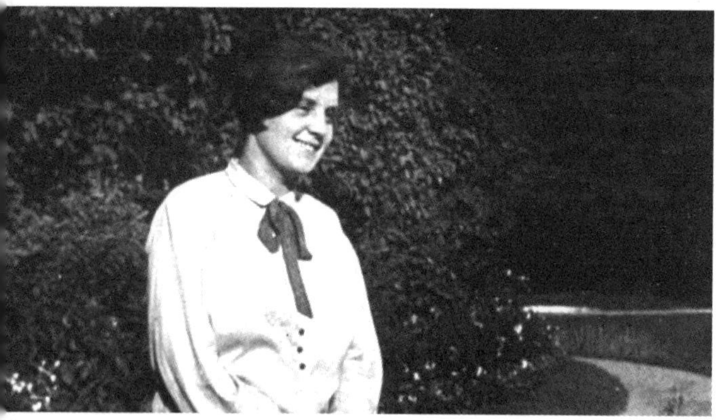

The young wife Hermína Dodalová, who had married Karel Dodal on 11 February 1928, poses in front of Elekta Journal's camera on 15 July 1928.

laboratories and editing rooms. Elekta's technical director was Jindřich Brichta, one of the leading experts in contemporary cinematographic technology, who could answer many of Dodal's questions, possibly except about animation, of which he had no personal experience.

The working conditions in Elekta Journal are, in many aspects, illustrated by the testimony of Jan Stallich, a cameraman who worked there between 1928 and 1930: "There were four of us cameramen there – me, Václav Vích, Karel Kopřiva and Josef Střecha who arrived somewhat later. So there were four of us and then some grips around. Every week, we filmed the common newsreel and, in addition, at least two to four commercials, which more or less helped finance the other matters done by Elekta Journal at that time. I, as a cameraman, worked with various directors (...), there was Dodal and there was Týrlová and all these people, the old party. And to me as a cameraman, these commercials were really important because they were not basically under any control; they were simply to serve their advertising purposes. The films were mostly made in the studio and each of them had forty to sixty metres. I could thus sample various methods of shooting, either contrast or soft ones, simply all kinds of film photography, and, on these commercials, practically every week

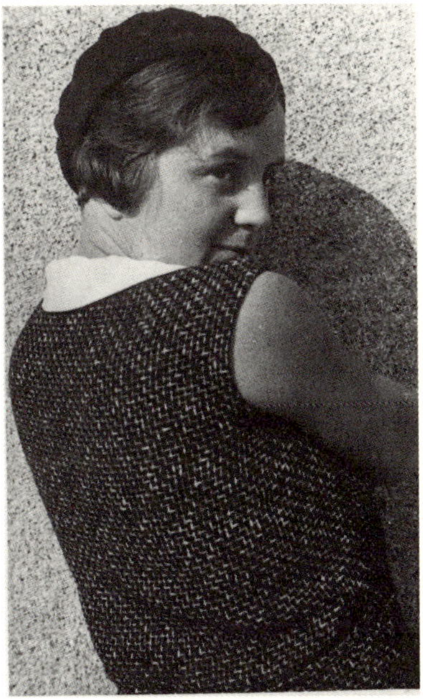

Hermína Týrlová, who chose the artistic pseudonym Tearlová, would write and draw in every spare moment from her early childhood. When she lived with Karel Dodal's parents, his mother Otilie complained that she was not the working kind, and threw all her drawings out after her departure.

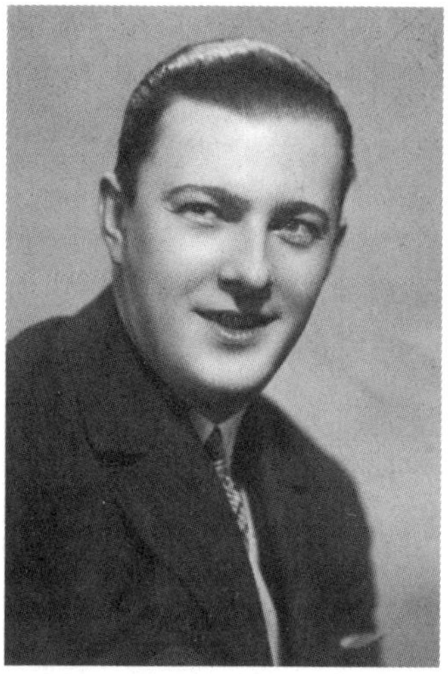

The film producer Karel Pečený, one of the founders of the Elekta Journal company.

I could test various things which would otherwise have been unacceptable."[6]

Like Jan Stallich, Karel Dodal learned trick technology on advertising commissions. As Hermína Týrlová recollected, "It began with drawing a logo or with a slogan for a commercial, say, 'Meinl Coffee – the real ambrosia'. Later came experimenting with cut-out sheets – every kid knows that this or that venture has this or that merchandise and that it is the best."[7]

Týrlová's mention about the cut-out sheets is also worth noting, proving that in this early stage they too employed the technology of cut-out film, which was easier to animate and was less time demanding. They learned to master cartoon technology by studying American cartoon comedies, watching cartoons stage by stage and over and over in a small viewer and exploring how to draw a figure, phase its motion and interlink the individual scenes and motifs. This is also how they gradually created the first copies of the motion of Felix the Cat, the popular character which Karel Dodal then appropriated and used in a commercial series.

Contrary to cut-out film, however, cartoon film required hundreds of drawings for shooting the phases, and in order to allow Dodal to manage the commission deadlines, the role of draughtsman and phasist was taken by his girlfriend. They shared a common household from 1926 and married two years later. Týrlová wrote about this in her memoirs: "I tried to assist him, but I did not know anything about it. There was no other way than to teach me. He would teach me quite patiently but sometimes indeed ran out of patience under the pressure of the workload. I would make mistakes from time to time, and then things would turn bad. It did not help at all that I was his wife. Perhaps, just because I feared his anger so much, I became his reliable colleague over time, a wheel of his work. But when I watched my own drawing in motion, I was overcome with a gonzo feeling of joy and pride and the work began to please me."[8]

When Týrlová later chose her artistic cognomen, she signed – and perhaps not accidentally – as Tearlová, since the tears spilled by the forbearing assistant must have been waters. The history of animated film is also a history of self-sacrificing partners and wives of the directors who not only tended to the heart and home and family finances but were also irreplaceable draughtswomen and phasists; even Ms Lillian Disney was no exception from this at the beginning of her husband's career.

The Czech Film Correspondent (Český filmový zpravodaj) in 1927 informed that Elekta Journal had established "a department working on cartoon trick films. This is an utterly new and yet uncultivated field of Czech film. The department is headed by the painter K. Dodal. The first comedies will be entitled *Ben's Troubles* [Alíkovy trampoty] and *The Adventures of Robinson* [Robinsonova dobrodružství]. Naturally, commercials are also filmed there. Making trick films is remarkably exhausting".[9] Týrlová recalled that the studio's equipment was very simple at that time: "The wooden table on which we drew had a metal frame with two fixed pegs, all inserted into the desk. We would dress the pegs with sheets of paper and these were then laid on a glass surface lit with a bulb from below. The so-called interphases were additionally drawn in between the initial and final phases of motion. A draughtsman thus spent his workday staring into artificial light which lit through the phases of motion the previous and the next drawing, including the one he drew in between. Shooting was even more laborious. We worked with the least sensitive material because black and white always stood out best on the slide. Yet, we thus had to use full lighting, and very bright light does not suit every eye. I never really minded artificial light, but Karel Dodal's sight was more sensitive. His doctor recommended to him that it would be better to give up his profession. But how could he give up all that which he had so strenuously attained and in which he endlessly believed?"[10]

The management of Elekta Journal apparently first viewed Dodal's work as promising. When it had its headed paper printed in 1927, the second place on the list of its production offer was taken by "trick, cartoon film". Other documents, however, seem to suggest that the hopes invested in this production did not come true – maybe because it was soon realized how demanding cartoon production actually was from the point of time and financing, and also because dealings with Dodal, who was very bad at deadlines, were not always easy. This turn in the management's approach is illustrated by the 1928 letter which Karel Pečený addressed to the Czechoslovak Ministry of Foreign Affairs, omitting Dodal from the list of significant filmmakers since he perhaps did not rate a person engaged in tricks and cartoons representative enough.[11] Another reason could be the increasing tension between the artist and Pečený, whose main production priority was the newsreel. The speculation is, to some extent, proved by Irena Dodalová, whose memoirs always mention only the other company owner, František Horký, in connection with Elekta Journal.[12]

Elekta's accounting books, on the contrary, clearly show that Dodal very soon gained a firm position in the enterprise. The oldest surviving information report that his wage during 1926 doubled from 400 to 800 Crowns. His regular monthly income in the next year was already 2,000 Crowns, raised to 2,500 Crowns in 1929. The given amount was occasionally upped by minor remunerations and his pay equalled the best cameramen working for Elekta Journal; in fact, the only person earning more (3,000 Crowns) was its technical director Jindřich Brichta. In comparison, an average white-collar salary at that time was between 800 and 1,300 Crowns and teachers prior to retirement were worth 2,700 to 3,900 Crowns at most, depending on their degree.[13]

Karel Pečený, a graduate from a school of commerce, very carefully kept the accounting books of all his companies. They today also help trace the work of the "painter" Dodal.

Únor 1926

				Kč	h
y	19.	Přenos		31198	38
y	"	p. Vilímek á conto		1000	-
y	"	p. řed. Kosek		1000	-
y	20.	Jóži Vich		400	-
A	"	" Zima		250	-
y	"	" Krejčír + přes oběd		170	-
y	"	" Kysel		20	-
y	X	materiál negativ ✓		385	56
A	"	benzin	✓	99	-
y	"	na elektriku Smolík		10	-
y	"	p. Schorsch za hon. Remed		150	-
y	"	F. Hostý á conto	⊕	200	-
y	22.	los pro firmu		80	-
A	"	pan Anton á conto	X	318	50
A	"	pan Anton á conto	X	7	50
y	"	kopírovací papír	✓	37	50
y	"	slč. Kalmárová za hon.		50	-
y	"	slč. Jenoušková " hon.		50	-
y	"	Vilímek á conto		1000	-
y	"	p. Dodal za hon.		50	-
TR.	"	p. Dodal á conto triku		200	-
y	"	F. Hostý á conto	⊕	200	-
y	X	A+B á conto ✓		300	-
y	"	A-B á conto		184	82
y	"	A-B á conto		40	80
y	"	Favorit za aparáty		230	-
A	"	benzin		66	-
A	"	benzin		82	-
A	"	nástavek	✓	1	20
y	23.	za laskavost slč. Vaškové		68	-
y	"	ing. Reichl lístek loterie		12	-
X	"	OO.F.H. ples		50	
		přenos		37911	26

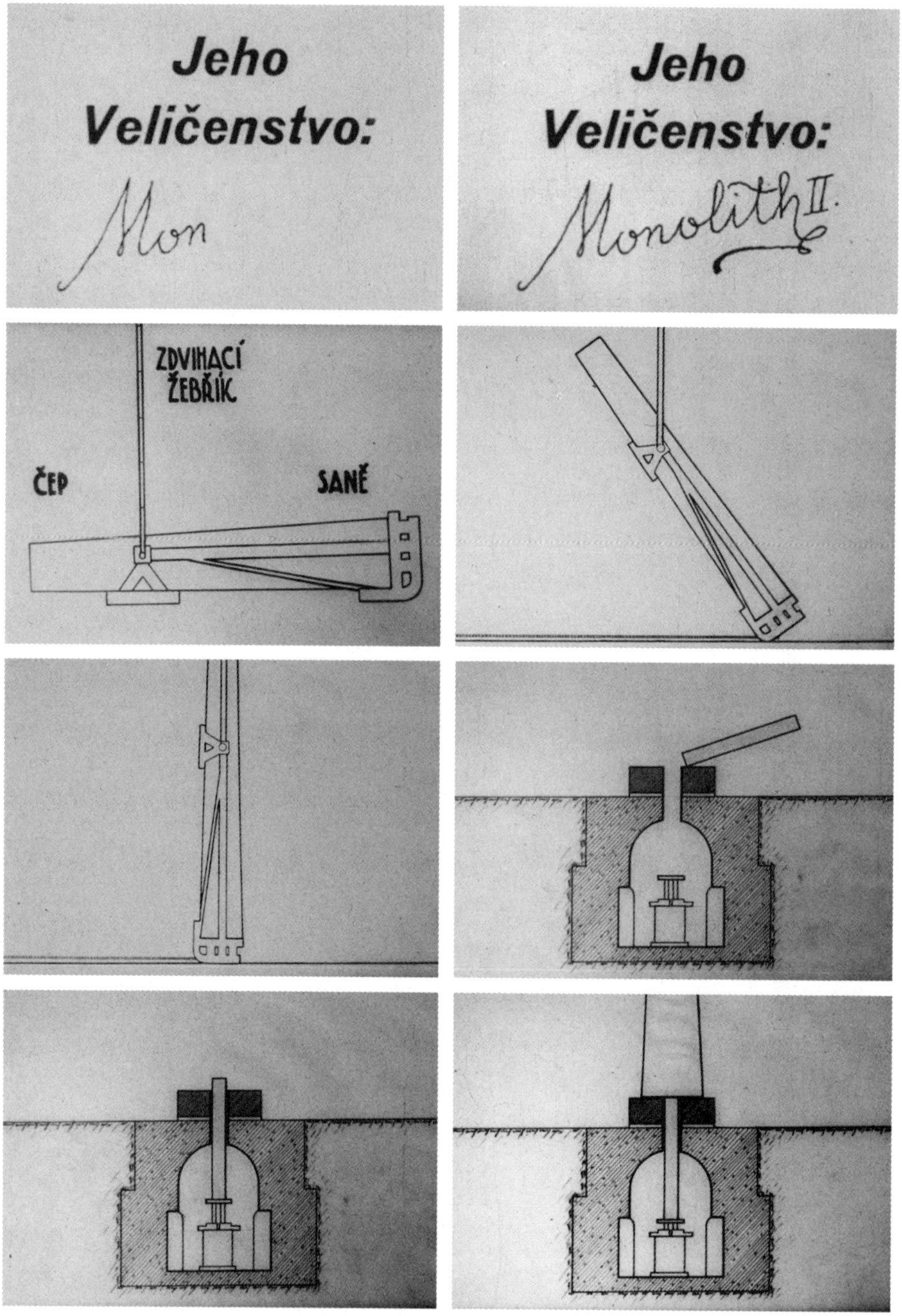
Jeho
Veličenstvo:
Mon
Jeho
Veličenstvo:
Monolith II.
ZDVIHACÍ
ŽEBŘÍK
ČEP
SANĚ

The main reason why Elekta Journal employed Karel Dodal was to have an expert in trick and animated passages in various commissions, whether it was commercials or educational films. The work was mostly anonymous and Dodal's name appeared in the credits only now and then. His collaboration was, for example, recorded in the *Monolith* (Monolit; 1929) by Jindřich Brichta, a film about installing a granite monolith in a courtyard of Prague Castle. Dodal here created the opening animated title as well as an array of static and moving schemes explaining the scheme of the construction. He also made diagrams for the medium-length picture *Demänová* (1928) which documented the krast formations in the Slovak cave of the same name and the work of the speleologists. The latter film, rather demanding from the point of production, then became one of the most representative works of Elekta Journal. Dodal's animated diagrams and schemes were moreover part of the films which described employing electrical discharges, car mechanisms, water drainages, railway development and the like.

Karel Dodal also was one of the filmmakers participating in the costly documentary *Prague in Shining Lights* (Praha v záři světel; 1928). In it, František Horký and the director Svatopluk Innemann departed from foreign models and conceived the film as a big-city symphony. Dodal's trick passages, evoking the rhythm and atmosphere of a metropolis with its glowing cafés, shop windows and neon commercials, undoubtedly contributed to the success of the picture – which is today ranked among the few Czech avant-garde films.

Even more, Elekta Journal made the best of its "painter" in producing feature films. Miroslav J. Krňanský and Ferry Seidl in the comedy *From the Czech Mills* (Z českých mlýnů; 1929) employed Dodal's short animated passages in the scenes from the heavens, and the artist also participated in several tricks there. He moreover had his share in the trick scene with ravens in the above-mentioned *Saint Wenceslas*, which is most probably abbreviated in the surviving version.

Takes from the documentary about placing a granite monolith at Prague Castle. Diagrams drawn by Karel Dodal were part of the film.

However, these minor and mostly anonymous works on commissions brought only little satisfaction to Dodal. Nor was his inventive soul fulfilled by the commercials featuring Felix the Cat because they had to follow the requirements of clients. The authorship films made in close collaboration with Hermína Týrlová, such as *A Water Sprite in Love* (Zamilovaný vodník; 1928), *Bimbo's Unfortunate Adventure* (Bimbovo smutné dobrodružství; 1930) and the now missing *Tommy and the Mermaid* (Tommy a mořská panna; 1930), took many months and were born in between commissions. The next chapter will discuss them in more detail.

The film *Prague in Shining Lights* ranked among the most costly projects realized by Elekta Journal, and Karel Dodal participated in its trick scenes. The picture also contains a montage from Dodal's now missing commercial, *Tea at Five...*

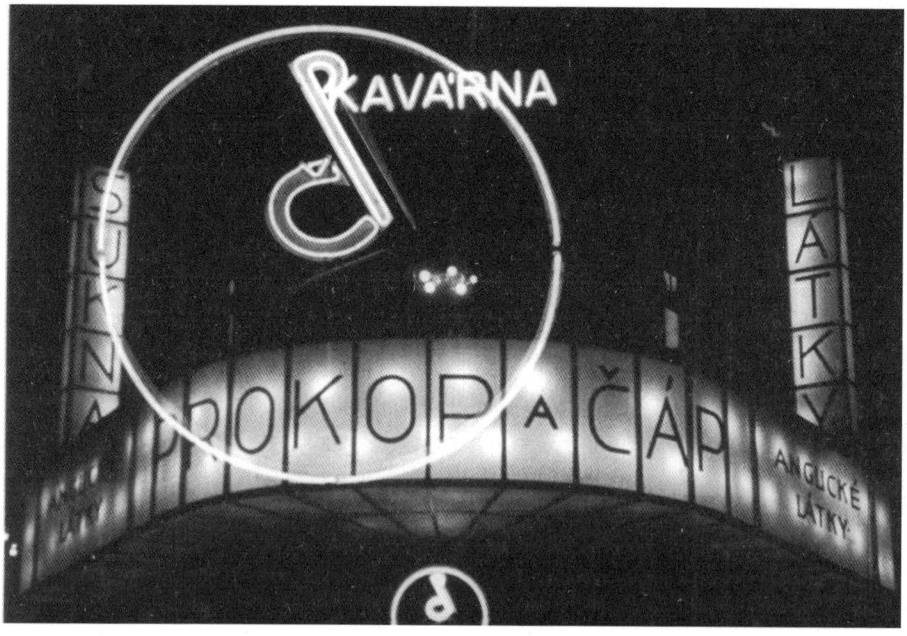

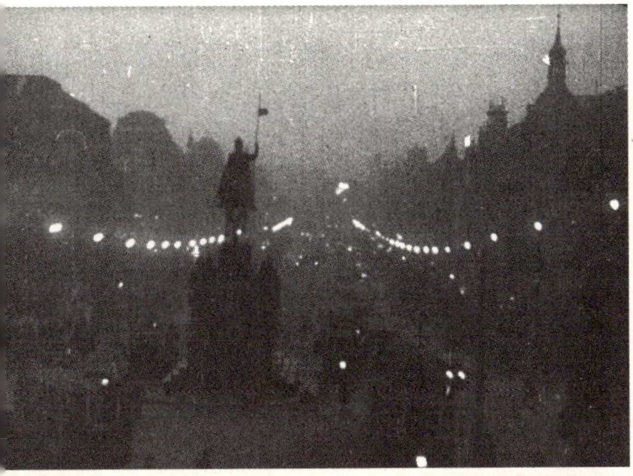

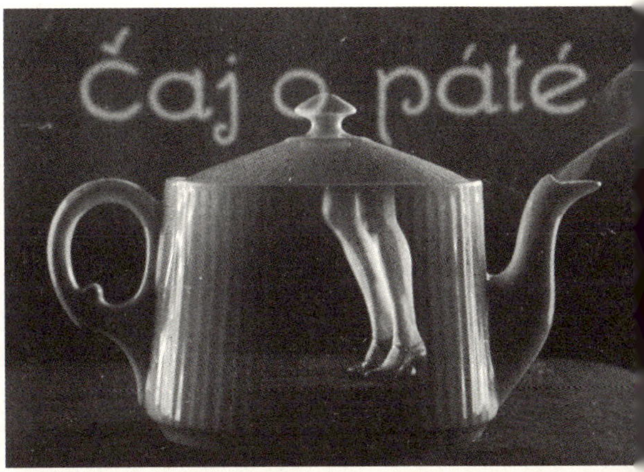
Čaj o páté

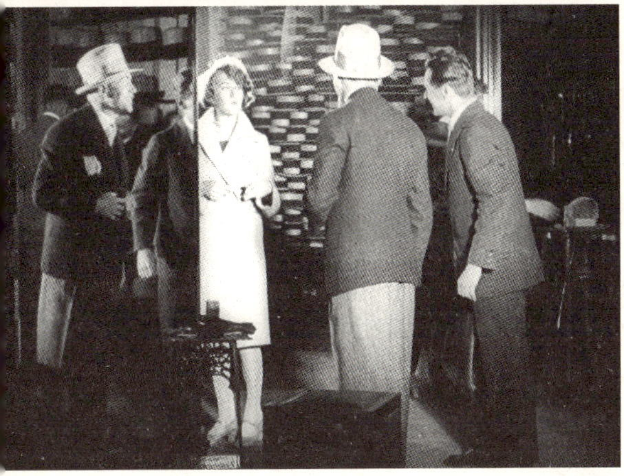

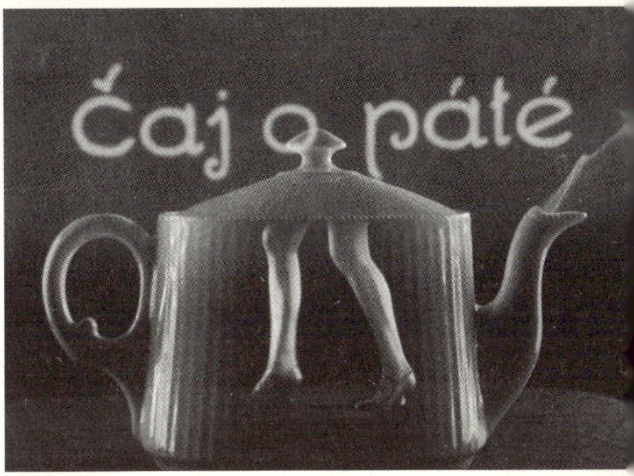
Čaj o páté

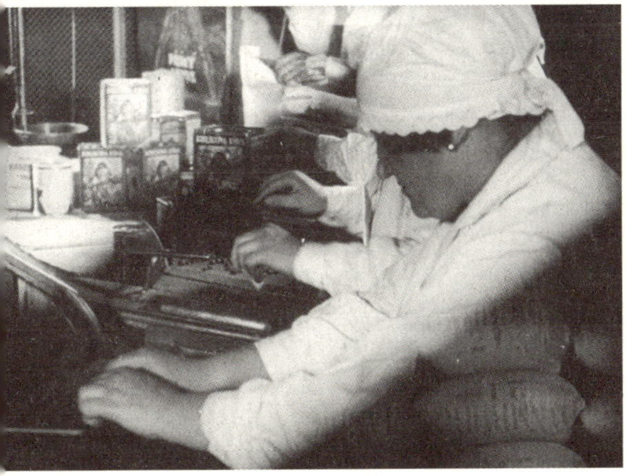

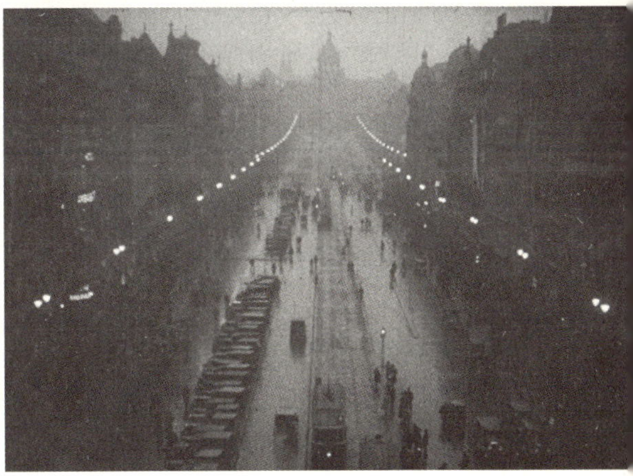

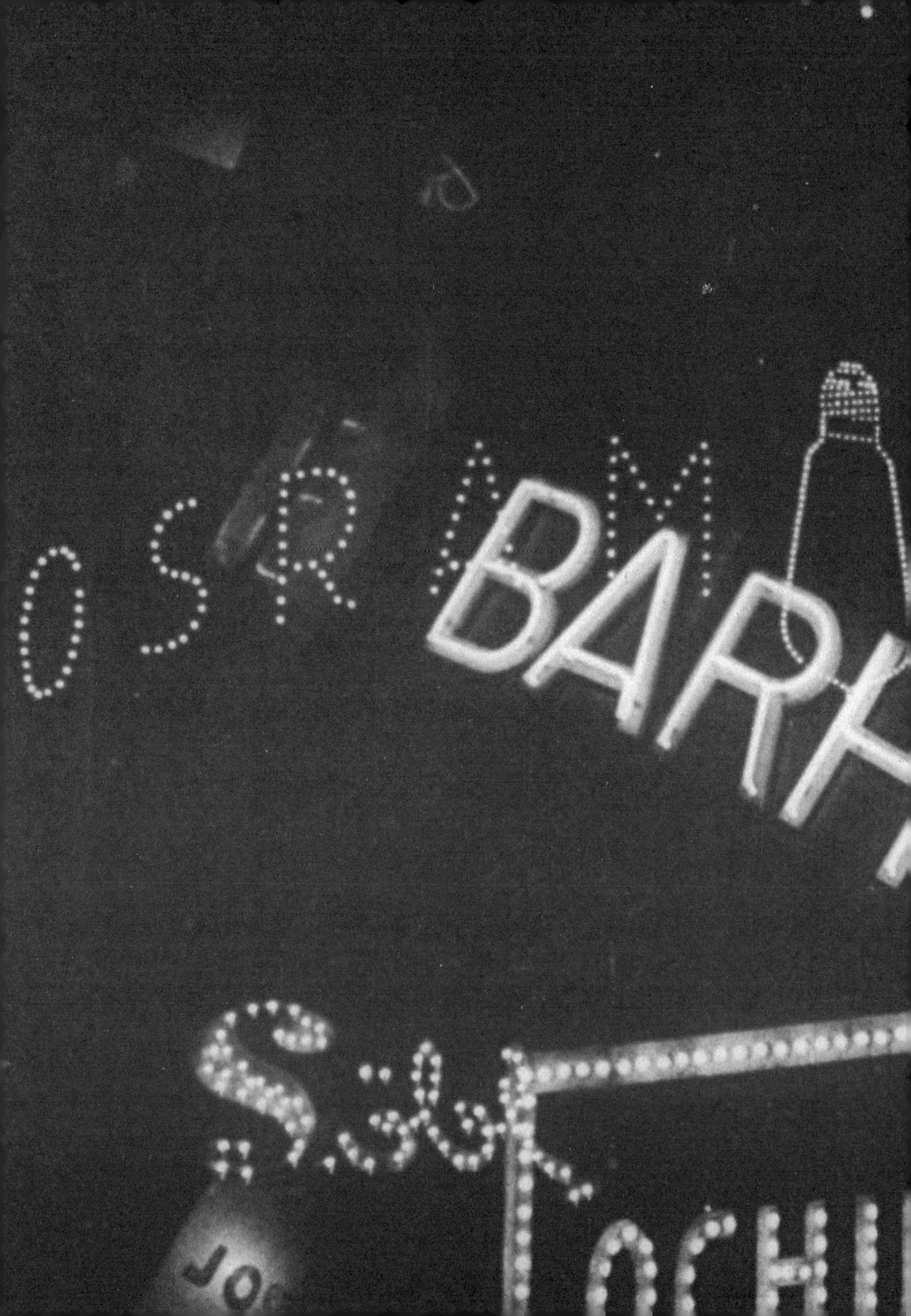

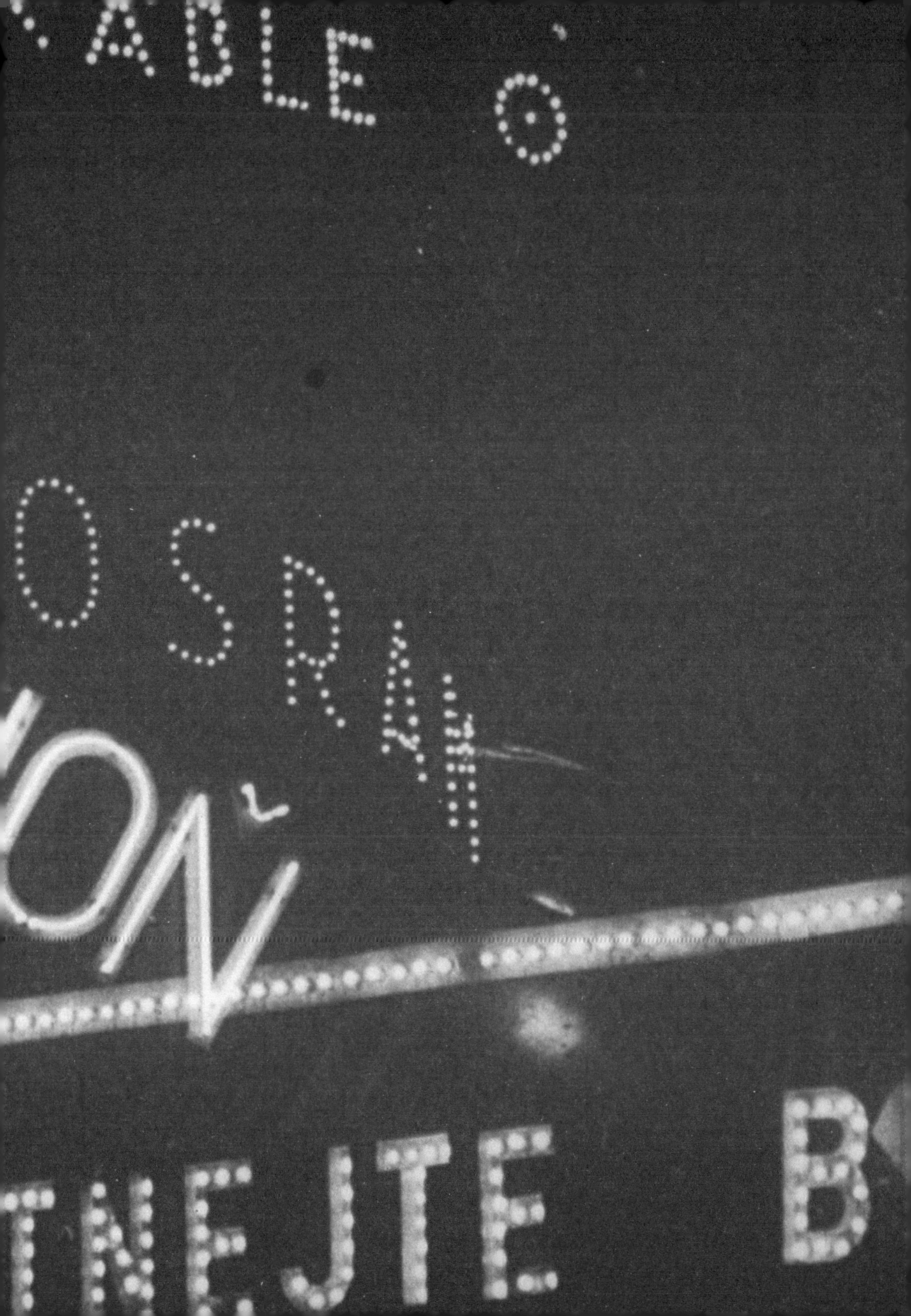

Little is known about Dodal's artistic plans and unrealized films. A notice in the 1929 *Film Correspondent* reads that Dodal and the cameraman Karel Kopřiva worked on a cycle entitled *Seasons* (Roční období), but the project apparently failed. Hermína Týrlová testified that "the working sessions and debates usually closed with Karel Dodal's frustration and his unfulfilled plans. He felt no more space for refining his talent and the acquired experience in Elekta Journal. He wished to make drawn supplements instead of the tiresome commercials that totally killed him. Elekta Journal had no understanding of this. Karel Anton had left the company and there was no one else left to support the development of cartoon film".[14]

Dodal eventually quit Elekta Journal in August 1929 and, only a month later, his position was taken by his wife.[15] The Elekta accounting daily journals testify that Týrlová-Dodalová started at 900 Crowns less than her husband, but the monthly wage totalling 1,600 Crowns was still pretty high for a woman at that time. Her responsibility was to finish several films and to work on other tasks, mainly linked with the newsreels.

Karel Dodal left Elekta Journal upon encountering some benefactor who promised to help him establish his own studio. Dodal invested in facilitating the drawing room for animated film, which included three drawing tables, colours, brushes, pencils, pens, papers, celluloid foils, trick table and trick camera, and acquired lighting equipment and film material. But the donor let him down and the entire plan resulted in a massive financial loss. His erstwhile wife later testified that her partner "almost had a nervous breakdown and it took him no less than a year to recover".[16]

The couple then lived on Týrlová's income from Elekta Journal. It, however, ran into crisis after the early 1930s' financial fiasco of the *Saint Wenceslas* epic. Many employees, Týrlová among them, were laid off and the company subsequently focused on publishing its newsreel. And although it kept producing short and commercial pictures, it never returned to cartoons.

The family's financial situation turned very tight when Hermína Týrlová lost her job in Elekta Journal. She also reported that Dodal's sight deteriorated at that time and the therapy drained a large part of their cash because they only later found out that the artist had no health or social insurance. They saw the only way out in launching a private film business. Dodal's instability

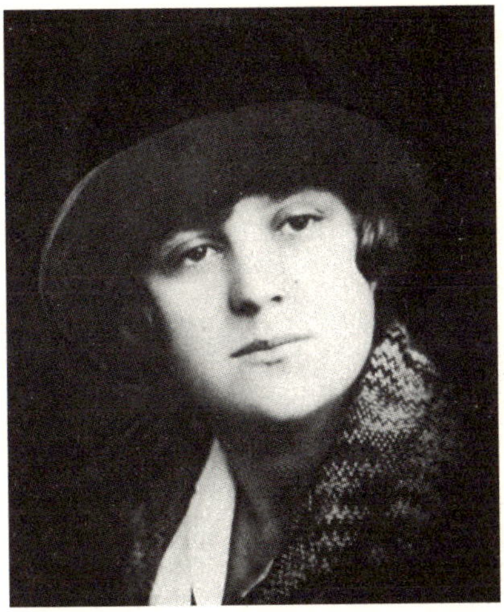

Hermína Týrlová
in the 1920s.

made Týrlová assume the initiative in finding a job, and she finally managed to acquire a commission from the Prague Real-Estate Institute to make a scientific film on amelioration. It turned out to be the first Czech full-length scientific film which, unfortunately, did not survive.

The problems of subsistence resulted in a marital crisis. As Týrlová wrote, "The failure of our own enterprise not only foreshadowed the end of my collaboration with Karel Dodal, but we moreover lost each other in the vicious circle of troubles. We broke up".[17]

This was a closure to one of the most significant chapters in the personal and creative lives of Karel Dodal and Hermína Týrlová. And the era of Czech silent cartoon was also coming to an end.

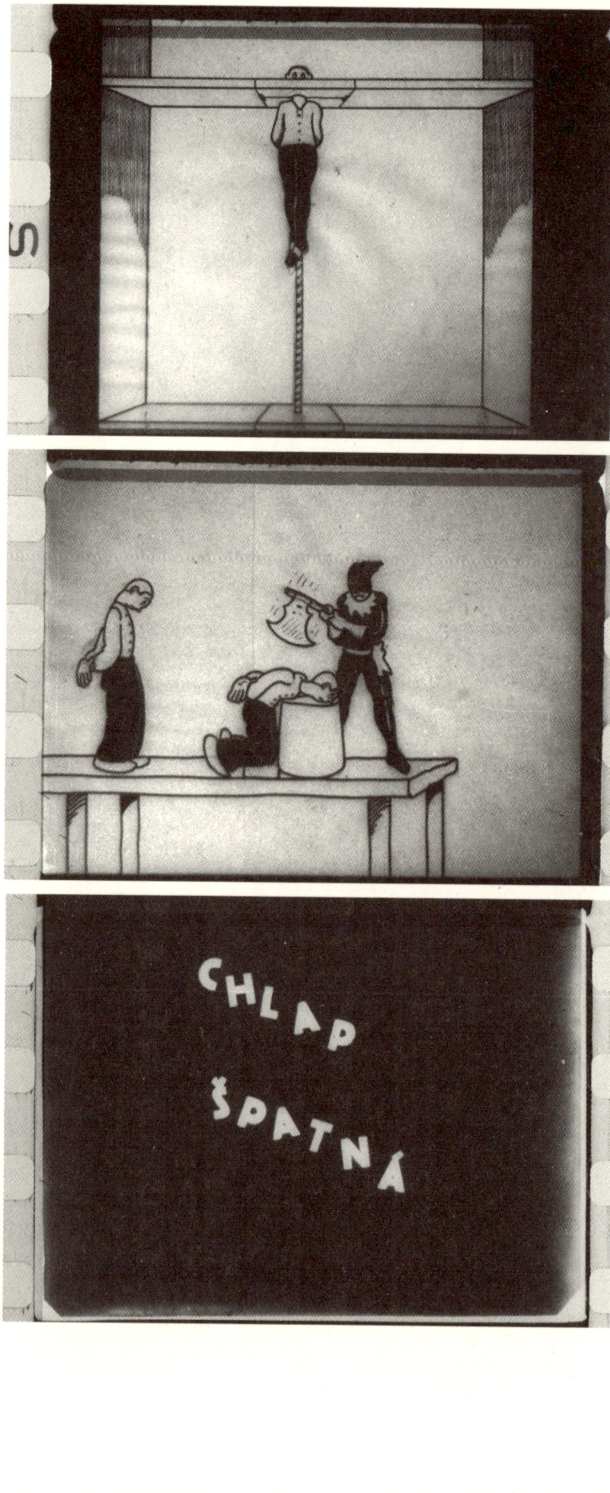

Takes from the film
From the Czech Mills.

1 Elekta Journal was led by K. Pečený, a graduate from an academy of commerce, who was responsible for the company's accounting and whose priority was news film. His partner was F. Horký, a technician who had not completed his studies but boasted literary and film ambitions and worked in Elekta Journal as its dramatic adviser and head of production; the associates in the initial stage were K. Anton, versant in theatre and film direction, the future producer of commercials J. Vilímek and the film entrepreneur O. Kosek, who financially supported Elekta in its beginnings. The position of the technical manager was held for several years by the experienced cameraman and expert in scientific cinematography, J. Brichta. Elekta Journal in the late 1920s also employed the future film historian K. Smrž as screenwriter, dramatic adviser and newsreel editor, and the future filmmaker, film theoretician and pedagogue J. Kučera launched his career in the company during his studies. The enterprise was founded as Ltd. under the umbrella of the AB company, but Pečený received his trade licence in 1927 and Elekta was recorded in the commercial register in 1928.

2 The titles which enjoyed the most favourable reception from both the public and the press were *The May Fairy Tale* (Pohádka máje; K. Anton, 1926), *Father Kondelík and the Bridegroom Vejvara I.* (Otec Kondelík a ženich Vejvara I.; K. Anton, 1926), *Ms Cathy from the Egg Market* (Paní Katynka z Vaječného trhu; V. Kubásek, 1927) and *From the Czech Mills* (Z českých mlýnů; S. Innemann and F. Seidl, 1929). A Czech-French co-production resulted in the now missing film *The Big City Jungle* (Džungle velkoměsta; L. Marten and M. Viel, 1929).

3 For more on this, see Klimeš, I. – Rak, J., "Idea národního historického filmu v české meziválečné společnosti" (The Idea of National Historical Film in Czech Inter-War Society), *Iluminace* (Illumination) 1989, No. 2, pp. 32–33.

4 Poster for the performance of *The Court Jester of George of Podiebrad*. The National Museum. fund Urania, No. 92.

5 Havelka, J., *Kdo byl kdo v československém filmu před rokem 1945* (Who Was Who in Czechoslovak Film before 1945). Praha: The Czechoslovak Film Institute, 1979, p. 240 (unpublished typed manuscript); the theatre beginnings are also mentioned in the monograph Benešová, M., *Hermína Týrlová*. Praha: The Czechoslovak Film Institute, 1982, p. 17.

6 J. Stallich in a 1968 interview with Z. Štábla, M. Frída and J. Brož. The National Film Archive, Collection of Sound Documents, No. 3.

7 Benešová, M., op. cit., p. 18.

8 Ibid, pp. 19–20.

9 "Čs. výroba trikfilmů" (Czechoslovak Trick Film Production). *Český filmový zpravodaj*, 1927, No. 31, p. 4; on Dodal's work on the cartoon *The Adventures of Robinson*; see also the article

"Československý film" (Czechoslovak Film), *Český filmový svět* (Czech Film World) 1927, No. 11, p. 6.

10 See Note 7, p. 20.

11 In the letter, K. Pečený listed J. Brichta, S. Innemann, J. S. Kolár, L. Marten, K. Kopřiva, V. Vích, M. Jonák and J. Blažek. See Dopis Karla Pečeného ministerstvu zahraničních věcí z 9. června 1928 (Letter of Karel Pečený to the Ministry of Foreign Affairs of 9 June 1928). The Archives of the Ministry of Foreign Affairs, fund III, section 1918–1939, box 405, Ref. No. 81277.

12 Dodalová, I., *Karel Dodal & I.R.E. FILM Praha. Datos o zrození kresleného filmu* (... Data about the Birth of Cartoon Film). The National Film Archive, Personal Fund of Irena Dodalová.

13 Accounting books 1926. The National Film Archive, fund Aktualita k.s., akt. No. 30.

14 Týrlová, H., *Klubíčko vzpomínek* (My Small Ball of Memories), p. 6. This typed manuscript is an unedited version of the director's memoirs intended for the book *Hermína Týrlová* by M. Benešová (see Note 5) and it contains several intimate statements which Benešová left out from the final, printed publication. The author of this book is grateful to J. Novotný from Zlín for providing the typescript.

15 As already suggested by the cameraman Stallich, she had frequented the studio much earlier. This is also proved by a film shot probably taken by Dodal on 15 July 1928 which Hermína Týrlová passed onto a student of the Film and TV School of the Academy of Performing Arts in Prague, H. Pinkavová, for her graduate work *Já tomu říkám nedrcat se o nebesa* (I Call It Don't Jog the Heavens; 1978). Years later, Týrlová said about the take – where she strikes a pose with a bunch of roses in a park – that Dodal insisted on her to "always be a lady" in the predominantly male studio as the right way to earn appropriate respect.

16 See Note 14.

17 Benešová, M., op. cit., p. 21.

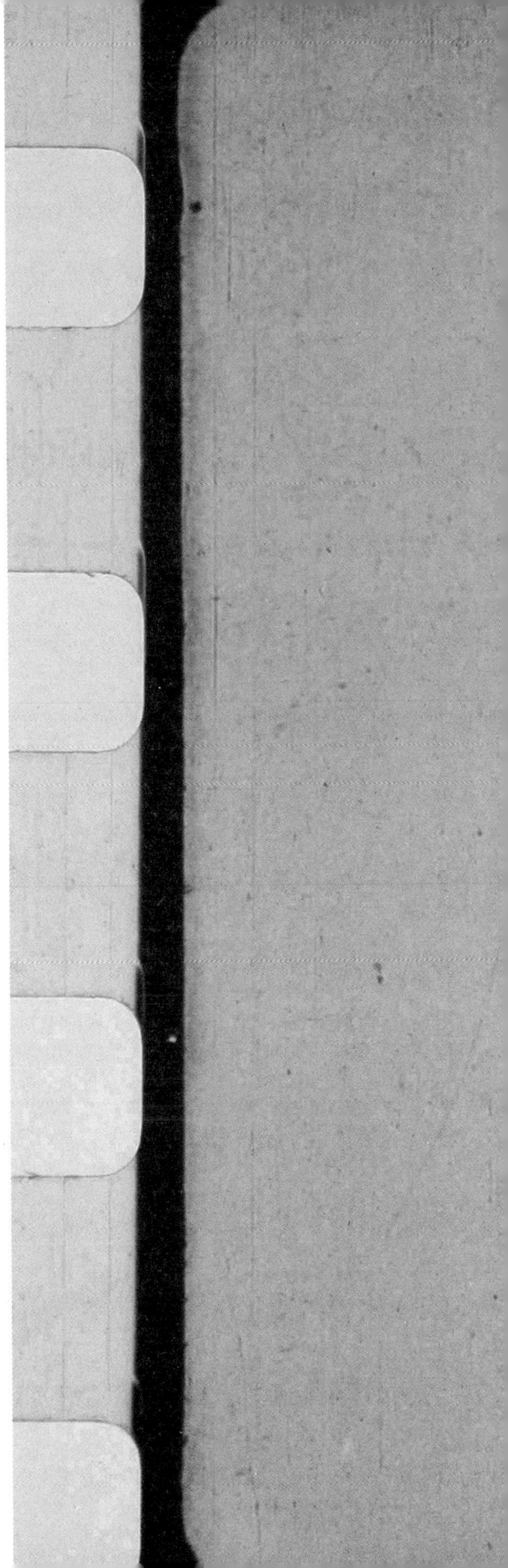

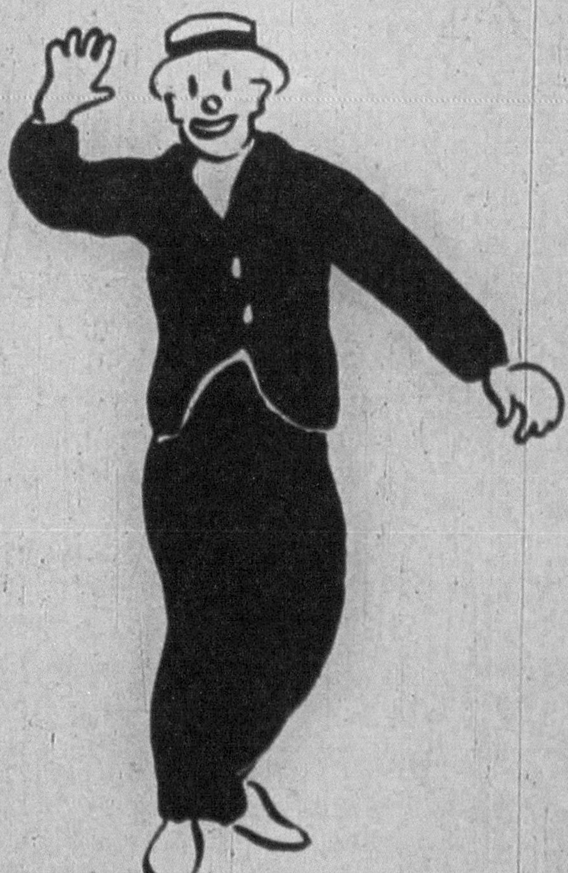

Felix, Bimbo and an Underwater Romance / The First Films by the Dodals

There is continuing uncertainty about Karel Dodal's real debut in cartoons, but one of the choices that might have been his first work in this genre was the 1925 commercial *See How Two Boys and a Dog Fool around These Days!* (Vizte vše, co tropí dnes kluci dva a jeden pes). The film opened in the same way as dozens of contemporary cartoons – a painter's hand appeared out of the blue, drawing two little boys, a tripe sausage and a dog named Ben and thus providing a basis for a conflict situation in the form of a crazy pursuit. The hungry boys were finally fed by a cook, which was followed by the commercial slogan "Good money-savers cook with Sana margarine". The film closed with a kinetic kaleidoscopic pattern with the emerging logo "Sana – Die Siegerin". The drawings of the "actors", remotely resembling the hand of the French animator Robert Collard, testified to a certain struggle in expressing the individual characters, but the figure and the animation of the dog were already convincing. It is interesting that the Propa company was credited as the producer, but there was no such firm at that time. We cannot verify any information here because the censorship sheet which should provide the real producer's name is missing and the original version of the film did not

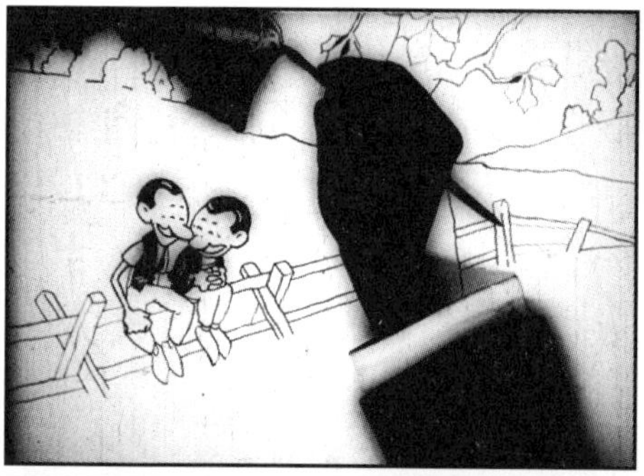

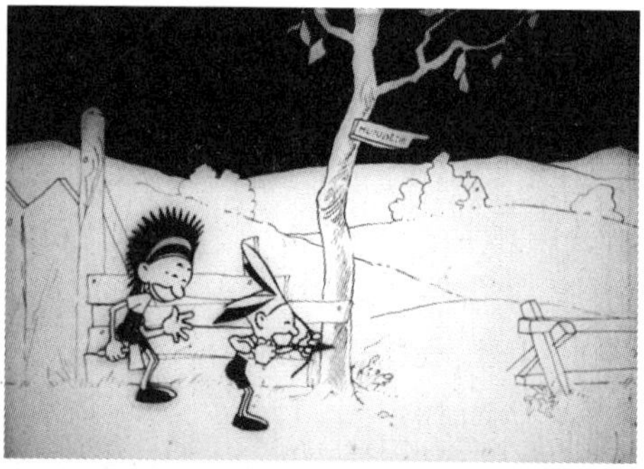

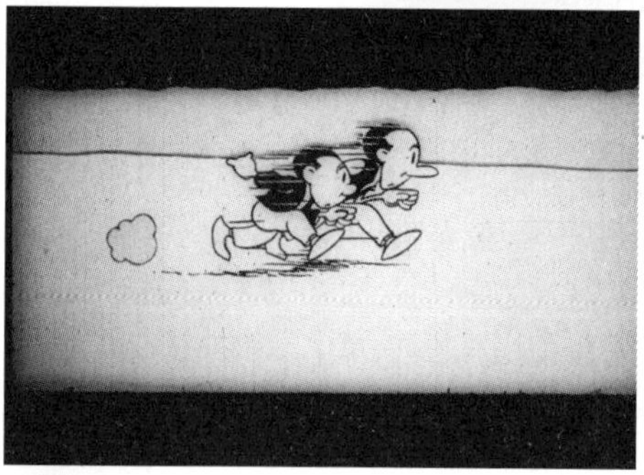

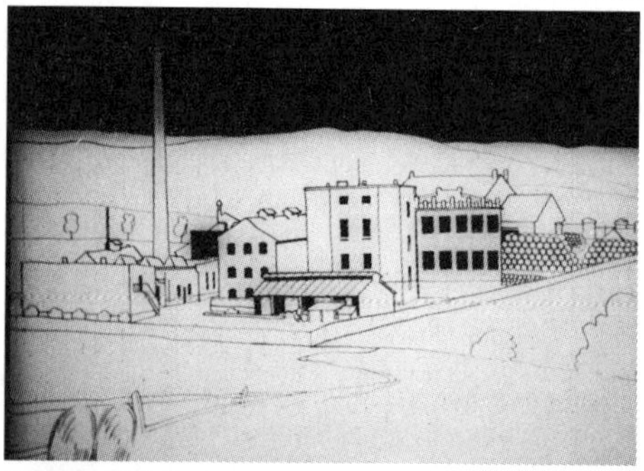

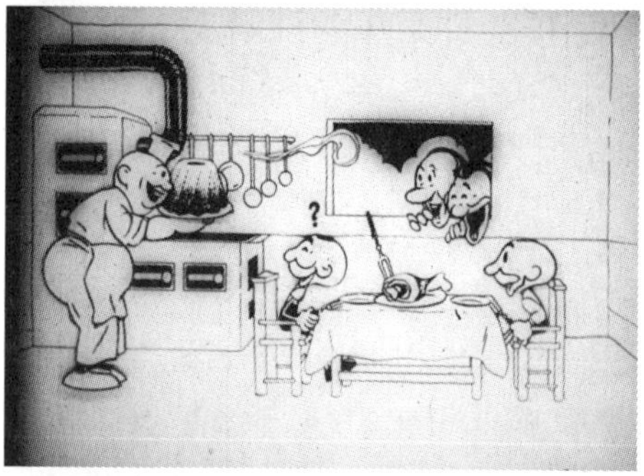

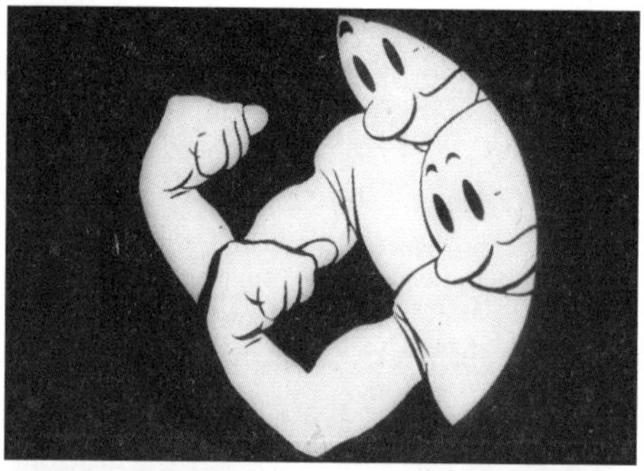

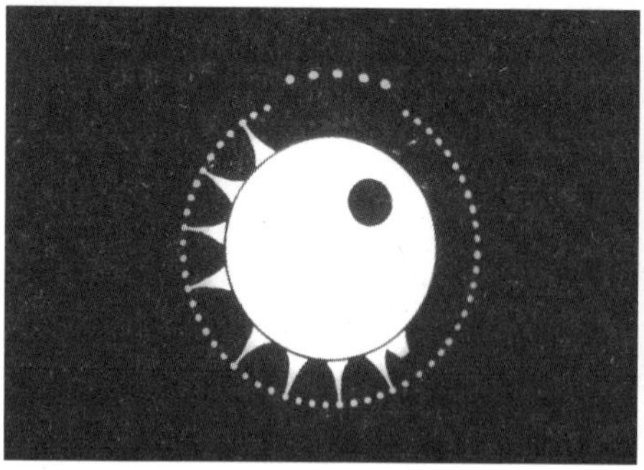

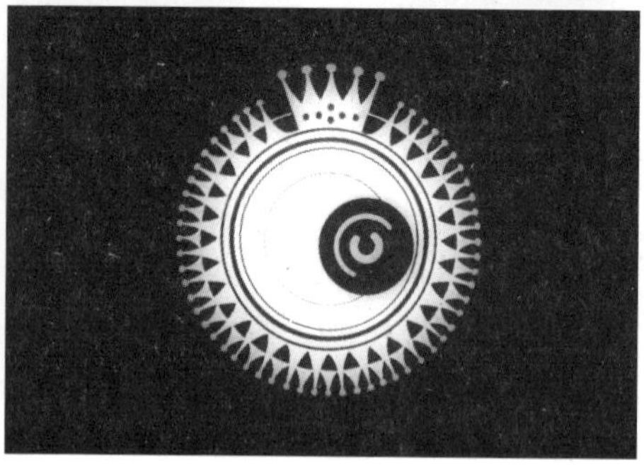

survive either. It is only known from its new version from 1931 when it was reintroduced to cinemas by Josef Vilímek, the owner of the Propa successor, Propaga. This circumstance makes us assume that it was Vilímek who helped Karel Dodal arrange the cartoon's production in the mid-1920s, i.e. before they both started at Elekta Journal.

Dodal's authorship is indirectly proved by an August report from *The Czech Film Correspondent* (Český filmový zpravodaj), informing readers about the planned cartoon comedy featuring Ben the dog and verses by Dodal's partner at that time, Hermína Týrlová. Her poem about Ben, entitled *Home* (Domov), also dates to the mid-1920s.[1] We eventually did not list the film in Dodal's filmography due to the absence of other sources.

We are, on the other hand, certain that Karel Dodal first introduced himself to the film public in 1927 when Elekta Journal presented his commercials made for the Savings Bank – *Felix the Cat Receives a Lesson* (Poučení Kocoura Felixe), *The New Adventures of Felix the Cat* (Nové dobrodružství Kocoura

Takes from the film *See How Two Boys and a Dog Fool around These Days!*, which are often attributed to Karel Dodal.

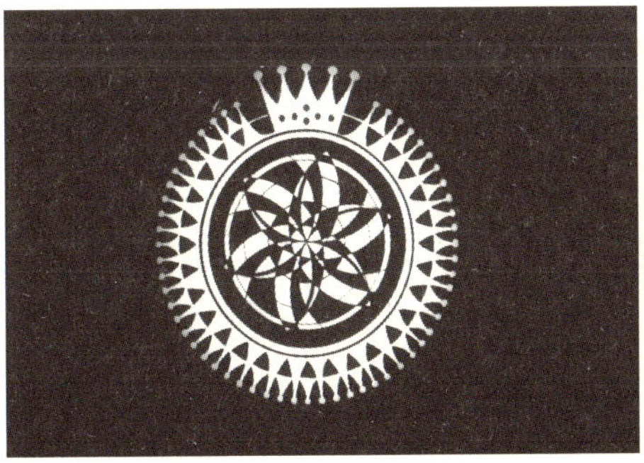

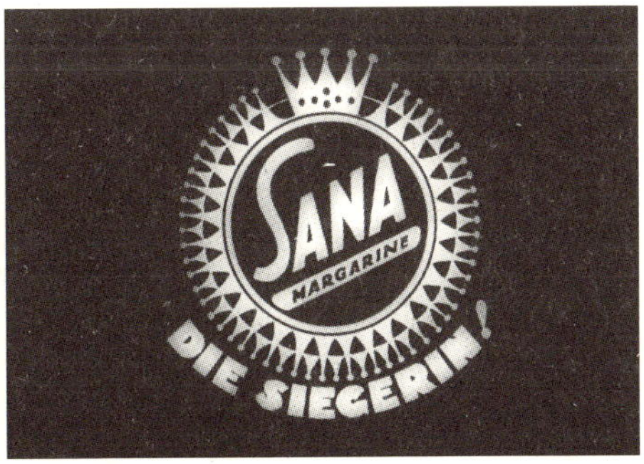

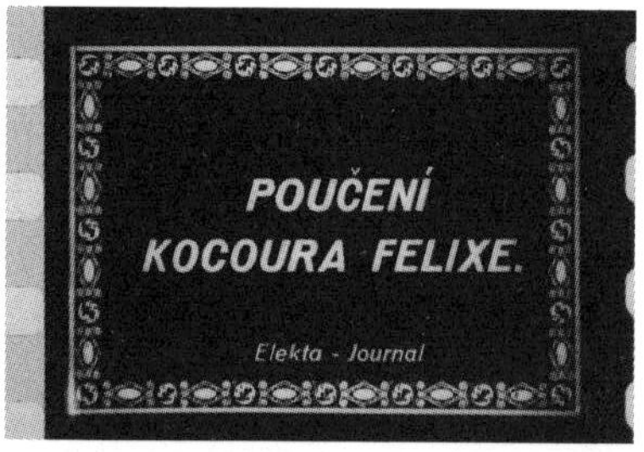

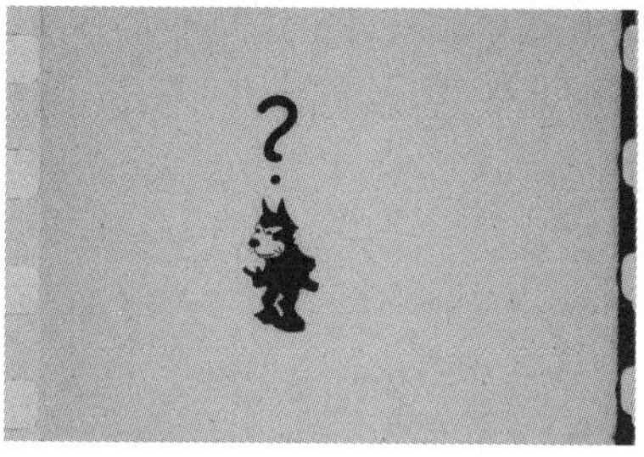

Felixe) and *Felix the Cat Has an Accident* (Nehoda Kocoura Felixe). Although these films have no opening credits, their authorship is clear from the above-mentioned article published in *The Czech Film Correspondent*.[2] The commercials illustrate how Dodal learned to embrace the style of American cartoon comedies. The first one, *Felix the Cat Receives a Lesson*, is simple to the point of naiveté. The cat paces impatiently back and forth in the empty space of the screen and seems to be troubled by something – until there finally appears the sign "Work and save!". He then produces some coins from his fur, depositing them in a nearby moneybox,

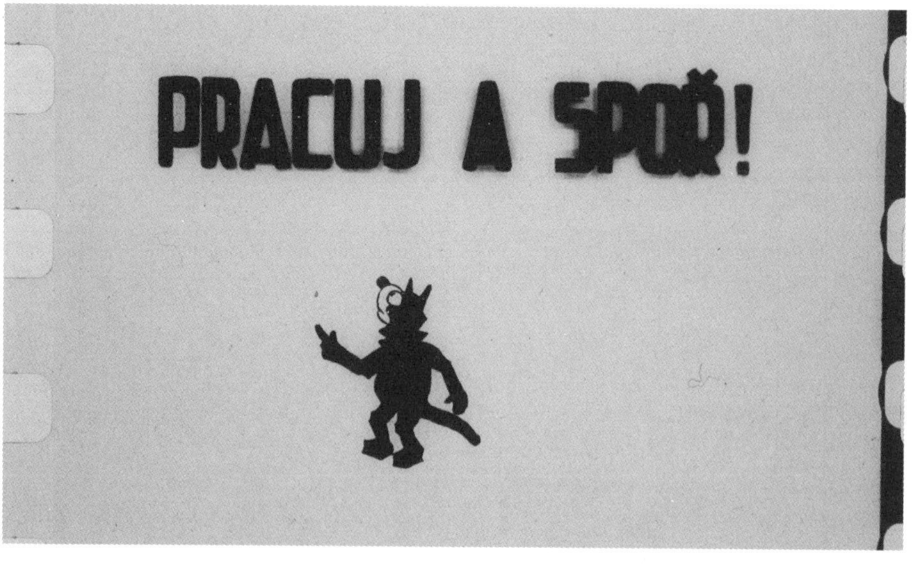

and the film closes with the slogan "Keep safe and best deposit your savings". The picture also features the characteristic question marks borrowed from the original by Pat Sullivan. The story of the next commercial, *The New Adventures of Felix the Cat*, became more intricate and narrative: it again opens with the scene of the strenuously contemplating Felix, but the background is occupied by a beehive. A swarm then flies out of the hive and the bees compose an inscription "Work and Save!". Felix immediately sets off to the outline of a city and runs to the building of the Savings Bank with his passbook. The following subtitles read

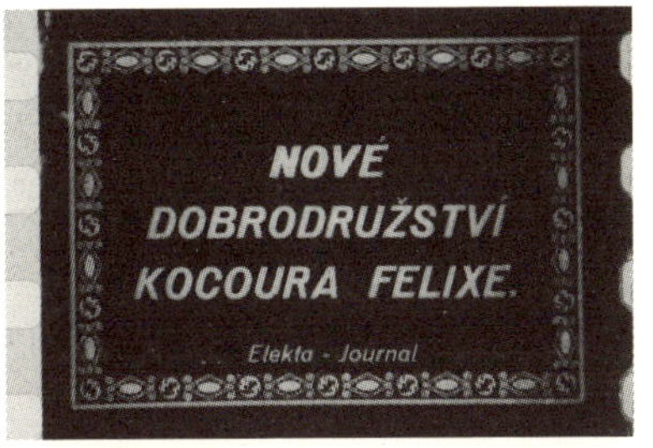

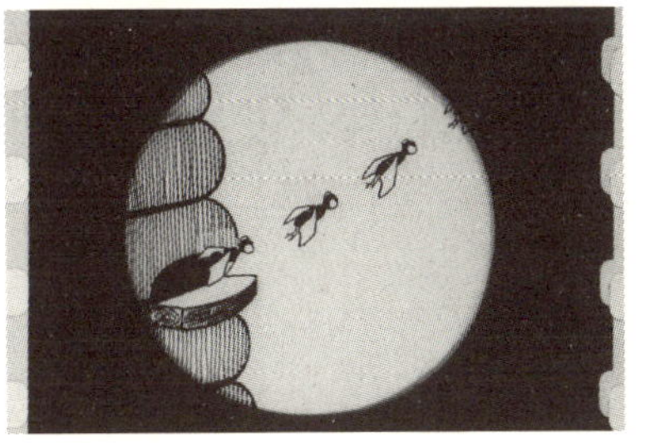

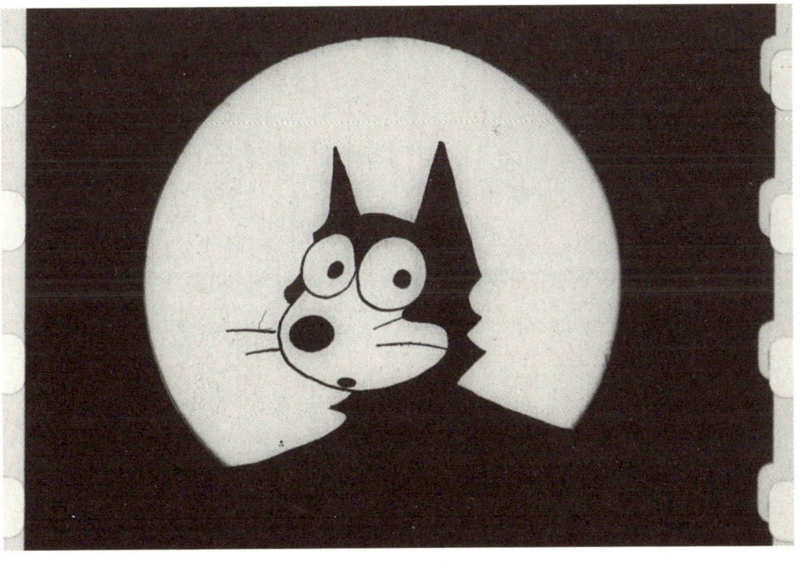

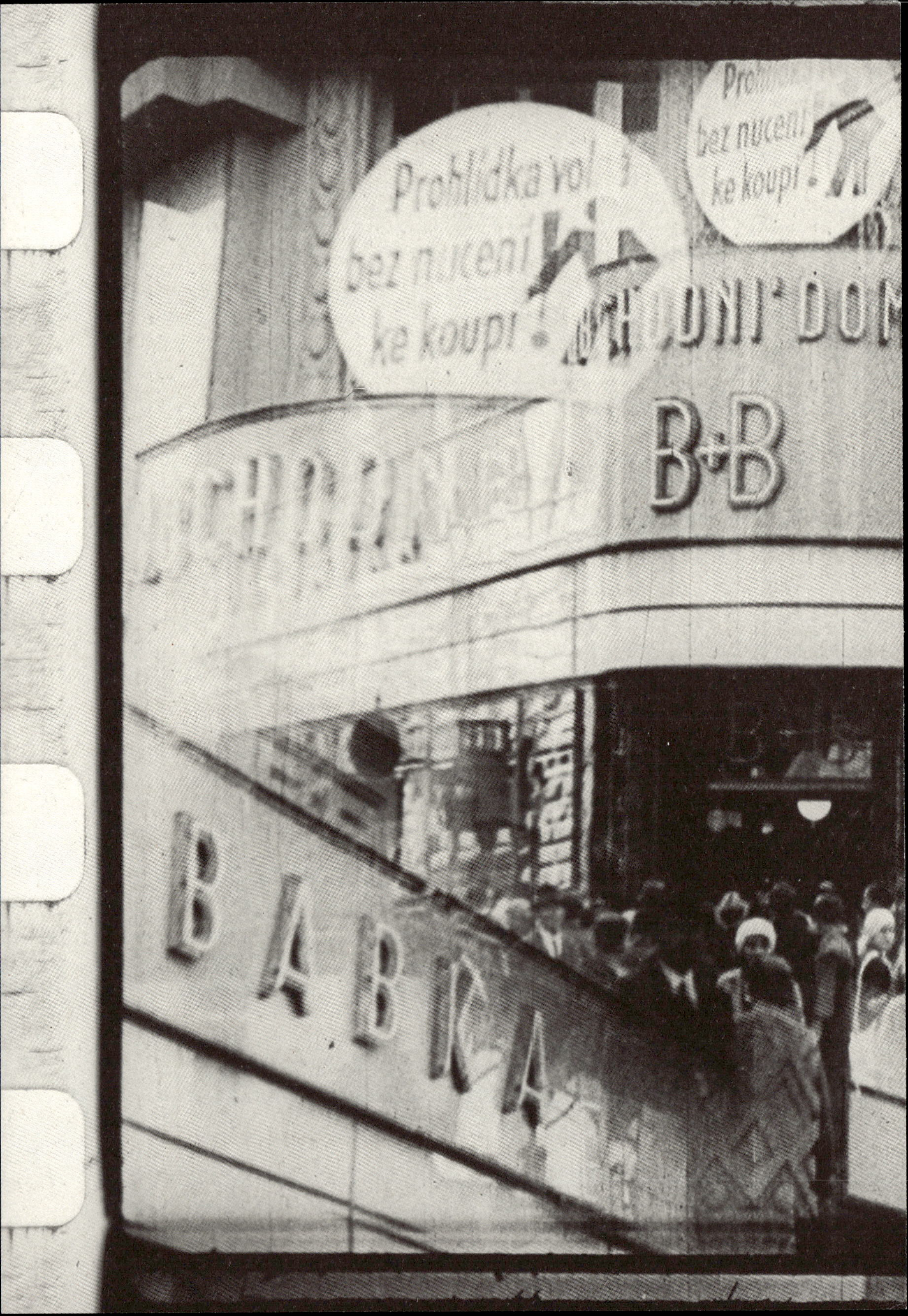
Prohlídka vol
bez nucení
ke koupi!
Prohlídka
bez nucení
ke koupi!
DNÍ DOM
B+B
BABKA

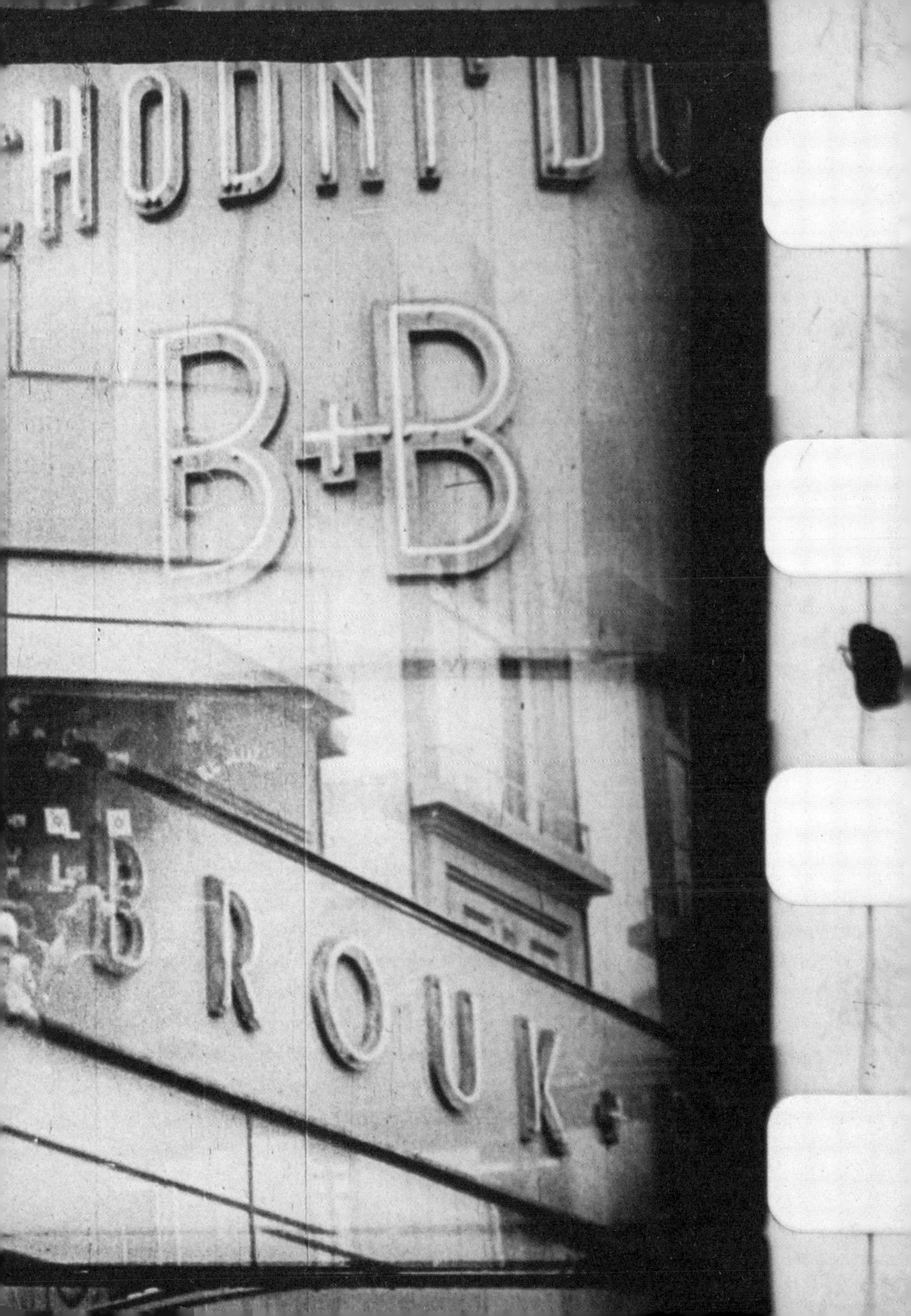
B+B
BROUK

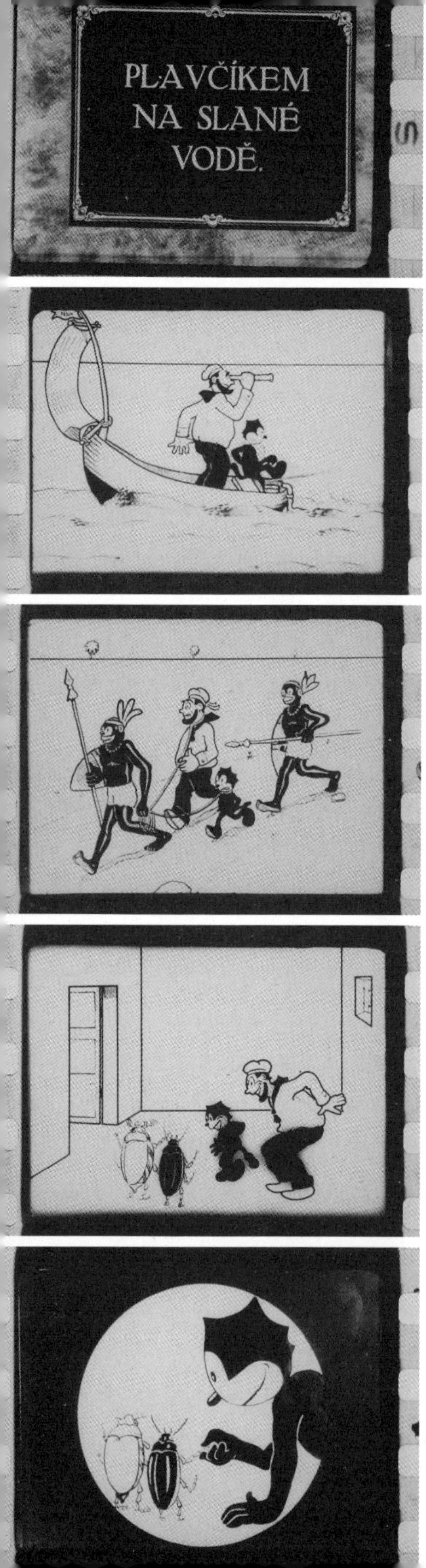

"Good that the bees reminded me..." and end with the appeal "Deposit your savings in the Savings Bank!". The third film from 1927, *Felix the Cat Has an Accident*, did not survive. During the next two years, Elekta Journal produced the commercials *What Felix the Cat Does Every Afternoon* (Co dělá Kocour Felix každé odpoledne; 1928), *Felix the Cat is Farming* (Kocour Felix hospodářem; 1928) and *How Felix the Cat Supported the Ostrava Region* (Jak Kocour Felix obohatil Ostravsko; 1929) which have not been found yet. We can also include the title *A Cabin Boy on Salty Water* (Plavčíkem na slané vodě; 1929) in this series due to the presence of the Felix character. It was a commercial promoting the Czech Brouk and Babka chain department store, although it is not a mere spot but a combined cartoon comedy which, from approximately two thirds in, is concerned with the advertising message. A documentary postscript attached to the end of the cartoon probably upon the client's demand demonstrates the hustle in front of the Brouk and Babka branches in Prague, Moravian Ostrava, České Budějovice and Plzeň whose cogency was to be underlined by multiple, albeit not too impressive, exposures. The filmmakers apparently wanted to meet the wishes of the commissioner even at the cost of a somewhat simpleminded plot:

Felix the Cat and a captain are shipwrecked on an island and the two survivors are saved from a cannibalistic tribe by little beetles(!) because they give the natives everything their crave, i.e. the wide assortment from their department stores.[3] Hermína Týrlová later recalled the business negotiations with the customer – who envisaged the commercial as a scene when his complete assortment would march from his store to the street – and noted that "it was

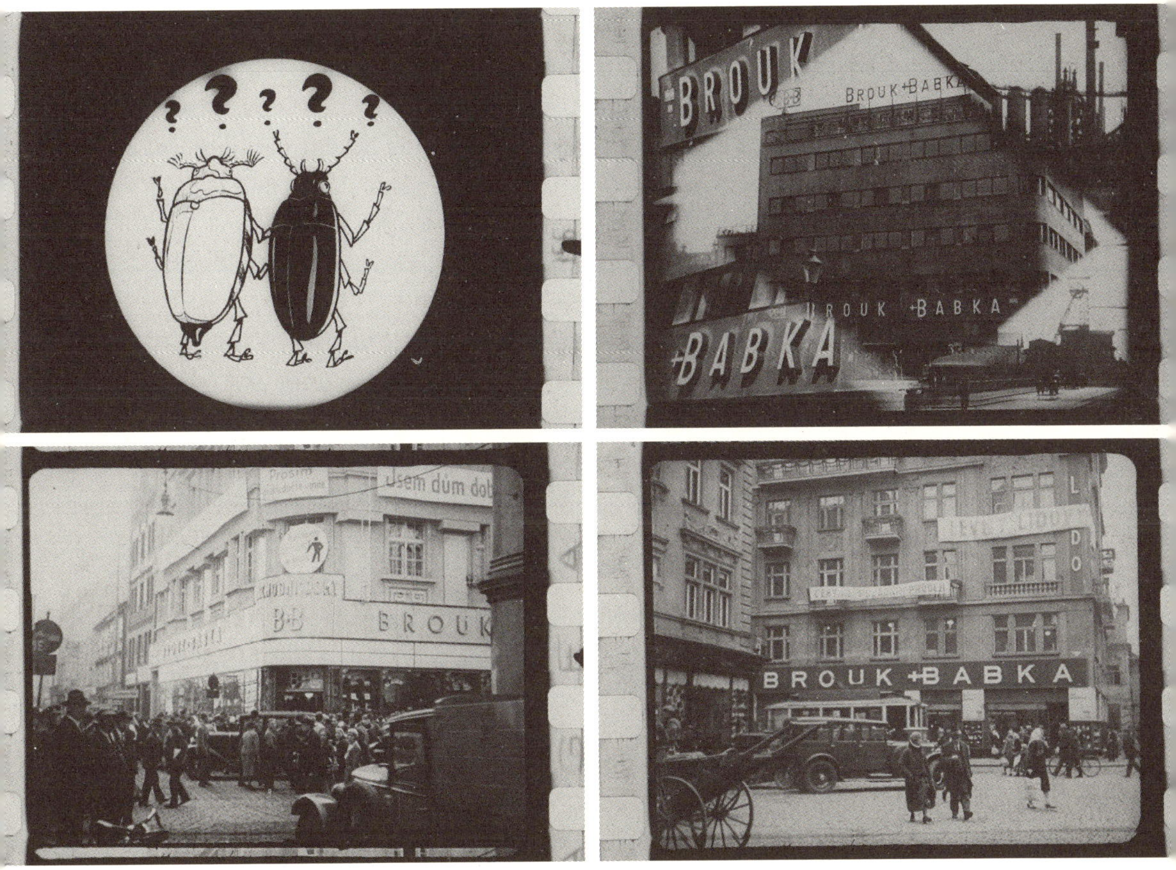

not even especially funny, yet tremendously laborious for those who would draw it and shoot it frame by frame on the reel".[4]

However, the mere fact that the film was a cartoon sufficed to attract contemporary attention. As Týrlová observed, "it was just enough to set a line or an ink splotch in motion – and the viewers were surprised and not at all appalled when the mysterious lines composed a logo of the recommended product".[5] But the Elekta Journal commercials featuring Felix the Cat came to offer something more: a popular hero running into many problems and eventually becoming the promoter of an advertising message. We can only regret that this first Czech commercial series did not survive complete.

The main ambition of Karel Dodal and his wife however was, in contemporary terminology, the "drawn supplements": that is, cartoon comedies. But since the given genre was not part of the Elekta Journal production plan, the Dodals could merely focus on their free work between commissions.[6] Their two films, which probably originated between 1927 and 1929, were offered for distribution only when they were about to leave the studio. The pictures *Bimbo's Unfortunate Adventure* (Bimbovo smutné dobrodružství) and *Tommy and the Mermaid* (Tommy a mořská panna) were introduced by Elekta Journal in 1930 while the third film, *A Water Sprite in Love* (Zamilovaný vodník), remained unfinished and never made it to the cinemas.

Bimbo's Unfortunate Adventure was the first cartoon "authored" by Karel Dodal. Fusing feature and animated film, it offered a local variant of the well-known and popular American series *Out of the Inkwell*, where an artist fights with the characters he has created, only to make them again vanish into an inkwell on his table. The American cartoonist Max Fleischer was substituted on the screen by Karel Dodal, while Bimbo, a cartoon character wearing a straw skimmer, replaced Koko the Clown (otherwise renamed Bejbl in Czech). The drawn Bimbo distracts the draughtsman from committing suicide caused by unrequited love and keeps inventing ways to cheer him up. He fulfils his wish and conjures him a "girlfriend" but, to Bimbo's disappointment, the drawing turns into a real girl in a birch grove. The draughtsman then sets off with her, having the betrayed and forlorn Bimbo again end up in the inkwell. The story was underlined by the touching verses written by Karel Smrž. Hermína Týrlová also participated in the film – and undoubtedly not just as the capricious girl

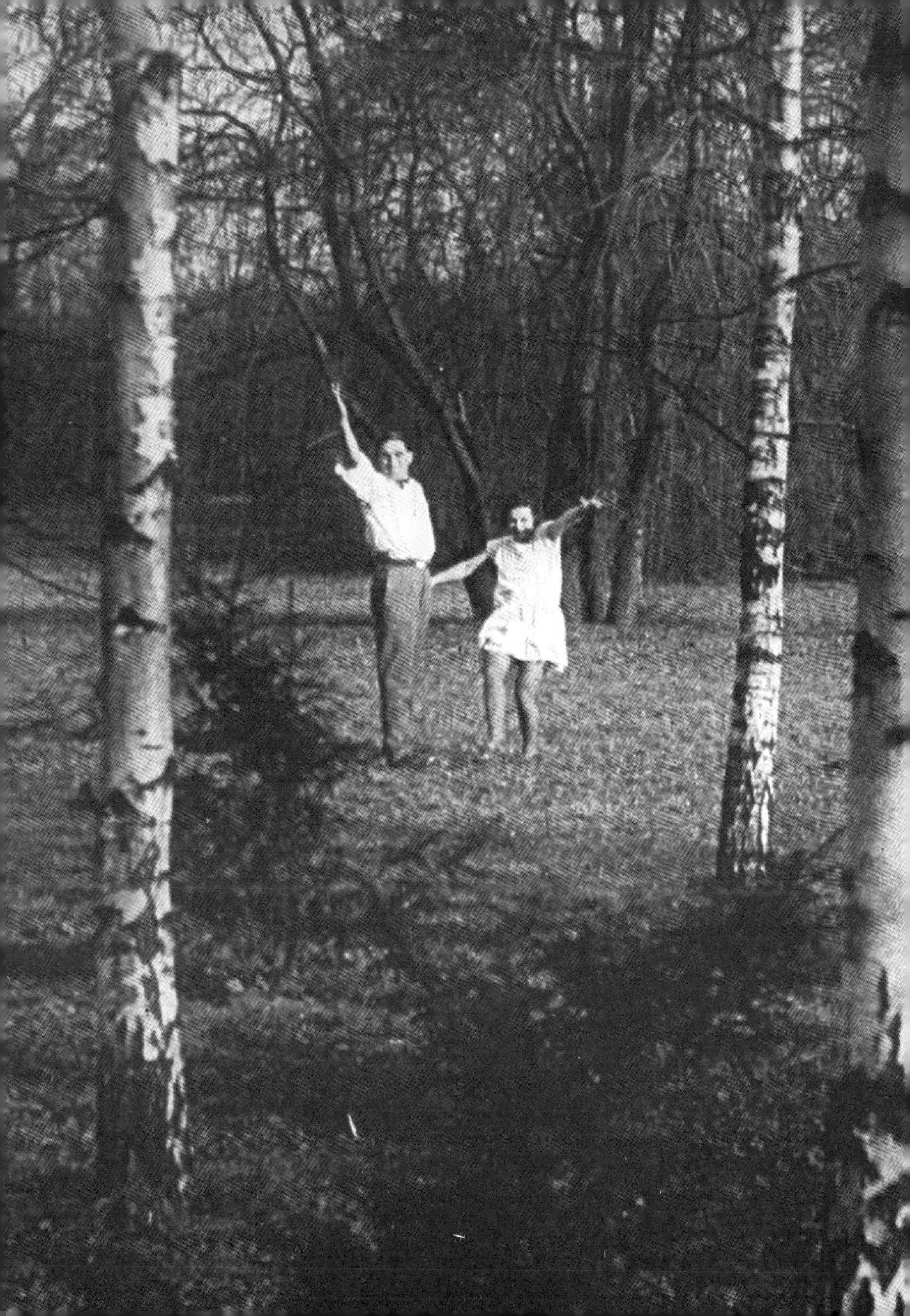

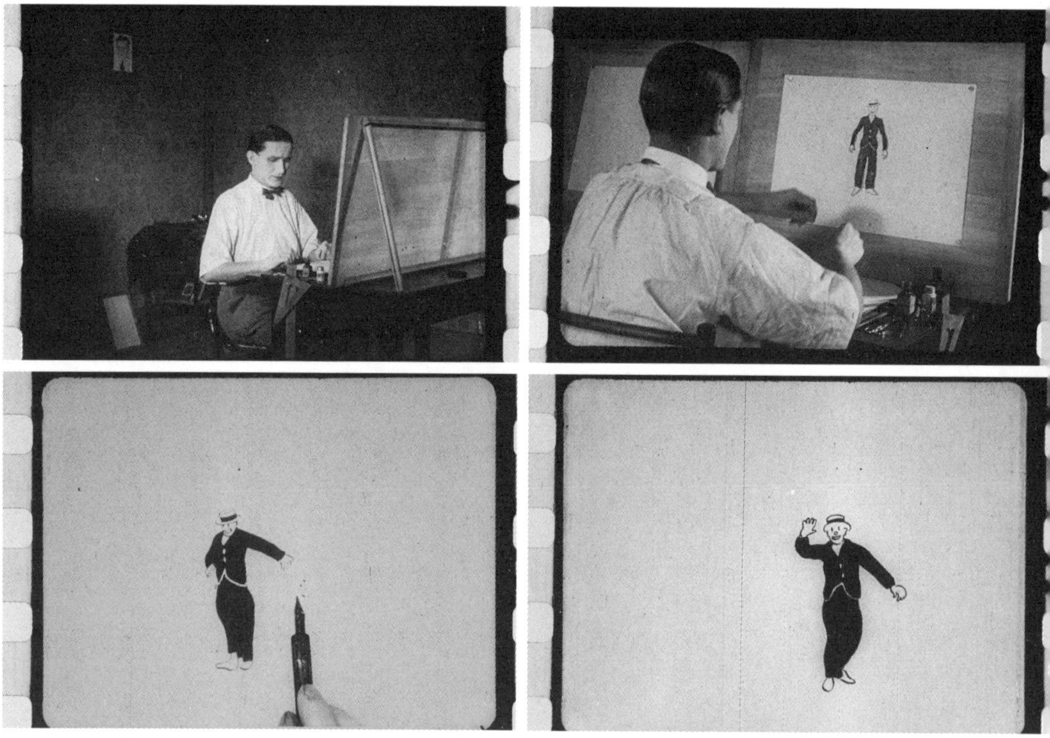

taking the draughtsman away. The final sequences with Karel Dodal also display another filmmaker, most probably from the ranks of the Elekta Journal cameramen. The Dodals here proved that they were perfectly capable of combining live action and cartoons and of appropriating many animation methods invented by the Fleischers. They, however, were not competent enough to approach the foreign original and its almost surreal poetics. The film nonetheless begs the question whether we should view it as plagiarism of the Fleischer brothers' works or a free, belated reflection of the "Fleischer style".

Another Dodals' "supplement" – *Tommy and the Mermaid* – was submitted for censorship soon after *Bimbo*. The records in one of the Elekta Journal

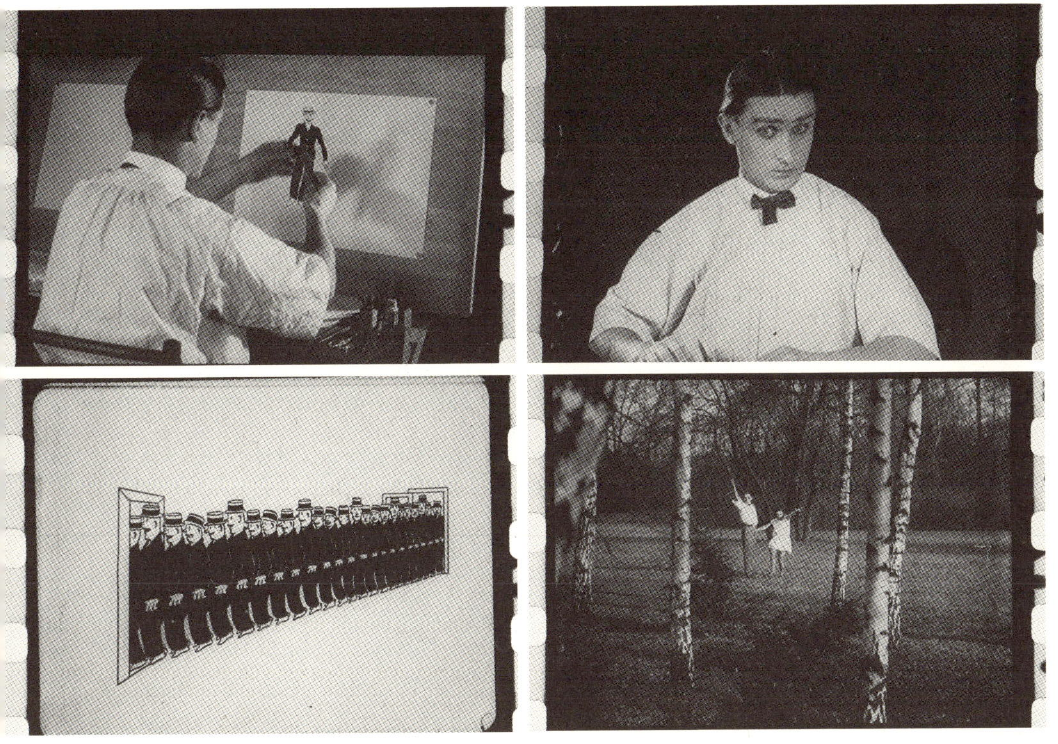

There is no doubt that the young Prague animator and his girlfriend used both the subject and an array of technological methods found in the oeuvre of the Fleischer brothers.

books show that Ms "Tearlová" charged her expenditures for drawing materials for this film in the amount of 39 Crowns in March 1930, probably at the time when she inserted the subtitles.[7] This perhaps was the reason why her name appeared in the captions for the first time. The description of the now missing film survived thanks to a conscientious and thorough clerk from the Ministry of Interior, who reported: "Tommy does not want to study. His father thus kicks him out and Tommy goes out into the world. He conjures himself an airplane, a balloon and a rocket while the latter becomes his means of transportation. He lights a cigar from the rocket and throws the stub inside. The rocket explodes, Tommy falls into some water and a fish throws him to the shore. He spots a flower, wants to cut it off and then sees that it is a lion which begins chasing him. Tommy climbs up a tree, catches a rope and notices that the lion on the other end is getting strangled. He climbs down again, wipes off the lion's tears and bandages his tail. He hears music, follows the singing and finds a dancing mermaid. Tommy plucks a flower and hands it to her. The mermaid watches him, completely amazed. Tommy gestures that he would like a kiss. The mermaid does not understand, but then there is a small boat which harasses the mermaid who flies into Tommy's arms. They sail away together. Tommy and the mermaid then fall down to a small church and receive the blessing. Years later, Tommy is a very old man surrounded by many grandchildren."[8]

The author of the text first slightly corrected it and then completely crossed it out. We must say in his defence that translating animated films into words is a thankless, almost impossible task. But the description is still an interesting and amusing testimony which well supplements the title sheet and provides more details about the missing film.

We can imagine the style of *Tommy and the Mermaid* if we compare it with another of Dodals' film, *A Water Sprite in Love*. The rolls of its negative were discovered in the early 1980s in the film archive of, what was then, the Czechoslovak Film Institute. The negatives lacked both the opening credits and subheads, were deposited in a Propagafilm box and had the title *Seed Cultivation* (Pěstování semen). It can well be that Týrlová asked her friend Josef Vilímek to keep the film for her before she left Elekta Journal because she did not want to take the highly flammable material home, and the Dodals moreover had neither any reason nor chance to return to the launched work. When the film archive keepers talked to Týrlová in the 1980s, she confirmed that it was jointly made with Karel Dodal from her script in 1928. She also stated that her partner was not satisfied with the picture, which was probably why it remained unfinished and was unfortunately not screened in the early 1930s along with the earlier *Bimbo* and *Tommy*.[9] To our regret, because the cartoon comedy about an enchanted water sprite retains its flair and appeal even to these days. It is a story about a philandering water sprite who enjoys himself playing love songs on his mandolin to a willow tree fairy while his wife rocks the little water sprites in a pond and pursues her husband. This film also had a happy ending: the water sprite faithfully returned to his horde. There are no surviving documents as to the succession of *Tommy* and the *Water Sprite*, but they probably originated during the same creative period and probably did not noticeably differ in their approach to drawing and animation.

The first stage of the Dodals' artistic collaboration described above is characteristic of the fact that their film technology was strongly influenced by the tradition of American cartoon comedies and that the two artists, albeit with alternating success, tried to employ the potential of metamorphosing drawings to the full. Their selection of subjects and styles largely departed from the local stereotypes widespread in popular sentimental readings of mediocre quality, which later also served as a foundation to Hermína Týrlová in her own titles. Despite some reservations, Czech film production could only benefit from the Dodals' contributions because the couple finally introduced professional-quality animation and the capability of mediating a story spiced with situation gags to Czech audiences.

lakes from the postponed film *A Water Sprite in Love*.
The author of the subject was reportedly Hermína Týrlová.

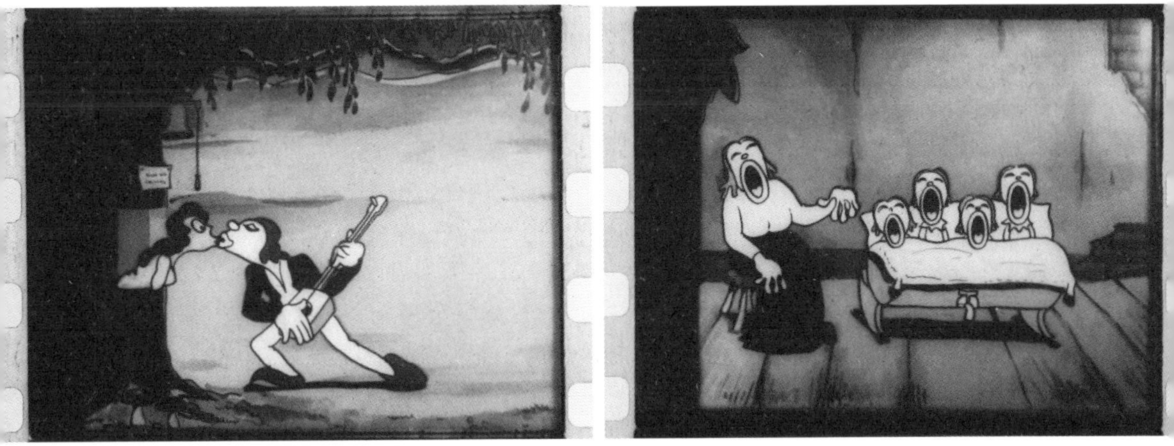

1 "Čs. výroba trikfilmů" (Czechoslovak Trick Film Production), *Český filmový zpravodaj*, 1927, No. 31, p. 4; the typescript of the poem *Home* is held in the National Film Archive, Personal Fund of Marie Benešová (yet incompiled).

2 Ibid.

3 The name of one of the department stores' owners, Brouk, means "beetle" in English.

4 Benešová, M., op. cit., p. 19.

5 Ibid.

6 Smrž, K., "I kreslený film má historii" (Cartoon Film Has Its History, Too), Filmová okénka (Film Frames), 1947, No. 9, p. 22.

7 Accounting books. The National Film Archive, fund Aktualita k.s., akt. Nos. 33, 35, 37. The books usually stated H. Dodalová as Tearlová.

8 *Tommy and the Mermaid.* The National Archives, Cinematographic Censorship Committee with the Ministry of Interior, Ref. No. 662/1930.

9 The films *Bimbo's Unfortunate Adventure* and *Tommy and the Mermaid* were submitted for censorship by the Elekta Journal's co-owner, K. Pečený, and were introduced to the cinemas by Gong, the company of the Horký couple. F. Horký was Pečený's associate. Both pictures were produced in six copies in view of the expected distributors' interest in Czech cartoon comedy.

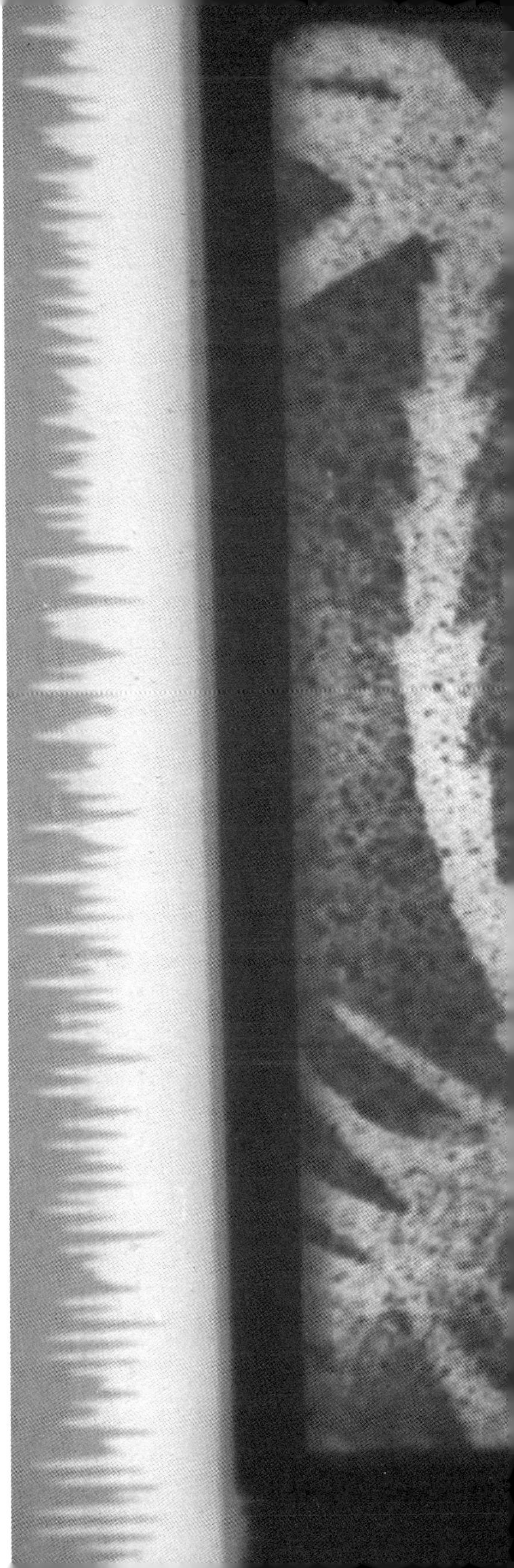

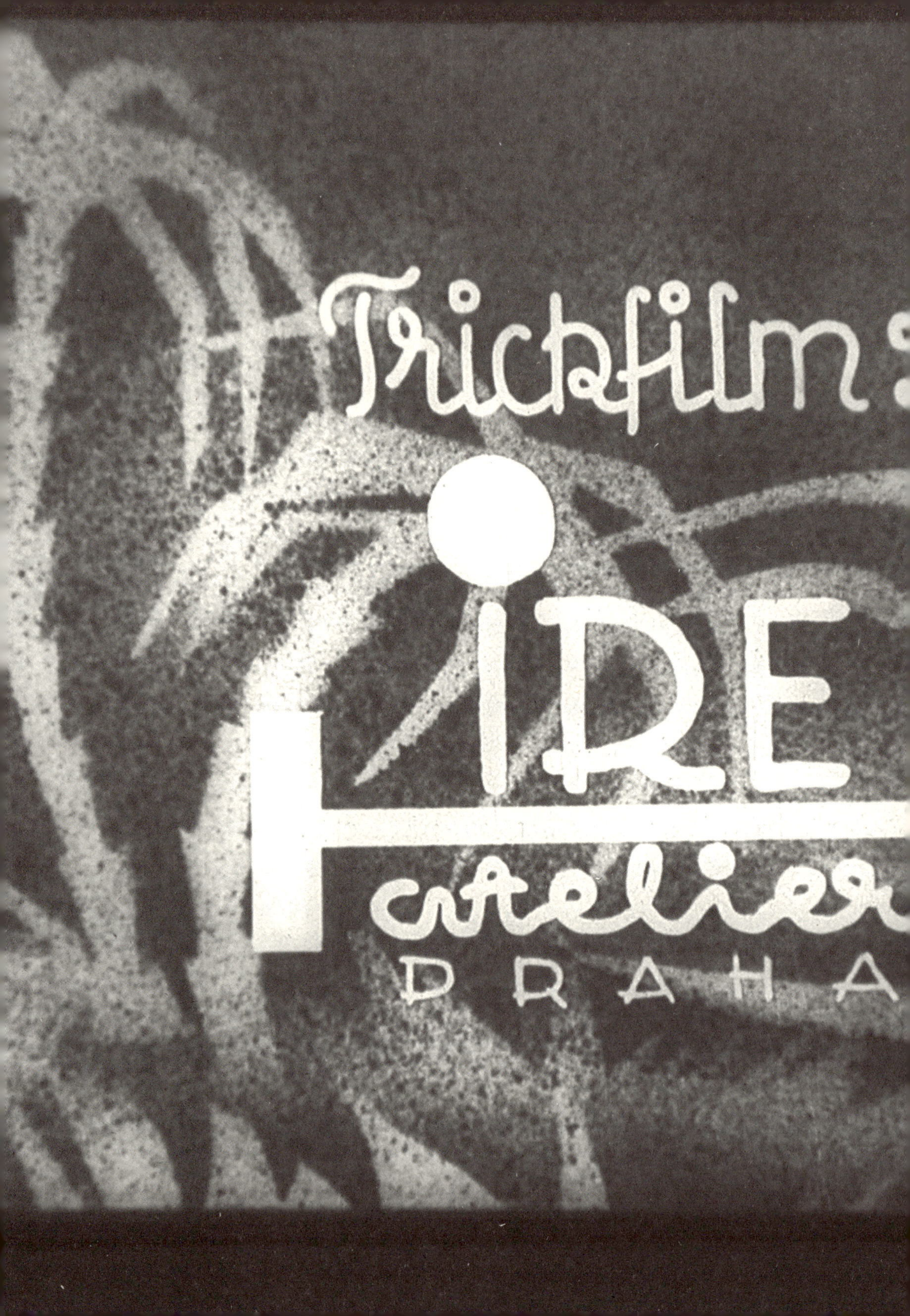
Trickfilm
IRE
atelier
PRAHA

The Fateful Encounter and the Birth of IRE-film

Just a few 1930s takes held by the National Film Archive suffice to take us back to the times when the Prague café Mánes radiated the relaxed atmosphere of the local jet set. The place was bustling and *en vogue* and it was adored by artists of all kinds as well as the metropolitan crème de la crème, all eagerly frequenting its tea parties, fashion shows and late-night concerts orchestrated by the flagship of contemporary easy-going elegance, E. F. Burian. And this is also where the "fateful encounter" occurred between the chic and divorced Ms Irena Rosnerová-Leschnerová and the handsome freelance filmmaker, Karel Dodal. The note inscribed on their photograph held in the inheritance of Karel Smrž informs us that the role of "fate" was played by this very film historian, publicist and repertory adviser. Both Leschnerová and Dodal, however, were not going through the happiest time of their lives when they met.

Irena Rosnerová was born to a family of a teacher of the Moses (Jewish) religion on 29 November 1900 in Ledeč nad Sázavou and she spent the most idyllic years of her childhood in the towns of Heřmanův Městec and Tábor, where she enrolled at a council school. After the First World War, the family lived in Brno where the father worked as a director of a Jewish orphanage. The surviving copies of Rosnerová's school reports[1] prove that the she received a rather prime education for that period; she attended a girls' school for two years and a school of commerce for a year. The 1920 register of citizens informs us that she also "trained for the profession of an opera singer".[2] She, however, left the opera chorus of the Brno German theatre[3] for Germany at the end of the 1920/1921 season. A year later, she wrote about it to her brother Rudolf:

„What you had told me about Elizabeth in Tannhäuser, Dich, teure Halle etc. – well, that is my beloved aria and I sang it countlessly at concerts and also in Germany for my opera engagement... I won the competition there with my voice and my rendering, but I had to think about my mother and brother and quit my artistic desires... it was very, very bitter... But it had to be... This is how I got the two of you to Prague, mum to stay with me, and you to a post where you did so well."[4]

Irena's parents parted sometime between 1922 and 1923 and Ms Rosnerová moved to Prague with her two children. Irena at that time described her profession in the register of citizens as "concessionaire" and "clerk". She married a bank officer, Leopold Leschner, in 1927 but the bond only lasted two years.

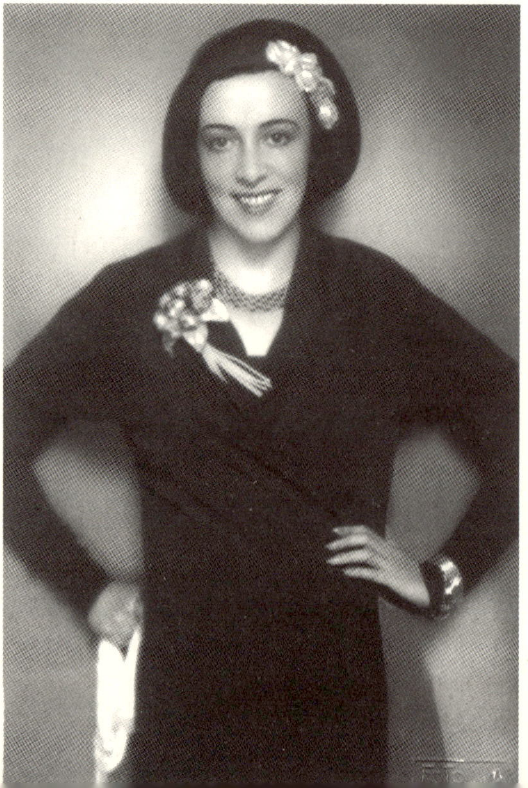

Portrait of Irena Rosnerová, probably from the period prior to her marriage to the bank officer, Leo Leschner.

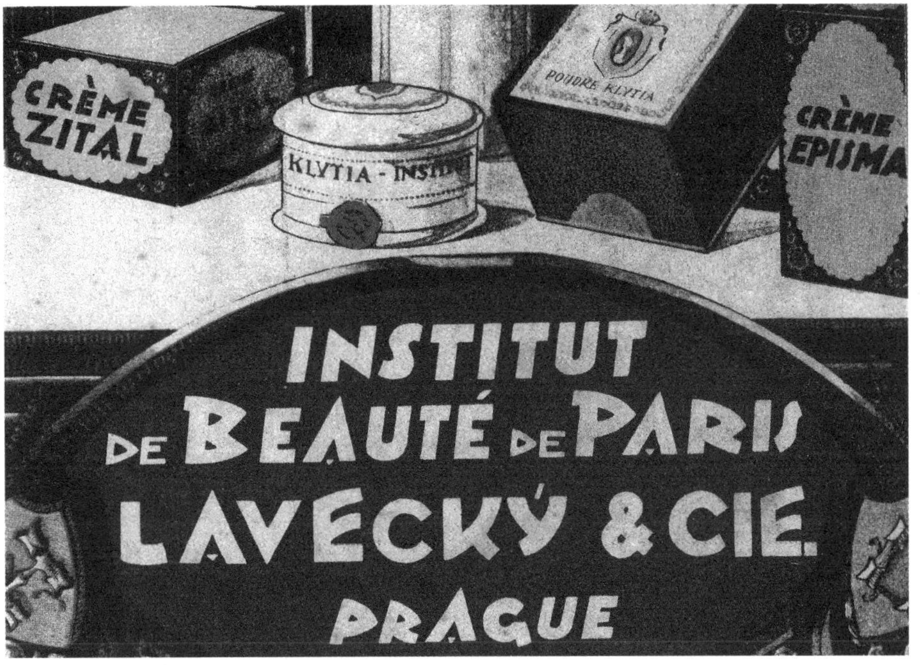

The Lavecký company offered exclusive hairdresser's, cosmetic and massage services in Prague and also ran wholesaling in perfumes and cosmetic products. Its hair treatment, Sorela, was almost legendary.

She returned to Paris in the early 1930s to pursue film production. The surviving mention in *The National Newspaper* (Národní listy) reports that Ms Irena "long studied in Paris with the distinguished painter Paul Peroff".[5] Although we have no detailed information about their relationship, it was probably Peroff who first opened the world of animation to her. When Leschnerová met Dodal in 1932, she was employed in the Prague leading cosmetic firm Lavecký & comp. as a "shop manager". The work certainly provided her a reliable financial and social background but it could hardly satisfy her cultural interests and artistic ambitions.

Karel Dodal was also still waiting for his opportunity at that time. He lived on occasional commissions, for example as a co-screenwriter for the picture *The Career of Pavel Čamrda* (Kariéra Pavla Čamrdy), based on the

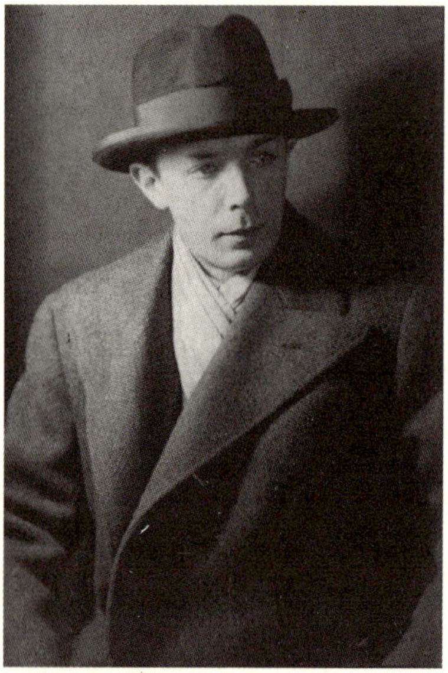

Karel Smrž, a film scriptwriter, dramatic adviser, pedagogue and film historian. He was in frequent contact with the Dodals from the mid-1920s, because he at that time also worked as script editor and author of subtitles in Elekta Journal.

novel by Ignát Herrmann. It is said that he assisted in film studios as a painter of backdrops and worked on animated film commissions which his wife managed to acquire. But at least the Prague professional circles already viewed him as a leading expert in trick and animated film thanks to his practice in Elekta Journal.

Soon after encountering Irena Leschnerová, Karel Dodal moved away from his former wife Hermína to stay with his father. In August, he left for France with his new partner and, in November, he registered in a flat in Karlova (today Seifertova) Street in the Prague suburb of Žižkov, where Irena lived with her mother Matilda Rosnerová.[6] They married in December 1935. This event probably also influenced the life of Dodal's ex-wife Hermína. Their separation was vindicated in August 1932 and she returned to her maiden name Týrlová in November 1935 when she was already employed in IRE-film, headed by Dodal's second wife.

There is no doubt that Irena Leschnerová offered Dodal help to realize his dream about his own studio soon after their met. Although she had no previous experience in film production, she possessed many of the preconditions for a private enterprise: she had studied at a commercial school, had worked as a shop manager, knew a lot about the film industry abroad, had many valuable social contacts and was also competent in negotiating. Her music and theatre education, interest in arts and culture and knowledge of animation learned from Peroff enabled her to translate well Dodal's ideas and subjects into tangible plans. She moreover had the merit of always assessing problems from a wider than just local viewpoint. The beginnings of her collaboration with Dodal clearly speak of this. Prior to launching a film company, Leschnerová organized their study trip abroad to gain experience in European trends and technologies and animated film production. We know their travels in detail since Irena, at that time Dodalová, described them more than fifty years later. She for example wrote:

"We left for Italy (Václav Vích), Cinecittà, and later for Germany. Karel became familiar with German professionals in shorts and cartoons: Fischinger, Max Fleicher, with films featuring cut-out paper characters, experimental films...This was a springboard for meeting artists working in short film in Paris. We visited the Russian pioneer Starevich, and Alexeïeff who, frame by frame, filmed shadows that threw needles stuck to the screen: *The Night at the Lysá Mountain* music by Musorgski: he met the photographer of genius: Man Ray..."[7]

Dodalová's testimony documents that they had encountered the most

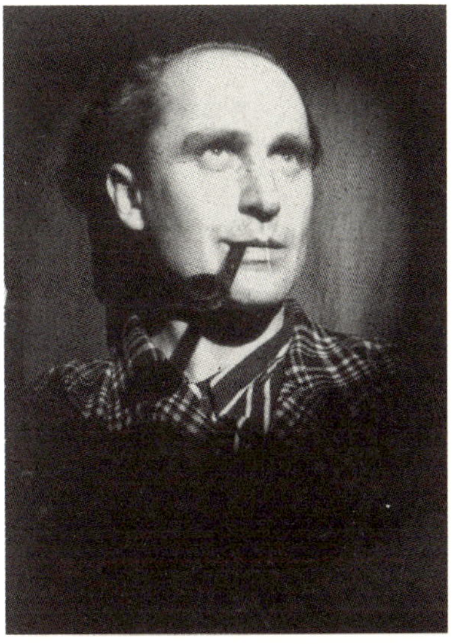

Karel Dodal with his indispensable pipe.

Irena Rosnerová (Leschnerová, Dodalová) performed as Irena Rosen during her opera beginnings.

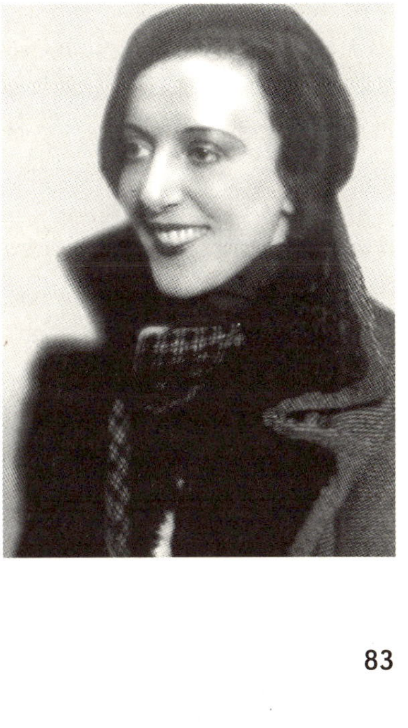

interesting achievements in European animated film and apparently some of their authors. One of the most significant professional impulses was meeting Oskar Fischinger whose concept of abstract film they later used in their *Fantaisie érotique*, *The Play of Bubbles* (Hra bublinek; both 1937) and *Ideas in Search of Light* (Myšlenka hledající světlo; 1938). They also became familiar with the colour film system Gasparcolor in his studio and later purchased the patent. Dodalová's mention about the cut-out films with paper figures was most probably linked with visiting the studio of Lotte Reiniger and her husband, cameraman Carl Koch, who made silhouette films. The category of cut-out film could at that time encompass paper cut-out film, the main field of, for example, the German Hans Fischerkoesen. An interesting experience for the two Czech visitors must have been the puppet animation seen in the studio of Vladislav Starevich, who had pursued it for almost 25 years; they later made the best of it in their 1936 films *The Secret of the Lucerna Palace* (Tajemství Lucerny) and *The Adventures of a Ubiquitous Fellow* (Všudybylovo dobrodružství). A unique opportunity to realize both the artistic and technical potential of animation was offered by the oeuvre of Alexander Alexeïeff and his partner Claire Parker who employed the unique, so-called pinscreen technology in setting their scenes in motion. Dodalová later described her impression of *The Night at the Lysá Mountain* (Une Nuit sur le Mont Chauve, Noc na Lysé hoře; 1933) in the journal *Cinema Review* (Kinorevue) although, with the lapse of time, she mistakenly stated the name of Max Fleischer in this context. Fleischer was indeed born in Vienna, but he and his family had lived in the United States since his childhood; she perhaps only meant encountering his films in German cinemas.

Certainly, one of the main gains of the couple's study trip was realizing the significance of sound and colour in European film advertising and animation from both the creative and commercial point. But their travels had yet another goal. As Irena Dodalová wrote, "Something must have happened to his sight... A French doctor recommended bathing his eyes in salty, sea water... we thus went south, to the sea... and it really helped Karel recover... And then we went back to Prague".[8]

Dodal had to complete several unfinished commissions upon returning from abroad. The first Czech scientific cartoon, entitled *Amelioration* (Meliorace

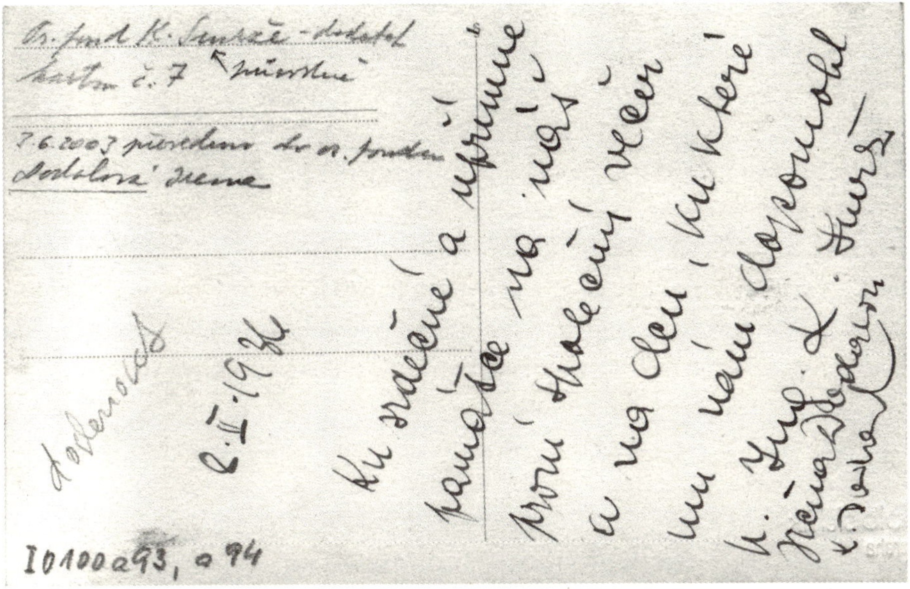

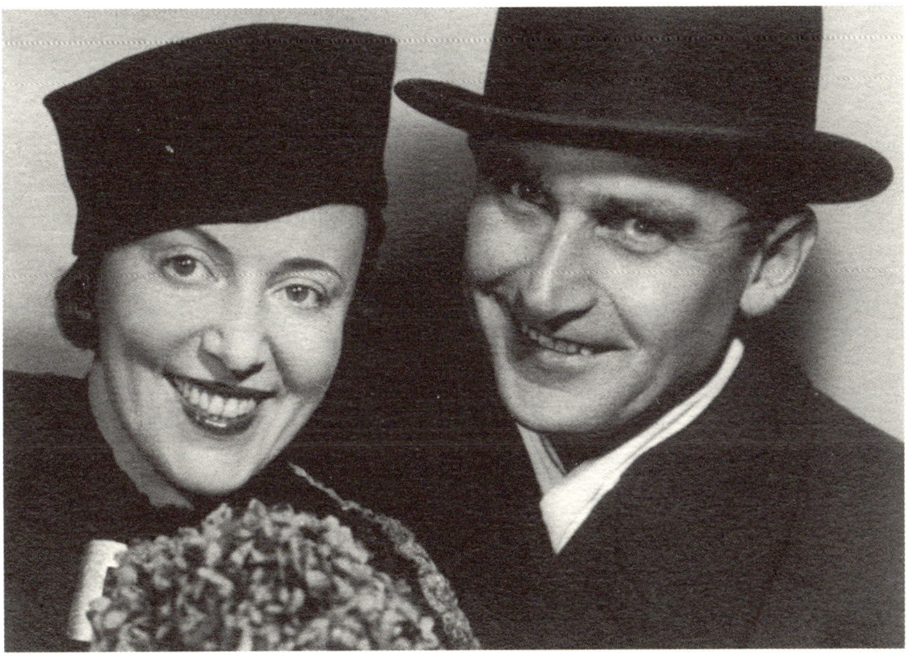

Photograph of the Dodals, who married in December 1935, which survived in the inheritance of Karel Smrž. The couple thanks him for introducing them to each other on the reverse.

půdy), on which the artist collaborated with the hydrology expert Otakar Solnař, was submitted for censorship in May 1933. It was financed by the land administration and the Czechoslovak Ministry of Agriculture and was introduced at the spring exhibition of the Agrarian Association. In June, Dodal finished the commercial *Little Eve Opens Her Little Eyes* (Evička otevírá očička), made for the Prague Creameries Association. The cartoon comedy about the importance of drinking milk also had its expert consultant named Božena Krůtová. Hermína Týrlová's memoirs suggest that it was her who gained these commissions and who also undoubtedly played the main role in realizing them. Her name is, however, totally absent in the written materials contained in the censorship files about the picture.

These works were simultaneous with Dodal's arrangements to launch his new studio. Its name, IRE-film, demonstrates the role played by Irena Leschnerová in moulding its future.[9] Dodal received his trade licence, which authorized him to work in advertising, in August 1933.[10] When he renewed the licence in 1936, he stated "producing films of all genres" as the purpose of his business, while in 1937, it was "producing films void of photographs".

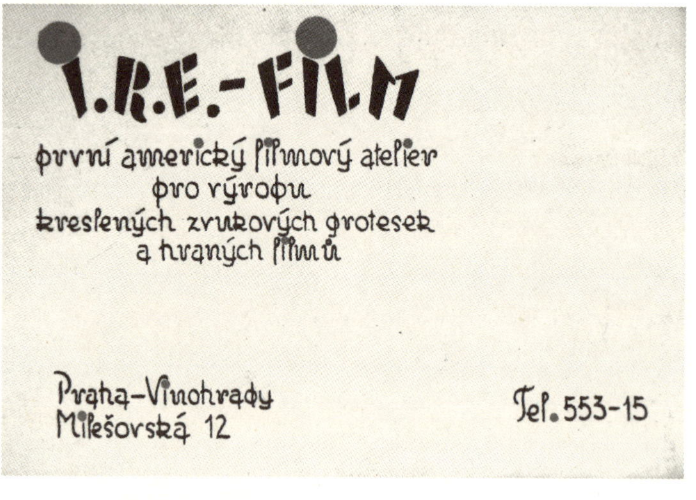

The choice of words proves that animated film at that time still lacked a comprehensive label. Official reports usually filed cartoons within the category of feature comedies or, eventually, shorts or the above-mentioned "supplements". They were distinguished after the employed technology (cartoon film, puppet film) or program focus (absolute film, abstract film). This genre, based on frame-by-frame shooting, became common in many languages under the summarizing name "animated film" (film d'animation, Animazionsfilm, multiplikacionnoje kino, etc.) only as late as during the 1950s and 1960s.

An apt illustration of the new film production studio's aims and developments is its gradually transforming logos. The title "IRE-film Studio" initially came with the slogan "The first American-style film studio producing cartoon and sound cartoon comedies and films". In 1937, the Dodals left out the "American film" reference and redesigned their activity as "The first artistic film studio specializing in animated and colour cartoon comedies – avant-garde shorts – films about industry and culture – Iréna and K. Dodal". The collocation "IRE-film" during the studio's existence kept reappearing in various forms: as "Atelier Ire", "IRE atelier", "IRE FILM", "I.R.E.-FILM" and "I.R.E-film".

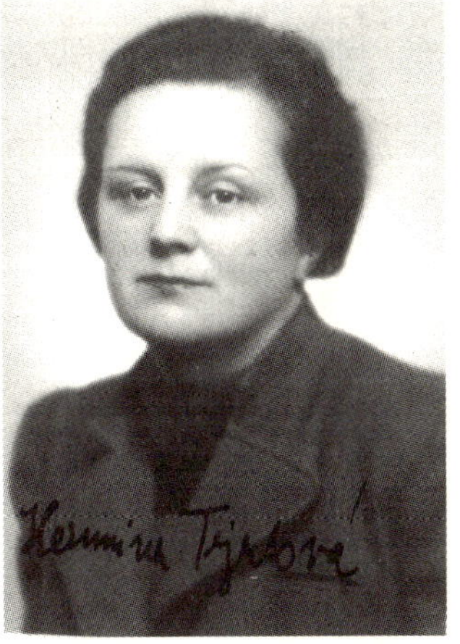
Hermína Týrlová

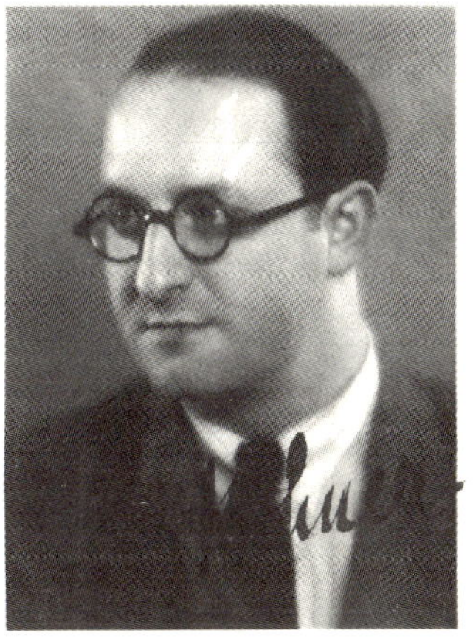
Bedřich Kerten

Eliška Ložková

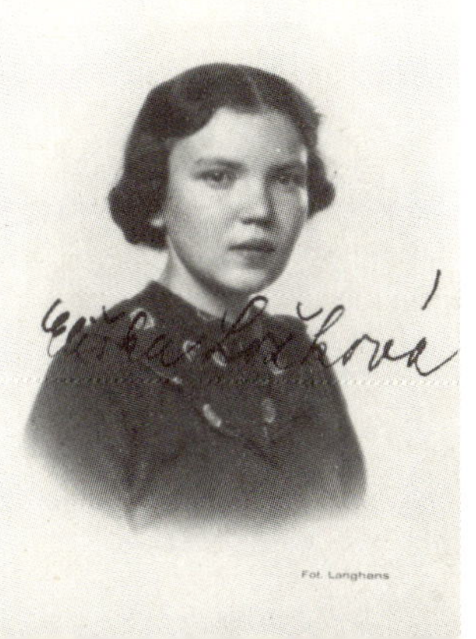

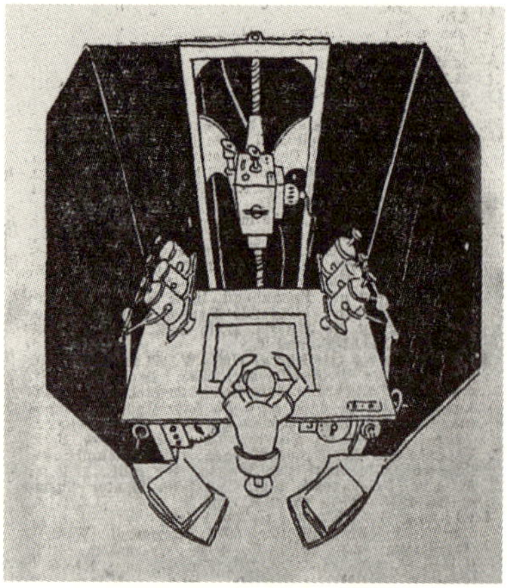

Trick table used in film animation.

In 1933, Irena Leschnerová, her mother and Karel Dodal moved to 12 Milešovská Street, an imposing block of flats on the border between the Žižkov and Vinohrady suburbs. Censorship files report that their new residence included a studio but the many subsequent renovations safely razed all traces of these tenants.

IRE-film was basically a family business, engaging not only Dodal but also his present and former partner and many other relatives. The first studio employee was Dodal's ex-wife Hermína. The offered position of "draughtswoman" gave her a way out of a difficult financial situation in which she found herself after parting with her husband, because there was no other Prague producer of animated film who would be interested in her profession. The studio also employed Dodal's younger brother Jaroslav Dodal and possibly Irena's younger sibling, Rudolf Rosner (Rohan). The position of accountant was taken by Rudolf Pick (most probably blood-related to Irena's mother Matilda Rosnerová, born Picková). An important co-worker was the 23-year old music composer Bedřich Kerten. The gradually growing production resulted in the arrival of Anna Čudová, Eliška Ložková, Pavla Weisová and Věra (whose last name is unknown).

The Evening People's Justice daily (Večerník Práva lidu) in 1936 ran a

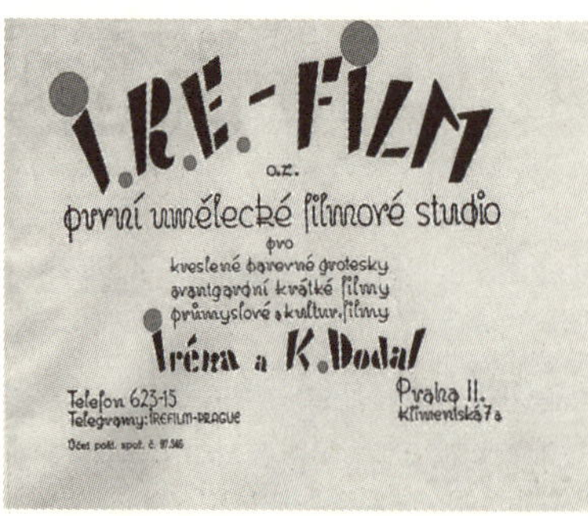

whole-page article about IRE-film, entitled "Cartoon Film – The Poetry of the Unreal. The Magic of a Thousand Pictures on a Reel: The Way Cartoons Are Made" (Kreslený film – poesie neskutečna. Kouzlo tisíců obrázků na filmovém pásku – Jak se dělá kreslený film). Irena Dodalová introduced the studio as follows: "What is IRE-film? It's a team of young people devoted to art who know no obstacles but draw, paint, shoot and create special films called *cartoons*. This enterprise is a small miracle of idealism in the otherwise realistic world of today, even more so that it is not supported by any bank capital, finances from the outside or any subsidies. The explanation is that those who collaborate with IRE-film do not shy from making sacrifice as to the work load, do not compromise either finances or art, and maintain their venture just because they *love* their work. The art director is the painter Karel Dodal. The lead draughtswoman, Mme Iréna, always has the task of inventing the idea, a section of a poetic story, a lot of girls' poetry. The technician and practitioner, painter K. Dodal, then constructs the framework and develops the situations and realizations. Four more colleagues step into the process and the next stages of the film with their ideas and subjects. Then there comes Iréna again to work on the first sketches. Dodal figures these poems and poetries, materializing them onto the celluloid plates. This is where the austere curves, calculated into precise lines, rhythms and motion, come to life. Two animators – Tearlová and Čudová – draw the motion interphases while the other two colour the figures, clean the plates and prepare them for the film machine."[11]

Several years later, the successfully developing production called for a new and more spacious place, which turned out to be the 7 Klimentská Street house in Prague. Because the Dodals worked with flammable material, they rented the fourth floor which suited fire regulations. One entrance led to the studio facilitated with a vast drawing hall of 12 × 6 metres and to four workrooms with telephones. There also was a projection room, a grand parlour room, and the producer's office. The residential part consisted of three rooms, a kitchen and a bathroom. Irena's mother moved to Klimentská along with the couple.

The studio walls were densely covered with drawings that, as one of the visitors observed, would easily make an exhibition in a museum of anatomy. The sketches of figures in motion and drawings of facial gestures in pronouncing

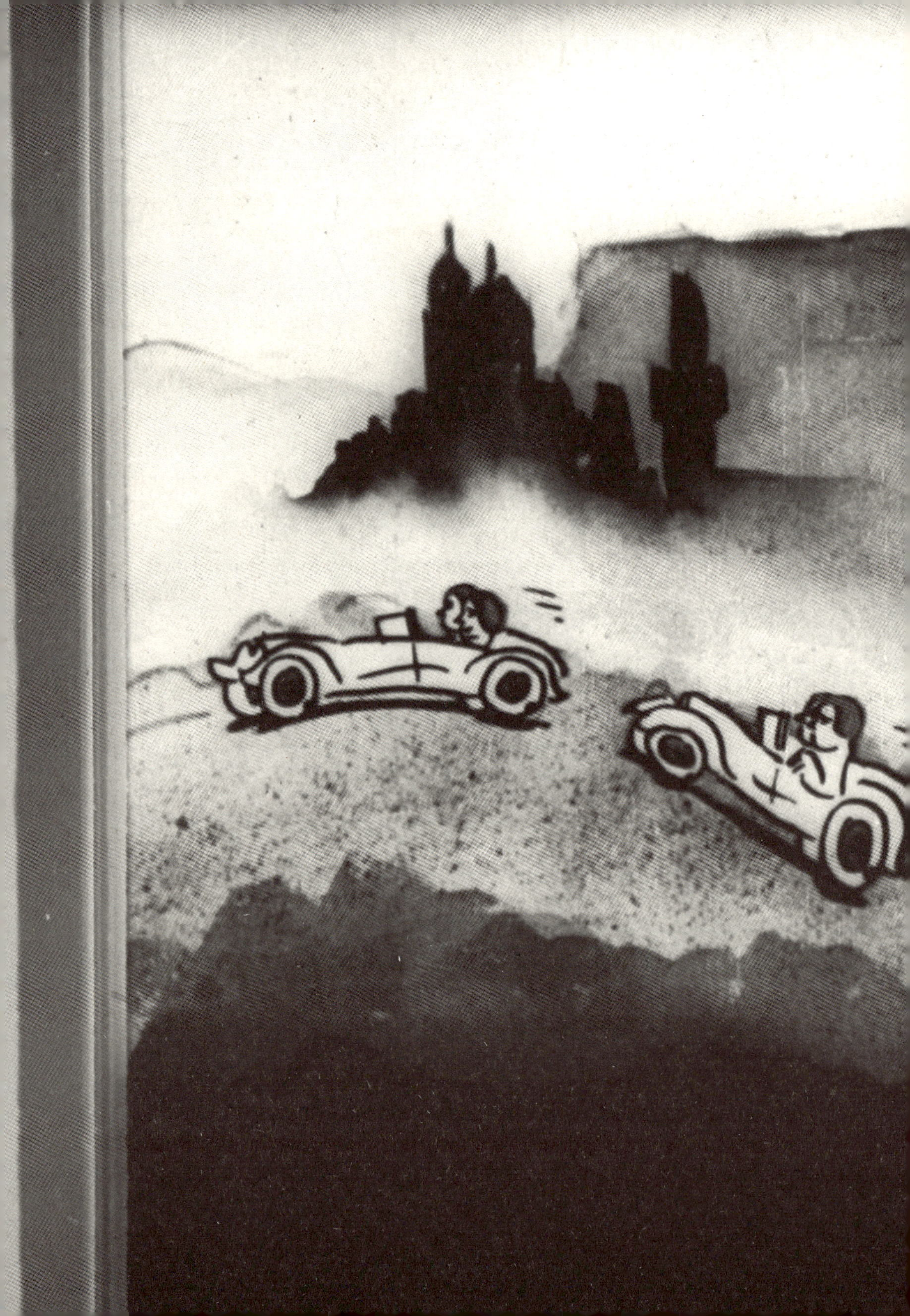

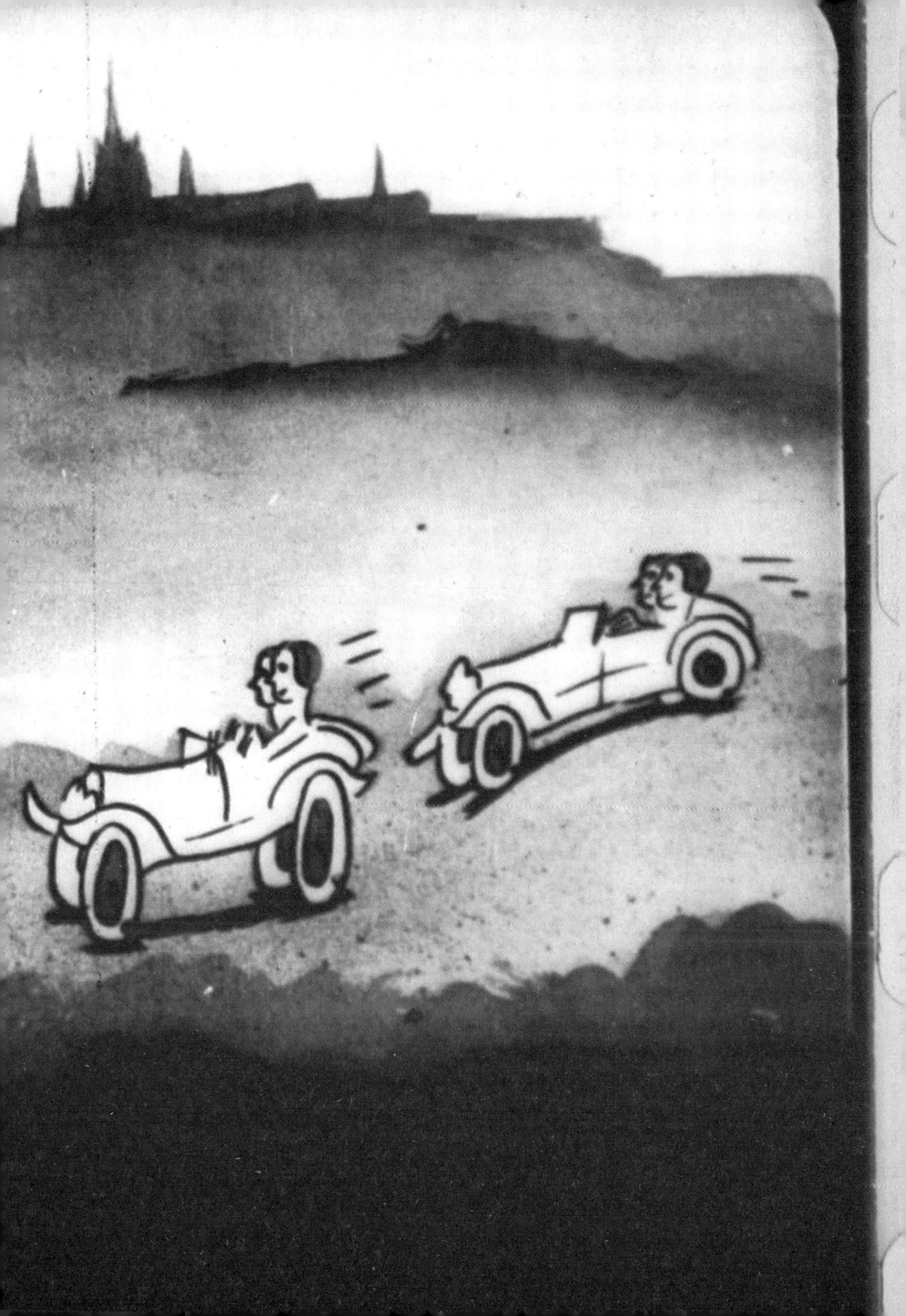

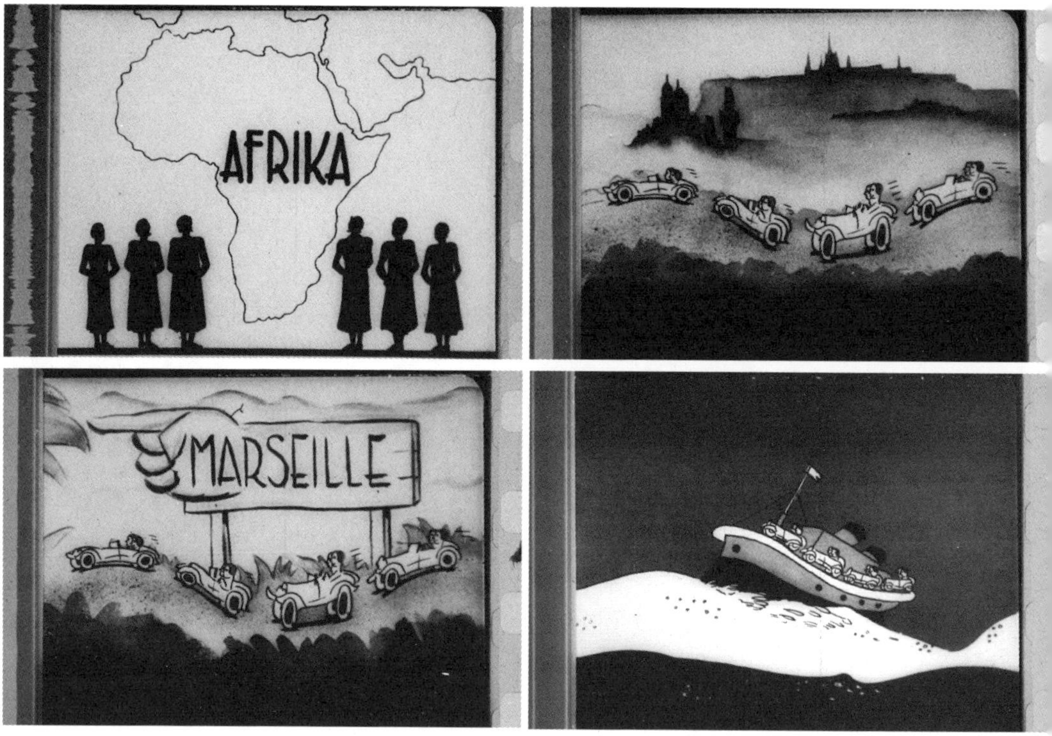

Takes from the promotional film *Six Women in Search of Africa*, directed by Leo Marten. It was about the trip of the Aero Blue Team through Germany, France and Algeria to the edge of the Sahara, through Morocco to the High Atlas mountains, through the mountains to the southern deserts, along the coast to the north of Spanish Morocco, and through Spain to Paris and Prague. The (often) lacking documentary shots were substituted by animated sequences by IRE-film and narration by the newscaster, Josef Laufer.

various phonemes and sounds served to control animation and to demonstrate the cartooning process to the lay visitors.

IRE-film legal matters were handled by the Doctor of Law, Alfred Popp, who had also arranged the rental in Klimentská Street. The surviving correspondence manifests that the young articled clerk befriended the Dodals to the extent of making them regular visitors to his archery club, since he ranked among the republic masters in the given discipline. Interestingly enough, the Dodal couple often used to arrive at the Academic League club escorted by Hermína Týrlová.

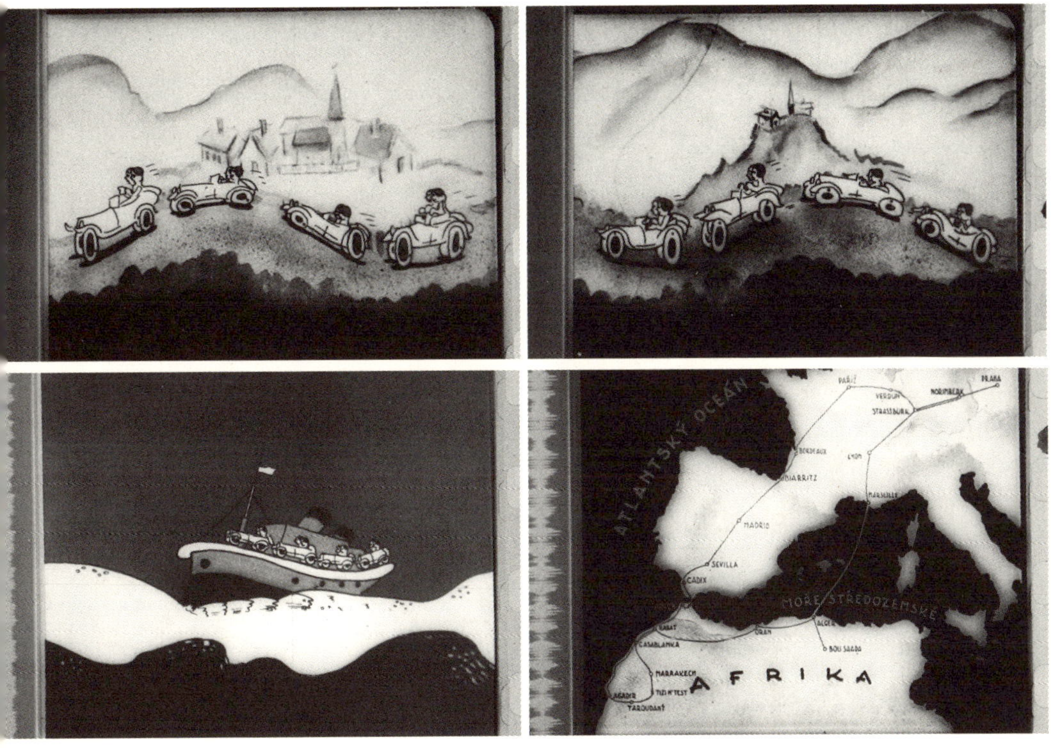

The studio staff changed over time, and it increased to eleven including the owners in the years of its greatest upswing, i.e. between 1936 and 1937. At that time, it employed two draughtsmen-animators of foregrounds, two draughtsmen-phasists of backgrounds and two colourists – but even such a cast did not suffice given the laborious process and extent of production. Working hours were often unobserved and the Dodals had to simultaneously master an array of positions and professions.

Irena Dodalová portrayed the studio's day-to-day operation in her distinctive staccato way: "What we lacked was the technical staff... I had to fill the gap myself: it was tons of work... inventing the idea... developing it for Karel...

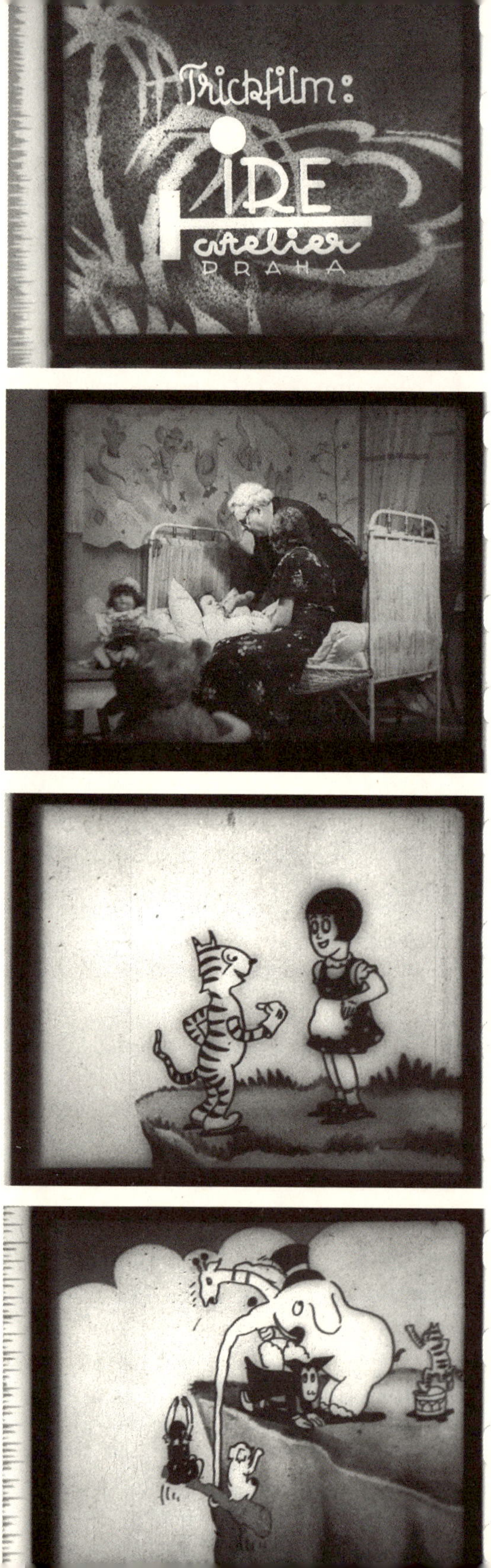

The combined staged and cartoon film *Elephant the Rescuer*, promoting Baťa rubber toys, represents the closing era of the company's advertising before the arrival of Elmar Klos in Zlín. It is also one of the first joint projects realized by Irena and Karel Dodal. The logo of their studio (see also the opening page of this chapter) later changed many times.

writing the dialogues and lyrics... the film script and the storyboards, the prep works for visual and sound recording... the montage of sounds and visuals... then filming on the film panel... and supervising the overall production... and meeting future customers... financial problems... presenting the pictures at European film festivals..."[12] Her testimony was supported by Alfred Popp who recollected that Dodalová held the multiple position of "topic-inventor, sound engineer and draughtswoman".[13] We know that she moreover served as the company's film producer, director and press spokeswoman.

Karel Dodal's roles overlapped as well. He was the artist, author of both visual and technical scripts and was responsible for lighting and camera. In addition, he was the studio lead and thus had to procure the technology.

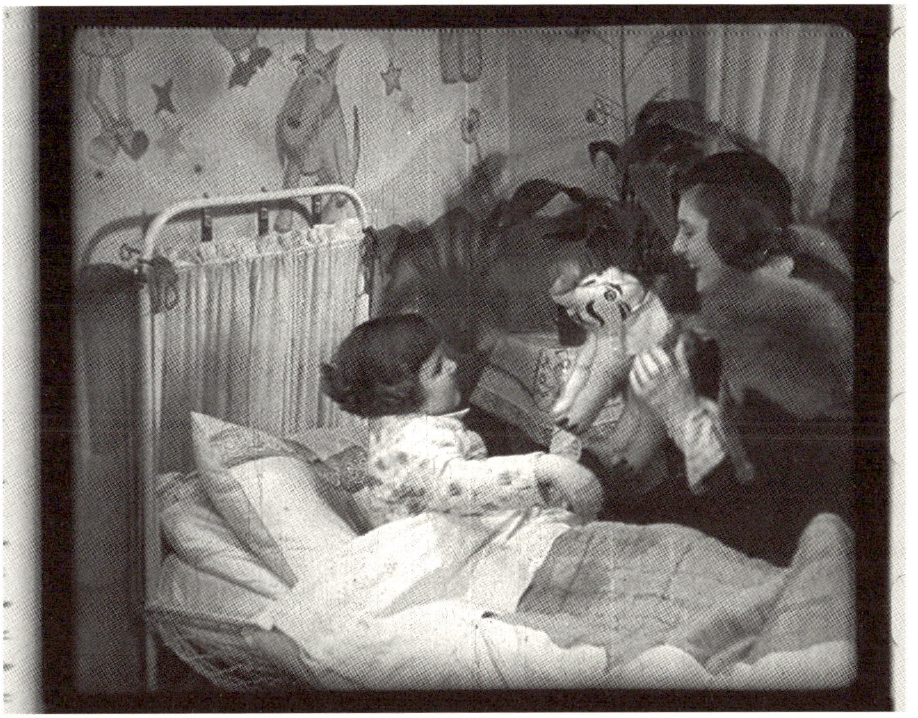

Although no contemporary photographs were found, two German journalists coincided in what was happening on the studio's trick table. One of them[14] claimed that Dodal would mount the camera above the trick table spread with the celluloid sheets with drawings. The table was set with spotlights to the left and right. The motion of the camera and the spotlights were controlled by an electric device personally constructed by the filmmaker. This testimony perfectly corresponds with the drawing published in the German daily *Neue Morgenpost*, illustrating an article by Hans Markert whose description of the studio works, beside other things, reads: "They first either compose their own music or adapt some existing pieces to their purposes; they design the basic plan for the animated drawings; one artist sketches the cartoon characters, another one draws the backgrounds and perspectives and the third one colours the pictures; celluloid sheets are used; then the visual part is supervised and the final drawings are shot: the pictures, spread horizontally on the trick table, are exposed with the automatically (electrically controlled) camera mounted above while the drawings are lit from both sides by six spotlights controlled by the cameraman via buttons situated under the desk of the trick table; the soundtrack is made in the recording studio with the assistance of the sound engineer, and the picture and the sound track are finally mixed on the editing table."[15]

As Hermína Týrlová recollected for the journal *Film Today* (Film a doba), the year 1954 brought new demands regarding the quality of equipment for the Gasparcolor film system:

"The shift of frames in the camera had to be absolutely precise because the system required triple shooting of each individual picture with three colour filters. The contours of the resulting three frames, shot one after another, had to match exactly... We urgently had to go from the thick celluloid sheets on which we had drawn the silhouettes to the thinnest and the most transparent ones which would not deprive the picture of its colour and light. And moreover, we had to modify the trick table. We needed to upgrade our equipment for the camera motion, and the new lighting of the sensitive material and the new cartooning tables were also desirable."[16]

Because IRE-film produced sound pictures from the very beginning, one of the most significant positions there was that of music composer. It was eventually taken by the very young Bedřich Kerten, a native from the North-Bohemian city of Teplice and a pop-music composer and arranger who arrived at the studio armed with some initial experience in film (which he later critically reviewed in two articles written for the *Prague Kurier*).[17] IRE-film gave Kerten the chance to learn composing for animated film which required an extraordinary sense of the timing and the rhythm of animated motion. Similar to the Walt Disney studio, the scores always came first, before the shooting, and were finalized after completing the given title. A stopwatch and metronome were irreplaceable in the studio.

Within a few years, IRE-film worked itself to a rather high standard from the point of technology and in the framework of contemporary Czech production. The Dodals came to form a creative unit in which they chimed and supplemented each other. This can be seen in the surviving film credits, always stating two authors: "Filmed by Iréna and Karel Dodal"; "Executed and drawn by Iréna and Karel Dodal"; "Libretto and drawing by Iréna and Karel Dodal"... The contemporary trick-film credits seldom mentioned directors, but anytime it happened here, it still went: "Libretto, directed and drawn by Iréna and Karel Dodal". Speaking to the press, Irena Dodalová always emphasized the crucial role of her husband in the studio as well as the active role of its employees. It should not be omitted that the enterprise also used external workers.

It is without doubt that Dodal's first wife Hermína Týrlová, the lead animator in IRE-film, experienced a difficult period of her life in the company. One of her testimonies summing up this stage of her life resounds with deep emotion and trauma: "Karel Dodal invited me to collaborate after some time. We re-established our former business connections and contacted our former clients via Karel's second wife. She was utterly illiterate in what we were doing but was good at selling it. Self-confident, impudent, ambitious, capable of unscrupulously pressing her goals to earn as much as possible, she was my absolute antithesis. She was quite good at that. After all, it just required six years and a twosome working under the utmost strenuous and unbelievable conditions, morning to night and without any Sunday rest. Nothing but piles and piles of celluloid covered with drawings, then colouring and shooting those sheets, and then washing them, and drawing and drawing again, day by day, almost nonstop and endlessly. Only later we received two more pairs of hands to disburden us a little. I have no words for how grateful I am for forgetting this most difficult and humiliating period of my life, and I mention this only because I want to be sincere and do not want to leave an empty gap in all those bitter six years."[18]

This suggests a forsaken woman forced to subordinate herself to the new wife of her previous partner. The wording shows the humiliation, and also the sacrifice. The plural used signifies that Týrlová, in spite of the divorce, was still convinced that she and Dodal formed a couple determining the IRE-film artistic profile. Her judgement of the conditions in the studio was certainly driven by the fact that she, due to her life condition, had to turn into nothing but labour, merely becoming a draughtswoman, phasist and animator. The surviving documents prove that her points were very subjective. She was nevertheless correct that working for IRE-film equalled extraordinary strain and exhaustion – but this held true for the rest of the employees as well.

Some working conditions in the studio were also illustrated by the radio show "Cartoon Superstar" (Hledá se hvězda pro kreslený film) whose script survived in the Czech Radio archives. The show was broadcast only in German and only in summer 1938, i.e. sometime after the Dodals had closed the studio. It was about the Dodals' earlier project linked with promoting *The Adventures of a Ubiquitous Fellow*, and it was initially planned to feature contemporary artistic celebrities such as the puppeteer Josef Skupa and the composer Jaroslav Ježek. But the swift change of conditions in, what was then, Czechoslovakia, turned the given program into a retrospective. Regardless of the pseudonym, the undoubted author of the series was Irena Dodalová. The surviving typescript to it, featuring the above-mentioned triangle Karel Dodal–Irena Dodalová–Hermína Týrlová, describes the life of the IRE-film studio in the utmost detail, such as "we grew accustomed to listening to the radio as we drew, because the almost unbearable staying up late would otherwise have been impossible".[19]

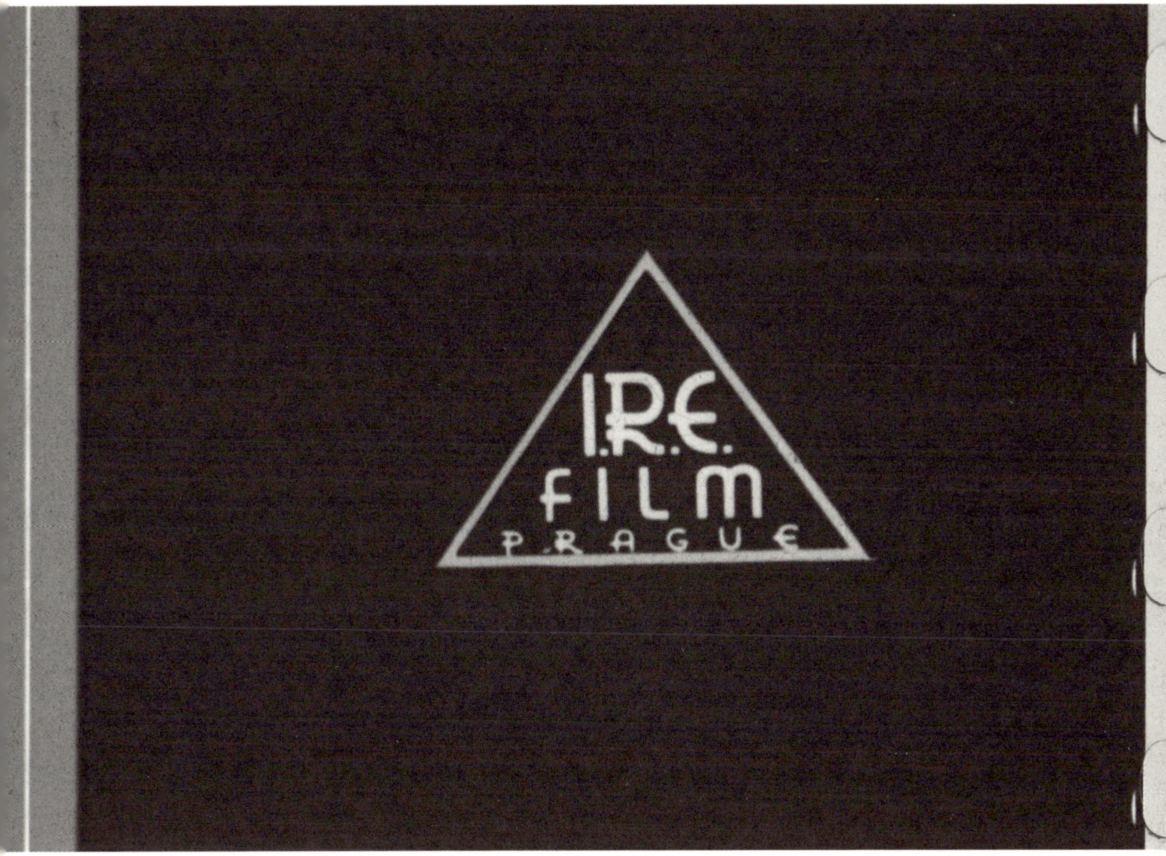
I.R.E.
FILM
PRAGUE

1 Copies of the school reports survived in I. Dodalová's idemnification request. In: *Amt für Widergutmachung in Saarburg, Irena Dodal*. Personal Fund of Irena Dodalová.

2 Census paper of 1921, Brno. The Brno City Archives.

3 The note about I. Rosnerová's opera activity is in the monograph Bondi, G., *Geschichte des Brünner deutschen Theaters 1600–1925*. Brün: Verlag des Deutschen Theatervereines, 1924, pp. 161, 173; and, as she stated in the indemnification request form (see Note 1), she privately studied with S. Pichler-Normann and T. Werner who also were part of the opera chorus of the Brno German theatre.

4 I. Dodalová in the letter addressed to her brother and dated 29 September 1983. The correspondence between Dodalová and her younger brother, R. Rosner (Rohan). Personal Fund of Irena Dodalová. R. Rosner (17 August 1902 – 29 August 1986) adopted the surname Rohan in November 1945. He worked as a train dispatcher and clerk and later probably assisted in IRE-film. He fought in the Czechoslovak foreign army during the Second World War. Thanks to his second marriage, he found himself in Záryby in the 1970s where part of his inheritance, including his correspondence with sister Irena, survived in the Cerha family.

5 Jarka, V. H., "Království paní Ireny" (The Realm of Ms Irena), *Národní listy*, 1937, No. 354, 25 November, p. 18. Peroff, however, was not French. The chequered life of this globe-trotter, which even included an American anti-Bolshevik expedition to Siberia, was reconstructed by J. Goergen in the 1990s ("Discovering Paul N. Peroff", *Animation Journal*, 1998, No. 2, p. 43). P. N. Peroff originated from St Petersburg but left for the United States prior to the First World War. He acquired US citizenship in 1918 and adopted the American style of advertising film. Upon his return to Europe, he continued producing animated films in France and mainly in Germany.

6 Data from the evidence of citizens. The National Archives, Prague.

7 Dodalová, I., *Karel Dodal & I.R.E. FILM Praha. Datos o zrození kresleného filmu* (... Data about the Birth of Cartoon Film). Personal Fund of Irena Dodalová.

8 Ibid.

9 A smaller film production company, Irefilm, existed at that time in Sweden but I do not assume that its name played any role in naming the Czech studio.

10 This is proved by the application of the Žižkov municipal government of the Capital of Prague of 10 August 1933, addressed to the Police Headquarters. The National Archives, Police Headquarters 1931–1940, D 707/6, box 5364, Dodal.

11 -nk-, "Kreslený film – poesie neskutečna...", *Večerník Práva lidu*, 1936, No. 179, 2 August, p. 3.

12 See Note 7.

13 Letter of A. Popp to The Czechoslovak Film Institute (ČSFÚ, Československý filmový ústav), 20 September 1985. Personal Fund of Irena Dodalová. The family of O. Popp donated the correspondence of their father, A. Popp, to the National Film Archive. A. Popp was already acquainted with the Dodals before the war. The branched Prague family of Dodal, on the contrary, held almost no documents concerning the artist; it was also because the distressed relatives used to destroy post-war correspondence. H. Týrlová, too, destroyed her personal correspondence before leaving for her rest home, explaining that she did not want any more people going through it.

14 I depart here from the copied clipping of the German article "Trickfilm in Prag", filed in the Personal Fund of Irena Dodalová without any detailed information.

15 Markert, H., "Monate Arbeit – fünf Minuten Vergnügen. Hinter den Kulissen' des tschechoslowakischen Trickfilms", *Neue Morgenpost*, 1937, No. 227, 26 September, p. 11.

16 Týrlová, H., "Kus historie našeho loutkového filmu" (A Piece of History of Our Puppet Film), *Film a doba*, 1954, No. 5, p. 866.

17 Kerten, F., "Musik zu Kurztonfilmen", *Prager Film-Kurier*, 1934, No. 74, 18 August, p. 2; ibid., "Der Librettist und Komponist", *Prager Film-Kurier*, 1934, No. 77, 25 August, p. 2.

18 Benešová, M., op. cit., pp. 21–22.

19 *Hledá se hvězda pro kreslený film*, untitled German typescript. The Czech cataloguing title is not original. Archive and Program Funds of the Czech Radio, Ref. No. 4532, p. 9. See Larsen, E., "Trickfilmstar gesucht / Hledá se hvězda pro kreslený film / Rozhlasové pásmo z pražského filmového atelieru" (Cartoon Superstar / Radio Show from the Prague Film Studio), *Radiojournal*, 1938, No. 32, 7 August, p. 5. Czech media mentioned the show as "Hledá se hvězda pro trickfilm" (Trick Film Superstar), *Filmový kurýr* (Film Courier), 1938, No. 32, 12 August, p. 2.

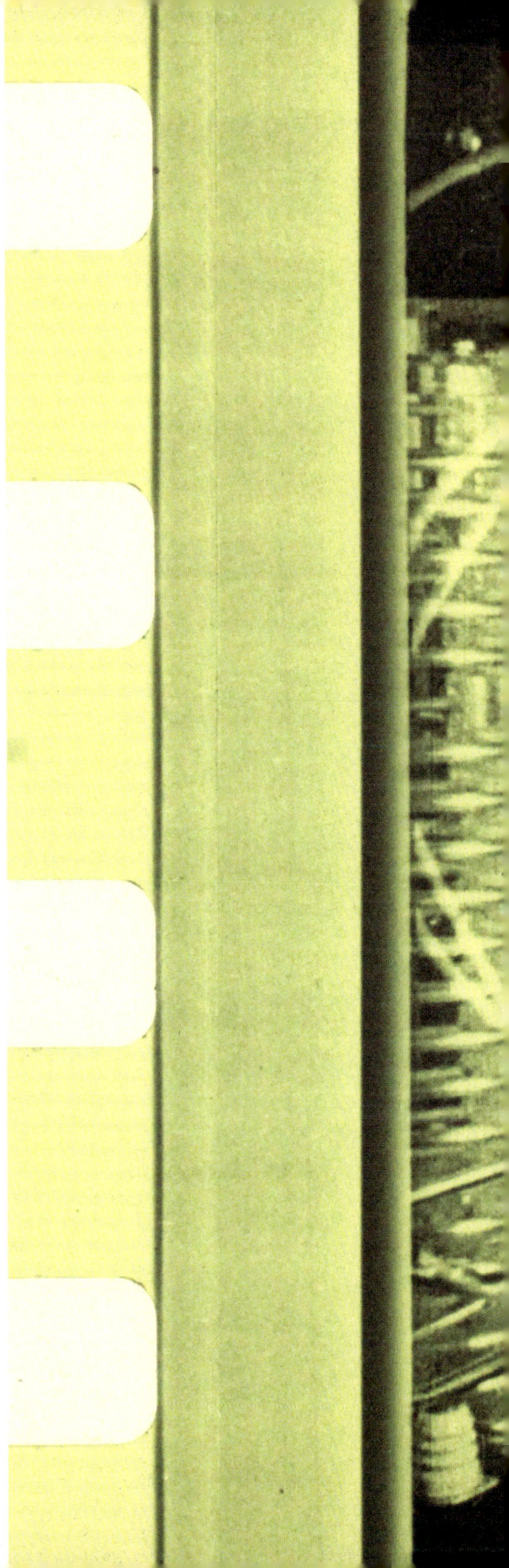

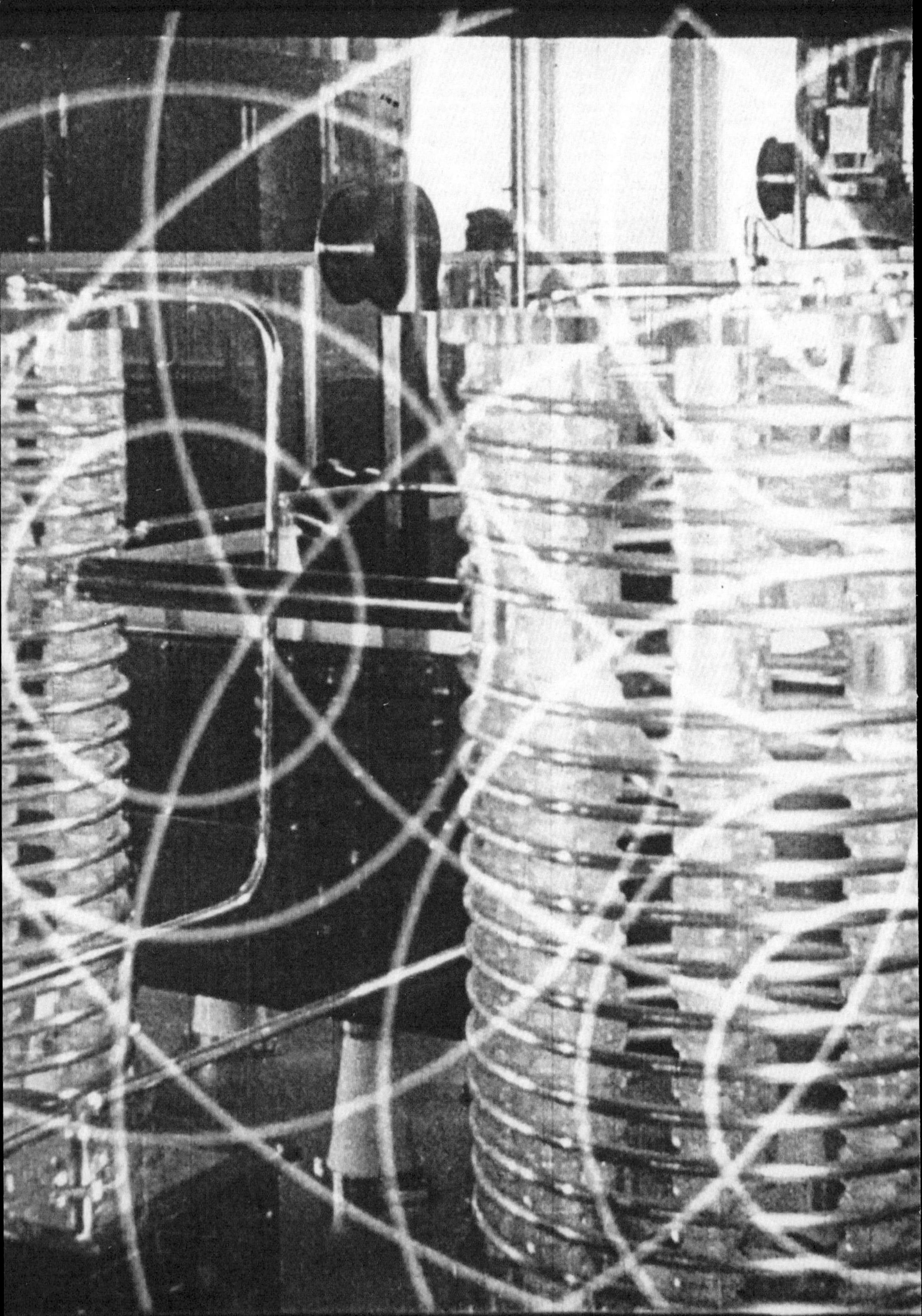

The Adventures of a Ubiquitous Fellow / Fusing the Czech Puppet Theatre Tradition and Film

Although the global economic crisis was slowly coming to an end and the economy was taking a turn towards recovery when Irena Leschnerová and Karel Dodal established the IRE-film studio, it required much optimism and courage indeed to launch a business in the demanding trick and animated film production in a country that lacked a continuous tradition in this field and its film market was rather tight. The authors, however, departed from their experience gained in France and Germany and assumed that they, too, would be able to procure sufficient financial means to follow their artistic dreams via working on commissions. They also undoubtedly gambled on acquiring support from the Film Advisory Board and, eventually, other institutions. The first years of their independent enterprise seemed promising.

The IRE-film's first significant and prestigious commission was a promotional film for the radio company Radiojournal. Czechoslovak Radio at that time was an influential institution holding as equally crucial a position as do TV and internet today. Its program range was rich and multi-layered; it aimed at varied strata of the population of many professions and interests, and its live broadcastings allowed the listeners participate in an array of sport and cultural events and performances. The radio not only focused on traditional culture but also contemporary modern music and the like. One of

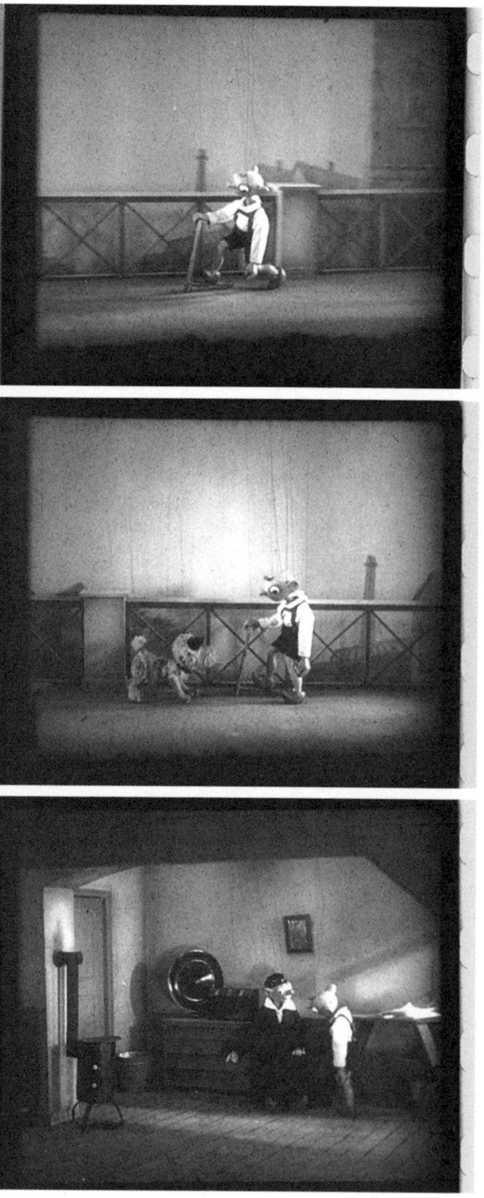

Takes from the picture *Spejbl's Fascination with Film*.

its most noticeable personalities was the Plzeň-based Professor Josef Skupa whose puppet theatre with the starring characters of Spejbl and Hurvínek were known by the listeners from the frequent radio shows and gramophone recordings as well as his tours throughout the republic. It was thus a matter of course that the preparatory works for the Radiojournal film included Skupa's name.

The puppeteer's experience with film prior to meeting the Dodals was not exactly the best. Although he, from the 1920s, rejected most of the offers from Elekta Journal, Legiafilm, Propagafilm and others, he eventually agreed to collaborate on two films: the silent comedy *Spejbl's Case* (Spejblův případ) and the medium-length *Spejbl's Fascination with Film* (Spejblovo filmové opojení). Works on a commercial for the Prague Association of Cast-Iron Bathtubs, produced by the Reklama Slavia company in 1930, made Skupa realize that shooting was extremely time consuming, that it collided with his work in theatre and that it even did not pay off financially.[1] It is therefore surprising in this context that he very soon, in 1931, filmed the puppet picture *Spejbl's Fascination*, and moreover with a totally unknown producer, Josef Fišer. The sound puppet film was medium-length and opened with a scene performed by a live actor: a monologue of the leading Czech actor Jindřich Plachta alias Ms Acetylene.[2]

In fact, Skupa's friendship with Jindřich Plachta could have been among the reasons why the artist gave the nod to re-sail the troubled waters of animation aimed at grown-ups instead of children. The film in question told the story of Spejbl searching for a financier to prompt his film career but finding himself

Jiřina Skupová, Josef Skupa and Gustav Nosek in the 1930s.

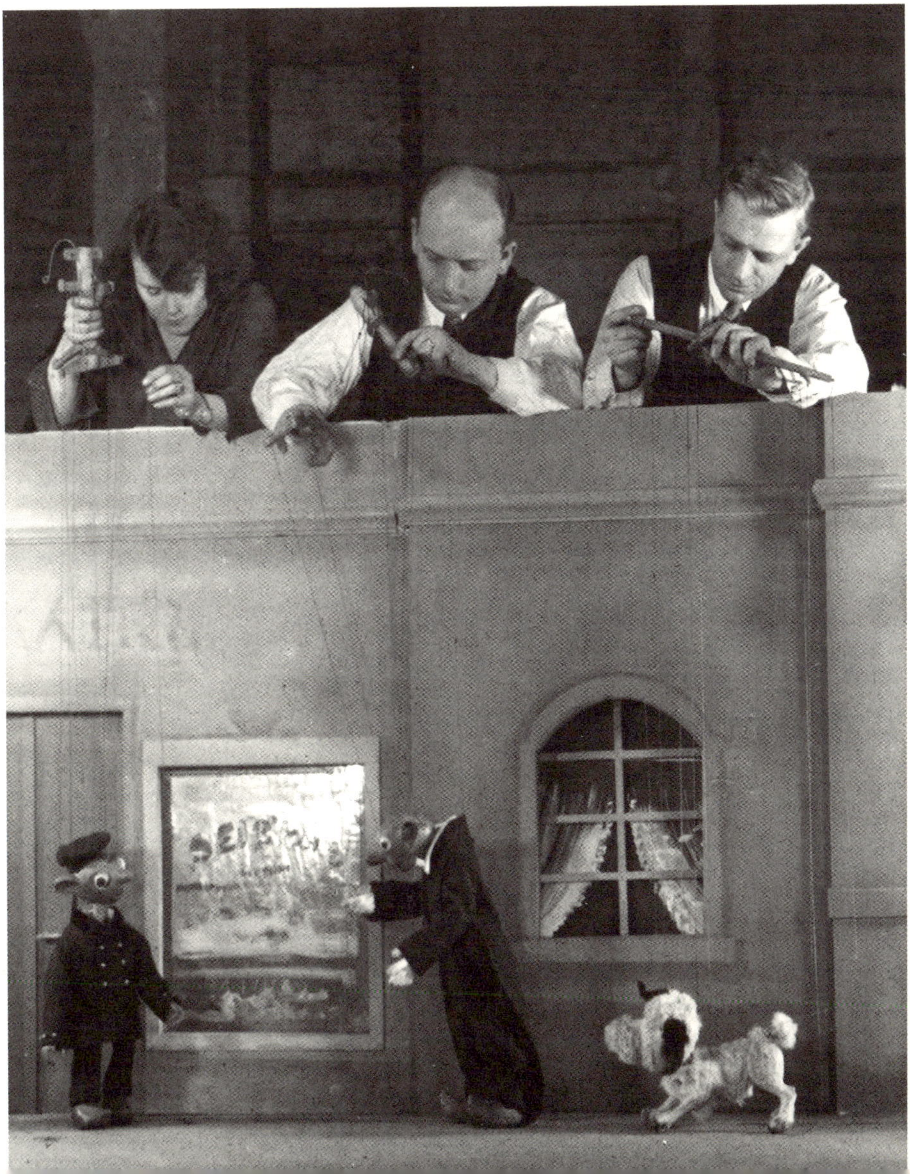

trapped in the clutches of a versant swindler. He is finally liberated by his son Hurvínek thanks to a Radiojournal warning broadcast. The surviving libretto proves that despite the square, almost simpleminded plot, Skupa was enormously focused on the project, also trying to supress the motionlessness of theatre stage and replacing it with film methods. He would note in the libretto which takes should be shot in whole or in detail or semi-detail, large detail (he wrote "premier plan"), he would insist on panoramic and moving camera (he called it "gadget") shots and on lap dissolve and fading of the takes, would use film montage in a succession of scenes and so on. It is apparent from the libretto that Skupa here pondered a new relation between a staged and filmed puppet, although the marionettes were still set to motion mechanically instead of via animation. Bringing Skupa's libretto ideas to life would certainly require a considerable amount of time and strain, but the production manager Fischer was able to arrange no more than half a day for Skupa and the cameraman Jan Stallich in the Vinohrady studios of the AB company. Only a small part of the promising project was therefore realized and the authors could incorporate puppets into the film space in merely a few places. *Spejbl's Fascination* – described as "the first Czech 100% spoken puppet film" and "the story of rags and sticks on 7 strings" in the premiere invitation – was previewed on 7 April 1931 in the Světozor cinema along with the film about Ms Acetylene. The censorship authorities ruled that the program was "for the adults only". It was therefore in no case a children's film as it is today sometimes mistakenly described. It was screened in April in Světozor for two weeks and simultaneously in two other movie theatres – in Kotva for five weeks and Radio for two weeks – and it later passed through several cinemas outside Prague.[3] Its flagship song "Handkiss, Missus", released by Ultraphon, soon became widely popular.

This work by Skupa undoubtedly occupied a significant place in the history of early animation, and *Spejbl's Fascination* can possibly be viewed as the first Czech puppet film, because the commercial *Spejbl's Case* was rather just a filmed puppet sketch. What is interesting – albeit not completely clarified – is the film's bond to Radiojournal. A month before the premiere, Skupa published a shot from the film in the magazine *Radiojournal*, noting that *Spejbl's Fascination with Sound* would soon be introduced to cinemas. The article, stating "sound" instead of "film" in the title of the picture, stressed that it would attract both viewers and radio amateurs because "radio plays an important role here. The story, for instance, starts with an announcement of our Radiojournal. The soundtrack was composed by a member of our orchestra, music composer R. Kubín".[4] This with the lapse of time provokes speculation that Skupa's film was actually a disguised Radiojournal commercial, which would explain much about why the puppeteer, who otherwise declined filming, took charge of the project. The hypothesis also seems to be supported by many attributes of the film, such as the dominant position of the radio receiver in Spejbl's home, the many lines about the radio program and mainly the construction of the plot where the happy ending is contributed by a Radiojournal announcement. In addition, the above-mentioned magazine notice not only drew attention to Skupa's forthcoming premiere but also his future radio program and his planned three-month tour through Czechoslovakia and to Vienna. It was an exemplary case of synergic use of multiple media such as radio, film, press and theatre and, in Skupa's case, often also the recording industry.[5] And although Josef Skupa would frequently make the best of this interactive effect, he would always verbally insist

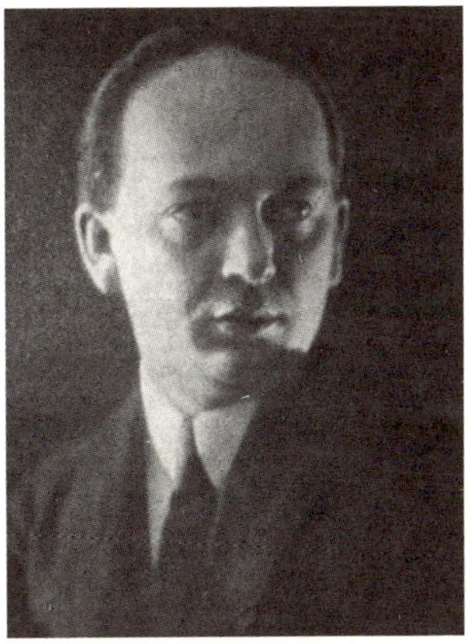

Josef Skupa was one of the most distinctive personalities of Czech puppet theatre during the inter-war period.

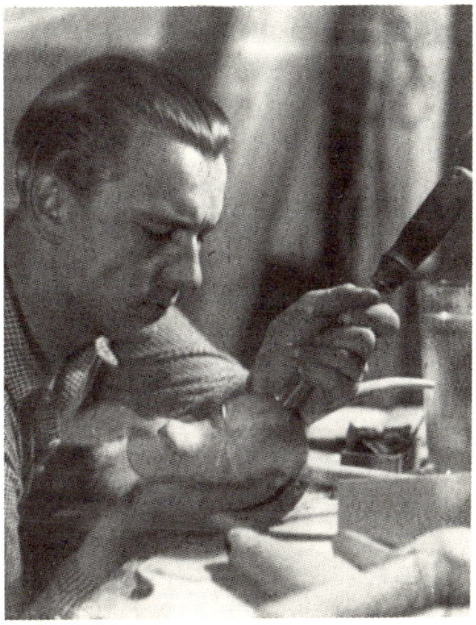

The beginnings of the puppeteering career of Jiří Trnka were closely linked with Skupa's puppet theatre, based in Plzeň.

that he was just a touring puppeteer. He would even urge Radiojournal in several letters to ban his gramophone recordings from being part of its program structure: he thought that they did not bring the proclaimed advertising effect but on the contrary considerably weakened the interest in his touring shows. His correspondence suggests that he was equally disappointed by his collaboration with film.

Skupa nevertheless later agreed to the Radiojournal offer that the Dodals would base the character of Hurvínek in a cartoon on the principle of radio broadcasting. The given choice had an undoubted marketing asset for all involved. From the point of Radiojournal, the share of Professor Skupa – very popular with the radio listeners – guaranteed a favourable reception of the film and facilitated its promotion. The Dodals imagined that the film transformation of the cherished theatre and radio character of Hurvínek could somehow become analogical to Mickey Mouse. And it also was an interesting challenge for Skupa because he thus had the first chance ever to collaborate with people professionally engaged in film animation whose renown largely excluded the danger of a flop. Skupa indeed took his collaboration on the film seriously to the utmost and closely supervised the entire process. One of the proofs of his approach is the letter addressed to IRE-film where he complained that the puppeteer and filmmaker Trnka had not finished his work yet, and claimed he would not "lend Hurvínek" without co-acting with him.[6] It also was Skupa who adopted the name Ubiquitous Fellow (Všudybyl) for Hurvínek's new, animated form from the 19th-century puppet theatre. He moreover generously permitted the filmmakers to feature his marionette for free, albeit for one-time use only; his correspondence testifies that all future collaborations would be based on "sharing the profits".[7]

The concept of *The Adventures of a Ubiquitous Fellow*, co-developed by Jan Černý as the head of the Radiojournal PR section, the Dodals and Josef Skupa, deserves attention for several reasons. Animation in advertising was far from new at that time and both trick and cartoon sequences had been appearing in school, instructional and scientific films from time immemorial, but the given picture was neither planned as instructional nor merely commercial: its purpose was to introduce the public to the most recent progress in the field of radio broadcasting and to achieve this in the most easy-going

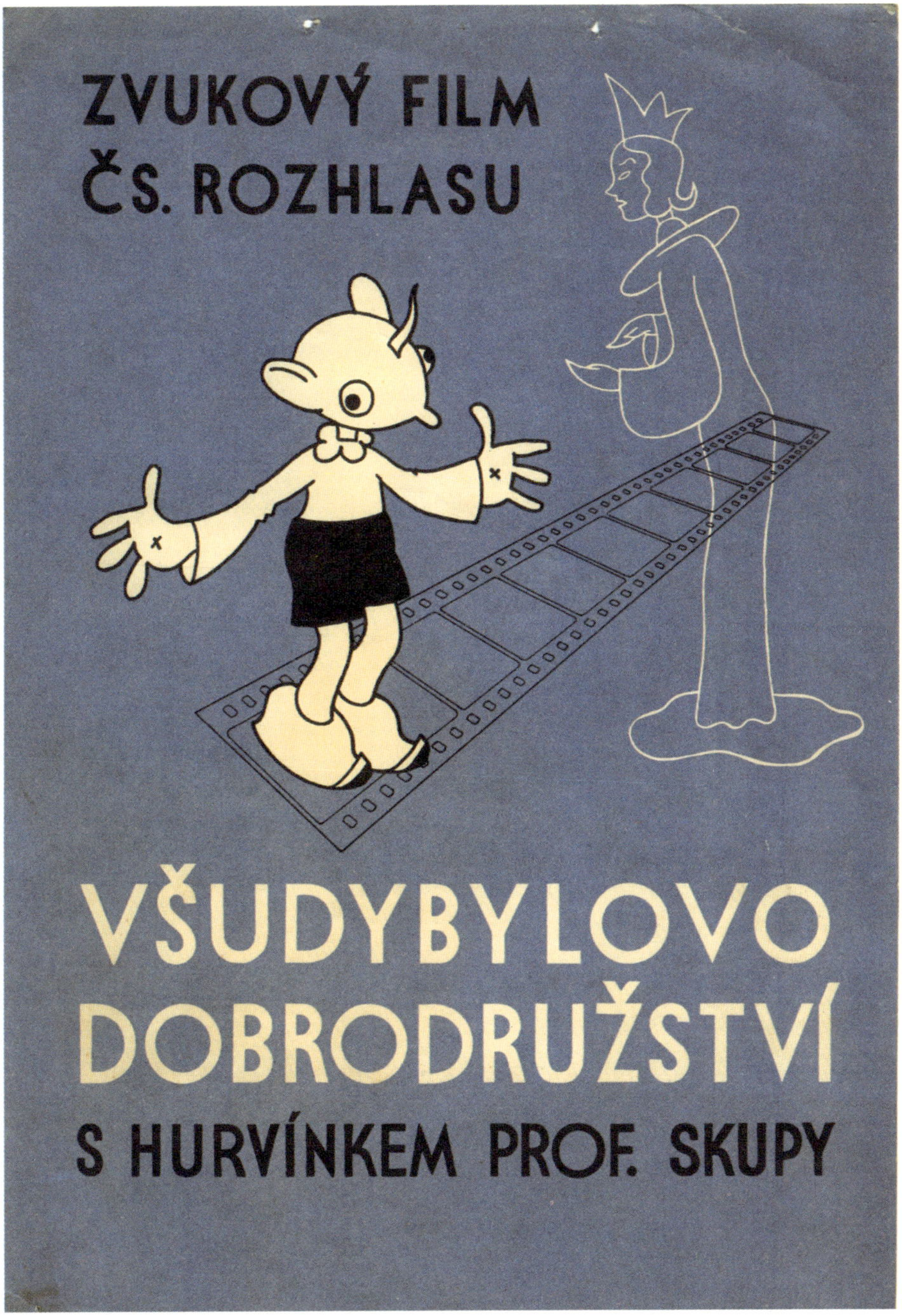
ZVUKOVÝ FILM
ČS. ROZHLASU
VŠUDYBYLOVO
DOBRODRUŽSTVÍ
S HURVÍNKEM PROF. SKUPY

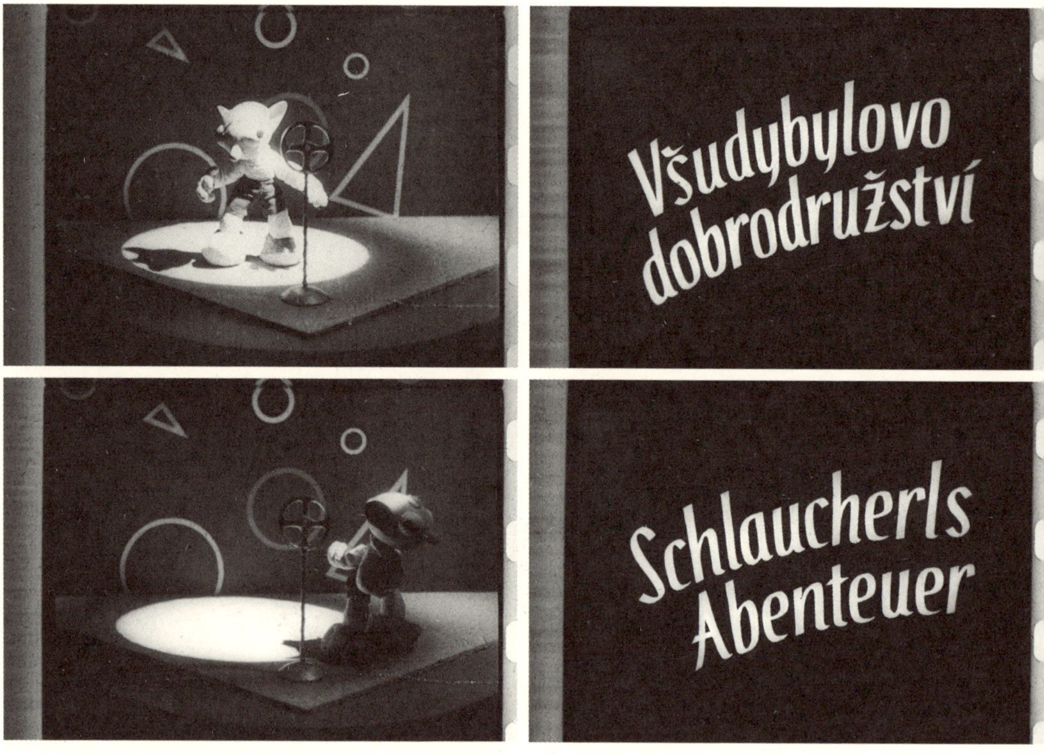

The Adventures of a Ubiquitous Fellow was shortened upon the recommendation of the Film Advisory Board, and it then arrived in cinemas in a new version with virage. Only the first part of this authorized adaptation survived. But another version of the title, containing Czech and German subtitles and new introductory music, was probably made from the originally black-and-white negative, although the Dodals did not participate on it.

and interesting manner. The aim was to make a popular and scientific animated title, howsoever this genre was rare in contemporary cinematography and the label "popular scientific film" did not exist yet.[8]

The authors developed a new type of a film narrative in *The Adventures.* They based it on the relationship between two fictitious characters – the curious Ubiquitous Fellow whose black-and-white outlines referred to both Hurvínek's looks and nature, and the Queen of Waves whose white, as if pellucid, pen-and-ink drawing evoked the invisible world of electromagnetic

waves. The core of the plot was the Fellow's resolution to find the origin of radio waves broadcast to outer space. The story develops linearly: the curious Fellow falls overboard from his space gondola and appears before the Radiojournal "skyscraper" building where he meets the Queen of Radio Waves and is shown around her entire kingdom including the radio studios and the Liblice transmitter. She explains to him the principle and technology of distributing electromagnetic waves and the informed hero finally sets off back to space with a radio broadcaster. The chosen teacher-student form of dialogue allowed for structuring the technical subject into questions and answers. Although it did not provide much space for employing cartoon gags (this requirement was perhaps met by, for instance, the shots of the greedy microphones), the appeal of rendering the story was mainly contributed to by the graphic and animation aspects and also the Skupa-like dialogues, maybe written with concern to school kids indulging in diminutives.

One of the stages of *The Adventures* genesis is captured by the libretto finished on 20 November 1935 whose main author was, according to the surviving typescript, Irena. Two colours of the typewriter ribbon (black and red, so fancied by the author) served to differentiate the description of picture and sound (right/left page of the script). Part of the film was to be made via animation in the studio, in other passages the heroes' dialogues were to be accompanied by visual montages borrowed from specialized films. The text on which the story was based – and which undoubtedly resulted from many previous negotiations – documents that the authors at this point already had a clear idea about the final picture, because it not only contained the succession of sequences but also stated many details of how to realize them. The film credits included the name of Jan Černý as the libretto co-writer, undoubtedly due to his collaboration on the expert contents of the film.

Future consultations probably resulted in attaching an introductory scene with the animated puppet of Hurvínek who stressed that Professor Skupa permitted him to appear in the cartoon as the Ubiquitous Fellow only after much persuasion. The authors thus created an interval and, simultaneously, a link between the theatre puppet and the drawn character, between Hurvínek's theatre and film existences. Skupa's student Jiří Trnka – a fresh graduate from the School of Applied Arts, an illustrator, commencing set designer and keeper of the Wooden Theatre (Dřevěné divadlo), who was already at that time a conspicuous personality of the Prague culture scene – was invited to adapt the puppet for the animation purposes. Since it was Trnka's first contact with film, the Italian historian of animation Giannalberto Bendazzi concluded that Trnka also animated the puppet.[9] We can imagine that Dodal minutely consulted him about the puppet's construction so that its motion could be phased, but we unfortunately have no information about the filming process and whether the busy Trnka participated in it at all.[10] The additionally incorporated Hurvínek's opening act is nevertheless one of the first Czech attempts at animating a puppet and these sequences demonstrate the problems brought about by the new technology, e.g. the issue of lighting.

The main designer of the film was Karel Dodal and it was one of his most distinct works from this period. He not only managed to translate the puppet of Hurvínek into a simple pen-and-ink line drawing suiting animation but also to create impressive designs for the scenes of Hurvínek's travels through outer space and to express, in a stylized short-cut, the modern nature of the new, recently opened radio facilities. It, however, was not a documentary drawing but a fictitious idea which in some details corresponded with the Radiojournal reality; for example, the large close-up of the face of the popular newscaster, František Havel, the microphones, the new organ, the Liblice transmitter and other features. The new functionalist building of Czechoslovak Radio was in Dodal's rendering transformed into a skyscraper surrounded by constructions resembling New York more than Prague.

The graphic quality of Dodal's drawings was proved by their frequent publication in newspapers and magazines, although their main purpose was to comply with the requirements of animation. Dodal in *The Adventures* developed an artistic solution whose traces can be found, for instance, in the

Ježek's musical score contains 74 sheets, including the instrumentation for piano, three violins, two trumpets, trombone, three saxophones, bass, celeste and guitar, as well as the adaptations of (supplements to) the individual parts which were probably created during the final synchronization of the film picture and music.

32 páginas

„Všudybylkovo dobrodružství"

propagační film Radiojournalu

Synchronní hudba

Složil

Jar Ježek

Schází:

~~Dýka~~
~~Lift~~
salon krásy (Fronty)
~~Příjezd městečk~~ 10. [illegible]
~~Koupání měst.~~ in Moll

Praha 1936.

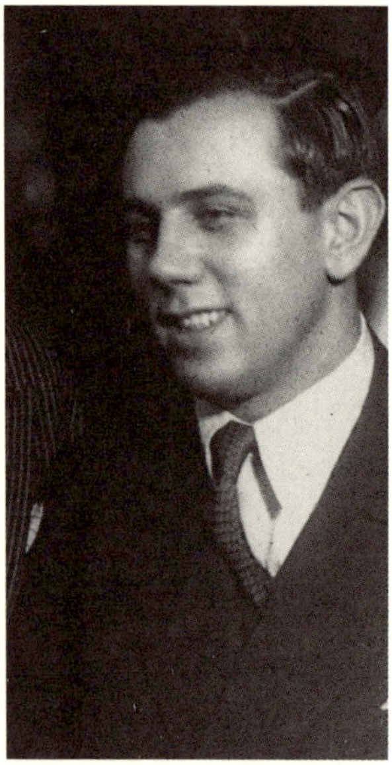

The pianist and composer Jaroslav Ježek also conducted the Liberated Theatre orchestra during the 1930s. His music, strongly influenced by jazz, became one of the most characteristic parts of 20th-century Czech musical culture.

earlier commercial *Mum's Trip to Heaven* (Maminčin výlet do nebe; 1935). He segmented the surface of the film picture into foreground and background layers, the main and side surfaces. He enclosed some scenes in some kind of cartouches – graphic spaces delineated by irregular trapezoids – subsequently locating the scenes with the main characters into them. The side surfaces were distinguished by "decoration" in the form of simple graphic signs, such as triangles and circles. Various modifications of these simple morphologies were subsequently employed in several following films. The aim of articulating the surface was clearly to develop new possibilities of the characters' motion in space. The figures of the Fellow and the Queen did not merely move frontally (horizontally) as it had been customary in Czech film, but newly could move in fictitious environments both due to the animation and the film "edit", represented by changes of takes or their size. For example, the deep view into the radio corridor with the accentuated perspective of the floor lines allowed for capturing the figures motion from foreground to background. The animation also had a sense for the grace of the female walk. The film in many scenes – such as Všudybyl's cosmic gondola cruise with stars whirling in the background – evoked a three-dimensional space. Dodal and his colleagues also achieved this quality by using two or three layers of foils.

The composer of the music accompaniment to *The Adventures* became Jaroslav Ježek whose name was at that time linked with The Liberated Theatre (Osvobozené divadlo) as well as with Czech film, and who also was a frequent Radiojournal guest. Ježek was apparently invited not only because the music was to be modern jazz which was his domain but also with respect to his high reputation in cultural circles. It was a new experience for both sides. The Dodals probably gave him very precise instructions as to where they required music. The score was divided into twelve parts (Hurvínek on the Moon, Falling, Organ, Light Bulbs...) and the music was synchronized with the animated picture in all passages that did not include the Všudybyl's and the Queen's dialogues. The latter were narrated by Josef Skupa as the Fellow and Anna Kreuzmannová as the Queen of Waves.[11] It seems today that combining a modern cartoon film with the theatrical diction of Skupa's puppet ensemble did not do any good to the result, but Hurvínek's voice in Skupa's rendering probably appealed to the contemporary public. The final synchronization of music and film was assisted by Bedřich Kerten who adjusted Ježek's music to the filmed material. Part of the

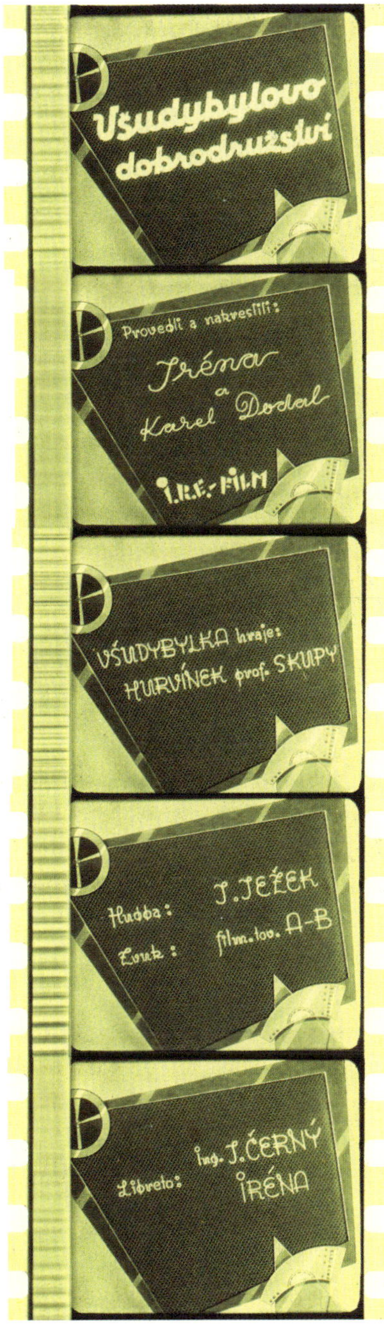

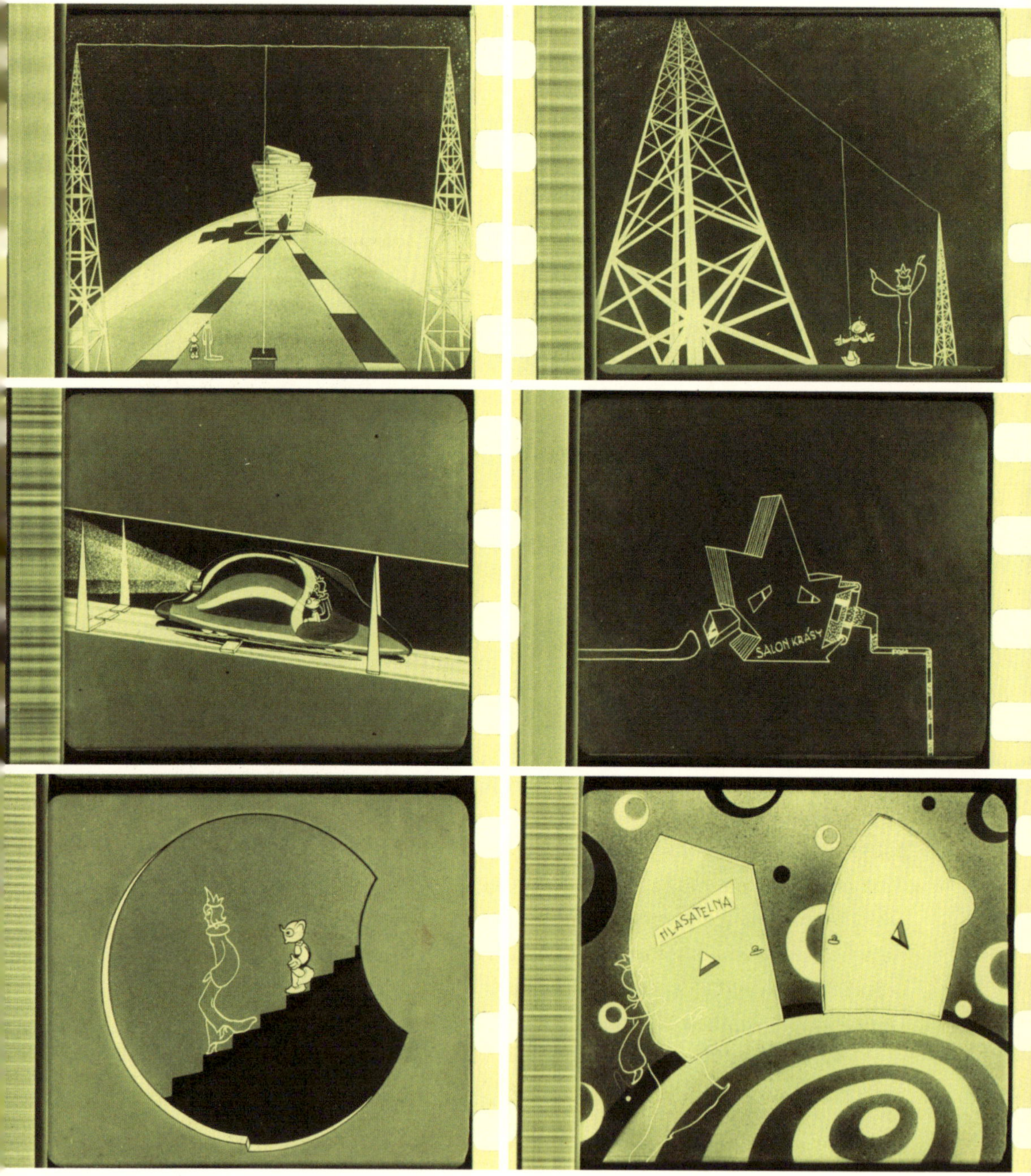
SALON KRÁSY
HLASATELNA

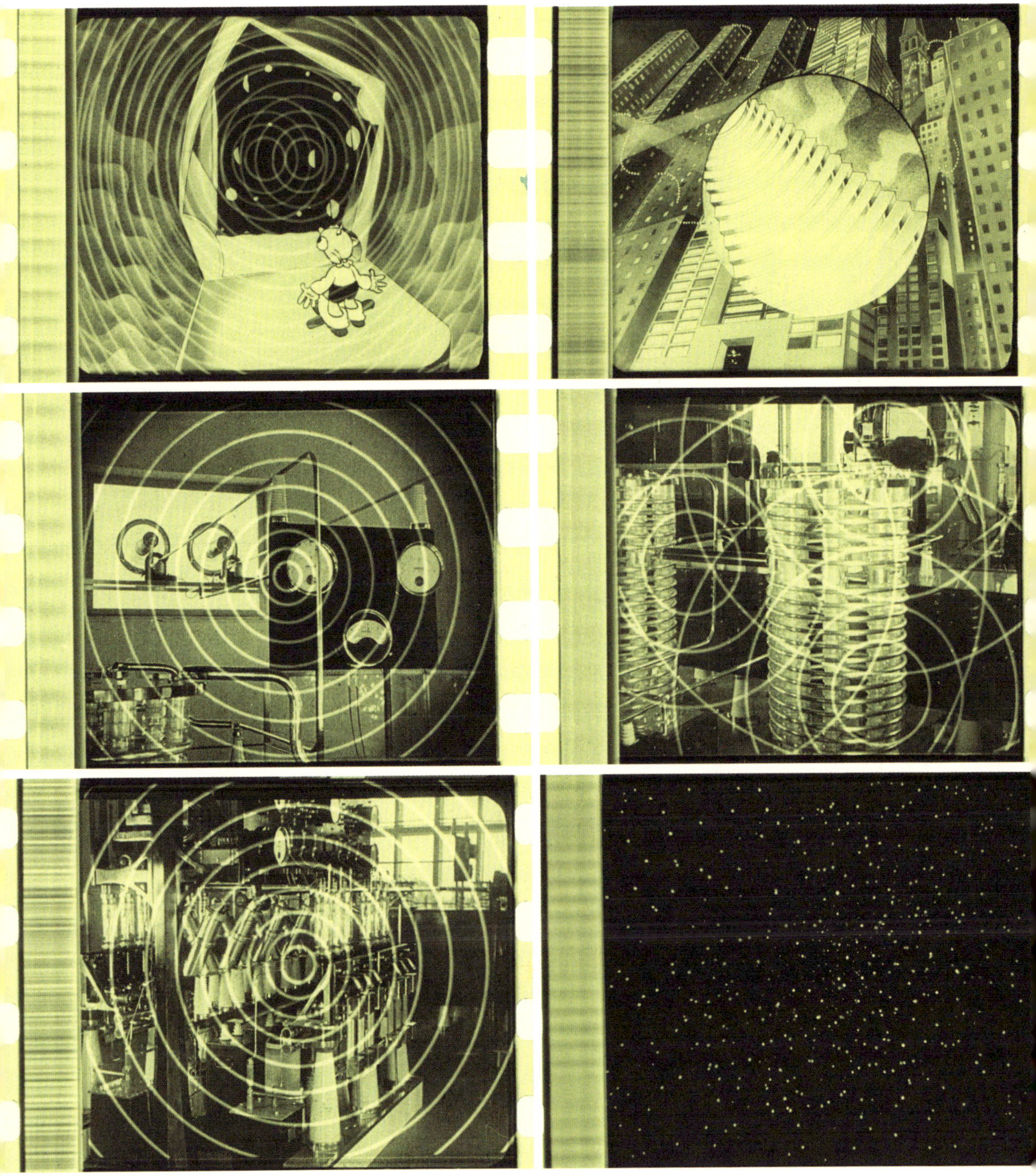

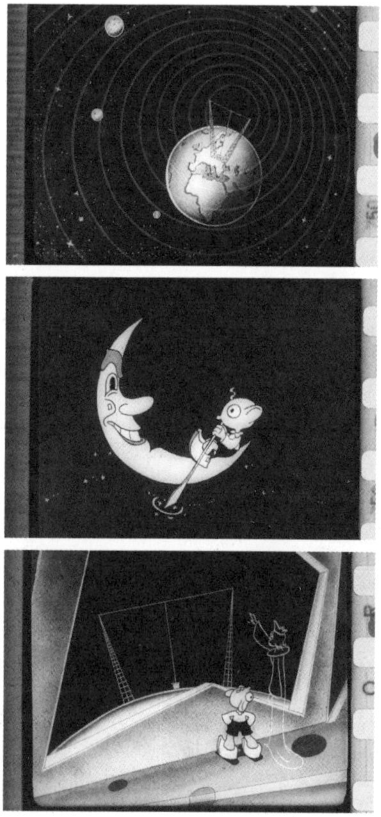

score was thus left out; it, however, illustrates the original intent of the authors.[12]

Certain problems arose from realizing the expert passages where the Dodals used a montage of takes from a film about the Liblice transmitter and the German animated film *Radio Technology* (Die Rundfunktechnik, Technika rozhlasu).[13] This fusion did not work out as the authors had imagined. The given method was advantageous from both the aspect of time and financing but the passages from the instructional films considerably collided with the popular and scientific style of the cartoon and its artistic concept. The recommendation of the Film Advisory Board then resulted in a 120-meter shorter virage version. The filmmakers accentuated the three-dimensional visual character of the introductory sequence and unified the

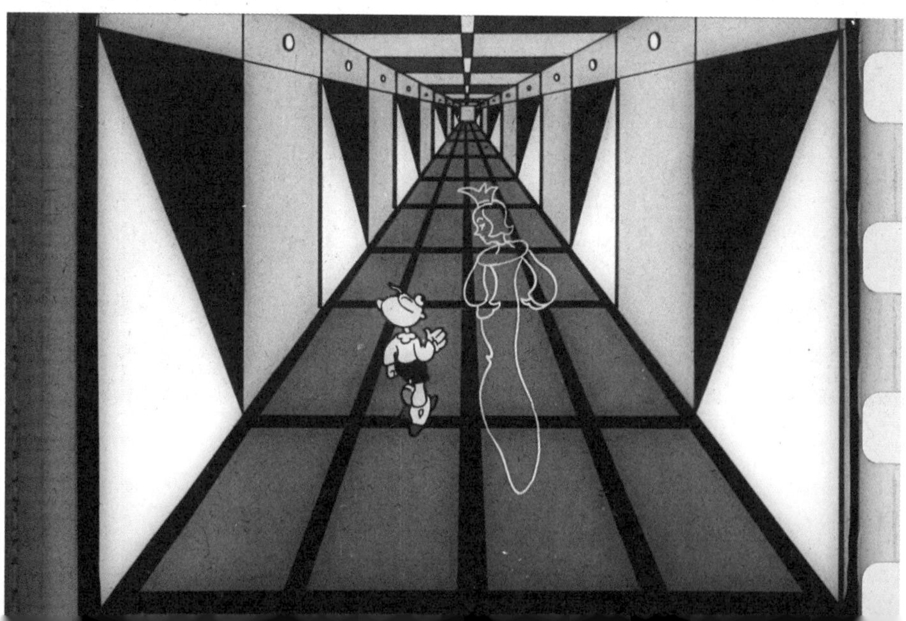

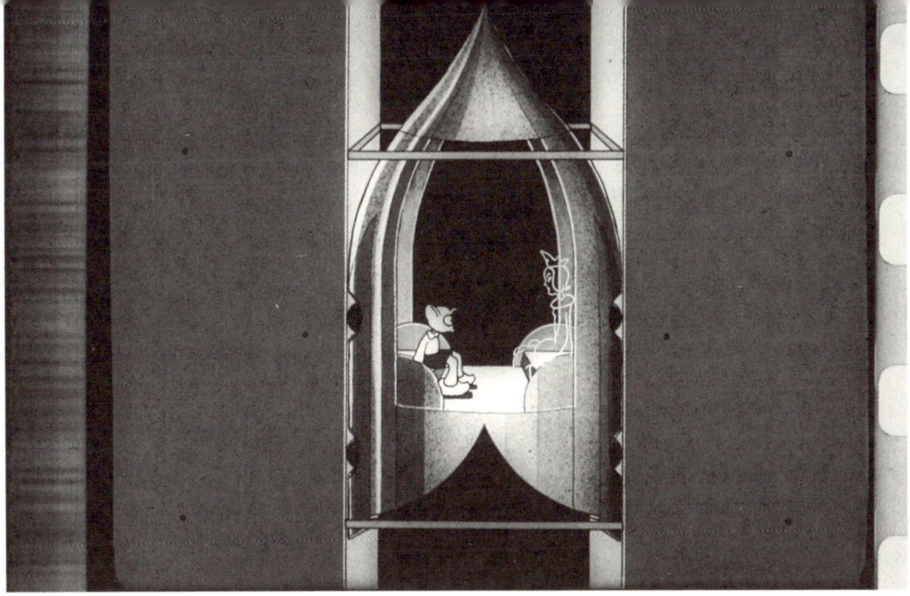

overall style by overlaying the documentary passages with dynamic circles. The yellow virage underlined the visual qualities as well as the cogency of the film, which made some journalists write that the picture was in colour. We can indeed regret that solely the first part of this version, which can be viewed as the original form of the work, survived.

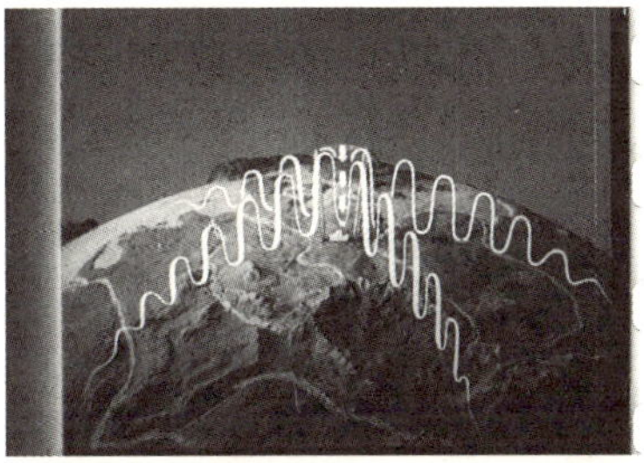

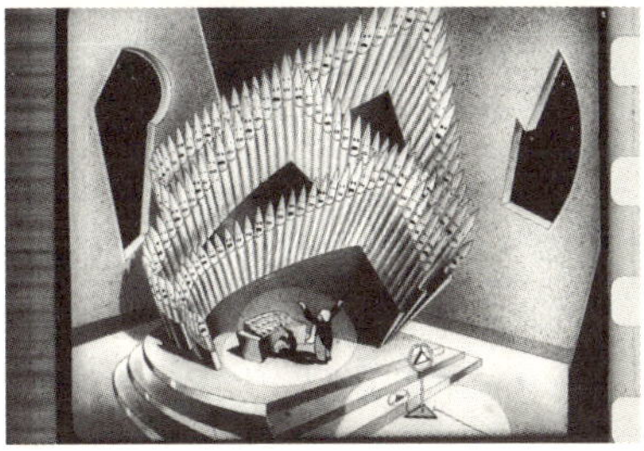

Dodal's designs of mainly the opening and closing passages are successful from both the artistic aspect and that of animation. Modern design, artistic shortcut and professional animation produced a new quality in Czech cartoon film. *The Adventures* represented an experiment in the contemporary context, and the moment when IRE-film brought Dodal's pen-and-ink line drawings of Hurvínek with his distinctive conduct, diction and verbiage to the movies can be perceived

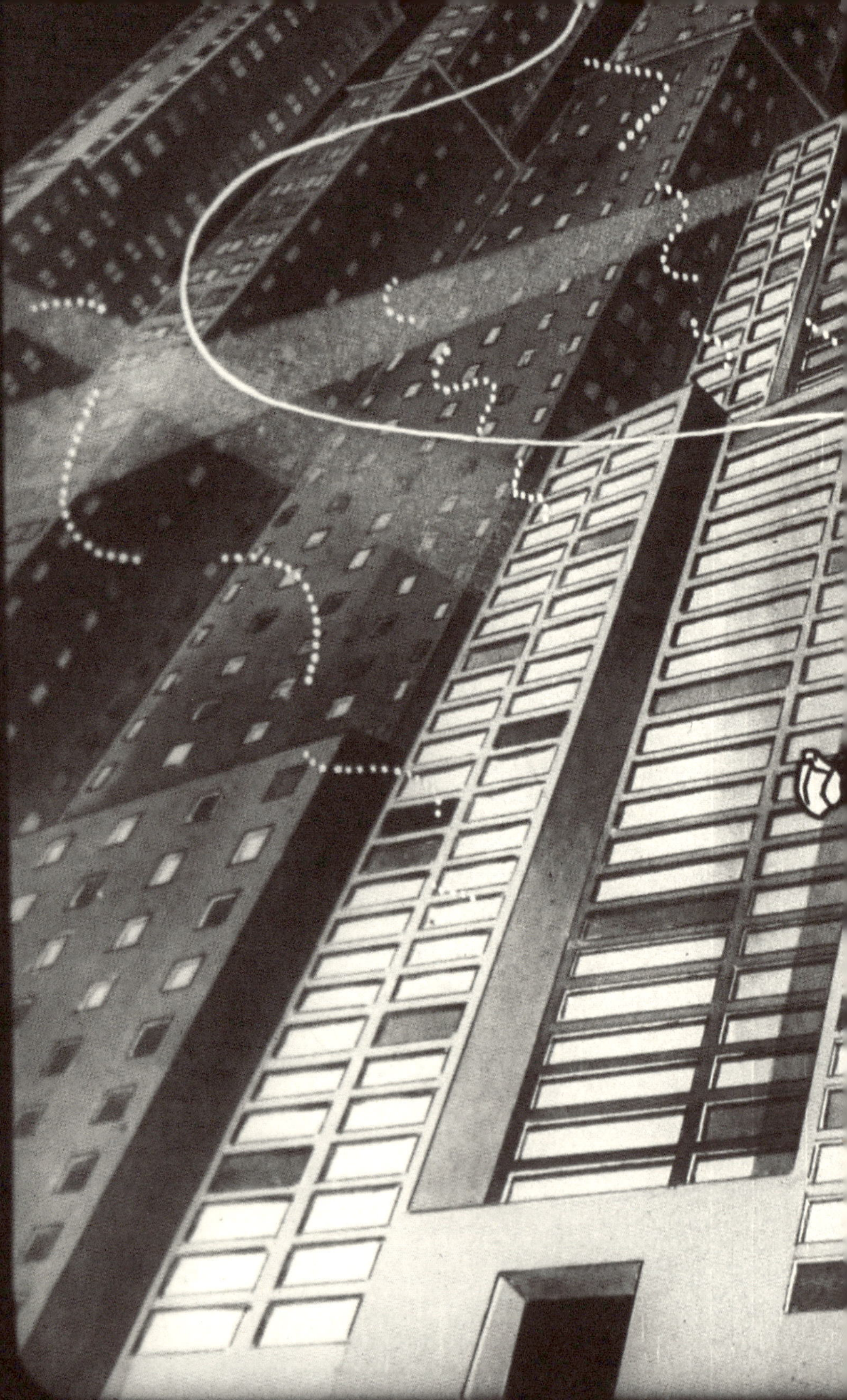

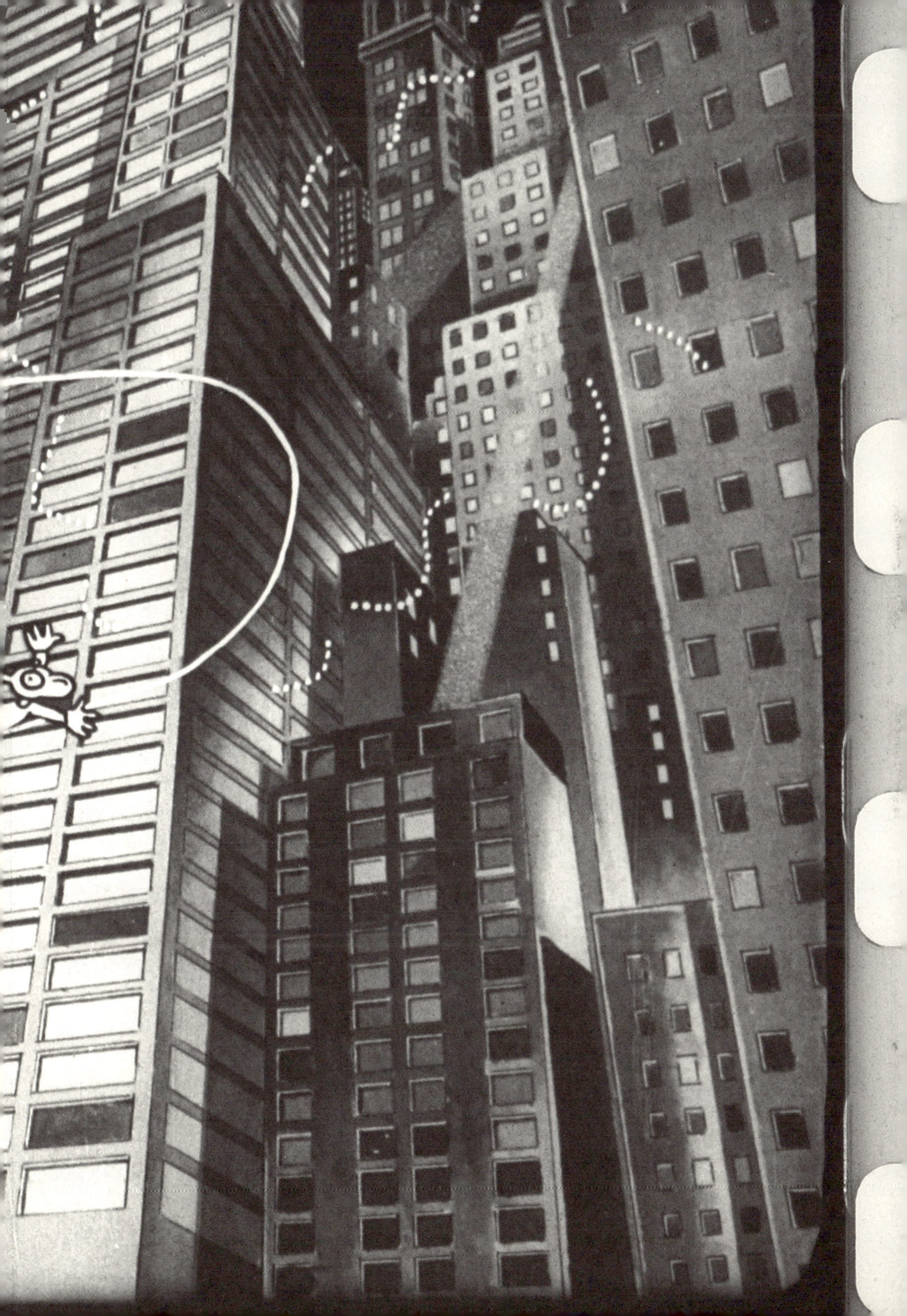

as the turning point when the tradition of Czech puppeteering, as represented by the modernist Skupa, and local animated film fused.

Filming *The Adventures* and introducing the picture went along with a systematic media campaign in newspapers and magazines and in Radiojournal broadcasting. It emphasized all the details of cartoon-making and effectively employed the well-known names of Josef Skupa, Jiří Trnka and Jaroslav Ježek. The distribution was procured by Radiojournal. The film was previewed at the Piešťany film exhibition in June 1936. There, the Dodals also presented the designs to *The Adventures* and the technology of processing colour film material at the art exhibition entitled "Theatre, Film, Music and Literature" (Divadlo, film, hudba a literatura).[14]

The red-carpet premiere for invited guests from the ranks of ministries, press, film companies and other institutions was held on 17 June 1936 at 10:30 p.m. in the Lucerna cinema in Prague. The reporter from *Film Strategy* (Filmová politika) wrote that the picture received a long ovation and "the parting present to everybody was playing the record with the music components of this film, composed by J. Ježek".[15] A selection of music was released by Radiojournal as a gramophone "soundtrack", used for promoting the film in the country and abroad. The film script also served as a basis for the radio series of the same name, aimed at school broadcasting. Irena Dodalová's plan to publish a corresponding book aimed at the young, however, was not realized.

Radiojournal postponed introducing *The Adventures* to the film distribution to autumn due to more favourable publicity options. A promotional sketch featuring Josef Skupa along with Jaroslav Ježek and the Dodal couple was planned for the same season.[16] The materials prepared by Irena Dodalová were rejected by Radiojournal, and the two clips for the broadcasting were made by Skupa alone. The first clip from late August 1936, opening with several beats of Ježek's music, was conceived as an interview of the radio newscaster František Havel with Spejbl and Hurvínek which revolved around the significance of radio, the collaboration between radio and sound film and mainly around *The Adventures*. In the second, somewhat shorter program shot in autumn, Hurvínek personally invited viewers to see the cartoon, which had already been successfully screened at the Venice Film Festival.[17] Professor Skupa wanted to help Dodalová, hurt by having been rejected, and suggested

Radiojournal make "a fictitious report from the IRE-film studio from where the promotional radio picture *The Adventures of a Ubiquitous Fellow* originated; it would explain to children how cartoons are made".[18] It was probably on the basis of this suggestion that Dodalová prepared the series "Cartoon Superstar" (Hledá se hvězda pro kreslený film) which, however, became part of German broadcasting only in summer 1938 (see the preceding chapter).

Radiojournal provided German and Italian subtitles to *The Adventures* and the film was then purchased by many countries. The 1937 Radiojournal annual report informs that it was screened in 300 movie theatres in Czech, Slovak and German versions. A year later, it was shown in 53 cinemas.

The Adventures of a Ubiquitous Fellow became one of the most significant works in the Dodals' oeuvre and it received favourable response from both Czechoslovak and foreign spectators. In the following years, it helped the Dodal couple present their work in the United States and Argentina. Information on its revenues did not survive. There is only a record from the proceedings of the Film Advisory Board where the Dodals applied for support because they had reportedly lost on the collaboration with Radiojournal. They eventually received a subsidy of 15,000 Crowns from the Board.

The friendly contacts between the Dodals and Josef Skupa did not cease with the discussed title. The two sides probably had an understanding for each other because they, among other things, shared a passion for employing puppet theatre and animated film as the means of socially engaged messages. In September 1937, Irena Dodalová wrote to Skupa about the filmmakers' wish to prolong their teamwork and to film a comedy with real puppets at their own expense. The events linked with the ending era of pre-war Czechoslovakia, however, did not provide enough possibilities to realize such a costly project.

The Adventures remained part of film distribution even during the Nazi Protectorate, albeit with new, Czech-German opening credits, and its executive producer was stated as Czech instead of Czechoslovak Radio. The names of its authors – an exile and a Jewish filmmaker – were left out.[19]

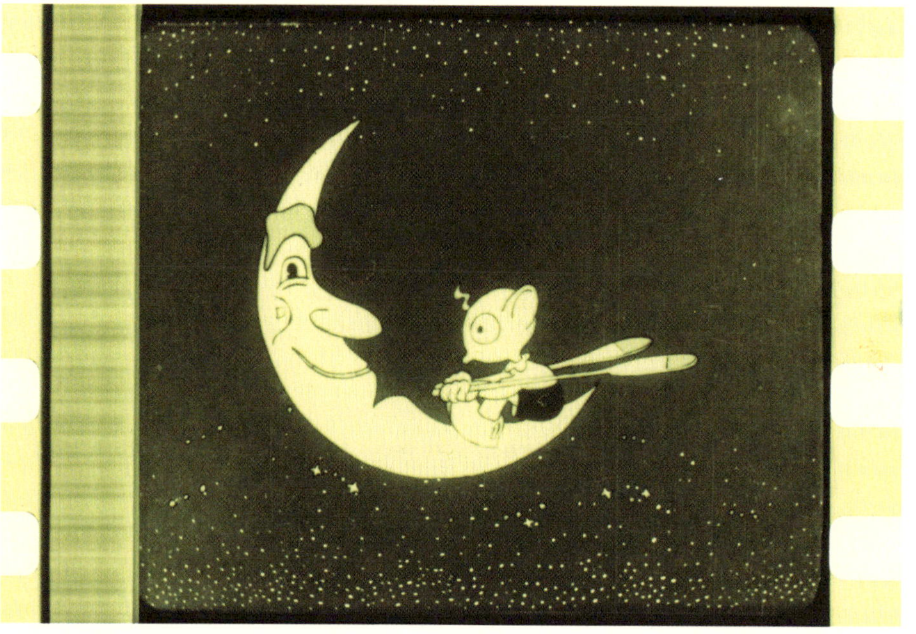

1 Skupa in his letters mainly complained that his royalty was inadequate to the laborious nature of the work. The Plzeň City Archives, Josef Skupa Literary Inheritance, box 34.

2 It was the lead role of the Prague gossiper, Ms Fragrance Acetylene, with which Plachta began in the cabaret Saturn in 1921. The character then reappeared in many variations on the scene of the cabaret Červená sedma (The Red Seven). The film passed the censorship proceedings on 25 March 1931 under the title *Slavná filmová hvězda paní Acetylínová jde do biografu na film Spejbl a Hurvínek* (The Famed Film Star Ms Acetylene Goes to the Cinema to Watch Spejbl and Hurvínek); its footage was 260 metres.

3 Havelka, J., *Čs. filmové hospodářství I. Zvukové období 1929–1934* (Czechoslovak Film Industry I. The Sound Period 1929–1934). Praha: Čefis, 1935, p. 183.

4 Correspondence between J. Skupa and Radiojournal, 9 and 11 March 1931; see Note 1. The edited version of the two letters was reprinted in the magazine *Radiojournal*, 1931, No. 12, 21 March, p. 5.

5 The subject of synergy is discussed in more detail by Szczepanik, P., K*onzervy se slovy. Počátky zvukového filmu a česká mediální kultura 30. let* (Word Cans. The Beginnings of Sound Film and the 1930s Czech Media Culture). Brno: Host, 2009, pp. 414nn.

6 Letter of J. Skupa to IRE-film, 2 February 1936; see Note 1.

7 Ibid.

8 Animated passages usually merely served to explain instructional and school films. A trick picture on Einstein's theory of relativity, filmed in the United States in 1924, was probably aimed at professionals.

9 Bendazzi, G., *Cartoons: One Hundred Years of Cinema Animation*. Bloomington (Indiana): Indiana University Press, 1994.

10 Skupa in his correspondence complained that Trnka was too busy to fully engage in the commission; he thus hardly would have had time to supervise the tedious work of animating the puppet.

11 The typescript of the subtitles submitted for censorship also stated the name of T. Lorelli, a member of Skupa's theatre troupe who reportedly performed the passages with the singing Queen of Waves. These sections are, however, absent in the film and Lorelli's name eventually did not appear in the credits.

12 J. Ježek, musical score to *The Adventures*. Personal Fund of Irena Dodalová. I thank M. Večera for his information concerning the use of the score in the film.

13 The film of four parts was made in 1930 in Germany. Radiojournal acquired it in the early 1930s and procured its Czech edition. The matinée screenings of the full version were held in the Prague cinema, Kotva, from 6 to 14 April 1931, and its several previews were on the cinema's program on 1 May 1931. The picture also premiered in the cities of Jablonec nad Nisou, Kolín and Banská Bystrica. The Czech version (subheads) was supplemented with some materials documenting the local conditions (e.g. the Liblice transmitter). The high quality of the detailed explanation accompanied by animated diagrams allowed Radiojournal to use the film for many years.

14 "Barevný film na výstavě v Piešťanech" (Colour Film at the Piešťany Exhibition), *Filmová politika*, 1936, No. 17, 19 June, p. 3.

15 "Český kreslený film" (Czech Cartoon Film), *Filmová politika*, 1936, No. 18, 3 July, p. 4.

16 Letter of Radiojournal to J. Skupa, 22 July 1936; see Note 1.

17 *The Adventures of a Ubiquitous Fellow*, plates RJ 182, RJ 183 (matrix Nos. 1314–1317), sound foils 0629, 586. The Czech Radio Archives. Apart from these recordings, the Archives also hold a working sound version of the same title, which documented a dialogue between Anna Kreuzmannová and Josef Skupa (16:32') about the film. It is on two plates, RJ 158, RJ 159 (matrix Nos. 1269–1272). The film represented Czechoslovak cinematography at the 1936 Venice Biennial. The film critic and publicist, S. Ježek, who attended the festival wrote that the film "attracted attention by the verve of its draughtsmanship and unleashed modern invention while the plenteous dialogues, dictated by the didactic nature of the work, were detrimental to its comprehensibility". In: *Panorama českého filmu* (Czech Film Panorama). Praha: Čs. filmové nakladatelství, 1946, p. 147.

18 Letter of J. Skupa to Radiojournal, 25 September 1936; see Note 1.

19 The Dodals in the early 1950s created a new version of the film in Argentina. For the Spanish script with the explication, see *Las aventuras de Busybody*. Personal Fund of Irena Dodalová.

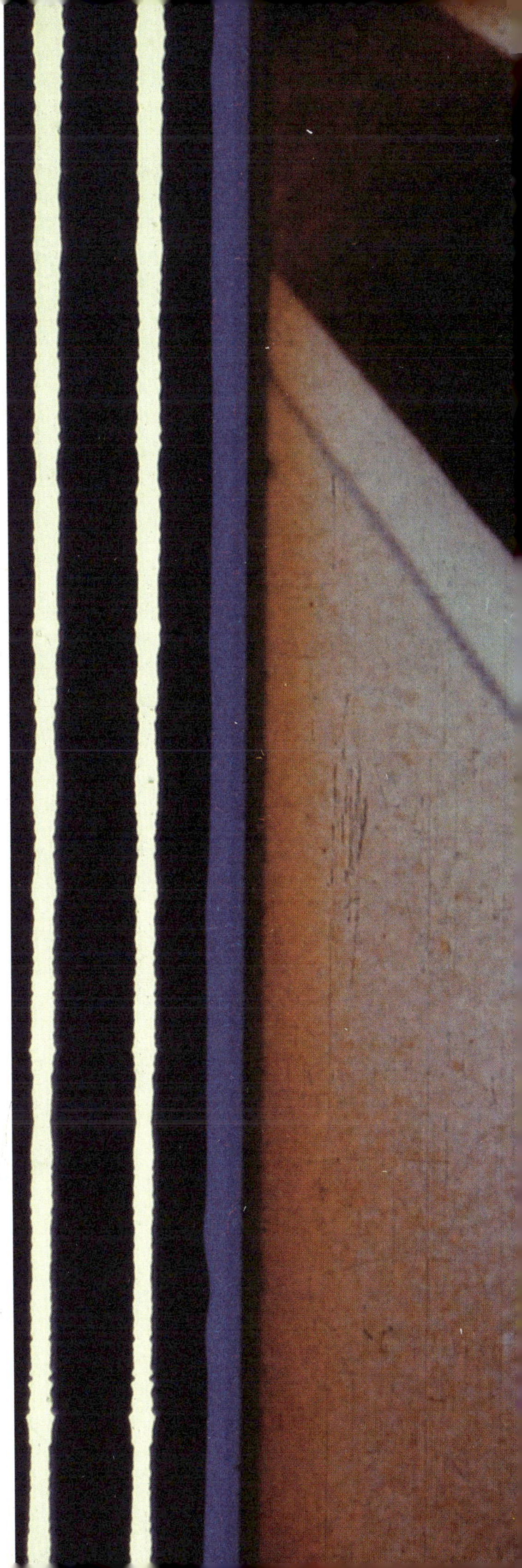

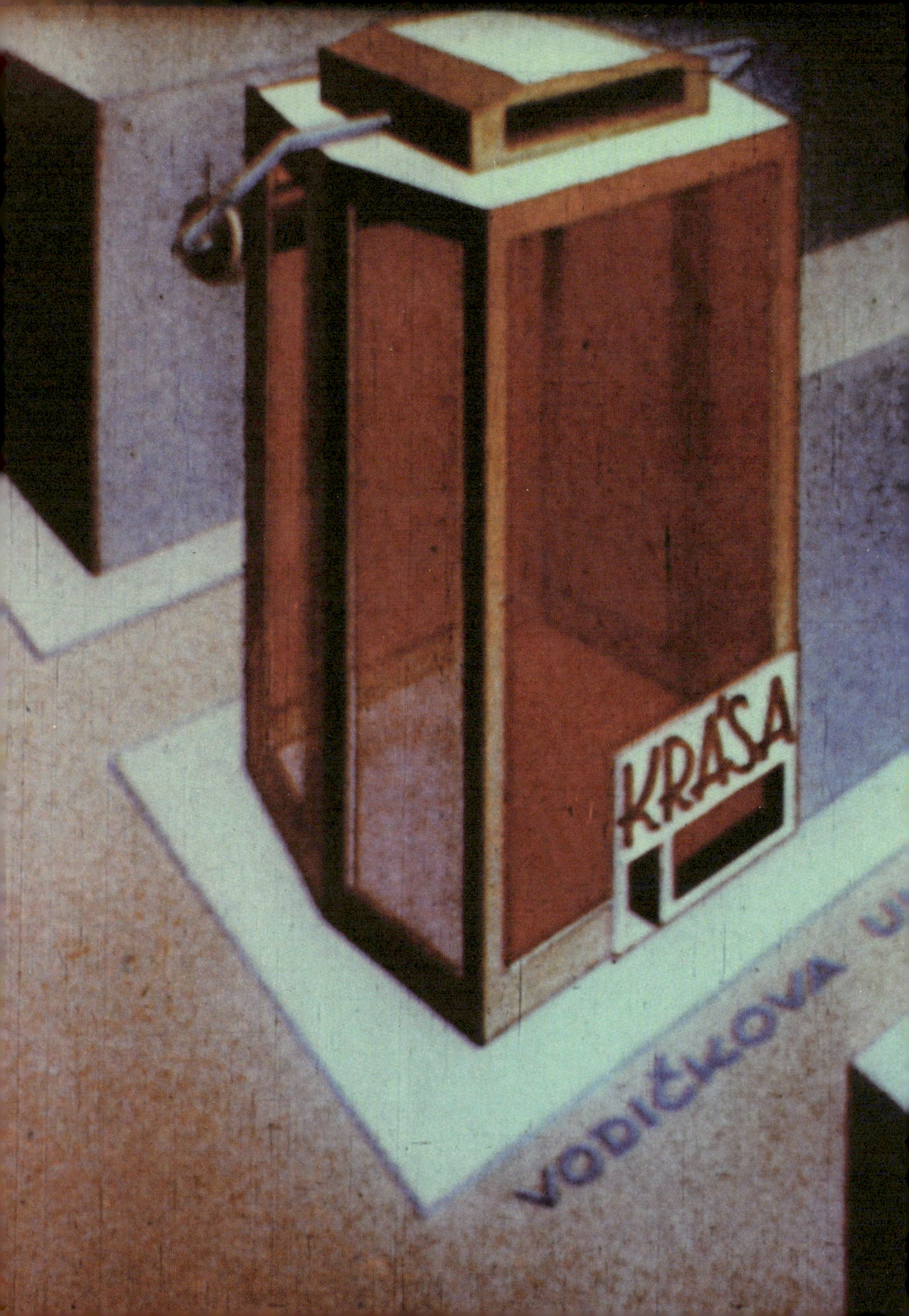
KRÁSA
VODIČKOVA U

Schicht, Baťa and the Rest / The Advertising Market in Inter-War Czechoslovakia

Pre-war advertising in Central Europe is inseparable from the name Schicht and the commercials promoting its Saponia, "the soap with the deer logo", Radion washing powder, the toothpastes Kalodont and Thymolin and the margarines Ceres and Vitello. Schicht's advertising items are still plentiful at collector's auctions today. The joint-stock company Jiří Schicht – part of the Unilever holding from the 1920s – had developed the most varied styles of commercials and advertising events since the late 19th century, aimed at the urban as well as rural audiences. Advertising became omnipresent in the metropolitan milieu and in newspapers and magazines; its diverse forms came to pervade households and bombed the public several times a year with seasonal campaigns designed by various companies. Cinemas also served advertising purposes, projecting black-and-white and colour commercial slides, later often followed by screening commercial films, prior to the main program.

Czech companies, too, were building their unmistakable image in the 1930s when Irena Leschnerová and Karel Dodal arrived on the film advertising market. The Orion chocolate products, fabrics by Prokop and Čáp, Kulík Coffee, the Brouk and Babka department stores, the assortment sold by Waldes – all these had their unique style, while the most noticeable commercials came from the Zlín-based Baťa. And although Schicht more or less mirrored the traditional style of imperial German advertising, Baťa followed the modern tendencies of American commercials.

When the avant-garde designer and artist greatly skilled in commercial graphics, Zdeněk Rykr, pondered poster design as one of the distinct advertising means, he noted: "A poster is like a young girl. It must be amusing, in fact even flirtatious, elegant and *chic*. No matter the seriousness of the subject. It should be effortless in presentation and refined in pathos. It has something of the 'gentleman rogue', something of a little white lie and something of social convention in it. – It floats above truth and dances above life. It lampoons heavy issues and ridicules virtues. And we vainly attempt it here. We are not enough airheaded for this. The dark cloud of Czechoslovak gloominess hangs above it with an almost suffocating surge."[1] The well-known author of the Orion brand logo precisely grasped one of the elementary maladies in Czech advertising during that period, which included the sphere of commercial film clouded by the "gloominess" from the 1920s to the beginnings of sound film.

Czechoslovakia and the world alike viewed the contemporary production of film commercials as marginal, as a matter condemned to short-run consumption, and most film producers merely tolerated it as a source financing their more important projects. With few exceptions, commercials were utterly anonymous works – they often lacked opening credits (similar to the TV commercial spots today); their producers provided their names only in the censorship proceeding documents, and also their authors usually remained anonymous to the grief of today's archive keepers. But had it not been for advertising commissions, Karel Pečený would not have published the first Czech newsreel *Elekta Journal* and many Czech feature films would not have been made. More or less all producers, including the AB company, were involved in commercial film. Those specializing in this field were, for example, the Degl Brothers, Poja, Elekta Journal (Karel Pečený from 1930), Favoritfilm, Josef Vilímek or, respectively, Propaga, Slavia (later Reklama Slavia) and, during the 1930s, Josef Kokeisl, Baťa Zlín (later FAB), Baal, Unionvox, Ludvík Guba, and Fišer and Lehner. The Brno-based companies active in this business were, for instance, Leopold Barič, Bruna Brno, Legia Brno and Terra film. One of the most significant producers in the Czechoslovak advertising film market was the Piras agency and its offshoot, Piras-Thalia, which produced most of the commercials for the

Schicht company, often in either German or Viennese studios. Commercials promoting Schicht products did not surpass conventional models, although some of them – such as the washerwoman fighting imps in the *Bublees* (Bublínkové) – are still charming even today.

We can distinguish several approaches to the advertising plan, the narrative, in the colourful mixture of these productions. The first type was short spots presenting a product and a brand and based on montaging either moving or static pictures. Another type employed the feature-film narrative, constructed with concern to the subject of the commercial. The latter usually comprehensively portrayed the peripeteia of the film's heroes, solved in the end easily, quickly and at a reasonable price thanks to the promoted products. These commercials were aptly described by the journalist Karel Poláček in one of his columns: "One can rarely guess from the story of such films which commodity would be advertised: the excellence and prime quality of the recommended article is only revealed at the end and one can never comprehend what the previous history was actually about and how it is associated with the subject of promotion."[2]

Yet another category of films somewhat combined methods characteristic

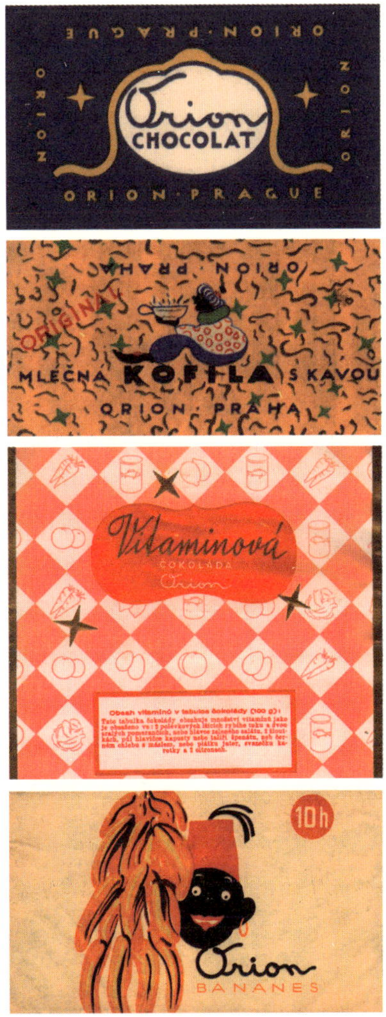

Posters by Zdeněk Rykr, who worked for Baťa, Kulík, Čedok and others. His most famous achievements are his Kofila and Orion designs, used to these days, while the latter (in the form of four-pointed star) gave name to the chocolate factory of František Maršner.

of instructional, promotional, industrial, educational as well as commercial films. These pictures were undoubtedly aimed at meeting the wishes of the customers who wanted the artists to treat miscellaneous information in a single work (and for a single payment). These commissions would usually result in prolonged film explications which, naturally, could not fulfil the planned advertising purpose.

Modern American commercials were only distant examples for the local producers, and only few in the film industry were able to appreciate their essence. The possibilities of advertising and the "cinematographic art"[3] in Europe at that time were mainly discovered by avant-garde filmmakers, utilizing the economic background of producers and companies to realize their experiments. Jan Kučera wrote in 1928 that "just cinematography alone will soon be able to fully perform the tasks assigned to advertising. [...] Freedom in rendering visual forms of our world, which authentic film artistry so demands, had first been proven in advertising. A director of a commercial need not fear making ultimate films, montages with no subject, a film with no subtitles".[4]

Kučera insisted that although a commercial was – and would always be – an utterly routine and mercantile product since its power was in the purity of its form, it nevertheless influenced and impregnated the art of cinematography. His treatise certainly reflected the discussions held in the contemporary community of young Czech filmmakers. We unfortunately have no proof of how these efforts to break through conventional approaches were realized in Elekta Journal, because most short spots are missing. The ideas of the future film theoretician were employed in Czech film only by the artists of the sound era, such as Alexandr Hackenschmied and Elmar Klos at Baťa or the Dodals in IRE-film.

The belated and prolonged development of Czechoslovak film advertising did not suit the local German business strata and the owners of German cinemas, well familiar with the more mature market in the neighbouring country,

Poster by Höns from 1932, promoting cloth sold by Prokop and Čáp.

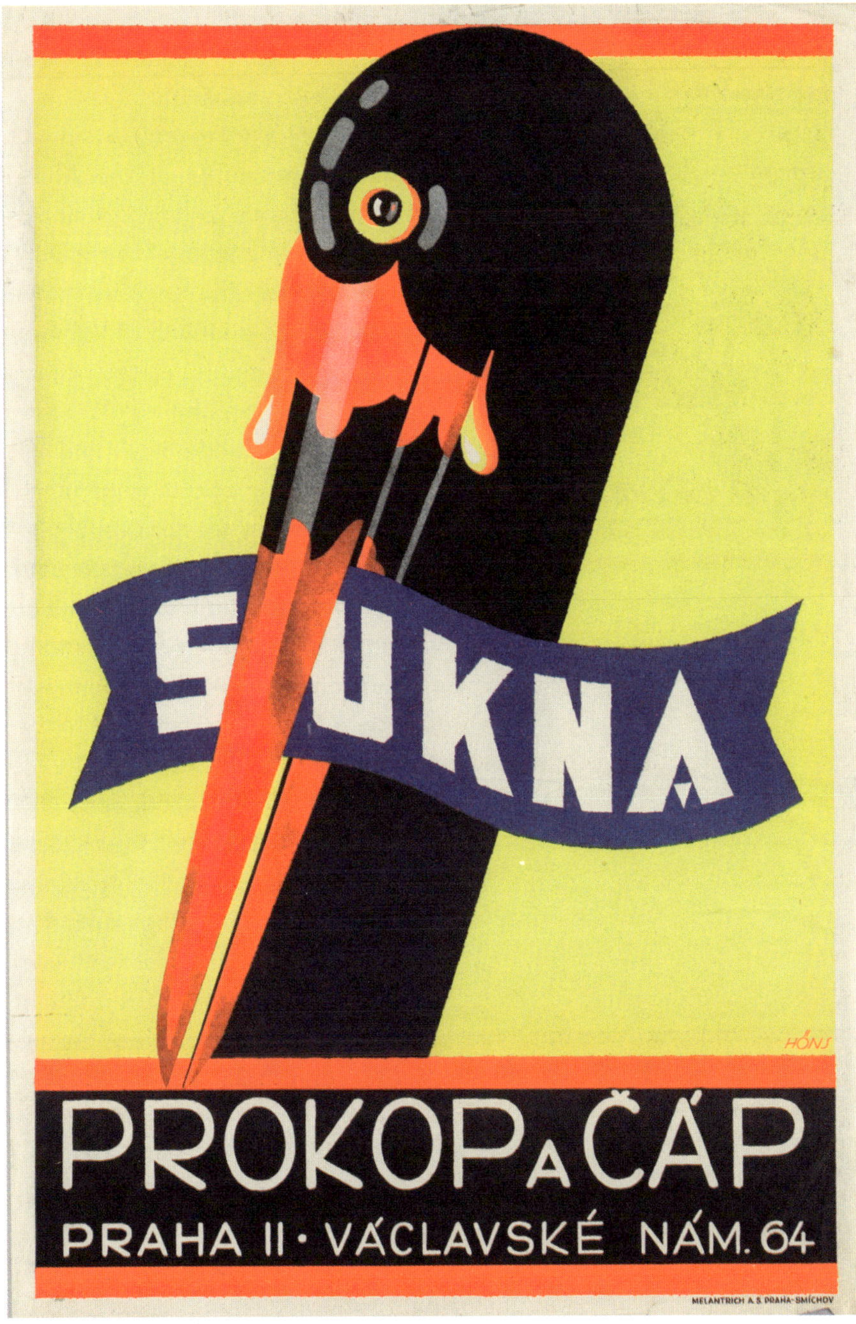
SUKNA
HÓNS
PROKOP A ČÁP
PRAHA II · VÁCLAVSKÉ NÁM. 64
MELANTRICH A. S. PRAHA-SMÍCHOV

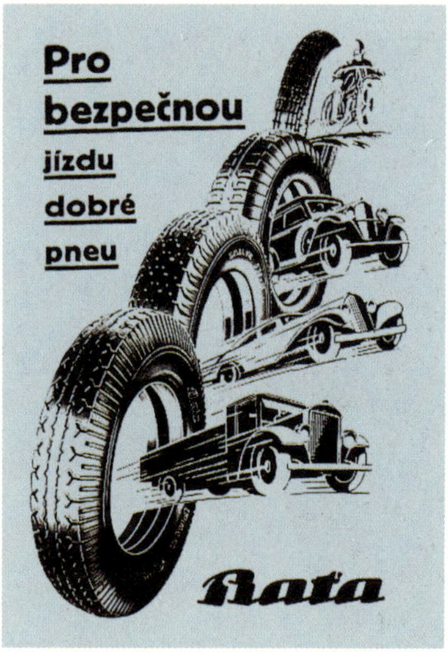

The film *The Road Singing* embodied a new approach to commercials as it was perceived by the group of young Zlín filmmakers, including Alexandr Hackenschmied (Hammid), Elmar Klos and Jan Lukas. The music was composed by IRE-film's collaborator, Bedřich Kerten.

thus addressed various politely phrased submissions and recommendations to Czechoslovak authorities.[5]

Modern film commercials in the Czech lands, departing from the American advertising style, began developing as late as in the latter half of the 1930s in the Baťa city of Zlín, i.e. almost simultaneously with the launch of IRE-film. The early Baťa commercials did not largely diverge from the commonplace production: they were made by various Prague producers on the basis of commissions assigned by the film and photography section of Baťa's advertising department, based in the 52nd building of the corporation in the given city. When Jan Baťa had a collection of these commercials screened for him in spring 1934, he was content neither with their quality nor the fee charged by the producers. He thus decided to establish an independent film department in Zlín, which mainly consisted of the scriptwriter and director Elmar Klos, the film producer Ladislav Kolda and the cameraman and film editor Alexandr Hackenschmied, at the turn of 1934 and 1935. The company came forth with a new production and financial concept, and the management soon approved building a new film studio and laboratories in Kudlov near Zlín. The first results of the changed management of the Baťa Film Studios (Filmové ateliéry

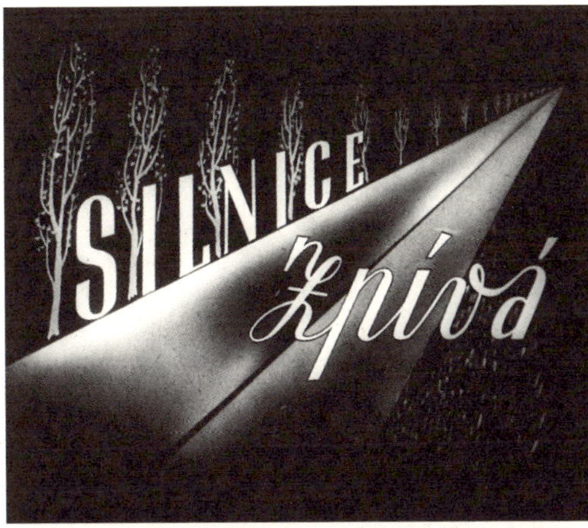
SILNICE
zpívá

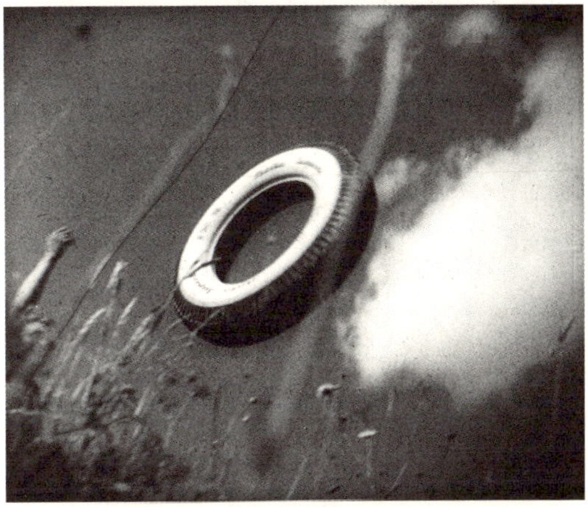

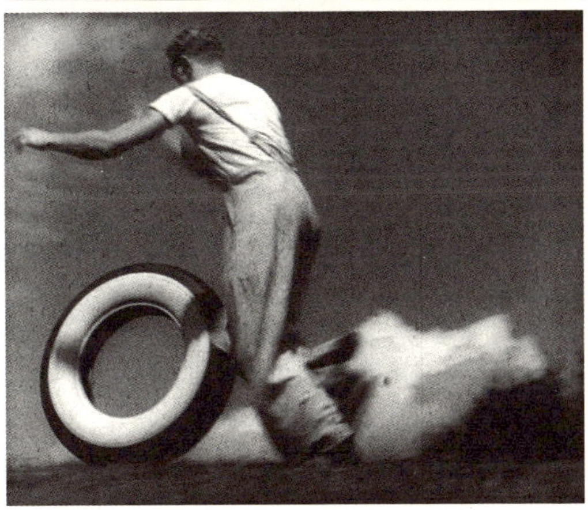

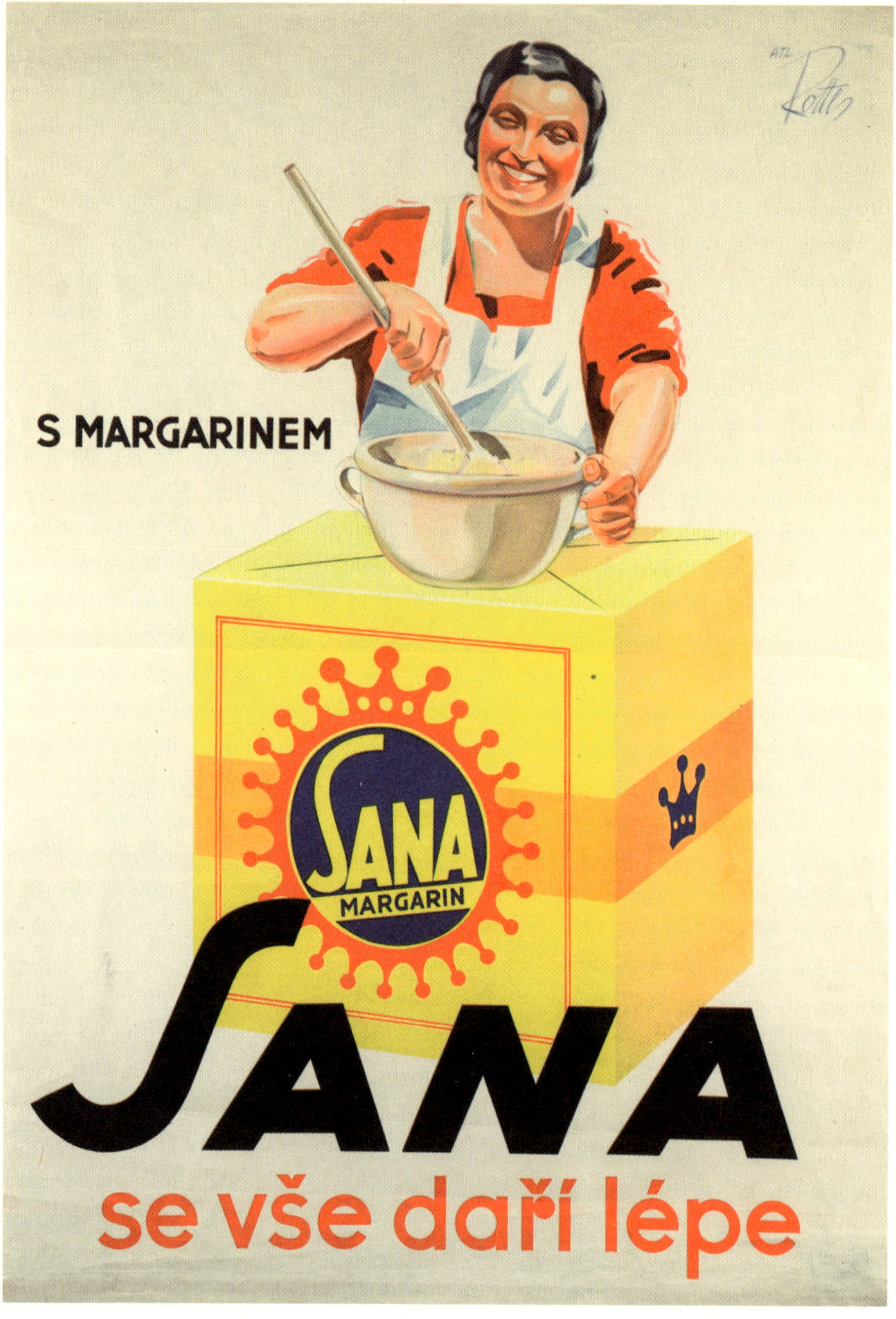
S MARGARINEM
SANA
MARGARIN
SANA
se vše daří lépe

Baťa; FAB) came in no time, although the films were made in Prague studios up to August 1936.

The innovative style of the Zlín group was foreshadowed by its 1935 commercial *The New Song* (Nová píseň), promoting Baťa rubber boots. Its main feature is the so-called *burlaks* – a Russian epithet for people hauling barges and other vessels upstream from the 17th to 20th centuries – wearing the traditional bast shoes. They march along a Czech riverbank to the accompaniment of their flagship song of the Volga Boatmen, "Yo, Heave Ho", performed by the Wise Teachers of Gotham, and as soon as they pass behind a Baťa advertising board, they begin jigging because they are now wearing Baťa wellingtons. The ad ingeniously combines a moment of surprise, wit and a convincing commercial appeal. As the final swift montage tells us, good shoes can ease everyone's work, be they a fisherman, postman, train dispatcher or labourer. The authors gambled on three efficient crutches: a film hyperbole recalling Repin's countlessly reproduced and thus widely known painting *Burlaks on the Volga*, a music paraphrase of a song which was, beside other things, frequently heard in Czechoslovak cinemas in the rendering of the exiled Don Cossacks, and the well-known Baťa billboard serving to magically transform the Russian serfs. The versatile filmmaker Alexandr Hackenschmied not only brought a modern visual film concept to Zlín but also, having been Plicka's film editor, enriched the studio's scope with the art of montage. The main example of the local team efforts in the field of modern film advertising then became the montage picture *The Road Singing* (Silnice zpívá). The story of 100-meter footage about Baťa rubber tyres, personified via a rhythmical comment in *ich-form*, was awarded a gold medal at the 1937 Paris World Exhibition.

Besides several exceptional commercials, the studio naturally produced pictures based on traditional methods where confused, intricate stories resulted in happy endings thanks to Baťa footwear. Worth mentioning from the studio's oeuvre, which also included instructional, industrial, promotional and documentary films, is the advertising newsreel *Window to the World* (Okno do

The Rotter studio,
a 1930 poster promoting Sana margarine.

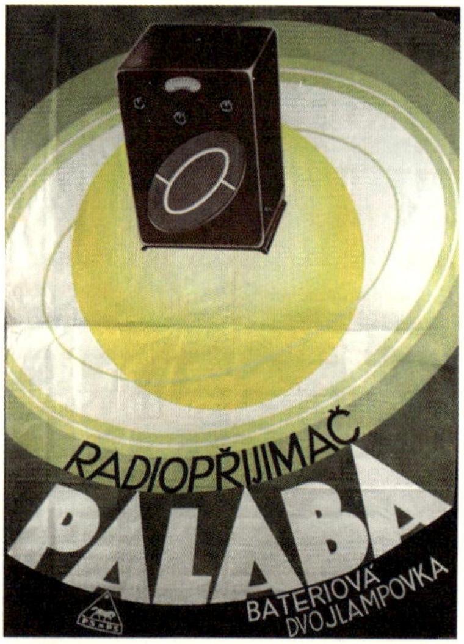

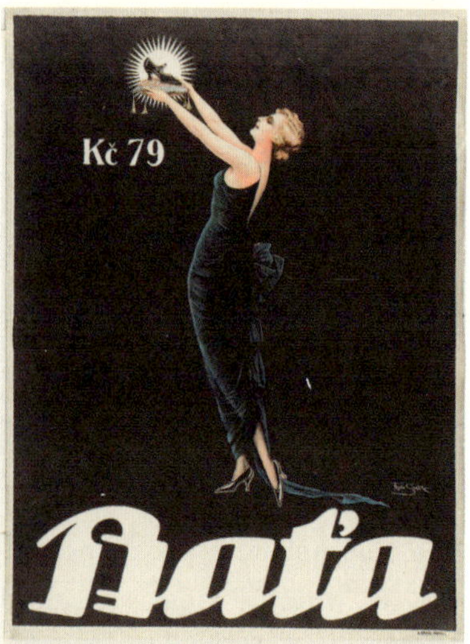

From the advertising oeuvre of Zdeněk Rykr (for the Palaba company) and Fráňa Smetek (for Baťa).

světa), designated for the entire chain of 800 Baťa stores. The fortnightly program, screened from 1937 to the beginning of the war, contained news shots and always closed with an overview of the Baťa new season collections. They ran on specially adapted projectors, activated directly by customers in the shops. The production of the Zlín studio held a specific place in pre-war Czech film since it formed an integral part of the holding's economic structure as one of the components of Baťa executive media network, which followed the marketing style and design of the company.[6]

Apart from Baťa, other manufacturers or, respectively, their advertising and publicity departments, sometimes also made their own instructional and promotional films and commercials. One of the most dynamic in this sense since the era of silent film had been the Sigmund Lutín company, a successful producer of globally exported water pumps. The Plzeň-based industrial complex, Škoda, also established its own film production.

An independent chapter in film advertising is the production for the joint-stock Jiří Schicht from Ústí nad Labem. Its commercials – very often trick and cartoon pictures – mainly promoted commonplace household commodities such as margarines and washing powders. Although Schicht was stated as the producer in several titles, most of them were commissioned from advertising agencies. The company had dozens of factories in various European countries and many commercials were thus made abroad, in Germany, the Netherlands and Great Britain, as well as other places. This advertising film production, reportedly also participated in by the leading representatives of European avant-garde, is yet to be documented. The National Film Archive is one of several institutions holding collections of Schicht's commercials aimed at the Czechoslovak market and shot by various producers.

A frequent mediator in commissioning films for Schicht was the Piras agency (Promotional Advertising and Commercial Joint-Stock Company [Propagační insertní a reklamní A. S.], previously known as Haasenstein and Vogler; the names of the founders were subsequently left out). With a wide promotional, advertising, commercial and publishing scope, the company was founded in the late 19th century in Hamburg. It was active in the European market and, from 1920, in Prague. Besides links to Vienna and many other European centres, it had branches throughout Czechoslovakia, for instance in Teplice-Šanov, Moravian Ostrava and Brno. The agency provided advertising services to local as well as foreign companies, such as Jiří Schicht (margarines,

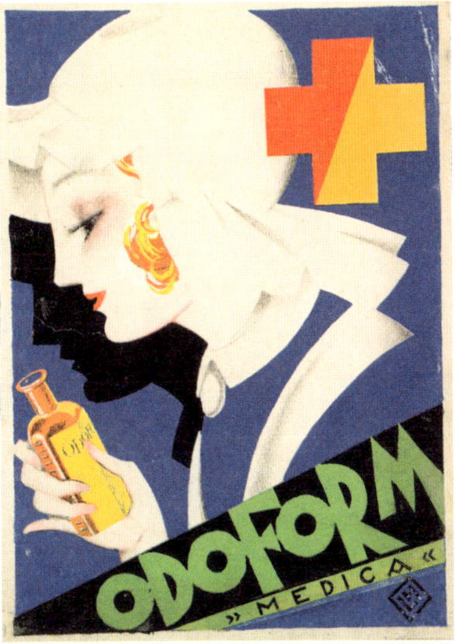

Graphic designs by Leo Heilbrunn, whose most successful advertising concept was the ad promoting Alpa menthol ointment.

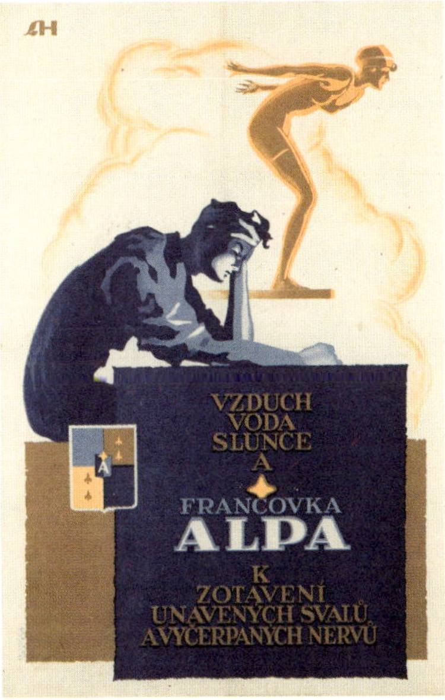

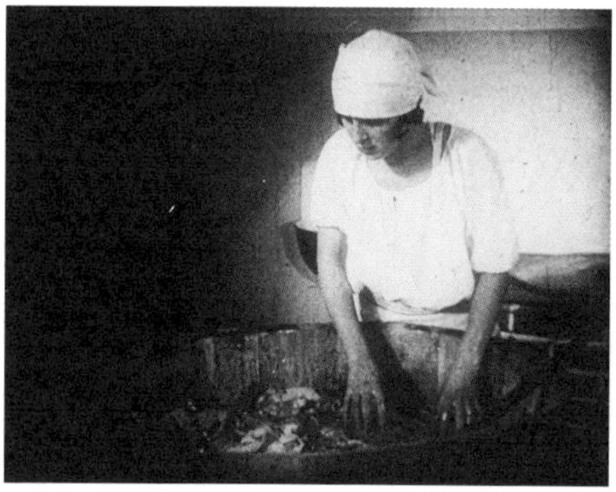

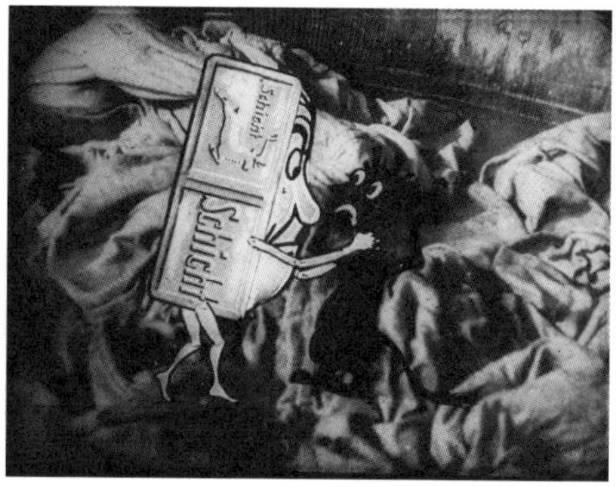

Takes from the film combining live action and tricks, *The White Deer* (Der Weisse Hirsch, Bílý jelen), from the early 1930s, well illustrates the style of ads promoting Schicht products and made in Berlin and Viennese studios.

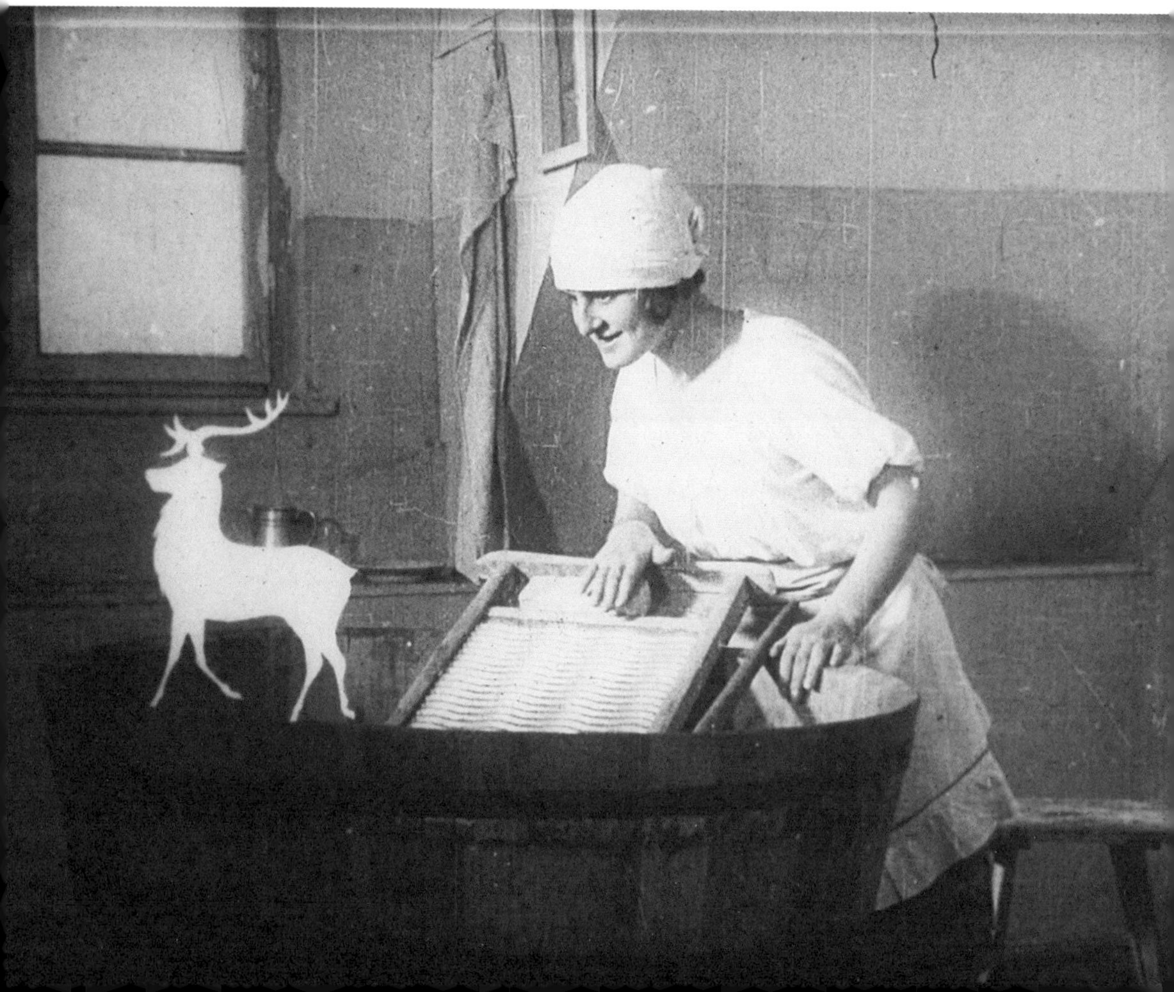

washing powders etc.), Orion (chocolate products), Pixavon (the Odol company), Aero (aircrafts), Fracillon & Co. (Swiss Longines watches), Gibbs (razors), Weber (velvet) and Liebig (fabrics).

Piras also took control of cinema advertising in the 1920s and produced an array of commercials partly shot in Germany and Vienna. It was linked with the Thalia-Kino company which it later took over. The studio, laboratory and copying works were provided by regular suppliers, for example AB, Favorit Film and Hera film, and the individual commercials were made by various hired scriptwriters, filmmakers and actors. Piras' own advertising production was long limited by its statute. The management thus extended it in 1935, and the new object clause allowed Piras "to conduct, either on its own or foreign cost, the production of advertising films as well as all works appurtenant to this production, to establish and/or acquire studios and laboratories for this purpose for both own use and the use of other parties, and to conduct trade of all kinds in the field of film advertising".[7] The dawning political situation, however, ruled out building the film studios and the company was, on the contrary, liquidated with the beginning of the Protectorate.

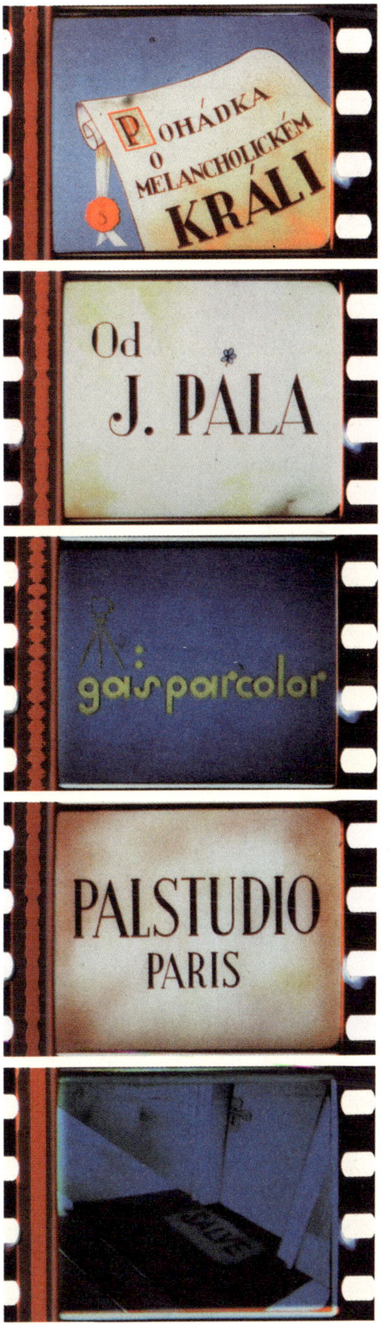

Czech cinemas not only introduced domestic but, occasionally, also foreign

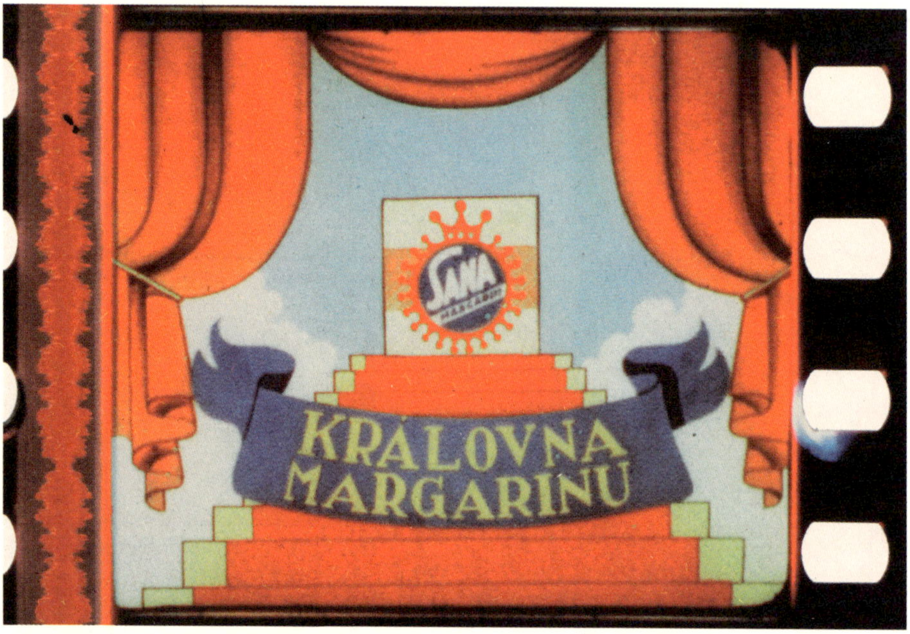

One of the alternatives to the so-called German Reich advertising style was the oeuvre of the Hungarian exile, György Pál. He began working on the commercial *A Fairy Tale about a Melancholic King* for the Rakovník company František Otta in Prague, but his limited work permit meant it had to be finished in Paris, in summer 1934.

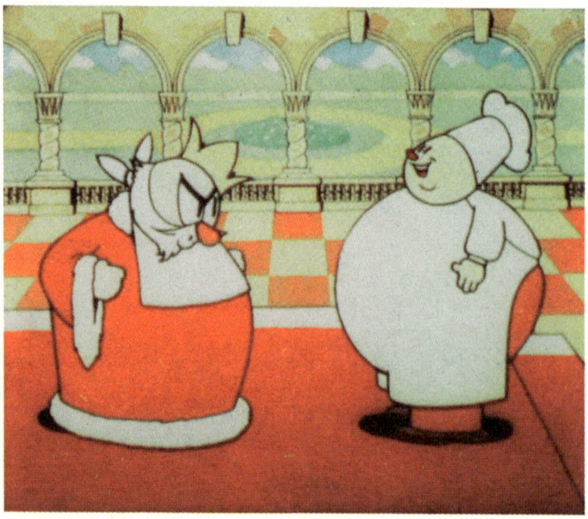

advertising production. For example, German films were imported by Excentric Berlin and Werbe-Kunst and, in the 1930s, Fischerkoesen and UFA. Part of these films was moreover adapted commercials from abroad – the films that initially recommended foreign commodities received new Czech subtitles to promote local merchandise. These products oftentimes were not even submitted for censorship.

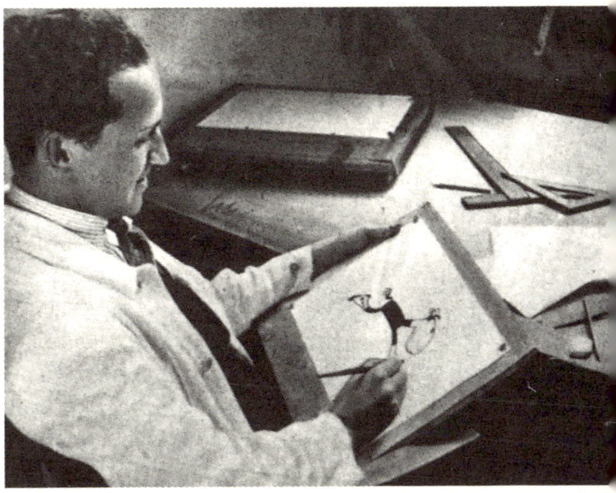

György Pál in Berlin in the early 1930s.

When the Dodals launched their IRE-film production, the German film industry was experiencing dramatic changes. The arrival of Nazism to power and its strengthening ideology was driving thousands of Nazi opponents and people endangered by the racial laws off their land, while Prague became the stop-gap for many refugees.

The Czechoslovak capital for example provided asylum to György Pál, a gifted Hungarian artist specializing in trick film.[8] The graduate architect briefly headed the section of animated film in the UFA studio and, in 1932, established his own company in Berlin – one of the first ones employing the colour system, Gasparcolor, in trick film. He came to Prague illegally from Berlin in March 1933 and probably received support from Miloš Havel who helped him continue with film animation. He shot two black-and-white commercials in the Barrandov AB studios:

Desider Gross.

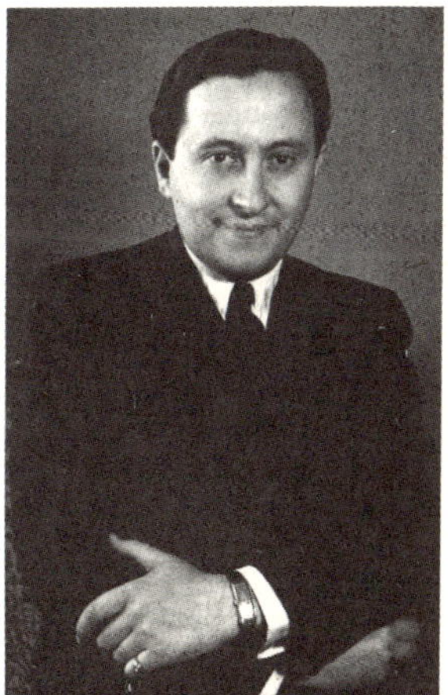

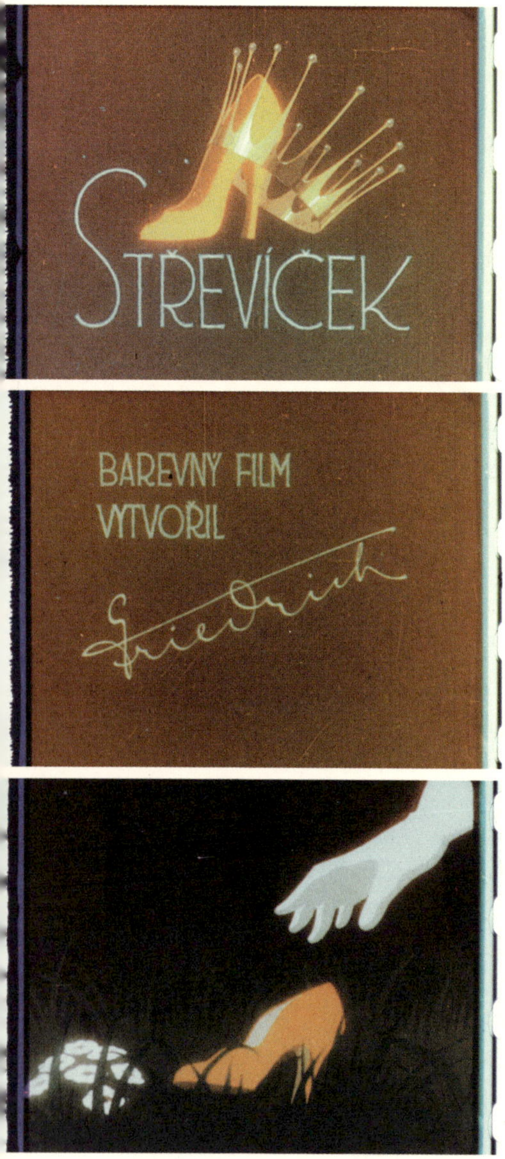

Takes from the film *A Little Shoe*, filmed by the German political exile Georg Friedrich in Prague for the Krása shoemaking company.

The Winner (Vítěz; 1933) and *Stop Drudging!* (Nedři se!; 1933).[9]

However, Pál had to leave Prague in March 1934 and his latest commission for Schicht, *A Fairy Tale about a Melancholic King* (Pohádka o melancholickém králi; 1934), was thus completed in Paris. Before he eventually had to escape from the Nazis for the United States, his situation was temporarily solved by the Philips company which invited him to the Netherlands. He established his own studio in Eindhoven where he brought up an entire generation of animators and draughtsmen and filmed a collection of animated commercials ranking among the golden fund of European pre-war advertising. He asserted himself through the excellent puppet commercials *A Ship on Air* (Loď v éteru; 1935), *An Air Symphony* (Symfonie éteru; 1935), *How Radio Tubes Are Made* (Výroba radiových lamp; 1935) and *In the Land of Shining Bulbs* (V zemi zářících žárovek; 1936). During the war, he became a significant Hollywood filmmaker in the United States.

Prague in late 1933 served as a provisional refuge to yet another Hungarian exile, Desider Gross, who had conducted business in Germany as a producer and distributor of film commercials for nine years. His correspondence with the Foreign Police Headquarters proves that Gross planned to make Prague the centre of his international trade in film advertising, i.e. an activity which had yet to become known in the country.[10] The core of Gross's activity was adapting the ends of his "standard commercial films" to the specific needs and requirements of particular companies from various countries. And although he did not acquire either resident alien status or a trade permit in Czechoslovakia, he maintained close business relations with many Prague film companies such as Piras, Grafo-film and Unionvox, and his technical base became the local film laboratories, Herafilm. Its owners, Josef Tušla and his wife Cyrilla, purchased the Norwegian patent of L. Eriksson for subtitling foreign sound films in 1931 and, four years later, they already had seven machines using this system, as well as a special machine for subtitling colour copies.[11]

Takes from the film *Nobody Likes Us Any More* by an unknown director and participated in the painter František Muzika and the composer Jaroslav Křička.

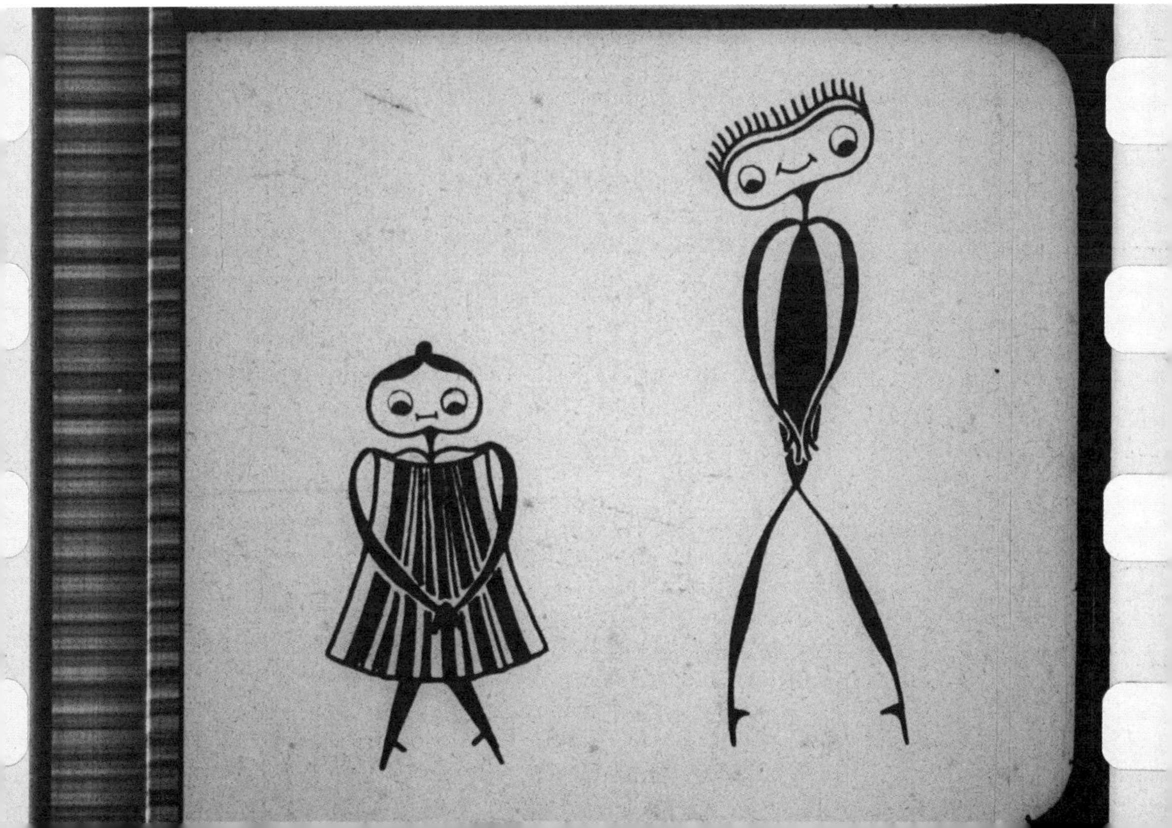

Gross as producer eventually introduced eight films to the Czechoslovak market during the 1930s, but the only surviving one, held in the National Film Archive, is the cartoon commercial *This Way or the Highway* (Jenom tak a ne jinak; 1933) promoting the Prague Gasworks. And although his films were part of the local production statements in 1933, it lasted only two years; Gross then had to apply for an import licence and his works were henceforth being declared as UFA products. His Prague activities kept focusing on international business: he exported his commercials to Switzerland, the Netherlands, Italy, Hungary and Scandinavia, especially Norway. The historian Gunnar Strøm found out that Gross's collaboration with Norway had already begun in Germany and continued during his exile.[12] Between 1934 and 1938, Gross applied for the censorship approval to introduce seventeen commercials in Norwegian film theatres, stating Czechoslovakia as the place of their origin.[13] The analysis of the available sources (not all the films survived) makes us assume that they were made by various artists throughout Europe and merely their subtitle copies were produced in Prague. The equipment of the Herafilm labs would correspond to this speculation. When Desider Gross appealed against his banishment from the Czechoslovak Republic in April 1938, his letter addressed to the Ministry of Interior summarized his hitherto life in the country. Gross stressed that he had managed to draw foreign markets to the local film industry, to acquire valuable foreign currency worth more than a million Crowns for Czechoslovakia and to create employment opportunities for film studios, laboratories, animators, actors and authors. He also justified the application for prolonging his residence permit by the fact that he had learned Czech and had become fully integrated into the domestic economic life. Czechoslovak authorities first dismissed the permit, but he eventually succeeded in prolonging it. Gross nevertheless left for Brazil in March 1939 where all traces of him vanish.

Georg Friedrich, an ex-citizen of the German Reich active as a graphic artist and filmmaker, also provisionally lived in Czechoslovakia for political reasons.[14] He filmed the commercials *Flying a Rocket* (Letíme raketou...) and *A Little Shoe* (Střevíček) in Prague in 1937, while especially the latter brought a new, subtle and fragile expression to the local film milieu. The picture was produced by the Czech company, Sunfilm, which employed Friedrich as an "instructor". The artist and his wife fortunately made it to Stockholm in spring 1939.

It is rather evident that a local producer who would exclusively specialize in animated advertising was non-existent in Czechoslovakia during the given period. If, then, someone indeed dared to make a cartoon commercial either in Propaga or Reklama-Slavia, it was silent, black-and-white and dilettantish – with one exception: the first noticeable Czech sound commercial *Nobody Likes Us Any More* (Nás už nemá nikdo rád; 1933), promoting the Šotek Hellada washing powder. Details about the picture of distinctive design, music and animation are unknown. The data found in the censorship files solely state that the team included the famous Czech painter František Muzika and the music was composed by Jaroslav Křička. The partnership between the promising artists and the company Slavia unfortunately ceased.

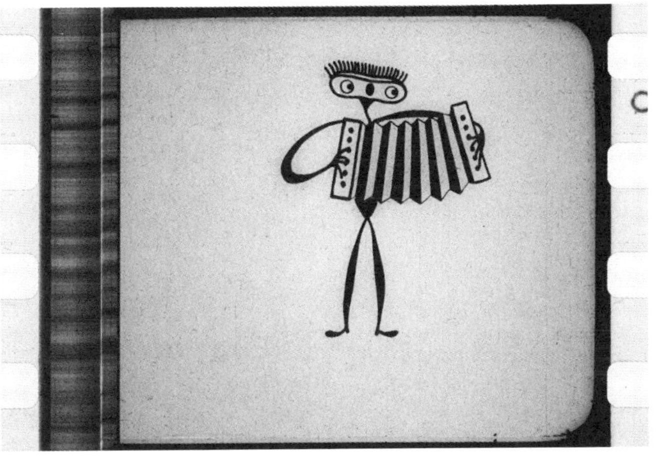

1 Rykr, Z., "Československý filmový plakát" (Czechoslovak Film Poster), *Tribuna* (Tribune), 1927, No. 220, 18 September, p. 4.

2 Poláček, K., "O filmové reklamě" (About Film Advertising), *České slovo* (Czech Word), 1930, No. 261, 6 November, pp. 1–2.

3 Kučera, J., "Reklama a umění kinematografické" (Advertising and the Art of Cinematography), *Filmový kurýr* (Film Courier), 1928, No. 29, 25 August, pp. 1–2.

4 Ibid.

5 For example, Pleyer's Kino Propaganda addressed its 1936 "Exposé zum Aufbau des Werbefilm-Wesens in der Tschechoslowakei" to the Czechoslovak Ministry of Commerce, recommending to increase the import of foreign commercials and thus support the development of making Czechoslovak commercial films as the most advanced promotional means. The pleading emphasized that film commercials bring cinemas an important side income and recommended not only screening these films in metropolitan but also provincial cinemas. A report about the pledge was provided by Z. Urban at a meeting of the Film Advisory Board on 16 November. The National Archives, Ministry of Enterprise, Commerce and Industry, Film Advisory Board, box 2754, pp. 1–2.

6 For more on this, see Szczepanik, P., op. cit.

7 *Protokol 15. valné řádné hromady Pirasu (19. června 1935*; Protocol from the 15th Piras Regular General Meeting of June 1935). The State Regional Archives Prague, Piras, a. s., box 1777, pp. 12–13.

8 The National Archives, Police Headquarters 1930–1940, M 734/24 Marczincsák Julius, box 8679, Ref. Nos. 1967 and 361754.

9 *The Winner* was a sound remake of the silent *The Champion* (Šampion; 1928), produced by Thalia-Piras. Pál had to adhere to the original, rather uninventive synopsis promoting the qualities of Ceres margarine via the results of a sport competition participated in by anthropomorphized comestibles, and although he added several gags and apt drawings of viewers, the film was too lengthy. Pál's second commercial, *Stop Drudging!*, did not lack wit. Combining live action and tricks, it presented several stories of clumsy people struggling with animated real objects to finally counsel on the advantages of the Radion washing powder. The music composer was E. Košťál. The author probably negotiated distributing his films during his Prague sojourn, and the works were submitted for the censorship proceedings by K. Pečený. M. Frída and J. Brož noted that their Czech versions were adapted by Dodal. See Frída, M. – Brož, J., *Historie československého filmu v obrazech 1930–1945* (A History of Czechoslovak Film in Pictures...). Praha: Orbis, 1966, p. 165.

10 The National Archives, Police Headquarters 1941–1951, G 995/8 Gross Desider, box 2615, Ref. No. 88543.

11 Štábla, Z., *Data a fakta z dějin čs. kinematografie 1896–1945* (Dates and Facts from the History of Czechoslovak Cinematography...), Vols. 2, 3. Praha: Československý filmový ústav (ČSFÚ, Czechoslovak Film Institute), 1989, pp. 486–487, 301.

12 Strøm, G., "Fumes From the Fjords", *Animation World Magazine*, 1997, No. 2, pp. 23–24. – Ibid., "Desider Gross and Gasparcolor, European Producers: Norwegian Products and Animated Commercials from the 1930s", *Animation Journal*, spring 1998, pp. 28–41. – Ibid., "Desider Gross and Gasparcolor in a Norwegian Perspective", Part 2, spring 2000, pp. 44–55.

13 The copy of the Czechoslovak films inventory, submitted for Norwegian censorship, is held in the archive of the author of the present book.

14 The National Archives, Police Headquarters 1931–1940, F 1673/9 Friedrich Jiří, box 5886.

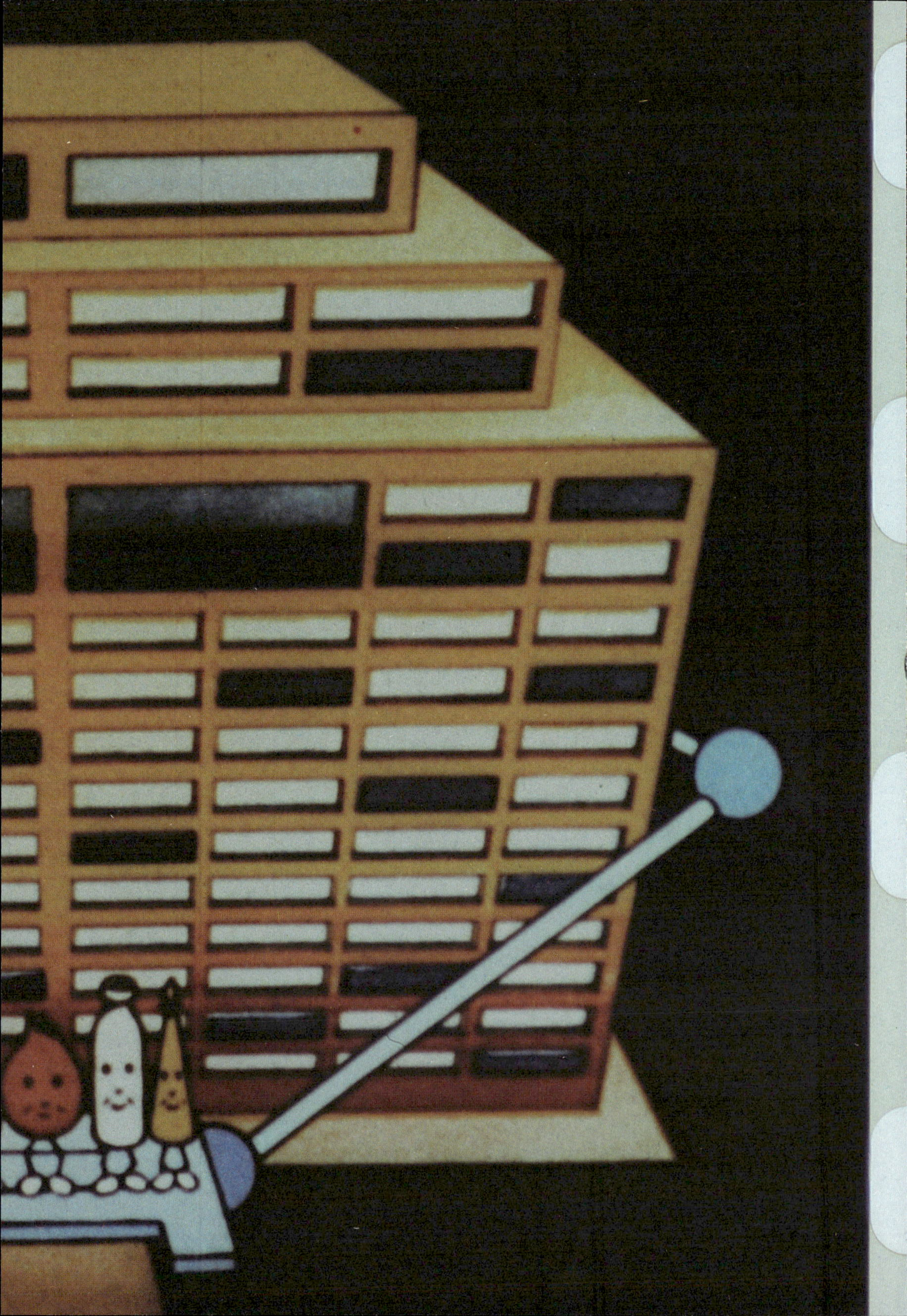

IRE-film and Seeking a Style of Czechoslovak Film Advertising

IRE-film was the first Prague production studio focusing on cartoon and animated commercials, but the absence of a competitor was not always beneficial since it was necessary to convince the local business circles about both the advantages of this type of advertising and the fact that a new company could make as equally attractive commercials as those arriving from abroad. The main problem in acquiring commissions, however, was money. If a commonplace film commercial at that time required between ten and fifteen thousand Crowns, the costs of animated commercials were double, and even around fifty thousand and more in the case of colour film advertising.[1] It was less than the foreign companies charged at that time but still only affordable by a narrow circle of Czechoslovak entrepreneurs. The tough business negotiations in IRE-film were taken over by "Ms Irena" who, as many recall, could pride herself on a remarkable gift for organizing things and conducting business, as well as on her indispensable charm, elegance and assertiveness. She certainly made the best of her knowledge from the school of commerce and her social contacts established in the firm Lavecký & comp., even though her position in the predominantly male business world was anything but easy.

Irena Leschnerová first tried to hook the studio into the Baťa holding, because working for this modern industrial complex was not only a matter of prestige but also a good business prospect. She managed to get a commission to promote Baťa rubber toys. The ensuing commercial *Elephant the Rescuer* (Slon zachráncem) combined a story featuring a little girl craving for a Baťa rubber elephant and a cartoon sequence of her dream. The credits state a director of a rather strange name, J. Ros-Aga. Pseudonyms were commonplace in the Zlín studios whose artists disguised as, for example, Klaus Hakon, A. H. Panthon, and Six. The exotic *nom de guerre* of the *Elephant*'s director probably resulted from Irena Leschnerová's maiden surname – Rosnerová – and the surname of the photographer and editor Jaroslav Pagáč, who at that time headed the film and photographic section in the Zlín advertising department and probably was both the commissioner and co-director of the picture.

Elephant the Rescuer was finished in early summer 1934, simultaneously with Jan Baťa in Zlín vigorously gearing to the issue of the company's film advertising and deciding to found a separate film department, Baťa Film Studios (Filmové ateliéry Baťa; FAB) within Baťa's Auxiliary Works (Baťovy pomocné závody; BAPOZ). Jaroslav Pagáč was removed and Irena Leschnerová began seeking a new partner for negotiations. She turned to the distinguished Czechoslovak filmmaker Elmar Klos who played an important role in establishing the studios. The dealings could have failed for more than one reason, including the unsatisfactory results of the hitherto collaboration with Baťa. Although *Elephant* was unique in the Czechoslovak production due to fusing feature and animated elements and its ambition, unmatched in the contemporary Czech advertising, it could be reproached for all sorts of things including the total absence of wit and the unfortunate casting of the corpulent daughter of Oldřich Kmínek in the lead role. The cartoon passage and the post-production dubbing moreover made the commission extremely expensive, which directly contradicted with the Zlín efforts to reduce its advertising expenses to the minimum. Elmar Klos and his colleagues at that time moreover moved within the genres of short feature and montage film and did not count on employing cartoon commercials.[2] Yet another determining element perhaps was that Klos deeply despised the ambitious and vigorous film producer. This is rather clear from his foreword to the book about Hermína Týrlová, published many years later and noting that all negotiations as to possible future

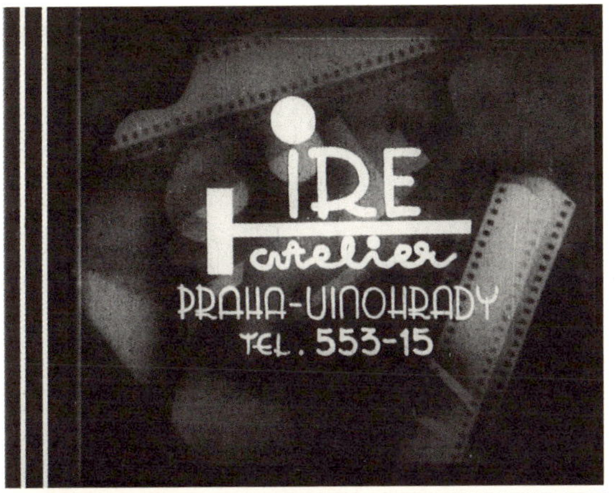
I.R.E
atelier
PRAHA-VINOHRADY
TEL. 553-15

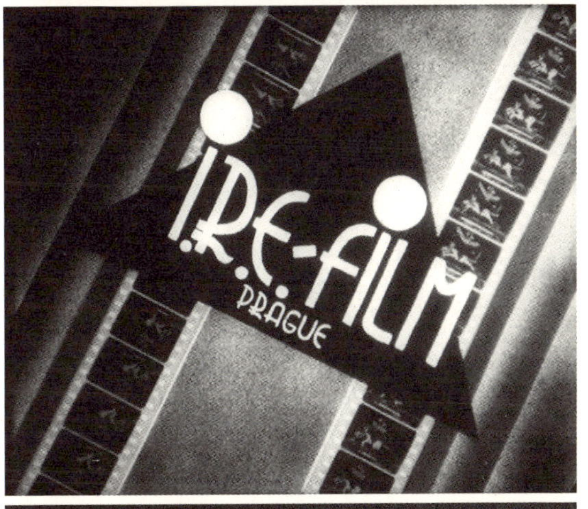
I.R.E.-FILM
PRAGUE

I.R.E.
FILM
PRAGUE

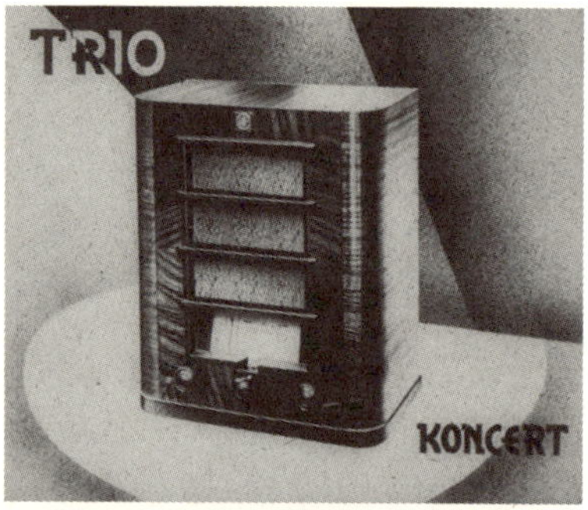

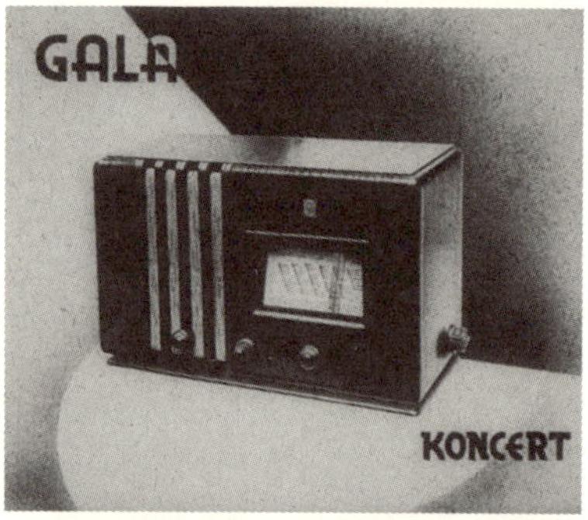

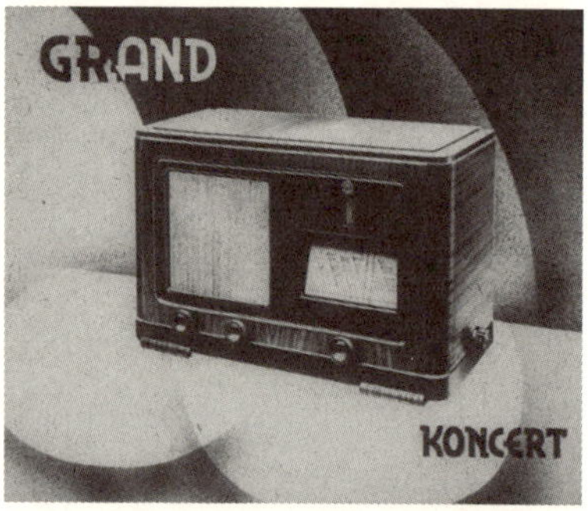

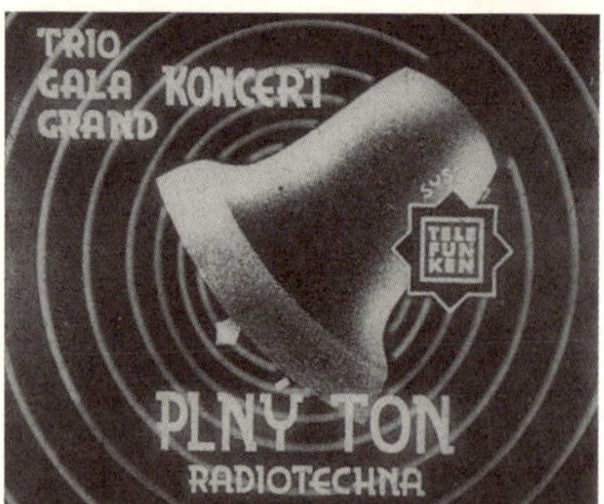

collaboration were, instead of Dodal, "led in an immensely horse-trading manner by his second wife, Irena Dodalová, who had come to tightly control both Dodal and the company bearing her name, IRE-film. This pushy lady, capable of ruling everyone out of discussion for long minutes, would miraculously find out about the time and place of my business meetings in Prague just upon my arrival to the city, and she pursued her acquisition pressure with a verve that made me at least twice abscond from her running down a rearward staircase in the House of Services. I think that this was one of the main reasons why I sided with Hermína Týrlová from the first day".[3]

It seems that Irena's negotiations with the Piras agency as yet another potentially serious partner on the Czechoslovak market were more successful. This can be judged from the fact that IRE-film in its beginnings delivered two commercials to the company – *The Mystery of the MK 204 Turning Point* (Záhada mezníku MK 204) and the now missing film promoting Gibbs razors. Two other IRE-film commercials from same period, *The Lady-Killer* (Dobyvatel srdcí) and *The White Magic* (Bílé kouzlo), were reportedly produced and commissioned by Justin Karpner and Son. Censorship files from a later period only state Karel Dodal as the main executive producer of IRE-film.

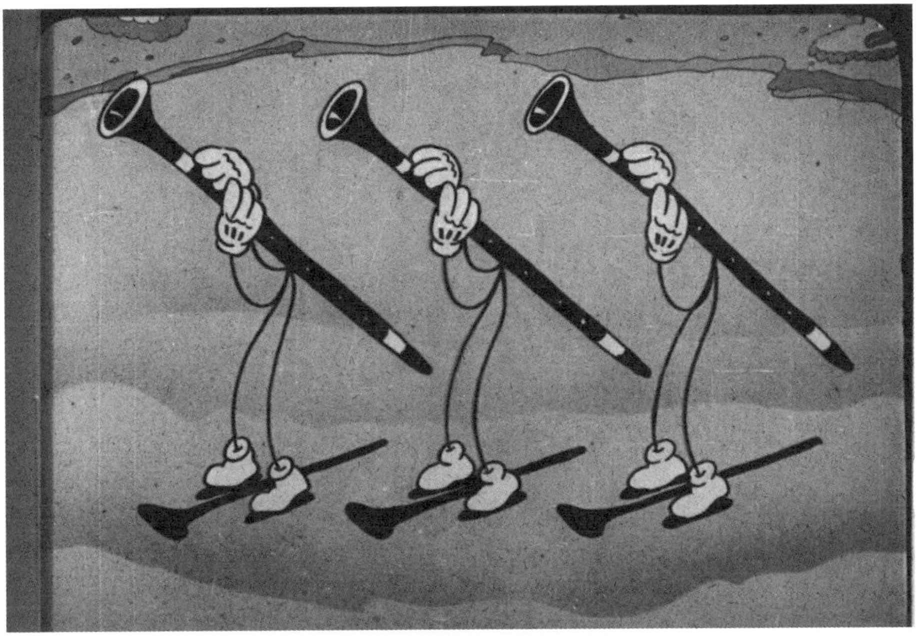

A Cheerful Concert tries to prove that only the sound produced by the new Telefunken radio receivers can provide a genuine experience of an orchestra's harmony. Personifying music via musical instruments allowed the filmmakers to present the metamorphoses of graphic, musical and sound images, and thus follow in the tradition of American film cartoon comedy.

The surviving subtitles and film surveys along with the appurtenant censorship files allow for the compling of an inventory of the IRE-film customers, the most important of which were the companies Telefunken, Elektro-Praga, Prokop and Čáp, Krása, Pilňáček, Ota Kollinský, Papež, Busch, Kosmos Čáslav and, last but not least, Jiří Schicht. The IRE-film commercials promoted a wide range of merchandise: soaps, fountain pens, washing powders, margarines, polishers, electric appliances, fabrics, shoes, radio receivers...

In contrast to the prevailing contemporary Czech short-film production, the studio from the very beginning made full use of the possibilities of the sound

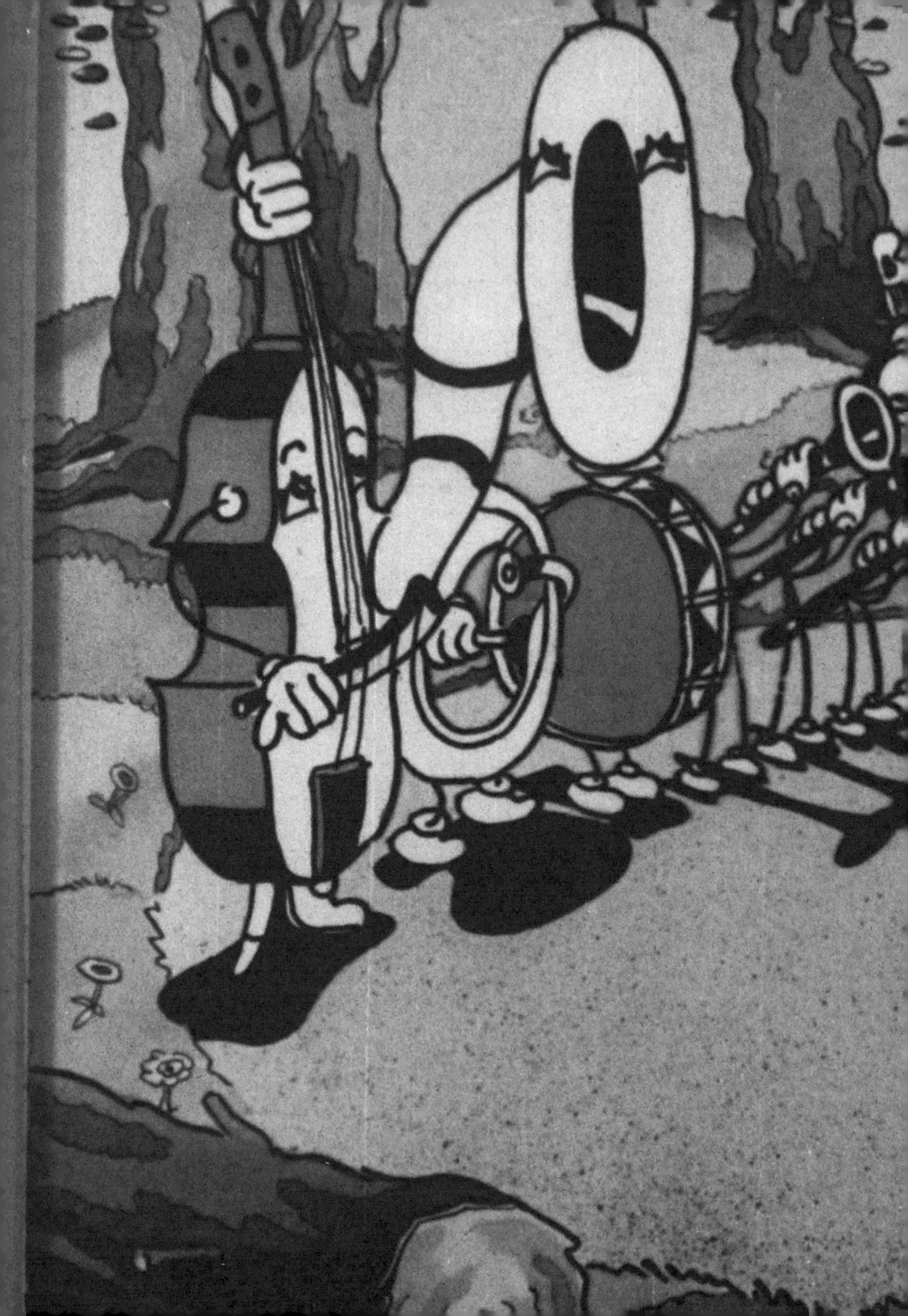

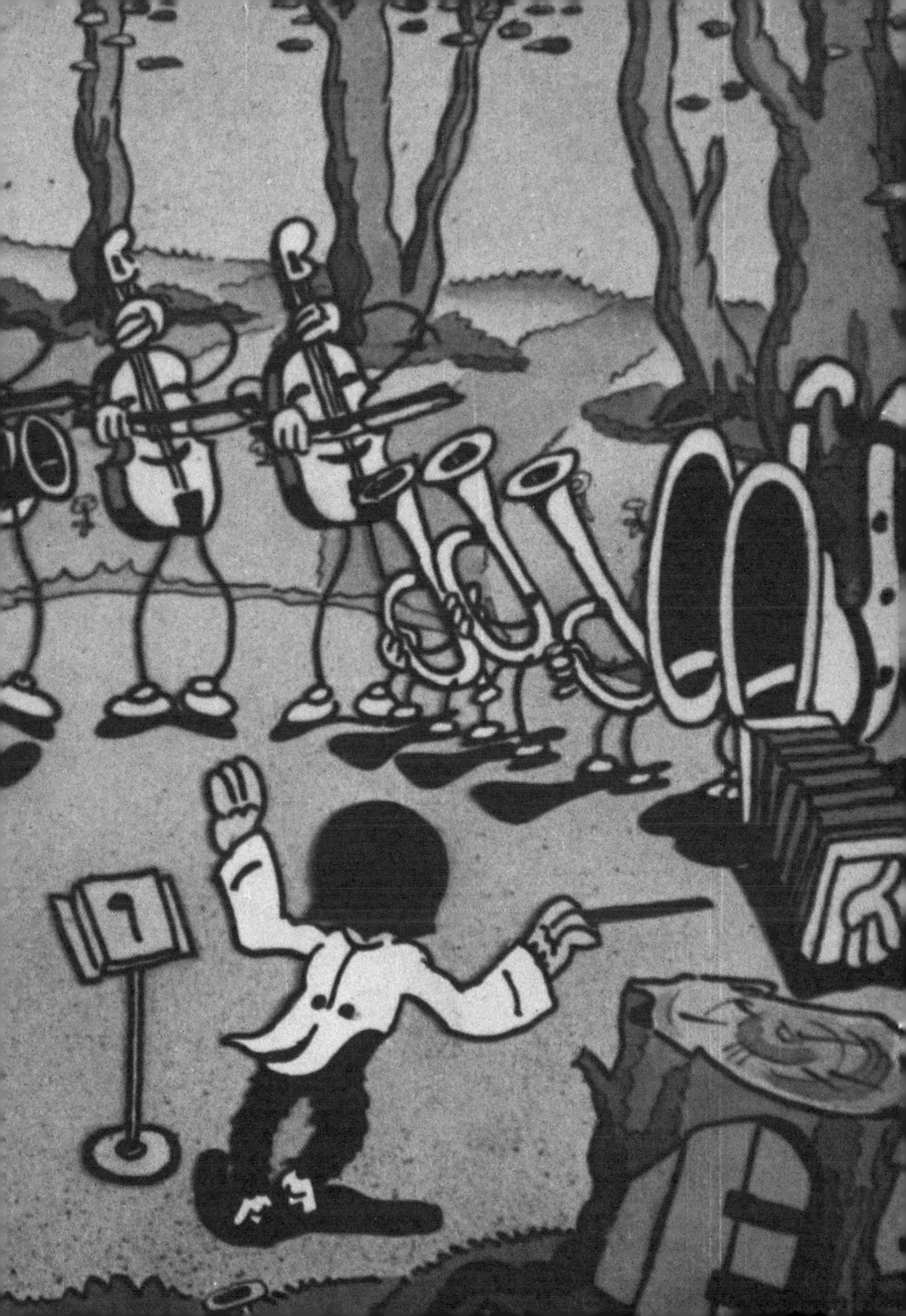

and, in the mid-1930s, also colour film.[4] The commercials naturally differed in footages. The longest picture was 140 metres, but a considerable number of the spots were capable of providing the advertising message on 45 to 65 metres (i.e. from two to three minutes). There is an interesting episode from 1934 when Karel Dodal asked the Ministry of Interior for permission to change the title of the commercial *Today and Tomorrow* (Dnes a zítra), promoting a formula fighting thinning hair, explaining that he had had to cut 40 metres from the initially 165-metre long picture because "cinemas are reluctant to accept films above 100 metres, a circumstance which had been unknown to us, and also the Sorela company does not want to pay for such an expensive screening and has asked us to shorten the film".[5] Although the picture did not survive, the corresponding documents inform us that the filmmakers left

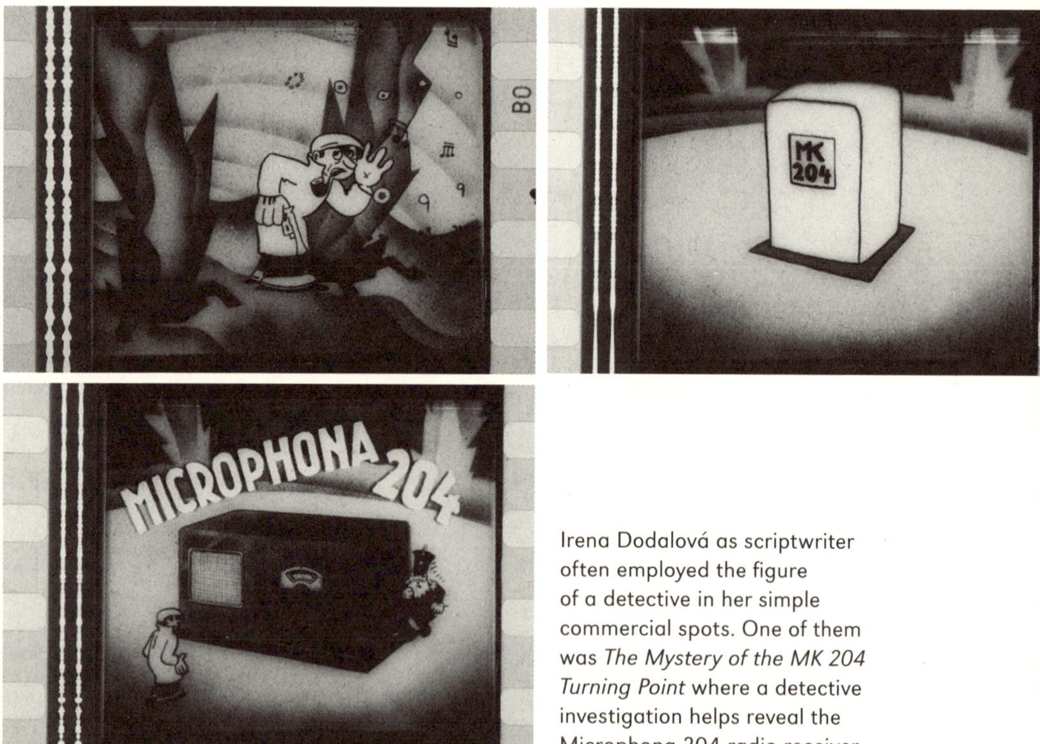

Irena Dodalová as scriptwriter often employed the figure of a detective in her simple commercial spots. One of them was *The Mystery of the MK 204 Turning Point* where a detective investigation helps reveal the Microphona 204 radio receiver.

out the opening sequence featuring an analogy of human age and the work received a new title, *The Duties of Life* (Životní povinnost). This proves how the requirements of the advertising film market at that time directly influenced the advertising contents and form.

The Dodals largely departed from foreign models and stereotypes in composing their commercials because local animation was almost non-existent at that time. Their main example became the stimuli arriving from avant-garde experiments, and the works by György Pál were their important inspiration. There are no surviving written documents about the encounter of the three in Prague but it is highly probable that they maintained close contact. This is indirectly proved by the fact that Karel Dodal made Czech versions of Pál's foreign films after the filmmaker's departure from Czechoslovakia.[6]

The IRE-film subjects and librettos usually came from Irena Dodalová. Her role as a scriptwriter was eased by the fact that she conducted the company's business negotiations and was thus familiar with the targets and preferences of the customers. Documents which would illustrate the process of approving the librettos and the extent of the agencies' participation are missing. We only know the results as they are reflected in the development of the IRE-film advertising oeuvre. By "development", we mean the shift from less skilfully conceived commercials to those whose advertising concept had some logic, humour and exaggeration. The increasing professionalism is evident if we compare the dramaturgies and artistic concepts of films aimed at equal products but created with a lapse of time – for example the 1934 and 1936 commercials promoting the soap Saponia (*Taming of the Black Giant* [Zkrocení černého obra], *The Play of Bubbles* [Hra bublinek]) and the commercials dating to 1934, 1935 and 1936 whose subject were radio receivers (*The Mystery of the MK 204 Turning Point, A Cheerful Concert* [Veselý koncert], *The Wizard of Tones* [Čaroděj tónů]). It is apparent that the films from around 1934 and 1935 were based on illustrative stories with cartoon gags and merely employed black-and-white film material. Many commercials created from 1936 already used the Gasparcolor colour palette and the initial illustrative narrative pattern was replaced by metaphor and artistic shortcut. But the concept of

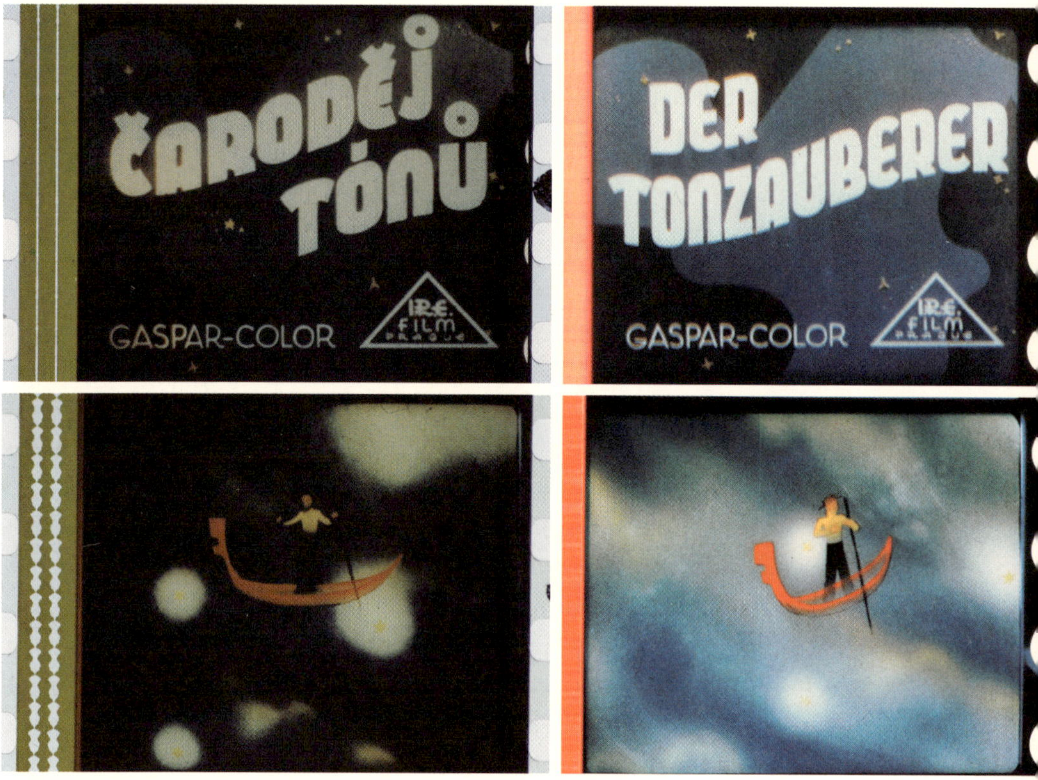

the ads was, however, influenced by many factors and not just by the filmmakers' ideas. Crucial in agreeing upon their content and style were the requirements and financial limits of the customers, and we must therefore view the "development" dimension as conditional. If commissioners wanted "traditional" commercials, which were moreover usually less expensive, the authors had to comply with their wishes. Exemplary in this sense are two commercials of similar style, originating from 1934 and 1937: *A Midnight Wedding* (Svatba o půlnoci), promoting Perola rye coffee and Karo chicory, as well as *Slattern and Glossie* (Šmudlík a Leskulinka) on the subject of Obé polish are characteristic examples of methods in sound cartoon comedy developing simple humorous situations that featured anthropomorphized

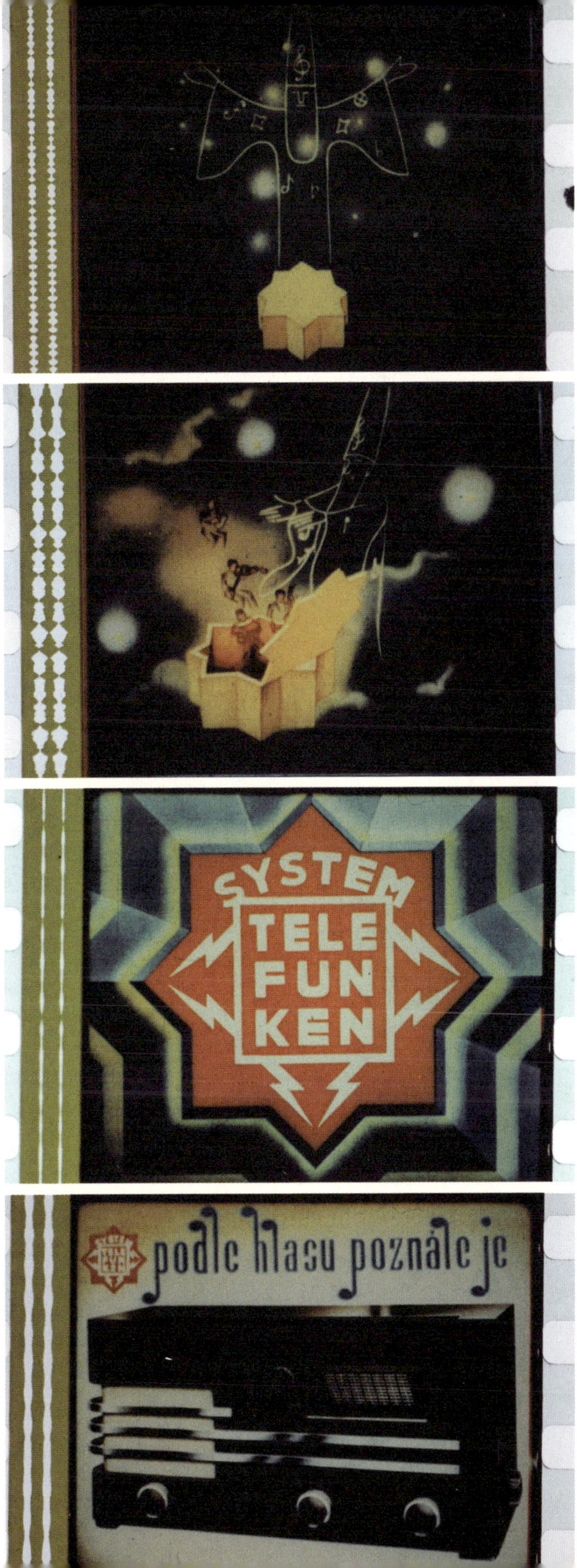
SYSTEM
TELE
FUN
KEN
podle hlasu poznáte je

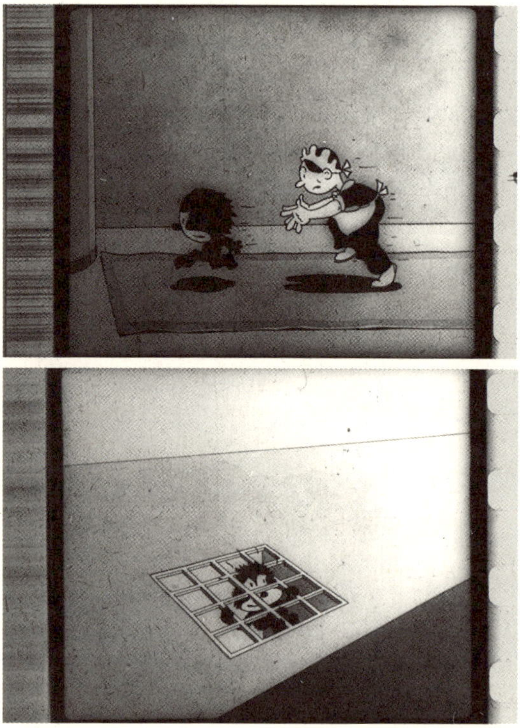

Takes from the sound cartoon comedies *Slattern and Glossie* and *A Midnight Wedding.*

products. And the abstract *Play of Bubbles* was in the process during the same time when Slattern was being chased by the little maid Glossie and fell into a sewer...

Between 1934 and 1938, IRE-film produced about 25 commercials which display three basic models of mediating the message. The first model focused on directly demonstrating the qualities and the uses of an offered commodity and laid emphasis on the informative aspect (*Everything for a Scrambled Pancake!* [Všechno pro trhanec], *A Brief View of the Future* [Malý pohled do budoucna], *The Sounds of Outer Space* [Znějící vesmír]). The second model was based on a constructed story (which often employed fairy-tale characters and motifs) whose happy ending was brought about by the promoted product (*The Taming of the Black Giant, The Mystery of the MK 204 Turning Point, Mum's Trip to Heaven* [Maminčin výlet do nebe],

A Midnight Wedding, A Cheerful Concert, The Secret of the Lucerna Palace [Tajemství Lucerny], *Three Men* [Tři muži], *The Unforgettable Poster* [Nezapomenutelný plakát], *The Protest* [Protest]). Constructing a story provided for gags and comedy techniques. The third model communicated with viewers via artsy images and metaphors, although it, too, contained product demonstrations and/or some attributes of a story (*The Play of Bubbles, The Wizard of Tones, An Autumn Song* [Píseň podzimu]).

An example of a purpose-built and informative commercial was the 1937 *Everything for a Scrambled Pancake!* for Vitello. It was based on explaining the qualities of the milk margarine by simplified diagrams and schemes, all introduced by the character of Uncle Bobby who was widely known to the audience from other Schicht commercials. The information was accompanied by a scrambled pancake recipe. This black-and-white film heavily departed from the "German Reich" advertising style of the Schicht spots, and it undoubtedly did so upon the customer's wish.

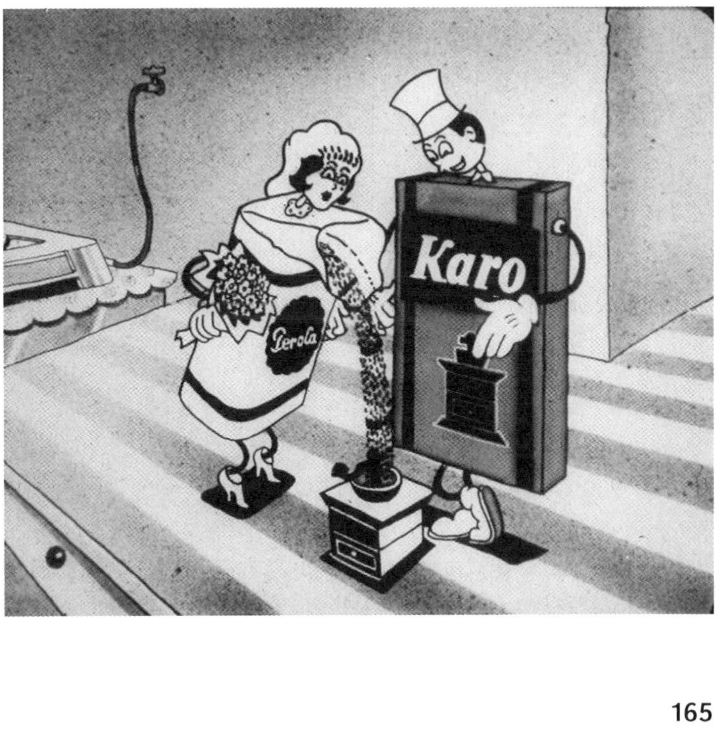

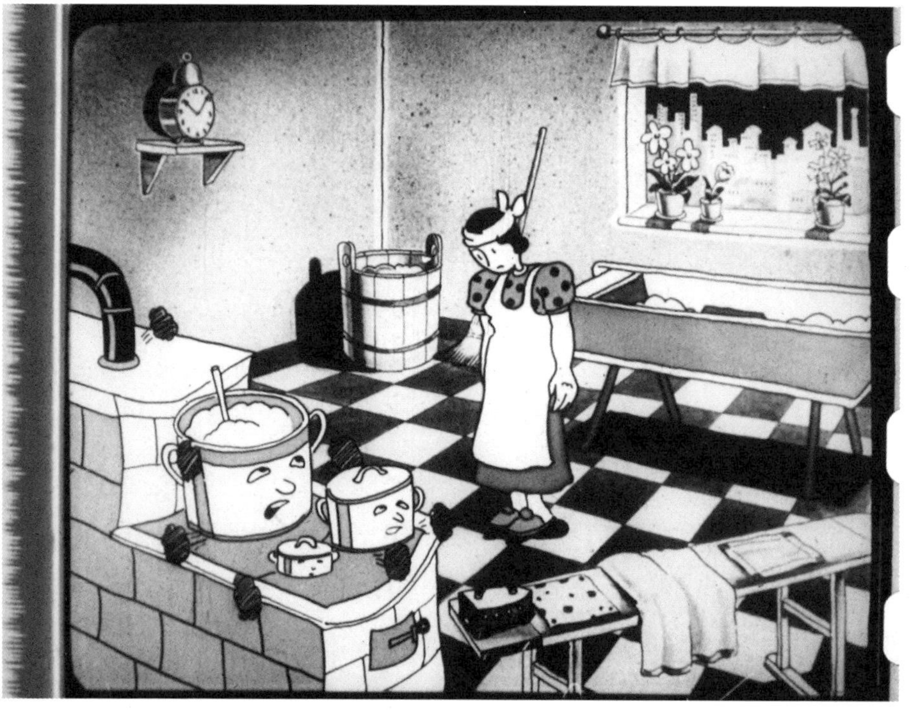

The Dodals received more creative space in the 1936 commercial *A Brief View of the Future* for the Ota Kollinský department store specializing in silk. Although it also was an informative spot, the result was highly spectacular thanks to the dramaturgy and the mixture of film cartooning and animated real objects, in this case ladies' dress fabrics. The film opened and closed with cartoon scenes featuring a presenter – a white-tied business agent – positioned on a theatre stage and inviting the viewers to visit the store and, outside the picture, commenting on the offered assortment of fabrics. The impressive character of the ad was further supported by the used animation methods, tricks and colour, and also by situating the beginning and the end on a stage which reminded the viewers of the upcoming

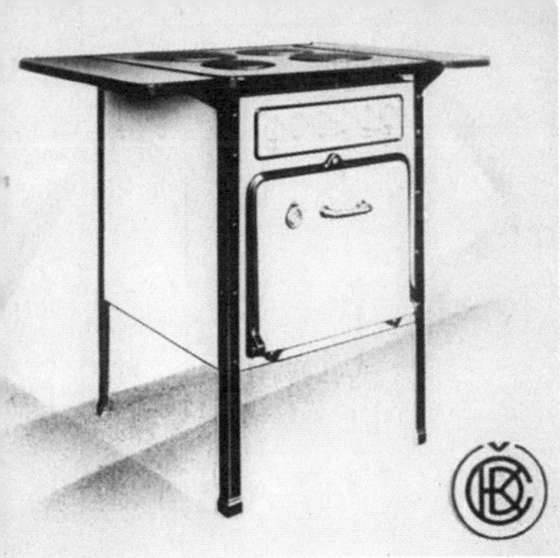

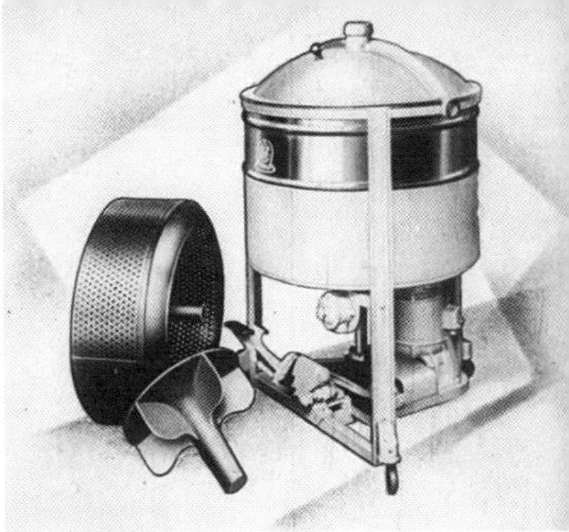

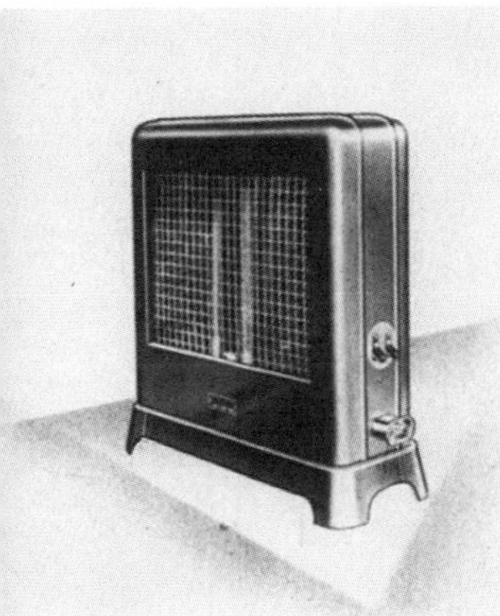

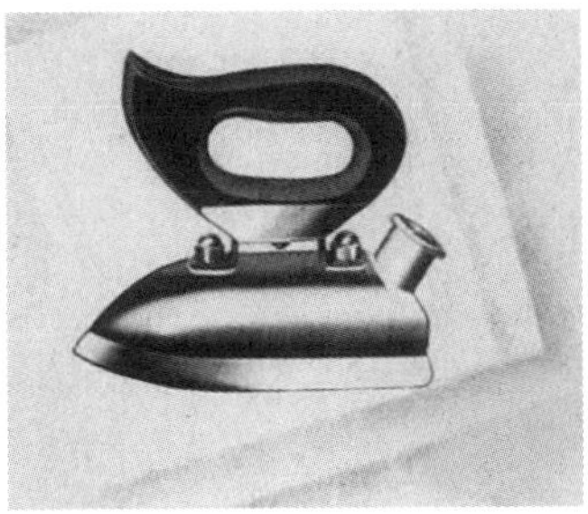

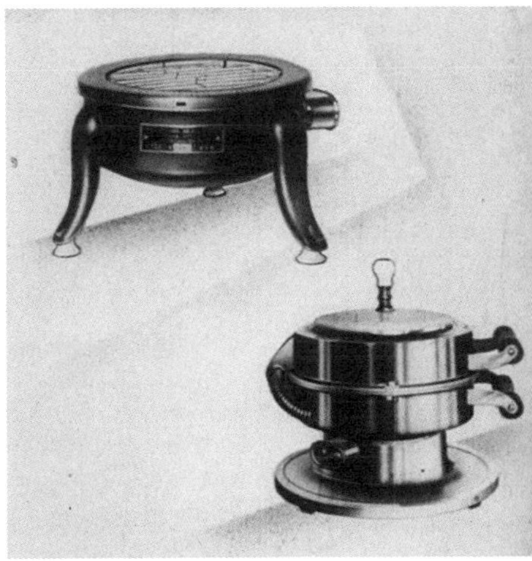

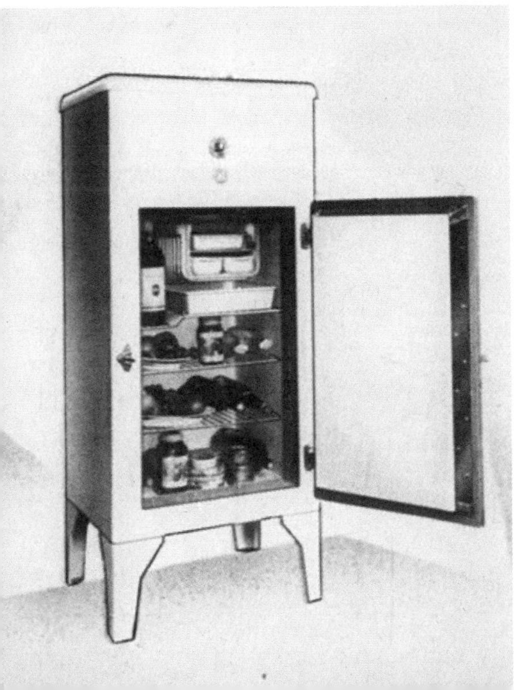

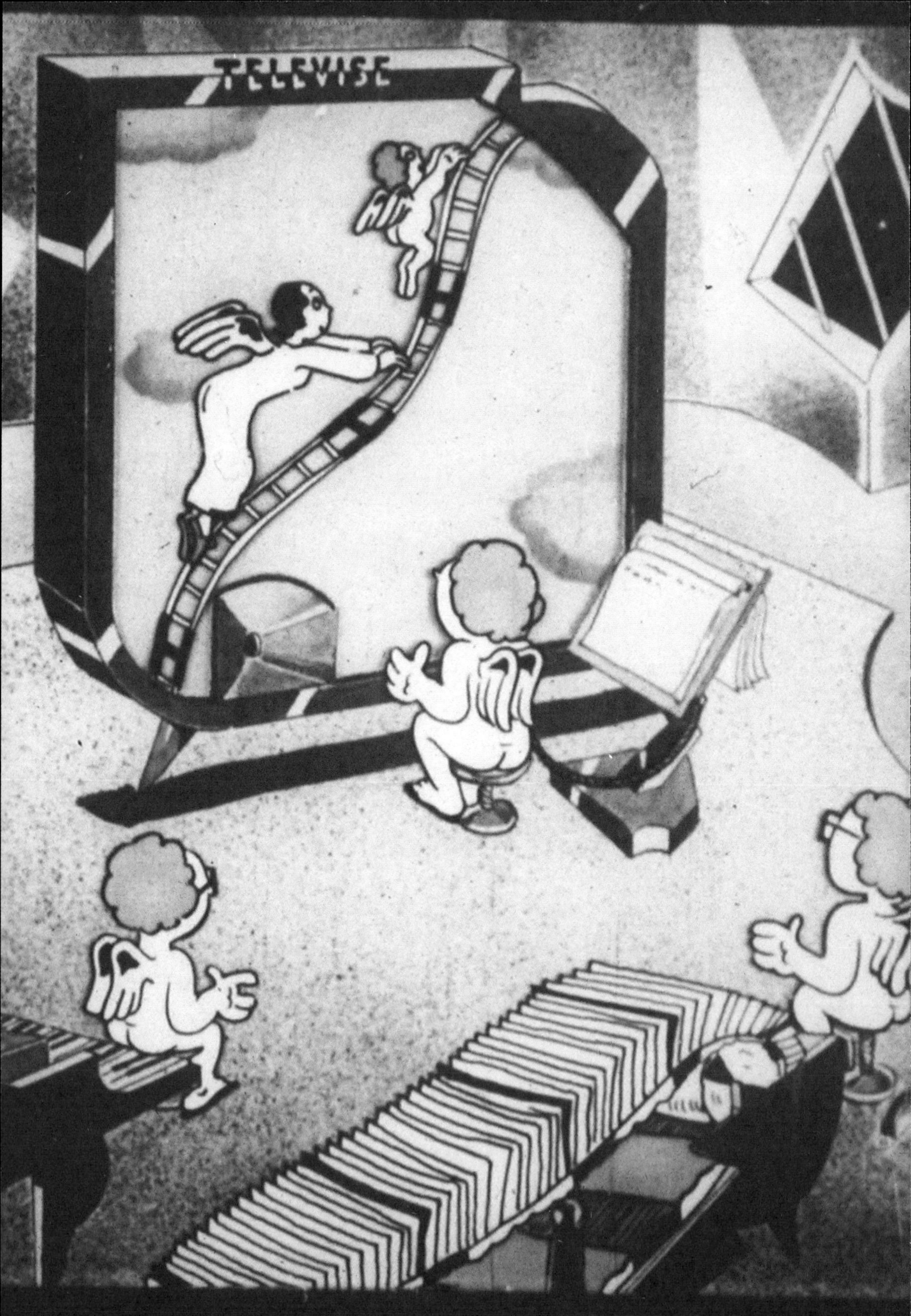
TELEVISE

social season and the urge to get a new evening gown, and thus underlined the subject of the commercial.

The second type of IRE-film's commercials followed in the tradition of sound cartoon comedy. The animation methods allowed for a free construction of the plot and the story which ensued in a happy ending thanks to the promoted, and often anthropomorphized, products. The commissions of IRE-film employed, for example, musical instruments, kitchenware, screws and margarine ingredients which turned into characters starring in various comic or quasi-dramatic stories. Frequent parts of them were laborious animations of the recommended products marching *en masse* through city streets or villages, which embodied the optimism, energy and power of the given brand and evoked their mass consumption and popularity.

The first IRE-film's successful attempt at a modern cartoon fairy-tale commercial was *Mum's Trip to Heaven* from 1935, presenting the wide assortment of electric home appliances from the Elektro-Praga company. It was a hard nut similar to which Karel Dodal had encountered in the 1920s' *A Cabin Boy on Salty Water,* whose commissioner also wished to promote the complete range of the Brouk and Babka department stores. The Dodals based the ad on a simple but effective proverb "to be on cloud nine" and sketched a story of a young wife dreaming about an effortlessly managed household. The heroine's trip to heaven (or, cloud nine) amused viewers with an array of gags including hints of paperworking angels and the use of television. The authors – mostly women in this case – gambled on automated work in the kitchen. The brief episode with the dog Spottie guarding heaven's door and marching back and forth before it with his little gun is especially worth noting. The given scene was rather irrelevant to the told story; it probably was Hermína Týrlová's contribution. When the heroine finally returned to Earth, a peddler-stylized female voice presented the Elektro-Praga catalogue of products to the viewers. *Mum's Trip*

Takes from the film *Mum's Trip to Heaven*. The Dodals solved the difficult task of promoting a very wide assortment in a single film by closing it with a presentation from the company's catalogue.

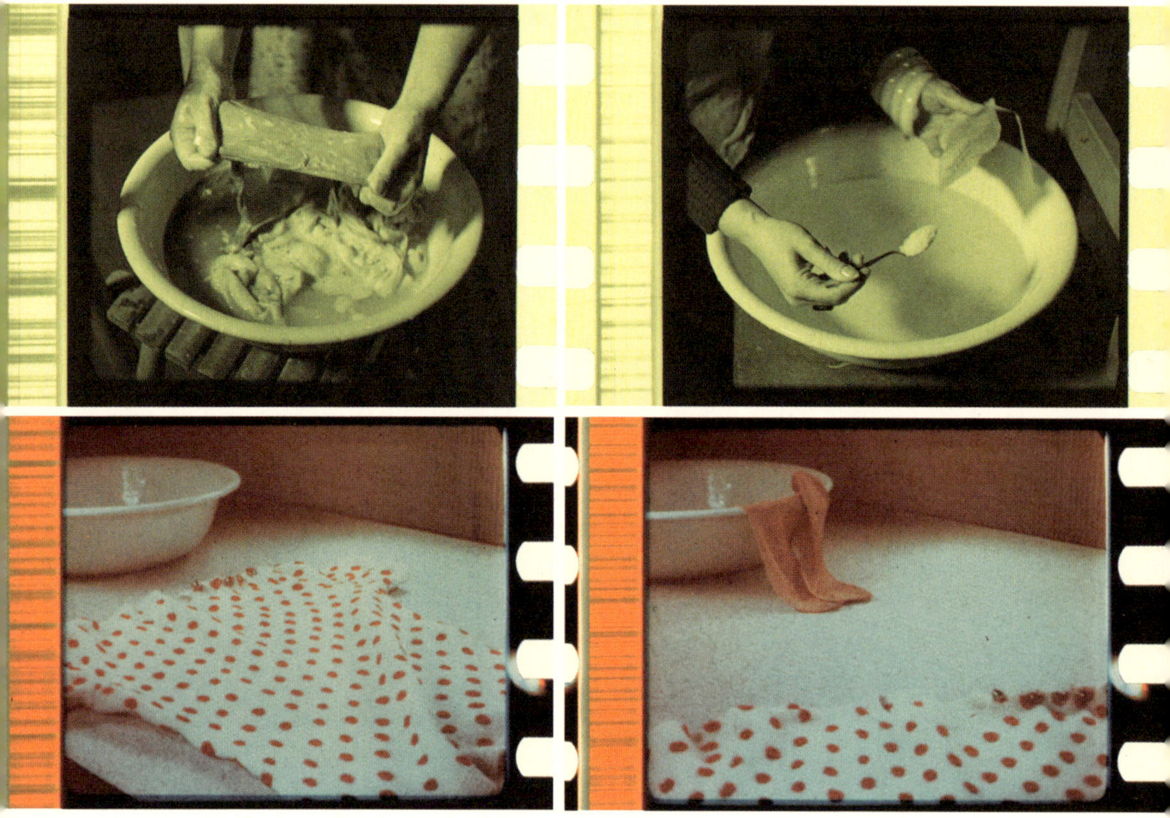

can be viewed as proof of the studio's increasing professionalism and the fact that it was already perfectly capable of fusing cartoon-comedy methods and the advertising assignment.

Using sound in a commercial is exemplified by *A Cheerful Concert* from the same year which developed a comedy story from the first tones of music, echoing with loud laughter at one point. The picture describes the trifles of anthropomorphized musical instruments: they produce sour tones, while bees or petite Mickey Mice, a frog, a caterpillar and the like fly and jump out of them. The conductor, however, eventually makes the orchestra

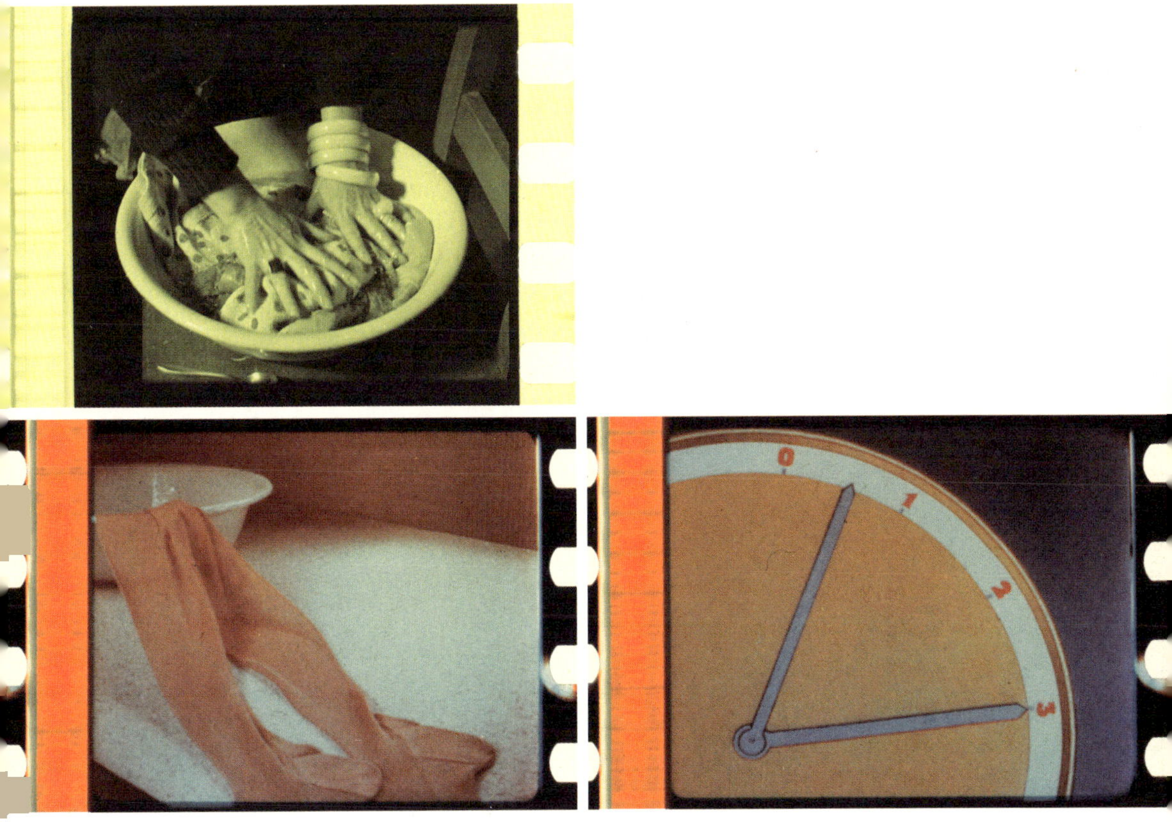

Takes from the combined, black-and-white virage and colour film *Perhaps Still Yesterday*. The quality of washing with the detergent which was "considerate" to laundry was most probably demonstrated by Irena Dodalová. The film survived in only several outtakes.

play cleanly and beautifully and perform a song "in full tune". The story and the music thus prepared viewers for the closing montage of spoken word and text promoting Telefunken radio receivers. There is no doubt that the Dodals devoted much time, strain and artistic potential to these commercials, and, for example, the harmonica and caterpillar scene from the *Concert* excels as a fabulous, graphic short-cut, animation and sound gag.

The Unforgettable Poster from 1937 proves that Irena Dodalová as the scriptwriter gradually managed to master her skills in constructing a plot. The Dodals originally planned to use the story about a billposter who falls

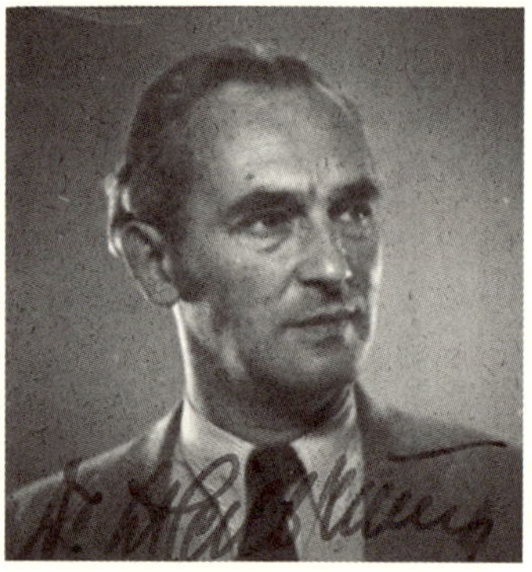

Leo Heilbrunn.

in love with Mona Lisa, as pictured on a new poster advertising film performances for the film *King Bluebeard and Mona Lisa* (Modrovous a Mona Lisa), and only subsequently turned it into a commercial promoting Sana margarine. The ad has often been mentioned in connection with *A Fairy Tale about a Melancholic King* (Pohádka o melancholickém králi) by Pál, because they both popularized Sana.[7] This case well illustrates the strategies of advertising departments which repeatedly exploited well-acquitted ideas and plots. Recycling characters, environments and methods for the sake of promoting a single product was in no case detrimental since the repetition helped strengthen the links built between a pleasurable experience and a promoted commodity.

The Dodals' *Poster*, however, was not a version of Pál's commercial; it offered both a new and distinctive artistic morphology and a new plot. Its heroes were not only the King, but also Mona Lisa as the Queen, and the story mover became the billposter who pasted posters for the films *King Bluebeard* and *Mona Lisa* on a corner with lanterns. As soon as the two characters came to life, they stepped out of the billboard and formed a (married) couple who, nevertheless, soon ran into trouble as Bluebeard was starving and the helpless Mona Lisa was drowning in tears. The couple's happiness was saved by anthropomorphized ingredients used for producing margarine and turned into bars of Sana in a modern machine unit. The advertising song "We bake, we boil, we stir-fry with Sana" was accompanied by an exemplary marbled cake, and the shot of the content ruler closed with the subtitle "The way to a man's heart is mainly through his stomach". Also important for the advertising message was the detail at the very end when the Sana logo came with a crown, "because Sana margarine certainly deserves the royal crown". This retrospectively associated the margarine with a royal dish. It was not actually the Dodals' idea but a requirement of the advertising experts – after all, Sana was crowned at the closing of Pál's film, too. The commercial was highly impressive due to

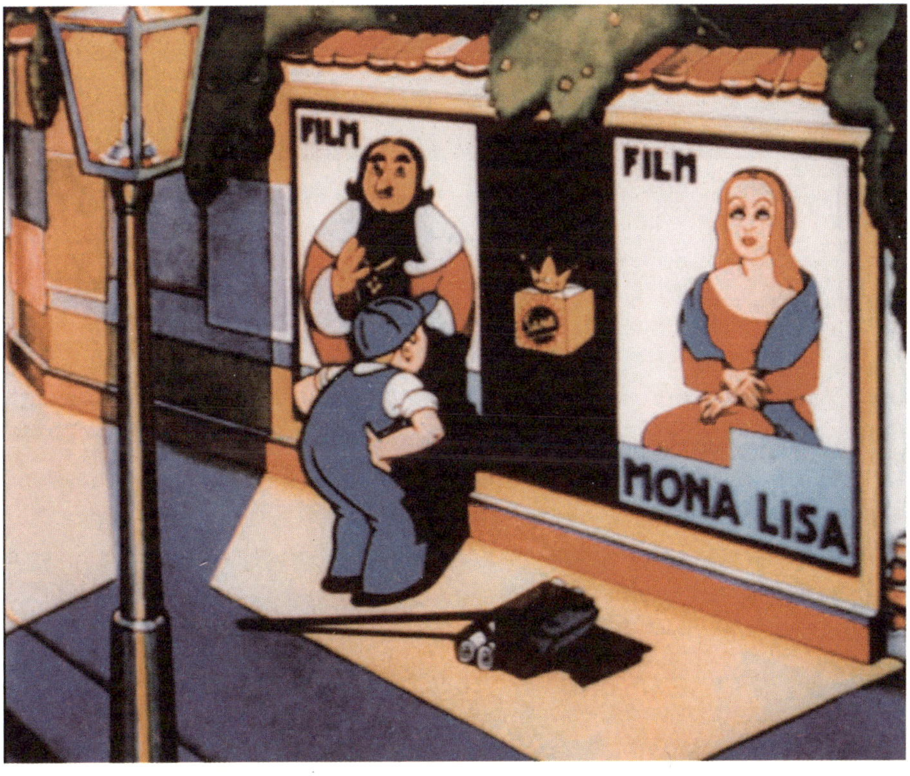

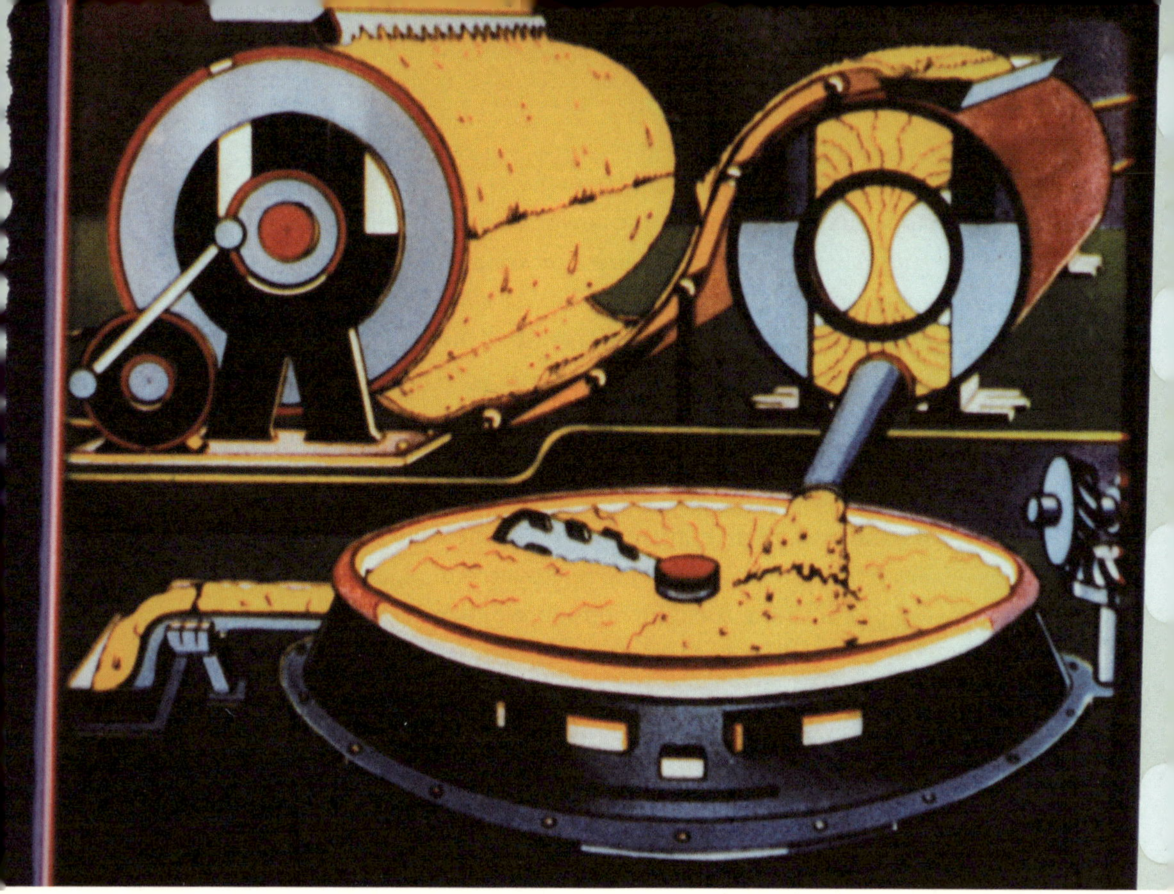

Takes from *The Unforgettable Poster*. The figure of the billposter was also characterized by the sound component of the film. Graphically simplified industrial objects and equipment were frequent "actors" in Karel Dodal's commercials.

the colour film material as well as the sound dramaturgy and the smooth fusion of image and message. If we compare it with the 1920s Sana ad *See How Two Boys and a Dog Fool around These Days!* (Vizte vše, co tropí dnes kluci dva a jeden pes), it is quite clear that Czech film advertising at that time had achieved a new level, and not only from the aspect of design and animation. It clearly shifted from simple demonstrations to smart audio-visual communication based on quoting various cultural signs.[8]

The group of films employing fairy-tale stories includes *The Protest*, the very last cartoon made by IRE-film in 1938. Even though it survived in only fragmentary form and low quality, the remains still suggest great design and dramaturgy and visually impressive scenes of the lamenting crowds. It departed from an affectionate story in which the metropolitan traffic stops and machines end up in scrapyards, with screws and spare parts calling out for oil. They are, naturally, saved by the new motor oil, Mogul.

The commercials leaning against a present-based feature story include two "detective" films, *The Mystery of the MK 204 Turning Point* (1934) and *The Secret of the Lucerna Palace* (1936). It seems that the subjects reckoned with the popular detective genre, mainly appealing to metropolitan audiences, while the detective character simultaneously presented quasi-mysteries which should be solved with the help of the promoted products. The first film features a detective trying to find the mysterious source of sound, a radio receiver in this case. The authors apparently tried to reflect upon the situation in neighbouring Germany when incorporating the scene with the dictatorial roaring commander. It nevertheless lacked any closer connection to the advertising message and thus totally missed the desired point.

On the contrary, Dodalová's return to the "detective pattern" in *The Lucerna Palace* enjoyed great success. It was of a combined type, containing a cartoon introduction[9] and a main part in the form of puppet film. The opening cartoon scenes, featuring the night lights in Prague's Wenceslas Square, did carry a subliminal message: the promoted shoeware producer, i.e. the main

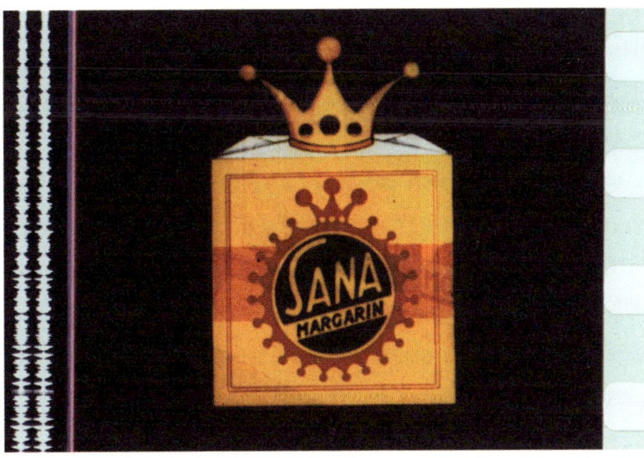

subject of the commercial, was "by chance" based in a Lucerna passage off the square. The film opened with a scene of a detective agreeing to find the source of a mysterious sound. It is worth noting that he was urged to do so by his commander through a TV screen.[10]

The detective eventually succeeded, revealing that the sound came from the hammers of shoemakers working in the Lucerna-based company. The charm of the commercial not only lay in the mixture of cartoon passages and the still stiff motion of the puppets, but mainly in the fact that the almost oversimplified plot was based on the harmony of sound, image and perfect timing. The playful communication with viewers also included confusing the name of the Prague Lucerna (Lantern) passage with the authentic lighting lantern which the filmmakers moreover inhabited with the shoemaking characters. The very favourable public response made the authors add a finale to the work, where a chorus of puppet cobblers staged the final advertising appeal dubbed by the Wise Teachers of Gotham. This new version fortunately survived with only the few last tones of its soundtrack missing.

Hermína Týrlová never ceased to emphasize that it was she who convinced Karel Dodal to base the commercial on puppets because she was at that time mesmerized by Aleksander Ptushko's Soviet film *The New Gulliver* (Novyj Gulliver; 1935). Without wishing to degrade her recollections, it must be said that the Dodals were at that time also closely familiar with the achievements of Starevich and Pál, and that there surely were many more sources of inspiration.

A specific place in IRE-film's body of commercials is occupied by a story of three washerwomen, presented in the 1938 colour ad *Three Men*. The credits state that the team included one of the Prague jet-set advertising experts, Leo Heilbrunn. The architect, who closely collaborated with the Piras agency, successfully developed the concept of the Czech flagship menthol ointment Alpa for many years and also designed film posters.[11] The presence of his name in the credits, stating him as "librettist", suggests close links between the Dodals and the milieu of Czech advertising. The impressive animation of this film departed from the frolicsome song sung by contemporary housewives, "Oh how jolly we are! We have no men, but if we had them, we would just weep". It is a pity that a considerable part of this chic film promoting the Three Men washing powder is now missing.[12]

The category of the "present-day" pictures also encompasses two films whose contents are today only known from the censorship files. A white woman in *Bambi and a Cactus* (Bambi a kaktus; 1934) disapproved of a dark-skinned (charcoal) man until Hellada soap turned him white. The 1934 *White Magic* (Bílé kouzlo) made a black kid dance so ardently that leaves around her hips shed and the issue was only solved by the Bambino company catalogue. It should be noted that similar subjects featuring black males and females and heaven with the omnipotent granny-God were not exceptional in advertising at that time.

An interesting option for the filmmakers was the model of art preview, presenting a product via metaphor and opening some space for creative imagination. A distinct embodiment of this

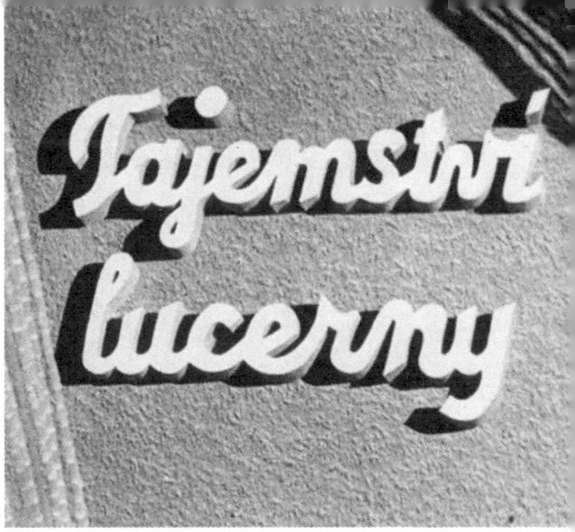

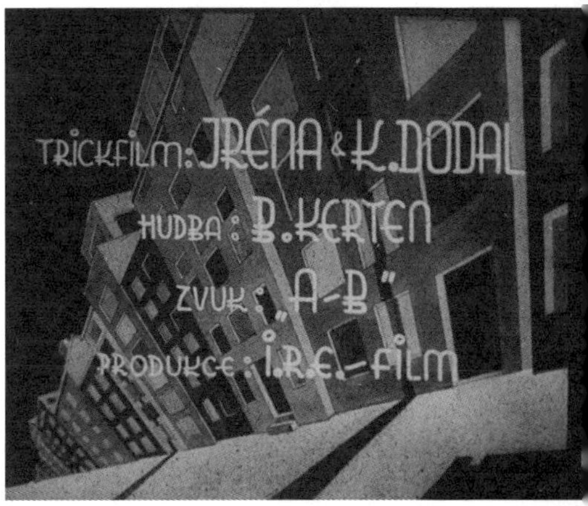

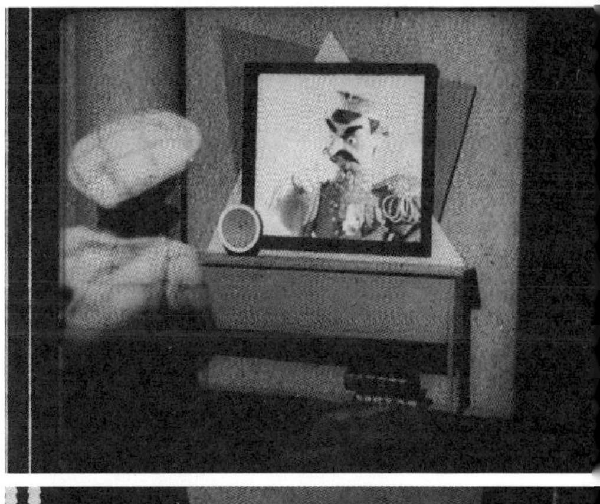

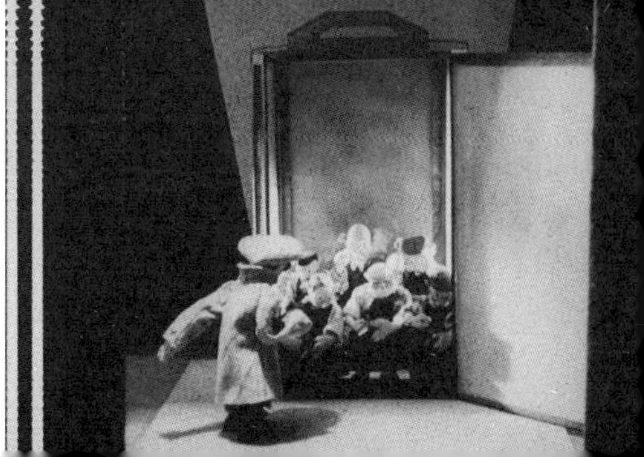

Hermína Týrlová always stressed that she had convinced Karel Dodal to employ puppet film in this commercial due to her impressions of Ptushko's full-length film *New Gulliver*. The Dodals' picture *The Secret of the Lucerna Palace* so thrilled the owners of the shoemaking company that the filmmakers were given the chance of finishing the closing scene with a sung advertising slogan.

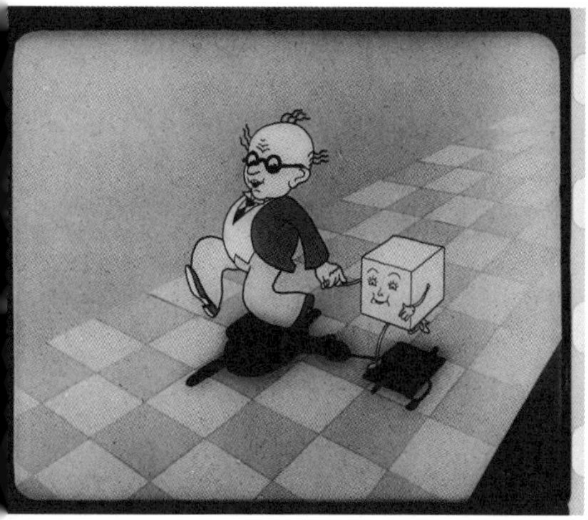

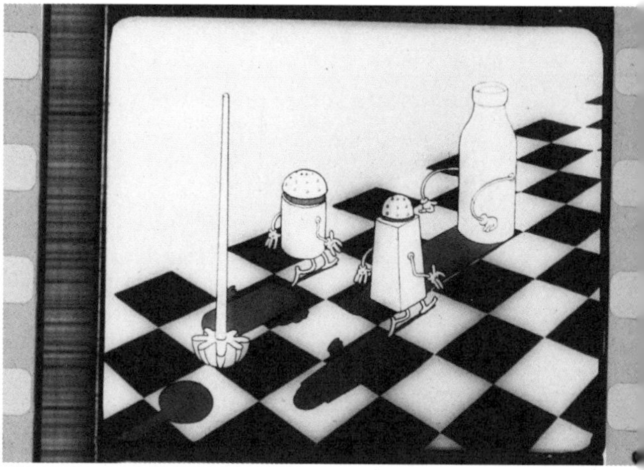

Takes from *Everything for a Scrambled Pancake!*, promoting Vitello margarine, prove that the authors here subordinated themselves to the style of Schicht commercials. They even adopted the character of Uncle Bobby who played a large part in the development of the Schicht image.

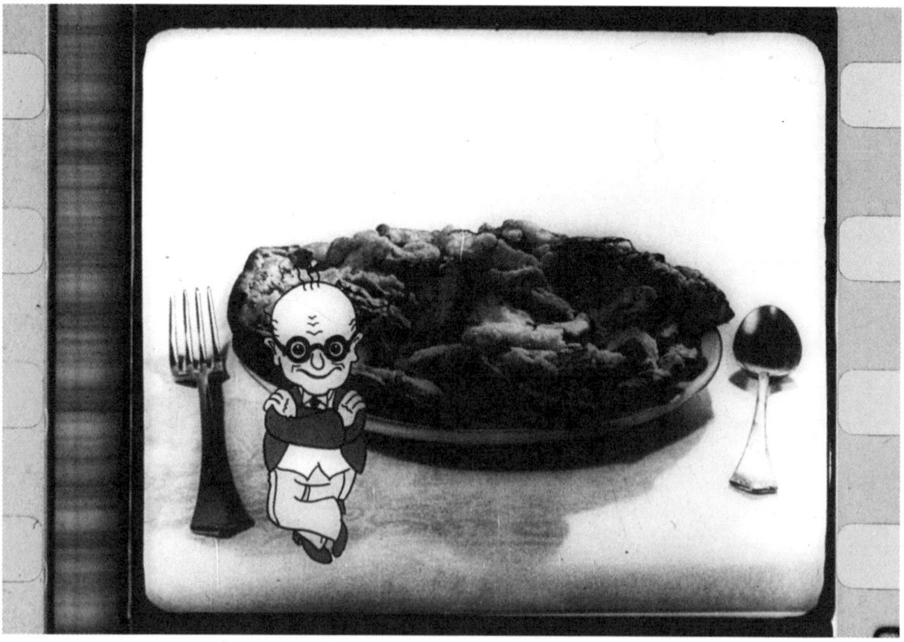

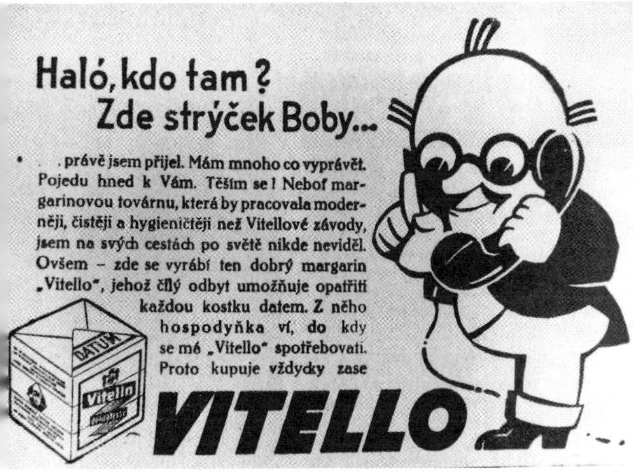

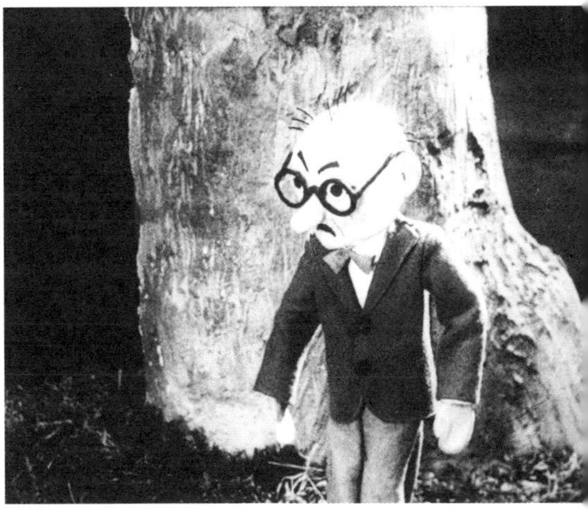

The character of Uncle Bobby in the film *The Transformations of Uncle Bobby* (Onkel Bobys Verwandlung, Proměny strýčka Bobbyho) from 1930, and an example of a contemporary press advertisement.

advertising style in Germany was Fischinger's commercial for the Toliraf agency, entitled *Circles* (Die Kreise; 1933/1934). Let us add that its author at that time filmed the colour abstract composition on musical motifs borrowed from Wagner and Grieg and closed it with the slogan "Alle Kreise erfasst Tolirag" (in free translation: Tolirag reaches all social circles). Fischinger's ad, introduced in December 1933 to great success, apparently served as an inspiration for the Dodals and their commercial *The Play of Bubbles*, promoting Schicht's Saponia soap. The kinetic play of abstract forms or a metaphor of floating, whirling and dancing, bursting and reappearing soap bubbles had a carefully made closing. The storks, which were part of the brand logo, flew off over a map of Czechoslovakia in all directions, holding the soap bars in their beaks. The interesting musical motif was accompanied by a voice-over appeal about the qualities of the refined turpentine soap "with a stork"[13]. Similar to Fischinger, the Czech filmmakers created two versions of the film. Some abstract parts of it remind several passages of the "authorship" *Fantaisie érotique*; they are, however, not identical. The latter picture will be discussed in the following chapter.

Yet another example of visual and musical metaphor in advertising is *The Wizard of Tones*, whose impressive visual image of musicians appearing and floating in space, underlined by the musical motifs, associated the wide offer of music arriving from space and mediated – magically – by the Radiotechna radio receiver. Dodal's "Chagall-like" composition, linked with conspicuous musical montage, resulted in an effective metaphor which closed with an economical advertising message. This IRE-film commercial, too, exploited some methods and metaphors connected with visualization of the sound qualities of radio receivers.

A testimony to the experimental character of IRE-film production is the commercial *An Autumn Song*, promoting the department store Prokop and Čáp and its assortment of fabrics and haberdashery and based on animated haberdashery objects: thimbles, dressmaker's tapes, pins, spools of thread, buttons and so on. The subject of autumn was introduced by old pages from a tear-off calendar falling on the floor and turning into vine leaves. The following trick procession of tailor's tools as if followed the beginnings of cinematography when viewers were stunned by the images of objects coming to life and motion. The trick technology serving to display a surreal world of buttons, needles, threads, and mainly snap fasteners can, for example, already be found in the 1912 commercial *Sewing Kit* (Der Nähkasten) by the German director and producer Julius Pinschewer. We can hardly expect that the Dodals would ever have seen his work. Nevertheless, both the assignment from the company Prokop and Čáp and the artistic and material character of the haberdashery opened to the Dodals a wide range of possibilities for using tricks and they consistently employed them throughout the film. The parade was followed by a preview from the department store's pattern book and a short scene with an animated stork with scissors. The style of this brief puppet scene, however, still indicated some confusion in using the appurtenant animation technology.[14] The film closed with falling leaves of cut-out fabrics, again recalling the subject of autumn, which represented a unique way of completing the required information from the advertising point of view. It seems that the company was well content with the result because it subsequently commissioned a cartoon commercial for the next season from the Dodals. The black-and-white picture with the final

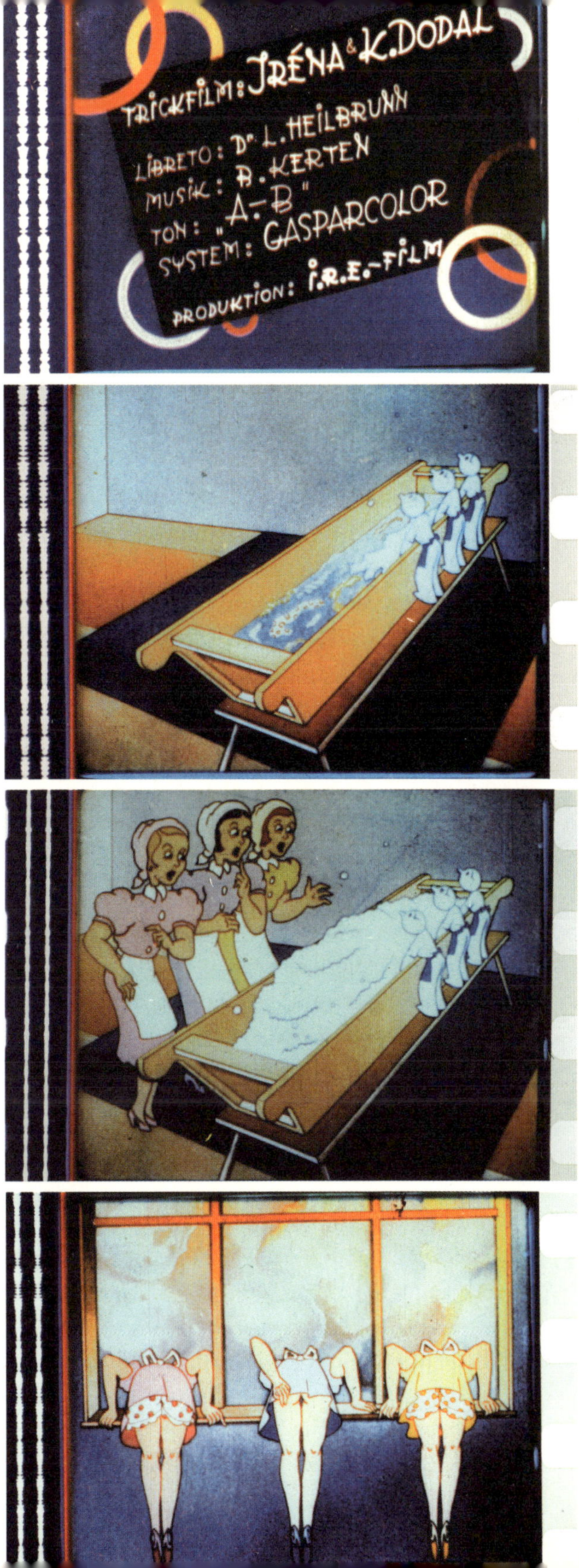

Takes from the film *Three Men*.

sequence in colour, *Spring Is Here* (Jaro je tady; 1938), unfortunately only survived in part.

IRE-film commercials always heavily relied on sound, which formed part of the advertising message along with the "pitcher's" diction and verbiage of the speakers. Such attention paid to the sound aspect was isolated in Czech film, and the studio's production can thus also be viewed as pioneering from this point. The young composer Bedřich Kerten worked with an array of motifs from various genres – from jazz to brass music, including the popular Wise Teachers of Gotham. The radio show "Cartoon Superstar" (Hledá se hvězda pro kreslený film) of 1938 suggests that Irena Dodalová played an important role in the studio's music dramaturgy and sound direction.[15] She would ask that the composer "at least once totally breaks away from the rules learned at the conservatory, from the prescribed intervals and from counting beats, from the harmony and counterpoint theories", and it was also she who supervised the completion of the pictures in the sound laboratories of the AB film studio. Not just the music but also the narrative – whether in the form of dialogues, rhymed slogans, advertising appeals or the song lyrics – were a firm part of the conscientiously elaborated sound and visual composition. The sound master Ivo Špalj confirmed this as he finished digitizing and restoring the sound reels of the Dodals' films, planned for DVD release: "The Dodals are amazing and it's unbelievable how thoroughly they considered everything!"

There are no written documents proving the Dodals' work with Kerten. The scope of production undoubtedly made IRE-film develop a standardized form of technical scenario and project their experience acquired abroad into it, and we can assume that Týrlová later brought this practice to Zlín. A certain testimony of the Dodals' technical groundwork submitted to composers is the script for *Ferda the Ant* (Ferda Mravenec) with music by Miroslav Ponc. The document[16] displays the script pages as divided into three columns. The first column described the content of the image including the required type of take. The second one was about the division of music into bars, the actions, sounds and noises and their onomatopoeic expression, and the third column provided numerical data about the number of frames to a given music bar.

A very effective component of film commercials at that time was colour. It was the commissioner and his financial possibilities which decided whether a film would be in colour or contain colour sequences, or would be black-and-white. The compromise thus usually combined a black-and-white film with a colour ending (for example in *A Midnight Wedding, Slattern and Glossie* and *Everything for a Scrambled Pancake!*). The first Dodals' picture which convincingly presented the emotional power of colour film was *The Tin Drum* (Tluče bubeníček), whose opening takes employed black-and-white film, but the entrance of the coloured Felix the Cat "lit up" the metropolis and introduced the Hellada soap. The commercial *Perhaps Still Yesterday* (Snad ještě včera), presenting the Trimin washing powder, even combined a virage part (takes of real hands washing clothes in a washbasin) and colour film, used for animating seductively surfacing dresses, stockings and slips whose colour underlined the verbal information about the fabulous effect of the detergent. The greatest asset naturally was to work with Gasparcolor only, however technically demanding the system was. But its colours were sharp and compact, and it was therefore used by numerous European authors of animated films as late as the early 1940s.

Looking at IRE-film's commercials in their entirety, they clearly speak of the creative energy, enthusiasm, invention and professionalism of the Dodals. Their activities stemmed from the tradition of European film advertising as well as the fruitful contacts with the oeuvre of György Pál. In addition, they brought a unique style to Czech film and designed prototypes of film commercials which were effective not only from the aspects of dramaturgy but also from the point of using sound, music and montage. They invented unique methods of cartoon comedy and abstract film and experimented in trick technology and colour film, in combining cartoon and puppet film and animating real objects.

The work of the studio certainly had a chance of asserting itself on the market and to keep developing – if only many conditions providing for this had not been missing at that time.

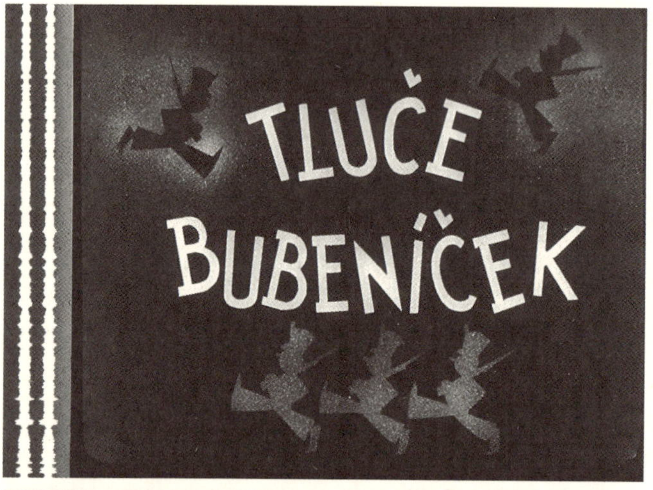

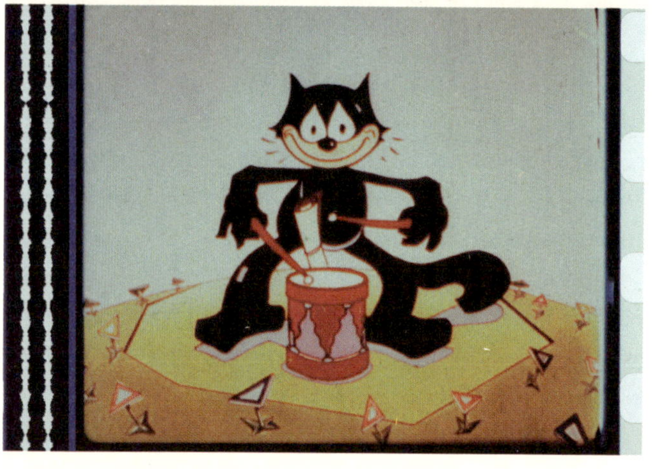

A colour take from *The Tin Drum*, which combined black-and-white and colour film material.

1 Documents relating to the studio's economic activity are missing. The given assessment of its expenses comes from information provided by the Czechoslovak Film Advisory Board.

2 Yet another Baťa cartoon commercial known from this period is *Our Children* (Naše děti; 1938), most probably commissioned by J. Pagáč. One of the collaborators was K. Müller, the music was composed by F. Kerten and the producer was Patriafilm. The latter also produced the today missing cartoon commercials *Death on the Hunt* (Smrt na lovu; 1934) and *The Maharajah's Wedding Present* (Svatební dar maharadžův; 1935). Müller worked with IRE-film as a scriptwriter on the films for J. Karpner, *The Lady-Killer* and *The White Magic*, in 1934.

3 Klos, E., "Běda ženám, které mužům vládnou" (Woe to Women Who Rule over Men), in: M. Benešová, op. cit., p. 8.

4 The given requirement seems to be natural but watching the contemporary documentaries, for instance, makes us realize that a considerable part of Czech shorts were still silent, and if they had sound at all, it was mostly an indifferent accompaniment to the subtitles. Films offering a mixture of narration, music and, eventually, sound were very rare.

5 Dodal's letter addressed to the Czechoslovak Ministry of Interior, undated and filed as part of the corresponding censorship documents. The National Archives, Cinematographic Censorship Committee with the Ministry of Interior, Ref. No. 21/1934.

6 Frída, M. – Brož, J., op. cit., p. 165.

7 The commissioner in both cases was, again, the Schicht advertising department. Sana Praha acted here as a separate company due to tax purposes, but it was still part of the holding into which it was incorporated in the early wartime years.

8 One of them is, for example, the billposter character. As J. Kroutvor noted, this figure "is often linked with a bizarre story and it replaced an angel with a speaking tube in a modern city". – Kroutvor, J., *Poselství ulice: Z dějin plakátu a proměn doby* (Message of the Street. From the History of Poster and the Changes of Time). Praha: Comet, 1991, p. 9. The billposter also referred to the very beginnings of Czech cinematography: to the film *An Exhibition Sausage Man and a Billposter* (Výstavní párkař a lepič plakátů; 1898) by F. Křiženecký.

9 The film intro survived in two versions, one of them containing several abstract kinetic patterns.

10 Television was at that time intensely written about and discussed, for example, in the circle of Radiojournal employees – and IRE-film pictures, such as *Mum's Trip to Heaven* and *The Secret of the Lucerna Palace*, already presented the TV screen as a functional part of the modern world.

11 Štembera, P., "Reklamní plakát v Praze ve 20. a 30. letech. Emil Weiss, Leo Heilbrunn, Höns" (Prague Advertising Posters of the 1920s and 1930s...), In: *63. Bulletin Moravské galerie* *v Brně* (63rd Bulletin of the Brno Moravian Gallery in Brno). Brno: Moravská galerie, 2007, pp. 153–163; *Český filmový plakát 20. století* (Czech 20th-Century Film Poster). Brno, Praha: Moravská galerie / Ex libris, 2004.

12 People in the studio apparently had fun working as is proved by the take of the housekeepers leaning out of the window; one of them is pulling her skirt down because she does not wear knickers. The take was so short that it would not bother the censors but viewers could notice it. Such a scene was quite unique in Czech films.

13 The brand still exists; it is active in Croatia where Schicht built one of his factories before the Second World War.

14 P. Štembera states that the graphic designer Höns developed the concept of the Prokop and Čáp brand between 1924 and 1935 and that this work was "one of the pinnacles of this sector in the entire inter-war Czechoslovakia". – Štembera, P., op. cit., p. 159.

15 *Cartoon Superstar,* untitled German typescript, 18 pages. The Czech cataloguing title is not original and was attached additionally. Archive and Program Funds of the Czech Radio, Ref. No. 4532. The show was broadcast on 7 August 1938 on the station Praha 2 (Mělník transmitter) from 6 to 7 p.m.

16 *Ferda the Ant,* technical script. The Czech Museum of Music, Prague, Inheritance of Jaroslav Paclt (yet incompiled).

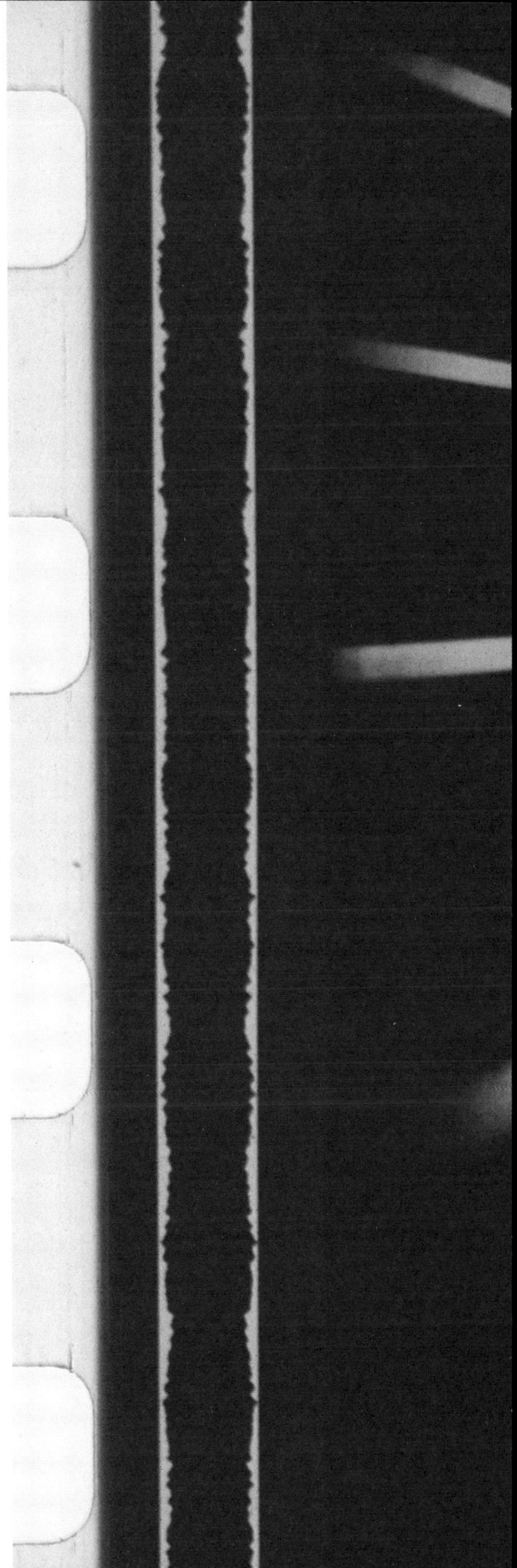

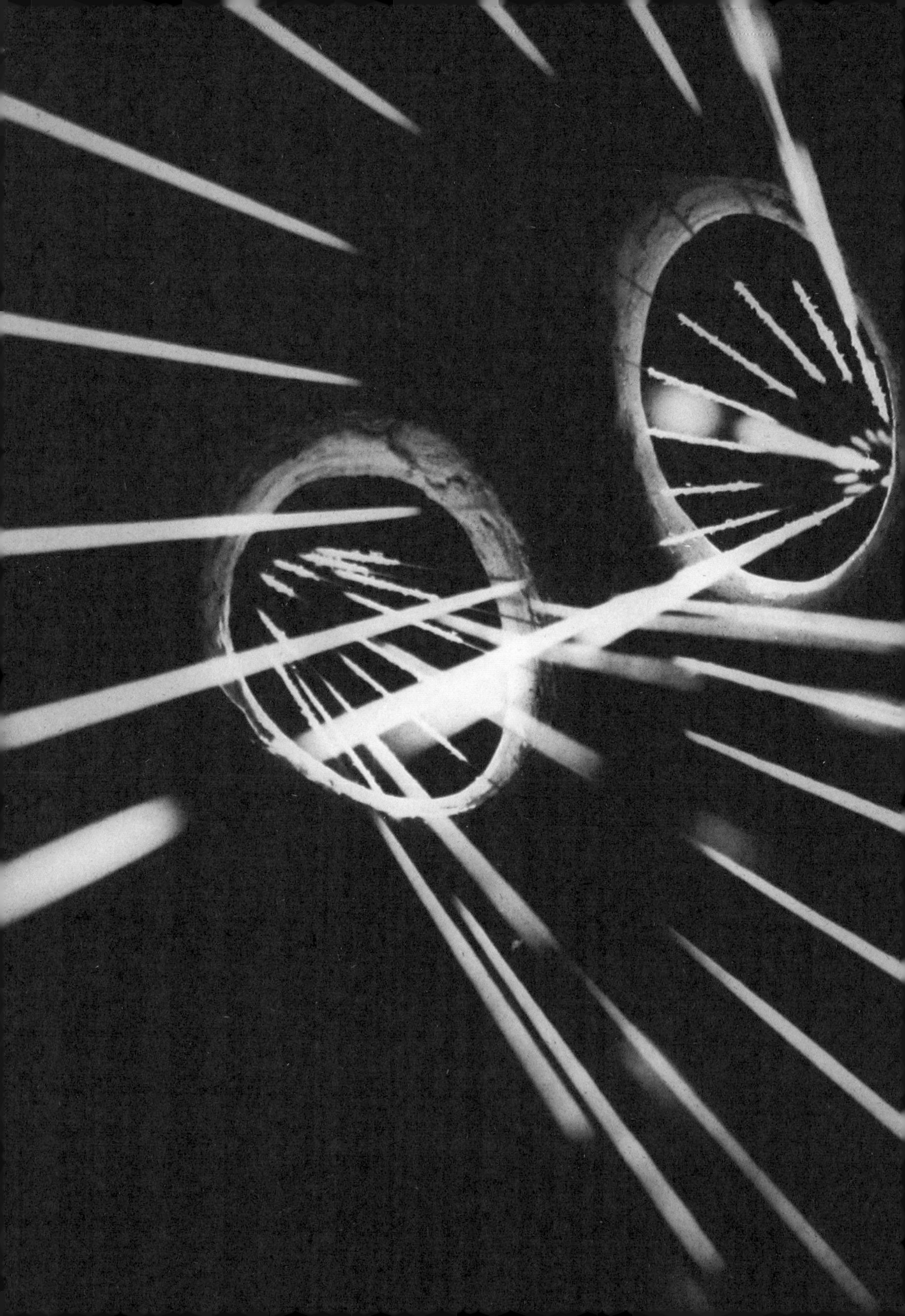

The Dodals' Czech Oeuvre / Their Program and Its Realization

In 1936, when the Dodals applied for the support for their animated films from the Film Advisory Board, the letter attached to the application summed up the projects which they proposed for realization. They were: *A Stone Fairy-Tale* (Kamenná pohádka); *Prague in Colours* (Barevná Praha), intended for the Paris exhibition; a film about Czech folklore; a personification of dance in the form of drawn pictures of undulating curves and colours; the film *Poem*; an adaptation of Karel Čapek's drama *R.U.R.* as a colour modern film with acting figures; yet another film adaptation on the motifs of Josef and Karel Čapek's drama *Pictures from the Insects' Life* (Ze života hmyzu), and finally, *Fireflies* (Broučci), an adaptation of the well-known children's book by Jan Karafiát.[1] The application is the only document capturing the dramaturgy concept of the studio although the couple, unfortunately, did not manage to realize any of the presented projects.

Other plans and intentions of the studio are known from the contemporary press. They included the film *The Rebellion of Shapes* (Vzpoura tvarů) dealing with social subjects, and the abstract fantasy, *A Little Ball in Love* (Zamilovaná kulička), quoting Dvořák's *Humoresques* (Humoresky). The Dodals also worked on a title about a billposter in love, and more...

The submitted projects were clearly demanding and the Dodals' program was clearly fanciful. Neither the state of development in Czech animated film nor the studio equipment sufficed for these intentions. Realizing the works would moreover have highly exceeded the financial possibilities of contemporary Czech film production even if the authors would have received the required state subsidy. We must, however, admit that all the subjects well fitted the technology of animated film. It is worth noting that the Dodals in the case of the *Pictures from the Insects' Life* speculated about puppet film, and their overall program was mainly aimed at adult audiences with the exception of the *Fireflies*. The couple considered introducing their production outside Czechoslovakia and some films, for example those about Prague and folklore, were also meant as a political representation of the country abroad. On the one hand, the program departed from kinetic and audio-visual possibilities of animation and avowed the line of avant-garde abstract films; on the other hand, it headed towards the narrative tendency in animation, following the oeuvre of Vladislav Starevich and others. The above-mentioned proposal can be viewed as the first dramaturgy program and the first vision of the potential in the Czech animated film production.

IRE-film's prestigious projects which the filmmakers tried to assert in the following period were the films about folklore and the film about Prague. Their concept is proved by the two surviving screenplays to *The Czechoslovak Republic in Colours, Dances and Songs* (Č.S.R. v barvách, tancích a písních), even though neither of them ever materialised.[2]

The film script to *The Czechoslovak Republic in Colours, Dances and Songs* was written early, in 1935, and was based on the idea of consonance between animated creations of folk art, such as ornaments found in embroideries, Easter eggs and pottery, all accompanied by motifs from Antonín Dvořák and folk music – i.e. on confronting the rhythms and structures of artistic and musical signs. The assigned authors were Karel Dodal (tricks, drawings), Irena (libretto, direction) and Bedřich Kerten (music). The press reported that the Dodals also worked on a version of the given subject under the title *Dances, Songs and Colours in the Czechoslovak Republic* (Tance, zpěvy a barvy v ČSR) where a combination of documentary and animated film would express the relations between landscape, folk songs, folk dances and folk costumes. It

I.R.E. - FILM

první americký filmový atelier pro výrobu kreslených i hraných zvukových groteser a filmů

Praha - Vinohrady | Telefon 553-15 | Milešovská 12.

Trik.filmu: Ak. mal. Karel Dodal | Zodpovědní spolupracovníci: Libreta a režie: Irena | Hudba: f. Kerten

Titl. 11.11.1936

Filmový poradní sbor,
při ministerstvu obchodu,
P r a h a II.,

Dovolujeme si sděliti, že máme zájem (při udělení objednávek) na zadání některého z dodatků pro kulturně výchovné, případně pro propagační filmy určené pro cizinu .

Zjistili jsme, že byl založen Svaz ze čtyř výrobců, kteří chtějí obstarati tuto výrobu sami a dovolujeme si proto upozorniti na naši spolupráci.-

V našem programu se nachází stále ještě neprovedený plán výrobní :

1./ Kamenná pohádka / barevná Praha / pro výstavu v Paříži / Můžeme nabídnouti nyní barevné kopie á RM 1.35 /za 1 m /

2./ film českého folkloru : a./ kraslice v orig.barvách
b./ výšivky ,,
c./ sklo ,,
d./ hračky ,,
/ máme barevný systém ,, Naturwahre Farben-Fotografie ,,který umožňuje orig.vzhled provedení a barvu předmětů /

3./ Taneční stělesnění / kresba vlnovek a barev/ ,, P o e m ,, dle známé hudební skladby a dle tanečního pojetí české taneční umělkyně Mme Š.

4./ R.U.R. / barevný figurkový moderní film / dle románu Karla Č a p k a schopný exploitace do celého světa /

5./ Ze života hmyzu detto

6./ Broučci, dle známé povídky .

atd.

can be that the authors' interest in folk art was evoked by the favourable response to Plicka's visual symphony *The Land Sings* (Zem spieva; 1933) but their plan to combine animation and various ethnographic forms and to link them with documentary passages opened an utterly new perspective to film. Folk art was one of the greatest passions of Irena Dodalová, which later found its way into her Argentinian folklore lyric epopees where she reportedly also used trick technology. She remained faithful to this interest till the end of her life; she even proposed to Vladimír Opěla from the National Film Archive in one of her last letters sent to Prague that she would present a lecture about folk art in the city.[3] The surviving preparatory works for the 1930s' folk pictures merely include several puppet and cartoon shots from the film material acquired from Argentina. The sound take of a doll representing a rural wife in folk costume standing by a cradle in a rustic chamber in part follows Pál's approach to styling a puppet, which departed from the style of wooden toys. Several frames of the reel as if anticipated the journey taken several years later by Jiří Trnka in *The Czech Year* (Špalíček; 1947). Some other outtakes of the film, too, show the attempts at combining folk songs and puppets.

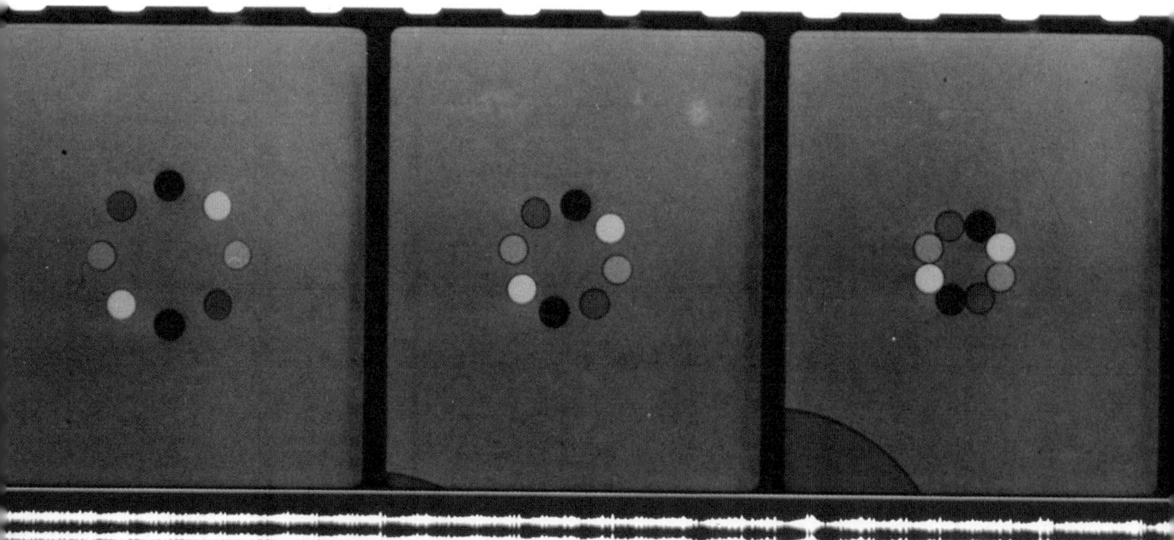

The Dodals very much fought for the animated project *The Heart of Europe* (Srdce Evropy), which they worked on between 1936 and 1938 and which fused artistic ambition and a deliberate business plan. It was designed as a poetic vision of Prague "where water, smoke, floating clouds and falling leaves and snowflakes are in fluid motion".[4] They also wanted it to present the Czechoslovak capital as the heart of historical architecture and a significant Central-European destination. The film was conceived so as to serve the promotional purposes of the Ministry of Foreign Affairs which would purchase a significant number of shorts from Czech producers from the 1920s. *The Heart of Europe* was to be based on animated watercolours of Prague by Jaroslav Šetelík, a middle-class painter of high renown. The artist presented his watercolour collection, capturing urban motifs during various seasons of the year, in the Prague Topič exhibition hall in 1932 and published them in a representative foreign-language book. His works were also known to the wider public from countless colour postcards. The idea of animating watercolours was unique at that time, even more so that the filmmakers wanted to employ the rather complex Gasparcolor system. It is also interesting that the painter would moreover

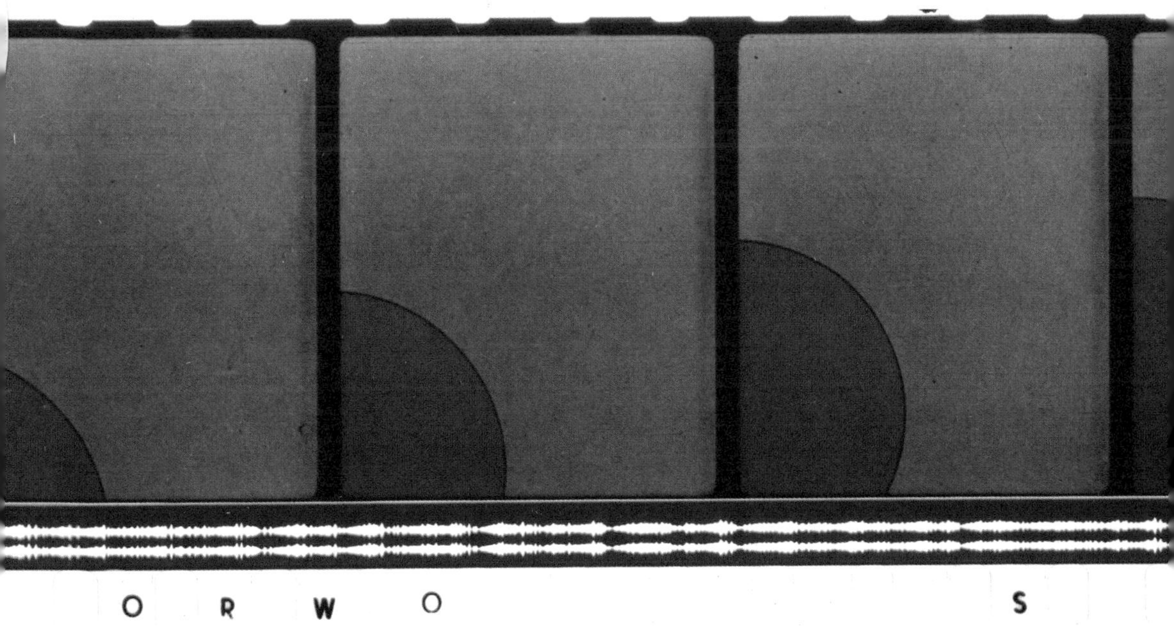

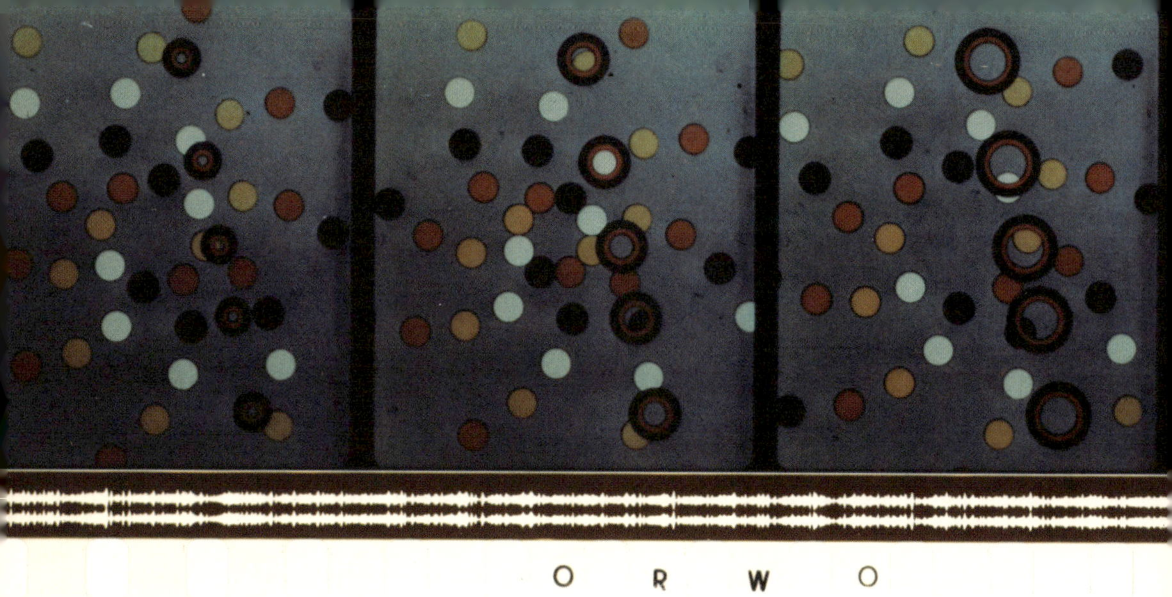
O R W O

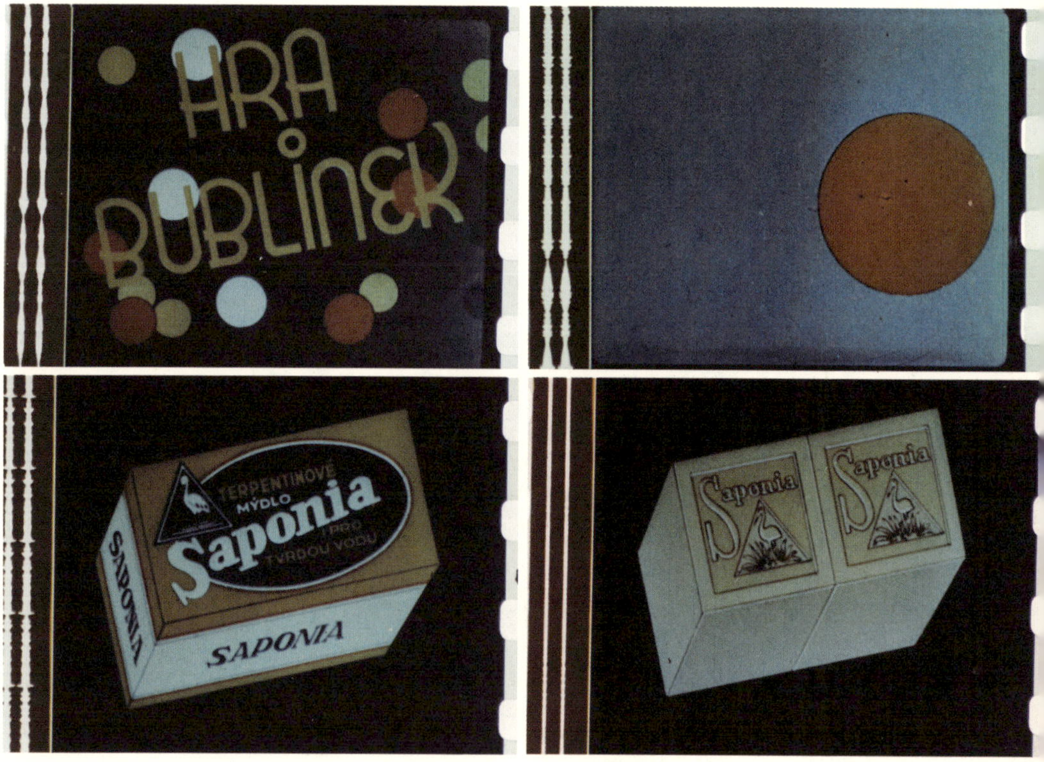
HRA
BUBLINEK
TERPENTINOVÉ
MÝDLO
Saponia
I PRO
TVRDOU VODU
SAPONIA
SAPONIA
Saponia
Saponia

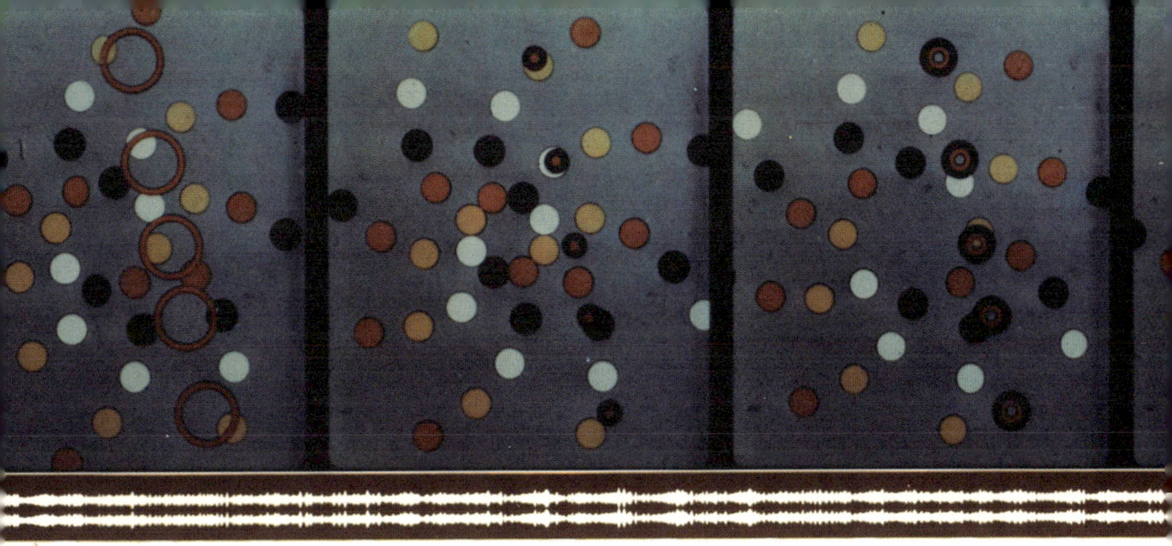

S 628

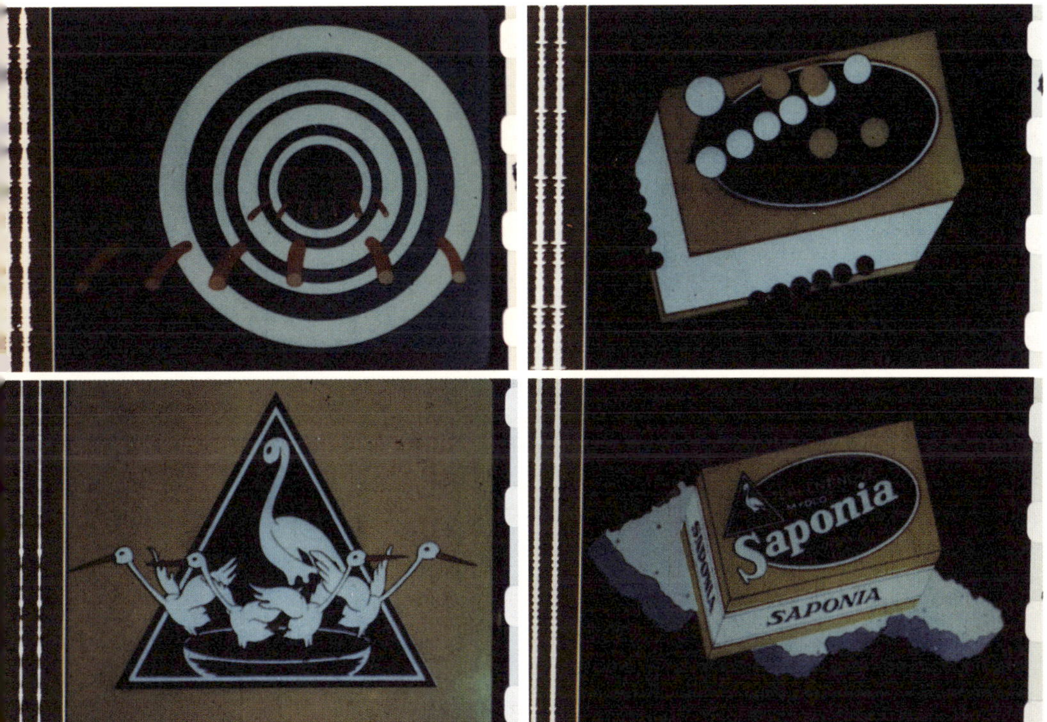

participate in the film's overall production. The contemporary composer and a famous radio orchestra conductor, Otakar Jeremiáš, was invited to be the music director. The popularity of the given collaborators was undoubtedly to serve the film's publicity, equally as the names of Josef Skupa and Jaroslav Ježek helped promote *The Adventures of a Ubiquitous Fellow* (Všudybylovo dobrodružství; 1936). An offer to financially support the production came from the banker and Elektafilm director, Josef Auerbach; he, however, later withdrew from the partnership. We can only speculate whether he feared that the distribution of an animated film would not cover the high production costs or whether he turned the project down because he had already begun shifting his activities abroad due to the unfavourable domestic situation and saw no good prospects in the Czechoslovak production.

As soon as the Dodals failed to reverse the decision of the leading Prague producer, there was no other choice but a state subsidy, and they thus turned to the Film Advisory Board in 1937. Their grant application, including the libretto, was then reviewed by the Supplementary Committee and Jindřich Elbl reported its standpoint in September. The committee arrived at the decision that the costs, amounting to one hundred thousand Crowns, were too high and the film could not be made without a new producer. In order to prevent false hopes, the body agreed that the support would cover one-fifth of the expenses at maximum.[5] It also negotiated with other financial sources via the City of Prague which eventually promised to support the film with fifty thousand Crowns provided that the Board would give an equal amount.

At its sessions held in January and February 1938, the Board again widely discussed the project, and the tangled negotiations resulted in an official appeal for the support from the Prague Municipal Office.[6] In March, the body debated the standpoint of the municipality's presidium which ruled that it had no additional means but was willing to take part in the project if it would be participated in by the Film Advisory Board and the Department of Tourism, i.e. the Ministry of Foreign Affairs. Jindřich Elbl suggested that the authors make a ten-meter test film to ease the decision process.[7] The same issue was brought up in April. It seems that the Dodals hesitated to invest in a film preview without a secure financial background. It was eventually suggested that the Board would release ten thousand Crowns to produce the preview and that its total investment would be 30 thousand Crowns. The proposal was, among others, supported by Miloš Havel emphasizing that "the company in question makes colour cartoon films using special technology which we do not have in the Republic yet".[8] The proposal was eventually approved but that did not equal the prospect of further financing as the Dodals had requested. And although it was already apparent that they would not find support for the picture celebrating Prague as the Czechoslovak capital, the authors met the requirement to produce the ten-meter preview.[9]

Out of the many plans and considered projects, the Dodals did not complete more than two authorship films, the abstract opuses *Fantaisie érotique* (1937) and *Ideas in Seach of Light* (Myšlenka hledající světlo; 1938). These were the first Czech titles reflecting foreign experimental works in this field. They, however, fulfilled their mission only in part since neither one made it to Czech cinemas and they were both largely inaccessible to film historians and publicists for a long time. And although abstract film was far from being unknown to the Czech avant-garde, these were very unique projects in the history of Czech cinematography.

The concept of abstract film as a new kinetic art was first introduced to the Czech public by Karel Teige in 1924 in his straightforwardly entitled book *Film*. The new abstract film production was represented in then-experimental works by artists such as Marcel Duchamp, Hans Richter, Werner Gräff, El Lissitzky and Viking Eggelling. Teige wrote that "these films despise anecdote, literariness and theme but want to profess poetry. They use shapes, lights and colours solely for the sake of emotion which they can evoke in viewers, for the sake of the sensual instead of portraying qualities. They clearly and precisely figure out the optical effect: they are physical organisms producing lucid emotions; they are a keyboard of shapes, almost a dictionary of shapes and colours. They are films living only through the play of optical forms in motion and having no practical purpose and sense; they are entertainment for soul and a pleasure for sensibility... these abstract films in their synopsis must bring pungent *optical surprises* in order to keep viewers' senses in the desired tension... pure film, *pure cinematography* – this is what is being created here".[10]

Teige's relation to experimenting with kinetic images was restrained. He mainly perceived them as a "lesson" in composing film picture and film morphology, insisting that abstract film injected aspects of artistry from a painting studio into film and lacked poetic emotion. The members of the Butterbur (Devětsil) art group mainly viewed their admired film medium as a spectacle of thrilling optical and photogenic qualities of "reality itself" and an exciting rhythm of film montages; a spectacle which was to whirl with optical metaphors and lyrical images as "art that is simultaneously optical and poetic".[11] If the members of the avant-garde movement employed the form of "film scores", "film poems" or "film librettos", their productions mainly pertained to literature and did not interfere with the milieu of Czech cinematography.[12] The authors, after all, did not even expect their works to be transferred onto the screen. Although, for example, Vítězslav Nezval's script *A Sensitive Bourgeois Strolling and what the Horse Says about It* (Procházka citlivého měšťáka a co tomu říká kůň) can today be read as an original subject for animation, this film genre was non-existent during that period, and not only in the Czech environment. The time of the surrealistically-toned films by the Belgian Raoul Servais was to come only half a century later...

In Prague, the ideas of abstract film were mainly close to visual artists. From among the Butterbur members, there was the music composer, visual artist and experimenter Miroslav Ponc, who pursued the relations between optical and acoustic expressions and also incorporated film into his explorations. However, he never realized his drawn sketches to the 1920s' abstract cinematographic compositions in the film medium. Abstract film theory was also followed by the Prague architects Arno Hošek and Zdeněk Pešánek.[13] The two shared an interest in the experimental tendencies of the European artistic avant-garde and in the Bauhaus movement. They also participated in the congresses of the German Society of Psychology, organized by Professor Georg Anschütz in Hamburg, where Oskar Fischinger presented his film experiments with the Gasparcolor system. Neither Hošek nor Pešánek expected that their more or less theosophical script to the film essay *A Healthy Life* (Zdravý život), written by the first, and the subject of the abstract composition *The Birth of the Universe* (Zrození vesmíru) by the latter would ever be filmed. And neither of them had any practical experience of filming; Hošek even dedicated his subject "to the future, when film is liberated from technical limits".

Thus the Dodals were the pioneering filmmakers employing the medium of film in abstract works in the latter half of the 1930s. Their first project was *Fantaisie érotique*, realized thanks to its simultaneous advertising version, *The Play of Bubbles* (Hra bublinek). It was long impossible to get a clear idea about the relation between the two versions because only the commercial stayed in Prague after the war and it was thought that it was one film only having two titles. The chance to compare the film material of both versions only arose in the late 1990s when *Fantaisie érotique* was returned to Prague from Buenos Aires.[14] The comparison shows that the pictures share the middle section but each has separately made opening credits and opening sequences. They also differ in the closing passages, albeit several of the last frames of *Fantaisie* are missing. Dodalová recollected that the end of the film copy was destroyed

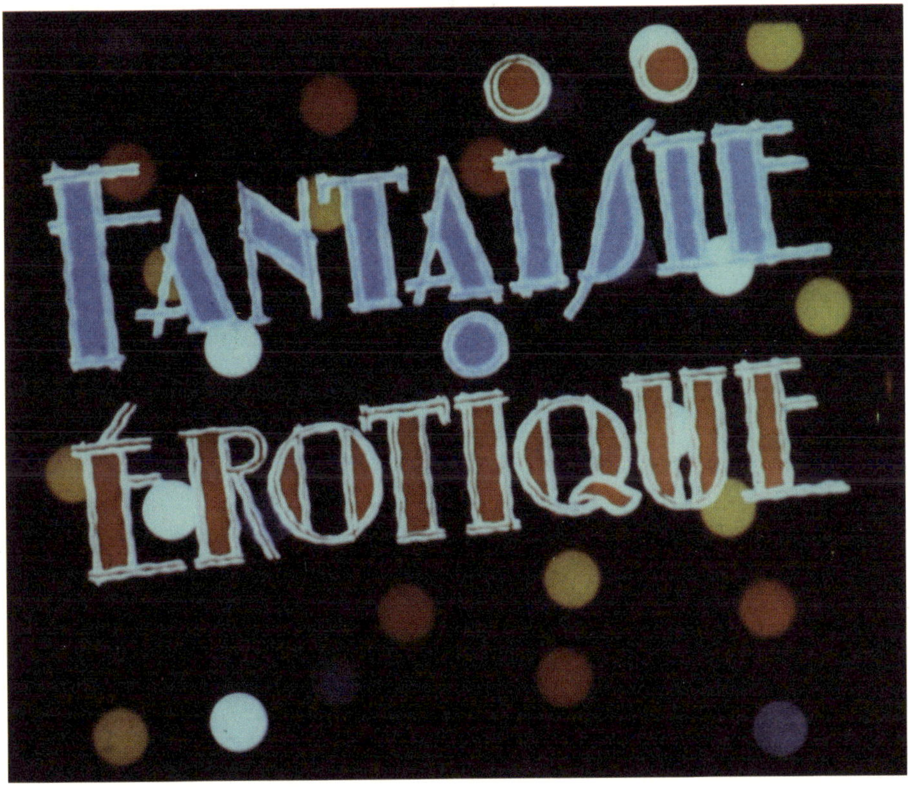

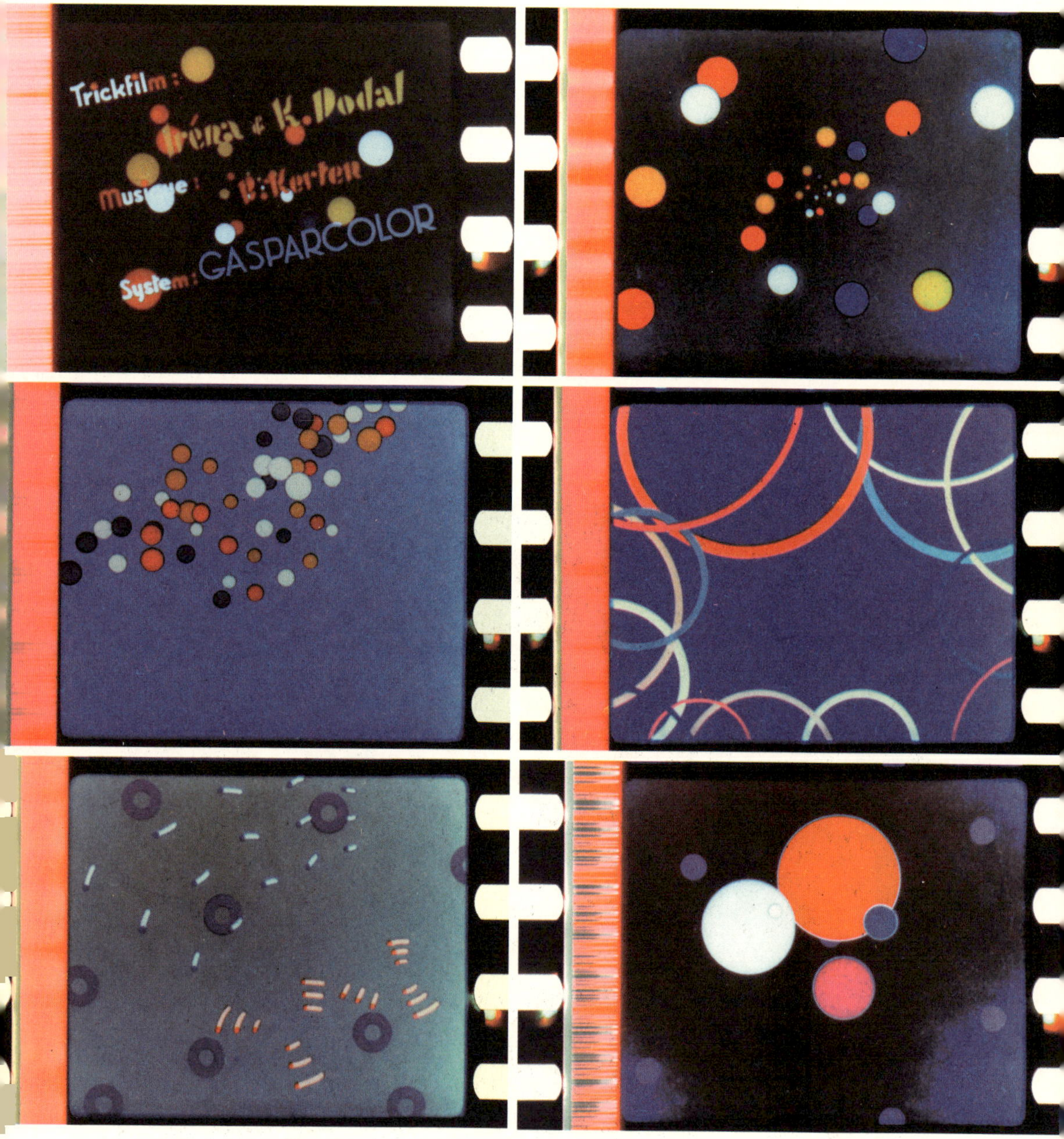
Trickfilm :
Iréna & K. Dodal
Musique :
E. Kerten
System : GASPARCOLOR

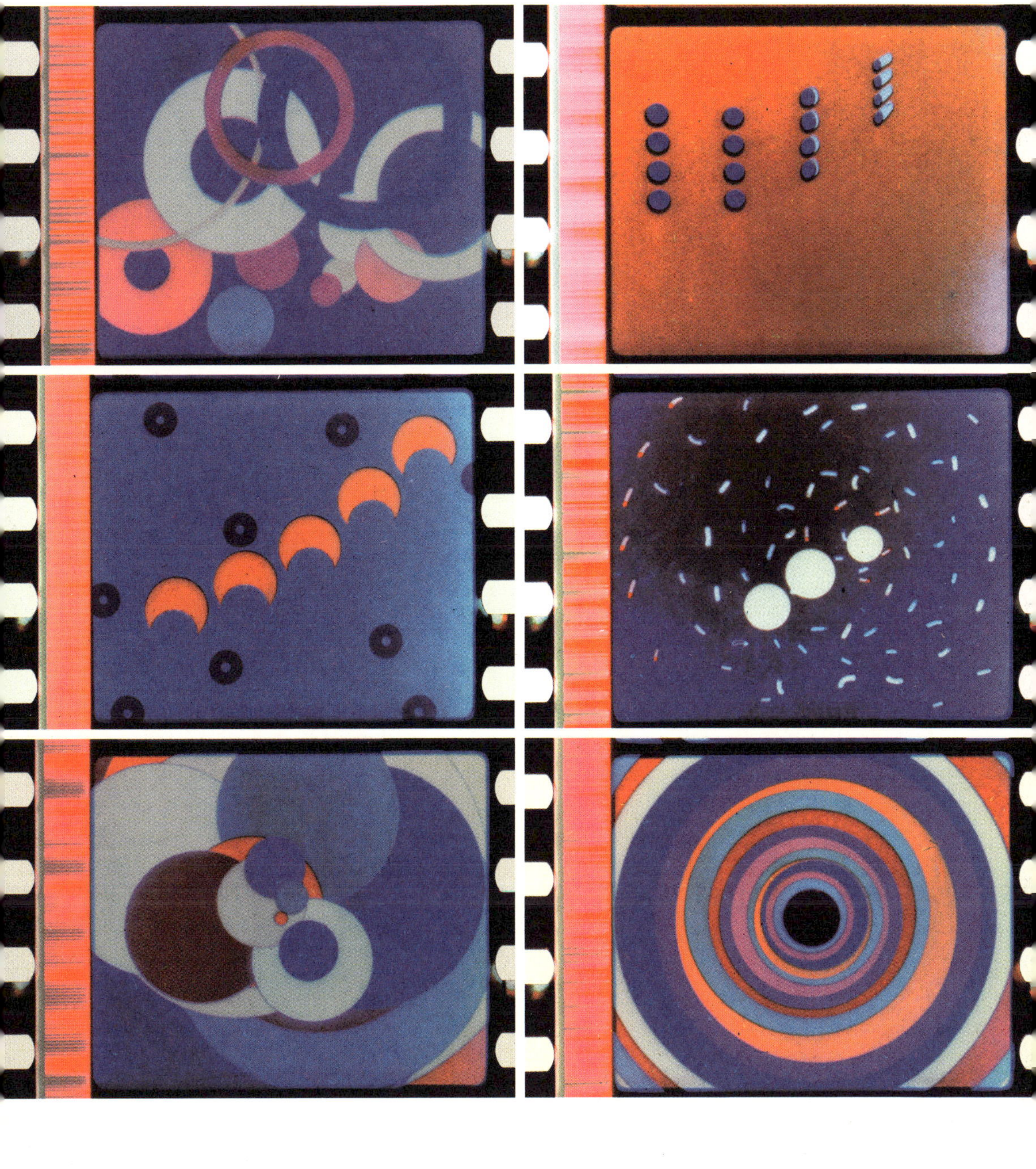

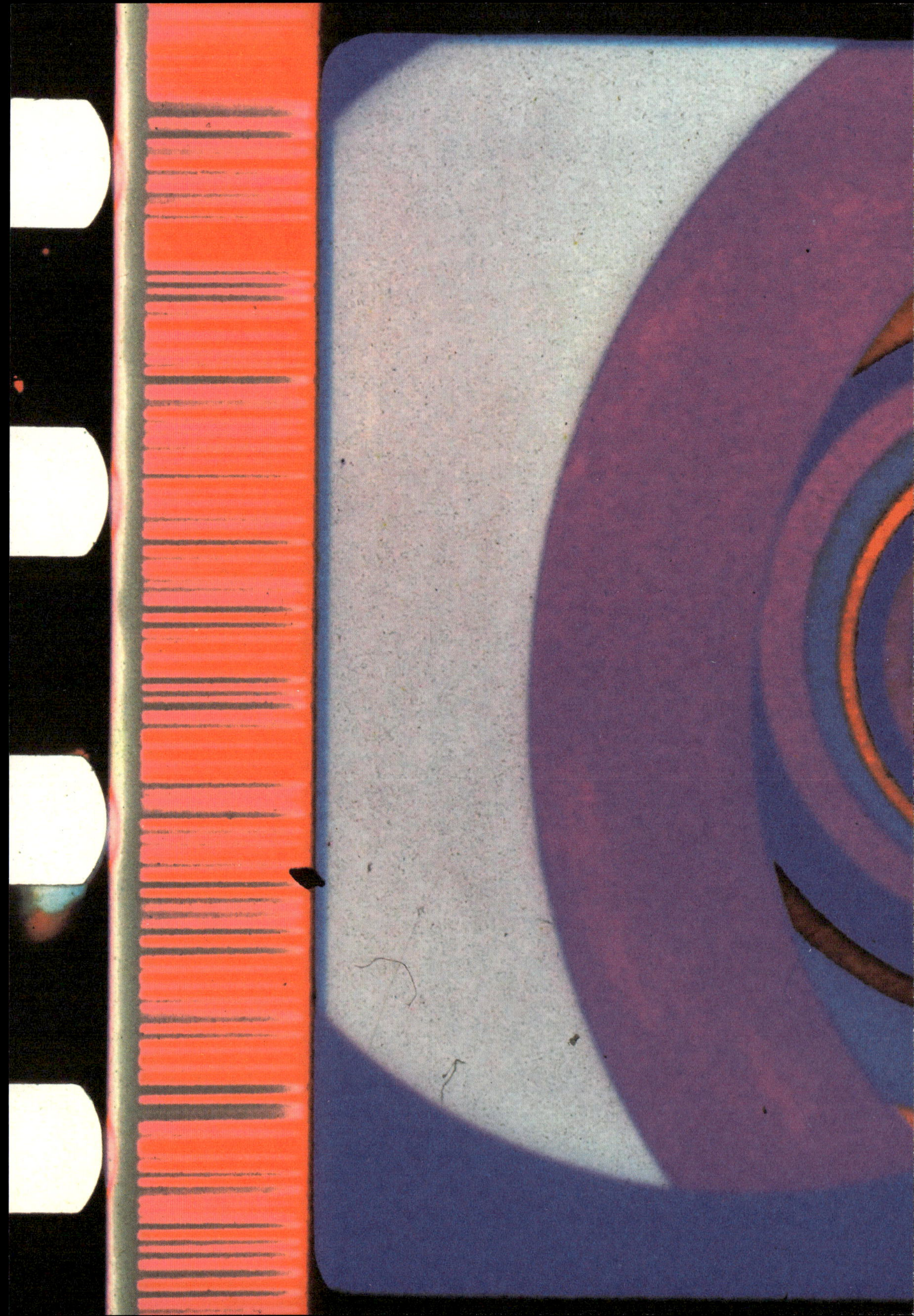

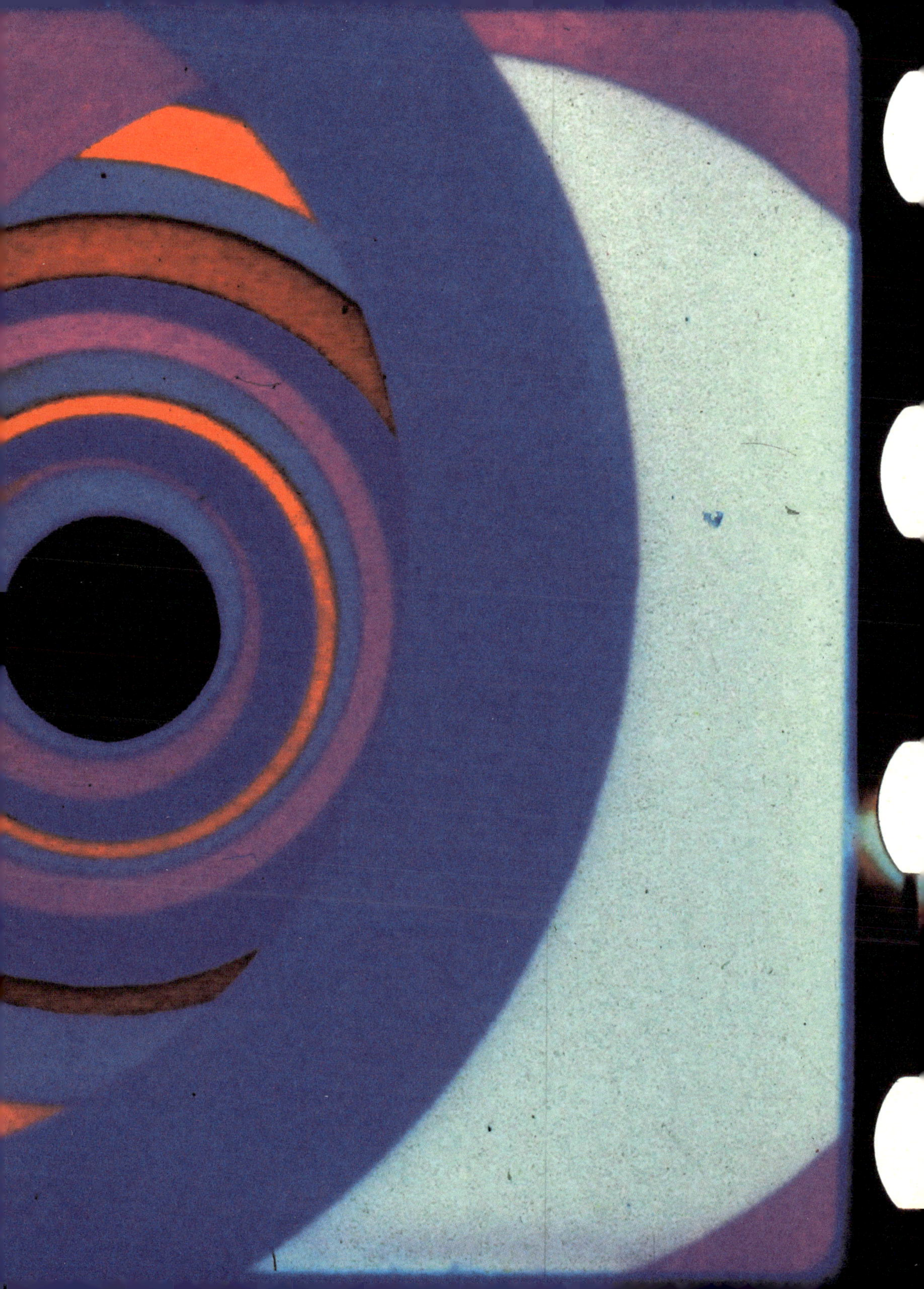

when Karel Dodal presented the picture in the New York Museum of Modern Art in 1939. We are fortunate enough that the sound reel with the complete musical record survived in her archive and allowed for reconstruction of the sound at the end.

As suggested above, the Dodals could make two versions of the jocose play of colour shapes thanks to Jiří Schicht's commission of a commercial with the soap Saponia which moreover allowed for using the Gasparcolor technology. We cannot convincingly prove the sequence of the works today. The only surviving document is the 1937 censorship record to the commercial *The Play of Bubbles*. *Fantaisie érotique* was never submitted for the censorship proceedings.

The Dodals here undoubtedly followed the experience of the German director Oskar Fischinger, who had demonstrated the appeal of abstract film for advertising, even though their projects differed in many aspects. Fischinger first made a commercial version for Tolirag, and as soon as he acquired the copyright to the material, he removed the advertising message and introduced the adapted version as a self-contained abstract film *Circles* (Kruhy) in July 1934.[15] In the Dodals' case, the film versions were created simultaneously. The question remains as to what the wording of their contract with Schicht was and whether it solved the given issue at all. It definitely was a precedent in the Czech film industry and it is well possible that the Dodals' client was utterly unacquainted with it. This circumstance would explain the subsequent tension in the disputes over the film *Kalodont* (see Chapter Thwarted Plans).

Coming from the context of IRE-film's work, everything had probably begun with the idea of *Fantaisie érotique* which as if embodied the current harmonious love affair between the authors. A quote from the contemporary press seems to largely prove this assumption. An article published in the *Global View* (Světozor) weekly from September 1937 quoted Dodalová that "the film begins with kettledrum strokes copying the human heartbeat and escalates the tone and motion of the multi-coloured forms as far as to the bacchanalia for eyes and ears, and proceeds to the liberating conclusion when the counterpoint motions amicably die away. The initial idea was that of eroticism, a matter of sensibility, not sense".[16] The colours of graphic structures were to correspond with the timbre of each instrument so that the kinetic images and the musical accompaniment brought a synesthetic experience. The sound of the saxophone was linked with yellow, the clarinet with blue, the kettledrum with ultraviolet and the trumpet with bright red. *Fantaisie* did not exploit the existing compositions – instead, the Dodals worked with Bedřich Kerten to create a new colour visually-sonic kinetic composition which was expressive, emphatic and provocative. It seems that Fischinger's process of leaning on renowned composers offered a better reception point for the audiences.

The Dodals probably screened *Fantaisie érotique* mainly in their studio to invited guests. The picture was also known to the members of the Film Advisory Board who recommended it to be part of the prestigious program of Czechoslovak film at the 1937 Paris World Exhibition and the Czechoslovak film collection intended for the Venice film festival.

The Dodals' second abstract film strikingly differed from the cheerful *Fantaisie* blaze of colours. The black-and-white picture (originally including virage according to some information) was made in IRE-film's own production and only in an English version under the title *Ideas in Search of Light* (Myšlenky v hledání světla or, respectively, Myšlenka hledající světlo) when the couple were already considering emigration. Their passport application stated that the purpose of their travel was a study trip...

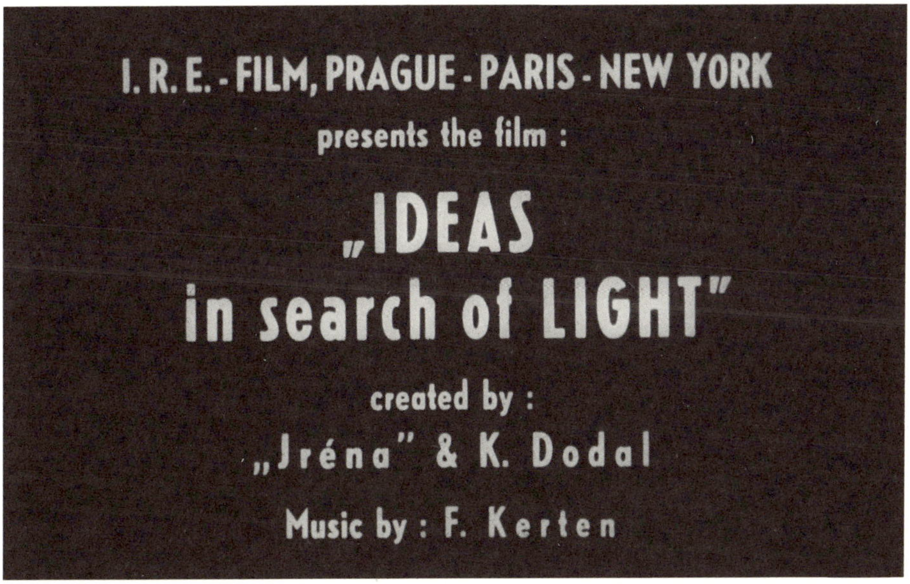

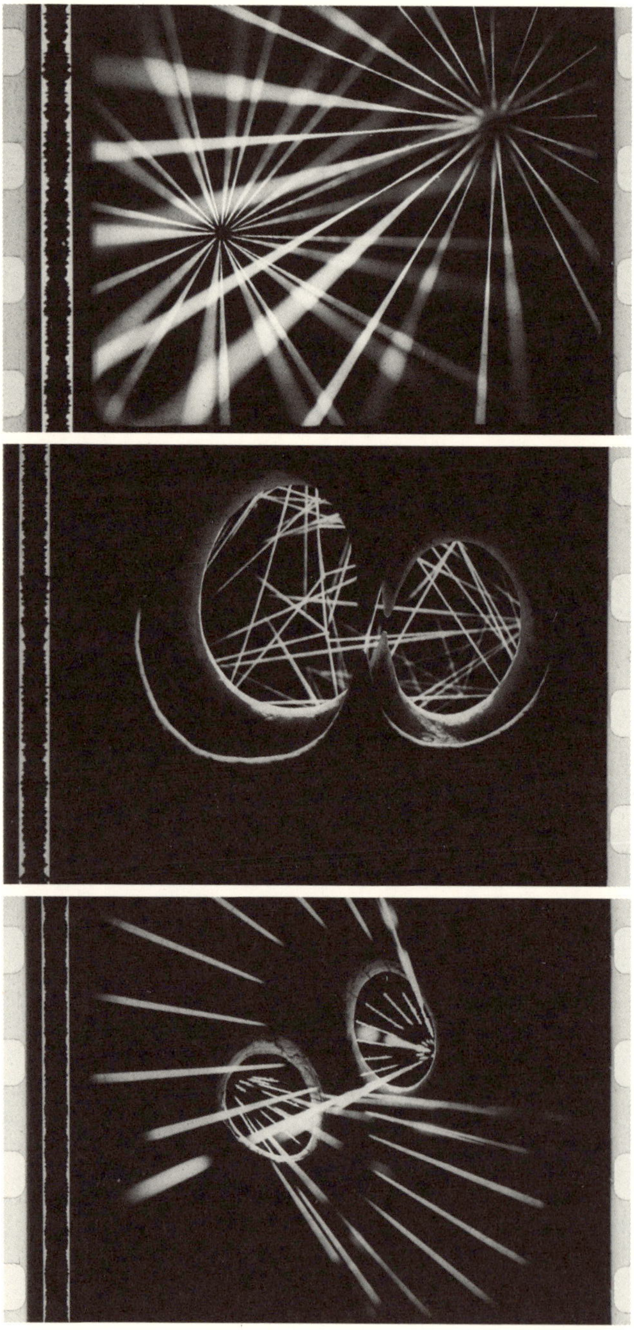

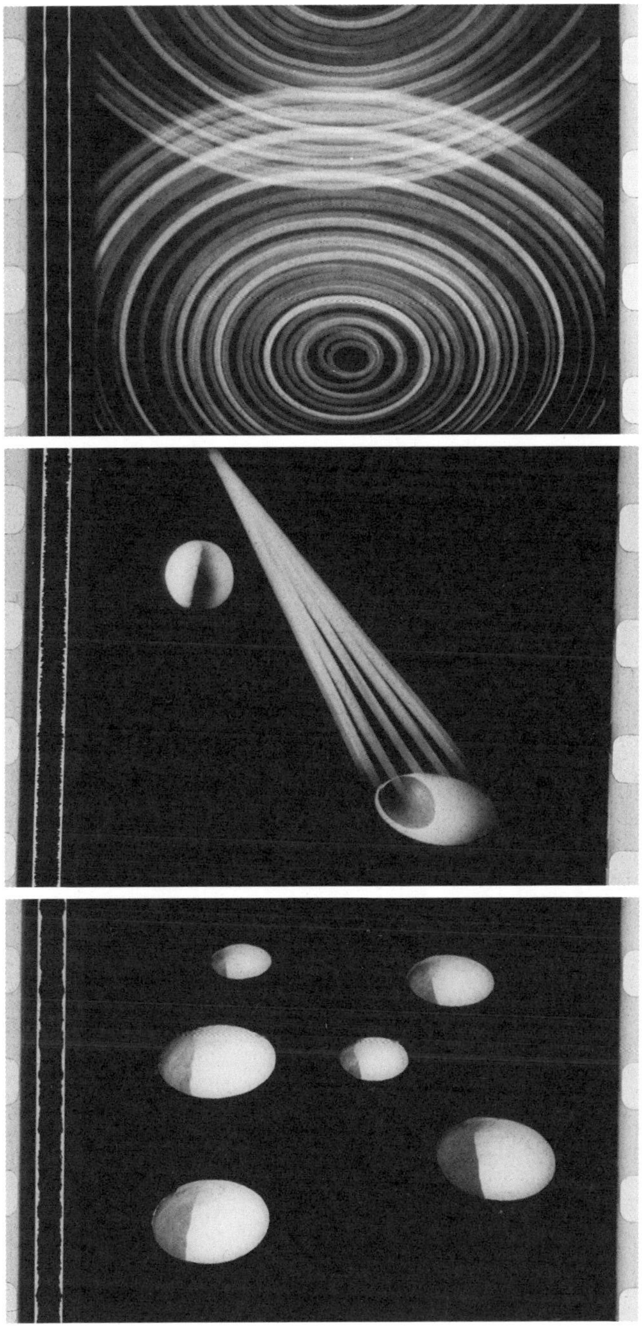

It was as if *Ideas* anticipated the catastrophe of the impending war; it spoke of the anxiety and imminent danger and tried to outline a certain way out, represented by Beethoven's *Ode to Joy* on the one hand and, on the other, by the symbol of the cross. It was not only unique in its intent but also in the selection of means of expression and the used technology. V. H. Jarka first reported about its filming in the *National Papers* (Národní listy) in December 1937 as follows: "I have, for example, found the painter Dodal in front of some fanciful miniature planetarium with stars shining through it. A laboratory technician was patiently sitting by this device and a net of threads, a perfect cobweb, was hanging behind her. And yet, these threads served no other purpose than to represent, after being lit and photographed – rays of light in this trick film whose title will be *Ideas in Search of Light*!"[17]

Abstract film images originated from combining animated three-dimensional objects made of wooden skewers, threads, plasticine or modeller's clay and shots taken via the methods of cartoon film. As follows from both Jarka's description and the film itself, a significant role was played by the lighting and illumination, which created space for the objects and, at the same time, simulated their motion. This Dodals' picture also referred in some signs to earlier black-and-white works by Oskar Fischinger – but it simultaneously followed a different path of abstract film because it embodied an attempt at combining abstract morphology and a philosophical message. Beethoven's composition did not work as a musical structure but mainly as a cultural reference serving to support the authors' idea in the beginning and closing of the title. The metaphorical portrayal of the genesis of harmony which is increasingly disturbed by the hostile forces of aggression and evil via the motion of abstract forms was illustrated by Kerten's music. The authors opened the film with a commentary so as to be able to connect the ambitious intellectual concept with the visual events occurring on the screen: the first part of the text emphasized that the film anticipated new cinematographic art, that it was not mere entertainment and that it symbolized the greatness of Humanity and Brotherhood, while the second part tried to verbally present the visual symbolism of the work.

Search of light as searching for hope ends in the film with the symbol of a cross which linked the closing with the introductory text and the subject of a prayer to God. The overall concept departed from the spirituality of Dodalová: her correspondence betrays that she believed in Jesus as one of the worshipped Prophets who "brought the doctrine of love and progress to humanity".[18] She also undoubtedly wrote the text; this seems to suggest the expressive style of the statement which is so familiar from her later correspondence. Translating the proclamation to Czech is rather tricky and since the original Czech wording is missing, we cannot tell whether the difficulty is an authorial or translation problem. In any case, using the opening commentary signifies certain authors' doubts as to the communicative potential of the kinetic symbols used in the film and it is often criticized equally as the short and rather clumsy rendering of the cross at the end.[19]

Although *Ideas in Search of Light* did not fulfil the invested expectations in full, it occupies an irreplaceable position in the history of Czech animated film because it followed Irena Dodalová's creed that trick/cartoon film was "predestined to higher than merely lyrically entertaining goals" and could have a "purely humanist mission".[20] It was a reflection of its era and a protest against the imminent aggression which incorporated it into the contemporary tendency of leftist, anti-war art.

The given title was the last one which IRE-film realized in Czechoslovakia. The places of its origins stated in the credits are Prague, Paris (where the Dodals had a studio at that time) and New York (where they planned to leave for a study trip). As mentioned above, it was screened in Prague for only a small group of guests and had never been introduced to Czech cinemas. It was only projected at the Venice film festival where it, however, passed unnoticed.

Making abstract films had always been the domain of painters, architects and avant-garde artists who experimented with the potential of film as a kinetic and audio-visual medium. Karel Dodal certainly was no avant-garde artist and abstract film was most probably introduced to the studio's program by Irena Dodalová. It is difficult to say today whether this focus embodied the couples' intrinsic consonance with abstract morphology or whether it aimed at boosting the artistic prestige of IRE-film. But since the studio planned more abstract etudes, we must allow for the option that the Czech filmmakers' interest in animating artistic signs was indeed somewhat deeper.

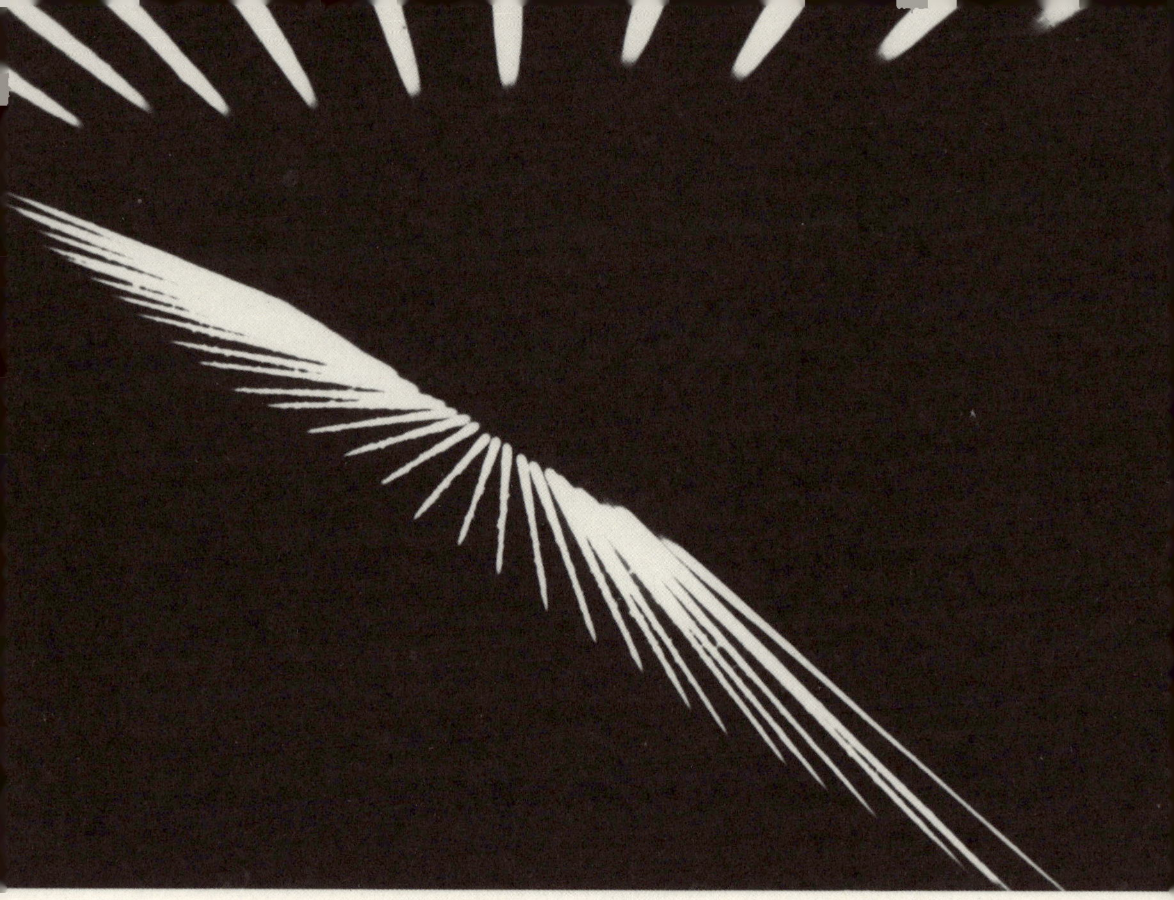

1 Letter of IRE-film to the Film Advisory Board, 11 November 1936. The National Archives, the Ministry of Enterprise, Commerce and Industry, box 2754, Ref. No. 112 317.

2 Letter of IRE-film to J. Auerbach with the attached libretto. The Archives of the Ministry of Foreign Affairs, fund 3rd Section 1918–1939, box 403, file No. 2, record Ref. No. 139458/III-2/35 of 31 October 1935. *Srdce Evropy, Manuscript pro barevný kreslený film v délce 200 m* (The Heart of Europe, Manuscript for a Colour Cartoon Film of 200 m Length). Appendix to IRE-film's application for financial support, addressed to the Film Advisory Board, 28 August 1937. The Military Historical Archives, box 12, Ref. No. 23308.

3 Letter of I. Dodalová to V. Opěla, 1–6 March 1989. Personal Fund of Irena Dodalová.

4 Iréna, "Trikfilm a jeho možnosti v Evropě" (Trick Film and Its European Possibilities), *Kinorevue* (Cinema Revue), 1937, No. 14, 24 November, p. 275.

5 Record from the 122nd session of the Film Advisory Board, 6 September 1937. The Military Historical Archives, the Ministry of National Defence, box 204, p. 7.

6 Record from the 137th session of the Film Advisory Board, 20 January 1938. Ibid., box 330, p. 9. Record from the 139th session of the Film Advisory Board, 3 February 1938. Ibid., pp. 5–6.

7 Record from the 145th session of the Film Advisory Board, 18 March 1938. Ibid., box 331, pp. 9–10.

8 Record from the 147th session of the Film Advisory Board, 11 April 1938. Ibid., pp. 4–5.

9 The atmosphere in the Board is well illustrated by its records from late 1938. During the October control of films to which the Board allocated money, someone wrote next to the title *The Heart of Europe* that the applying company had moved to Paris, and the wording betrays the apparent dislike of some present members. At the December session, IRE-film was advocated by K. Smrž who stressed that although "the company had already produced more than what the Board supported (10,000 Crowns for 10 metres), it could not make a living in Prague and thus left for Paris". Record from the 163rd session of the Film Advisory Board, 27 October 1938. Ibid., pp. 4–5. Record from the 166th session of the Film Advisory Board, 1 December 1938. Ibid., p. 3.

10 Teige, K., *Film*. Praha: Václav Petr, 1925, p. 99.

11 Ibid., p. 112.

12 Hradská, V., *Česká avantgarda a film* (Czech Avant-Garde and Film). Praha: Československý filmový ústav (ČSFÚ, Czechoslovak Film Institute) 1976, p. 39.

13 Strusková, E., "Arno Hošek", *Iluminace* (Illumination), 2003, No. 4, pp. 117–133. The name of Z. Pešánek, one of the leading founders of multimedia art, mainly appears in the film in connection with the title *The Light Penetrates the Dark* (Světlo proniká tmou). The silent black-and-white picture, only underscored by music and made by O. Vávra and F. Pilát in the early

1930s, is based on abstract play of lights which, however, is not the result of trick technology but a record of Pešánek's kinetic sculpture decorating the headquarters of the Prague Electric Enterprises at that time.

14 For more on this, see the end of Chapter Irena and Karel Dodal in the United States.

15 With regard to the ban on abstract art in Germany, Fischinger used the number of the censorship approval to the Tolirag commercial. The year of production of *Circles* is therefore given as both 1933 and 1934. For more on this, see Moritz, W., *Optical Poetry. The Life and Work of Oskar Fischinger.* London: John Libbey Publishing, 2004, p. 220.

16 ELA, "V ateliéru kresleného filmu" (In the Studio of Cartoon Film), *Světozor*, 1937, No. 36, 9 September, p. 583.

17 Jarka, V. H., "Království paní Ireny" (The Realm of Ms Irena), *Národní listy*, 1937, No. 354, 25 December, p. 19.

18 I. Dodalová was also interested in theosophy and anthroposophy which is clear from several sources including her correspondence with her brother Rudolf. Personal Fund of Irena Dodalová.

19 See, e.g., Čihák, M., "Absolutní film" (Absolute Film), *Kino-Ikon*, 2004, No. 2, pp. 16–17.

20 Iréna, "Trikfilm a jeho možnosti v Evropě", *Kinorevue*, 1937, No. 13, 17 November, p. 253.

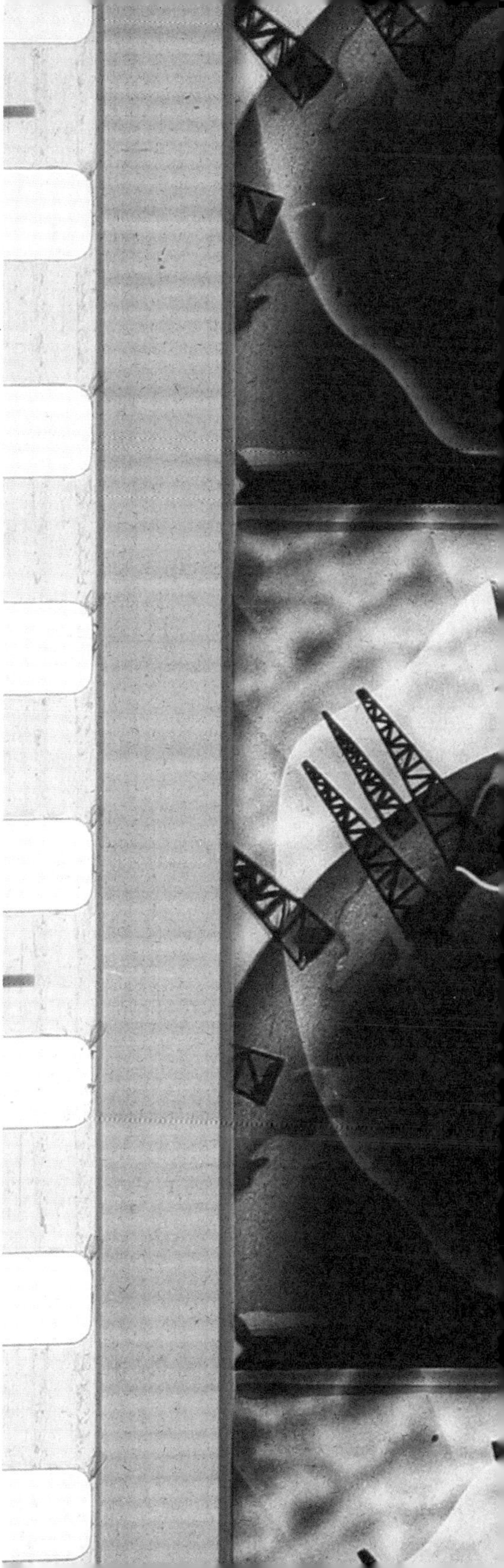

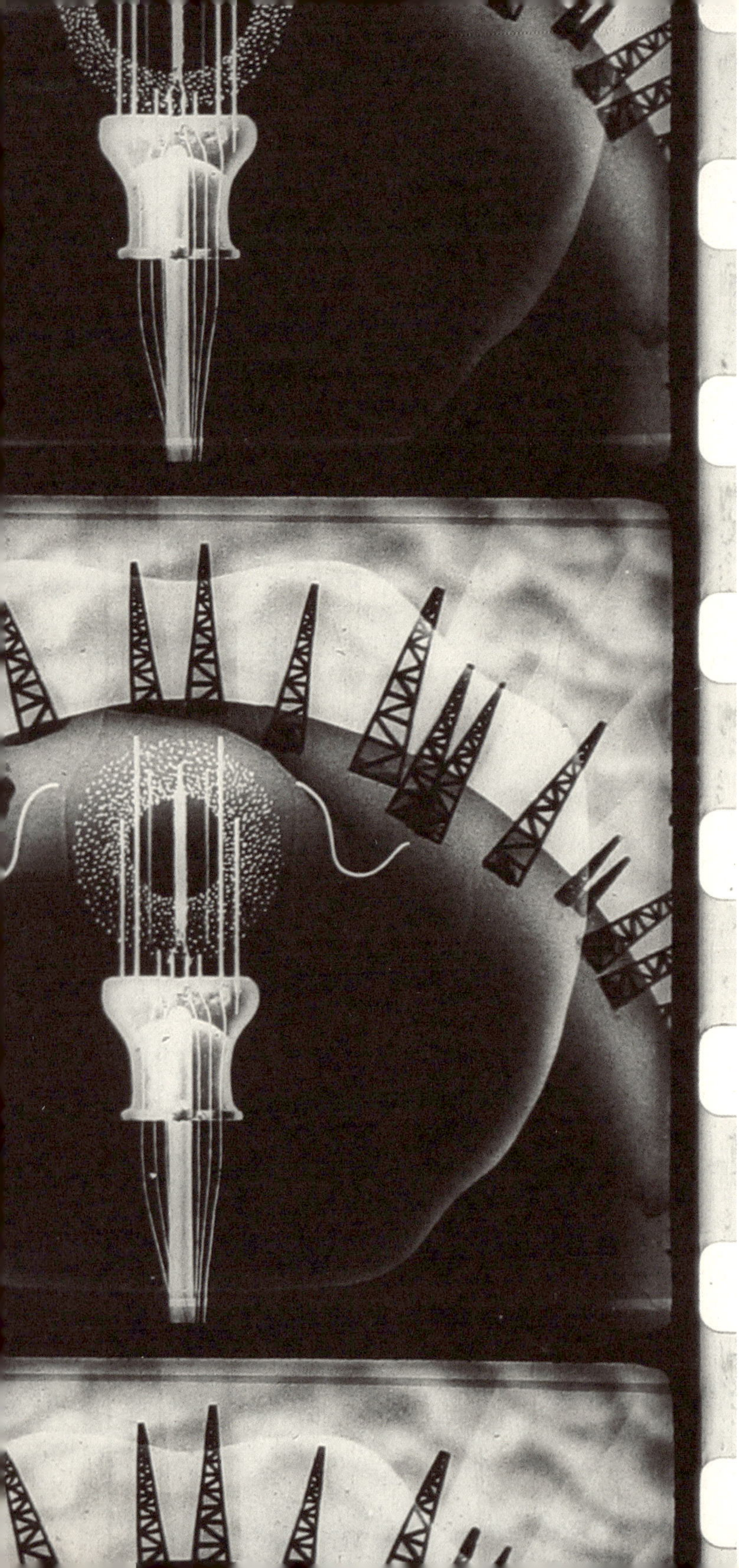

Irena's Public Relations and Film Reflections

During the 1920s and 1930s, the Czechoslovak press rarely reported about the screened film "supplements", usually only on the occasion of the premiere of a feature trick films, such as Ptushka's *New Gulliver* (Nový Gulliver) or Disney's *Snow White and the Seven Dwarfs* (1937). From time to time, the press ran an article describing the methods of making cartoon films or mentioning some anniversary at Disney. The subject of Czech cartoon film was pushed to the newspapers by Irena Dodalová, since her husband – the artist and designer – probably lacked the required aptitude for such activity. The overviews of the contemporary press prove that "Ms Irena" became the spokeswoman of the studio and systematically informed journalists about events in IRE-film.[1] This "public education", in this sense synonymous with public relations, helped preserve the picture of the studio's activities and plans in the media. The promotion and marketing also included organizing press campaigns which accompanied the film screenings at various ventures both at home and abroad.

The most extensive campaign, mediated by Radiojournal, was run in 1936 in connection with *The Adventures of a Ubiquitous Fellow* (Všudybylovo dobrodružství). The commercial promoting the film at that time also appeared on the radio.[2] The studio moreover published newspaper ads in the film-related

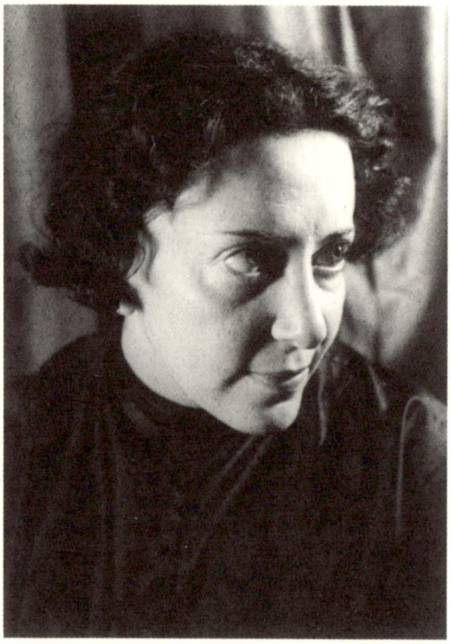

Undated portrait photograph of Irena Dodalová.

press and in the magazine on modern advertising, *Type* (Typ), albeit only in its beginnings; it later withdrew from print ads probably due to their low effectiveness.

Irena Dodalová not only informed the press about the work of the studio, but also tried to turn the public's attention towards the entire field of cartoon and animated film. She consistently tried to convince audiences that this area both had its history and could acquit itself well in many spheres of film and that there indeed was an alternative to the concept of American film cartoons.

In the jubilee issue of the *Film Courier* (Filmový kurýr) weekly, which looked back at most of the various fields of film culture, Dodalová published an article with the provocative title "What Do We Do with Czech Trick Film?" (Co s českým trikfilmem?).[3] She conceived it as a response to three elementary questions. The first question – "what was the local situation in the trick history?" – was answered by remembering the first attempts of Karel Anton and Karel Dodal in this field and highlighting Dodal's efforts to break free from American models. The question as to the present situation in Czech trick film provided a chance to sum up the main plans of the IRE-film's young team which, as

Kreslený film - poesie neskutečna

Kouzlo tisíců obrázků na filmovém pásku — Jak se dělá kreslený film

-nk- Viděli jste už někdy při návštěvě biografu kreslený dodatek? Jistě že ano. Zvykli jsme si na kreslené barevné dodatky k celovečerním programům a těšíme se na ně. Bývají velmi vtipně řešeny a jsou nejenom veselým dodatkem filmu, nýbrž často skutečným uměleckým dílem, zasluhujícím obdiv a ocenění.

Zájem o kreslený film roste. Škoda, že zatím jen v řadách filmového obecenstva a nikoli také náležitou měrou mezi filmovými producenty a půjčovnami.

Jako vždy, s kresleným filmem přišla první Amerika. Americké výrobky to byly, které nám ukázaly, čeho lze dosíci za použití technických prostředků a jak je možno mrtvé hmotě dát život. Ale málokdo z diváků, kteří s radostí shlédnou několikaminutový dodatek kresleného filmu, ví, jak se takový film dělá. A málokdo ví, že máme v tomto směru také dokonalý domácí výrobek, který se může směle měřit s výrobkem americkým.

Navštívili jsme včera atelier pro výrobu kreslených a barevných filmů. Jmenuje se IRE-FILM a vyrábí krásné filmy, které by zasloužily větší pozornosti našich filmových kruhů.

Zastihli jsme tu paní Dodalovou, uměleckou vůdkyni IRE-FILMU a požádali jsme ji o rozhovor pro své čtenáře.

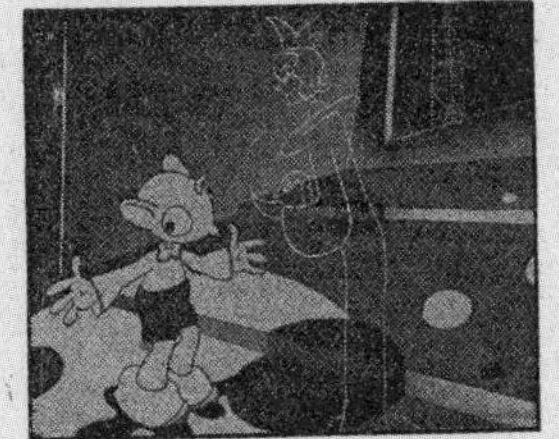

Z kresleného IRE FILMU: »Všudybylovo dobrodružství«. Hurvínek v rozhovoru s královničkou. Tato fotografie skládá se ze 3 obrázků: 1. Scéna (pozadí), 2. Hurvínek, 3. Královnička. Položením celuloidových destiček na sebe dostaneme teprve tento obrázek.

KDO JE IRE-FILM?

To je umělecky cítící kolektiv mladých lidí, kteří neznají překážek, ale kreslí, malují, filmují a vytvářejí speciální filmy kreslené. Tento podnik je v dnešním realistickém světě malým zázrakem idealismu, tím spíše, že se udržuje bez bankovního kapitálu, bez cizích finančních podpor a bez jakýchkoliv subvencí. Vysvětlení je v tom, že spolupracovníci IRE-FILMU se nelekají pracovních, časových, finančních a uměleckých obětí a svůj podnik udržují proto, že svou práci milují.

CO JE TO KRESLENÝ FILM?

To je — jedním slovem — vášeň. Je to živelná touha neskutečné učiniti hmotným. Tuto touhu možno nazvat cestou v noci, cestou v neznámé, divoké krajině, v níž každý krok je dobrodružstvím. Ale pozor. Nejen to. Kreslený film je také vysilující, velmi složitá a nad pomyšlení unavující práce, vyžadující bezpodmínečně celých lidí, houževnaté trpělivosti a vytrvalosti. Jenom školení, cvik a léta vytrvalé práce daly tvůrcům kresleného filmu dnešní lehkost a ladnost ve tvoření.

JAK SE DĚLÁ KRESLENÝ FILM?

To ... tázka, na níž málo lidí dovede dáti odpověď. Je to tajemství, které až dosud bylo skryto zrakům nezasvěcenců, obestřeno ilusí, klamem a krásou pohybů neživých hmot na plátně biografů.

Matkou každého díla je — jako vždy — myšlenka. Myšlence se musí postavit dějová a důvodová kostra, která se vloží do zvláštních situací a krásné poesie. Je to, řekněme, jakási elipsa tvoření. Začátek je koncem: Napřed poesie myšlenky, namáhavá práce a její výsledek — poesie hotového díla, schopného uchvátit oko divákovo.

VLASTNÍ PRÁCE.

Kolektiv IRE-FILM pracuje vždy společně. Šest lidí se sejde k přátelskému hovoru, šest lidí hledá náměty. Není o ně nikdy nouze. Lidé, kteří milují svou věc, dovedou vždy najít představu své příští práce. Dovedou si práci najít, i když se jiným zdá, že jí není.

Z přátelského hovoru vyjde námět. V hlavách umělců je rychle zpracován, základní myšlenky vtěleny na papír a již se začne. Bez otálení, není kdy na dlouhé studie.

Zakrátko tu je připraven celý scénář s přesnými, do nejmenších milimetrových podrobností jdoucími rozpočty a světlo světa spatřují první nákresy. Zrodí se osoby děje, dějiště a ze všeho vychází konečná forma filmu.

A ZAČNE SE KRESLIT.

Ze základních posic přichází se k dalším. Kreslí se na absolutně čistý, bezbarvý celuloid. Ovšem, ne bez pomůcek. Atelier v té chvíli vyhlíží jako velká výstava jednotlivých fází denního života člověka. Máte tu velkou tabuli, na níž jsou zakresleny různé tvary úst při vyslovování samohlásek, souhlásek i slabik, nebo zachyceny různé fáze pohybů člověka a pod. To jsou jakési předlohy, z nichž se bere život.

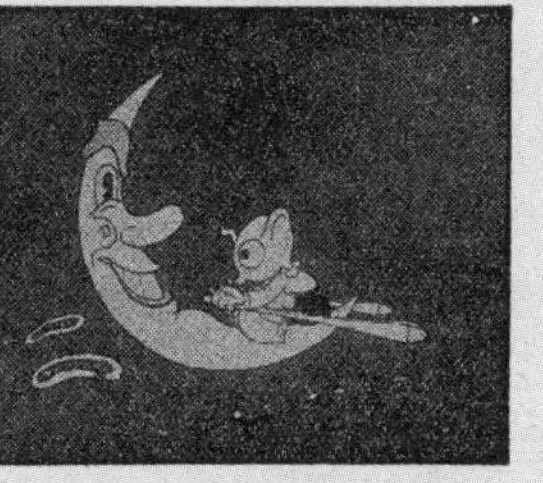

Z filmu »Všudybylovo dobrodružství«: Hurvínek na gondole. Opět tři obrázky: 1. Obloha, 2. mraky, 3. Hurvínek.

TITĚRNÁ PRÁCE.

Každý pohyb figurky ve filmu je přesně vypočítán. Kreslíř si postaví dva body: základní a výslední pohybovou posici. Myšlenou křivku pohybu rozdělí na několik dob a pak mezidoby podrobně vykresluje tak, až celek splývá v jediné máchnutí rukou, krok či otevření úst a pod. Kolik dělicích bodů, tolik obrázků.

Každý z těchto obrázků se kreslí na zvláštní celuloidovou plotnu. Plotny se čislují a pozorně skládají, po straně popisují čísly scén a mluvenými slovy. Po úžasně namáhavé práci, když celý děj filmu je vykreslen, přikročuje se po několika kontrolách k vlastnímu filmování na normální filmový pás.

ÚKOL FILMOVÉ KAMERY.

Z jednotlivých celuloidových ploten se sestavují obrázky scén. Jeden obrázek či fotografie, tak, jak je vidíme na reprodukcích, skládá se ze tří až pěti celuloidových, průhledných destiček, které složeny na sebe, dávají teprve výsledek — konkretní hotový obraz.

Tyto obrazy přijímá poté filmová kamera ve zvláštní kabině. Každý obrázek tvoří samostatný záběr, samostatné okénko. Spíše než filmováním možno nazvat tuto práci fotografováním. Jeden pohyb ruky či úst vyžádá si vždy několik okének, aby celek při promítání působil dojmem jednolitého pohybu. Aby si čtenář mohl učiniti představu o této práci, prozrazujeme, že nejnovější kreslený barevný film »Všudybylovo dobrodružství« s Hurvínkem, který je majetkem Radiojournalu a je právě na filmovém festivalu v Benátkách, měří 500 metrů. Těchto 500 metrů filmu skládá se z 25.000 fotografií, které musily být každá samostatně filmovou kamerou přijaty. A každá z těchto 25 tisíc fotografií se skládá ze 3—5 obrázků, které teprve ve své vzájemné kombinaci dávají vlastní kompletní scénu s hrajícími osobami. Možno tedy říci, že pro tento film bylo zapotřebí nejméně 75.000 celuloidových ploten a na každé z nich zvlášť nakreslený obrázek.

BARVY A HUDBA.

Barevný film se vyrábí stejně, jako film kreslený, pouze tuší. Po nakreslení kontur se plochy velmi opatrně pokrývají barvami, k tomu účelu zvláště připravovanými.

Horší je to s hudbou a slovním doprovodem. Při normálním filmu má komponista možnost tvořit pro dlouhé scény a může komponovat široké motivy, kdežto při kresleném filmu je metráž velmi omezena a komponista musí komponovat motivy i jen na 4 metry filmu. Ozvučování hotového filmu je velmi složité. Ozvučují se postupně jednotlivé obrázky a na přijímání zvuku pro film, který se promítá 4 minuty, pracuje až 25 lidí v ateliérech A-B.

SPOLUPRACOVNÍCI IRE FILMU.

IRE FILM má šest spolupracovníků. Umělecké vedení je svěřeno malíři Karlu Dodalovi. Prvá kreslířka Mme Iréna má vždy za úkol stvořiti myšlenku, kus poetického děje a hodně dívčí poesie. — Technik a praktik, malíř K. Dodal staví kostru, situace a realisace. — Další 4 spolupracovníci doplňují práce a pokračující fáze filmu svými nápady a idejemi. Pak pracuje Iréna na prvých nákresech. Dodal tyto básně a poesie vypočítává a technicky zhmotňuje na celuloidových plotnách. Rostou zde strohé křivky pohybů, vypočítané do přesných čar, taktů a pohybů. Dva animatoři Tearlová a Čudová kreslí mezifáze pohybu a ostatní dva vyplňují figurky barvou, čistí plotny a připravují je pod přijímací filmový stroj.

DALŠÍ PRACOVNÍ PROGRAM IRE FILMU.

V první řadě je to barevný kreslený film, representující Prahu. Má to být kamenná pohádka, hýřící jemnými barvami v ucelených barevných náladách, v nových záběrech s pohybem mraků, vody, s obdobným střídáním jarních, letních, podzimních i zimních nálad.

Pak je tu propracovaná myšlenka a scénář na krásný barevný film o našem folkloru, který má zachytiti tance, zpěvy a barvy v současném zpracování barevnou stylisací květin, výšivek, kraslic atd. pod názvem *»Tance, zpěvy a barvy v ČSR.«*.

VELIKÉ MYŠLENKY.

IRE FILM má však předně nové, snadno realisovatelné myšlenky se sociální a satyrickým postřehem, myšlenky evropské, které by musely přinésti i obchodní úspěch tomu, kdo by je podchytil. Tyto však bude moci asi kolektiv IRE realisovati až v cizině, ježto se mu zde neposkytuje ani filmovými, ani státními útvary pomocná ruka. A bez peněz a bez objednávky lze těžko i tu nejlepší a nejhodnotnější myšlenku uskutečniti.

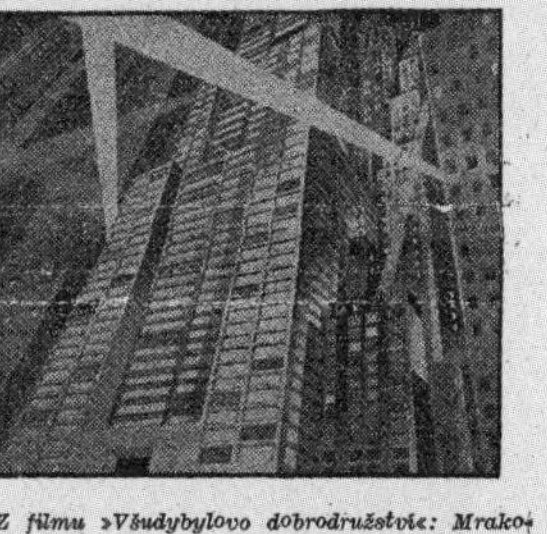

Z filmu »Všudybylovo dobrodružství«: Mrakodrap, do nejmenších podrobností prokreslený. 3 obrázky: 1. Kontura mrakodrapu, 2. okna, v nichž se občas rozsvítí světlo, 3. světlomety.

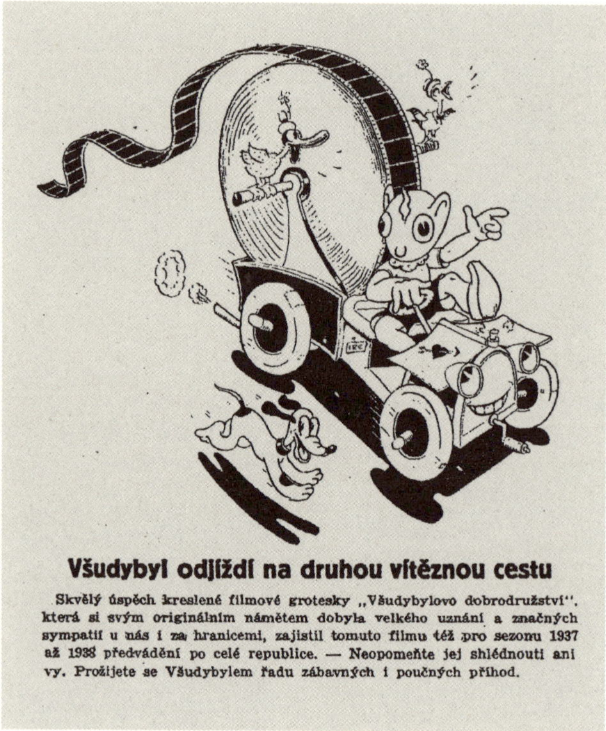

Všudybyl odjíždí na druhou vítěznou cestu

Skvělý úspěch kreslené filmové grotesky „Všudybylovo dobrodružství", která si svým originálním námětem dobyla velkého uznání a značných sympatií u nás i za hranicemi, zajistil tomuto filmu též pro sezonu 1937 až 1938 předvádění po celé republice. — Neopomeňte jej shlédnouti ani vy. Prožijete se Všudybylem řadu zábavných i poučných příhod.

From the *Radiojournal* weekly, 16 October 1937, No. 41, p. 11.

Irena wrote, strived for new artistic and genuine, characteristic Czechoslovak cartoon film. In order to gain its firm place on the market, the studio began making promotional titles. The short footage of these "little films", however, condensed both the work and the story of a feature film. The writer mainly underlined the care given to matching sound and picture as completely equivalent components. She then noted about colour film: "Sound and colours! What a lovely century. What a pleasure for the highly intellectual audience but – what new obstacles for such a small studio..."[4] The conclusion of the article turned to the future and reasoned that cartoon film was not merely humorous cartoon comedy but could be useful in technical and abstract sciences, education, warfare and research institutions, and could also play a role in feature films. The essay closed with an imperative: the future depends on the understanding of the film audience and the "relevant places".

LA "CINEMECCANICA"

Lunedì 17 Agosto 1936 - XIV - Ore 21.30

AVE MARIA

Produzione: Itala Film - Germania - Regia: Johannes Rieman

Interprete principale: Beniamino Gigli

Tino Dossi, famoso cantante, acclamato dalle platee di tutto il mondo, vive solo, senza donne, senza distrazioni, senz'altri amici che il suo fido suggeritore Apollonio e il suo cane Barry che lo accompagnano nelle sue «tournées». Sul suo pianoforte è la partitura d'un canto ch'egli ha composto per la sua fidanzata e che s'intitola al suo nome: Maria. Dal giorno in cui ella è morta, egli non l'ha più cantata.

Ogni anno, nell'anniversario della morte di Maria, egli si reca a Parigi e fa celebrare un ufficio funebre. Allora, accompagnato da un coro di fanciulli, egli canta il suo mirabile «Ave Maria». Nessun estraneo dev'essere presente nella cappelletta del cimitero a turbare quel rito. Ma un giorno il destino è più forte di lui. Mentre le note dell'Ave Maria salivano nell'azzurro cielo, una giovane donna, sorpresa da uno svenimento, giaceva accoccolata sui marmi del peristilio. Il sagrestano ne dà notizia a Dossi chiedendo perdono e scusandosi col non aver saputo come far fronte all'imprevisto incidente. Il cantante si avvicina all'intrusa e vede una giovinetta semplicemente vestita, dal viso bellissimo ma patito. E' Claudette, canzonettista di ritrovi equivoci, alla quale Apollonio ha raccontato sotto l'influsso dell'alcool la storia del celebre tenore e che d'accordo con l'amante del cuore, Michel, ha organizzato il trucco nell'intento di sedurre Dossi e ricattarlo. La commovente storiella che ella racconta, trova nel tenore un ascoltatore compiacente e credulo: veniva dalla provincia, spiega, per pregare sulla tomba del fidanzato, il primo e l'unico amore e si chiama Maria. La vicenda, che rassomiglia così stranamente alla sua, commuove il tenore che cade nella rete. La presunta provinciale lo accompagna in una visita alle bellezze della metropoli mostrandosi ammirata ed estasiata ed accogliendo, infine, con gratitudine, la proposta di Dossi di ricondurla in macchina nel suo villaggio di provincia. Claudette ha fertile la fantasia e pronta l'inventiva e si fa condurre in un povero paesello della Francia meridionale dove indica al cantante una miserabile capanna: la casa di mio zio, dice, che mi ha allevata come figlia. Il tenore si commuove al pensiero dell'esistenza che attendeva la giovine in quel tugurio e la convince ad accompagnarlo in Italia, sua patria. Nella villa di Dossi, davanti al grande quadro di Maria, la fanciulla sente un'onda di rimorsi salirle alla gola e quando il tenore rievoca la storia del suo amore perduto e di quella dolce canzone chiusa per sempre nel suo cuore, non sa più trattenersi. Il suo pianto lieve e sommesso commuove il cantante, che crede di averla involontariamente ferita e ricambia il suo bacio. Senza avvedersene egli è preso da un sentimento profondo che lo trasforma e gli ridà la gioia della vita.

Anche Claudette non è più quella, ma sull'amore nascente prevale un senso di orrore e di vergogna. Dossi si propone di aprirle il suo cuore e di chiederle di diventare la compagna della sua vita: ha già telegrafato, anzi, ad Apollonio notificandogli il suo imminente fidanzamento. Apollonio è atterrito e viene immediatamente in Italia, accompagnato da Michel. Animati da opposti intenti, i due fanno ogni sforzo per impedire il matrimonio. Sforzi inutili, finchè Apollonio si decide a rivelare a Dossi ogni cosa: il tenore vede crollare il suo edificio di speranze e di illusioni e prende congedo da Claudette e dal suo amore in una scena commovente.

Il giorno seguente apprende che Claudette è rimasta vittima di un incidente stradale e giace gravemente ferita all'ospedale. Dimentico di tutto, si precipita alla clinica, ma non viene ammesso al capezzale della fanciulla che lotta con la morte. Passano i giorni, i mazzi di fiori che egli le invia quotidianamente si accumulano nella stanza di Claudette, la quale sente un mattino nell'attiguo salone la voce fremente del tenore che canta l'Ave Maria in un concerto da lui offerto agli infermi: si fa condurre in lettiga nella corsia dove echeggia il nostalgico canto d'amore e dove Dossi, che la scorge, canta per lei, canta come non ha mai cantato. Pallida e bella, gli occhi pieni di lagrime di gioia, Claudette beve, grata e commossa, l'onda dei suoni, lo sguardo fisso sull'uomo che ama. Tino Dossi ha ritrovato la sua Maria.

Precederà **GIORNALE L.U.C.E.**

Seguirà **Grotisky** (Le avventure di Vsudybyl - Cartone animato Cecoslovacco)

Dodalová later followed her ideas with an essay "Trick Film and Its European Possibilities" (Trikfilm a jeho možnosti v Evropě). Its parts were consequently published in the *Cinema Review* (Kinorevue) weekly and reviewed the author's opinion on animated film which she perceived as a "world of its own".[5] She emphasized that it was the oldest film culture and that Reynaud's drawings as brought to life by his invention, the praxinoscope, still retained their charm even with the long lapse of time. Perfect animated film with its continuous production and guaranteed export was possible due to the financial background in the United States. Its problem, however, was the one-sided focus on cartoon comedy which had become synonymous with the genre of cartoon film. Soviet production, then, might have served higher aims, but its deficiency was the absence of experiment. In Europe, cartoon film scraped along under the indifference of state and exhausted itself in commercial projects: "And so, as we watch the life journey and the eventual success of such an European artist who had busily strained and worked for six or ten years, we find out that he might have made about fifty great promotional films but only about three art films, those which he wanted and had to create out of the inner duty towards himself, and that he either financed them from his own sources or even still owes for them."[6]

The writer thus steered attention towards the conditions of IRE-film's existence. And as if she wished to rehabilitate and justify the studio's activity in the advertising business, she noted that Oskar Fischinger, for example, worked himself up on good promotional pictures, and praised his successful commercial for the cigarette brand Muratti (*Muratti greift ein*; 1933), emphasizing that Fischinger financed it alone with much difficulty, but that it nevertheless opened the door to the North-American market for him. Dodalová also recollected screening his avant-garde films in Prague[7] and especially acknowledged his *Composition in Blue* (Composition in Blau; 1935). György Pál in her opinion "has perfectly mastered cartoon film and has created modern stylized puppets after these cartoon figures; puppets whose expression and motion

Dodal's trick table as featured in the German press within the article "Drei Monate Arbeit – fünf Minuten Vergnügen. Hinter den 'Kulissen' des tschechoslowaskischen Trickfilms", *Neue Morgenpost*, 26 September 1937.

he had simplified to the utmost austereness. And since he is also an excellent photographer and has well embraced the entire film *metier*, his promotional films had softness, delicate poetry and perfectly harmonized colours".[8] She moreover returned to the Dodals' encounter with Alexander Alexeïeff in Paris and explained his unique pin-screen technology to Czech readers.

Irena Dodalová saw the basic "predestination" in short film "of either avant-garde or folkloristic or even clearly satiric character".[9] The main thing to her was "the beautiful, mysterious, exciting field of new tendencies – trick film which is avant-garde, expressionist, surrealistic; in short, purely artistic. Such film does not already work with only the possibilities given by the methods of a painter, but seeks and finds other and yet unknown possibilities, a new imaginary world".[10]

Dodalová's articles, which apparently chimed with the ideas of her husband, opened new horizons to the local public. Her texts can be viewed as the first reflection upon the subject of cartoon and animated film in the Czech environment. Even though she was neither a film theoretician nor critic, in

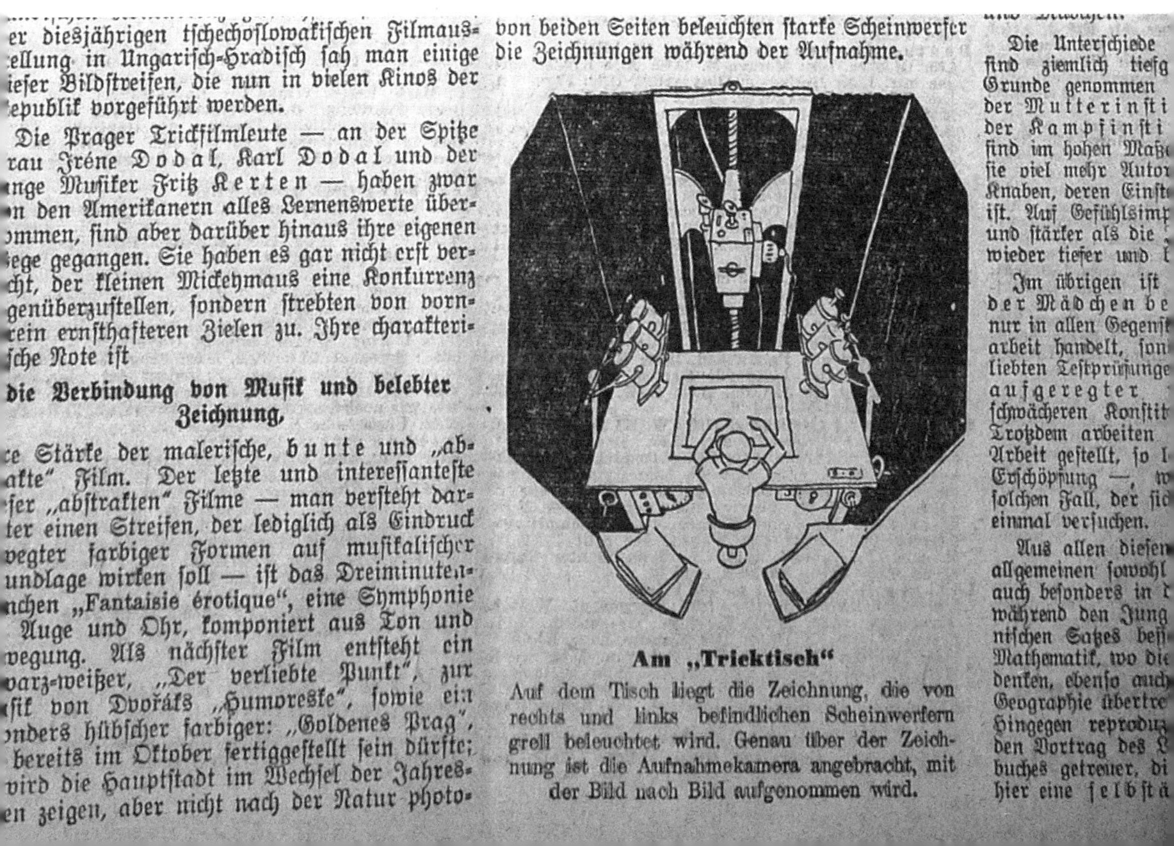

er diesjährigen tschechoslowakischen Filmaus-
:ellung in Ungarisch-Hradisch sah man einige
iefer Bildstreifen, die nun in vielen Kinos der
epublik vorgeführt werden.

Die Prager Trickfilmleute — an der Spitze
rau Iréne Dodal, Karl Dodal und der
nge Musiker Fritz Kerten — haben zwar
n den Amerikanern alles Lernenswerte über-
mmen, sind aber darüber hinaus ihre eigenen
ege gegangen. Sie haben es gar nicht erst ver-
cht, der kleinen Mickeymaus eine Konkurrenz
genüberzustellen, sondern strebten von vorn-
rein ernsthafteren Zielen zu. Ihre charakteri-
sche Note ist

die Verbindung von Musik und belebter Zeichnung.

e Stärke der malerische, bunte und „ab-
akte" Film. Der letzte und interessanteste
ser „abstrakten" Filme — man versteht dar-
ter einen Streifen, der lediglich als Eindruck
vegter farbiger Formen auf musikalischer
undlage wirken soll — ist das Dreiminuten-
chen „Fantaisie érotique", eine Symphonie
Auge und Ohr, komponiert aus Ton und
vegung. Als nächster Film entsteht ein
varz-weißer, „Der verliebte Punkt", zur
sik von Dvořáks „Humoreske", sowie ein
nders hübscher farbiger: „Goldenes Prag",
bereits im Oktober fertiggestellt sein dürfte;
vird die Hauptstadt im Wechsel der Jahres-
en zeigen, aber nicht nach der Natur photo-

von beiden Seiten beleuchten starke Scheinwerfer die Zeichnungen während der Aufnahme.

Am „Tricktisch"

Auf dem Tisch liegt die Zeichnung, die von rechts und links befindlichen Scheinwerfern grell beleuchtet wird. Genau über der Zeichnung ist die Aufnahmekamera angebracht, mit der Bild nach Bild aufgenommen wird.

Die Unterschiede
sind ziemlich tief
Grunde genommen
der Mutterinsti
der Kampfinsti
sind im hohen Maße
sie viel mehr Autor
Knaben, deren Einst
ist. Auf Gefühlsimp
und stärker als die
wieder tiefer und

Im übrigen ist
der Mädchen be
nur in allen Gegenst
arbeit handelt, son
liebten Testprüfunge
aufgeregter
schwächeren Konstit
Trotzdem arbeiten
Arbeit gestellt, so l
Erschöpfung —,
solchen Fall, der sie
einmal versuchen.

Aus allen diesen
allgemeinen sowohl
auch besonders in
während den Jung
nischen Satzes bei
Mathematik, wo die
denken, ebenso auch
Geographie übertre
Hingegen reprodu
den Vortrag des
buches getreuer, di
hier eine selbstä

her distinctive style she formulated certain principles of animation on the basis of her own scriptwriting and directing practice and experience. She pointed at the differences between conceiving the scripts to feature and cartoon films while the dramaturgy of the latter had to be exclusively solved via optical means instead of dialogues. She also stressed that music and sound in animated film were of equal importance and cogency as the image. The cardinal aspects in her view were the artistic shortcut and the precise timing of the story.

As a film producer, Dodalová also used the newspapers when fighting for support from the "relevant places". By this, she undoubtedly meant the Film Advisory Board which subsidized Czech cinematography. But not even the expressive tone of her article "Does State Support of Film Have a Right to Keep Quiet about Its Folklore?" (Má státní filmová propagace právo pomlčeti dále o svém folkloru?), published in the *Film Courier* in 1937, helped IRE-film receive the grant it had applied for.[11]

Dodalová appeared in the press for the last time in February 1939, in the daily *National Work* (Národní práce). A journalist signed as -vp- interviewed the filmmaker and producer, who had just returned from her travels abroad, and let her summarize her experience with animation in the article "Across European Trick Film" (Napříč evropským trikfilmem). The five hectic years she had spent in the cartoon film studio convinced Irena that the local market was too small and that it was therefore necessary to organize both the production and distribution on a wider international framework. Omitting the contemporary political reality, she saw the perspective in establishing a large European cartoon studio based in Prague and producing films "of such artistry and ideological contents which would allow for their export throughout Europe".[12] These films would not compete with the North-American production but would attract the audiences' interest precisely by differing from the Hollywood standards, i.e. by their focus on "satirical and social subjects". It seems quite evident that building a Central-European studio had been an unvoiced wish of the Dodal couple since the very beginning of their enterprise, but their work "collapsed" at the given moment. The end of the article suggested that the idea of establishing an extensive film production of cartoon films could be pursued by their followers.

I.R.E.-FILM

první americký filmový atelier pro výrobu kreslených i hraných zvukových grotesek a filmů

Praha-Vinohrady Telefon 553-15 Milešovská 12.

Trikfilm: Ak. mal. Karel Dodal
Zodpovědní spolupracovníci: Libreto a režie: Iréna
Hudba: f. Kerten

Praha. 29.X. 1935

L i b r e t o.

„ Č.S.R. V BARVÁCH TANCÍCH A PÍSNÍCH...„

Ouvertura : Směs Dvořákovy hudby / Humoreska/

Titulky : Podloženy barevnými duhovými měkkými vlnami vzájemně se prolínajícími.....

Po titulkách se otvírá scéna do zajímavých mráčků a obláčků.......
Mezi těmito tančí naše zeměkoule.....
Řada hvězd mizí v dáli....... proplouvají mráčky a míjí zeměkouli....
Pomalu mizí také obláčky ....Přibližujeme se k naší zemi.....

S námi současně pěští se k zemi bílá holubice.....ztrácí se naším zrakům ......jeví se co bílý bod, který se usazuje uprostřed světadílu Evropy......

Evropa se zbarvuje a je nyní pestře sestavena z barevných ploch evropských zemí......Přibližně ve středu těchto barevně oddělených zemí vyrůstá rudě červené srdce:Republiky ....

Ve středu srdce sedí naše bílá holubice s rozepjatými křídly ......
Ta nyní roste a roste ....Pod jejími bílými perutěmi uniká rudá barva a ztrácí se tak, že tvoří pak přirozené hranice našeho státu...

Nyní spatřujeme na sceně bílou plochu utvořenou z bílých perutí holubice a kolem dokola červené hranice , které se při přiblížení mění v řady rudých růží....

To již slyšíme národní nápěvy naší vlasti.....

Bílá plocha Republiky se mezitím ponenáhlu mění v zelenou pláň......

Přibližujeme se opět, takže vnímáme pouze jeden zelený úsek a seznáváme při dalším přiblížení, že zelená plocha sestává vlastně z nesčetných zelených lístků a lístečků........

II.

Z těchto lístečků vyhlédnou najednou na něžných stonkách červené, modré, bílé květinky , které se na svých stonkách počnou malebně pohoupávati dle zvuku zvonkové hudby ......

Obraz jest nyní malebný a pestrý......Vidíme modré zvonečky ...... červená srdíčka .....fialověmodré chrpy ......bílé sedmikrásy ..... rudé máky ....

V hudbě slyšíme nyní známý národní nápěv v rytmickém pojetí.......

Květinky opustí své místo...... Utvoří malé skupinky a počnou tančiti známé lidové tance a dětske reje......Současně slyšíme nápěvy písní...

Ponenáhlu vyniká ojedinělý nápěv beze slov a současně se uvolní skupinka květinek z reje a počne tančiti solový výstup............. Pak scena skončí v stilisovaném ornamentu pestrých barev, který předvádí lidovou výšivku toho neb onoho kraje ......

Po několika těchto ukázkách vyskočí stilisované květiny z motivů a utvoří pestrý koberec květů , který pokryje celou Č.S/R., mezitím co se od obrazu opět vzdalujeme ......

Vnímáme opět celou Republiku v pestrých barvách, ve kterých převládnou barvy: červená, modrá a bílá......

Tyto barvy utváří ponenáhlu velký praporec , který se opět zmenšuje, až tvoří malou, pohyblivou vlajku, která se postavuje a svým zaostřeným koncem žerdě zapichuje do středu Republiky , kde počíná živě vláti co červenomodrobílá státní vlajka ....

Vzdalujeme se za zvuků národní hymny od obrazu až vidíme opět jen plastickou Evropu, ve středu naší Republiku, ze které vlaje plynule a vesele vlajka našich národních barev.....

- k o n e c -

Délka asi 180 metrů. Provedení 3 barevným systémem...... Provedení v nejlepší umělecké a technické úrovni za spolupráce našich nejznámějších odborníků ve Folkloru.

The personal archive of Irena Dodalová, which she sent to Prague from Argentina, unfortunately holds none of her pre-war scripts. Archive research eventually discovered her three "librettos": to *The Adventures of a Ubiquitous Fellow* (the Plzeň City Archives), *The Heart of Europe* (the Central Military Archives) and *The Czechoslovak Republic in Colours, Dances and Songs* (the Archives of the Ministry of Foreign Affairs). All these synopses clearly demonstrate the artistic, animation and sound concepts of the titles in question.

Irena Dodalová certainly earned the respect of the local professional public and was viewed as an expert in animated film. This is proved by the fact that she was invited to lecture at the 1937 and 1938 seminars organized by The Film Studio – which can be perceived as a predecessor of the Prague Film and TV School of the Academy of Performing Arts. Its program, systematically introducing the issues of the particular areas of film art and aesthetics, film production and technology, production and distribution, was presented by leading personalities in the field, such as Jan Mukařovský, Bohuslav Havránek, Vladislav Vančura, Otakar Vávra and Jindřich Elbl. Irena Dodalová, too, lectured there about European animated film at a seminar held in December 1937.[13] She also had a presentation about trick film origins and developments in Europe and America in the Social Club,[14] Reklub – a respected Czechoslovak association of advertising professionals – and in the Club of Czech and German theatre and drama experts. In May 1938, she introduced the history of cartoon film to members of the International Culture League and the PAX club in the hall of the United Association of Private Employees.[15] Her lectures were always accompanied by projections.

It is apparent from a distance that Irena Dodalová, even despite all her efforts, had not managed to raise the IRE-film brand to the awareness of the wider public. The phenomenon of film was at that time embodied by feature film and its mythology of film stars and, exceptionally, by American cartoon comedies. When Jaroslav Brož summarized the development of animated film in his 1938 article "From Mickey Mouse to Avant-Garde Art" (Od myšáka Mickyho k avantgardnímu umění), he observed that "hardly anybody knows that there is also a studio equipped for producing colour cartoon sound films

here in Czechoslovakia" and ranked the Dodals next to Cohl, Iwerks, Disney and the Fleischer brothers.[16]

The only book text which acknowledged the Dodals' oeuvre as part of the Czech film industry was the non-numbered spread in the German version of the yearbook *Czechoslovak Film* (Der tschechoslowakische Film) of August 1938. The brief text with several photographs, headlined "Der Trickfilm in der Tschechoslowakei", informed readers about the "pioneer" of Czech trick film, the painter Karel Dodal, and his close colleague Irena Dodalová.[17] It mentioned *Fantaisie érotique, The Adventures of a Ubiquitous Fellow, Ideas in Search of Light* (Myšlenka hledající světlo) and *The Unforgettable Poster* (Nezapomenutelný plakát; under the title *The Unforgettable Mona Lisa* [Nezapomenutelná Mona Lisa]) and the "attempt" at capturing the myth and poetry of the Czechoslovak capital as seen through a painter's eyes, *The Heart of Europe* (Srdce Evropy; under the title *Golden Prague* [Zlatá Praha]). The contribution was probably incorporated into the book thanks to Karel Smrž who co-organized the yearbook. He, however, succeeded in doing so only in the German version.

A take from the film *A Brief View of the Future*, which invited the viewers to visit the Ota Kollinský department store.

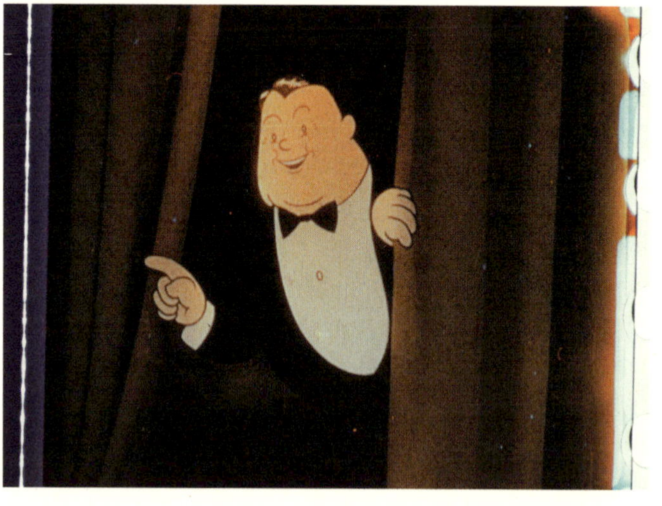

1 Although we have mainly followed the Czechoslovak press, Dodalová would also often address German journalists, as is apparent from the outtakes filed in the Personal Fund of Irena Dodalová.

2 *The Adventures of a Ubiquitous Fellow.* The Association of Pension Funds of the Czech Republic, plates RJ 158, EJ 159; plates RJ 182, 183.

3 Iréna, "Co s českým trikfilmem?", *Filmový kurýr,* 1937, No. 25, 18 June, p. 55.

4 Ibid.

5 Iréna, "Trikfilm a jeho možnosti v Evropě", *Kinorevue,* 1937, No. 13, 17 November, pp. 252–253; 1937, No. 14, 24 November, pp. 274–275.

6 Ibid., p. 274.

7 The cartoon sound studies by O. Fischinger on the program of the second and third weeks of avant-garde, held in the Prague Kotva cinema in 1931 (16–22 January and 13–19 February).

8 Iréna, "Trikfilm a jeho možnosti v Evropě", p. 274.

9 Ibid.

10 Ibid.

11 Iréna, "Má státní filmová propagace právo pomlčeti déle o svém folkloru?", *Filmový kurýr,* 1937, No. 52, 24 December, p. 3.

12 -vp-, "Napříč evropským trikfilmem", *Národní práce,* 1937, No. 48, 17 February, p. 6.

13 The lecture was held on 6 December 1937. In: *Seznam přednášejících ve filmovém semináři* (The List of Lecturers at the Film Seminar). The National Film Archive, fund Filmové studio (Film Studio), Inv. No. 35.

14 -k-, "Světoví umělci mezi námi" (World Artists among Us), *Filmový kurýr,* 1937, No. 50, 10 December, p. 2.

15 -h-, "Dějiny kresleného filmu" (A History of Cartoon Film), *České slovo,* 1938, No. 110, 11 May, p. 4; also the *Rudé právo* (Red Law) daily, 1938, No. 110, 11 May, p. 4.

16 Brož, J., "Od myšáka Mickyho k avantgardnímu umění", *Právo lidu* (People's Law), 1938, No. 43, 20 February, p. 17.

17 "Der Trickfilm in der Tschechoslowakei". In: *Der tschechoslowakische film,* Bd. III. Prag: Filmové studio, 1938.

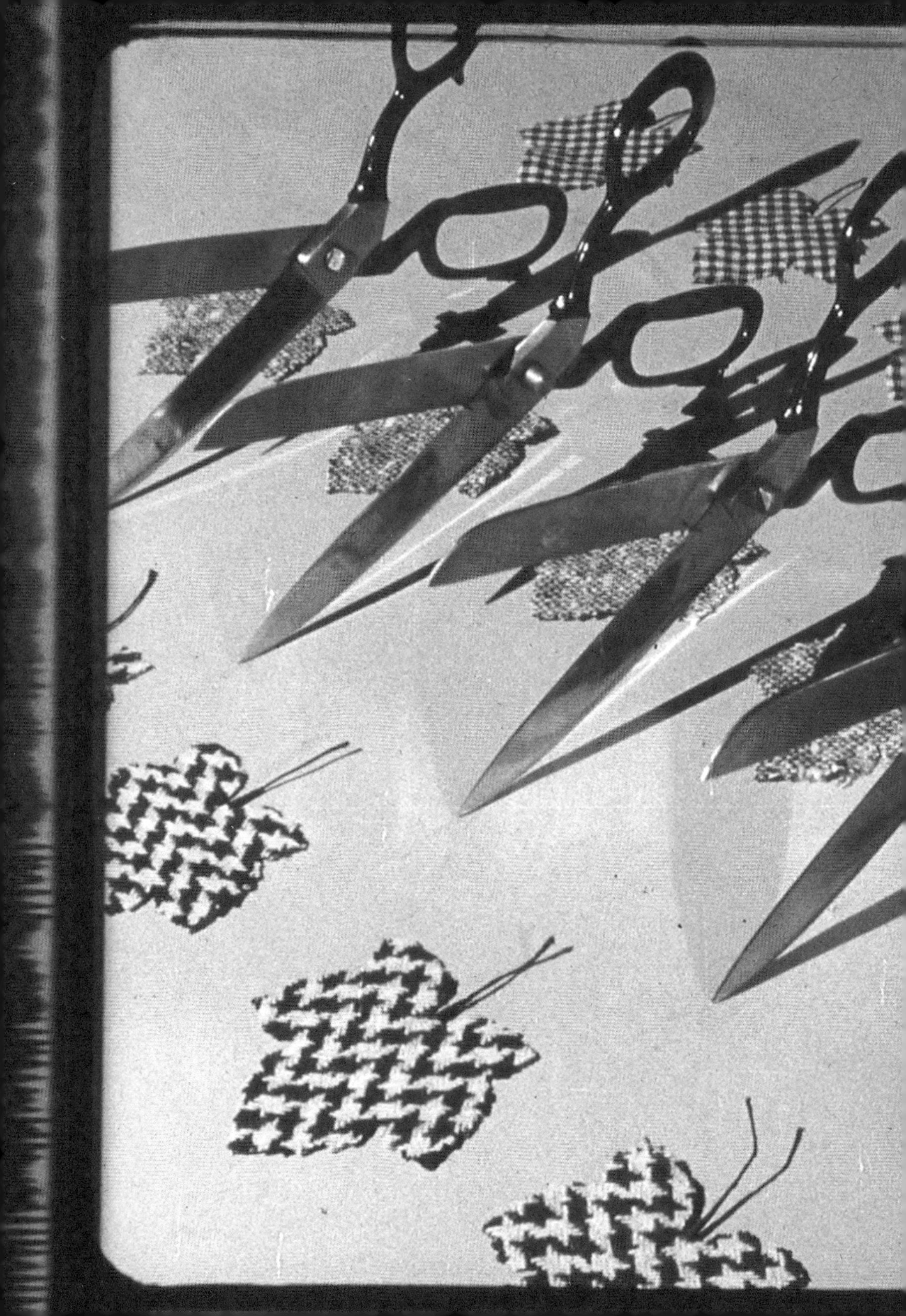

Thwarted Plans / Closing IRE-film

The most detailed testimony describing the position of IRE-film in the Czech cinematographic milieu, its supporters and sympathizers as well as its fights with various institutions is the records from the sessions of the Film Advisory Board. This body of a rather representative "cast" was constituted in November 1934 and served an array of functions: it distributed grants for the local production, was involved in legislation and in organizing film activities, acted as a central dramatic adviser and actively accommodated international presentation of Czechoslovak films. The records document that the majority of the Board's members watched the development of the new studio fondly, especially in its beginnings. In spring 1936, the Board ratified the proposal submitted by a representative of the Ministry of Foreign Affairs to support IRE-film's cartoon promotional supplements by a fifth of the approved real production costs.[1] In June of the same year, the studio received a subsidy of 15 thousand Crowns for *The Adventures of a Ubiquitous Fellow* (Všudybylovo dobrodružství) on the basis of its complaint that it had lost 27 thousand on the Radiojournal commission.[2] The Board also subsidized the presentations of the Dodals' studio at both local and foreign shows and, in the case of introducing *Fantaisie érotique* in Paris and Venice in 1937, it provided 4,405 Crowns to IRE-film to make its colour copy.[3]

Another important role played by the Board was to protect the national interests of Czechoslovak film industry. IRE-film won exclusive rights to produce animated commercial and promotional films. Irena Dodalová later recalled that the decision was signed by the section councillor Zdeněk Urban from the Ministry of Enterprise, Commerce and Industry, and the body thus advocated IRE-film's exclusivity many times. For example, in March 1936 when the Haas company applied for approval to import the film *Fig Coffee* (Fíková káva), the Board declined the request, noting that the promotional film could be assigned to IRE-film.[4] This recommendation, however, did not guarantee that the Dodals would indeed get hold of the order.

An illustrative example of the conditions in which IRE-film conducted its business and of the Board's scope of influence is the documents on the commission of a commercial promoting the Kalodont tooth-paste, and we will therefore pay more attention to this "case".

The intense negotiations lasted from April to June 1937. They began with a letter of 14 April in which the advertising department of the General Perfumery Authority, the limited liability company Elida, Střekov (part of the joint-stock syndicate Jiří Schicht or, respectively, Unilever),[5] asked the supreme councillor Zdeněk Urban from the Ministry to approve the import of a commercial for the tooth-paste which would be filmed by the Lintas company in Berlin under the participation of Elida, based in Vienna, Warsaw, Osijek and Budapest. The colour and sound trick film was to be 100 metres long and its production costs were to total about 6.5 thousand German Reichsmarks. The correspondence included a typewritten Czech translation of the screenplay to the film *The Man Who Failed to Remember* (Muž, který na to zapomněl). The professionally compiled script deftly employed cartoon film to portray the experiences of a drunken man whose world transmutes and doubles and the colours of objects change, and who finally discovers the beneficial effects of the given mouth hygiene. Elida stressed in the letter that if the picture was produced by a Czech company, it would result in problems with purchasing the literary original, owned by the Berlin advertising company Lintas.[6] The chairing Miloš Havel proposed that the picture could be made by IRE-film, and offered to find out about the relevant conditions. He used Josef Tušla as his intermediary who provided the script by a German

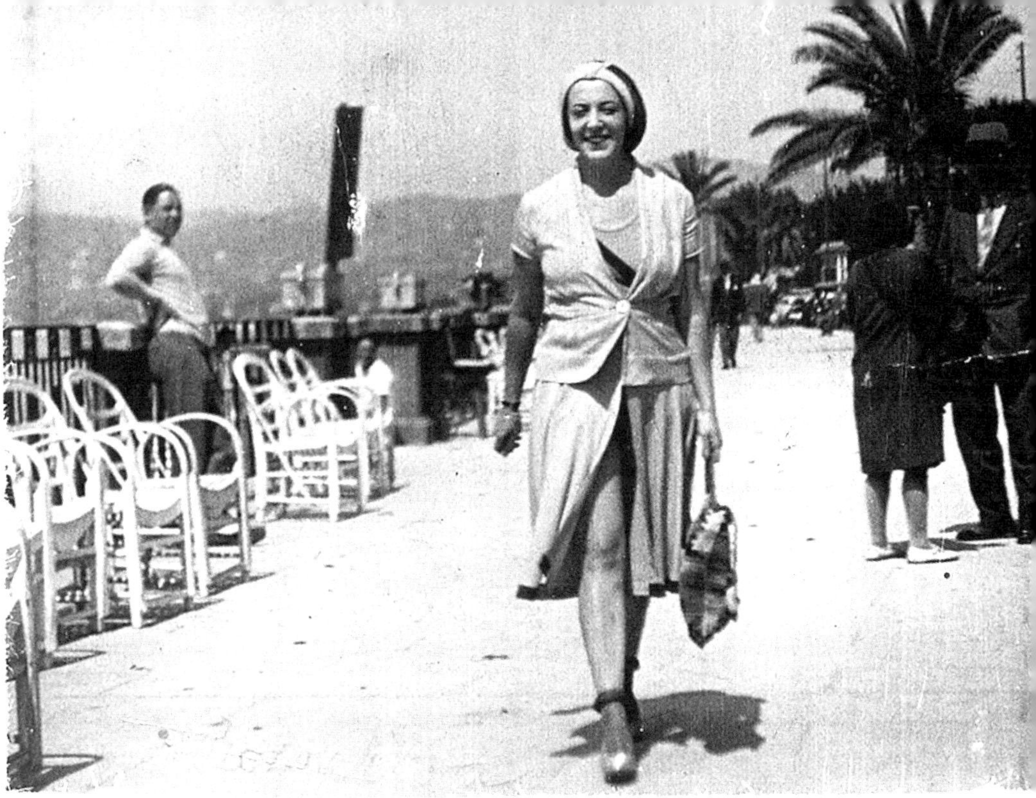

Irena Dodalová abroad (undated).

writer to the Dodals. We quote their subsequent reply in full since it contains interesting economic data:

"In response to the kind inquiry of your member, Mr Josef Tušla, as to the discreet matter of importing the Kalodont colour cartoon film for the Schicht company, based on the provided script, we take the liberty of offering you such a film fully based on the given contents.

The flat price for the first version including the first copy: 57,000 Crowns without sales and turnover tax.

We also take the liberty of pointing out on this occasion that the price list issued by the German UFA and by Gasparcolor states that making one colour metre of a sound cartoon costs from RM 100 to 150 and the price of a 50-metre colour film therefore ranges from RM 7,000 to 10,000 which approximately equals 80,000 to 110,000 Crowns.

The script which we had received to assess suggests that the film in question is of 'standard' character, i.e. that it can serve to promote various

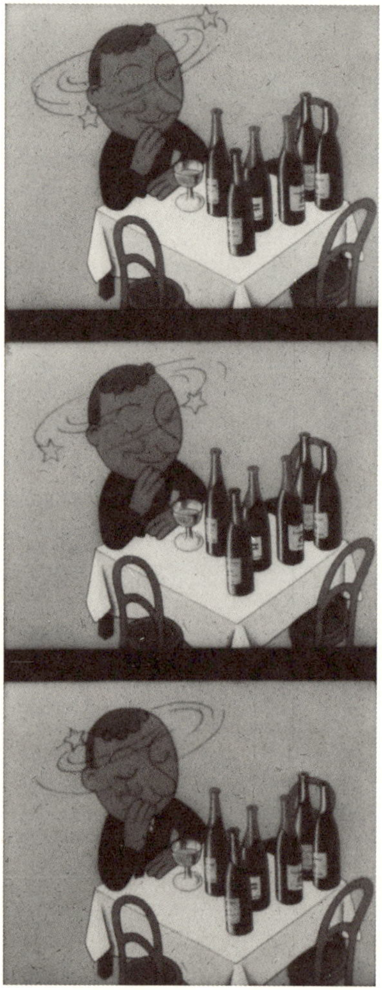

The Dodals fought for making *The Crucial Two Minutes* for two years. The picture was eventually filmed by Hans Fischerkoesen in Germany.

commodities depending on the commodity for which the closing is adapted. We thus do not think that it would be a film produced exclusively for the Kalodont brand; we instead think that it is a universal film which merely needs to receive a new drawn ending and this condition would considerably lower the costs on such a work.

Regardless of this circumstance, we are of the opinion that we would still be cheaper than the foreign competition. It would therefore be apposite if the Schicht company first considered our offer or, eventually, our collaboration.

Yours faithfully, Irena and Karel Dodals, returning one copy of the libretto."[7]

The Dodals sent another letter to the Board on 10 May 1937.[8] It reads that they had learned from a collaborating German laboratory that Schicht intended to import a colour cartoon film into Czechoslovakia and that they wondered why Schicht was refusing to work with them. They asked the Board for protection and attached extracts of complimentary references on their production (Gasparcolor, Sagor, Paris, Dr Bruno Fuerst, Lektor der Masaryk-Volkshochschule, Moderne Theater- und Kinoreklame Palast Berlin, Martin's Hollywood, Marten, Rio de Janeiro, Myzet – Hollywood, Cinema illustrazione – Milano).

On 26 May 1936, the Piras agency stepped into the negotiations with a letter[9] again addressed to Zdeněk Urban. It advocated the right of its customer, Jiří Schicht, to produce and import the given film and informed that the company would provide 200 thousand Crowns for its distribution (it later came out that the amount represented cinema revenues). Piras further noted that Schicht planned to order the Czechoslovak picture, *The Housewives' Praise* (Franenlob, Chvála hospodyněk), from it. If the import of the film was proscribed, it would thus impair the interests of Czechoslovak cinemas. The closing of the letter then quite maliciously pointed that in any case, colour films were not made in Czechoslovakia because they were developed and copied in Germany.

The Piras letter was debated at the Board's session of 3 June 1937.[10] The record from the meeting only briefly noted that a discussion developed around the case, especially around the 200 thousand Crowns provided for the distribution of the Kalodont film. Jindřich Elbl nonetheless suggested that Schicht should consult the Supplementary Committee (i.e. the committee for short films). The board members unanimously voted against producing the film in

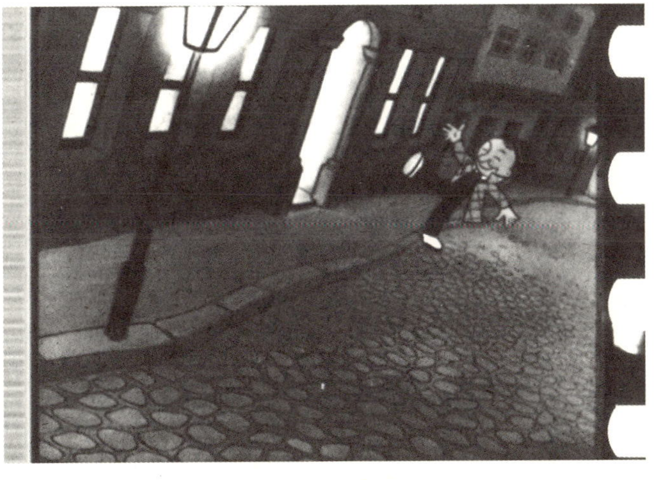

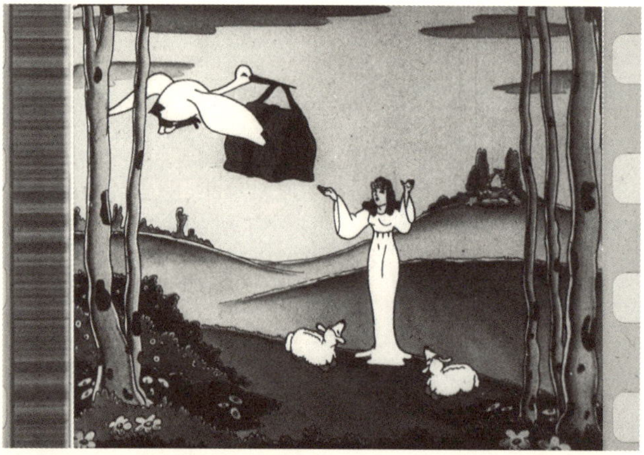

The picture *Spring Is Here* and the combined title *An Autumn Song* were made by IRE-film for the Prokop and Čáp company.

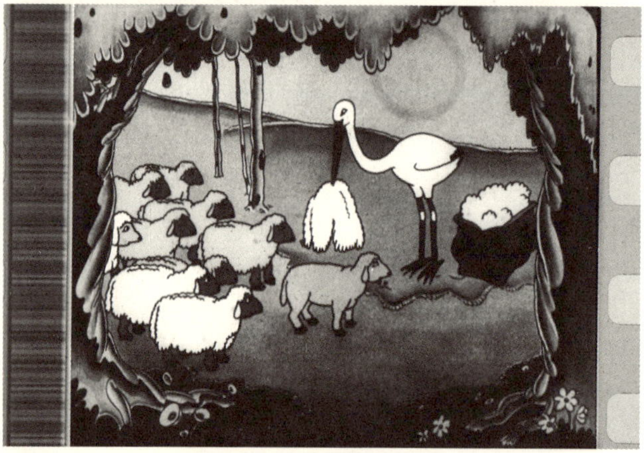

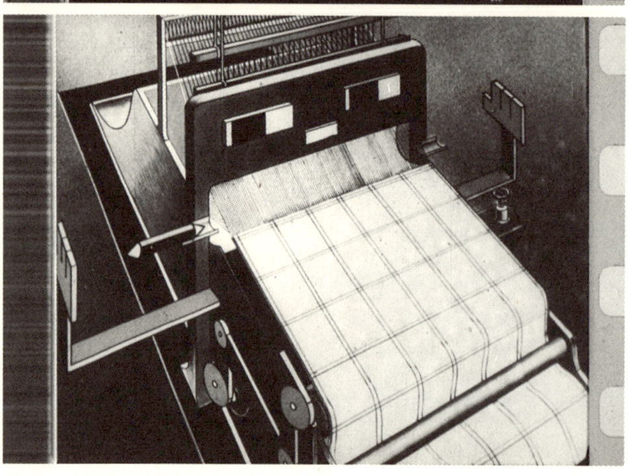

The outtakes sent by Irena Dodalová from Argentina include several colour frames, which probably formed the closing of the film, as is proved by the text of the song found in the censorship file.

Piras whose main role should be cinema advertising and slides instead of film production.

Piras objected to this standpoint in a letter of 9 June 1937.[11] They protested that "the by-laws and the trade permit of Piras as a promotional, advertising, commercial and publishing joint-stock company state the production of commercials and promotional and supplementary films as the field of its activity" and stressed that the firm had been part of the industry for eighteen years, supporting the claim with a list of its hitherto collaborating filmmakers.[12] They also referred to their appeal of 26 May, stating that "if the Jiří Schicht company from Ústí nad Labem is permitted to import a colour trick film, even though such production in this country is non-existent, Piras will reciprocally give it a feature commercial film which had already been commissioned and which is underlined by the above-mentioned import. Both films will subsequently be exploited in Czechoslovak cinematographs and will result in a total turnover of c. one million Crowns, an amount to be passed on in favour of the cinematographic industry".[13]

The Kalodont case returned to the Board's agenda on 10 June. Ignoring the previous standpoints, the members agreed to import the commercial provided that it was filed in the "D" index

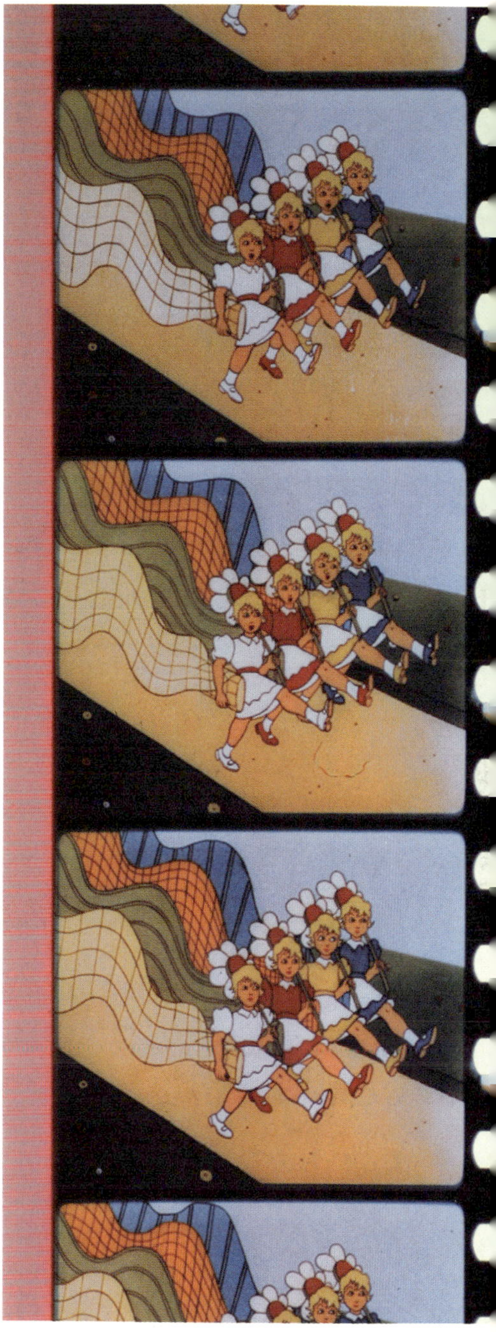

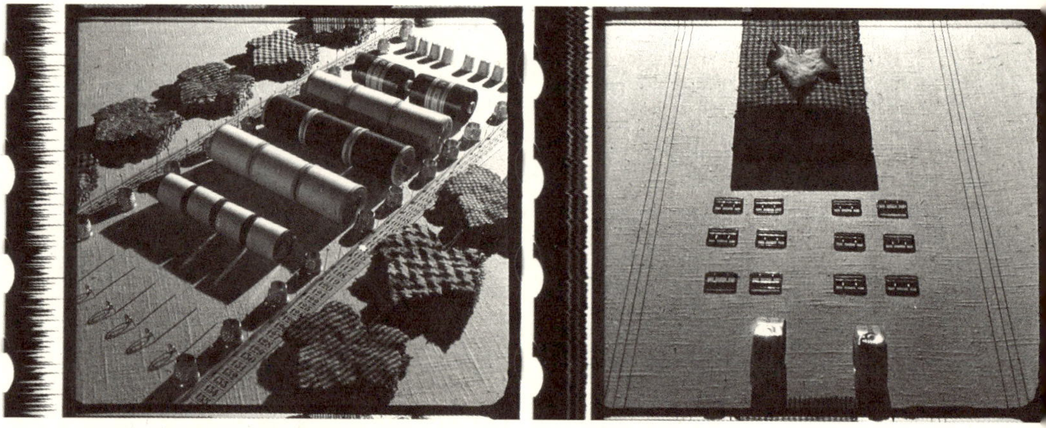

An Autumn Song commercial employed animating real objects (tailor's tools in this case). It closed with stylized puppets representing St Procopius and a stork and finalized with images of falling leaves cut out from the company's autumn fabric collection.

of the Association of Czechoslovak Film Industry and Trade in Prague. The ordained registration fee was ten Crowns per regular film metre. The justification reasoned that the approval was issued considering that a new commercial was ordered from a local company. The clause wrapped up on 19 June at the appurtenant Ministry of Enterprise, Commerce and Industry under Reference Number 63 268, IV. A.

The records along with the surviving correspondence prove that although the Board members did their best to support Czech film production, they were unable to compete with the economically powerful and successful partners such as the Piras agency and the Jiří Schicht company. In the given case, IRE-film also had to wrestle with heavy foreign competition. The Kalodont-hygiene ad, filmed by Hans Fischerkoesen who was one of the most experienced advertising filmmakers of Germany of that time, was approved by the local censors very soon, in 1938, under the tile *The Crucial Two Minutes* (Důležité dvě minuty) and it ranks among the most successful titles of German film commercials.

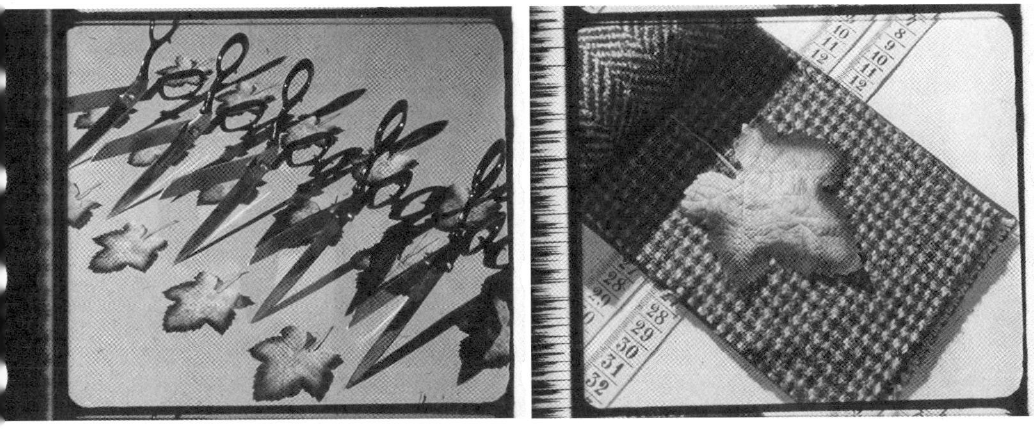

Quotes from the contemporary sources also testify that IRE-film's situation was tricky and its "exclusive" position in the Czech market of commercial films was only conditional. In spite of the difficulties, the studio asserted itself in the local advertising market, and it undoubtedly managed to do so thanks to the yet unseen quality of its films and production scope. Its ten commercials made in 1936 elevated it into the position of one of the largest producers of animated commercials in Czechoslovakia during that period. The next summer, the Dodals' work received due recognition as their *Fantaisie érotique* was introduced at the Paris World Exhibition along with the film *People on an Iceberg* (Lidé na kře; 1937) by Martin Frič. The gala was attended by the Czechoslovak ambassador in France, Štefan Osuský, and the couple was also present. The *Fantaisie érotique*, produced by an utterly unknown Prague studio, attracted much attention and helped the Dodals establish contacts with French filmmakers which they subsequently employed in founding their Paris studio. During their Paris sojourn, the couple moreover participated in the

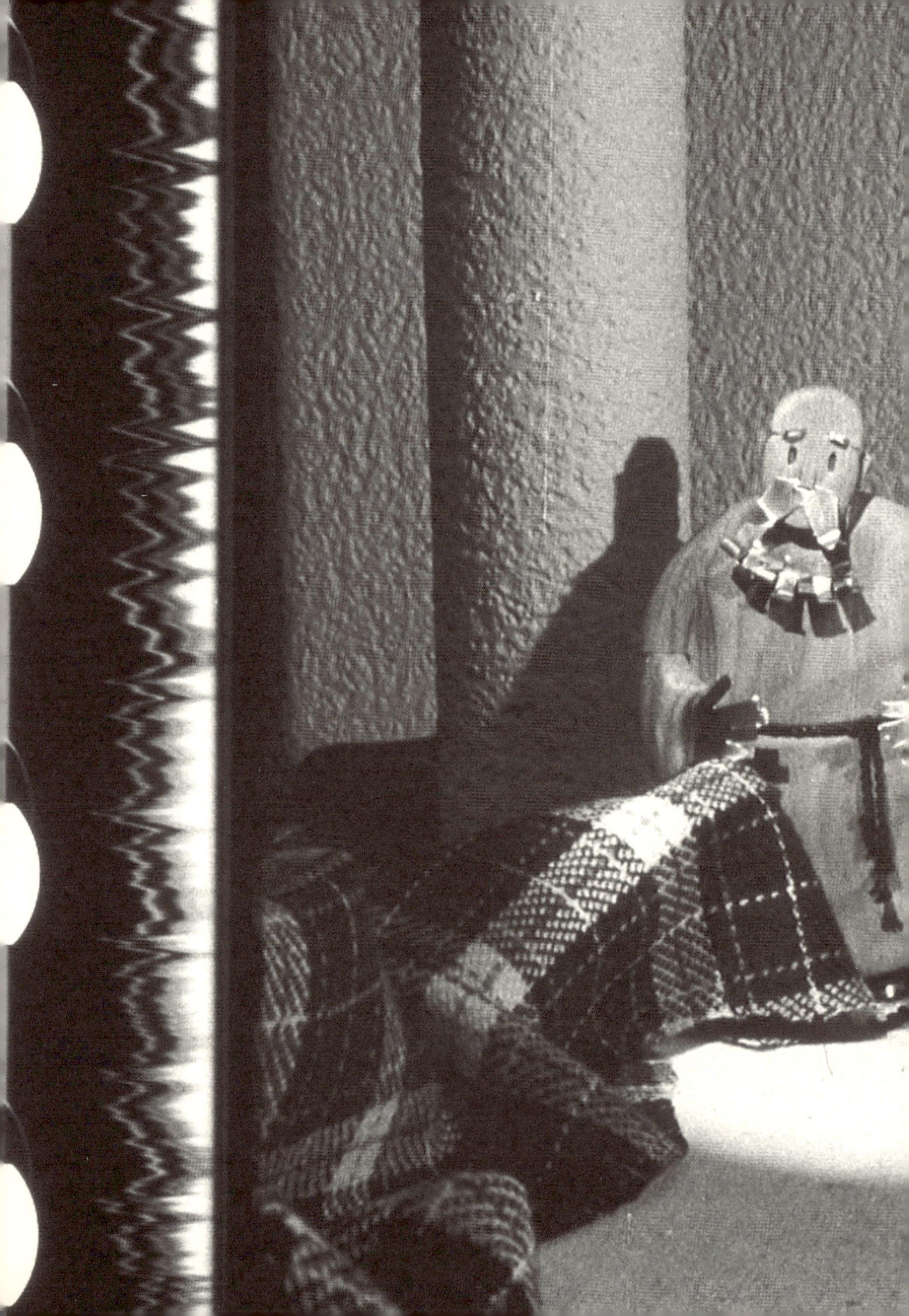

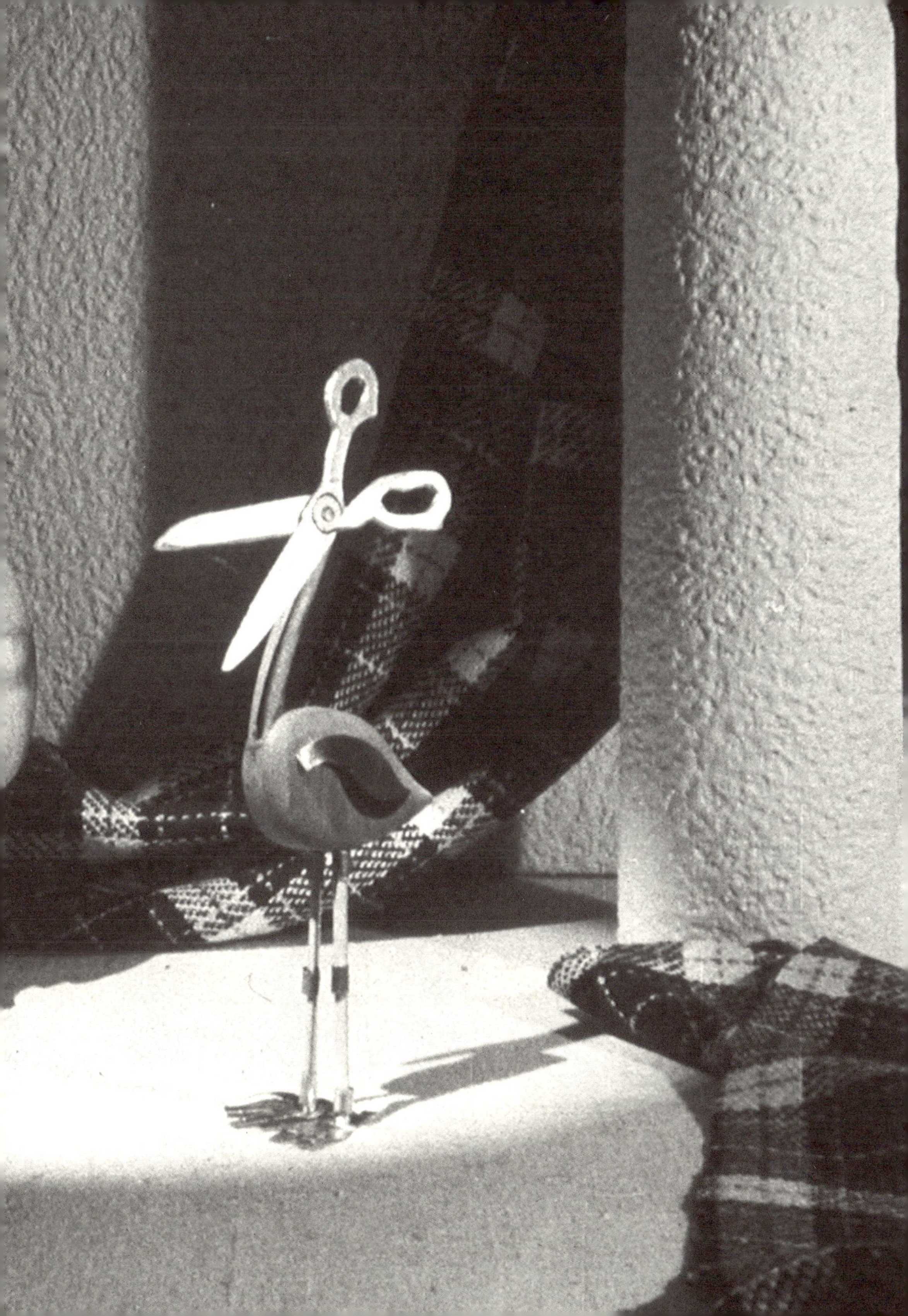

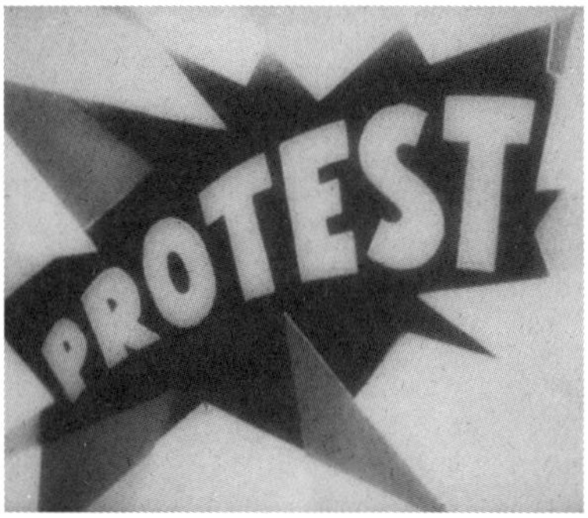

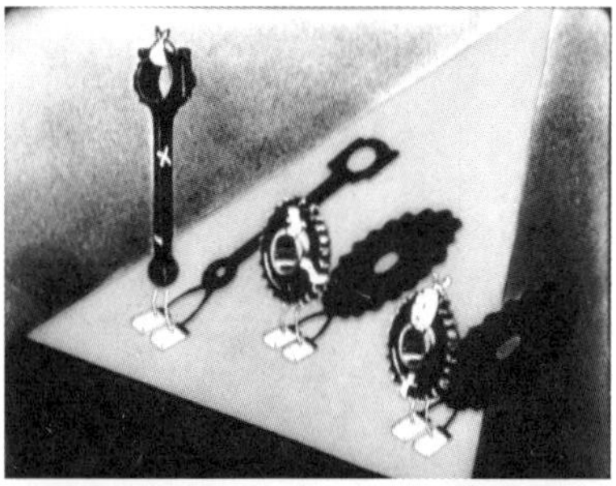

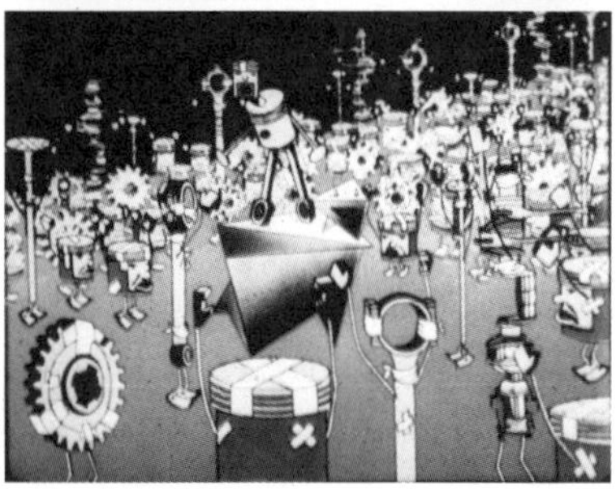

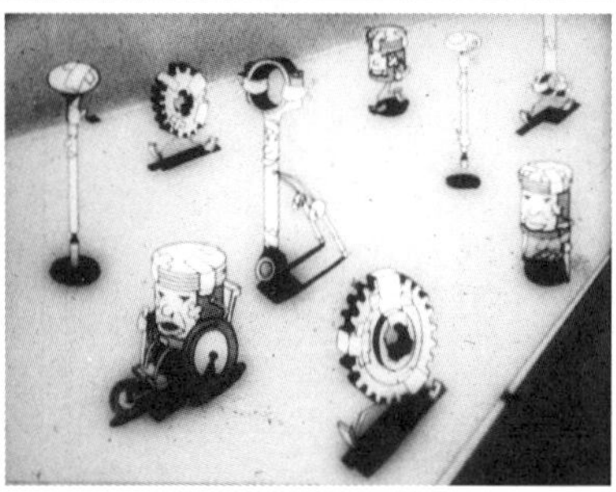

international film congress whose opening was held on board the Normandie ocean liner.

The year 1938, however, progressed under the looming economic crisis which severely affected most film productions focused on advertising. This lucidly revealed the limits of the Czechoslovak film market, along with the fact that a small private company was plainly unable to compete with well-established advertising agencies powered by influential economic groups. The Kalodont negotiations were a telling example of this. The political and economic conditions in Czechoslovakia were pressured by events in Germany and the explosive international situation. Many potential business partners moved abroad or at least pondered doing so. The customer circle willing to invest in Czech cartoon commercials was far from expanding and very close to dramatically shrinking.

IRE-film's 1937 production dropped by a half as compared to the previous period. In 1938, the studio made just two animated commercials, *The Protest* (Protest) and *Three Men* (Tři muži). They both excelled in design and animation, as well as in obliging the advertising assignment. But more commissions would not arrive and even *The Heart of Europe* (Srdce Evropy), a title in which the couple invested many hopes, did not receive a subsidy. In August 1938, the Dodals finished their project *Ideas in Search of Light* (Myšlenka hledající světlo), produced from their own sources and prepared with regard to its future screening abroad. Their passport application from the same time reads that they were ready to leave for the study trip to the United States, and Hermína Týrlová applied for her passport, too.

Although little is known about the Dodals' pre-war life in Prague, they certainly played a unique role in the Central-European filmmaking community and had a considerable share in prompting its development. And while Karel Dodal was already kindred with an older generation, his wife swiftly established new social contacts and befriended younger artists. The couple was also in close contact with their exiled colleagues living in the capital – György Pál, Desider Gross and others. There are no direct documents to prove this but it is supported by many indirect testimonies. Dodalová's publishing activity shows that she was well familiar with Pál's oeuvre and highly respected it, and Dodal stood behind the Czech versions of his films.

Irena Dodalová also maintained contacts with theatre professionals fleeing from Germany and Austria, and eagerly joined their activities. The end of her appearance in the Club of Czech and German Theatre and Drama Experts in late 1937 was described by V. H. Jarka in the *National Papers* (Národní listy). She said there, in her characteristic bursting style and with idealistic zeal, that "at a time of the winning machines and weapons – also live film must fight for truth, and it must speak to all those who still can reason and think. It is necessary, even at the cost of one being financially underestimated, to put a hand to the plough and work; and work hard."[14]

Pre-war development in Czech advertising film as well as the IRE-film studio closed with the Protectorate of Bohemia and Moravia. Karel Dodal, Irena Dodalová and Hermína Týrlová were 37 years old at that time. Most of their dreams and hopes did not come true. They were part of a tragic generation. Fully identified with the ideals of the First Republic, they merely managed to lay the foundations to their work which they could not follow up with in their country. But they, naturally, could not anticipate that.

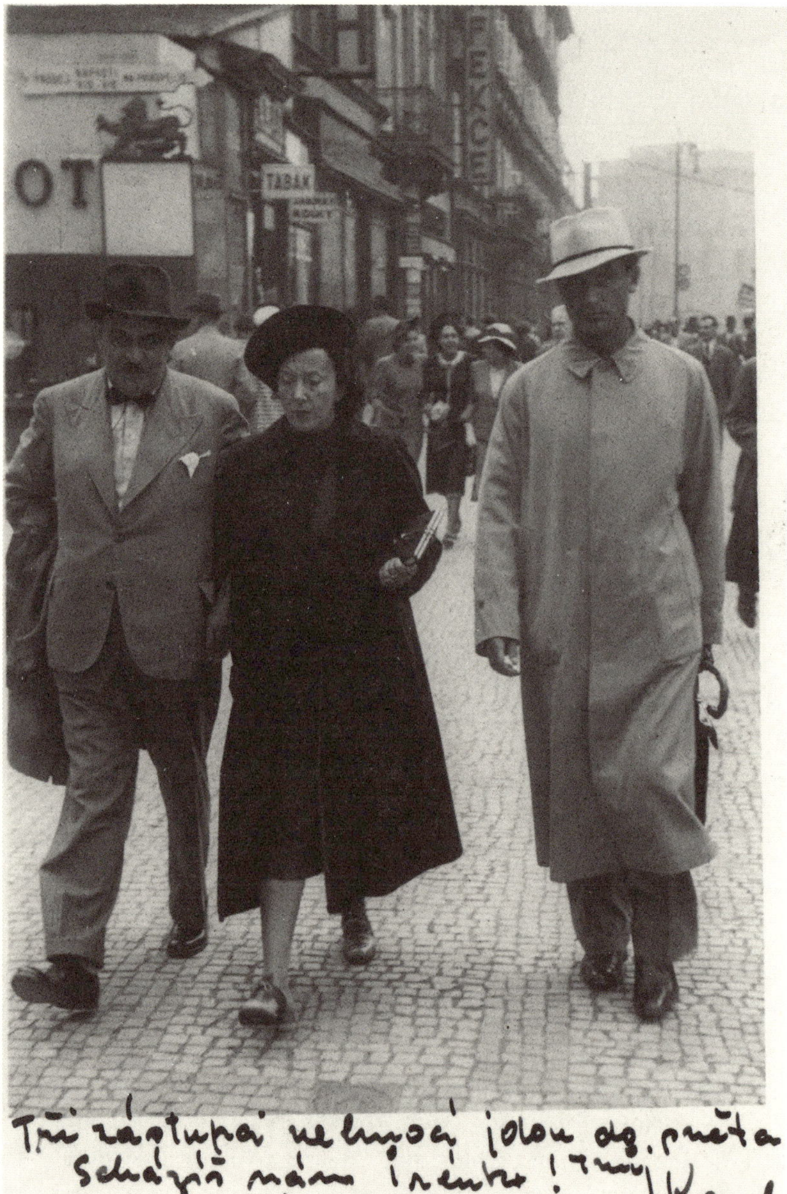

Tři zástupci velmocí jdou do světa
Schází nám Irénka! Tvůj Karel

Irénko zlatá, dlouho to trvalo
než se jsme sešly! Nezklamu Tě!
[illegible]

1 Record from the 65th session of the Film Advisory Board, 15 April 1936. The National Archives, the Ministry of Enterprise, Commerce and Industry, box 2345, No. 5.

2 Record from the 74th session of the Film Advisory Board, 26 June 1936. Ibid., p. 3.

3 Final account of the *Fantaisie érotique* colour copy production. The National Archives, the Ministry of Enterprise, Commerce and Industry, box 2754, Ref. No. 77900. According to the document, the copy was made by Gasparcolor in Berlin.

4 Record from the 61st session of the Film Advisory Board, 16 March 1936. The National Archives, the Ministry of Enterprise, Commerce and Industry, box 2345, Ref. No. 29163, p. 5.

5 Letter of Piras to the Ministry of Enterprise, Commerce and Industry, 9 June 1937; it is part of the file Žádost fy Schicht, Ústí n. Labem, o dovoz reklamního filmu (Application of the Schicht Co., Ústí n. Labem, to Import an Advertising Film). The National Archives, the Ministry of Enterprise, Commerce and Industry, box 2756, Ref. No. 63268.

6 Record from the 108th session of the Film Advisory Board, 22 April 1937. The National Archives, the Ministry of Enterprise, Commerce and Industry, box 2756.

7 Letter sent by the Dodals, 26 April 1937. Ibid.

8 Ibid.

9 Ibid.

10 Record from the 112th session of the Film Advisory Board, 3 June 1937. The National Archives, the Ministry of Enterprise, Commerce and Industry, box 2756.

11 Letter sent by Piras, 9 June 1937. Ibid.

12 Ibid.

13 Ibid.

14 Jarka, V. H., op. cit., p. 2.

The Dodals on Na Příkopech Street in Prague in 1938. The man on the right is Richard, a family friend and also the author of the inscription below the shot.

The Wartime Anabasis / 1940s

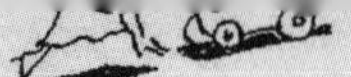

is all right.
"...nt" from amer studio are for
all right. I have for both every
...g this salute: 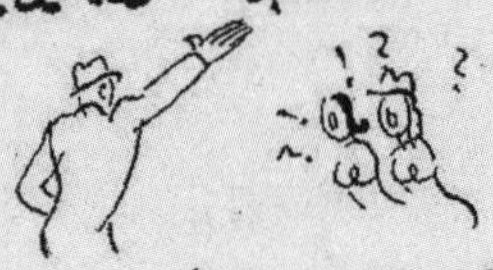

...n all. Thank you for your speach with
... and others.
I only know this: in this field will
possible make many <u>good</u> things.
Kinnack like to go South in end of
this month find something – possibility...
He promise me write to Hoorn but
this have little time. May will be for
... time also good go to Army Civil S.
... spoke to him about this and he don't
... here about this speaking about women
... ally. But when will be nothing better
in this new time, he answer: „the by!!?"
is there everything more exchausting? Have you
...pasio? Are you drawing something in
free time. or only: 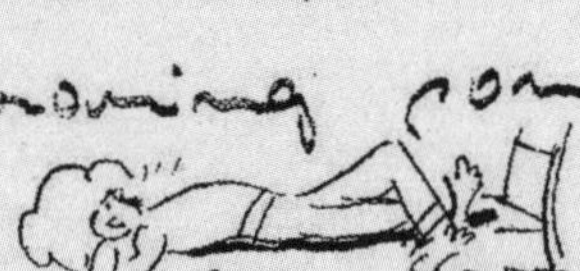 or: 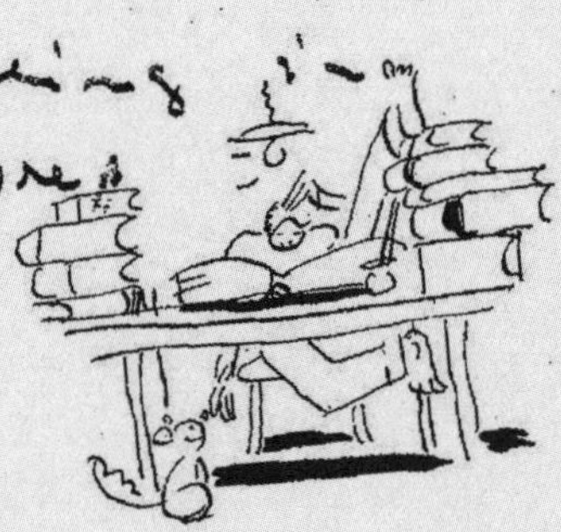

With best wishes:

K.D.

Zbraslav, Paris, Minneapolis, New York / In Search of Asylum

The small town of Zbraslav, a charming summer resort frequented by the higher middle class during the Czechoslovak First Republic, also became one of the Dodals' leisure residences. When they left their Prague studio and the Klimentská apartment in summer 1938, they rented a three-room flat in a private villa there. In autumn, however, they left for their Paris cartoon film studio. It was in 11 Villaret de Joyeuse, just off the Arche de Triomphe, and at that time it employed five draughtswomen. No detailed information about the studio's activity and the duration of its existence were found. We can only assume that the Dodals established it in the latter half of 1937 at the earliest and closed it in autumn 1938. It is also possible that they sent some film materials from Paris to the United States and used them in New York after the war.

The couple spent the time of the Munich Treaty events in France and Karel Dodal set off to the United States at the end of the year. He travelled alone while his wife was supposed to follow him as soon as she had settled all business and family matters in Prague. Although it was officially a "study" trip, the Dodals actually planned to transfer their animated film production to America. The reason underlying the exile was not only their production problems

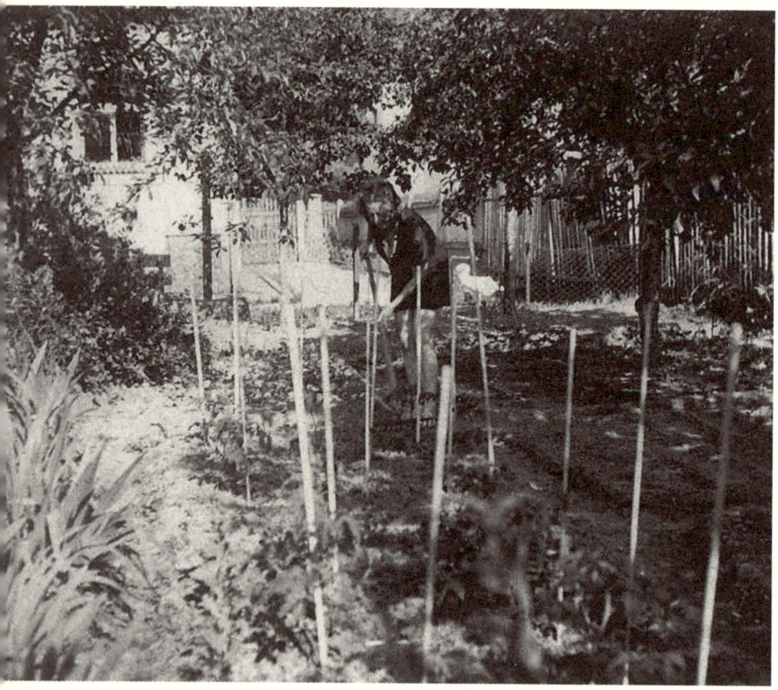

Irena Dodalová in her Zbraslav garden, growing vegetables the selling of which to Jews was already strictly prohibited.

described earlier but also the worsening international political situation heading towards the war.

Irena Dodalová had to return to Prague in the early 1939. Her presence in the capital was forced by administrative issues and family commitments – her mother at that time lived in the shared apartment at Zbraslav and her brother Rudolf was on his way to Palestine to enter the Czechoslovak foreign army.

Irena also coped with a rather intricate problem of how to send the studio's technical equipment and the films to her husband overseas. She told this almost unbelievable story from the Protectorate beginnings many years later in Argentina to her friend, Ms Voldánová, who reproduced it as follows:

"He wrote to her asking for his apparatus and she needed approval from the 'protector'. She told me that she set off to Prague Castle sporting a violet hat and high heels. The guards supposedly let her in, thinking she was visiting someone of high rank: she stormed a staircase, not knowing which one, she knocked, not knowing where, and there she was, face to face with the

KAREL RISINGER NÁST.
B. B. ČERNÍK
ZASILATELSTVÍ
PRAHA
KANCELÁŘE - II., HAVLÍČKOVO NÁM. 3
TELEFONY: 21462 - 21461
TELEGRAMY: ZASILATEL ČERNÍK PRAHA
ÚČET POŠTOVNÍ SPOŘITELNY - 18004
BĚŽNÝ ÚČET - ČESKÁ PRŮMYSLOVÁ BANKA V PRAZE

EXPEDICE: PRAHA X., JUNGMANNOVO NÁM. 11
TELEFON 38389
SKLADIŠTĚ: PRAHA VII., NA MANINÁCH 20.
TELEFON 72212

Praha, dne 1. července 1939.

P.T.

Korespondenční oddělení

Policejního ředitelství,

PRAHA I.,

Byl jsem pověřen panem Karlem Dodalem, nar. 27. ledna 1900 v Praze a bytem v Zbraslavi II./čp. 187, abych obstaral převoz jeho svršků z Prahy do Spojených států severoamerických.

Za tím účelem předkládám v příloze seznam stěhovacích svršků se třemi průpisy a prosím o jeho laskavé potvrzení. Dále přikládám potvrzení Okresního úřadu v Praze pro politický okres Praha-venkov.

Děkuji předem za laskavé vyřízení a poroučím se

v dokonalé úctě:

Blok č. 2341
(Em. 1938.) 364.89 7/8.
Juxta Čís. 000071
na dávku za úřední úkon ve věcech správních dle saz. pol. .... sazby .... nařízení č. 248/35, Sb. z. a n.
10 Kč (deset Kč)
Malý konceptní 5a. Přísně súčtovatelné.
Min. fin. 10.129/38-V/14b.

13a

14/9 80/38 - III 9988/38

S E Z N A M

předmětů provozního zařízení k výrobě kreslených filmů, patřících malíři <u>Karlu D o d a l o v i</u>, tč Universita ve státu <u>M i n n e s o t a, M i n n e a p o l i s ,</u> U.S.A. k bezcelnému odbavení tam, za účelem dočasného přesídlení do U.S.A.

1./<u>železný stůl s příslušenstvím</u>
pro výrobu trickfilmů, reostat atd.
celkem . . . . 24 kusy

2./<u>pracovní filmové doplňky</u>
stativní vzpěry, ruční projektor atd.
celkem . . . . 6 kusů

3./<u>kreslířské doplňky</u>
malíř. stojan, 2 prázdná mal. plátna,
4 dřevěné podstavce /kozy/ papírové
instrukční obrazy 2, kresl. prkna atd.
celkem . . . . .14 kusů

4./<u>osvětlovací doplňky ve .... 3 bedýnk</u>.
stínidla, lampy, taktoměr, chronometr,
motorek k pistoli atd...... 13 kusů

5./ <u>malířské potřeby ve 2 balíkách a
1 bedýnce</u>
malířské drobnosti, kaseta, stříkací
pistole, měřič světla, skleněné okénko
barevné tisky Šetelíkových předloh,
staré celuloid. desky na kreslení a
kovový rámeček, reklamní publikace,
korkové desky atd........ 20 kusů

6./ <u>věci pracovní rázu osobního</u>
<u>1 krabice</u> s geometr. dřevěn. tělesy
<u>1 bedýnka</u> s odbor. listy a film. kritikami
<u>1 bedýnka</u> s filmovými kresbami
<u>1 bedýnka</u> s knížkami o filmu a fotograf.
<u>1 bedýnka</u> s zápisky o film. pracích
<u>1 bedna</u> s starými notami a knihami

7./ <u>1 cestovní gramofon s deskami</u>
ve 4 částech, staré, His Mast. Voice

8./ <u>1 ruční fotografický přístroj</u>,
starší model IHAGE EXACTA, v brašně

9./ <u>Camera Šlechta</u>, starší model opravený,
s 2 stativy, 4 objectivy, motorkem,
s casetami, drobným příslušenstvím,
asi celkem . . . . 21 kusů
ve . . . . <u>3 bedýnkách</u>

10./<u>50 krabic filmových výstřižků</u>
starých reklamních filmů ve versi české,
neprodejné, ukázkové, k učení pohybů,
ve váze asi 140 kg netto, bezcenné

I N V E N T O R Y

of objects of equipment for the production of cartoons animated, belonging to <u>Mr. Karel D o d a l, now at the University Minneapolis Sate of Minnesota U.S.A.</u> to be admited duty free to the U.S.A. for the purpose of temporary residence in U.S.A.-

1./<u>metaltable with full equipment</u>
for cartoons animated-production, reostatic etc. in all . . . . 24 pieces

2./<u>production accessories</u>
statics, handprojector etc.
in all . . . . 6 pieces

3./ <u>drawing accessories</u>
painter-stand 2 old linens paint.
4 wooden supports, paper-paint. instruct. 2,
drawing boards etc.
in all . . . . 14 pieces

4./ <u>illumination accessories in 3 small cases</u>
lamp-shades, lamps, tactometer, chronometer,
motor for the pistol, etc .... 13 pieces

5./<u>Painters accessories in 2 packets and
1 small case</u>
other small articles in a small case,
painters cassete, spraying pistol gun.
Light metr. glass window form, old coloured
prints of Šetelik forms, old celluloid
desks for drawing, metal frame, advertising
publications, corks for padding etc.
in all about add. . . . . 20 inarticl.

6./<u>personal effects for work. and. stud.</u>
<u>1 box</u> with geometr. wood articles
<u>1 case</u> with film periodicals. critics etc
<u>1 case</u> " film drawings
<u>1 case</u> " books of film & photography
<u>1 case</u> " notes of film-works-stud.
<u>1 case</u> " old music notes and books

7./<u>1 portable gramaphone with desks in</u>
4 pieces, old, His Masters Voice,

8./1 <u>Hand Photo Apparatus, older model</u>,
IHAGE EXACTA, in a small box

9./<u>Camera Šlechta,</u> older model, renovated
with two stands supports, 4 objectives,
motor, camera-cassetes, small accessories,
articles belonging to the camera, about
21 pieces, in . . . . <u>3 cases</u>

10./ <u>50 boxes film-clippings of</u>
old advertising film-copies in Czech
language, without price, without worth,
<u>unsalable</u>, used for learning purpose only,
total weight about 140 kg netto

'protector'. She told him what the case concerned – the sending of the apparatus to her husband. He asked: 'Is he Aryan?' She went: 'Natürlich.' And he gave her the approval. She left but collapsed at the Castle Stairs. The apparatus then went by ship on the Elbe."[1]

The narration is undoubtedly based on the real course of events and is supported by the correspondence of Alfred Popp. In addition, it well illustrates Dodalová's disposition. A surviving list testifies that the shipment was indeed quite sizeable.[2] Dodalová smartly summed up the shipped IRE-film archive as "50 boxes of film outtakes, old film commercials in their Czech version, unsalable, demonstrative, made to design the motion, approximate weight 140 kg, priceless".[3]

Dodalová also applied for approval to travel to the United States upon the invitation of Robert A. Kissack from the University of Minnesota, but it was already impossible to leave the Protectorate.[4] Probably thanks to the

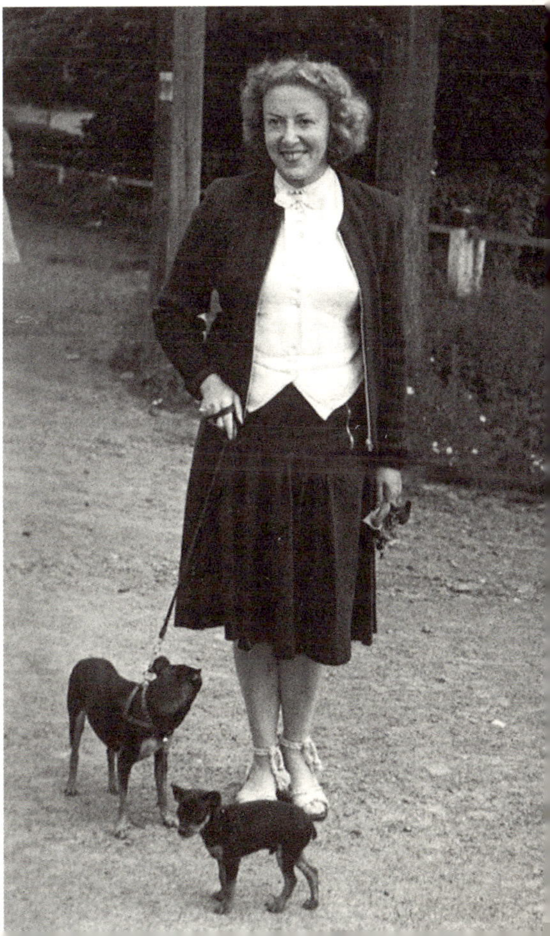

Undated photograph of Irena Dodalová.

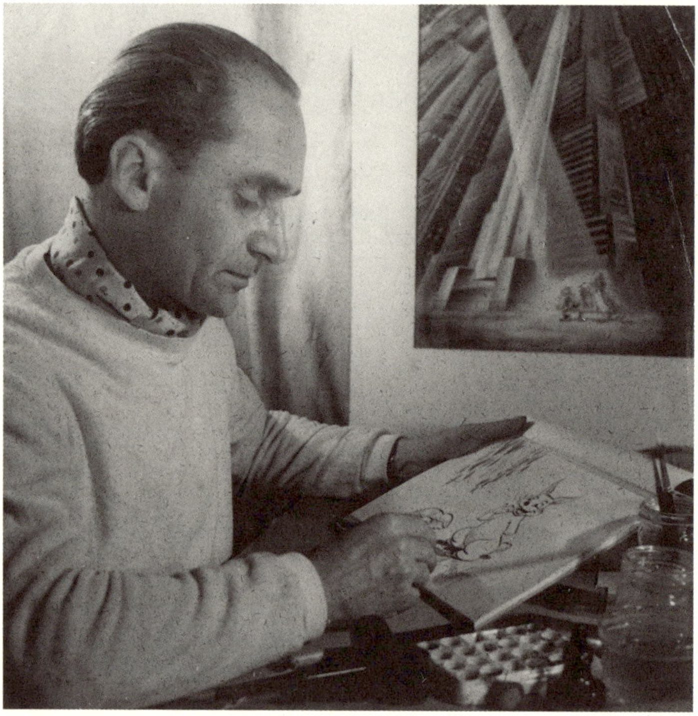

Karel Dodal in the United States in the early 1940s.

intercession of the film producer Miloš Havel, she found work in the photographic studio of Arno Pařík who was employing Jews from mixed marriages.[5] She first stayed in a Zbraslav hotel and later commuted to Prague from the Zbraslav villa. Outside Prague, she established new social contacts, taught a neighbourhood boy German, befriended a little girl from the villa who still remembers the charming lady and the distinctive clothes she wore, she gardened (as is documented by a period photograph), and even found a female companion there who took in her dog when Irena, as all Jews, was forbidden to keep pets. The Zbraslav period closed with her 1942 imprisonment during the Nazi campaign following the assassination of the Reischprotektor Heydrich and with her being transported to Theresienstadt (see the next chapter).

In summer of the same year, the deserted Zbraslav apartment was occupied by two German women with several children. They partly kept and partly discarded the furnishings of the previous owners. The IRE-film archive ended up in a laundry room where it served to stoke the fire and boil the kettle.[6] The written documents and photographs which Dodalová cherished the most were, luckily, safe with Karel Dodal in the United States.

Dodal's beginnings in North America can at least in general features be captured thanks to research carried out by the Rockefeller Archive Center in the early 1990s[7] and the documents and memories of his one-time, sixteen-year younger friend, Richard Pavlicek.[8]

Dodal spent his first months in the States in the company of Otto Rádl. This drama adviser to the Prague branch of Paramount, screenwriter and, from 1937, London correspondent of the *People's Papers* (Lidové noviny) who became interested in cartoon film already before the war, most probably interpreted and translated for Dodal in the beginning of his journey and helped him become acquainted with the unfamiliar milieu. The two jointly sought work in animated film, preferably in a scientific or university institution. Their future was discussed at the School of Fine Arts at Yale University in February 1939. The head of the local department, Professor Allardyce Nicoll, wrote to John Marshall, a significant representative of the Rockefeller Foundation, asking him to help find employment for the two exiles. Marshall's first response was slightly embarrassed, but the favourable reception of their films eventually made him recommend the two to the Visual Educational Service of the University of Minnesota. Karel Dodal stressed during the negotiations that he was expecting more financial means from his wife in Prague and owned the professional technology to produce 35mm films.[9]

In February 1940, Dodal wrote to the composer Jaroslav Ježek about his work at the university as follows:

"I am working here on a film along with ten draughtsmen. It is a scientific film, but right now I am doing sketches for another picture about Paul Bunyan. That's something like our Krakonoš.[10] But Krakonoš is a serious old buddy, whereas this man is only busy with Canadian jokes. And what jokes! Anyway, as soon as I finish this scientific film, it will be Paul Bunyan's turn."[11]

By mentioning the scientific title, Dodal most probably meant his work on the *Iron Ore Film* (Film o železné rudě), which he gained upon his arrival at the university where he was employed as an animator with the meagre monthly wage of 100 dollars. He apparently also received other assignments in the department, as can be seen from the animated sequences in the instructional picture *The Teeth of Your Own* (Tvůj vlastní chrup; year of production not given).[12] His main project was the animated *Paul Bunyan*, based on the screenplay by Otto Rádl. The works were headed by Robert A. Kissack and the crew, such as the draughtsmen, phasists and colourists, consisted of the university students. The ten-minute title was filmed on colour material and it was widely publicized in the local press. It is known from the correspondence that Dodal unexpectedly left the university sometime in autumn 1940 – i.e., in the midst of shooting. When he returned in early 1941, the university management solved where to get students for finishing the film in the next term and at the same time viewed the Czech filmmaker's conduct as, at least, violating the established customs. In addition, the grant from the Rockefeller Foundation was to expire that year.

This must have been the period when Dodal travelled with Richard Pavlicek to Chicago and New York to seek new advertising commissions for animated films; we know about the journey from the latter's correspondence.[13] The family of the accountant Joseph Pavlicek, who had moved to the United States in 1907, took Dodal in shortly after his arrival in Saint Paul in Minnesota. Their twenty-two year old son Richard then became Dodal's interpreter at the university and occasional driver. The trip, unfortunately, did not work out well. During the screening of Dodal's cartoons, filmed back in Prague, for the representatives of the Brick Manufacturers Association, held in one of the prestigious hotels in downtown New York, the incorrectly connected projector caused a short circuit and the venture turned into a debacle.

When Dodal gave up finishing the university film, Vee Quital Pearson – the head of the team – became one of its draughtswomen. They, however, did not manage to complete the picture without the main author and no shots of the animated takes were tracked down.[14]

As it follows from the available documents, the university was merely a temporary place of activity to Dodal for he still hoped for a donation from Czechoslovak exile institutions to make his authorial film. He also unsuccessfully applied for work at Disney's. The repeated intercession of John Marshall probably helped him to the position of trick cameraman for aircraft

Minneapolis Sunday Tribune and STAR JOURNAL

MARCH 22, 1942

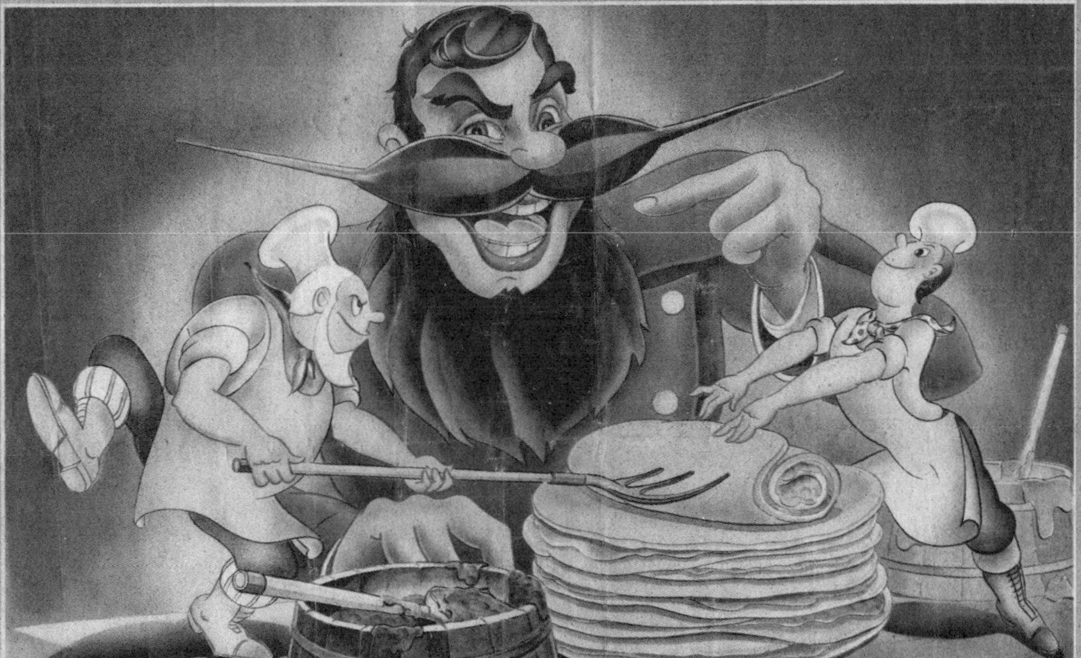

Giant Paul Bunyan—in the University of Minnesota's animated cartoon—wolfs down stacks of giant flapjacks.

PAUL BUNYAN

'U' ANIMATED CARTOON TELLS STORY OF MINNESOTA'S GIANT LUMBERJACK

Paul Bunyan, mythical giant of Minnesota's boom-day lumber camps, felled whole forests with one sweep of a saw. Tall tales about him have long been told in the Northwest. Now they're being put on the screen by a University of Minnesota artist, a Czech refugee named Karel Dodal. His 10-minute animated cartoon will show how tough, [illegible] Paul met Babe, the Great Blue Ox, in the Winter of the Blue Snow (when it was so cold that words froze in air, noisily thawing out the next Fourth of July). It will show the marvelous efficiency of Paul's logging camps, where, in almost one motion, lumberjacks jumped into shirts, pants and boots, washed their faces, ate, grabbed their axes and ran to work. These are highlights of the Bunyan legend, as drawn by artist Dodal.

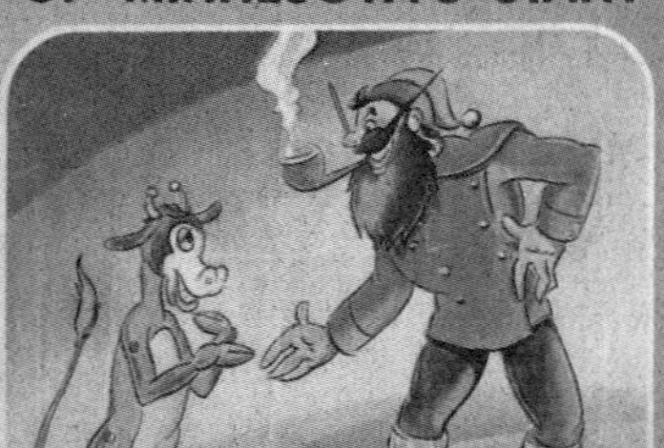

1 Paul meets Babe, who measured 42 axe handles and a plug of chewing tobacco between the eyes.

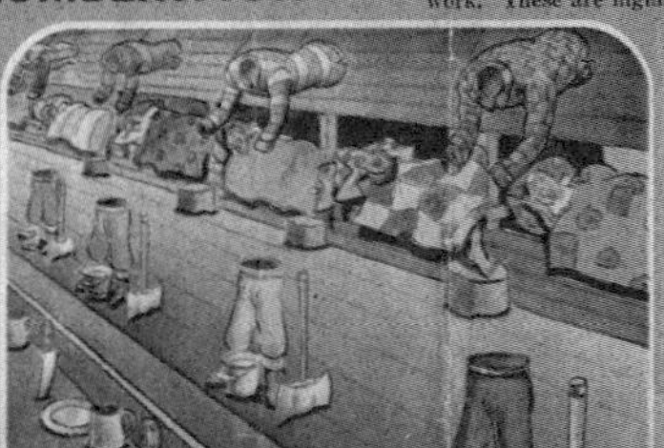

2 Paul's lumberjacks jump from bed into their clothes. They logged No. Dakota clean in a winter.

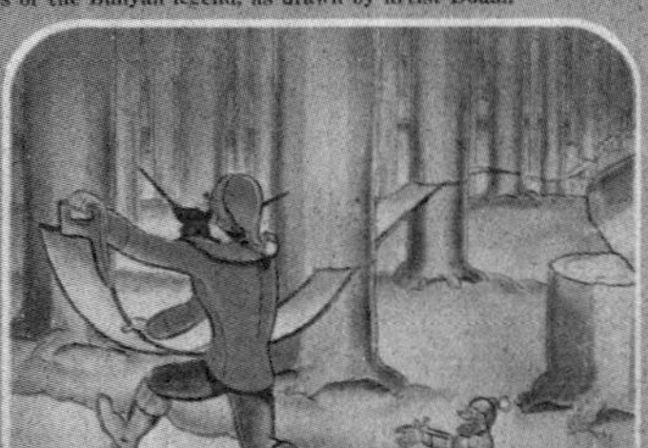

3 By himself, Paul could cut down a forest. He used mammoth pine trees to pick his teeth.

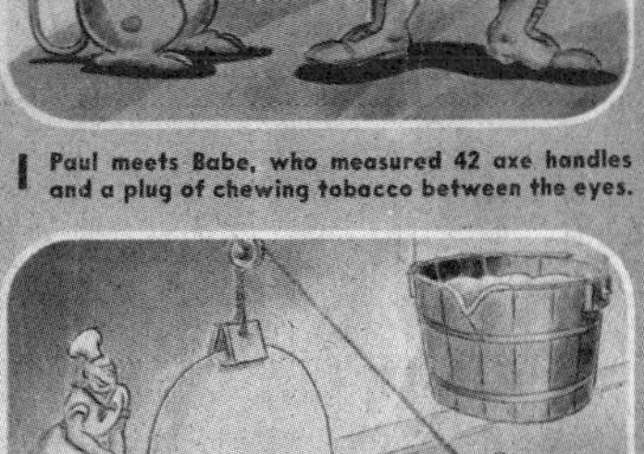

4 It took two cooks to flip over one of Paul's jumbo flapjacks. His appetite was enormous.

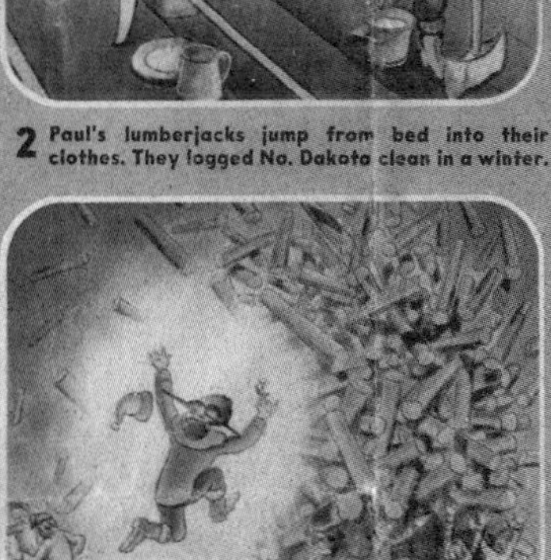

5 Accidentally sneezing, Paul broke up a monster log jam that had stumped his best lumberjacks.

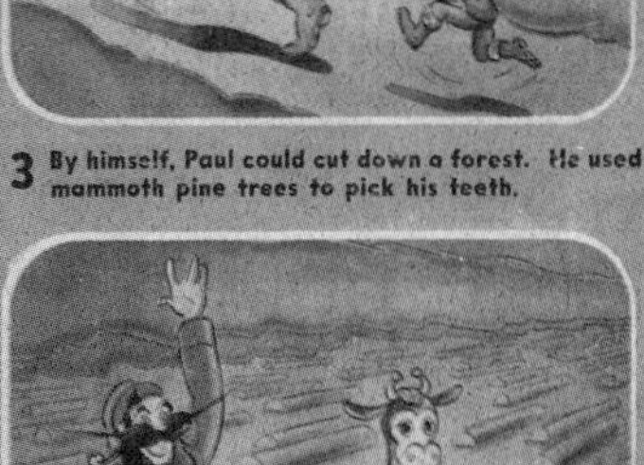

6 When the logs went down the river in the spring, Paul and Babe went with them.

TURN THE PAGE TO SEE HOW THE UNIVERSITY'S 'PAUL BUNYAN' FILM IS MADE

Paul Bunyan (Continued)

Here's How the Paul Bunyan Film Is Made

Creator of the University of Minnesota version of Paul Bunyan is Karel Dodal, talented Czech. When the university's visual education department got a Rockefeller foundation grant to make the Bunyan animated color cartoon, he was picked to do the work.

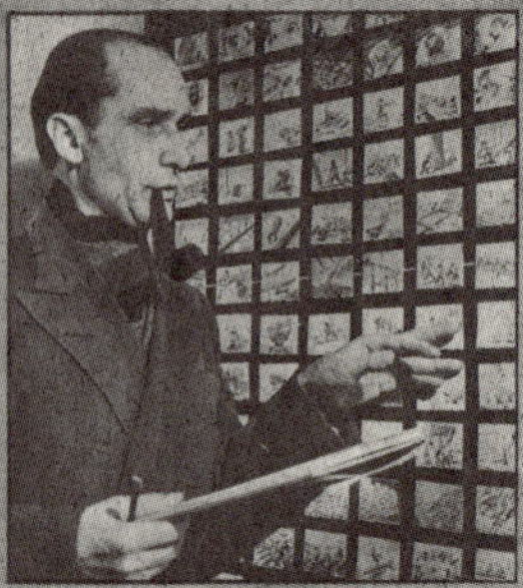

These sketches were drawn by Dodal (shown) after long research and story conferences with department heads. They indicate the cartoon's plot and guide Dodal and his assistants in working out details of the film.

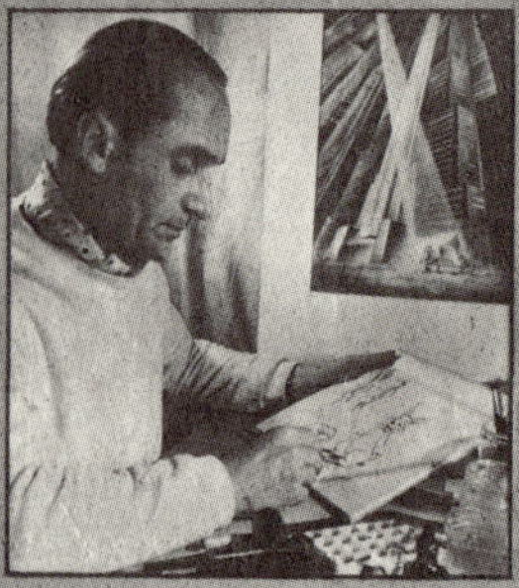

Dodal himself draws only master sketches. NYA assistants, as many as 24 workers at a time, draw the many pictures needed for in-between action. They are learning to animate government cartoons for soldiers' training.

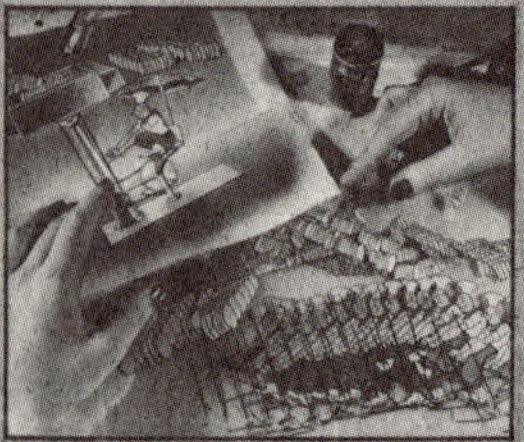

This is in-between action: each drawing carries action ahead a trifle. Flashed one after the other, they give the impression of motion. Twenty-four complete pictures are needed for one second's time on the screen.

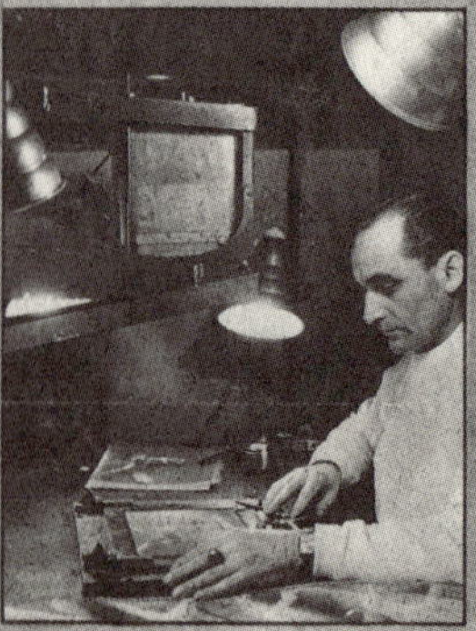

Each picture, some 15,600 altogether for the 10-minute movie, is photographed separately, and each consists of as many as five transparent sheetings, one over the other, each containing a part of the scene.

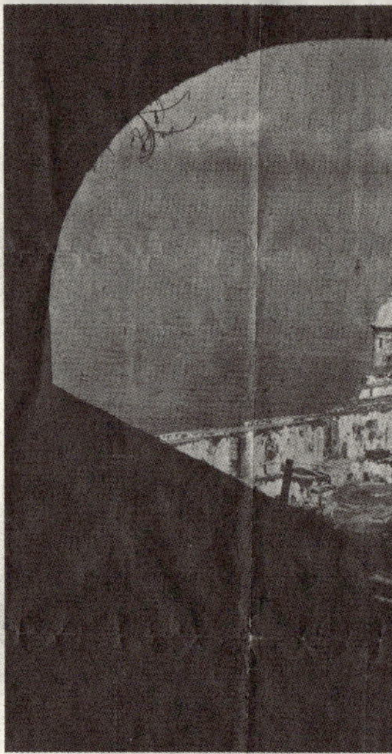

A YANK STANDS GUARD IN PUERTO RICO FORT

Guarding the approaches to the Panama canal are American soldiers in the Caribbean. This sentry is silhouetted in an archway of the ancient Fort San Cristobal at San Juan, Puerto Rico.

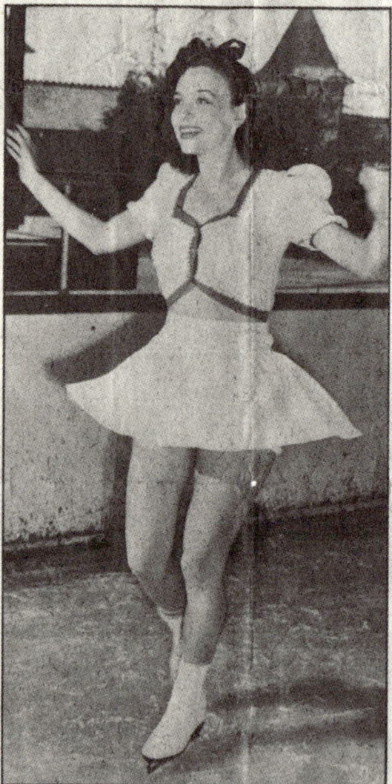

'AMERICA'S BEST-BUILT GIRL'

"Best-built girl in America," according to famous magazine illustrator John LaGatta, is young Hollywood actress Renee Hall, shown cutting a curve or two on the ice. Since Renee, a former New York model, joined the film colony, RKO Radio, her studio, has started calling her "the perfect curve girl."

instructional films. Richard Pavlicek stated that he was employed in the Secorski Helicopter in Rochester and then in the Department of Instructional Film of the Bell Aircraft Corporation in Buffalo where he, among other things, developed moving models and diagrams for Norman Mathews's title *Flying the P-39* (1939). Towards the end of the war, the recommendation of the Rockefeller Foundation helped him get a place at the Department of Educational Films with the American Film Center.

According to Dodal's letter to Ježek, the filmmaker tried to find an intercession for his wife's US visa. "She's such a great girl, and although I have very influential friends here, I haven't found the right way of getting her here. If you know about something helpful, I'd reward you gratefully."[15] The right way eventually was not found and Dodal reunited with his wife in New York only after the war.

1 Letter of H. Voldánová to the author of this book, 4 October 2000. Personal Fund of Irena Dodalová.

2 The inventory of the shipped items was attached to the letter of the forwarding company Karel Risinger nást. B. B. Černík, 1 July 1939. The National Archives, Police Headquarters 1931–1940, D 707/6, box 5364, Dodal.

3 Ibid.

4 Letter of R. A. Kissack to I. Dodalová, 18 April 1939. Personal Fund of Irena Dodalová.

5 Dodalová's neighbours at Zbraslav thought she was at that time working in the Barrandov studios. See the author's interview with K. Krčilová at Zbraslav of 11 October 2004. The National Film Archive, Collection of Sound Documents, No. 1004. Although there are no available documents proving Dodalová's Barrandov activity, her work in the studio of A. Pařík was confirmed by photographer J. Skála during several phone conversations (26 February 2006).

6 Interviews with K. Krčilová (see Note 5) and R. Vodičková (30 November 2005). The National Film Archive, Collection of Sound Documents, No. 1067.

7 The results of the archive research, initiated by V. Konečný, are deposited in the Personal Fund of Irena Dodalová.

8 R. J. Pavlicek (born 13 March 1916, St. Paul, Minnesota), an architecture graduate from the Institute of Design. At the time of his first encounter with Dodal, he had studied at St Paul School of Art, a New Bauhaus, in Chicago. He was Dodal's colleague at the University of Minnesota between 1938 and 1941 and later, till 1946, worked in the Training Film Preparation Unit of the Army Air Force. The 2012 correspondence with Mr Pavlicek, mediated by his care person N. F. DeMars, is deposited in the Personal Fund of Irena Dodalová. Pavlicek provided the National Film Archive with five of Dodal's hand-written letters from the early 1940s, some newspaper clippings and two 35mm film rolls with Dodal's photographs published in papers and magazines on the subject of President T. G. Masaryk and the Czechoslovak army. Employing the snaps, made for the Sokol association, was forestalled by the war events.

9 Letter of A. Nicoll to J. Marshall, 22 February 1939. Personal Fund of Irena Dodalová.

10 A mythical mountain spirit who protects the Giant Mountains (Krkonoše) against greedy treasure hunters, poachers and other light-fingered villains.

11 Letter of K. Dodal to J. Ježek, 19 February 1940. The Czech Museum of Music, Prague, Correspondence of Jaroslav Ježek, p. 224, Inv. No. 70.

12 For more on this film, visit http://www.ebooksread.com/authors-eng/elizabeth-armstrong-mrs-reed/the-educational-screen-volume-23-24-hci/page-39-the-educational-screen-volume-23-24-hci.shtml [quote of 28 December 2012].

13 Letter of R. Pavlicek to the author of the present book, 6 June 2012. Personal Fund of Irena Dodalová.

14 R. D. McHattie, *My Comic Mom!! Golden Age Artist Vee Quintal Pearson!!!* Minneapolis: Zyxalon Press, 2012.

15 See Note 11.

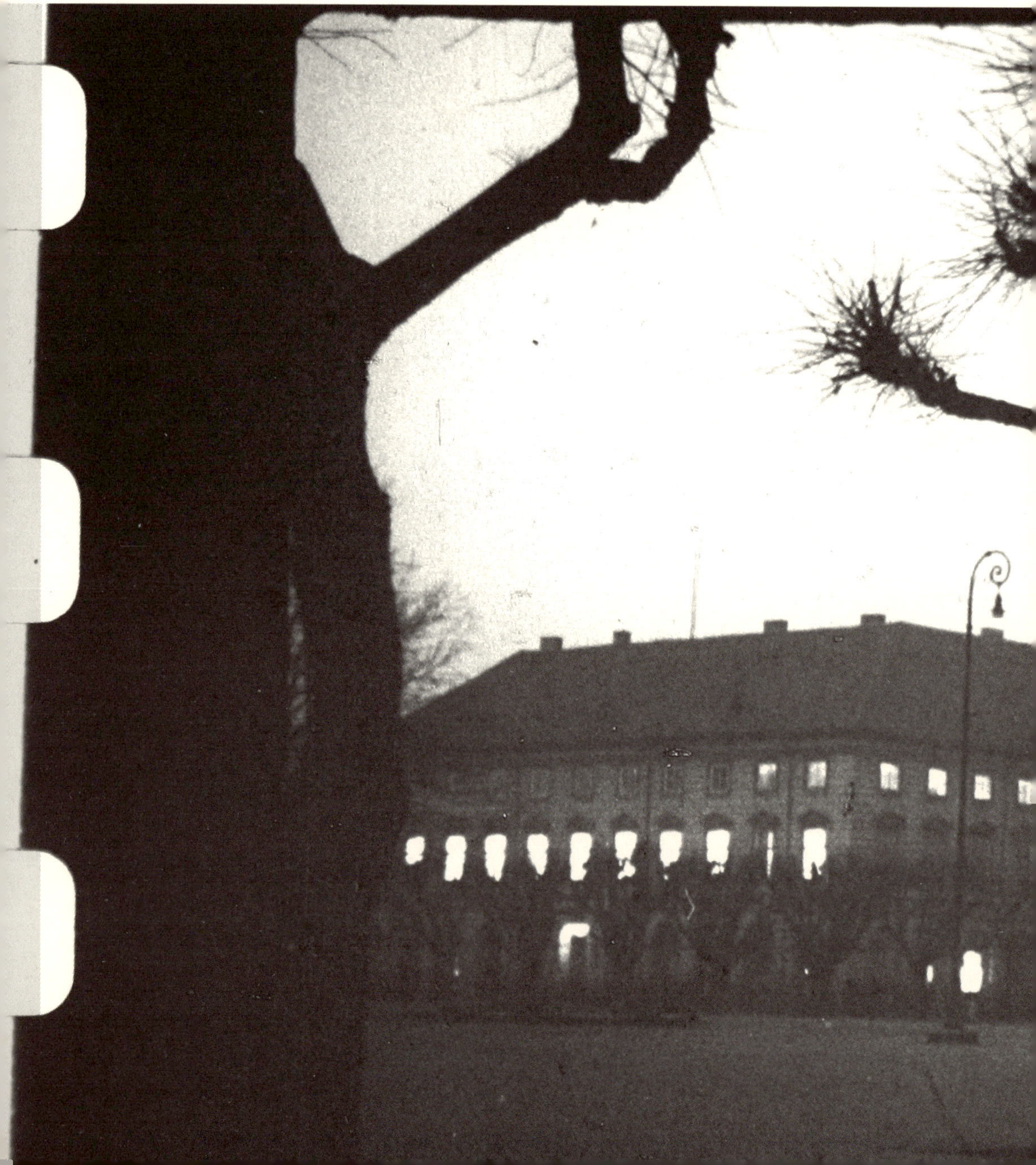

The Theresienstadt Years of Irena Dodalová and the Story of the Stolen Outtakes

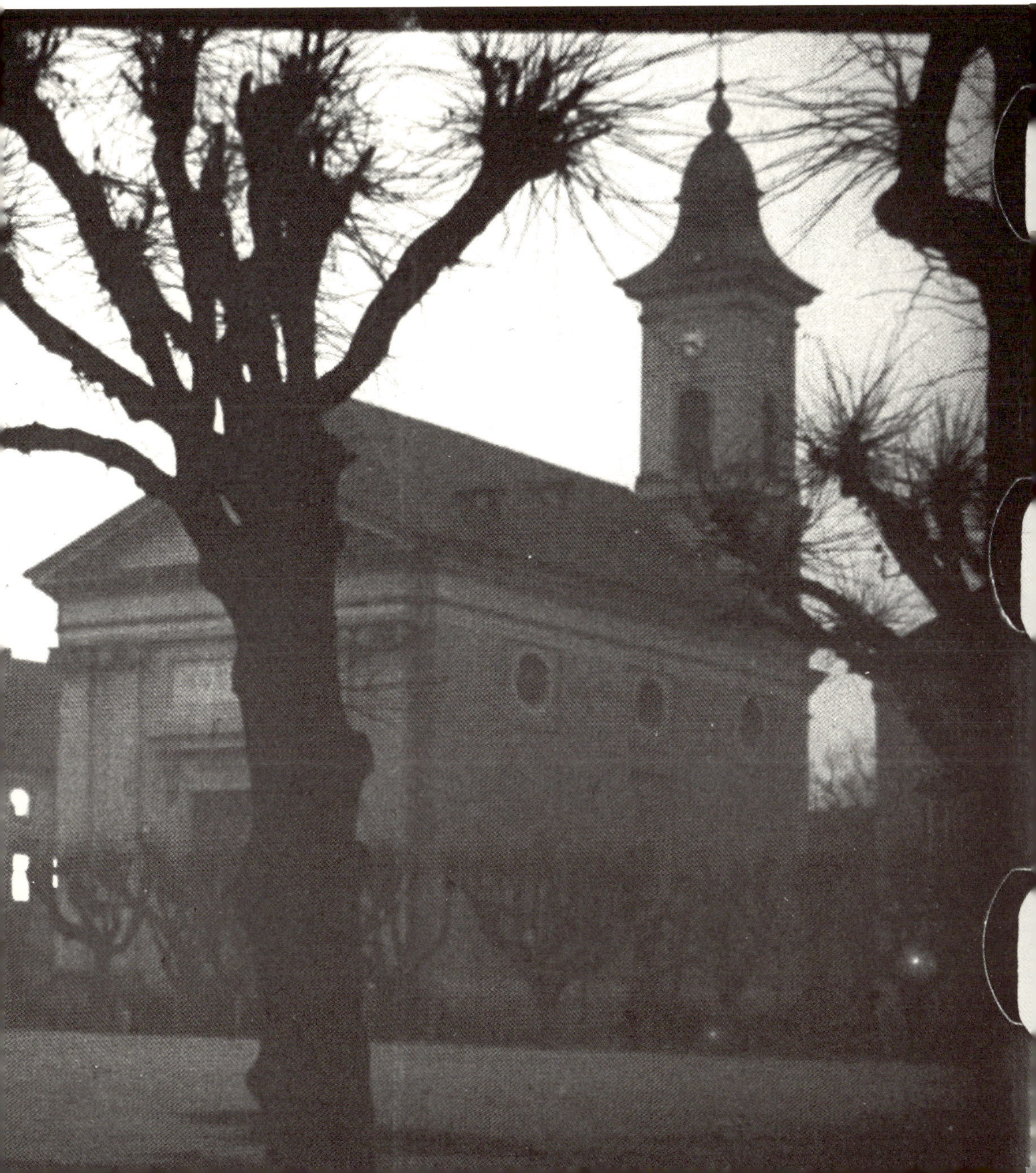

When Irena Dodalová moved to Zbraslav in the late 1930s and began working in Pařík's photographic studio, she cut herself off her former colleagues[1] and the Prague milieu, and many actually thought that she had gone abroad with her husband. This opinion prevailed among both film professionals and historians even during the post-war period – since those who knew about her several-year imprisonment in the Theresienstadt ghetto kept silent about it.

In the 1970s, the name of Dodalová as a Theresienstadt theatre director was remembered in a book by Eva Šormová.[2] In the 1980s, the hitherto unknown chapter of Dodalová's participation in the late-1942 ghetto filming[3] was opened by the Dutch historian Karel Margry. Starting from the memories of eyewitnesses, he judged her rather negatively, as the ambitious wife of a filmmaker who overrated her capabilities. Such an opinion could easily be disproved with regard to Dodalová's pre-war work in animation which neither the eyewitnesses nor Margry knew – but the issue of her activities in the ghetto could not be bypassed. The surprising identification of the 1942 film outtakes, then, raises even more questions which require answers.[4]

Copies of the *1942 Theresienstadt* outtakes. 4/ The sheep herd was transferred to Theresienstadt from Lidice.

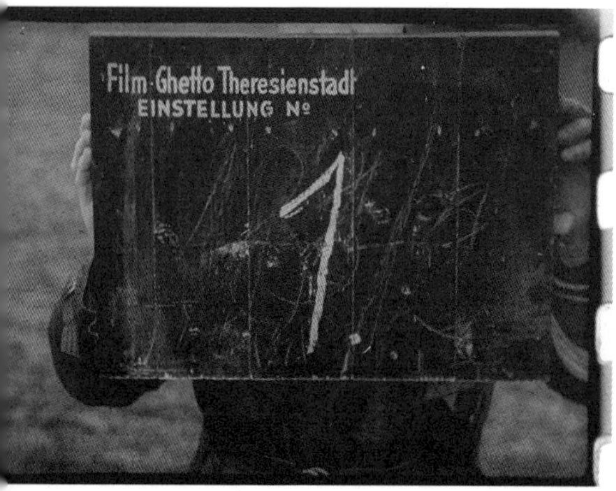

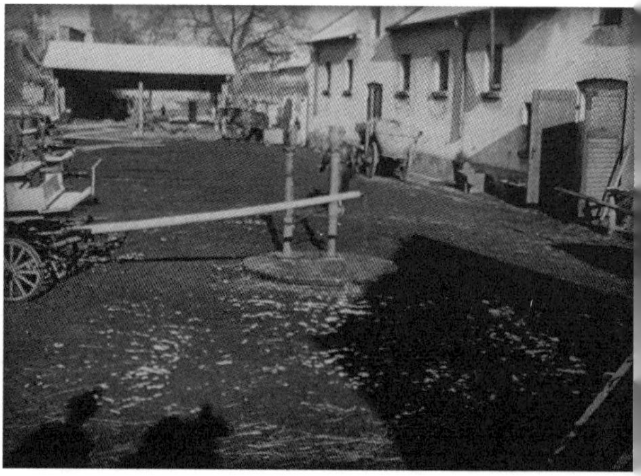

By the end of 1941, the Nazis had turned the late 18th-century fortress and garrison of Terezín into a reception and transit camp for Jews from the Protectorate *en route* to Auschwitz and Treblinka. The city, which all the inhabitants had to abandon, moreover served as the so-called *altergetto* for German and Austrian Jews, and also Jews being transported from other European countries passed through it. Part of the Theresienstadt complex was the Small Fortress used by the Nazis as a prison for Protectorate political inmates and a place of execution of the ghetto Jews. About 33 thousand people died in Theresienstadt between 1941 and 1945 and another almost 87 thousand were further sent to the annihilating camps in the East.

The 1942 film shooting in the ghetto is often associated with "Gerron's" propaganda film known as *The Führer Gives the Jews a City* (Der Führer schenkt dem Juden eine Stadt, Hitler daroval Židům město) whose title was, according to the surviving credits, *Theresienstadt* (Theresienstadt. Ein Dokumentarfilm aus dem jüdischen Siedlungsgebiet).[5]

But the ghetto actually inspired three titles between 1942 and 1945. In November 1942, a short documentary about it was made there under the

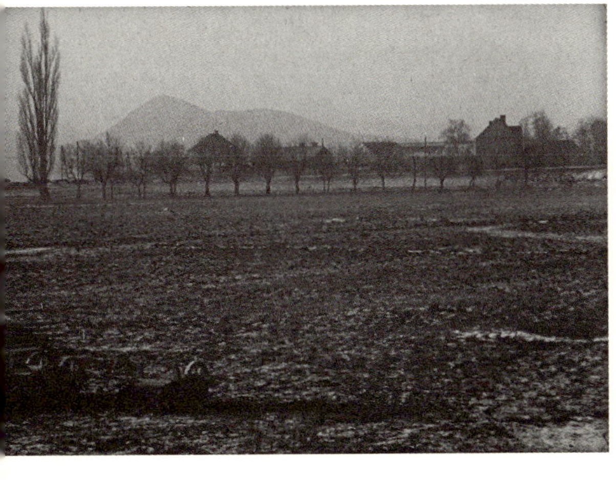

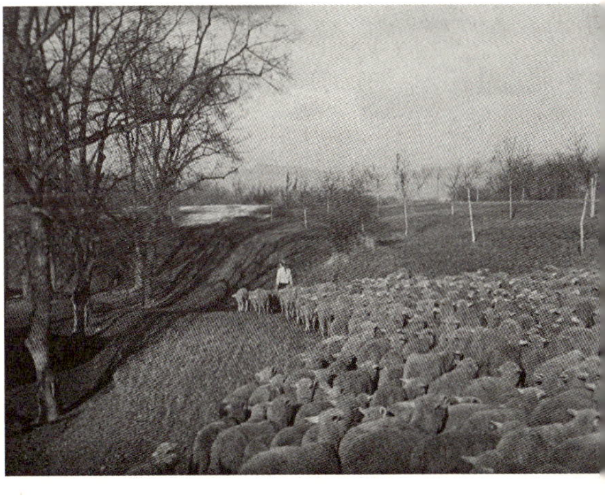

"conduct" of Irena Dodalová. The second title, a clip about the arrival of the Dutch Jews, dates to January 1944, and the works on the above-mentioned propaganda *Theresienstadt* lasted from autumn 1943 to March 1945. The takes from it are widely known from countless film compilations focusing on the ghetto and holocaust. Contrary to most Nazi film undertakings in other ghettos and concentration camps, the Theresienstadt headquarters ruled to not only engage the inmates as a crowd but also as members of film crews. The projects were on the outside shielded by personalities of considerable artistic renown, and Dodalová was selected as the first one; after all, no other professional filmmaker was available there at that time. The second project involved the well-known German theatre and film actor and director, Kurt Gerron. But it was clear that the shootings were in fact operated and "directed" by the superior institutions – the Prague and Berlin SS and the Theresienstadt commander's office. The three projects differed in many aspects. The 1942 film was shot by a group of German cameramen from the ranks of the SD and SS, i.e. the *Sicherheitsdients* as the Nazi secret police and the *Schutzstaffel* as the defence corps (the share of the imprisoned Czech Jews will be discussed

1/ and 2/ Takes filmed by Hanuš Král, featuring the transport forced to march from Bohušovice to Theresienstadt.

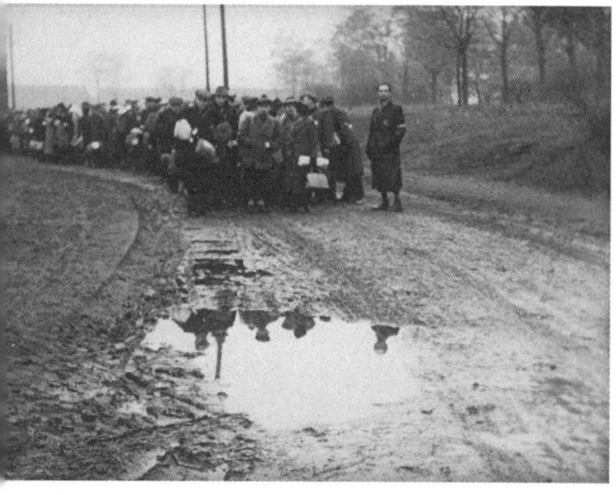

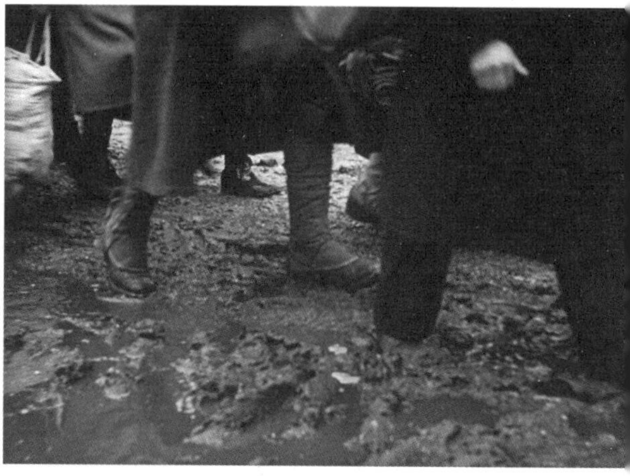

later), while the 1944 crew were Czechs from the Aktualita company. The first film was silent; the next ones already employed sound. The first two pictures had short-film footage; the third propaganda and "representative" work was full-length. The major part of the given material is missing. The 1942 film is today believed lost and only about one hundred short outtakes (with a total footage of four minutes)[6] and a sequence from the 16mm documentary about its making (eight minutes long)[7] survived. The clip from January 1944 was destroyed immediately after its developing[8] and only one third of the original footage of *Theresienstadt* is available.

But let us return to the beginning of Dodalová's Protectorate story. Switching addresses naturally could not save her from being transported since her name was already on the list of Zbraslav Jewish residents. She, however, arrived at the ghetto very early – upon an eager denouncement of her having taken a bus, an activity already strictly prohibited to Jews.[9] First detained and interrogated in the Prague Pankrác and Střešovice prisons and sentenced to death, she was eventually sent to Theresienstadt along with her mother in June 1942. "It's a miracle I escaped when Heydrich was assassinated and

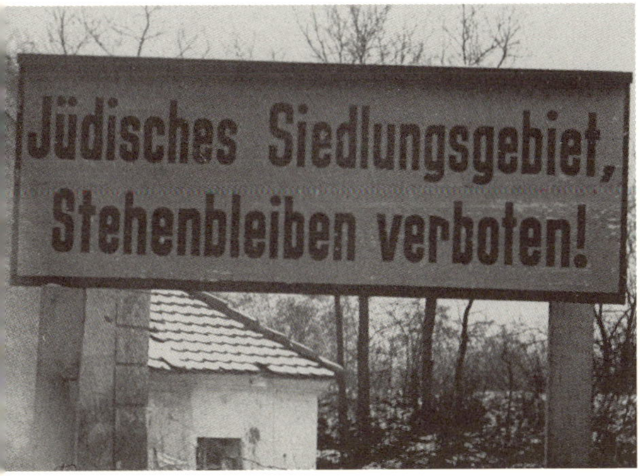

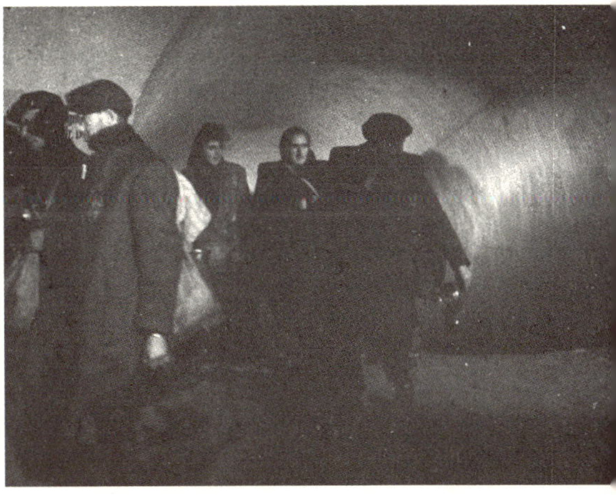

all intellectuals were shot. Everyone in Prague thinks me dead," was how she described her situation to her husband in a letter of April 1945.[10] Other circumstances of her imprisonment and the forces behind the "miracle" are unknown; there are merely some details pointing at potential explanations.[11]

Theresienstadt was indeed a merciless place. The Council of Jewish Elders struggled hard to cope with the chaos, starvation and outbreaks of diseases in the over-populated city with more than 50 thousand people squashed in. In April 1945, Dodalová wrote to her husband about how she had felt at that time: "I took pains to figure out why this ordeal had come upon me. I always did my best to be a good person. And yet, there was no answer no matter how hard I tried." But she, too, had to conform to the rules and do the assigned works; she farmed and later became a forewoman of the female mica-processing group. One of the few ways out of the despair was the cultural activities organized by the leisure-time camp section. Soon after her arrival, Irena thus began adapting the performance of Villon's ballads, introduced by E. F. Burian in his Prague D34 theatre before the war as *Paris Plays First Fiddle* (Paříž hraje prim!). The rehearsals were nonetheless halted

1/ to 4/ Takes from the so-called *Schleissung*, where all personal belongings were subjected to being searched.

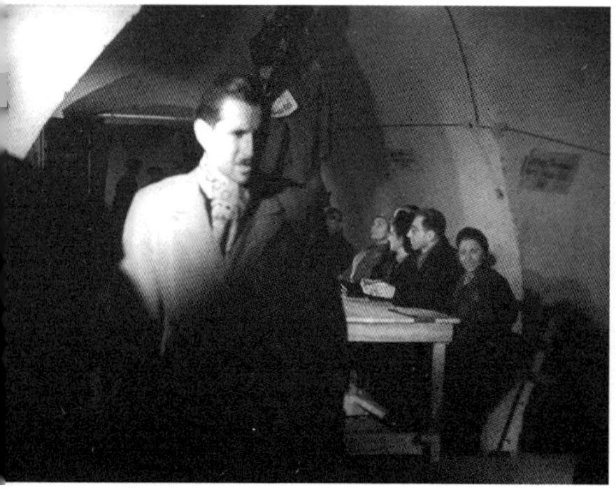

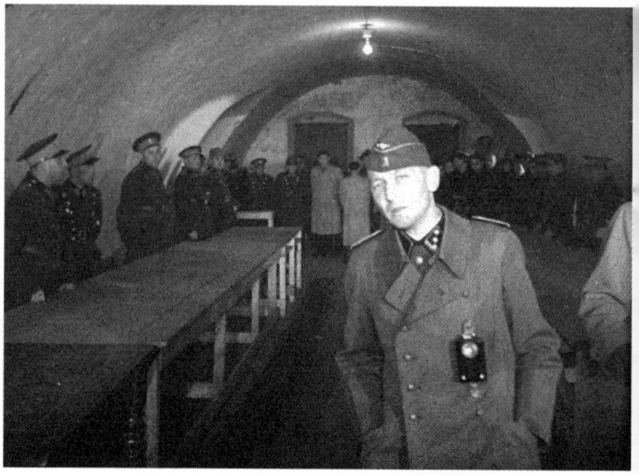

in late August or early September as Irena was ordered to write the screenplay about the ghetto.

The preparations for the film are documented by the surviving synopsis *Ghetto Theresienstadt:. A Brief Outline of a Film Report* (Rohentwurf einer Filmoreportage, Stručný návrh filmové reportáže).[12] Margry later wrote: "If [the screenplay was] used, the film would have given a true picture of the severe and godforsaken life in the ghetto: the trapped inmates; the extreme density of population; the utmost starvation and deprivation; the poorly equipped medical facilities; the misery of the old and ill; the frightening death rate; the despotic orders yelled; the abysmal fatigue from the work – it had it all. The script's undertow was so grim and the anticipation of downfall gushing from it so strong and heavy; nothing could ease the dreadful conditions in the ghetto; the imprisoned community was on the verge of collapsing. And although Theresienstadt was officially a terminal station, the script clearly betrayed the most nightmarish fear omnipresent in the ghetto life: being crammed onto a train heading east."[13]

The synopsis not only gave an unbelievable picture of the ghostly atmosphere in the ghetto but also was interesting from a filmmaking aspect, for it

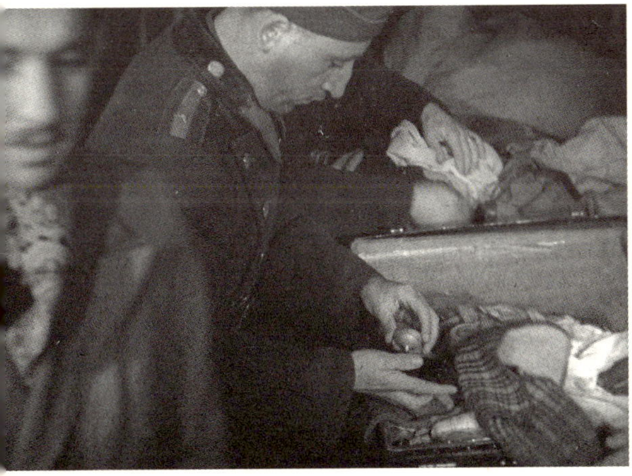

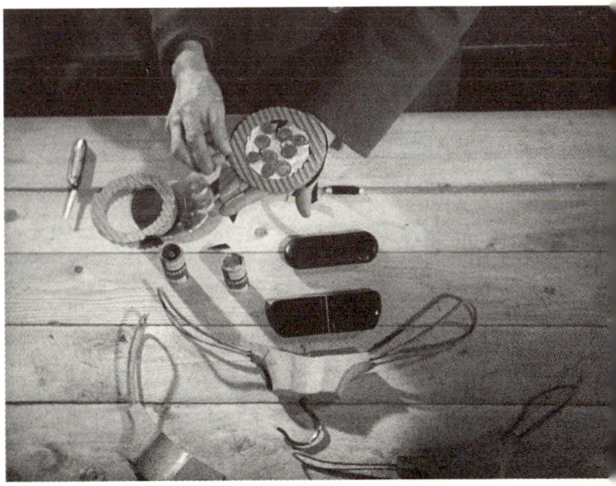

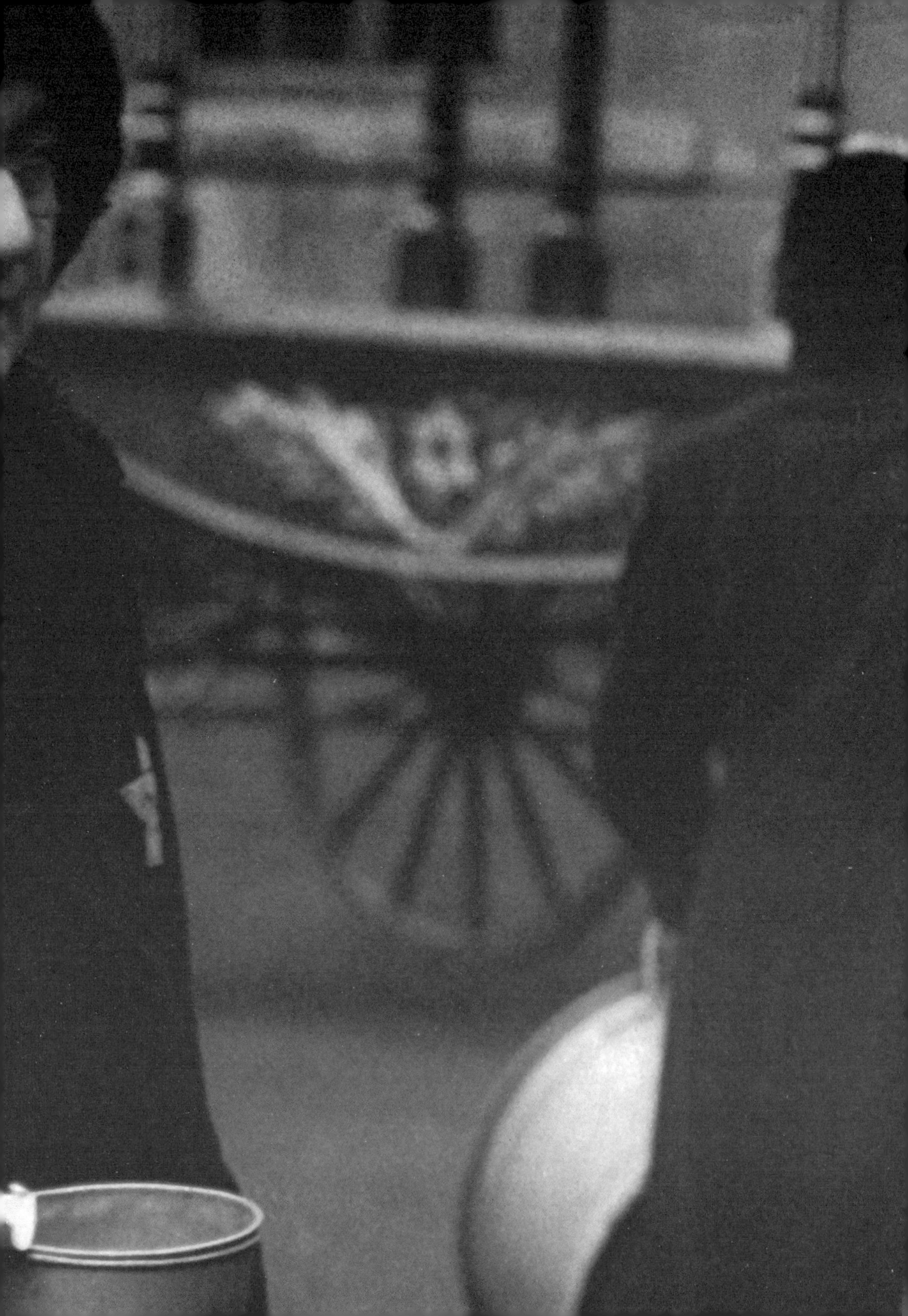

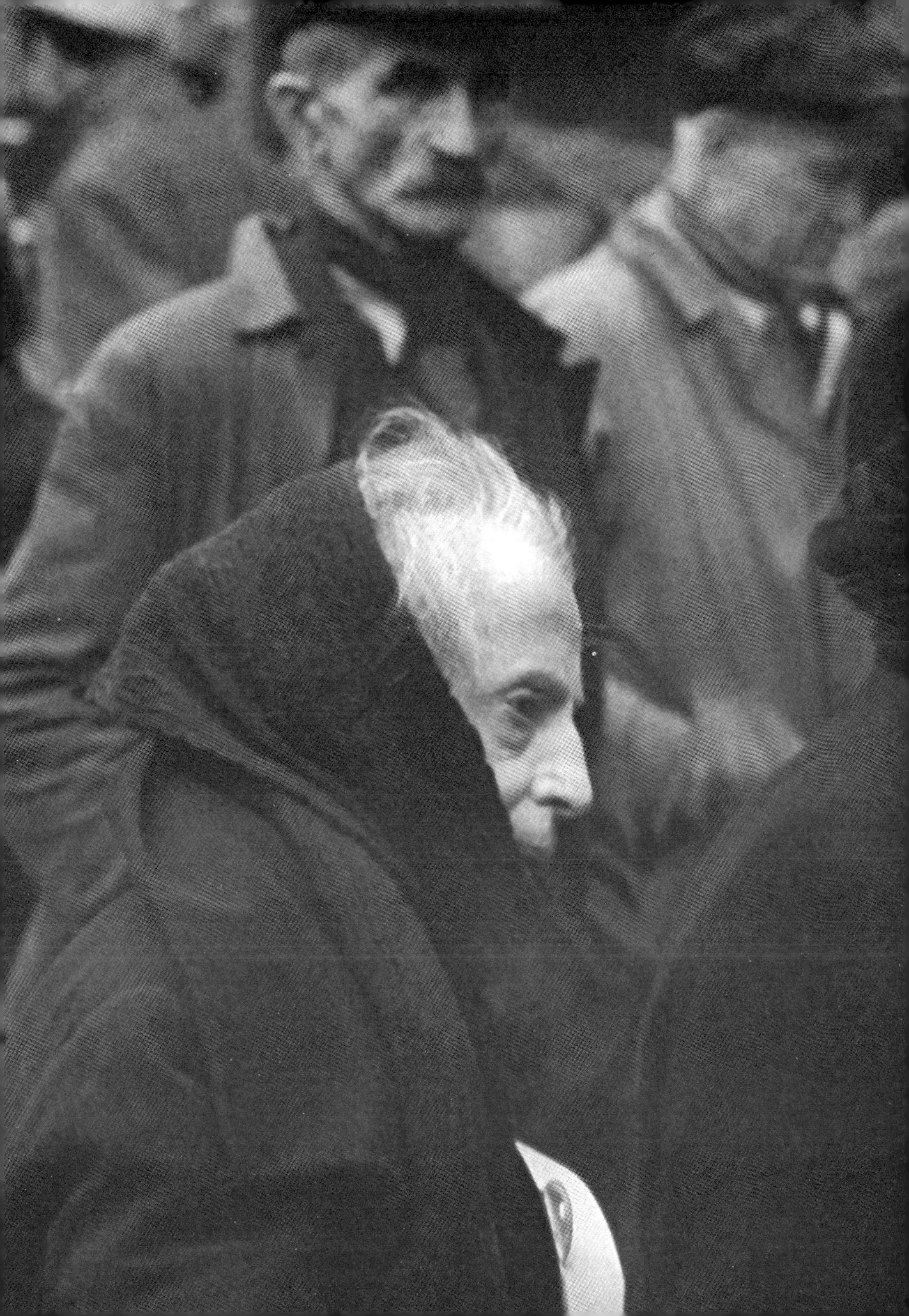

captured reality via montage and fast-cut metaphorical images and scenes. The closing overview of the Theresienstadt regular stats submitted to the commander's office by the local Council of Elders, then, was a sarcastic comment on the miserable ghetto conditions and was based on trick and simple animation. It thus comes as no surprise that Berlin dismissed the manifestly provocative material no matter the flawless and professional execution.

Margry thought that the author of the anonymous typescript was most probably "a young and German-speaking Czech skilled in film technology that had arrived at Theresienstadt with one of the first transports",[14] and Dodalová was apparently outside his focus for many reasons. Recent research nonetheless makes us assume that the lead in the synopsis was none other than this bi-lingual, forty-two-year old Prague filmmaker and experienced screenwriter well familiar with the tricks of the trade. The testimonies of the then-partaking crew seem to prove this. The letter which Dodalová wrote to her husband sometime in April 1945 reads: "The Himmler himself ordered a documentary film to be made of Terezín. Several of us were told to prepare scripts. They chose my script."[15]

1/ to 4/ From life in the Theresienstadt ghetto.

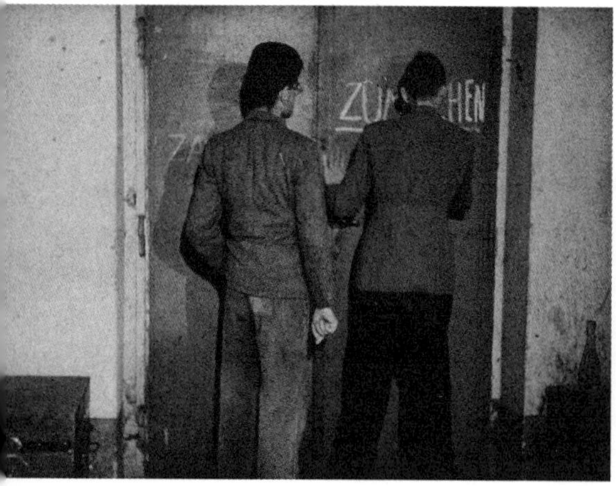

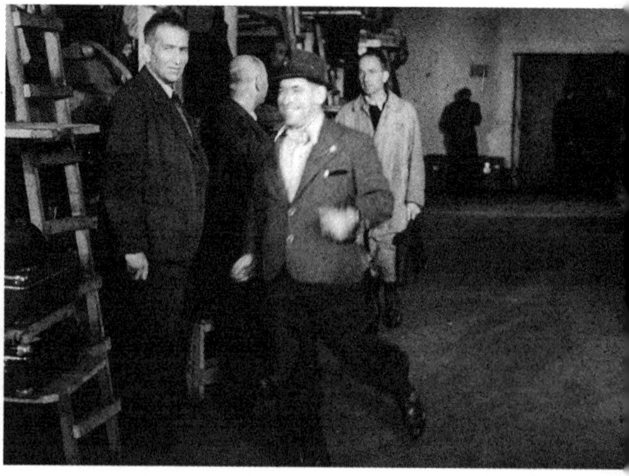

Hans Hofer, who participated in the filming, observed after many years in his "Belated Report" (Opožděná reportáž) that "The director Von Otto invited the Prague film director Irena Dodalová and officially ordered her to write a synopsis to the so-called culture film in eight days. Ms Dodalová designated a former assistant director and a young cameraman as her aids and, with them, the draft met the deadline and could be presented".[16] Dodalová as the author of the first documentary version of the script was also mentioned in the memoirs of another Theresienstadt survivor, the Viennese actor Eugen Preis.[17] The comparison of the archive documents allowed for the assumption that the two collaborators were an apprentice cameraman, Jindřich Weil, and Adolf Aussenberg, an engineering student with artistic talent as proved by his Theresienstadt stage designs.

The triad Dodalová–Weil–Aussenberg, however, did not develop the synopsis alone. An event of such significance for the ghetto life could not escape the attention of the Jewish Elder Jakob Edelstein and the Council of Elders. It remains unknown whether they dealt with the authors directly or through the drawing room, ordered to collaborate on the shooting by the commander's

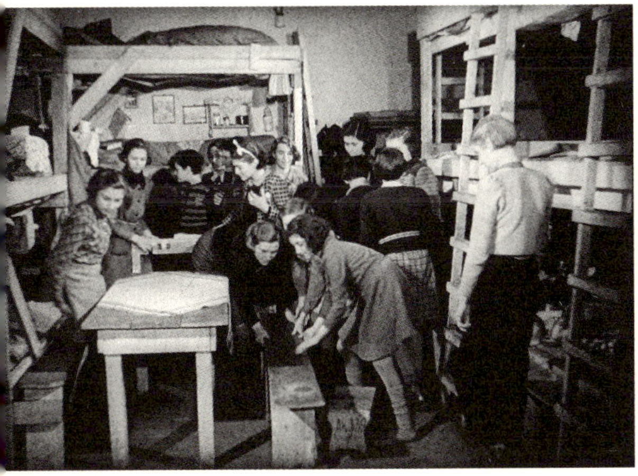

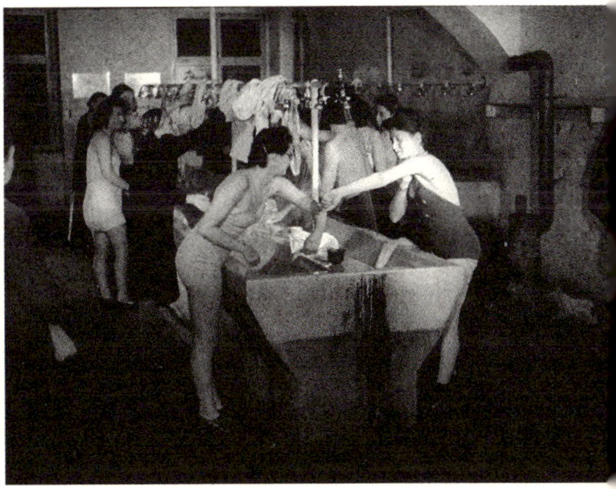

office. We believe that Dodalová from the very beginning worked with Petr Kien, who she had known from Prague when she had lectured at the film seminars and when the gifted young man had studied painting with Willi Novak. A member of the drawing room, he also undoubtedly provided her with the stat diagrams regularly produced by the Council of Elders for the head of the commander's office, Siegfried Seidl. It is worth noting that the discovered outtakes include a scene capturing Edelstein as he submitted one of these statements to the Theresienstadt commandant.

The drawing room fell under the technology department and its official task was to facilitate different art commissions for the Jewish self-government and the Theresienstadt commander's office and other SS units. Unofficially, it allowed its employees plus other gifted people such as architects, artists, designers, draughtsmen and the like to use the otherwise unavailable paper and drawing tools for capturing life in the ghetto. This was the only chance to visually document the conditions in which they were caught, no matter how risky it was.[18] Owning a camera, let alone a film camera, was a capital offence. The autumn 1942 filming nonetheless prompted the drawing room,

3/ Takes documenting that the filming was not only participated in by SS-men but also captive Jews.

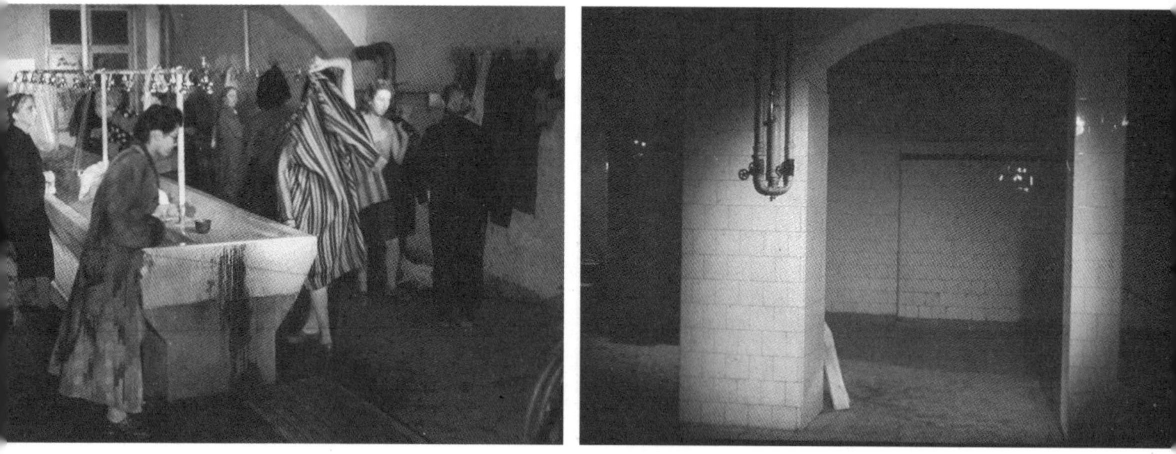

headed by the charismatic Bedřich Fritta, to an utterly new situation from which it could benefit.

The works on the film were managed by SS-Obersturmfürer Herbert Otto who, in the early 1940s, ruled a special commando unit in the Chełmno extermination camp and later had some special missions in Prague, Theresienstadt and Rhineland, but had absolutely no idea about filming.[19] However, the surviving takes from Prague, where he disputes with the architect František Zelenka, show that he apparently enjoyed the role of film director. Margry remembered him as an annoying, perverse person harassing women.[20] The camera crew consisted of members of the SS security units. All these circumstances suggest that the project was not a professional Reich production and the picture was instead designed to serve the internal purposes of the SS units commanded by Himmler.

The filming began in Prague and was naturally unassisted by the Theresienstadt prisoners. Information about the November 1942 arrival of the Nazi crew to the capital appeared in the record of the local Jewish Religious Community.[21] The surviving outtakes show that they worked at the Community, in the Old-New Synagogue and in front of the entrance to the Jewish Town Hall. One of

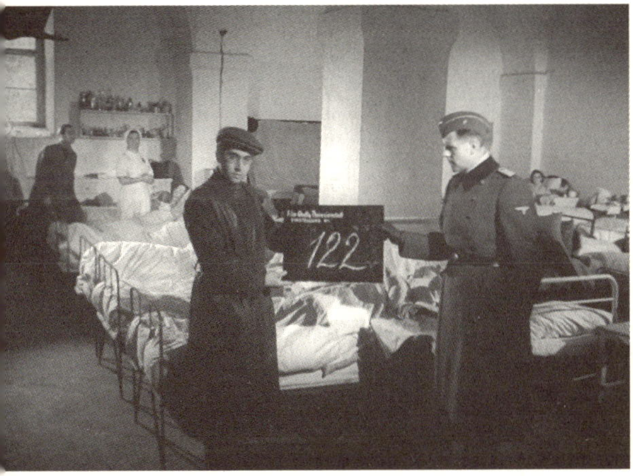

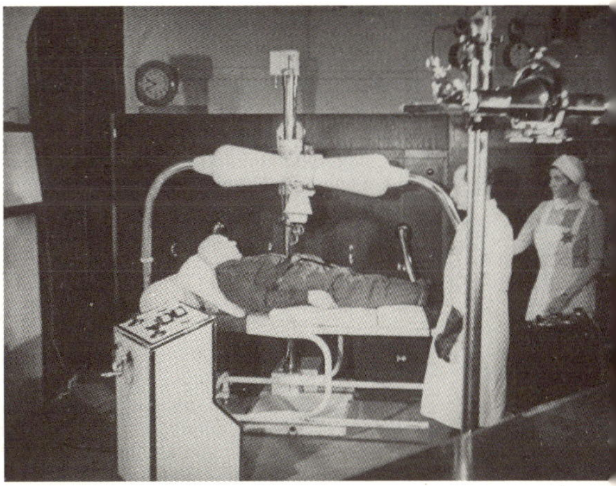

the "actors" was a young boy, Karel Roubíček, who much later said that they had sent him "from the Jewish Religious Community to be part of crowd at the *Zentralstelle* in [the Prague suburb of] Střešovice. I would again and again climb up and down the first-floor stairs in the spotlight with the other extras, accompanied by the chortling SS-men. And when I once stupidly gazed into a reflector, some Hauptsturmführer thought I was laughing, summoned me and asked: *'Kommst Dir wohl komisch vor...?'* And he slapped me across my face. I guess the cameraman was Hauptsturmführer Otto whom I later saw in Terezín where he would film us boys in the showers or would just wait there for the women's turn."[22]

As soon as the SS filmmakers finished in Prague, they switched to the ghetto, and the commander's office provided them with a crew of prisoners, mostly those from the drawing room. Dodalová, too, was ordered to partake and to coordinate the works as a head of production. Jews at that time were already completely excluded from all activities in the film industry and were even outlawed from going to cinema, and letting them professionally participate in the film was thus rather paradoxical.

3/ and 4/ The Theresienstadt outtakes both contain unofficial shots and takes intended for the planned propaganda film (the woman at the microscope is Doctor Gertruda Klepetářová-Adlerová).

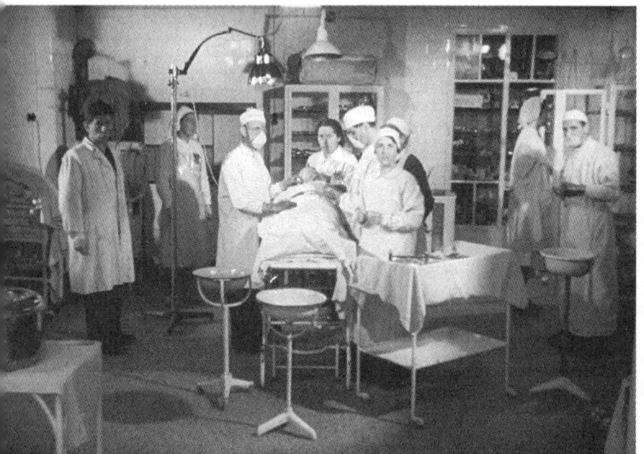

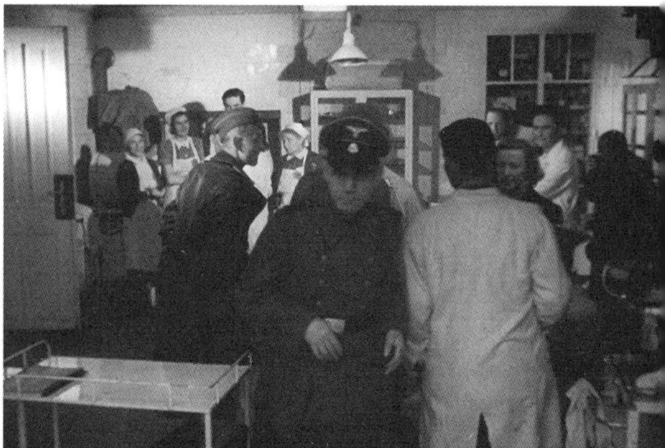

According to Hans Hofer, Herbert Otto ordered the emptying of one room in the so-called Hamburg barracks and labelled it "The Office of the Theresienstadt Film" and "Entry Strictly Prohibited" (*Kanzlei des Theresienstädter Films; Eintritt strengstens verboten*). Hofer also said that the atmosphere during the works was relatively calm although the overseeing SS-men punished even peccadillos physically.[24]

The filming took merely a few days and the group of SS-men then rushed out of the ghetto. The exposed material was most probably sent to some Prague film lab and then again returned to Theresienstadt for editing a service copy. This rather unusual post-production process, too, testifies to the special regime of the entire undertaking: a negative of a film made by the Wehrmacht propaganda (*Propaganda Kompanie*) would be sent directly to Berlin for further processing.

The picture of the today unknown title apparently remained unfinished and is believed lost. Hofer later described its story as follows: "Mr Holländer [...] and his wife are due to be transported. Holländer goes to the Jewish Community. We can see the Jewish Town Hall, the session of the Council of Elders and Holländer packing, then the way to the assembly point at the fairground

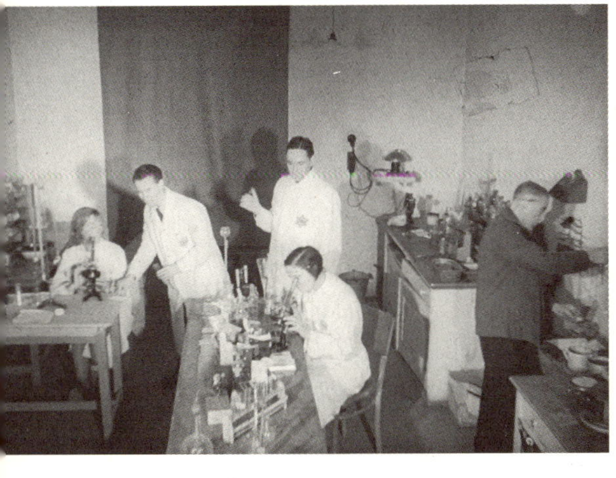

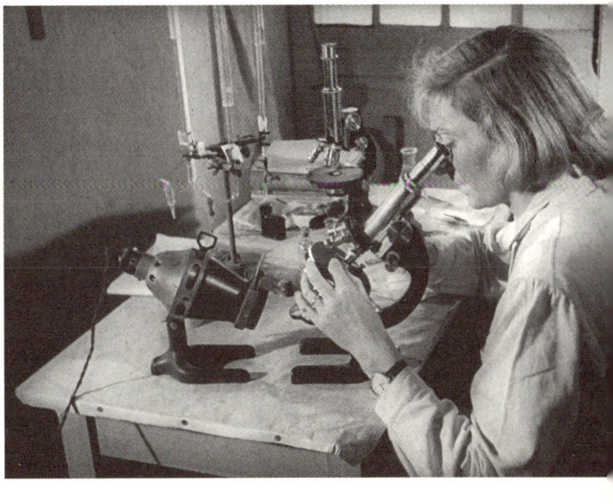

[before the Prague Trade Fair Palace], the three days in a barrack there, the food distribution, sleeping etc. Then there is boarding the train, the arrival at Bohušovice, the march to Theresienstadt, the arrival at the ghetto. – Holländer at the *Schleissung* [body search], the accommodation, the work assignment, working in a wood storehouse, on the way to get food, the cabaret entertainment, reposing to sleep – fadeout. Plus some takes of gloomy streets, filthy children's asylums etc. in between."[25]

Peter Schauer, who claimed to have watched the film after the war in Prague at Jindřich Brichta's while tracing his lost relatives, remembered that the last takes of the hopelessly overcrowded barracks with the three-storey bunk beds mercilessly evoked the forlorn and sinister atmosphere in the camp.[26] These testimonies prove that the title was discontinued and laid off – i.e. it did not receive credits and sound – mainly because it was utterly unfit for the propaganda purposes. More details about the fate of the service copy after its shipping to Berlin are unknown, but it still might be part of some archive or private collection.

Back in the filmmakers' presence in Theresienstadt – not all inmates were actually happy with it. The filming certainly brought either some distraction

1/ and 2/ Takes from a session of the Council of Jewish Elders. 3/ Obersturmführer Siegfried Seidl, the Theresienstandt camp commander. 4/ Jacob Edelstein, head of the Theresienstadt Council of Elders, reporting to the Commander's Office.

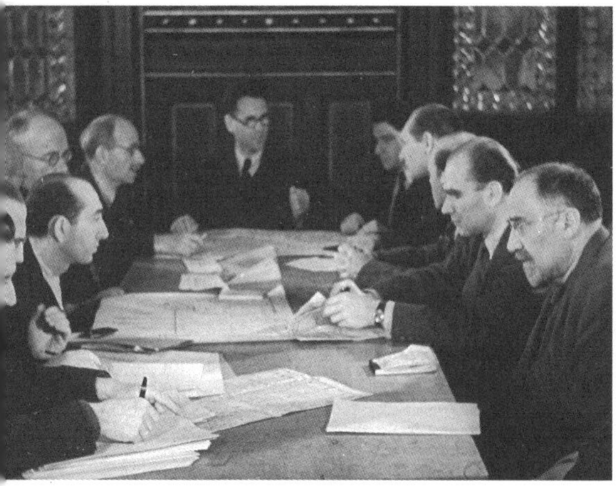

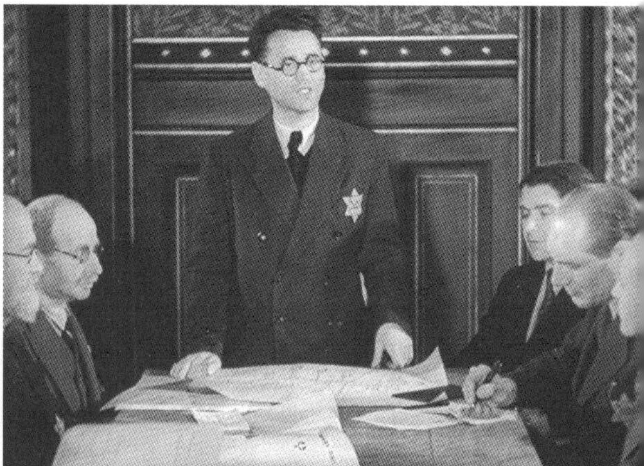

and/or surplus food supplies to some, but the majority was alarmed.[27] The single fact that the commander's office privileged a Jewish group to day-to-day contact with those in SD and SS uniforms understandably provoked suspicion of quislingism. The only source as to how the shooting actually went and how the Jewish part of the crew seized the opportunity for the sake of their better survival is the 1970s' testimony of its member, Hanuš Král, recorded for the Prague Jewish Museum. The attorney, photographer and then-ghetto cameraman, who also worked in the drawing room, witnessed that "the works were assigned to the Jewish prisoners Irena Dodalová, Jindřich Weil, Hanuš Král and others... The project was launched in summer 1942. The group agreed to undermine its designed purpose and, among other things, they decided to slow down its progress to the utmost. Irena Dodalová persuaded the Germans that the film required lighting from Barrandov studios and makeup stuff from Düsseldorf (from Co. Schminka). They were given everything."[28]

One of the remarkable aspects of Král's testimony is that they viewed themselves as a *group* waving its own strategy. In any case, the mere fact that the Theresienstadt commander's office dealt with the issue of importing make-up

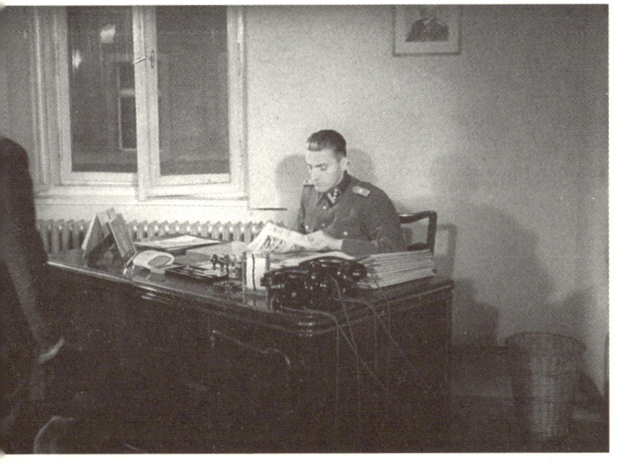

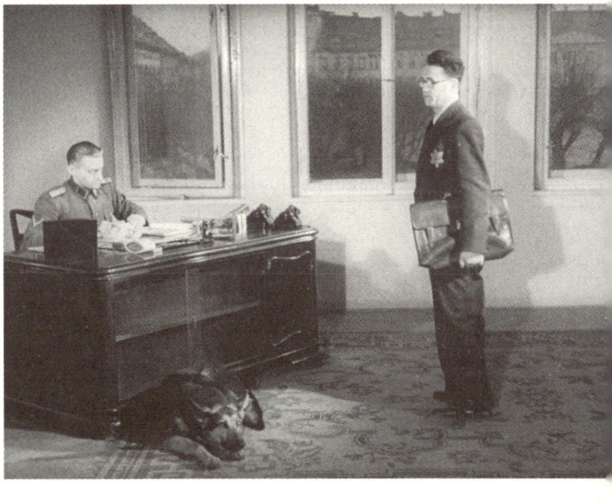

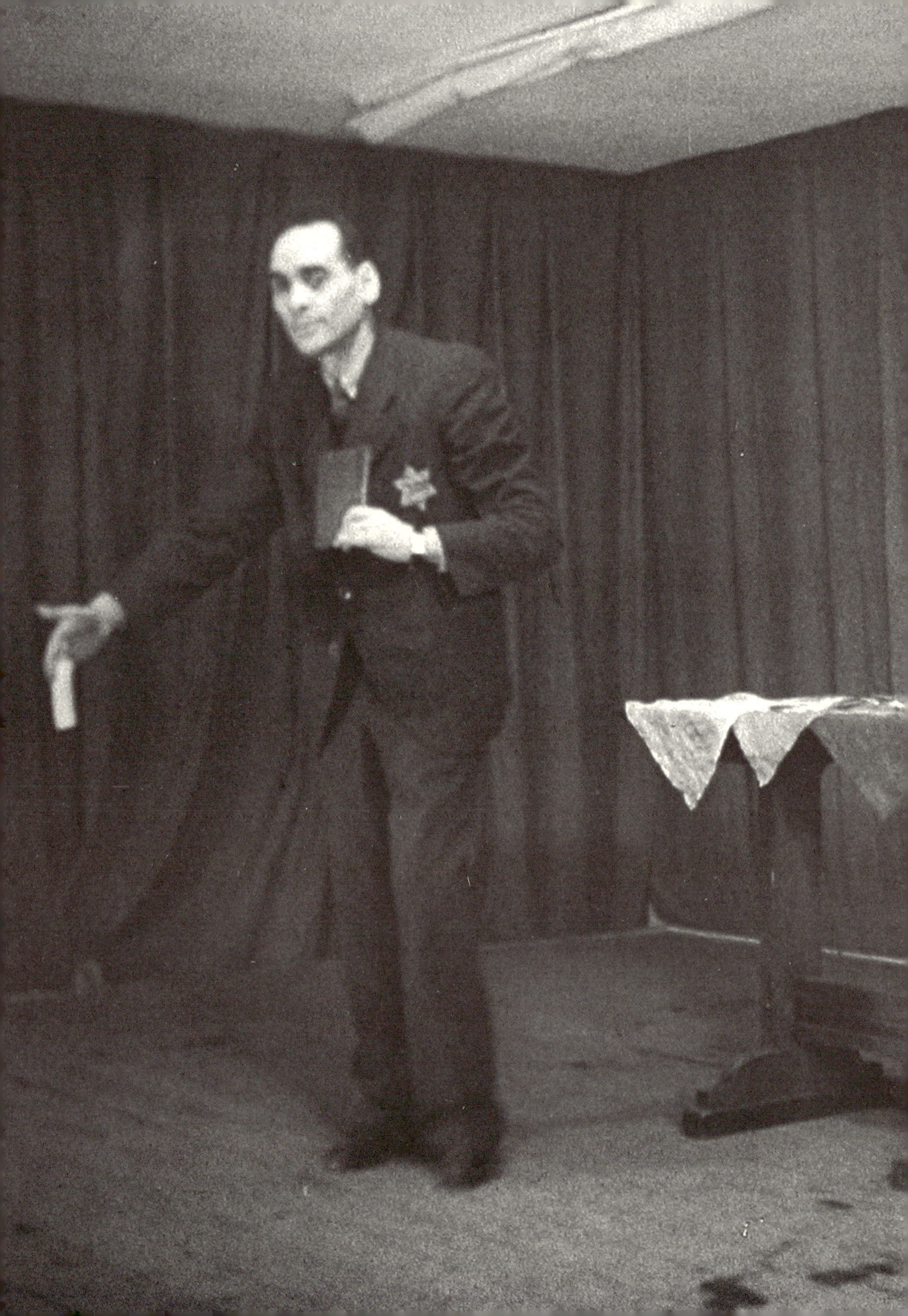

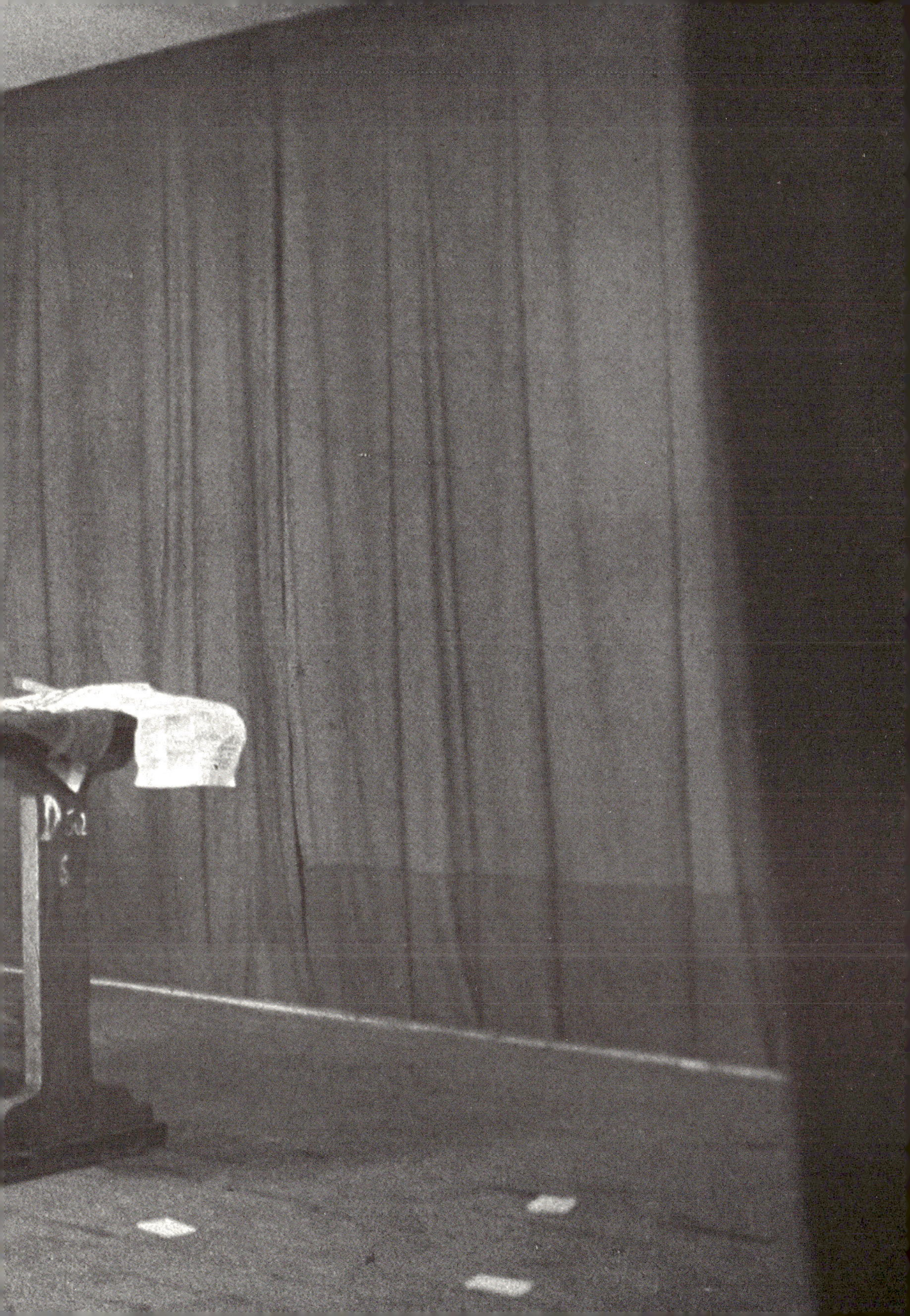

from Düsseldorf, moreover claimed by a Czech filmmaker, and moreover in June 1942 – i.e. at the outcome of the Battle of Stalingrad – well illustrates the irony of the situation. When the group could not hinder the filming any longer, they at least tried to influence it from behind the camera. (The surviving takes prove that the Propaganda Kompanie filmmakers used three 35mm cameras and one 16mm camera.) As Král added, "We tried to alter the contents based on the Nazi script as much as we could. The Germans, for example, required a *streicher* Jewish specimen, but the group would always take average Jewish types. One scene captured the arrival of a transport heading to Bohušovice. The group managed to shoot several people heavily struggling with their luggage and wading in mud. Another scene, made in the ghetto, included a background with the local hearse usually serving to transport bread, corpses and immobile people, and so on."[29]

The attorney's interpretation of the filming conditions with inmates having regular access to the camera seemed both unreal and hardly viable for technical reasons. It thus came as a great surprise to discover the given motifs in the newly identified 1942 outtakes from Theresienstadt, which proved him true.

1/ and 2/ The ghetto café was accessible upon production of an entrance ticket.
3/ The detail not only captured the daily menu but also the date of filming.
4/ Irena Dodalová holding some keys and the script.

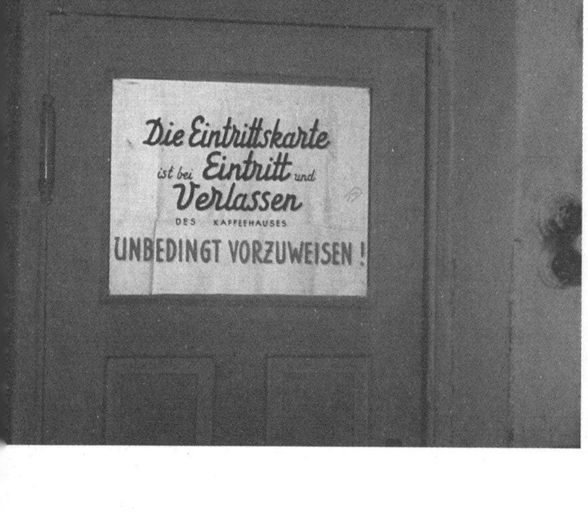

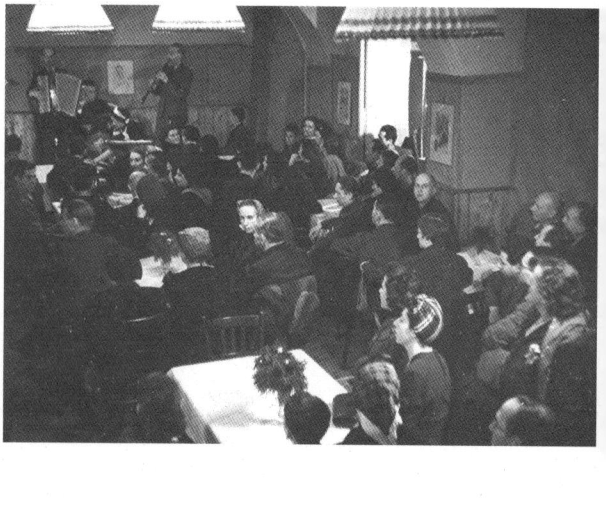

Král also noted that the group tried to hinder the deadline, i.e. the editing of the filmed material, under the pretext of Dodalová's illness.[30] A phone call from Berlin, however, ordered it to be finished immediately. "They were given this ultimate deadline of the next morning. Spending all night in the commander's office over the working copy, they managed to cut out and hide two frames from each important scene and to smuggle them out in film boxes. Irena Dodalová later passed them on in Switzerland, but no one knows who to. The film was never completed."[31]

This part of Král's text provided a new and essential piece of information – that despite the omnipresent surveillance and risk, the Jewish members of the crew in late 1942 indeed stole parts of the given film material from the SS and hid them in the depths of the ghetto! Král thus indirectly confirmed Dodalová's words about the seized shots: "I managed to dispatch many takes out from Terezín. They are now in a Prague archive.[32] I had to edit the film in the commander's office behind the locked door. It was more than 25 reels. I kept many scrolls in the ghetto, believing they were safe there. I could not take any with me – not even my notes. That would have meant my death."[33]

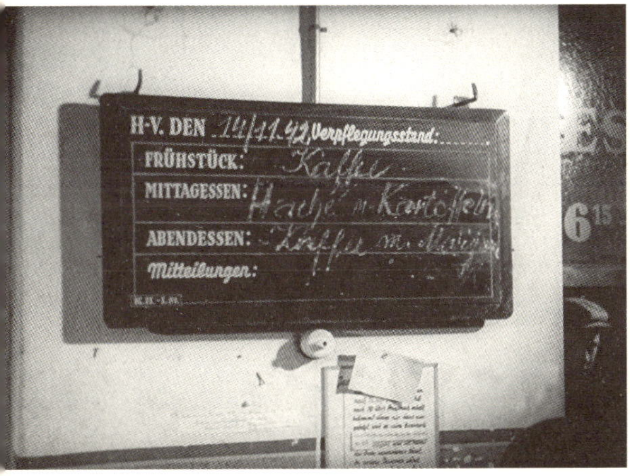

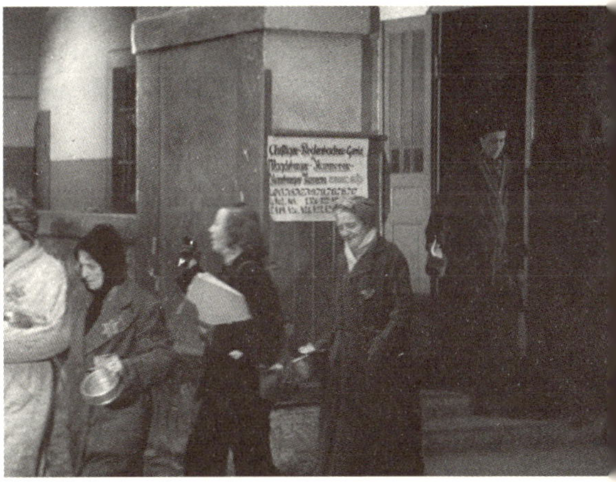

This quote from Dodalová's letter sent to her husband from Switzerland in April 1945 exemplifies the ways how she would usually utter on her holocaust experience. Conceived as a "remembrance", the given piece of writing must be judged from the perspective that she wrote it knowing that albeit it was the end of the war, the camp was still in German hands, which also might be a sound reason to carefully tiptoe around the hidden film materials. This part of the letter has long been perceived as spurious for no one assumed that things like this would ever have been possible under the Theresienstadt conditions.

Many lucky coincidences steered us from Král's testimony to the actual outtakes, although we have as yet been unable to pinpoint their journey from the ghetto to Switzerland and then back to Prague. We have merely tracked them to the late 1960s when an anonymous person arriving from Switzerland brought a box with the film and handed it over to Artur Radvanský at the Jewish Community. Radvanský then asked two young filmmakers, Zeno Dostál and Lubor Dohnal, to take care of the film, and they had the 35mm inflammable scroll copied in the Barrandov Film Laboratories. The person tending to the material, composed of numerous pasted fragments, in the following years was

1/ The man in the background is the head of the drawing room, Bedřich Fritta.
2/ to 4/ Takes of works documented for the Nazi propaganda film.

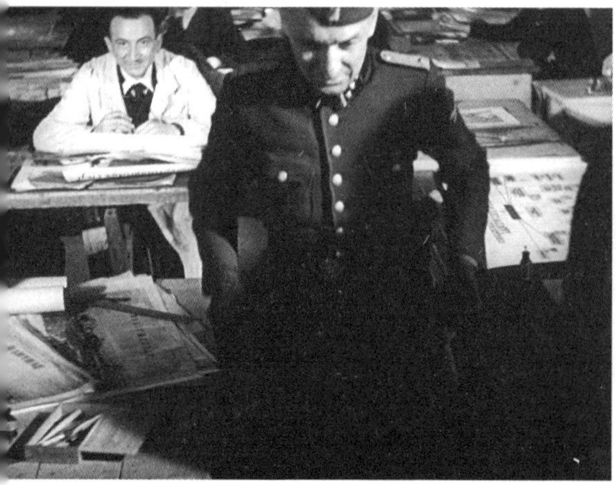

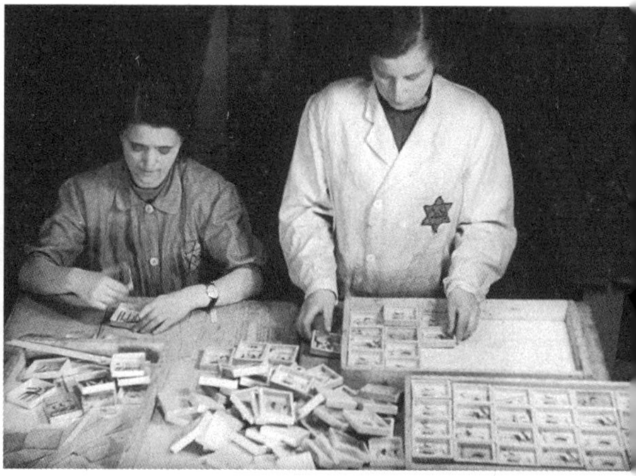

Lubor Dohnal who had it copied in the Munich Irra labs in the early 1990s for he thought that it was related to the Gerron's filming.[34]

When our research in 2004 identified the material as the *Theresienstadt* outtakes mentioned by Hanuš Král and Irena Dodalová, Lubor Dohnal donated it to the National Film Archive in Prague. It is today part of the Archive's collections and filed as *Theresienstadt 1942 (Film Outtakes*; Terezín 1942 [Filmové výstřižky]).

But there is yet another, and unedited, record of the 1942 Theresienstadt undertaking, entitled *Theresienstadt 1942 (Dreharbeiten).*[35] It was shot on 16mm film and was identified years ago in Poland by Karel Margry as he researched the local archives. It apparently was not a commonplace amateur "family picture". Several eyewitnesses agreed that it was an unofficial account made by S-Hauptsturmführer Olaf Sigismund who personally documented the course of the shooting on his private camera. The comparison of the two materials revealed that the "anonymous" author filmed the same scenes as did the cameramen with their 35mm camera and that many takes were moreover complementary.

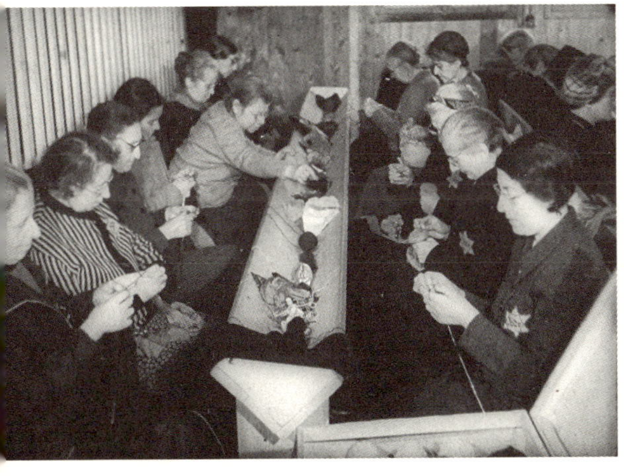

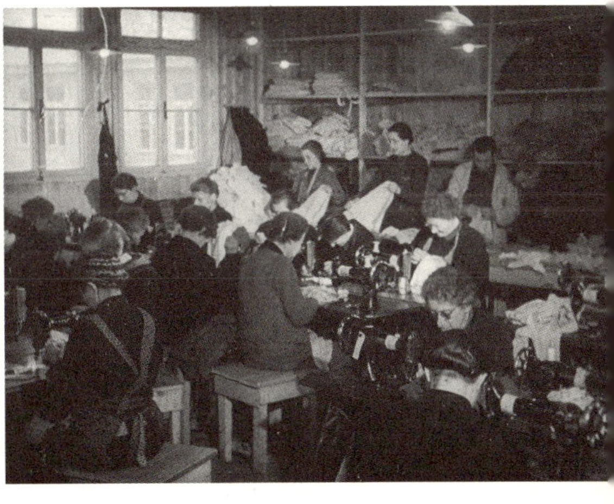

Sigismund's film is twelve sequences on several subjects, and while his material is more or less continuous which allows for its smooth screening, the individual outtakes from the National Film Archive pasted together into a single reel are so short that their projection is almost impossible. Their unique value lies in the fact that they represent about a hundred authentic motifs from the Theresienstadt ghetto.

The above-mentioned surviving film material can be divided to three groups. The first one is the sequences which were most probably created for the planned film. The second group is, like the Sigismund work, shots from the filming while many of them were certainly made without the awareness of the SS-men. The third group is takes which can be interpreted as a message of the trapped Jews to the people outside the ghetto, such as the pictures of the transport from Bohušovice to Theresienstadt and the detail of the old people against the hearse, described by Hanuš Král. But there are many other frames to be read as a message from hell. The 122 take from a hospital room is a freezing comment on the film's situation in itself: the two people jointly holding the clapboard here are a Jewish inmate and an SS-man. The building

While the takes 1/ and 3/ were apparently made for the propaganda film, the takes 2/ and 4/ clearly captured unofficial life in the ghetto.

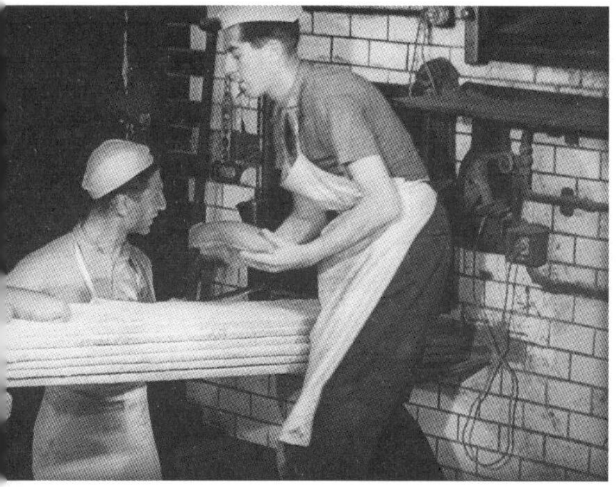

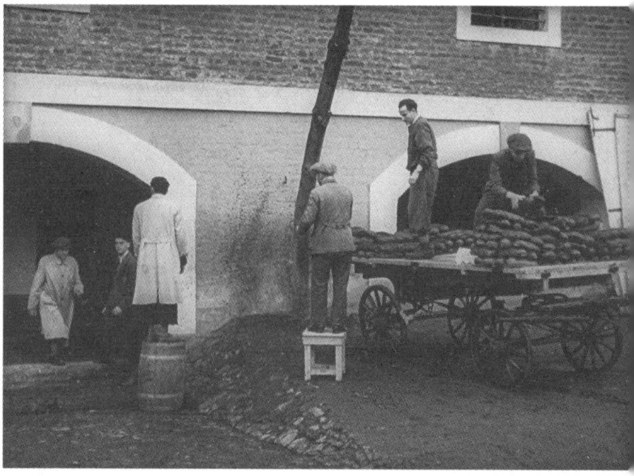

of the Theresiendstadt commander's office with its windows ablaze with lights – a symbol of the main source of fear and danger – is captured against the dark plaza with trimmed trees. The date of filming is presented via a small board featuring the daily menu. And there also is Bedřich Fritta, backing up in the drawing room and smiling at someone behind the camera who he apparently knows. Very impressive and telling are the details of the boards with inscriptions, such as the warning instruction to produce an inmate card when entering and leaving the local café, and so on.

In addition, several outtakes from the Theresienstadt title along with the Sigismund documentary caught Irena Dodalová in person. In view of the circumstances of making the film, she definitely cannot be viewed as its director as she is oftentimes described. On the other hand, her role in both making the film and stealing and smuggling its parts out was certainly crucial. All the accomplices must have assumed that no one was going to particularly control a box containing mere "scraps". The filmmaker clearly leaned on her early Protectorate elegant hit of smartly declaring part of the IRE-film archive, shipped to her husband to the United States, as priceless outtakes.

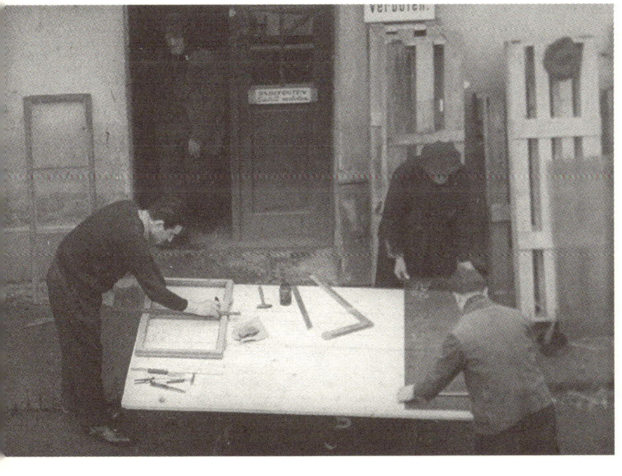

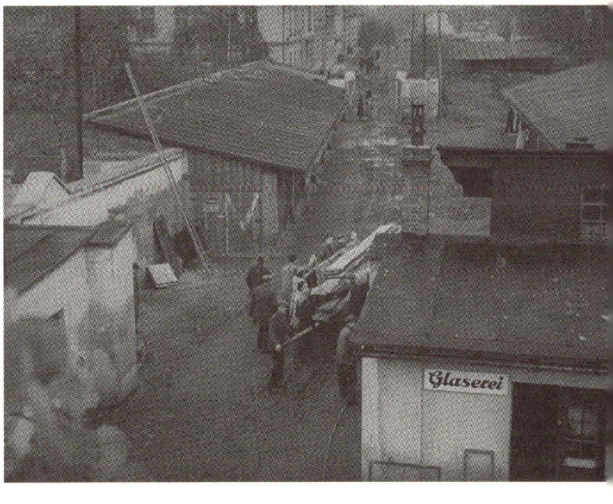

With the end of the filming, Dodalová continued in her *François Villon* in spring 1943. The ballads raptured by the 15th-century rebel and bohemian seemed perfectly relevant to the ghetto reality, and she staged them claiming that "here and now, deliberately and out of my innate urge to protest against injustice, derogation and lie, I pay tribute to some boys who were left behind in here".[36] In this, she certainly referred to the closing scene with the silhouettes of five hanged figures against the rising sun, which insistently recalled two Theresienstadt executions of January and February 1942. The music was composed by Viktor Ullmann, choreography was assisted by Kamila Rosenbaumová and two other participators were Irena's friends with whom she had collaborated on the film: Adolf Aussenberg took charge of the design and Jindřich Weil of the lighting. The performance had about forty repeats. From July 1943, it was staged in the theatre hall of the Magdeburg barracks and was later transferred to the new theatre space in the C III loft under the title *Betlerballade* (Beggar's Ballad, Žebrácká balada). The theatrologist Eva Šormová opines that the show surpassed the character of other Theresienstadt productions not only by its form but mainly by "the pessimistic somberness

1/ Staged conflagration with firemen. 4/ A take filmed during the Bohušovice–Theresienstadt railway construction.

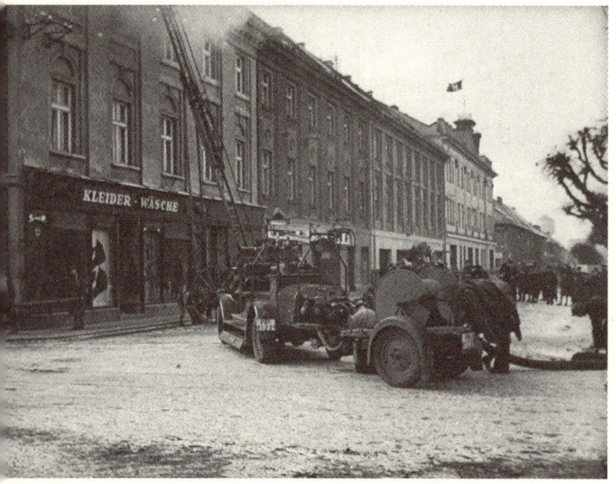

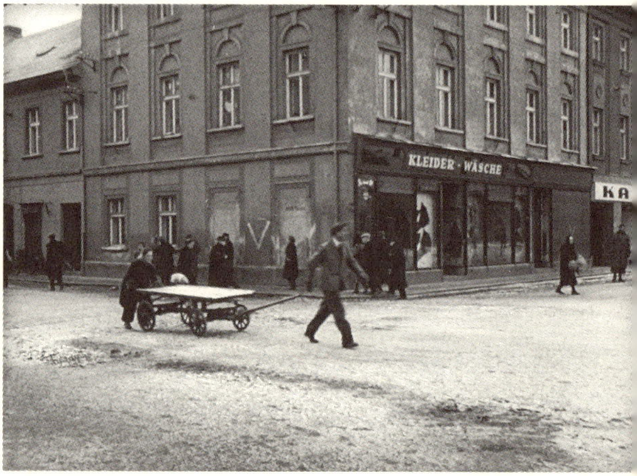

and balladic tune", and thus in a way followed in the line of the unrealized film synopsis.[37]

Dodalová's other activities in the ghetto are summed up in her typewritten notes which she prepared in 1944 for Karel Heřman who at that time began collecting documents about Theresienstadt culture.[38] They state that she, among other things, became involved in the program of reading in old people's homes and sick bays, and the list of extracts from poems by, for example S. K. Neumann, Jaroslav Vrchlický, Jaroslav Seifert, Vítězslav Nezval, Jiří Wolker, Antonín Sova and František Gellner, gives clear evidence of her literary preferences. She also continued in her pre-war education activity, preparing lectures about film for the co-inmates and the young in the ghetto.[39] Many plans, however, remained unrealized. The Department of Leisure Time in 1944 for instance declined her proposal to establish a Russian-style "independent scene".[40]

The ghetto artistic scene was not without various clashes and fights. This aspect of the local personal relationships is reflected in the memoirs of the theatre expert Ota Růžička, where Dodalová became one of the targets of

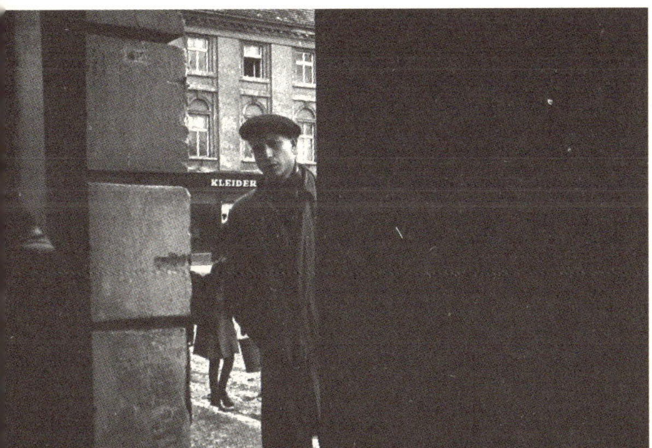

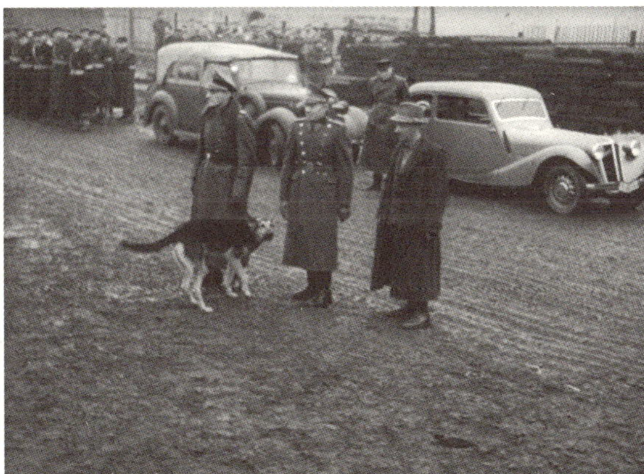

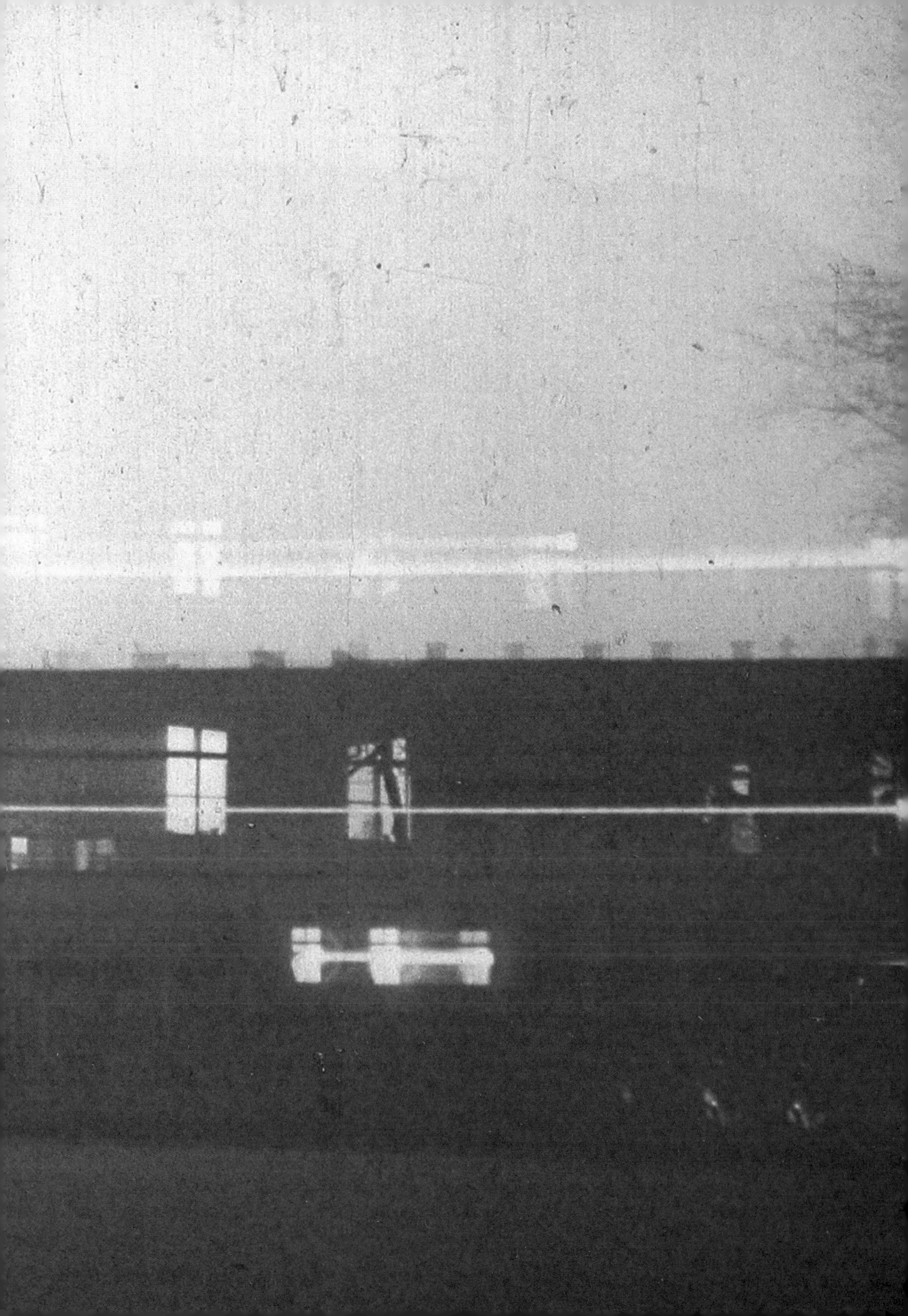

his spiteful comments. The author resolutely opined that "the poor staging of Villon's poems" was re-run merely due to her contacts with the head of the leisure-time department, the architect Otto Zucker, who feared her because she had directed the first Theresienstadt film and could have been a worry in the commander's office. This was a harsh and totally groundless allegation. The author also criticized the so-called "shalomiades", i.e. the Zionist activities and Yiddish theatre performances in which Dodalová participated and no one was allegedly interested in them.[41]

The fact that Irena Dodalová became close to the local circle of the Brno Zionists and directed two Yiddish performances in the ghetto certainly had several reasons. She had many bonds to Brno via her memories of her studies, the architect Zucker indeed impressed her, she even befriended his sister, the opera singer Tamara, and there were undoubtedly multiple other corresponding personal relationships which unfortunately cannot be supported by any surviving documents. It is, however, clear that her focus was most crucially influenced by her childhood and youth spent in an orthodox Jewish family. Her deeply embedded memories of the Scripture remembering the significant

1/ to 3/ SS-Obersturmführer Herbert Otto, who headed the filming in Prague and Theresienstadt, with the set designer František Zelenka. 4/ A shot from a Theresienstadt corridor.

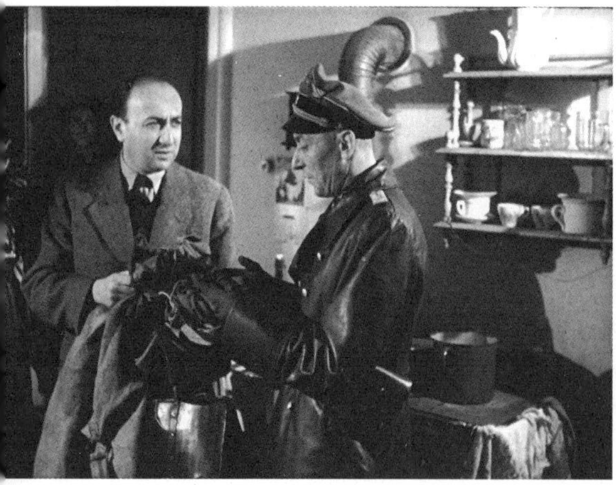

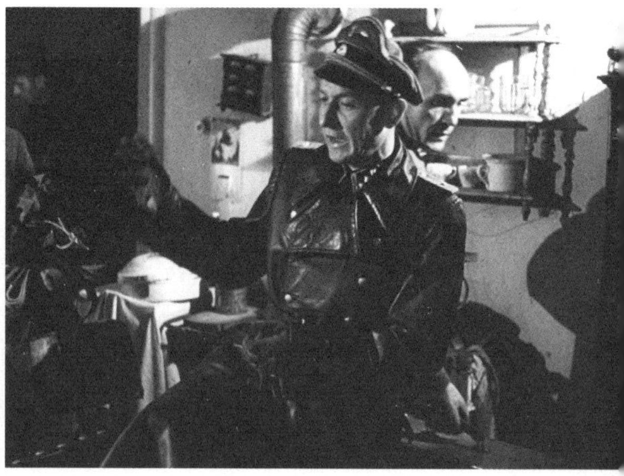

events of Jewish history and resounding in the Jewish prayers and religious rituals and holidays, such as the sabbath, rosh hashanah, yom kippur, passover, chanukka and purim, received utterly new meanings in the situation of peril. Dodalová's past as the daughter of a Jewish religion teacher distanced her from the young Czech secularized Jews and drove her to the company of people occupied by the past and the future of the Jewish nation. Her Yiddish performances reflected these issues. Dodalová apparently could not speak the language of the East-European Jews but it might be that her ghetto existence brought back her subconscious childhood memories when her Bratislava-born father was often visited by foreign delegations arriving from distant places.

The first program, entitled *Jewish Motifs in Songs and Poetry* (Jüdische Motive in Lied und Vers, Židovské motivy v písni a poezii), which Dodalová prepared for autumn 1943, illustrated the Jewish contribution to both East- and West-European culture. The second staging, *Half-Way* (In Mit'n Weg, Uprostřed cesty), was based on the motifs from J. L. Perez's *Golden Chain* (Die goldene Kette) and Sholem Aleichem's *Tevye the Dairyman* (Tevye der milkhiker). The team of associates consisted of, for instance, Eugen Weisz, Viktor Ullmann

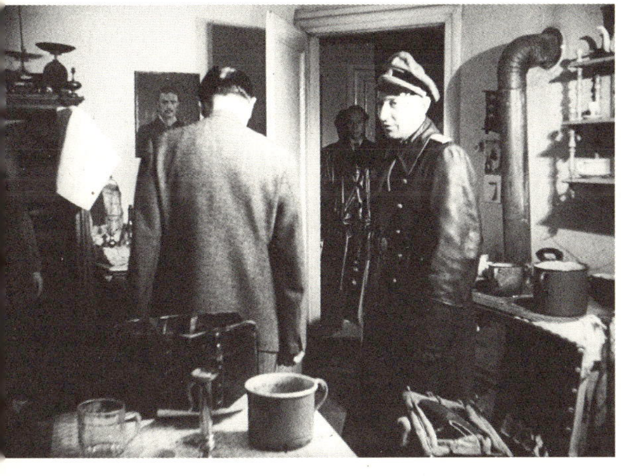

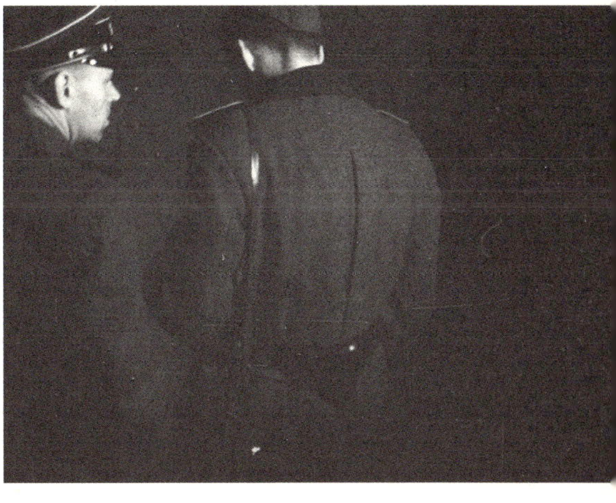

(music) and Bedřich Fritta (stage design). The surviving Dodalová's introduction to the performance is dated 28 November 1943 and states: "During its life in exile and the pursuit, oppression and pogroms related with this, the Jewish nation in all these eras longed to escape the tragedies. In the early 20th century, it was the mystics of the Kabbalah by which the Jewry tried to preserve its attitude to life and whose messianism promised in the worst period of the century new, more just times with no social and national differences, but with reconciliation and peace. This motif is captured in a fragment of Perez's *Golden Chain*. The way out which the Kabbalah tried to provide by escaping to the unreal became unfit for our nation in today's real time, real oppression and enslavement. And so we strive to also find a new and realistic way. It is a craving to fulfil the age-long desire for our own land, a liberated life which would allow for the development and a future freely flowing through the space of history for the new generations. Only the forthcoming period will show if this desire comes true, and if it does, whether it is the right point of departure. And because the Jewish nation is still only half of the way there, we have entitled today's evening, featuring two stages of our history, *In Mit'n Weg – Half-Way.*"[42]

1/ The film's "side" cameraman, SS-Hauptsturmführer Olaf Sigismund. 2/ Close-up of Sigismund, found in the National Film Archive. 3/ The group of filmmakers approaching the crematorium was probably also shot by Sigismund on his 16mm camera (the presented takes are from the 16mm Polish title *Obóz koncentracyjny v Teresinie* from the archives of Filmoteka narodowa).

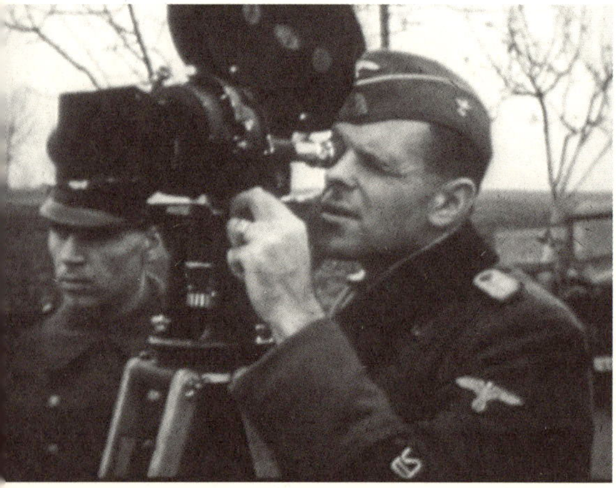

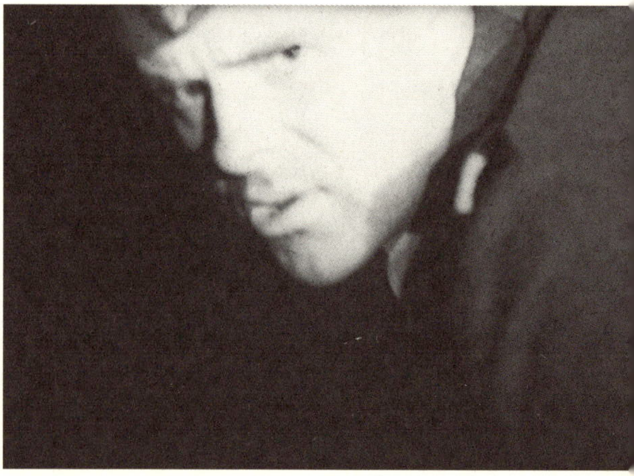

The introduction also outlines the concept of the stage adaptation: "The falling perspective of the walls, the dim atmosphere lit only with two candles, the dismal faces of the Hasideans and the prophetic face of an old rabbi evoke the atmosphere which should help understand the Hasidism of that time."[43]

When the feature propaganda film was made in Theresienstadt in 1944, Dodalová was not originally assigned to be part of the crew. The filmmakers from the production company Aktualita, however, were ordered to film several scenes from her expressively conceived *Half-Way*. Ivan Frič who partook in the film's final editing recalled his plan to close this "cheerful cinema" with the tragic shots from Dodalová's staging.[44] Although the Nazis eventually rejected such an ending for rather understandable reasons, at least one take from the performance survived thanks to Frič: the picture of a dying Jew.

There remains a question why some of the survivors interviewed by Margry were so critical about Dodalová. The childless, smart and emancipated but also authoritative and oftentimes exalted director defied the average and certainly had many disputes with both the members of other theatre groups and the management of the leisure time department. Ota Růžička in his memoirs

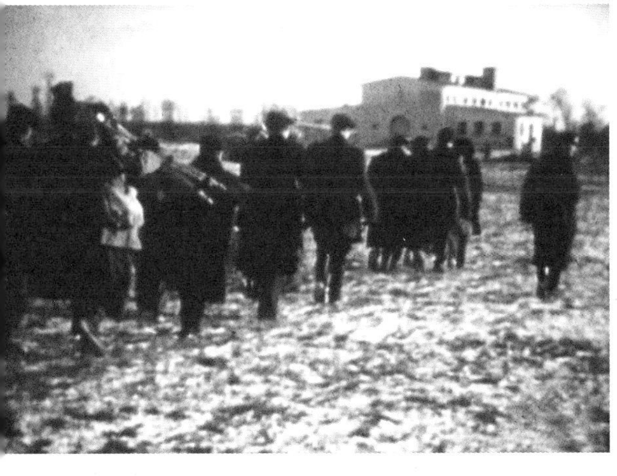

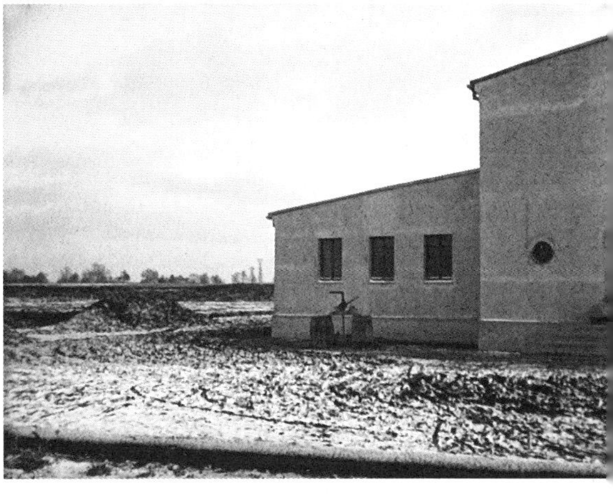

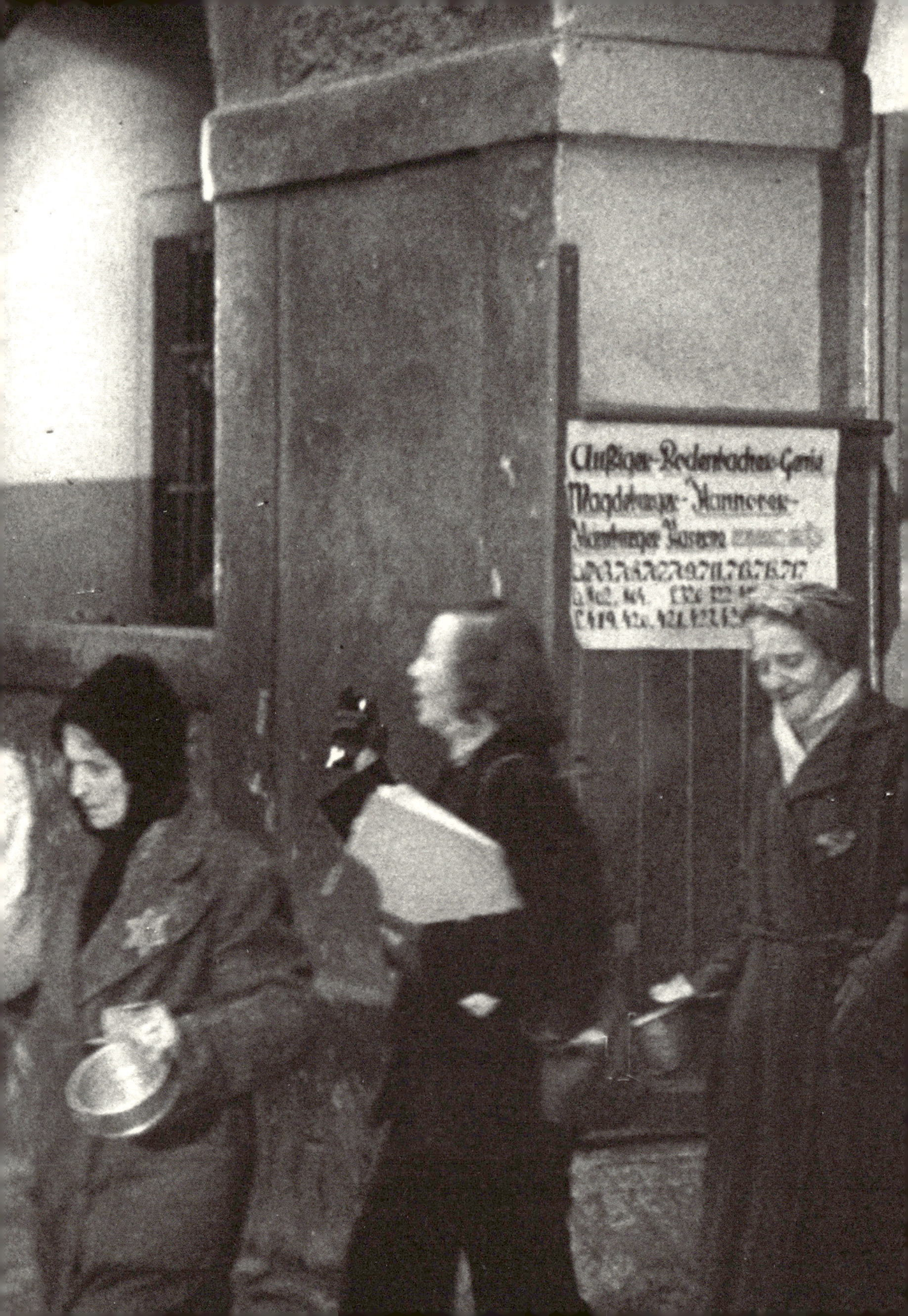
Aussiger-Bodenbacher-Genie
Magdeburger-Hannover-
Hamburger Kaserne

moreover wrote that neither her close relations with the members of the Brno Zionist group nor her Yiddish performances met with understanding by the Czech Jews.[45] Her relationships with young men were also disliked,[46] while the gender aspect must have played a considerable role in the case of this attractive woman. As one of the eyewitnesses remembered, Dodalová was even in the ghetto conditions able to look as if she was on her way to a café, which naturally not only evoked admiration but also envy and indignation.[47] The surviving photographs from the 1942 filming, nevertheless, do not capture a woman of the world but a tired and aging person.

Dodalová in Theresienstadt once briefly met her father, with whom the family had not lived since the 1920s and who died in the ghetto along with all the relatives from her mother's side. Matilda Rosnerová only survived the years of imprisonment thanks to her daughter who even managed to save her from being transported. This unbelievable action is known from two of Irena's versions.[48] Dodalová herself escaped death in the East especially due to her work in the mica-plating workshop, whose members were not selected to be transported.

She and her mother left Theresienstadt in February 1945 in a transport of 1,200 prisoners heading to Switzerland. In autumn of the same year, she set off for an adventurous journey through Spain and Portugal to her husband in the United States.

Irena Dodalová always avoided discussions about her life in the ghetto. There are merely a few hints in her correspondence with her brother Rudolf, and the only emphatic answer she would ever give to her last friend in Buenos Aires, Helena Voldánová, was: "Please don't ask."

Although the circumstances of Dodalová's *1942 Theresienstadt* project do not allow for entitling her as the director of the film, she undoubtedly played a crucial role in both organizing the filming and acquiring and hiding the outtakes in the ghetto.

1 The last document about the presence of H. Týrlová in the Dodal family dates to 1938 when she substituted for the absent Dodalová and negotiated with some company about unpaid for newspaper clippings. See the police file held in the National Archives, Police Headquarters, 13 January 1939, Ref. No. 020962.

2 Šormová, E., *Divadlo v Terezíně 1941–1945* (The Theresienstadt Theatre...). Ústí nad Labem: Severočeské nakladatelství, 1973.

3 Margry, K., "The First Theresienstadt Film (1942)", *Historical Journal of Film, Radio and Television*, 1999, No. 3, pp. 309–337; in Czech: "Zajímavý předchůdce – první terezínský film (1942)" (An Interesting Predecessor – The First Theresienstadt Film...). In: *Terezínské studie a dokumenty 1998* (Theresienstadt Studies and Documents). Praha: Academia, 1998, pp. 205–231.

4 For more on this, see the texts written by E. Strusková: "Film 'Ghetto-Theresienstadt 1942': Poselství filmových výstřižků" (... The Message of the Film Fragments), *Iluminace* (Illumination), 2009, No. 1, pp. 5–36; "Ghetto Theresienstadt 1942: The Message of the film Fragments", *Journal of Film Preservation*, 2009, Nos. 79/80, pp. 59–79; "Film 'Ghetto Theresienstadt': Die Suche nach Zusammenhängen". In: Loewy, R. – Rauschenberger, K. (eds.), *Der Letzte der Ungerechten. Der "Judenälteste" Benjamin Murmelstein in Filmen 1942–1975.* Frankfurt am Main: Campus, 2011, pp. 125–157.

5 On this, see Note 3 and other texts by Margry: "'Theresienstadt (1944–1945)': The Nazi Propaganda Film Depicting the Concentration Camp as Paradise", *Historical Journal of Film, Radio and Television*, 1992, No. 2, pp. 145–162; "Das Konzentrationslager als Idylle: 'Theresienstadt', ein Dokumentarfilm aus dem jüdischen Siedlungsgebiet". In: *Auschwitz: Geschichte, Rezeption und Wirkung. Jahrbuch 1966 zur Geschichte und Wirkung des Holocaust.* Frankfurt am Main–New York: Fritz Bauer Institut, 1997, pp. 319–352.

6 The fragments consisting of several frames and pasted to a single reel are held by the National Film Archive under the title *Terezín 1942* (Výstřižky [... Fragments]), ZF 1681.

7 Three reels of the 16mm film are filed in Poland under the title *Obóz koncentracyjny v Teresinie* and in Germany as *Theresienstadt 1942. Dreharbeiten.*

8 The second short film from spring 1944, made by the cameraman I. Frič, was allegedly viewed as trial material (*Probefilm*) preceding the propaganda film; the result was reportedly unsatisfactory and was destroyed upon Himmler's order. – Felsmann, B. – Prümm, K. (eds.), *Kurt Gerron – Gefeiert und Gejagt, 1897–1944: Das Schicksal eines deutschen Unterhaltungskünstlers: Berlin, Amsterdam, Theresienstadt, Auschwitz.* Berlin: Hentrich, 1992, pp. 140–144. Frič also talks about the filming, from which he preserved many photographs, in his testimony made for the Jewish Museum in Prague (Holocaust, Inv. No. 033).

9 Dodalová in her correspondence with her brother Rudolf stated the names of the informers who were already dead at that time. Personal Fund of Irena Dodalová.

10 I. Dodalová in the letter to K. Dodal of April 1945. In: *The Black Book. The Nazi Crime against the Jewish People.* New York: The Jewish Black Book Committee, 1946, pp. 292–297.

11 Her arrest is also proved by the memories of two Zbraslav eyewitnesses. See the author's interviews with K. Krčilová (11 October 2004) and R. Vodičková (30 November 2005). The National Film Archive, Collection of Sound Documents, Nos. 1004 and 1067. In a letter of 4 March 1981, addressed to her brother, Dodalová mentioned that she had been given the informers' names during her interrogation in the Střešovice prison. This note makes us assume that the Nazis at that time maybe tried to persuade her to collaborate. Her own name, however, was never part of the quisling list. Personal Fund of Irena Dodalová.

12 *Theresienstadt – Rohentwurf einer Filmreportage.* New York: Yivo Institute.

13 Margry, K., "Zajímavý předchůdce – první terezínský film (1942)", p. 210.

14 Ibid, p. 212.

15 *The Black Book*, p. 294 [original wording of I. Dodalová's quote in English].

16 Hofer, H., "The Film about Terezín. A Belated Report". In: Heitlinger, F. – Otis, O. – Ehrmann, R. (eds.), *Terezin 1941–1945.* Prague: Council of Jewish Communities in the Czech Lands, 1965, pp. 181–184. Hofer testified that another version of the script was written in Berlin and its completion was the responsibility of Kien who complemented the originally documentary depiction of the ghetto life with a story of a fictitious Holländer family.

17 Schauer, P. A., *Filmarbeit in Theresienstadt.* Wien: [internal print], 1993.

18 When the drawings by Fritta, Haas, Troeller, Ungar and Bloch were found in summer 1944, the artists and their families were arrested in the Small Fortress where F. Bloch was beaten to death. The group was deported to concentration camps, and Ungar and Fritta never returned from there.

19 Information from the letter written by his wife, E. Otto, dated 20 March 1945 and addressed to Himmler. BARCH Ludwigsburg, V 505 AR 2158/67 Herbert Otto (Zentralamt f.d.Reg.d. Judenfrage i.B.u.M.).

20 The filming of naked girls in a pool, mentioned by several eyewitnesses, was most probably Otto's private initiative.

21 Information provided by F. Weidmann to the staff of the Jewish Central Museum. The National Museum Archives, fund Anna Volavková, boxes 44, 744.

22 From K. Roubíček's e-mail addressed to the author of the present book (23 June 2006).

23 Hofer, H., op. cit., p. 181.

24 Ibid.

25 "After the war, I was at Jindřich Brichta's and watched two reels of 35mm film kept in paper boxes inscribed Secret Reich Matters: one reel with scenes from Dodalová's and Kien's film, about 150 meters long, silent, yet unedited and untitled, and a reel from 1944, also silent, unedited and untitled, as well as other film fragments whose copies Mr Brichta gave me. They are one of my most precious belongings. About 150 meters from Dodalová's and Kien's work showed the transportation of a married couple to the yet 'unadorned' camp and their integration into it. The second reel with the 1944 film, of approximately 500-meter footage, overlaps with the meanwhile lost and then again found edited material." From the author's correspondence with P. A. Schauer.

26 When R. Brösslerová returned from the filming to her parents with some make-up on, her father was first angry but calmed down as soon as he learned that she had been given food on the shot. R. Brösslerová in an interview with the author (24 May 2006). On the contrary, see the notes of E. Redlich. In: *Zítra jedeme, synu, pojedeme transportem. Deník Egona Redlicha z Terezína (1. ledna 1942 - 22. října 1944)* (Tomorrow We Go, My Son, We Will Be Transported. The Diary of Egon Redlich from Theresienstadt. [1 January 1942 - 22 October 1944]). Praha / Brno: Ústav pro soudobé dějiny (Institute of Contemporary History) / Addendum, 1995, pp. 157, 164.

27 H. Král, Jewish Museum in Prague, fund Holocaust, Inv. No. 80.

28 Ibid, p. 4.

29 It is not clear whether it was erysipelas or another disease, since the surviving documents vary on this (e.g., the documents for the Amt für Wiedergutmachung in Saarburg, Verwaltungsakce VA 284 089, or Dodalová's letter to her husband of April 1945.)

30 Král, H., op. cit., p. 3.

31 Dodalová in this case could mean the Jewish Central Museum in Prague which, however, filed no films. It instead kept photographic documentation of the collections where the film reels could easily have been hidden. Some representatives of the Central Institute for Coordinating Jewish Matters in Bohemia and Moravia, too, could have been interested in the given film documentation. This possibility is supported by the fact that J. Lauscher found a reel with a part of the propaganda film *Terezín* in a Střešovice villa after the war. He copied several photographs (today held in the Terezín Memorial), and the found section of the film was then taken to Jerusalem.

32 *The Black Book*, p. 295.

33 The film band (footage 137.4 meters) with a copied-in sound track contains about 100 fragments, some consisting of merely one or two frames. Most fragments are pasted together by stickers; in some cases, the stickers merely connect two parts of a single motif.

34 See Note 7.

35 Dodalová, I., *Balada Protest; Žít v komfortu, ach, na to v světě není!* (Protest Ballad; O, Nothing Compares to Living in Comfort!). Theresienstadt 1942, 1943, 1944. 20 July 1944. The Terezín Memorial, Karel Heřman Collection, No. 103.

36 Šormová, E., op. cit., p. 43.

37 The Terezín Memorial, Karel Heřman Collection.

38 "Divadlo a film" (Theatre and Film; August, September 1943), "Svět filmu, sociologie filmu, poslání filmu" (The World of Film, the Sociology of Film, the Mission of Film; April–June 1944), film lectures for youths in the L 218 barrack which also included a passage about trick film.

39 The main partner of this rather foolish idea was Bedřich Graus, 19 years old at that time, whose two performances were, along with Jaroslav Žák's play *Škola základ života* (School, the Basis of Life), among the proposed titles of the new troupe. Akademie recitace (české) (Czech Recitation Academy). The Terezín Memorial, Karel Heřman Collection.

40 The author also was extremely critical about the "shalomists" and the Zionist activities. In: *Ota Růžička 1972. Památník Terezín, Paměti* (The Theresienstadt Memorial, Memoirs) 834, pp. 12–13.

41 Irena Dodalová, the Terezín Memorial, Karel Heřman Collection, No. 3919.

42 Ibid.

43 "Interview mit Ivan Frič, Kameramann des Films 'Der Führer schenkt den Juden eine Stadt'", Prag, Sommer 1991. In: Felsmann, B. – Prümm, K. (eds.), op. cit. Frič gave several more interviews and also assisted Margry.

44 See Note 40.

45 This criticism of the Theresienstadt male eyewitnesses who would gather in Vienna after the war was soundly expressed by P. A. Schauer in his correspondence; see Note 25.

46 Hájková, A., "Strukturen weiblichen Verhaltens in Theresienstadt". In: G. Bock (ed.), *Genozid und Geschlecht: Jüdische Frauen im national-sozialistischen Konzentrationslagersystem.* Frankfurt am Main: Campus, 2005, pp. 202–219.

47 Dodalová described the scene with the SS-men almost identically in two letters, one addressed to K. Dodal and dated April 1945 (see *The Black Book*, op. cit.) and the other to her brother Rudolf and dated 23 November 1980 (see the Personal Fund of Irena Dodalová).

48 The transport was a result of the negotiations between the Swiss politician J.-M. Musy and Himmler, organized upon the request of the Jewish orthodox organization of Isaac Sternbuch. No one initially reported to the transport since its destination was unclear. According to the set criteria, the transport did not concern, for instance, people holding significant civil positions and having contacts with foreign countries, which also was Dodalová's case. Her letter to K. Dodal of April 1945 describes the wild way of how she got onto the transportation train, although the survivors question her testimony. The only certain thing is that it was not easy to include her in the transport.

Living in Exile / 1940s–1980s

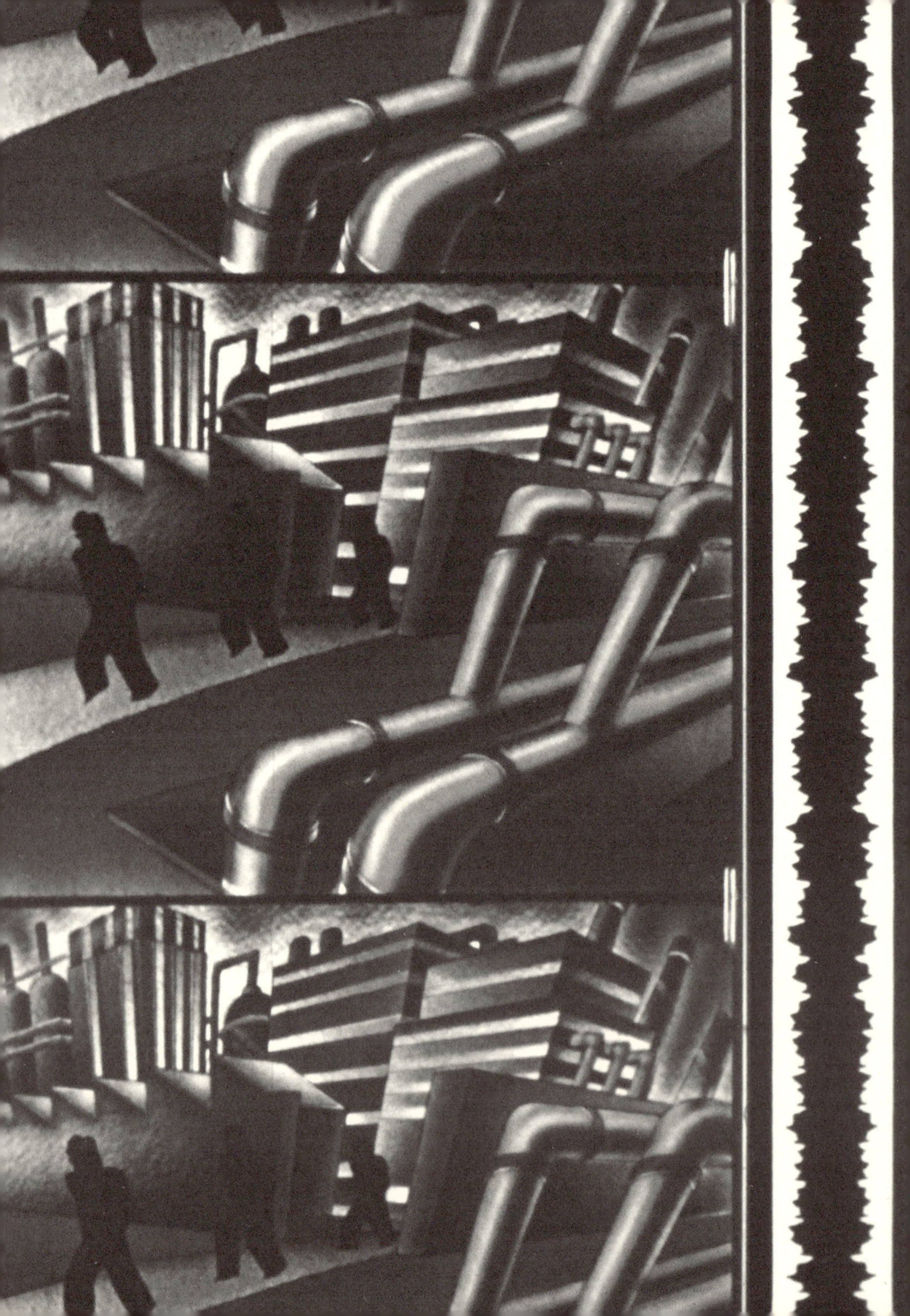

Irena and Karel Dodal in the United States and Argentina

The Dodals' first weeks after the war, when the couple reunited in New York, are captured in a comprehensive letter sent by Irena to her Prague friends, the Popps, and written with short interruptions between August and December 1946. Karel Dodal, too, attached a brief addendum. The letter opened with a summary of Dodalová's first overseas experiences, provided in her characteristic staccato style:

"I came here rejuvenated from Switzerland and Portugal where I had waited for the boat for six weeks. Many ideas I had; encounter, rest, acclimatization, new style of work, focus on art, life... Everything went otherwise. Already during the first days upon the arrival, I've become overwhelmed with worries. I didn't speak the language and, after the four years of isolation, found myself in the unbelievably oceanic labyrinth of that city, with its elevated railways, skyscrapers, thousands and thousands of cars, omnipresent noise and lights, people of all nations, colours and shapes clad in most various attires; it all was different, wild, bouncing and swelling, rapacious, rushing forward and forward...

I had no time to take all that in, to put myself into that place, to hook in – Karel would work on a film in his studio till night. He was too busy to explain anything to me and I was left isolated and forlorn during the first days. And

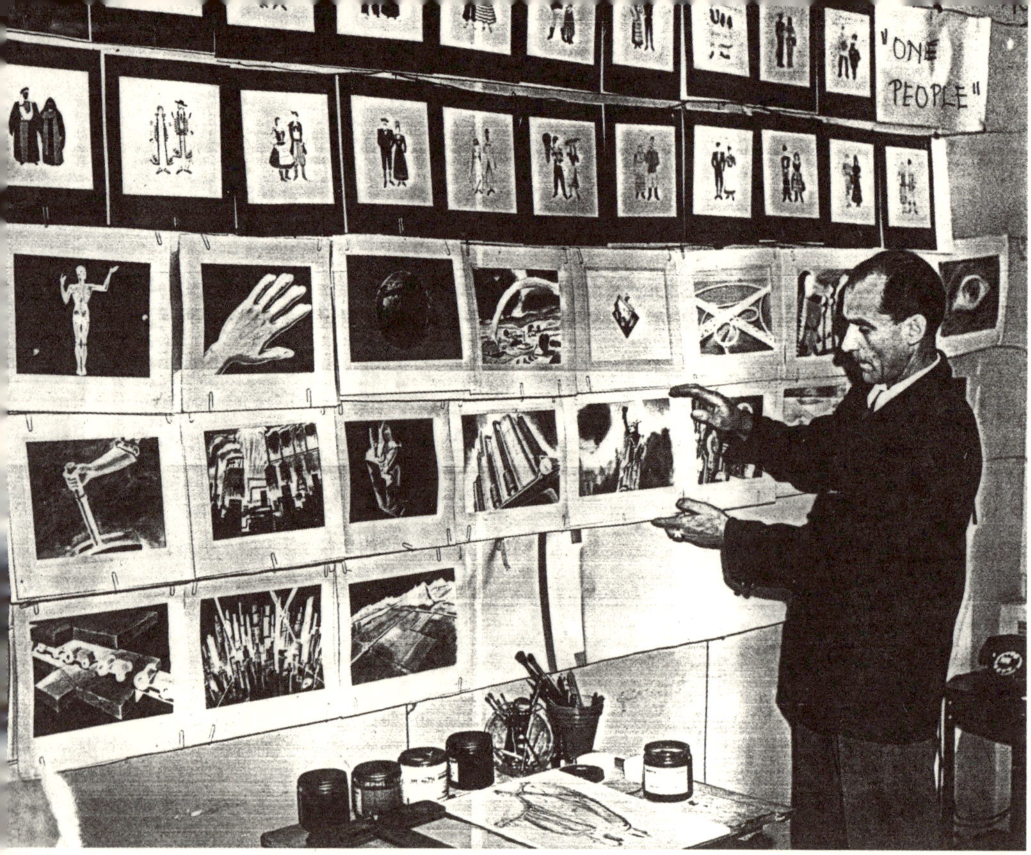

Karel Dodal finishing the film *One People* in New York in 1946.

then, more trouble came – the company for which Karel was working went bankrupt, he lost his job, right on my birthday, I had been in the USA for just a week. And right after, he had to move from the studio owned by the school and the school wanted it back instantly... A new studio had to be found so that Karel's film could be finished, and that had to be whitewashed and adapted for film purposes, let alone that New York does not really abound in vacant places available for rent, neither apartments, nor studios."[1]

Karel Dodal in the mid-1940s worked in the Department of Educational Films with the American Film Center which, after the war, ran into financial troubles. He was laid off in November 1945, shortly before the Center's abolishment. In order to continue making animated films, he established his own film production – Irena Film Art – which would follow on from the experiences from IRE-film and where, as its title suggests, a crucial role was again played by his wife. As Dodalová wrote to the Popps, the new studio was situated "close to Broadway and Times Square, downtown, and it's not as nice as our Klimentská. We employ six artists during the day and others at night, till 11 p.m. They're of all imaginable races and nationalities".[2] Her husband complemented the information with an apology for being silent: "Because I really have no spare time: our draughtsmen wait for my sketches and simply chase me to work. Every time I stop, they are idle and that costs a fortune. Everything is about Unions here, and as soon as one launches one's own studio and wants to make it through, there's no other way but... to keep on racing. We do day shifts and then night shifts, from 6 to 11 p.m. Then we ride home, that's midnight, we're in bed at one a.m. and then it's over and over again the next morning."[3]

It was rather difficult for the couple to follow in their pre-war life after all those six years, and not only for existential but also personal reasons. Dodal had already achieved a certain status in the new world and was, as always, already surrounded by pretty young ladies, which Dodalová could not abide from mentioning in her correspondence. She, on the other side, struggled hard to make her way in the unknown and hectic environment after her Theresienstadt misery. In addition, she was totally illiterate in English and was thus eliminated from many negotiations, which put her into an unprecedented inferior role. If her husband looked up to her in Prague, she became his burden in New York. But her description of their local life from December 1946 was already along much more cheerful lines: "Thank God that many things have changed for the better! We've moved from Brooklyn (because of my weak lungs) to the country, to another state, Connecticut-Darien, but the great conditions provided by the American railways allow for just an hour (!) of daily commuting to our New York studio. We've rented a small wooden, American-style villa, with a large garden and a tomcat which, true, was not contracted, but he eagerly frequents both his food bowl and my bed. We have five different heating stoves here (for water, for heating the place, for cooking, for baking and for the kitchen), so Karel is pretty preoccupied on Sundays, trying to keep the fires going and doing all the cooking. I never cook; I just eat all those delicious Czech meals (on Sundays) for we merely peck at something like

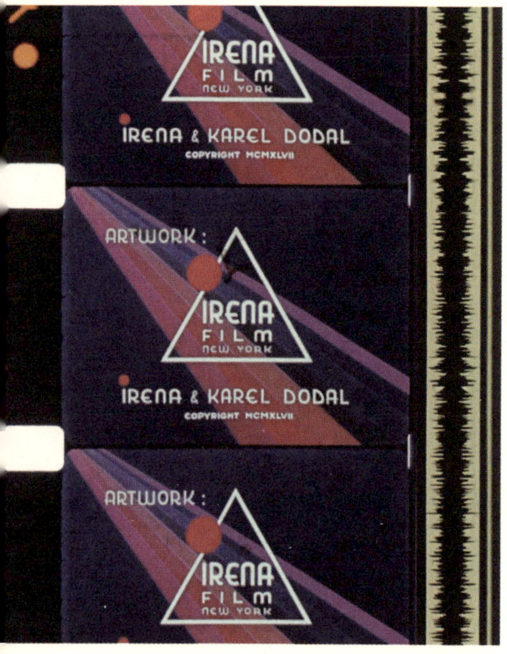

The archive of Irena Dodalová still holds a copy of the 16mm film *There Were Three Men*, promoting cooperative farming.

sparrows during the week, having neither rest nor time for a bite".[4]

In the following months, the couple intensely indulged in producing filmstrips and educational and promotional pictures. In 1946, they shot a title on the history of the dairy business, *The Inside Story of Milking*, and also the film *One People*, from which they expected a lot.[5] The colour cartoon told the dramatic story of North America having been populated by many races, religions and nationalities where no one can be excluded. According to the ending narrated by the famous actor Ralph Bellamy, it was "the solemn duty of each and every American to live in friendship and work in harmony so that we can reciprocally create a more successful and more united America".[6] It was a tribute of the grateful asylum applicants, and its focus against racial intolerance moreover deeply resonated with the authors' conviction. The film was distributed by The Anti-Defamation League which also probably participated in its production. The expenses were in part covered by the American Film Center where Dodal had begun working on the picture.

In 1947, the Dodals finished the film *There Were Three Men* for The Cooperative League of the United States of America and labelled it artwork, suggesting that it was not a commonplace promotional picture. It survived thanks to Dodalová's archive, and even though its colours have degraded over time, it is still interesting proof of the couple's post-war orientation and the development of Karel Dodal's style.[7] Its genre can most aptly be described as agitprop of Dziga Vertov type. Its aim was to clarify and promote the advantages of the cooperative system, illustrated by the story of a worker and a farmer who realize that they can effectively face a capitalist creaming off of the profits if they build a parallel cooperative. The growing curves reflecting the success of this enterprise show that the chosen way has been correct and the movement, where revenues are distributed justly, spreads around the globe. The asset of the script was the synoptic explanation combining picture, text in the picture and narration. Dodal designed the figures of stylized shapes whose duplicated outlines evoked three-dimensional illusion. The simplified drawings of the worker and farmer were distinguished by the colours of their overalls (blue and green) and minute details (the worker wears a cap, the farmer sports a hat); the capitalist was featured in the classical cartoon style as fat. The symbolically indicated industrial environment loosely drew from modern fine art (e.g., Lyonel Feininger). The film images employed the potential of metaphors and connotations:

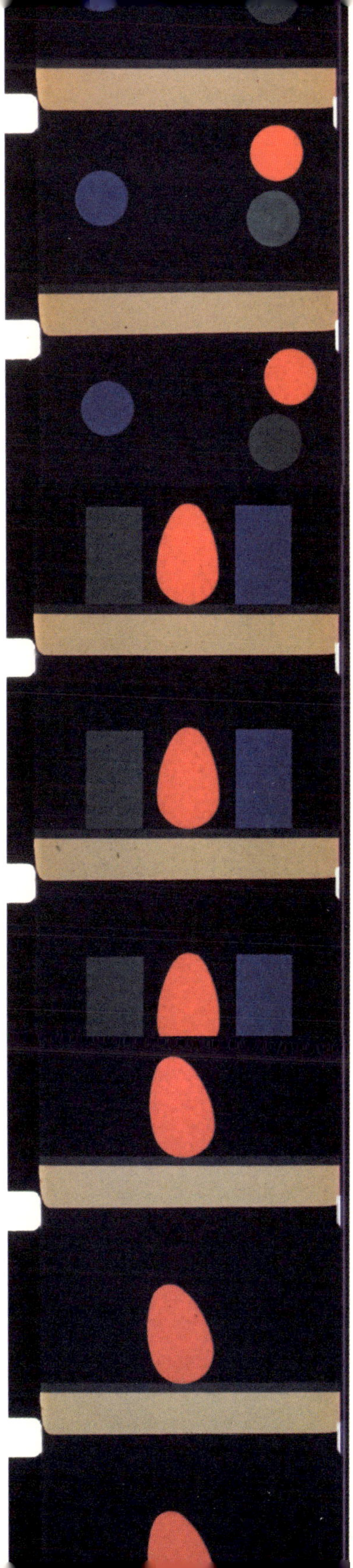

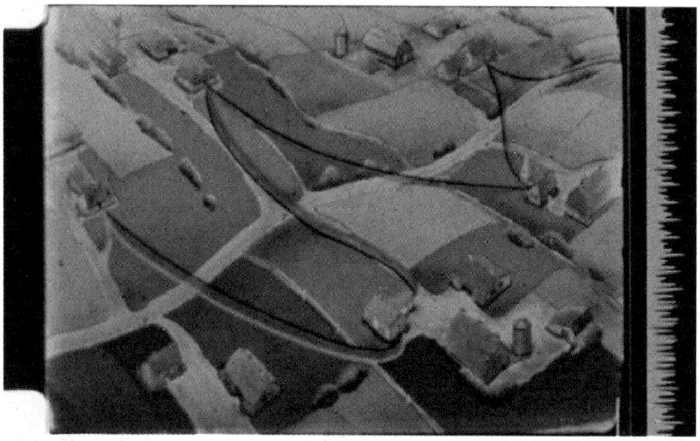

Karel Dodal the artist arrived at a distinctly stylized form and characters in his film *There Were Three Men.*

wealth was represented by warehouses stocked with money; the "enlightenment" dawned on the working couple under a tree like the apple landing on Newton's head; the capitalist machinery was expressed via shadows moving within industrial complexes (the artistic rendering of these passages is rather unique); the view of the circle of chairs, taken from above, evoked the movement's communality, and so on. Like the pre-war IRE-film works, the title contained an image of a TV screen, which here worked as a connecting medium serving the world of capital. And equally as in the preceding films, there is a loose paraphrasing of a scene from another artist's work, in this case Jiří Trnka's. The scene with the farmer pampering a plant and struggling with the caprices of nature remotely evokes the introduction to Trnka's *Grandfather Planted a Beet* (Zasadil dědek řepu; 1945). It is assumed that Dodal was familiar with the oeuvre of this artist, most probably via Josef Auerbach who launched the American distribution of the films by The T-Shirt Brothers (Bratři v triku) studio shortly after the war.[8] The music to the film was composed by Robert Strassburg, a new composer and pedagogue who later asserted himself at prestigious Jewish universities. The commentary was narrated by William Adams, the speaker well-known from the popular weekly broadcast *The March of Time*. The subject of the cooperative agitprop

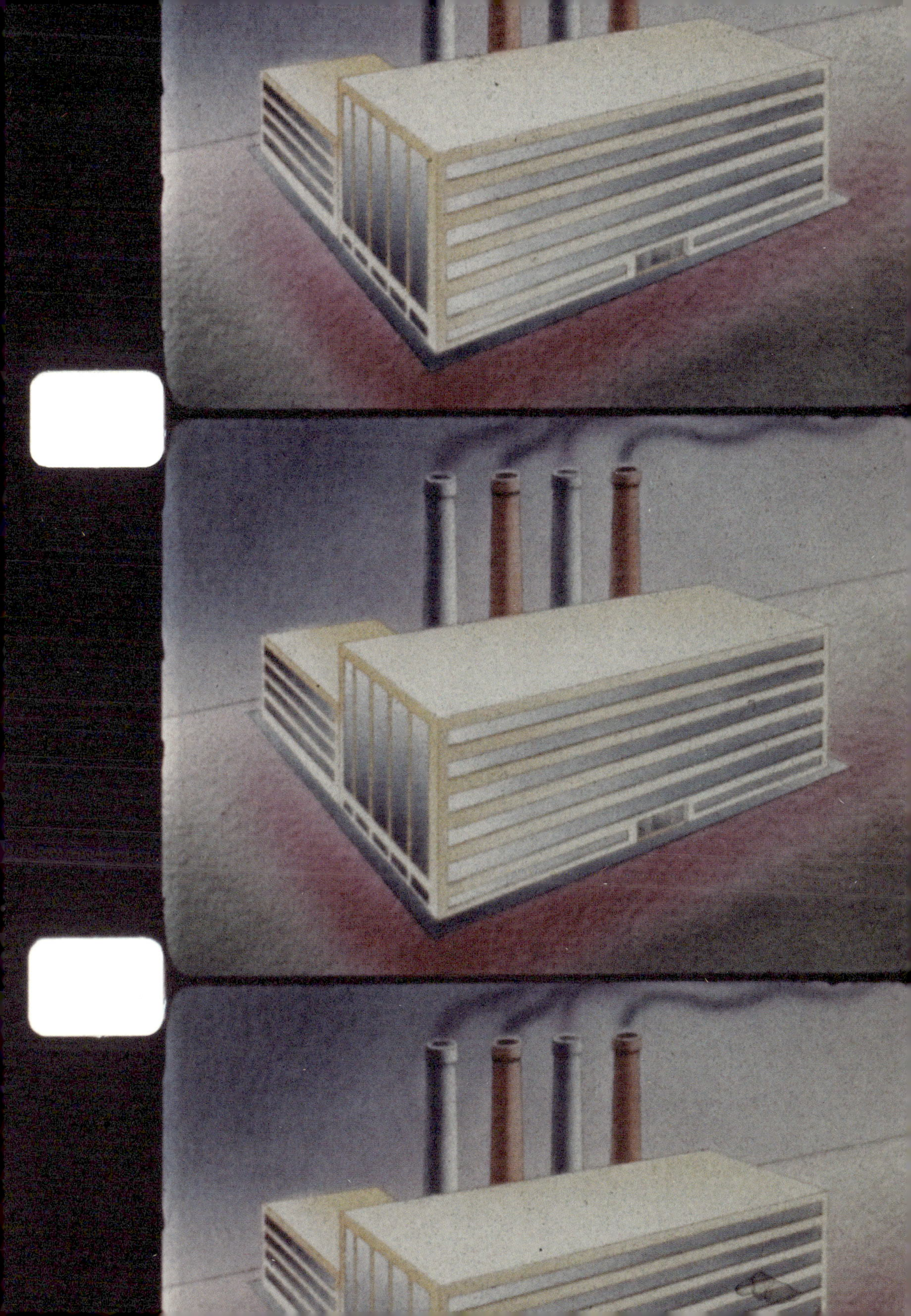

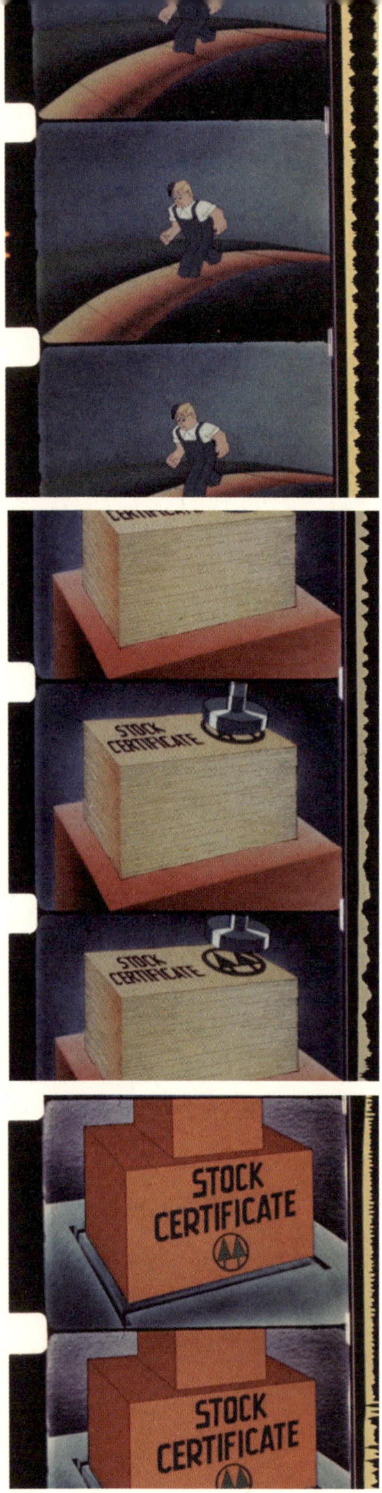

was certainly close to Central-Europeans accustomed to their credit unions from the 19th century, but its collectivist tune was far off for the American audience, which clearly limited the scope of its distribution in the States. Both its contents and style, however, widely anticipated the post-war tendency of the Canadian, British, as well as European, animated films introducing the public via metaphorical shortcut to socially topical subjects, such as the partnership of nations, the anti-war movement and the fight for social progress. This heavily resonated with the program of The T-Shirt Brothers, mainly Duba's *Atom at the Crossroads* (Atom na rozcestí; 1947) and Miler's black-and-white title *The Millionaire Who Stole the Sun* (O milionáři, který ukradl slunce; 1948).

The film *There Were Three Men* was first presented to invited representatives of the United Nation's Department of Information, Film and Research and the press in a private Broadway studio in September 1947, and the event was described by Josef Šrych in an extensive article "Creators of the Tradition of Czech Cartoon Film" (Tvůrci tradice českého kresleného filmu), published in the *New York Papers* (Newyorské listy). It informed readers that the film was to be screened in England, France, North-European states, Switzerland, Australia and

FEB 11 1948

IRENA FILM ART

STUDIOS · 781 EIGHTH AVENUE · NEW YORK 19, N. Y.

IRENA & KAREL DODAL
CIRCLE 5-9158

N.Y. February 9th,1948

The Museum of Modern Art
on the 53th Street
NEW YORK CITY

FILM LIBRARY

Dear Miss Iris B a r r y,

we would like, if possible, to get your attention for 2 - 3 short animated films in 35mm and 16 mm(colors) which - we feel- could be of interest for your audience and eventually , the film library. The screening time would afford from 20 to 25 minutes of your time.

The pictures are :
"THE SEARCH for LIGHT" an abstract 35 mm black & white film developing the 4th Paraphrase of the IXth Beethoven Sypmhony to the idea : Salvation of Mankind through Love . (10 min.)
" FANTASIA" 35 mm abstract film developing colors and forms to original music (5 min.)
" ONE PEOPLE" 16 mm color film dealing with the idea :Building America (6 min.)
" THERE WERE 3 MEN " 16 mm color film dealing with the Co-Op idea.
The two first are created in Europe 1938, Paris
The others in New York 1946 and 1947

They already are enjoying a good acclamation in the U.S.A. and other countries.

Our references are : Dir.Arthur DE BRA The Motion.Pict.Ass.
Mr. Dickinson with the UNITED WORLD
445 Park Ave
Alexander HAMMID
Franz STAPP
and the outstanding Film Producers in N.Y
We both are having membership in the M.o.M.A.

We hope, it would be possible to get your attention to this screening,which could be arranged any time, you like, in the Museum .

Veru Truly Yours :

Irene Dodal

Arthur R

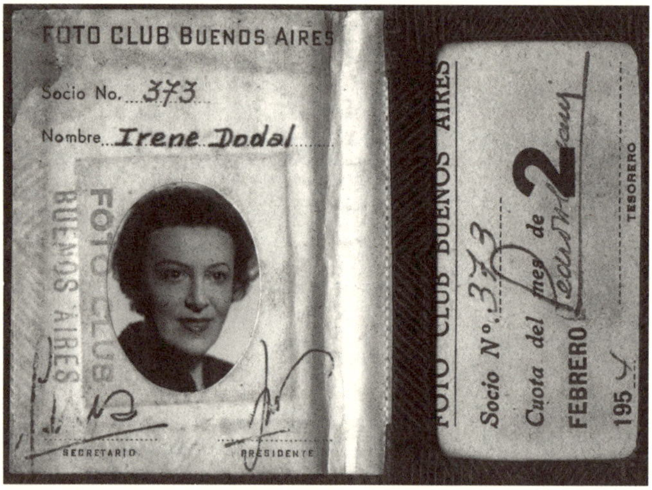

Irena Dodalová soon associated with many theatre and film companies in Buenos Aires.

Canada, but it remains unclear whether this reflected the already settled distribution or merely the couple's plans. Apart from the Czech natives in New York, the article was mainly aimed at Prague institutions, especially through the lines about Karel Dodal's wish to directly talk to the filmmakers from the T-Shirt Brothers about future collaboration on a film for the United Nations.[9]

Regardless of the initial start, the Dodals' situation in the United States was far from simple and easy. This is documented by the travel report of the Czechoslovak State Film delegation in New York, issued after visiting the couple in June 1947: "The Irena-Film studio makes four cartoon and four puppet films a year. It temporarily employs up to twelve draughtsmen who were on vacation during our visit, and were laid off afterwards due to lack of work. The production cost of a 10-minute picture, whether cartoon or puppet one, is one million Czechoslovak Crowns. The films they produce are mainly aimed at cultural and educational organizations. The advertising commissions are either made by large film companies or their cartoon-film department."[10]

The delegation visit proves that the Dodals were in contact with their homeland. They even at one point asked their friend, the Prague attorney Alfred

Popp, to arrange their return and the possibility of working in animation.[11] Their plan failed because they were offered a work in Zlín instead of Prague, which they had to decline for many reasons. They nevertheless maintained liaisons with the Czechoslovak State Film, for they were interested in co-producing a picture for the United Nations, entitled *We, The People*.[12] The United Nations representative, Hans H. Burger, welcomed their storyboard and promised international distribution in early 1948, but no guarantee of financial support came with that.[13] The Dodals' further negotiations with Prague were thwarted by the Czechoslovak Communist putsch of February 1948.

Karel Dodal (far right) and Irena Dodalová (far left, wearing flower-pattern dress), testing aspirants for film animation in Buenos Aires. It is worth noting that the Argentinian Ministry of Education simultaneously recommended developing the local production of animated educational films.

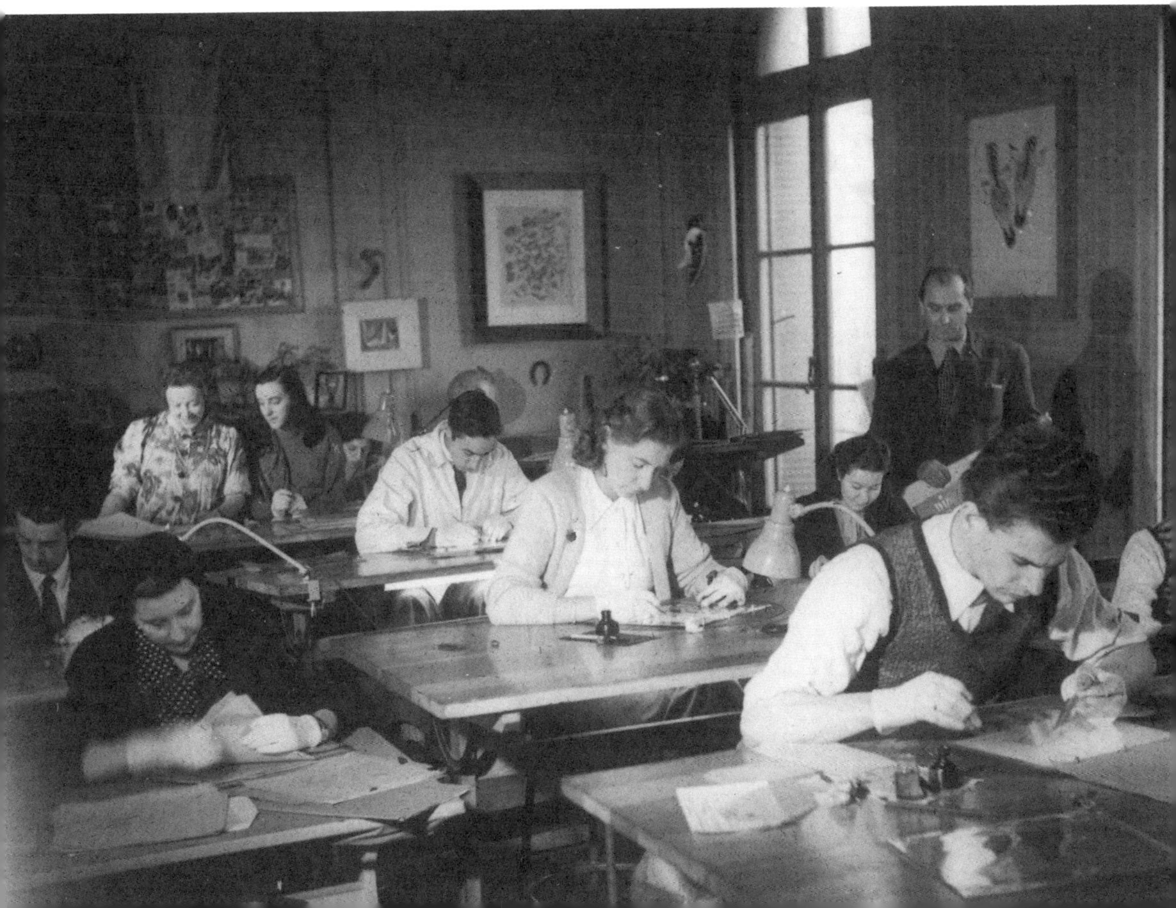

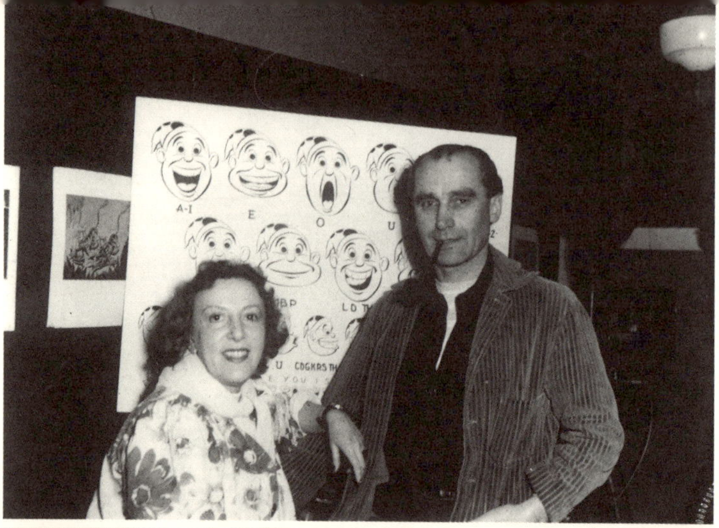

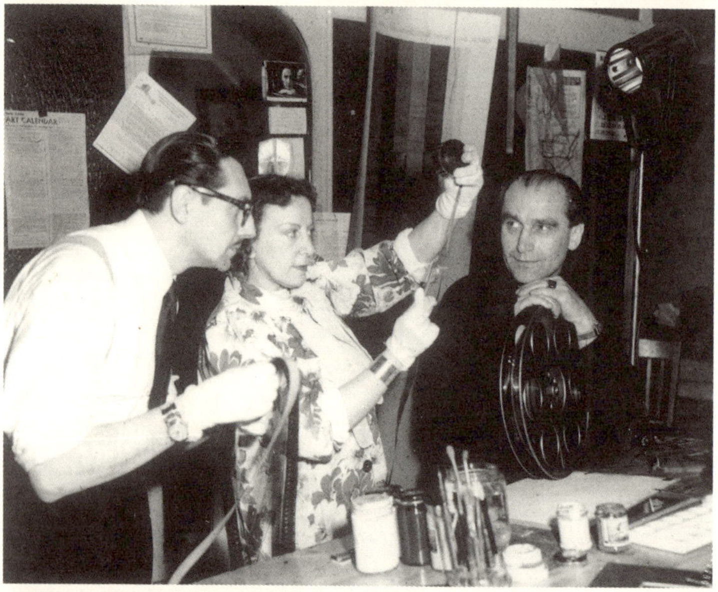

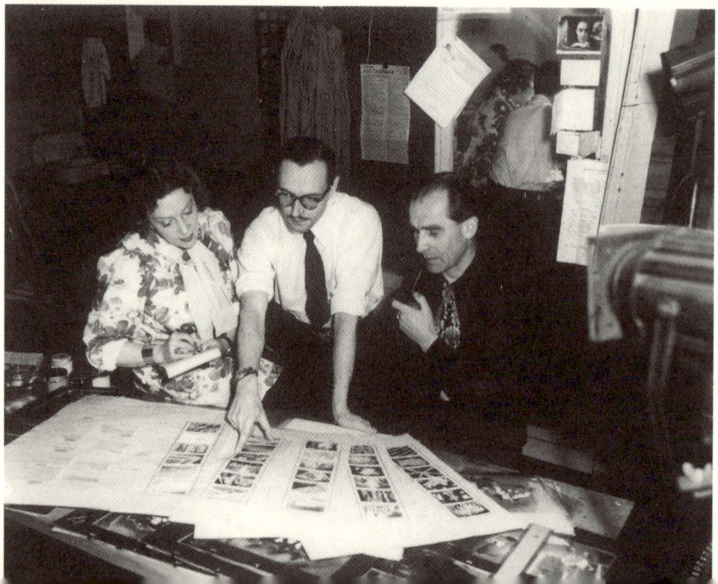

Undated photographs from Irena Dodalová's archive. The man wearing glasses remains anonymous.

The above-mentioned report also testifies that the couple would not find more commissions. It was a result of stagnating film production, and the arriving McCarthyism era was not a favourable prospect for the almost fifty-year old artists from Central Europe. Karel Dodal therefore earned a little by lecturing at American universities.

A solution to the uncertain situation came from the Argentinian Minister of Education, Oscar Ivanissevich, with his offer to build the production of animated educational films in Buenos Aires. Irena Dodalová described the beginnings of the collaboration, based on a two-year contract, as follows: "The terms are miserable, but Irena and Karel decided to depart for Argentina for the two years of their contract's duration... They both set foot on Argentinian soil with their Czechoslovak passports (Karel's American passport was not a definite issue yet). These two Czechoslovak passports then unleashed an array of persecutions and brought many enemies, the more so that they came with ten cases of film equipment and also their car... Their life turned into hardship, pursuit, deceptions, accusations... They finally signed the contract with Doctor Ivanissevich, the Minister of Education... Their knowledge of Spanish equalled browsing through a dictionary... But Karel was anyway appointed a professor to twenty draughtsmen and Irena the head of a department."[14]

The Dodals were not the only animation experts in Argentina. The country already boasted two primacies in this field: the cartoonist and animator Quirino Cristiani made the very first full-length facet film *El Apóstol* (Apostle) in 1917, and his first full-length animated title *Peludópolis* dates to 1931. Argentinian film history moreover records dozens of other artists pursuing animation over the years, but no large specialized studios had been established there. The Dodals did not occupy a more significant place in this history mainly because their films did not survive. The Argentinian film historian Alejandro R. González noted in his summary that the Dodals established the studio Argencolor in Buenos Aires, mentioning their films *Día del árbol* (Arbour Day), *Cuento de Navidad* (A Christmas Story) and *La reina de las ondas* (The Queen of Waves) which, nonetheless, soon fell into oblivion as a result of the local political turbulence.[15]

So, what is known about the above-mentioned titles? Irena Dodalová remembered that birds danced the zamba folk dance in trees in the animated *Arbour*

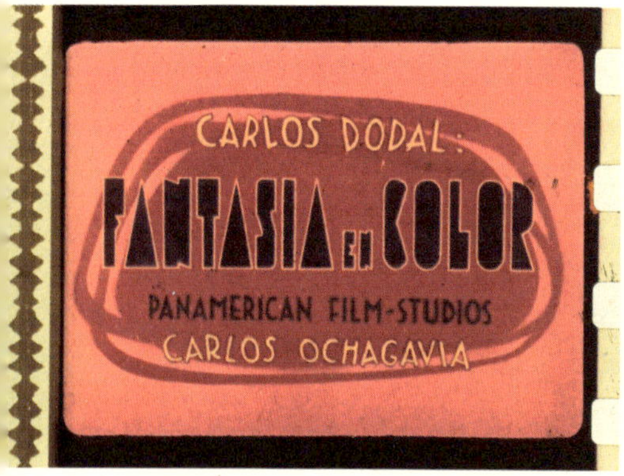

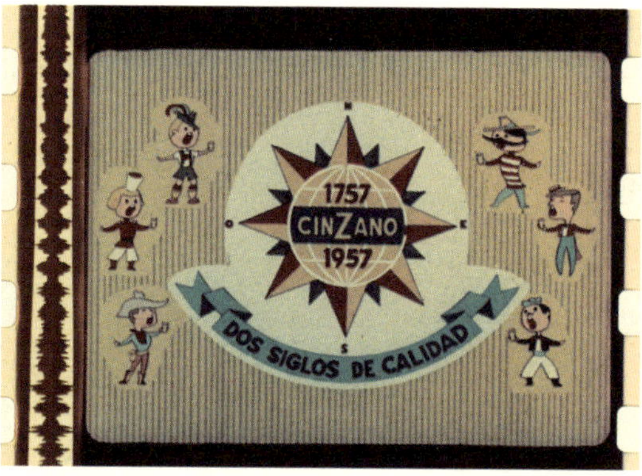

Day. It could well be that the picture is still hidden in some Argentinian archive. The *Christmas Story* was a puppet film inspired by *The Nativity* (Betlém) on which Karel Dodal worked in the 1950s, but he left the country before its completion. His wife had the still silent visual material copied and even in the late 1980s considered adding a soundtrack, but that never happened. She merely sent a few frames from its ending to Prague in 1989. It remains a question which version of the film the Argentinian historian actually had in mind and where the given film materials are today.[16]

The unfinished copy of the third picture was acquired by the National Film Archive in Prague thanks to Irena Dodalová. Its title conceals a new version of *The Adventures of a Ubiquitous Fellow* (Všudybylovo dobrodružství) where the authors left out the opening sequence with Hurvínek the puppet, changed the logos of the radio stations and removed the sketches of the Liblice transmitter, instead adding original scenes with the sea and grain (these were part of the Ježek's musical score, although they are missing in the Protectorate copy) and replacing several sections of the technical explanation with new ones in a more "modern" design. The adaptations were definitely not detrimental. The fund of Irena Dodalová also contains two Spanish scripts to the picture along with an explanation entitled *La aventuras de Busybody*, although it was distributed as *La reina de las ondas*.[17] Dodalová stated that the studio also produced educational films, such as the *Plantacion de arbol* (Tree Planting) and *Gigante Bueno* (A Good-Hearted Giant).

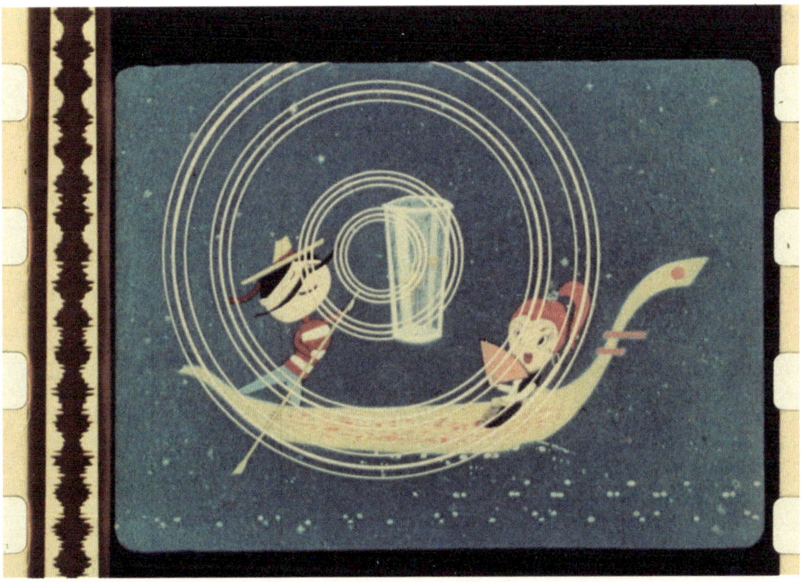

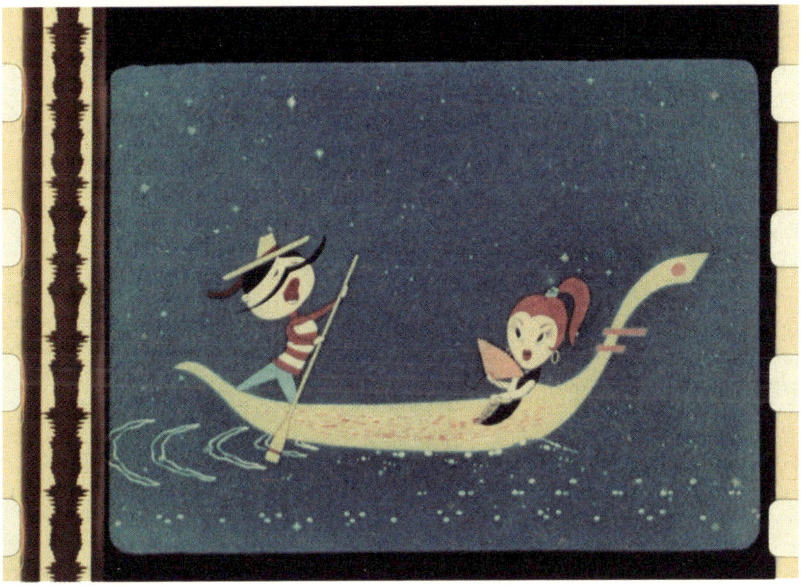

According to Irena Dodalová, the larger part of the Dodal's archive was destroyed by fire, and she was thus able to send only several outtakes to Prague. The frame of the opening credits to the film *Fantasia en color* also contains the name of Dodal's co-worker, Carlos Ochagavía. The takes with the gondola are from a commercial promoting Cinzano vermouth.

The auspicious Argentina beginnings were again followed by difficulties as the Ministry of Education closed the cartoon film studio after two years and the two exiles faced uncertainty again. It is not quite clear why they did not leave the country under such circumstances. It might be that they were delayed by a police investigation when their studio was robbed and part of its equipment vanished. Dodal then returned to advertising and eventually made over 33 animated commercials for the companies Muro, Cinzano, Dosio, Colgate, Radio Aparato, Toddy and others via the Panamerican film studios.

In the mid-1950s, Dodal – already first-named Carlos – met his namesake Carlos Ochagavía. The native Spaniard, who had studied in the United States and pursued many activities as a surrealist artist, advertising professional, film director and TV producer, became interested in animation thanks to Dodal. Unfortunately, the Czech filmmaker did not utilize the encounter which would

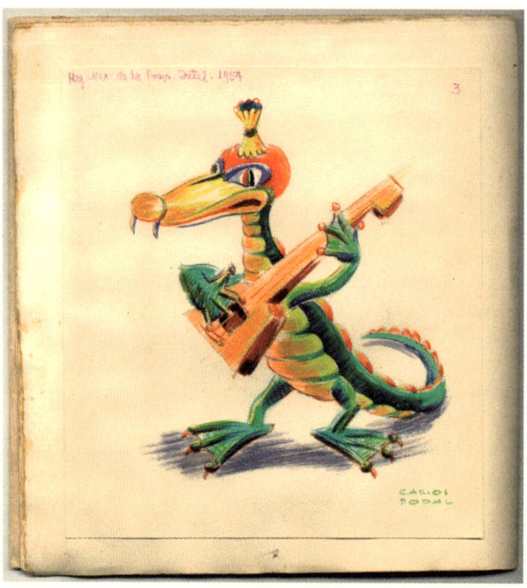

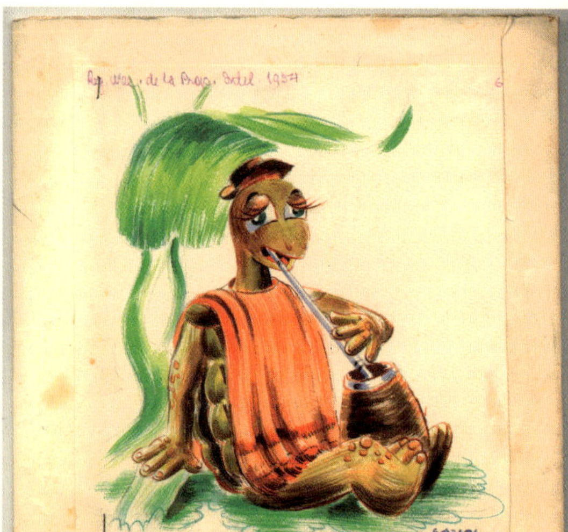

have opened doors for him to the new cultural environment. This episode was described by the art historian Enrique Martínez Glera: "Carlos learned a lot from Dodal, the Czechoslovak film director specialized in animated films, in 1955 and 1956. Dodal sported a Polish camera [which the author still thinks to be the original Czech device] and kept it in Carlos' studio. Carlos was the artist and Dodal the filmmaker. And even though Dodal would not lend him the camera, Carlos, totally inexperienced in filming, picked up many things by just watching – and he perfected his skills in that field, especially when he began working for the Lowe company. Dodal's animated films were somewhat static but Carlos was able to achieve much smoother motion."[18]

The relationship between the two artists was later compromised by Dodal's entanglement with Carlos' wife, Phyllis. As soon as Carlos found out about it, he threw him out of the studio. And while discarding his things, several

Karel Dodal's illustrations to the planned film *Concert* (El Concierto) are in the form of a folding picture-book.

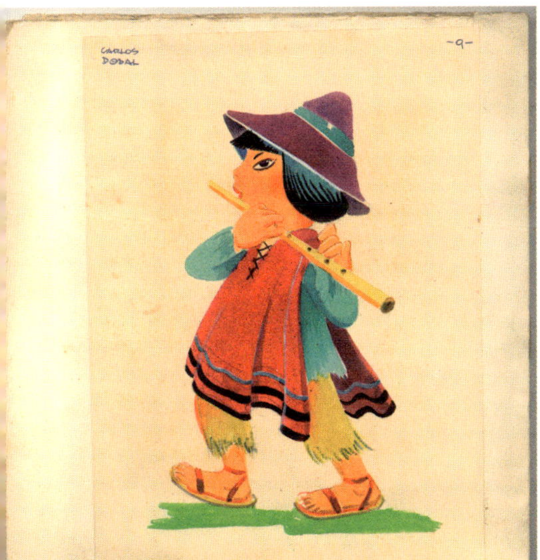

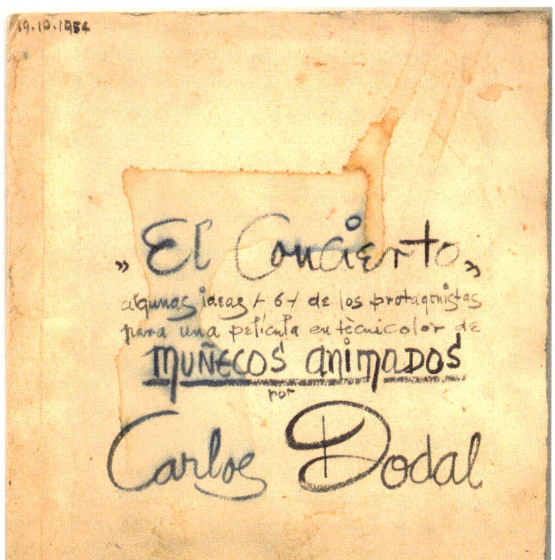

incriminating letters made it clear that Dodal had registered the films as his ownership without even mentioning the author of the drawings.

Although meeting Dodal affected Ochagavía's personal life adversely, it opened the world of animation to him. Several years later, he made the animated picture *La escoba de Lucinda* (Lucinda's Broom; 1961) which received an award at the Annecy festival. During the 1960s, Ochagavía also worked as animator and even became a distributor of animated films. He mainly focused on painting and illustration towards the end of his life.

Ochagavía certainly worked on many of Dodal's films as designer and animator. This is proved by his name surviving in the credits to several com-

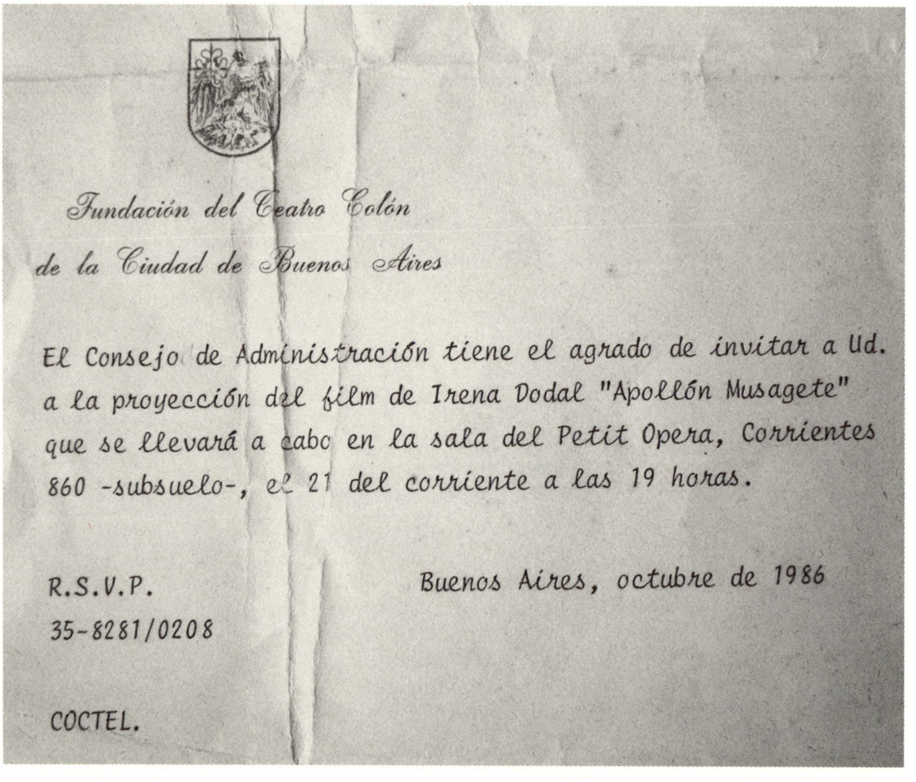

Fundación del Teatro Colón
de la Ciudad de Buenos Aires

El Consejo de Administración tiene el agrado de invitar a Ud. a la proyección del film de Irena Dodal "Apollón Musagete" que se llevará a cabo en la sala del Petit Opera, Corrientes 860 -subsuelo-, el 21 del corriente a las 19 horas.

R.S.V.P.
35-8281/0208

Buenos Aires, octubre de 1986

COCTEL.

mercials sent by Dodalová to Prague. It, unfortunately, were just fragments since the major part of Dodal's films was destroyed by fire.[19]

The significance of this encounter to Dodal is apparent from the folding picture-book to the film *Concert* whose palette evokes the bright and contrasting colours found in the paintings by the Catalan artist.[20] We, still, do not know whether Dodal actually finished the film. In any case, the figures from the picture-book appeared in an undated photograph from Dodal's exhibition held, as the stamp on the reverse suggests, in Paraguay. The black-and-white photo captures the considerable stylistic variety of the models used in his cartoon films and also quite aptly illustrates his gloomy mood. Dodal never – maybe due to the described unfortunate social incident – acclimatized to the Argentinian environment, parted with his wife in 1960 and left for the United States for good.[21] His letter from the same period, written to Hermína Týrlová in Zlín (at that time, Gottwaldov) speaks of his frustration and dreams about a house with large windows. Almost as if he was probing the situation... Týrlová reportedly said that this amused her being in her ground-floor little house.[22]

Contrary to her husband, Irena Dodalová soon established close contacts with the Buenos Aires artistic crowd and even won herself the possibility of independent film work.[23] In 1948 and 1949, she collaborated with the foundation Fondo National de las Artes which allowed her to make pictures about ballet and classical dance, i.e. fields that she had loved since her early years. As she wrote in her memoirs, she had had "previous schooling in singing, dancing and theatre... Sang operas in the Brno City Theatre for two years... When her contract expired, she decided to study feature-film production... Was recommended to a film centre in Berlin-Babelsberg: there, she became familiar with and assisted on the productions of Fritz Lang, G. W. Pabst (*3 Groschen Oper*), Max Reinhardt (*Theatre experimental*), and practiced in the Geierswerke laboratory, Berlin: simultaneously studying at the school *De Leon Kulechov: Technical Realization Cinematography*, with references to S. Eisenstein production... From there she was recommended to a production in Paris where she met Jean Renoir, René Clair (*Million*), Julien Duvivier (*The Great Waltz*), the photographer Man Ray y otros..."[24]

We cannot say how (and whether) Dodalová's foreign excursions ever came into existence, but being well orientated in the European inter-war world of art clearly prompted her contacts with the ballet scene of the Buenos Aires Columbus Theatre (Teatro Colón) as the most significant drama institution in Argentina. Her subsequent lyric epopees were symbioses of music, ballet and film and featured the most prominent dancers of that time. The testimony of her art is the 1951 *Apollon Musagete* – her hitherto only available title from this field. The fifteen-minute adaptation of an Igor Stravinsky ballet choreographed by Balanchine was not merely a record of a performance. The filmmaker liberated the dancers from the stage; they moved against a black background and only light pulled them out of the imaginary space and shaped their bodies. The individual dance positions were shot in various sizes of takes and from various angles, and their final montage included impressive large-dimensional close-ups. Fading was used to gradate the motion. *Apollon* was screened at many festivals during the 1950s and it still ranks among the works that have a firm position at various screenings of experimental film.

Dodalová's two other ballet films were *Don Juan de Zarissa* (1956) with music composed by Werner Egk, and *Dos danzas contemporaneas* (Two Contemporary Dances; 1956) to music by Modest Mussorgsky.[25] She also made the *Titres* (Puppets) with the prima ballerina Olga Ferri and the *Violin Magico* (The Magic Violin) with the Catalan violinist Xavier Turull. Several films were devoted to Argentinian folklore which she loved as much as the folklore of her homeland.[26] In addition, there are her film synopses in Spanish surviving in her archive fund, including a lot of material relating to the colour semi-documentary *La legendaria ciudad de los Cesares* (The Legendary Town of the Incas), on which she worked from the late 1950s to 1965 and which was to be co-produced with Peru. Her last realized film was the short colour picture *La tierra canta* (The Land Sings; 1965), produced by Guion cinematografico, whose script is also part of the given fund. Films by Dodalová were introduced at numerous Latin-American shows and represented Argentina at international film festivals held in Europe. It may well be that Argentinian film historians

Undated photograph of Karel Dodal. The stamp on the reverse suggests that the exhibition was held in Peru.

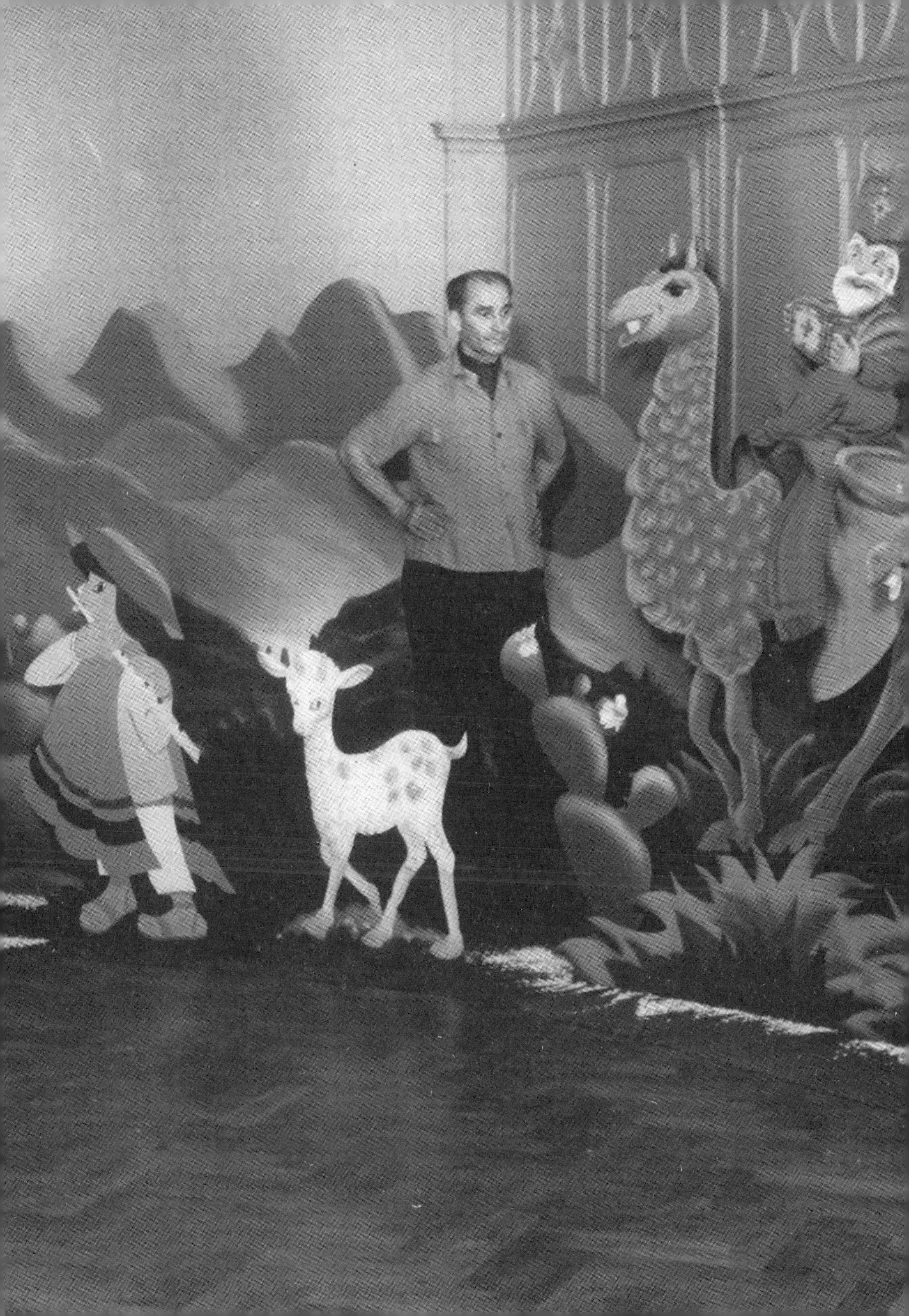

will manage to map out more comprehensively the filmography of the Czech native, who became one of the first female directors in Latin America.

The aging artist could not assert herself in Argentinian film production in the next years and, as she later wrote, she thus found her early theatre training useful. She began to pursue a teaching career. In 1959, she established her first theatre ensemble Primer Teatro Experimental Argentino de Cámara (The First Argentinian Experimental Chamber Theatre) and composed the next one in 1972 from the aspirants who responded to a newspaper ad. But it was more theatre seminars than a theatre stage for which Dodalová acquired the status of a cooperative. She wrote about this: "I had to train youths in

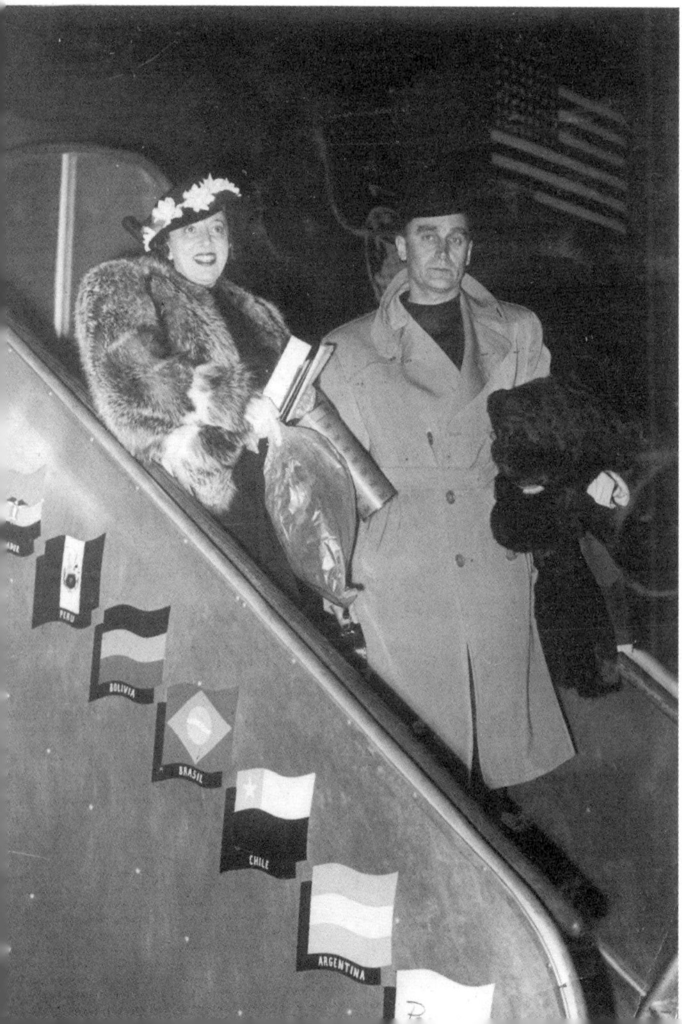

Undated photograph of Ms and Mr Dodal.

singing, in the dance *diccion*, in bodily expression, in music... it was desperate work because these were young people without any culture... they were from Yugoslavia, Africa, Russia, Germany, in short, 'Naciones Unidas' on a small scale... all was in the style of the Berlin experimental theatre which I discovered at Reinhardt's..."[27]

The ensemble gathered regularly twice a week, would go to cinemas together and Dodalová would lend them her theatre subscription card. The group performed now and then at various stages[28] and festivals, in clubs and even in the subway, and these presentations introduced impulses from 1920s and 1930s European avant-garde drama to the Latin American environment. During the rehearsals, with improvised costumes and minimum backdrops, Dodalová was a pedagogue, director, music arranger, occasional lighting engineer and often even author of the adapted texts. She learned with her students, for example, Paul Claudel's *Jeanne d'Arc* (Joan of Arc), James Joyce's *Exiles* and *Jedermann* by Hugo von Hofmannsthal. She also returned to Villon (*François Villon, Baladas, Testamento, Epitafio*, 1969) whose ballads she had first adapted in Theresienstadt. Notably her montage of music and choreography, entitled *Hola, Metropolis* (1974), which reflected the hectic life in the urban centre and used music from Disney films, enjoyed great success.[29] The performance was introduced at an international festival of pantomime and became part of a TV program.[30] Dodalová moreover staged variety shows based on Walt Whitman's poetry, programs departing from Argentinian folklore and so on. And even in her theatre activities, she protested against tyranny, lack of freedom and dictatorship. She wrote and staged the program *Carta al mundo* (Letter to the World) on the subject of co-existence and peace, performed by her ensemble at the First International Congress of Women in 1975. Nilio Omar Armas remembered that Dodalová integrated the song of a pampas gaucho, "Cuando tenga la tierra" (When I Have Land),[31] to the show although many students disagreed with it due to possible political persecution.

Dozens of young people passed through the troupe and some, such as Nilio Armas, Claudia Shifres, Oscar Sandoval Martínez,[32] later became art professionals. One of them also was Martin Barreiro, today's master and stage director of the Buenos Aires theatre El Convento who returned to the

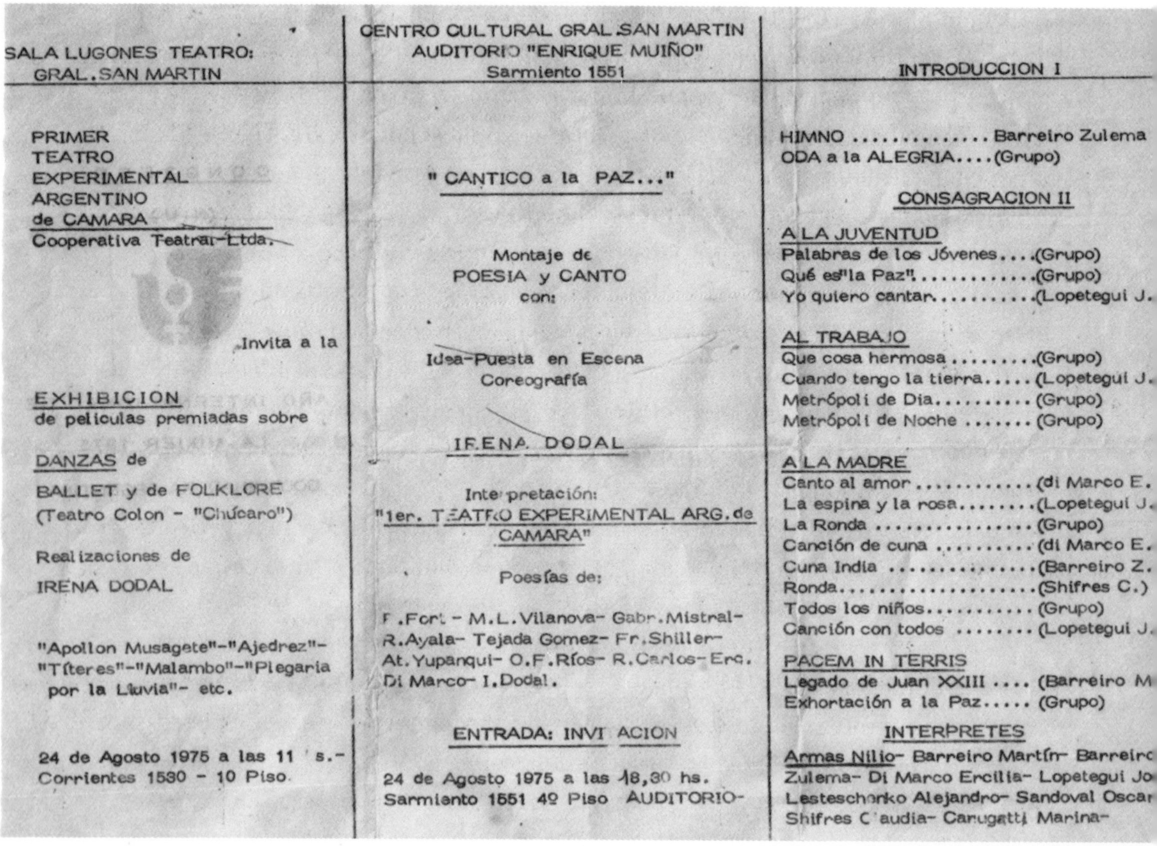

SALA LUGONES TEATRO:
GRAL. SAN MARTIN

PRIMER
TEATRO
EXPERIMENTAL
ARGENTINO
de CAMARA
Cooperativa Teatral Ltda.

Invita a la

EXHIBICION
de peliculas premiadas sobre

DANZAS de

BALLET y de FOLKLORE
(Teatro Colon - "Chúcaro")

Realizaciones de
IRENA DODAL

"Apollon Musagete"-"Ajedrez"-
"Títeres"-"Malambo"-"Plegaria
por la Lluvia"- etc.

24 de Agosto 1975 a las 11 's.-
Corrientes 1530 - 10 Piso.

CENTRO CULTURAL GRAL. SAN MARTIN
AUDITORIO "ENRIQUE MUIÑO"
Sarmiento 1551

" CANTICO a la PAZ..."

Montaje de
POESIA y CANTO
con:

Idea-Puesta en Escena
Coreografía

IRENA DODAL

Interpretación:
"1er. TEATRO EXPERIMENTAL ARG. de
CAMARA"

Poesías de:

F. Fort - M. L. Vilanova- Gabr. Mistral-
R. Ayala- Tejada Gomez- Fr. Shiller-
At. Yupanqui- O. F. Ríos- R. Carlos- Erc.
Di Marco- I. Dodal.

ENTRADA: INVI ACION

24 de Agosto 1975 a las 18,30 hs.
Sarmiento 1551 4º Piso AUDITORIO-

INTRODUCCION I

HIMNO .... Barreiro Zulema
ODA a la ALEGRIA....(Grupo)

CONSAGRACION II

A LA JUVENTUD
Palabras de los Jóvenes....(Grupo)
Qué es "la Paz"............(Grupo)
Yo quiero cantar..........(Lopetegui J.

AL TRABAJO
Que cosa hermosa.........(Grupo)
Cuando tengo la tierra.....(Lopetegui J.
Metrópoli de Dia..........(Grupo)
Metrópoli de Noche ....(Grupo)

A LA MADRE
Canto al amor............(di Marco E.
La espina y la rosa........(Lopetegui J.
La Ronda ....(Grupo)
Canción de cuna ....(di Marco E.
Cuna India ....(Barreiro Z.
Ronda....................(Shifres C.)
Todos los niños...........(Grupo)
Canción con todos ....(Lopetegui J.

PACEM IN TERRIS
Legado de Juan XXIII .... (Barreiro M
Exhortación a la Paz..... (Grupo)

INTERPRETES
Armas Nilio- Barreiro Martín- Barreiro
Zulema- Di Marco Ercilia- Lopetegui Jo
Lesteschenko Alejandro- Sandoval Oscar
Shifres Claudia- Carugatti Marina-

heritage of his teacher in the early 21st century and staged Villon's *Le Testament* and Von Hofmannsthal's *Jedermann*. He arrived to the group at the age of fourteen. "My artistic career began with her and I was her student as long as to 1984 when she decided to retire and urged us to go our own way. She had held this opinion since the time when I first met her. She was an excellent mentor. The fascinating thing about her was that she was able to retain her penetrating mental youth and admirable physical condition and health. Her approach to the world and her opinions were so authentic and believable that they deeply influenced all her students."[33]

Oscar Sandoval Martínez, a student of Irena Dodalová's theatre seminars, has been collecting written and photographic materials about the activity of his teacher for several years, depositing them in the Prague National Film Archive. Dodalová's theatre activity has not been summarized and compiled yet.

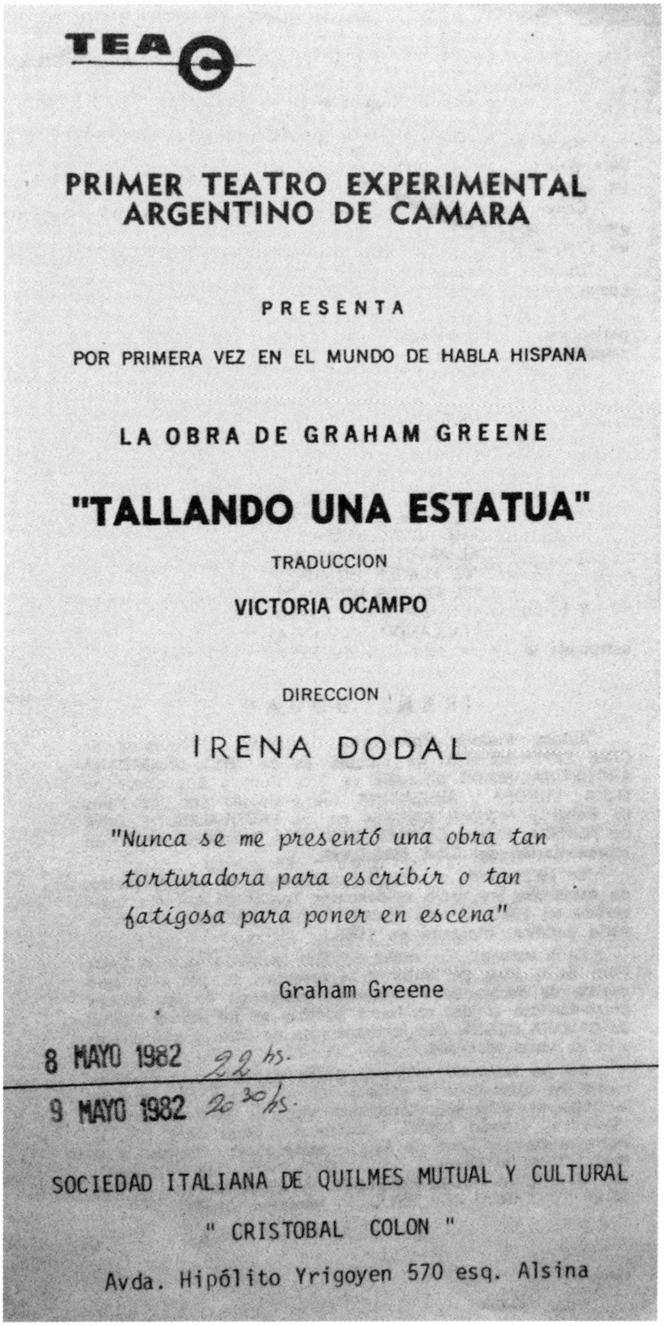

TEA C

PRIMER TEATRO EXPERIMENTAL
ARGENTINO DE CAMARA

PRESENTA

POR PRIMERA VEZ EN EL MUNDO DE HABLA HISPANA

LA OBRA DE GRAHAM GREENE

"TALLANDO UNA ESTATUA"

TRADUCCION

VICTORIA OCAMPO

DIRECCION

IRENA DODAL

"Nunca se me presentó una obra tan torturadora para escribir o tan fatigosa para poner en escena"

Graham Greene

8 MAYO 1982 22 hs.

9 MAYO 1982 20 30 hs.

SOCIEDAD ITALIANA DE QUILMES MUTUAL Y CULTURAL

" CRISTOBAL COLON "

Avda. Hipólito Yrigoyen 570 esq. Alsina

Working with young people in the theatre groups substituted for the missing family background to the Czech exile and allowed for realizing her artistic ideas and employing her teaching talents. Her personality was full of opposites. She was authoritative, but also had a sense of the magic of artistic work. Her friend, psychologist Helena Voldánová, judged her as follows: "Irena was intelligent, very spiritual; she meditated... and painted. She had enormous vitality and artistic verve. She always sought admiration and mainly had the importance of her own work on her mind, but had not much understanding for the work of other people."[34]

When she fought for things which she considered right, such as asserting Dodal's work, her organizational skills were mobilized and she became unyielding and tireless, but on the other hand often lacking both the strength and will to arrange her personal matters; her things in suitcases and boxes from the time when Dodal left her remained unpacked for years. But she retained a good memory till the end and knew precisely where which part of her belongings was and which key would open which suitcase. She was not a scholar type but had a wide scope of cultural knowledge and was interested in art and philosophy. Her idea of human existence and of sense of life included God, Jesus, Mother Theresa as well as the spiritual worlds of theosophists discussed in the writings by Blavatská, Steiner, Brenner and others.

Her letter of the early 1972, written to her brother Rudolf, reads: "Life is beautiful... every single flower, every bird, every little animal is a miracle of creation and intelligence... everything is part of a chain which, in all its components, is perfect... man is the only creature of free will (but, in a certain sense, of the choice to either build or wreck and destroy); man can choose between the two universal principles: plus or minus... To create or to destroy...

In order to draw ourselves nearer to the intelligence of the universe (to God), we must only suffer pain, and our tears will force us to think, will force us to meditate; only despair and solitude will bring us to the fullness of living and to the conviction that we are not alone; we will learn to love solitude, meditation, smile, nature..."[35]

Music was an irreplaceable part of her life to the end – she would even sing Dvořák's *Biblical Songs* to Professor Voldánová in her nineties.[36] When reading the diary of Anne Frank with her students, she would not talk about

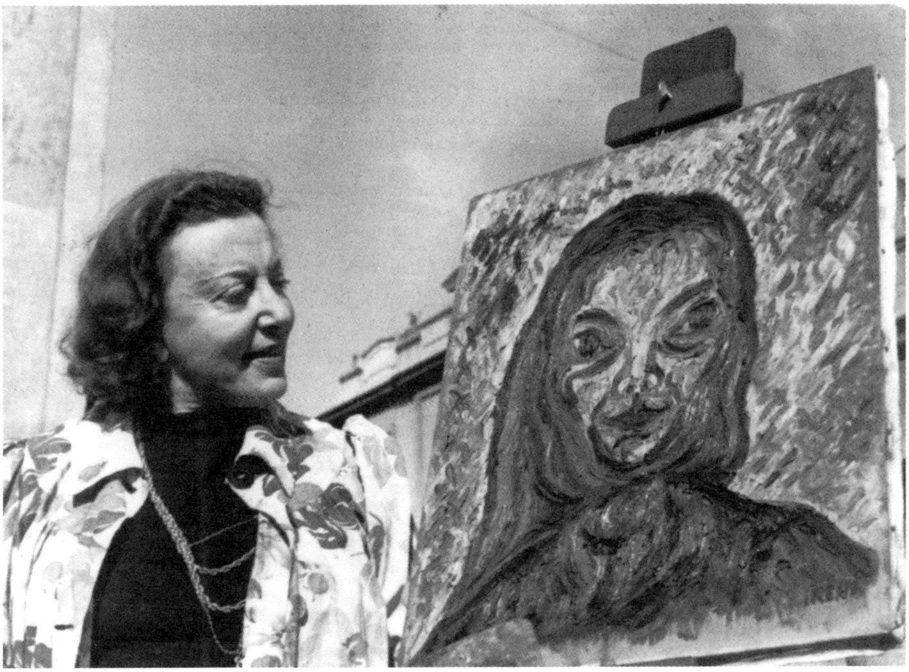

Irena Dodalová also painted and her inheritance moreover contains her musical compositions for her stage adaptations.

the war but about philosophy, evil, human arrogance and the need to steer all young people toward creating positive things, even though the negative always prevails and is stronger. She believed that each of us arrives in this world with a mission and that art fulfils the human soul. She would tell her students: "Well, girls and boys; look, you may have a friend, you may have a husband, life separates you but you must go on. And that's why you must always remain attached to theatre. True, your heart will grieve for a while, but then it maybe again falls for someone else, while theatre will always be here for you and will always be faithful. Sometimes you'll be really down, but theatre will always get you out."[37] These words apparently reflected her subjective experience and conviction.

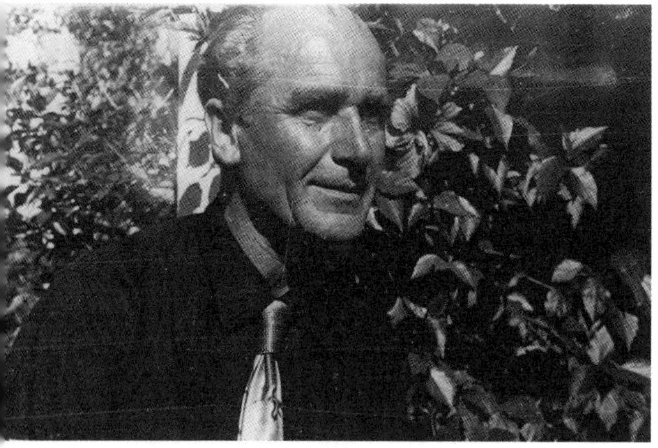

Undated photograph of Karel Dodal.

When the Dodals resolved to take the work in Argentina after the war, they naturally could not anticipate the consequences of their decision. The complicated post-war developments in their new country, with its successive dictatorships, oligarchy and military putsches going hand in hand with political persecution and mass murders, were a source of serious troubles for them as exiles for years. These events directly influenced everyday life. Informing thrived, transportation and post services very often did not work, the opportunities for traveling abroad were limited and equally limited was access to foreign currency; from time to time, it was impossible to go out because of gunfights... The fear of persecution was so strong that Dodalová gave up writing home for many years. As she wrote to her brother in 1985, "A Czech person with an Israeli background flounders like a fish out of water here..."[38]

Dodalová also long struggled with financial troubles. When her husband left, she moved to a woman exile from Germany for quite unclear reasons and fostered her for years.[39] Her situation only changed in the late 1960s when the West-German authorities awarded her damages for the years spent in Theresienstadt. She then purchased two flats on 1591 San Benito de Palermo Street where she established a studio for her students on the third floor and kept her private apartment on the fifth. Apart from her work for theatre, she painted, organized film classes and prepared several appearances on TV.

She maintained her contacts with Karel Dodal in the United States; she would write him on a regular basis and would call him on Sundays. She watched over his life, discussing with him and advising, while their dialogue was sometimes interrupted for weeks. Dodal's return to New York was not as he had imagined since most of his former protectors and patrons were out of their positions. The desired help came from the producer Robert Gross who, prior to the era of computer-generated animation, successfully interceded for his job in a NASA program. Dodalová reported that he actually received American citizenship for his drawn model of the 1965 landing of a module on the Moon. When Dodal's American guardian died (he reportedly had a stroke upon learning about the republican victory in the elections), the Czech exile was taken in by the producer's wife, Ruth Gross.

The separated couple, however, also frequently ran into quarrels. Irena, for example, complained in her letter to Rudolf that "Karel was an atheist when I first met him, but fell for experiments with the occult in the fourth dimension over the years in the States, and now he's a Catholic devoted to the Vatican and my letter infuriated him so as to call me a 'witch' worshipping demons, and he broke away from me definitely: all letters where I tried to provide a scientific explanation returned unopened with a note claiming that he didn't want my religious mystification to infect him... And now, he doesn't even want to hear about me".[40]

The Dodals last met in 1984. Irena at that time set off to the United States for Karel kept lamenting over his health. She found him in the Holy Name hospital in New Jersey and indeed managed to improve the patient's condition during her stay. She was only troubled by the presence of Dodal's new partner, Ruth Gross, during most of their conversations. And it also was Ruth who informed Irena two years later that Karel Dodal died on 6 July 1986."[41]

Even though the two had not been together for years, Dodal's departure was a great loss to Irena. She did not wait to send a message about this to Hermína Týrlová to Zlín, because the former professional threesome was in some contact for decades – they mutually (and sometimes jealously) watched their professional careers and turns of fate, and Dodal's death closed a very significant chapter in the lives of the two women.

In the years prior to her own death, Irena Dodalová strived to coin the name of Karel Dodal and their IRE-film activities to the history of Czech cinematography and to return her private archive, deposited in the city of Martinéz near Buenos Aires, to Prague. As soon as the Argentinian home affairs slowly quieted, she asked her long-time friend, the Prague attorney Alfred Popp, to help her transport the films and written documents. The negotiations related to the shipment, participated in by the Argentinian embassy and the Czechoslovak State Film, got complicated and prolonged – before the materials finally came to the Czechoslovak capital in summer 1989. But Irena did not get to open the letter informing her of their safe arrival.[42] She died in Buenos Aires in July 1989, just as she was getting ready to attend the performance of the visiting Prague Black Theatre.

Irena Dodalová with a drum. A shot by the Argentinian photographer Ricardo von Tschirnhaus, who visited her in her studio in the mid-1980s.

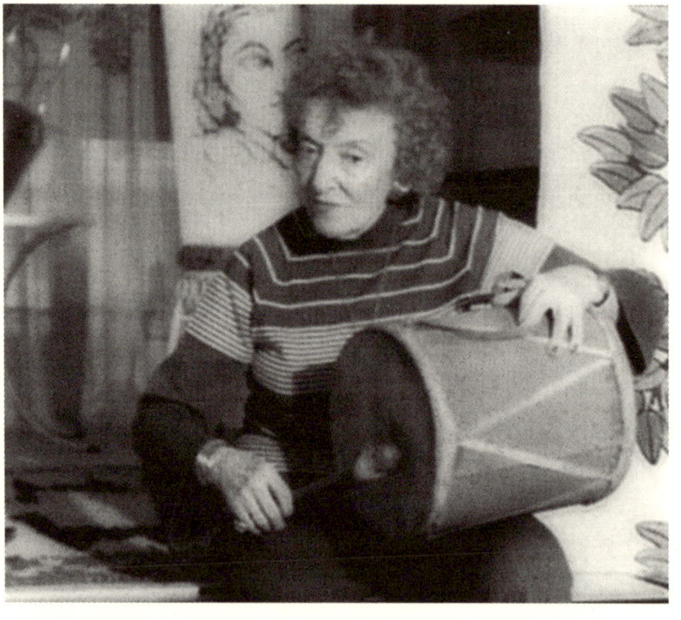

1 Letter of the Dodals to A. Popp family, August–December 1946. Personal Fund of Irena Dodalová.

2 Ibid.

3 Ibid.

4 Ibid.

5 Dodalová also introduced these films under the titles *The Inside Story of a Cow* and *One World.*

6 See the supply list to the film. Personal Fund of Irena Dodalová.

7 The film was sometimes introduced under the title *Once Upon a Time. There Were Three Men.*

8 The National Film Archive, fund Československý státní film (Czechoslovak State Film), R 9/A I./4P/4K.

9 The article, departing from Dodalová's information, also contains an abstract of the film's synopsis and mentions the pre-war activity of the Prague studio, while it not quite precisely describes the Dodals' complicated fates during the war. See Šrych, J., "Tvůrci tradice českého kresleného filmu", *Newyorské listy,* 9 October 1947.

10 "Zpráva československé technické delegace o kinematografické technice ve Spojených státech amerických" (Report of the Czechoslovak Technical Delegation about Cinematographic Technology in the United States of America). Filmový technický sbor (the Film Technical Board), Prague, October 1947. II. Kreslený film (Cartoon Film), p. 1. Collection Barrandov Studio, a. s., fund Barrandov – history, box 1947/13. Petr Dodal, the director's great-nephew, told the author that the Minister of Information at that time, Václav Kopecký, invited the Dodals to return to their homeland.

11 Comp. letter of A. Popp to Československý filmový ústav (ČSFÚ, Czechoslovak Film Institute), 23 July 1984. Personal Fund of Irena Dodalová.

12 Šrych, J., "Tvůrci tradice českého kresleného filmu", *Kino* (Cinema), 1947, No. 46, 14 November, p. 908.

13 Letter of H. H. Burger to I. Dodalová, 27 January 1948. Personal Fund of Irena Dodalová.

14 Dodalová, I., *Karel Dodal & I.R.E. FILM Praha. Datos o zrození kresleného filmu* (Data about the Birth of Cartoon Film). Personal Fund of Irena Dodalová.

15 González, A. R., "La animación en Argentina Los pioneros: Cristiani y Ducaud bajo el ala de Valle". Available [on-line] at: www.miradas.eictv.com.cu [quote of 17 October 2005].

16 The Personal Fund of Irena Dodalová contains the Spanish script to this film which is, however, dated 1968 when Dodal had already been living in the United States for several years.

17 See Note 14.

18 E. M. Glera in his e-mail to the author of the present book.

19 The fragments were related to the films *Sinfonia "C", Que acha disto?, Oru le Parece, Coci nero Vivo* and *Fantasia en Color.*

20 Dodal, C., *Concert.* I. Dodalová donated the folding picture-book to the daughter of J. Rippel who was arranging the dispatch of her archive to Prague at the Czechoslovak embassy in Buenos Aires.

21 The affair with Ochagavía not only had a family but also a court finale. Dodalová's bitter words in the letter to her brother Rudolf of 4 March 1981 were most probably related to this: "I can't even tell how I destroyed myself here in Argentina, because I fought as a tigress with the court and attorneys when they took his equipment as he once again was unable to meet a deadline and once again chased women instead of prompt work on his mind..." She divorced her husband in 1952 but the two were in contact till the end of his life, albeit living separately from 1961. Personal Fund of Irena Dodalová.

22 Information provided by Ms Komárková who helped Týrlová in her household. She also reported that the filmmaker destroyed her correspondence before leaving for an old people's home towards the end of her life.

23 According to N. O. Armas, her friends were the actors I. Marga, S. G. Cou and L. Vehil and the playwright R. Tálice. O. S. Martínez reported that she was also friends with dancers from the Columbus Theatre, for example D. Garcia, I. Borowski and J. Serrano, the theatrologist C. Mansa, choreographer H. Lobato and others.

24 See Note 14. This paragraph from Dodalová's correspondence more describes her interests during that time than reality. Her participation in filming can be doubted. It is, however, possible that she indeed worked in film laboratories (Geyer-Werke) in the 1920s, which would explain her competence later shown in IRE-film and in Pařík's studio. Although she never studied with Reinhardt, to whom she very often referred during her teaching, her Brno teacher was reportedly his student.

25 *Catalogue. Ten Years of Films on Ballet and Classical Dance 1956–1965.* Paris: UNESCO, 1968, pp. 15–16.

26 E.g., *Suite Argentina* (Argentinian Suite) and films devoted to the folk dances – *Baguala, Carnavalito, Malambo, Pericón* and others.

27 See Note 14.

28 According to information by N. O. Armas, these were, for example, Teatro Municipal General San Martín de Buenos Aires, Teatro del Centro, Teatro Estrellas and Teatro de Argentores.

29 Interview with O. S. Martínez in Prague in 2009. The National Film Archive, Collection of Sound Documents.

30 "El Show de Elio Roca", Canal 9. Interview with N. O. Armas, member of the Buenos Aires ensemble headed by the Argentinian publisher and writer, M. Reznik.

31 The two-part lyric epopee about the historical figure of gaucho M. Fierro (1872, 1879), written by J. Hernández, ranks among the basic works of late 19th-century Argentinian and Latin American literature and part of the text served as the basis for a popular folk song today performed by M. Sosa.

32 Partial documents relating to Dodalová's theatre activities are contained in the Personal Archive of Irena Dodalová. Other written and photographic documents about her work in Argentina were acquired for the National Film Archive from the initiative of O. S. Martínez. For more on this, visit [on-line]: http://irenadodal.blogspot.cz/2012/10/virginia-guedes-y-oscar-sandoval.html [quote of 28 December 2012].

33 Letter of M. Barreiro to the author of the present book.

34 Letter of H. Voldánová to the author of the present book, 4 October 2000.

35 Letter of I. Dodalová to her brother Rudolf, 31 January 1972. Personal Fund of Irena Dodalová.

36 See Note 34.

37 From the interview with the author of the present book with O. S. Martínez (Prague, November 2009).

38 Letter of I. Dodalová to her brother Rudolf, 18 October 1985. Personal Fund of Irena Dodalová.

39 The correspondence with her brother betrays that she missed her mother greatly. It seems that tending to the old German (who would allegedly poison her cats after every successful theatre premiere) served as a substitution for what she owed her own mother who was at that time dying in a facility of a Jewish Community in Poděbrady.

40 Letter of I. Dodalová to her brother Rudolf, 21 January 1980. Personal Fund of Irena Dodalová.

41 K. Dodal wrote a last will and testament during Dodalová's visit to the United States, bequeathing 35 thousand dollars to his ex-wife. In the hospital, however, he gave the disposition right to his property to R. Gross who then arranged his cremation and informed Irena that he had left nothing behind and that she had donated his last four unrealized storyboards to a New York museum of cartoon film. Such an institution has never been traced.

42 For more on this, see correspondence between I. Dodalová and V. Opěla. Personal Fund of Irena Dodalová.

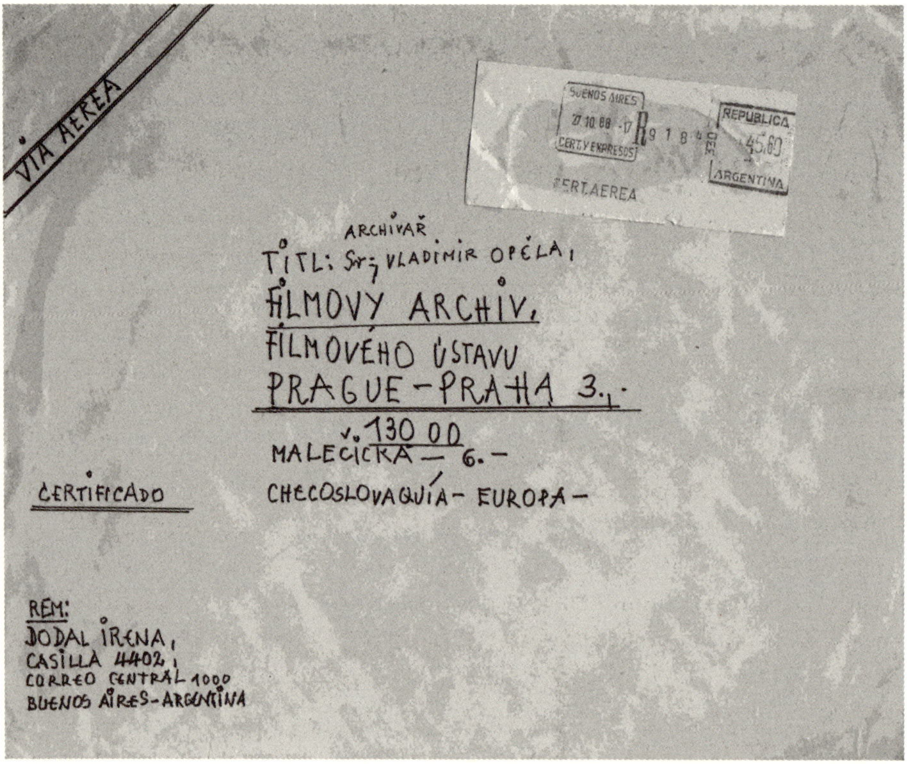
VIA AEREA
BUENOS AIRES
27 10 88 -17
CERT Y EXPRESOS
REPUBLICA
ARGENTINA
CERT. AEREA
ARCHIVÁŘ
TITL: Sr.: VLADIMIR OPĚLA,
FILMOVÝ ARCHIV,
FILMOVÉHO ÚSTAVU
PRAGUE - PRAHA 3.,.
v. 130 00
MALEŠICKÁ - 6. -
CHECOSLOVAQUÍA - EUROPA -
CERTIFICADO
REM:
DODAL IRENA,
CASILLA 4402,
CORREO CENTRAL 1000
BUENOS AIRES - ARGENTINA

Conclusion / The Discontinuity and Continuity of Czech Animated Film

Closing of IRE-film meant the termination of the only professional animated film production in Prague. The Nazi occupation of Czechoslovakia generated a strange gap between the local pre-war and post-war animated film production.

By a twist of irony, the Protectorate of Bohemia and Moravia subsequently became one of the main centres of German animated film production since the Third Reich needed to replace the widely popular Disney cartoon comedies with its own films in cinemas. The management of the production places dispersed throughout Germany and the occupied territories was gradually centralized, and the company Deutsche Zeichenfilm GmbH (German Cartoon Film) was eventually established upon Goebbel's order.

The Nazis first took a small Prague pre-war studio of film subtitles and tricks, AFIT, and the Austrian Richard Dillenz rebuilt it into a specialized cartoon film centre employing more than a hundred people. It was supervised by the compulsory administrator (*Treuhänder*) Josef Pfister, and the young Czech workers, banned from attending universities during the Protectorate, were introduced to the tricks of the trade by the classical German animator, Louis Seel. Dillenz began making the full-length colour *Orpheus and Eurydice* based on Gluck's opera of the same name, but, having no previous experience with cartoon film production, he frequently ran into conflicts with the Czech employees and the disputes even swung to Berlin. The project was eventually halted and the only finished title was the cartoon *The Sorcerer's Apprentice* (Zauberlehring, Čarodějův učeň; 1943), inspired by the symphonic scherzo by Paul Dukas based on Goethe's poem. However, only a black-and-white copy of the picture, originally shot on the colour material Agfacolor, survived. During the conflicts with Dillenz, the Czech head of production Zdeněk Reimann began enticing the graphic designer Jaroslav Benda to become the studio's art director. Benda agreed and joined a group of Czech employees on the preparatory work for the film *The Adversaries in the Depths* (Soupeři v hlubinách). But the German management soon rejected him and most of Dillenz's studio was incorporated into the Pragfilm company as a special Cartoon Film Department. The studio, headed by Horst von Möllendorf, produced three pictures: it made *A Wedding in the Coral Sea* (Hochzeit im Korallenmeer, Svatba v korálovém moři; 1944), based on the previous *Adversaries in the Depths*,[1] and finished *The Mischievous Bunny* (Klein aber Oho, Neposlušný zajíček; 1944) and *A Meteorological House* (Wetterhäuschen, Povětrnostní domeček; 1945).

The Baťa Film Studios (Filmové ateliéry Baťa; FAB) in Zlín initially did not make cartoons; they merely had a Department of Animated Diagrams filming trick takes for educational and instructional pictures. The Zlín director Ladislav Kolda, who had visited the Walt Disney Studio before the war, allowed for cartoon production in the early 1940s and its new employees included graduates from art schools. The designer Ladislav Zástěra was allocated to director Jiří Lehovec in order to realize animated abstract sequences for the film *Rhythm* (Rytmus; 1941); Stanislav Šulc, a graduate from the School of Applied Arts, began filming the cartoon *The Postman's Tale* (Pošťák Kolbaba), based on Karel Čapek's short story, with a newly established group of draughtsmen and future animators in 1941. At the same time, a crew including the Prague animator Hermína Týrlová began working on the puppet film *Ferda the Ant* (Ferda Mravenec), adapted from Ondřej Sekora's story, in the studio.

Conditions in the studio radically changed a year later when the Zlín film traffic was taken over by the German company Deschag (Deutsche Schmalfilmgesellschaft), a monopoly producer of narrow films in the framework of the Tobis holding. To meet the German requirements, the activity of the Zlín studio and laboratories mainly focused on producing foreign-language versions and 16mm copies of Nazi newsreels designated for the European territory controlled by the Third Reich. Ladislav Kolda, who acquired a temporary autonomy for the studio via his pre-war contacts with the director of the company Deschag, Johannes Eckhardt, agreed to cut down the production of documentaries and to preserve animated film production. The work on the film about Mr Kolbaba the postman, however, was halted because the studio was instead commanded to focus on the German cartoon series *Fritz und Fratz*.[2] About forty young employees, with Josef Kábrt and Zdeněk Miler among them, were trained in animation there on the simple graphics for cartoon comedies. The Germans also permitted the studio to continue producing puppet films, which launched with *Ferda the Ant*. Subsequently, the authorities approved the realization of *A Christmas Dream* (Vánoční sen), based on Hermína Týrlová's story.

The available archive documents prove that some Czech producers, too, were interested in animated film. In the early 1940s, Josef Skupa received an offer from Vladimír Pošusta, a quite unsuccessful entrepreneur in film industry, to arrange the production of a puppet film whose script was reportedly to be written by Jan Malík.[3] Skupa's answer summed up all the problems faced by potential puppet film makers: "I am again returning to the reasons why I keep being reluctant to make a puppet picture. Something like *Gulliver*, which cost loads of money and the army of people working on it had lots of time and all technology available, can never be our guideline. Other films with puppets acting directly through motion mechanisms require limited space. Strings cannot be prolonged endlessly. A puppet can only act close to the background because someone must always stand behind it, pulling the strings. If we film a theatre as it is performed on the puppet stage, it won't be a film but instead a filmed theatre and the critics will tear us to shreds. If we solve everything by filmmaking means, a roughly carved figure all over the screen won't look good; it will come out as a monster. And the close-ups can be even worse if the puppet lacks facial gestures."[4]

Although Skupa in his pre-war film scripts tried to break the barrier between the poetry of theatre and film, his excursions through film studios were too brief to allow him to more intimately adopt the possibilities offered to puppets by film. The Dodals, on the other hand, never had to solve the issue of using marionettes and large details in film since they, from the very beginning, used film trick technology which can set static images or three-dimensional objects in motion.

Our search for traces of the Dodals in the memories of the generation of the then-commencing filmmakers[5] led us to conclude that the young Czech employees[6] who worked in producing German and Czech animated films in Prague, Brno or Zlín were largely unaware of IRE-film and the Dodals. The less than five years of the studio's existence, during which only *The Adventures of a Ubiquitous Fellow* (Všudybylovo dobrodružství) was more widely distributed, was too short a period to develop an audience. The consequences of losing IRE-film were rather realized by the Dodals' coeval colleagues and the culturally oriented journalists who, at least in the early 1940s, tried to keep their name in the common awareness. An example of this is the information from *The Czech Film Correspondent* (Český filmový zpravodaj) from early 1941 where an anonymous author reporting about the Tobis attempt at making a cartoon reminded readers that although European animated film was in worse condition than that in America, "the painter Dodal had nice results in our country".[7] A reviewer of the *Film Courier* (Filmový kurýr) of April of the same year, writing about Brenten's failed cartoon film evening in Brno, observed: "We must admit that our film production is deprived of cartoon film which recently underwent sweeping improvement and has literally become the most complex film form. It is deprived because IRE-film, which had introduced several successful pictures of this kind (you certainly remember the witty *Adventures of a Ubiquitous Fellow*, amusingly explaining the principle of radio broadcasting) and even made colour films, is today non-existent. It thus cannot be said that we do not know Czech animated film. His creator was Karel Dodal, the founder of IRE-film. But it no longer exists."[8]

One of those who well sensed the abyss in Czech film production which had emerged with IRE-film's extinction was the film producer Miloš Havel. It was he who had helped György Pál temporarily work in the AB studio in Prague and who had consistently followed the developments at IRE-film, as is proved by the records from the sessions of the Film Advisory Board. When Trnka in 1941 created the illustrations for Karafiát's *Fireflies* (Broučci), Havel suggested he make its puppet film adaptation. It was a rather technically complicated task at that time and Trnka turned the proposal down. He, however, also negotiated with another producer, Karel Feix from Nationalfilm. These meetings resulted in Trnka's subject for the cartoon *Grandfather Planted a Beet* (Zasadil dědek řepu; 1945) which became the first post-war work by The T-Shirt Brothers (Bratři v triku) studio. Later, in the 1960s, Trnka noted about the Protectorate period that "the local cartoon film was in view then".[9]

The foundations of the new system of Czech animated film already began forming on Revolution day of May 1945. The post-war cartoon and puppet film production, represented by Jiří Trnka, Hermína Týrlová and Karel Zeman, and later also Břetislav Pojar, surprised many with original subjects, artistic concepts as well as animation, and won Czech cinematography renown and recognition at international film festivals. The main reasons for this rapid development were, to many, the conditions of the nationalized cinematography industry which resulted in centralizing the production to Prague and Brno (to the early 1950s) and Zlín (later renamed Gottwaldov) and facilitated the financing and distribution of pictures in an extensive cinema network. When Antonín Martin Brousil in 1948 evaluated Czech animated film, he stressed that there was "no conscious creative connection" between the contemporary (i.e. post-war) artists and the Dodals; he only admitted that Hermína Týrlová had brought certain technical knowledge from the Dodals.[10] He thus opined that the post-war heyday of Czech cartoon and puppet film equalled a new beginning which had nothing in common with the previous development; a conviction which in a certain sense still continues.

The figure of Hermína Týrlová undoubtedly represents a link between the pre-war, Protectorate and post-war cinematography. It is, however, a question whether she had only brought technical knowledge from the Dodals. Let us therefore again return to her story in more detail.

Týrlová in the late 1930s found herself in an extremely difficult situation for the second time in her life, since there was no work for her in Prague. If she wanted to continue animating, there was no other chance but to find a new producer and new place for her profession. After a number of unsuccessful negotiations, she received help from Karel Dodal's namesake friend Smrž, who recommended her to the head of the Zlín studio, Ladislav Kolda. She offered to debut with a film adaptation of the popular children's book *Ferda the Ant*. It is well probable that employing these illustrations in either a cartoon or a puppet film had already been discussed in IRE-film in 1936 when the book first came out. In 1940, Týrlová moved to Zlín where she first lived on her savings and then became the studio's employee. The studio at that time was a small, almost family, enterprise mainly associating young people ready to pursue new things where films were made collectively. And even though Kolda equipped Týrlová with many assistants, the picture's filming (and re-filming) took as long as seventeen months. It was difficult to make because the studio lacked elementary experience with animating puppets and organizing such a production. Problems also arose due to the vivid imagination of the inexperienced screenwriters inventing the plots who did not foresee the strenuousness of their technical realization. The crew managed to finish the film only when Ladislav Zástěra was appointed its co-director and brought some order to the process. After *Ferda the Ant*, Týrlová and her team began making *A Christmas Dream*, a story about a rejected rag boy puppet who is reunited with a whimsical little girl. This laborious and basically unrepeatable work was destroyed when the Zlín cutting room caught fire in 1944. This resulted in the filmmaker's nervous breakdown and her former phasist, Karel Zeman, created a new version of the picture during her recovery. Týrlová, however, refused to be the co-author and this event affected their relationship for decades.

Ferda the Ant was simultaneously distributed in a German version as *Der brave Slim*, provided in both wide and narrow formats. Irena Dodalová once bitterly commented that Týrlová as the former IRE-film animator had sold its expertise to the Germans. This was more or less understandable of a former Theresienstadt inmate. On the other hand, Týrlová's life in Zlín was anything but easy. She struggled hard to assert her ideas, the work would often stall, and she had to participate on the foreign versions of Nazi newsreels when the filming of the puppet pictures was in downtime.

The filmmaker's post-war position in Zlín was no less difficult. Her first realized subject was the combined picture *The Toy Rebellion* (Vzpoura hraček; 1947). As in the past, she brought the subject and animation concept to the studio. The film was born of the joint effort of the local team of scriptwriters and designers, the cameraman, editor and music composer and many others. František Sádek, appointed to Zlín from Prague, took hold of directing the acted parts with Eduard Linkers as the SS-man. Elmar Klos, then, had a considerable share in the film's success as he recommended replacing a thief in the toy fight by the given Gestapo person, which gave the picture a topical twist. Týrlová was not just an animator but also a demiurge there: her phenomenal memory and inexhaustible patience allowed her to set dozens of types of toys into action, to link them with live human action and to moreover employ many gags. The masterly direction and up-to-date message won the film great success both in the Czech lands and abroad, it received awards at the festivals in Brussels and Venice and the studio management expected the filmmaker to keep the line of engaged subjects. She would, however, keep submitting lyrical subjects which the management rejected. Týrlová eventually employed her pre-war experience from doing business with the Dodals

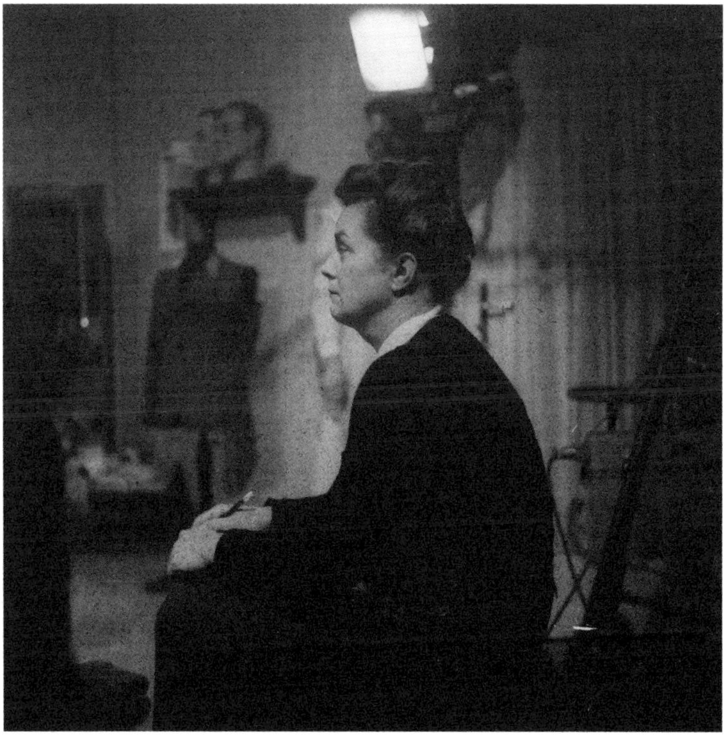

Hermína Týrlová in the post-war years.

and began filming commercial, at that time called "recruitment", pictures. The result was the film about shoe mending, *Why Do They Wither* (Co jim schází; 1947), the commercial *Lullaby* (Ukolébavka; 1947) promoting toys, the film *Collision* (Karambol; 1947) explaining the necessity of observing traffic rules, and the *Night Romance* (Nočná romanca; 1949) for the Slovak shoe factory Svit, where little male figures made of jersey wool helped two shop-window dummies meet. The titles were rather clumsy from an advertising point of view, but the author at least gained space for her unique animation. The faith in the power of this genre finally brought Týrlová unexpected success when her *Lullaby*, originally a commission for the Fatra Napajedla factory, was introduced at the Venice film festival and awarded a gold medal. The picture was globally distributed by UNESCO and the artist's name gained international renown. It was successful not only due to the coordination of the little figure and a live suckling, but also the sound montage employing the baby's laughter and weeping and the composition of colour and sound. The success eventually made the studio realize that Týrlová's domain were neither political nor social subjects but simple, plain stories with a happy ending and a moral lesson, mainly aimed at child audiences. These chamber etudes with minute humorous episodes were, after all, very close to her nature.

Elmar Klos in his recapitulation of the Zlín/Gottwaldov studio history wrote that Týrlová never took the path of difficult experimenting as, for example, Karel Zeman did.[11] But when he enumerated the objects which were seemingly impossible to enliven and enact in her films, he as if turned contradictory since Týrlová was actually an untiring experimenter, although of a different kind than Zeman. She was capable of bringing not only rag figurines and various children's toys but also wood, plastic, wool, stone, glass from Železný Brod, the famed Vizovice bakery products and other materials to life. She moreover successfully continued in her previous textile animation. Her experience from the pre-war advertising showed her that everything, including a bar of soap and an envelope, could be anthropomorphized. The titles of her post-war films, *The Toy Rebellion* and *A Marble* (Kulička; 1963) reverberate with the unrealized IRE-film projects *The Rebellion of Shapes* (Vzpoura tvarů) and *A Marble in Love* (Zamilovaná kulička), while the films *Kalamajka* (1957)[12] and *The Star of Bethlehem* (Hvězda betlémská; 1969) as if followed in IRE-film's erstwhile efforts to use folk art in animation. And, in her *Two Small Clews* (Dvě klubíčka; 1962) she returned, after many years, to animating sewing kits which had once acted in *An Autumn Song* (Píseň podzimu).

It therefore seems that Hermína Týrlová brought more than technical knowledge from Elekta Journal and IRE-film. The fact that she usually kept silent about her former experiences was natural to her: she was very friendly and kind, but the part of her personal life affected by pain and disappointment usually remained concealed. She was also not in the habit of sharing her expertise; first because she did not need to formulate the animation issues, which she solved intuitively, via theory, and second, because her generation, which had gained the related knowledge in such a hard way, did not exactly like to simply give it away.

The story of the Dodal couple long remained unattended by the professional public for many reasons which we have already mentioned, and if these reasons were ever published, it was from a critical distance. The film critic and essayist Jaroslav Boček in the early 1960s thought that Dodal was not a great artist but "a skilful imitator, a technological speculator rather than anything else. He did not have the pathos of a musically gifted person. He was not a poet of his field in the creative sense of the word".[13] Boček's view at the same time resonated with the contemporary conviction as to the low level of Czech inter-war animation.

How, then, to cope with such a pejorative opinion of the renowned critic and later author of animated films? We can agree with Boček that Dodal lacked the timeless imagination of Alexander Alexeieff, Oskar Fischinger, Lotte Reiniger and other experimenters. There is no doubt that he was just an average artist and dexterous draughtsman, but we must admit that every time he drew inspiration from foreign authors, he did so with the ease of an improviser and his many artistic solutions were utterly original. After all, copyright was perceived somewhat differently than today – advertising approaches and ideas at that time migrated throughout Europe, although not always without being noticed.[14] Dodal was not an epigone. Evaluating him must take the contemporary filming context into account and simultaneously admit that we are, alas, looking back on the basis of only few documentary materials. For example, the film sketches and technical scripts are missing, and Dodal's American and

Argentinian films are not available, either. We nevertheless cannot deny that the titles from the IRE-film production enriched Czech cinematography with a new and unique, multifaceted style and design.

Dodal's primary point of departure in cartoon film, however, was not artistic impulses (apart from perhaps his abstract creations) but his fascination with animation and trick. He was, first and foremost, an intrinsic film animator who had mastered several professions, being the trick cameraman, lighting engineer, writer of technical scripts, animator, film editor, director... He managed all the roles himself which were usually done by an array of experts in other studios. It was precisely Dodal's versatility which made him, under the given circumstances, a founder of cartoon and puppet film production – for no other, however gifted, academic painter would ever have asserted himself in the contemporary Czech film industry. Dodal moreover was a competent studio head who developed the first system of animated film production in the Czech lands. His versatility and professional zeal in trick filming and animation held considerable creative potential even despite the above-mentioned artistic and perhaps also intellectual limits.

Assessing Dodal's contribution to film, it should be noted that an essential role in his artistic career was played by the two lead women in his life who assisted the handsome, rather neurotic and unpractical man, as far as business issues were concerned, in solving the matters of both life and art work. They developed his plans and helped him realize them; they pushed him to finish his plans and observe his deadlines. They were his muses, although each of them ushered him along different paths. But it was this collaboration that helped Dodal make his most interesting pictures – and there is no reason to doubt that the unfinished American project *Paul Bunyan* would probably have been completed if they had been present.

The figure of Hermína Týrlová receives new facets in our context. The commencing theatre walk-on scribbling simple jingles gradually turned into a conscientious and patient animator for whom the field of animated and then puppet film became her employment and lifetime profession. Had it not been for her devoted and forbearing collaboration, Dodal would never have succeeded in Elekta Journal. Even though she was, as she would repeatedly emphasize, only little energetic and self-assertive, she always stood the test of difficult life situations with admirable vigour. She was able to manage her husband's work in Elekta Journal (as the first woman of this profession in the Czech lands) and, when necessary, she solved the family's existential problems on her own. Her role in IRE-film was also irreplaceable, because her qualified and tireless work of animator and phasist allowed the production to observe the commission deadlines. In addition, she certainly contributed to the production prosperity with many ideas.

In his second wife Irena, Dodal not only acquired an efficient film producer and manager but also an educated, smart and ambitious collaborator of a wide cultural horizon who enriched his hitherto rather provincial work with new impulses and challenges. Karel Dodal at that time accepted her opinions and proposals as his own and it is thus difficult, almost impossible, to differentiate between their individual creative investment. It seems that Irena Dodalová was aware of her husband's restricted creative potential: we know that she also negotiated with other artists. See, for example, her plans to employ Oscar Jacobson's illustration, the folklore morphology or Šetelík's watercolours, while the contact with one of the talented Prague advertising designers, the architect Leo Heilbrunn, was expected to bear fruit, too. She, however, never doubted either Dodal's irreplaceable role in the studio or his filmmaking talent.

It is therefore clear that the fundaments of Czech professional cartoon and puppet film were laid by Karel Dodal and his two wives. Dodal and Týrlová in the latter half of the 1920s mastered the tricks of the animation trade, creating the preconditions for the following development stage of the 1930s when IRE-film already aspired to achieve higher dramaturgy and technical goals. During that period, an array of draughtsmen and colourists was trained in this first specialized studio, the productivity of labour raised, and the titles made received a new quality thanks to the modern sound dramaturgy as well as the Gasparcolor palette.

Although independent, the studio continuously lacked financial strength and did not bring any creative freedom to the Dodals. It turned out over time that procuring stable and profit-making animated film production on the territory of, what was then, Czechoslovakia was an arduous or rather an impossible task even provided that the larger part of the production was commercials. The success of *The Adventures of a Ubiquitous Fellow* unfortunately remained isolated for there was no other public institution willing to invest in film animation. Yet another problem was that the Dodals were reluctant to take the path of American cartoon comedy and instead followed in the footsteps of European avant-garde filmmakers, at the same time wishing to employ animation not only for formal experiments but also for translating serious social subjects. Their avant-garde abstract opuses – *Fantaisie érotique* and *Ideas in Search of Light* (Myšlenka hledající světlo) – had no prospect of being introduced in cinemas and could only work as solitaires at special film events and presentations abroad. Also film history has been viewing their works as merely solitary artefacts whose only context is documentaries classified as Czech avant-garde. Abandoning the path of cartoon comedy and trying to follow in the tradition of modern European film deprived the artists of the chance to address wider audiences and children. In this sense, their enterprise was a failure. (Hermína Týrlová, on the contrary, later focused her career otherwise, on puppet films for children.)

On the other hand, there was a section of the Dodals' oeuvre which won the couple a primary place in a field viewed as secondary, and that was film commercials. Their works of this kind rank among the best achievements created in the Czech lands during the given period. Their studio turned into an experimental workshop where a new form of film advertising was born from the point of dramaturgy, design and animation – as well as sound and music. IRE-film thus became a brand with a well-grounded potential to enter the international market. And it was not the Dodals' fault that this never happened.

Looking at the development of Czech animated film, it is apparent that its individual stages in Elekta Journal, IRE-film and Afit, as well as in the Brno and Zlín studios, had their own stories, their own beginnings and ends. The loss of the film productions, however, did not mean their definitive ending – because the impressions from encountering the cartoon and puppet films undoubtedly lived on in the memories of audiences long after the pictures vanished from the cinema repertoires and after their titles, too, fell into oblivion. Also, Irena Dodalová's message about the mission of animated film and the necessity to develop a unique program of European animation, as published in the pre-war press, exceeded its period and helped create a concept which contributed to the establishment of The T-Shirt Brothers after the war. It was undoubtedly in the Dodals' studio where Jiří Trnka first came across Pál's films and the new approach to setting puppets in motion and where he, among other things, heard the ideas of Ms Irena about the chances of employing folk art in either cartoon or animated film – i.e. the subject which was so substantial in his post-war oeuvre. The issues as to the continuity or discontinuity of Czech cartoon and puppet film are not as easy to solve as they may seem at first sight. Exploring the inheritance of the Dodals can certainly contribute to their more precise formulation and to finding answers to the questions raised.

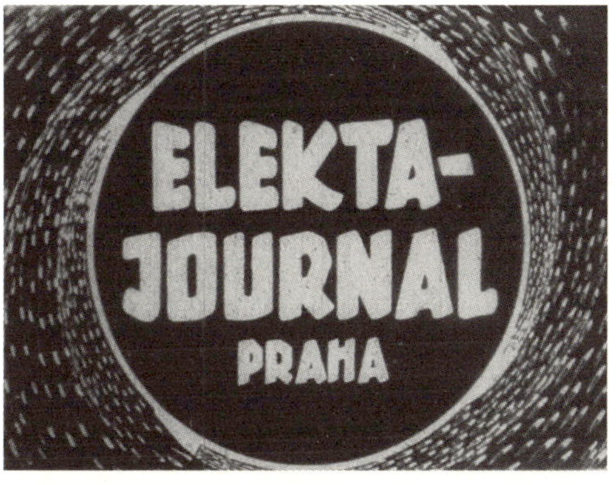

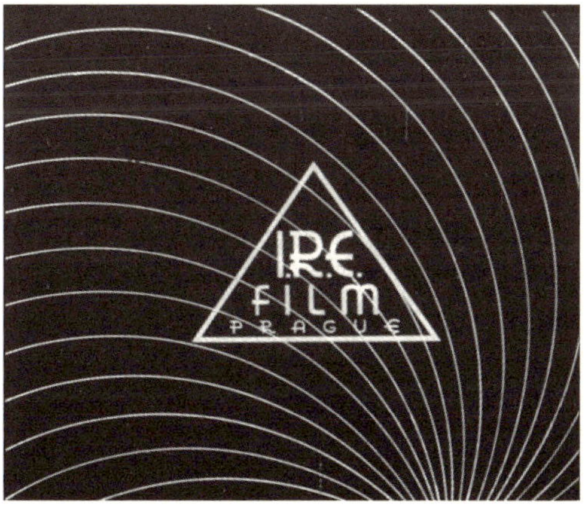

1 This working stage of the Czech employees is documented by the existence of the black-and-white copy of the film, deposited in the National Film Archive as *The Adversaries in the Depths* (Soupeři v hlubinách).

2 The employees at least tried to continue working on *The Postman's Tale* in secret. After the war, the unfinished black-and-white picture was taken in by the Brno studio, but it was never introduced to cinemas. The author of the series *Fritz und Fratz*, filmed from 1939 to 1945, was the Austrian J. Weichberger.

3 Letter of V. Pošusta to J. Skupa, 21 January 1941. The Plzeň City Archives, Josef Skupa Literary Inheritance.

4 Letter of J. Skupa to the Zdar-film company, 2 June 1941. Ibid.

5 Interviews of the author of the present book with professionals in the field of animated film. The National Film Archive, Collection of Sound Documents (F. Blahout, Č. Duba, S. Malý, B. Masník, B. Pojar, V. Schmiedová, F. Skřípek, Z. Skřípková, B. Šejda, M. Šindlerová, F. Vystrčil).

6 The Germans also appointed a compulsory administrator to the Brno villa where a technician working for the Zbrojovka Brno company, O. Blažek - a nerd adoring Disney and known under the cognomen Brenten – attempted to make cartoon films. The Brno administrator, however, in no way interfered in the Brentens-Production, Zeichenfilms enterprise, realized in the kitchen of Blažek's mother. Blažek was lucky enough to employ three young assistants: the later pedagogue J. Broskva, J. Fiala, one of the post-war directors of Barrandov Film Studios, and F. Vystrčil, the future designer and director of animated films. In 1944, the group finished the commercial *Cinderella* (Das Märchen vom Aschenbrödel, Pohádka o Popelce).

7 "Zajímavosti týdne" (Weekly Highlights), *Český filmový zpravodaj* (The Czech Film Correspondent), 1941, No. 4, 22 February, p. 3.

8 -ksž- [K. Smrž], "Jak se to nemá dělat čili representační večer kresleného filmu" (How not to Do It, or the Representative Evening of Cartoon Film), *Filmový kurýr*, 1941, No. 15, 11 April, p. 2.

9 "Dvacet let čs. trikfilmu. Vypovídá Jiří Trnka" (Twenty Years of Czechoslovak Trick Film. A Testimony of Jiří Trnka), *Film a doba* (Film Today), 1965, No. 6, pp. 284–291.

10 Brousil, A. M., "Československý kreslený a loutkový film" (Czechoslovak Cartoon and Puppet Film). In: *Malý filmový slovník* (Small Film Dictionary). Praha: Čs. filmové nakladatelství, 1948, p. 87.

11 Klos, E. – Pinkavová, H., *Historie gottwaldovského filmového studia v pohledu pamětníků, očima současníků a v dokumentech* (History of the Gottwaldov Film Studio from the View of Eyewitnesses and Contemporaries and in Documents). Praha: Československý filmový ústav (ČSFÚ, Czechoslovak Film Institute) 1984, p. 66.

12 Kalamajka – an Old Czech folk dance.

13 Boček, J., "Cesta Hermíny Týrlové za loutkovým filmem" (Hermína Týrlová's Journey to Puppet Film), *Film a doba*, 1960, No. 3, p. 159.

14 E.g., the German magazine *Die Reklame* at the turn of the 1920s and 1930s ran a section "Plagiat-Spiegel" (Plagiarism Mirror) where an author under the pseudonym Sapiens published examples of German ideas being appropriated by foreign press, while Czech and Slovak items were no exception.

Filmography 1927–1938

The presented list includes the animated films by Karel Dodal, Hermína Týrlová and Irena Dodalová from between 1927 and 1938 which the artists in question made in the Elekta Journal company and in their own studio, IRE-film. It also contains films in which either Karel Dodal and/or Hermína Týrlová participated as experts in trick technology. The filmography is provided in chronological order and according to subjects.

The basic information departs from the database of animated films held by the National Film Archive, which not only contains data on the archived films but also the results of researching the films which did not survive. The written information about the given films was further confronted with the censorship files and the information published in the Bulletin of the Ministry of Interior of the Czechoslovak Republic. The latter two sources allowed for verifying the production and technical data as well as the contents of the missing pictures. The files often also included transcripts of dialogue sheets, lyrics of songs, commercial appeals and the like. Other documents were found in the written and visual archives of the National Film Archive, especially in the archive of the company Aktualita which moreover contained the Elekta Journal accounting books. Research was also carried out in the National Archives, mainly in the archives of the Czechoslovak Ministry of Enterprise, Commerce and Industry (part of which was the Film Advisory Board), the Ministry of Foreign Affairs, the Municipal Council of the Capital of Prague and in the Central Military Archives, because the former Ministry of Defence had its representative in the Film Advisory Board. We also employed the contemporary press in issuing the lists of films and verifying the information. In addition, they paid attention to the commemorative texts written by Hermína Týrlová and Irena Dodalová, while the filmography lists compiled by Jiří Havelka again proved to be a valuable and reliable source.

Besides researching written archive records, we also used the information contained directly in the films. It is worth noting that these pictures in the time of their origination very often lacked credits informing about the authors and/or the production studio, many films only survived in an incomplete version and the existence of some is merely manifested by few film frames.

Alas, not even the present filmography can be viewed as a final one with regard to the incomplete foundation of sources and the above-mentioned condition of the surviving films. We have left many issues open. It can also be assumed that the list of films containing cartoon sequences and trick passages did not encompass some minor works by Karel Dodal and Hermína

Týrlová, made for various documentary and instructional pictures of Elekta Journal and, eventually, other commissions. We, on the contrary, managed to extensively reconstruct the IRE-film production. The collections of the National Film Archive hold twenty-two films of the total thirty titles produced by the studio, while eleven of them survive in a complete version. And since our research continues in other archive funds and identifications are also being carried out in other film archives, it can be hoped that we have managed to supplement and particularize our results to date.

In compiling the filmography, we also had to consider that the description of many of the followed categories used in feature films with actors does not correspond to the field of animation where the particular professions have different contents and different meanings in the hierarchy of the film work and production. Moreover, the credits of the pre-war films usually did not include many professions, such as the name of the director, cameraman, editor, animator and others.

Animated films did not have a standardized form for decades, or they eventually only provided the name of the "draughtsman" or "draughtswoman", i.e. the director. Moreover, the corresponding credits often were not set into the films at all either because the pictures were commercials, or they simply did not survive. The presented inventory draws from the information given by the film credits and also takes account of other written sources and mainly of the present-day terminology. The authors of the films from the IRE-film production usually provided the authorship information in the form "libretto – direction – drawing". In the case of Karel Dodal, this *de facto* not only encompassed his creative but also technical work because he was simultaneously the cameraman, trick-maker, lighting engineer, editor, and so on. As concerns Irena Dodalová, for example her role of sound engineer and her activity as a producer were explicitly not given. We do not add any information to the original version in the filmography; it is only translated to the 21st-century terminology – i.e., we use the categories "screenplay by", "directed by" and "designed by", and we do so even in the cases when this information is missing. The name of Irena Leschnerová-Dodalová is always given as Irena Dodalová in spite of the contemporary sources stating that she most often presented herself under the artistic cognomen Iréna. She accepted the last name Dodalová only as late as in December 1935. With few exceptions, the name of Hermína Týrlová was never part of the credits. Her position as a cartoonist, phasist and animator was recorded by the filmography only subsequently, under the category "animated by". We also consistently give the title of the Dodals film studio as IRE-film, although it changed in the course of time many times: from Atelier IRE, IRE atelier and IRE FILM to I.R.E.-FILM or I.R.E-film.

Karel Dodal and Hermína Týrlová
– films produced by Elekta Journal / 1927–1930

1927

Felix the Cat Receives a Lesson / Poučení Kocoura Felixe
production: Elekta Journal, *dates of censorship:* October 1927, October 1934
footage: original 35 m, surviving 26.4 m
directed by: Karel Dodal, *animation:* Hermína Týrlová
silent, black-and-white
A commercial promoting money saving.

The New Adventures of Felix the Cat / Nové dobrodružství Kocoura Felixe
production: Elekta Journal, *date of censorship:* October 1927
footage: original 40 m, surviving 42.1 m
directed by: Karel Dodal, *animation:* Hermína Týrlová
silent, black-and-white – virage
A commercial promoting money saving.

Felix the Cat Has an Accident / Nehoda Kocoura Felixe
production: Elekta Journal, *date of censorship:* November 1927
footage: original 59 m, the film material is believed lost
silent, black-and-white
Information about the commercial did not survive.

1928

What Felix the Cat Does Every Afternoon / Co dělá Kocour Felix každé odpoledne
production: Elekta Journal, *date of censorship:* March 1928
footage: original 70 m, the film material is believed lost
silent, black-and-white
Felix the Cat makes himself coffee from roasted chicory produced in the Czech town of Kolín.

Felix the Cat Is Farming / Kocour Felix hospodářem

production: Elekta Journal, *date of censorship:* November 1928

footage: original 130 m, the film material is believed lost

silent, black-and-white

A commercial with Felix the Cat, promoting merchandise from the seed-producing company, Jindřich Vaněk, based in Prague.

A Water Sprite in Love / Zamilovaný vodník

film material held in: the Czechoslovak Film Institute – Film Archive 1982–1984

footage: surviving 305 m

directed by: Karel Dodal, Hermína Týrlová, *animation:* Hermína Týrlová

silent, black-and-white

A film about a reckless water sprite and his jealous wife.

1929

How Felix the Cat Supported the Ostrava Region / Jak Kocour Felix obohatil Ostravsko

production: Elekta Journal, *date of censorship:* February 1929

footage: original 50 m, the film material is believed lost

silent, black-and-white

A commercial with Felix the Cat, promoting the new department store Brouk a Babka, based in the Moravian city of Ostrava. This film was also made in a German version entitled *Wie Kater Felix das Ostrauer Gebiet bereichte.*

A Cabin Boy on Salty Water / Plavčíkem na slané vodě

production: Elekta Journal, *dates of censorship:* August and October 1929

footage: original 205 m, surviving 240 m

directed by: Karel Dodal, *animation:* Hermína Týrlová

silent, black-and-white

A commercial promoting the Czech Brouk and Babka department store and its branches in the Czech towns of Prague, Plzeň, Ostrava and České Budějovice.

1930

Bimbo's Unfortunate Adventure / Bimbovo smutné dobrodružství

production: Elekta Journal, *date of censorship:* January 1930
footage: original 370 m, surviving 276 m
directed by: Karel Dodal, *animation:* Hermína Týrlová, *subheads:* Karel Smrž
cast: Jára – Karel Dodal, Máňa – Hermína Týrlová
silent, black-and-white
The story of the draughtsman Jára and the clown Bimbo.

Tommy and the Mermaid / Tommy a mořská panna

production: Elekta Journal, *date of censorship:* April 1930
footage: original 280 m, the film material is believed lost
silent, black-and-white
Funny stories of Tommy who went out into the world seeking adventure.

Karel Dodal and Hermína Týrlová
– collaboration on film diagrams and tricks produced by Elekta Journal / 1927–1931

1927

Then and Now / Dříve a nyní

production: Elekta Journal, *dates of censorship:* November 1927, new versions 1929, 1932
footage: original unknown, new version 895 m, the film material is believed lost
directed by: Svatopluk Innemann, *story:* Antonín Kratochvíl, Jan Pražák
technological part of the film: J. Čech, E. Guth, *tricks:* Karel Dodal
silent, black-and-white
A picture with feature-film framework about the origins and developments of Moravian farming cooperatives. Its new version was submitted for censorship proceedings in 1929.

Milk – Humanity's Nourishment / Mléko, výživa lidstva

production: Elekta Journal, *dates of censorship:* 1927, February 1929, July 1932, April 1935
footage: original 1,170 m, the film material is believed lost

directed by: Svatopluk Innemann, *story:* Antonín Kratochvíl
technological part of the film: J. Spisar, *tricks:* Karel Dodal
silent, black-and-white
A promotional film about processing and selling milk in the past and establishing milking cooperatives and creameries in Moravia.

1928

Electricity in the Service of the Countryside / Elektřina ve službách venkova
production: Elekta Journal, *date of censorship:* 1928
footage: original 1,513 m, surviving 560 m
directed by: Svatopluk Innemann, *screenplay:* František Horký, *tricks:* Karel Dodal
silent, black-and-white
An educational film about employing electric power in agriculture.

Their Icon / Jejich ideál
production: Elekta Journal, *date of censorship:* May 1928
footage: original 85 m, the film material is believed lost
silent, black-and-white
A commercial promoting Indian motorcycles.

Demänová
production: Elekta Journal, *date of censorship:* June 1928
footage: original 1,010 m, surviving 928 m
directed by: Jindřich Brichta, *screenplay:* František Horký, *director of photography:* Václav Vích, *tricks:* Karel Dodal
silent, black-and-white
A popular scientific film about the Slovak Demänová cave system.

Prague in Shining Lights / Praha v záři světel
production: Elekta Journal, *date of censorship:* June 1928
footage: original 830 m, surviving 629 m
directed by: Svatopluk Innemann, *story:* František Horký, *directors of photography:* Jaroslav Blažek, Max Jonák, Václav Vích, *tricks:* Karel Dodal

silent, black-and-white

A city symphony – the life of Prague inhabitans from dusk till dawn.

Electric Waves / Elektrické vlny

production: Elekta Journal, *date of censorship:* September 1928

footage: original 415 m, surviving 433 m

directed by: J. Tuma, *directors of photography:* Václav Vích, Karel Dodal

animation: H. Pettera, Karel Dodal

silent, black-and-white

An educational film about radiotelegraphy. The film was also made in a German version entitled *Elektrische Wellen.*

Tea at Five... / Čaj o páté...

production: Elekta Journal, *date of censorship:* October 1928

footage: original 120 m, the film material is believed lost

silent, black-and-white

A commercial about tea at five in the Prague club Alhambra with a fashion show of fur coats made by the company Fichl. The trick take by Karel Dodal also became part of the simultaneously produced film *Prague in Shining Lights* (Praha v záři světel).

MD Hons: The Significance of Nutrition for Human Growth / MUDr. V. Hons: Význam výživy při vzrůstu

production: Elekta Journal, *date of censorship:* October 1928

footage: original 400 m, the film material is believed lost

directed by: Jan S. Kolár, *director of photography:* Jan Stallich, *tricks:* Karel Dodal

silent, black-and-white

A film about the influence of healthy nutrition on the growth of animals and humans. The film was also made in a German version entitled *MUDr. V. Hons, Die Bedeutung der Ernährung Während des Wachstums.*

1929

The Monolith / Monolit

production: Elekta Journal, *date of censorship:* March 1929

footage: original 910 m, surviving 587 m
directed by, directors of photography: Jindřich Brichta, K. M. Paspa, Karel Smrž, *tricks:* Karel Dodal
silent, black-and-white
A film about installing the Mrákotín monolith at the third courtyard of Prague Castle.

From the Czech Mills / Z českých mlýnů
production: Elekta Journal, *date of censorship:* April 1929
footage: original 1,840 m, surviving 2,504 m
directed by: Miroslav J. Krňanský, Ferry Seidl, *screenplay:* Eduard Šimáček, *director of photography:* Jan Stallich, *tricks:* Karel Dodal
silent, black-and-white
A comedy from a miller's environment with short animated passages.

1931

The Career of Pavel Čamrda / Kariéra Pavla Čamrdy
production: Elekta Journal, *date of censorship:* December 1931
footage: original unknown, surviving 2,643.1 m
directed by: Miroslav J. Krňanský, *screenplay:* Jan Reiter, Karel Lörsch, Karel Dodal, *director of photography:* Jan Stallich
sound, black-and-white
A film fiction based on the novel of Ignát Herrmann.

Karel Dodal
– collaboration on film diagrams and tricks produced by other companies / 1933

1933

Amelioration / Meliorace půdy
production: Zemský úřad v Praze, *date of censorship:* May 1933
footage: original 410 m, surviving 211 m
screenplay, directed by: Otakar Solnař, *tricks:* Karel Dodal

sound, black-and-white

The result of establishing controlled water management near cultivated fields is the radical improvement of the quality of the soil.

Little Eve Opens Her Little Eyes / Evička otvírá očička

production: Blažena Krůtová, Karel Dodal, *date of censorship:* July 1933

footage: original 400 m, the film material is believed lost

set designer, directed by: Karel Dodal, *story:* Blažena Krůtová

sound, black-and-white

A cartoon comedy emphasizing the positive health effects of milk.

Karel Dodal and Irena Dodalová – films by IRE-film / 1934–1938

1934

Bambi and a Cactus / Bambi a kaktus

production: IRE-film, *date of censorship:* October 1934

footage: original 90 m, the film material is believed lost

screenplay, set design, directed by: Irena Dodalová, Karel Dodal, *animation:* Hermína Týrlová

sound, black-and-white

A commercial promoting the children's clothing brand Bambino.

Do Not Get Angry, Man / Člověče, nezlob se!

production: IRE-film, *date of censorship:* November 1934

footage: original 115 m, the film material is believed lost

screenplay, set design, directed by: Irena Dodalová, Karel Dodal, *animation:* Hermína Týrlová

sound, black-and-white

A commercial promoting the Vademecum Parker fountain pen and employing the popular board game.

The Mystery of the MK 204 Turning Point / Záhada mezníku MK 204

production: IRE-film, *date of censorship:* December 1934

footage: original 110 m, surviving 100.6 m

set design, directed by: Karel Dodal, *screnplay:* Irena Dodalová, *animation:* Hermína Týrlová, *music:* Bedřich Kerten

sound, black-and-white

A commercial promoting Microphona 204 radio receivers.

1935

The Duties of Life / Životní povinnost

production: IRE-film, *date of censorship:* January 1935

footage: original 125 m, the film material is believed lost

set design, directed by: Irena Dodalová, Karel Dodal, *screenplay:* Irena Dodalová, *animation:* Hermína Týrlová, *music:* Bedřich Kerten

sound, black-and-white

A commercial promoting Sorela hair products.

Gibbs Toothpaste / Gibbs zubní mýdlo

production: IRE-film, *date of censorship:* January 1935

footage: original 165 m, the film material is believed lost

screenplay, set design, directed by: Irena Dodalová, Karel Dodal, *animation:* Hermína Týrlová

sound, black-and-white

A commercial promoting Gibbs toothpaste.

Taming of the Black Giant / Zkrocení černého obra

production: IRE-film, *dates of censorship:* April 1935, 1937

footage: original 135 m, surviving 125.3 m

screenplay, set design, directed by: Irena Dodalová, Karel Dodal, *animation:* Hermína Týrlová, *music:* Bedřich Kerten

sound, black-and-white

A commercial promoting Saponia turpentine soap.

A Midnight Wedding / Svatba o půlnoci

production: IRE-film, *dates of censorship:* May 1935, March 1938

footage: original 135 m, surviving 138.1 m

screenplay, set design, directed by: Irena Dodalová, Karel Dodal, *animation:* Hermína Týrlová, *music:* Bedřich Kerten

sound, black-and-white, colour

A commercial promoting Perola rye coffee and Karo chicory, both produced by the company Franck and Son.

Mum's Trip to Heaven / Maminčin výlet do nebe

production: IRE-film, *date of censorship:* July 1935

footage: original 140 m, surviving 130.7 m (Czech version), 134.3 m (German version)

screenplay, set design, directed by: Irena Dodalová, Karel Dodal, *animation:* Hermína Týrlová, *music:* Bedřich Kerten, *collaboration on set design:* Jiří Weiss

sound, black-and-white

A commercial promoting home appliances produced by the ČKD Elekro-Praga company. The film was also made in a German version entitled *Mütterchen als Gast im Himmel.*

A Cheerful Concert / Veselý koncert

production: IRE-film, *date of censorship:* September 1935

footage: original 125 m, surviving 110.6 m (Czech version), 119 m (German version)

screenplay, set design, directed by: Irena Dodalová, Karel Dodal, *animation:* Hermína Týrlová, *music:* Bedřich Kerten

sound, black-and-white

A commercial promoting radio receivers produced by the Telefunken company. The film was also made in a German version entitled *Das lustige Konzert.*

1936

The Tin Drum / Tluče bubeníček

production: IRE-film, *date of censorship:* April 1936

footage: original 100 m, surviving 90.9 m

screenplay, set design, directed by: Irena Dodalová, Karel Dodal, *animation:* Hermína Týrlová, *music:* Bedřich Kerten sound, black-and-white, colour

A commercial promoting Hellada soap.

All Day Long in the Papež Amazing Shoes / Od rána do noci ve skvělých botách od Papeže

production: IRE-film, *date of censorship:* April 1936

footage: original 50 m, the film material is believed lost

screenplay, set design, directed by: Irena Dodalová, Karel Dodal, *animation:* Hermína Týrlová

sound, black-and-white

A commercial promoting footwear produced by the Papež company, based in the National Boulevard in Prague.

The Adventures of a Ubiquitous Fellow / Všudybylovo dobrodružství

production: IRE-film, *dates of censorship:* May, December 1936

footage: original 480 m (1st censorship), 350 m (2nd censorship), surviving virage 228.2m (3rd censorship, [1939?]), surviving 350.5m

screenplay, set design, directed by: Irena Dodalová, Karel Dodal, *story:* Jan Černý, *animation:* Hermína Týrlová, *music:* Jaroslav Ježek, *adjustment of the puppet:* Jiří Trnka, *voice of Hurvínek the Ubiquitous Fellow:* Josef Skupa, *voice of the Queen:* Anna Kreuzmannová

sound, black-and-white – virage

An explanation of the principle of radio broadcasting. The film was also made in a German version entitled *Schlaucherls Abenteuer.*

What's New on TV / Co nového v televisi

production: IRE-film, *date of censorship:* September 1936

footage: original 140 m, the film material is believed lost

screenplay, set design, directed by: Irena Dodalová, Karel Dodal, *animation:* Hermína Týrlová

sound, black-and-white

A TV commercial promoting the autumn line of the fashion brand Busch.

A Brief View of the Future / Malý pohled do budoucna

production: IRE-film, *date of censorship:* October 1936

footage: original 40 m, surviving 35.4 m

screenplay, set design, directed by: Irena Dodalová, Karel Dodal, *animation:* Hermína Týrlová, *music:* Bedřich Kerten sound, colour

A commercial promoting fabrics produced by the Kollinský company.

Perhaps Still Yesterday / Snad ještě včera

production: IRE-film, *date of censorship:* October 1936

footage: original 50 m, surviving 23.8 m

screenplay, set design, directed by: Irena Dodalová, Karel Dodal, *animation:* Hermína Týrlová

sound, colour, black-and-white – virage

A commercial presenting how to wash silk and wool in Trimin.

Three Men / Tři muži

production: IRE-film, *date of censorship:* November 1936

footage: original 90 m, surviving 60.4 m

set design, directed by: Irena Dodalová, Karel Dodal, *screenplay:* Leo Heilbrunn, *animation:* Hermína Týrlová, *music:* Bedřich Kerten

sound, colour

A commercial promoting the Three Men washing powder produced by the company Pilňáček, based in the Czechoslovak city of Hradec Králové.

The Secret of the Lucerna Palace / Tajemství lucerny

production: IRE-film, *date of censorship:* November 1936

footage: original 70 m, surviving 60.4 m (virage copy), 67 m (black-and-white copy)

screenplay, set design, directed by: Irena Dodalová, Karel Dodal, *animation:* Hermína Týrlová, *music:* Bedřich Kerten, *vocals:* The Wise Teachers of Gotham

sound, black-and-white – virage

A commercial promoting hand-made shoes produced by the Czech company Krása.

The Sounds of Outer Space / Znějící vesmír

production: IRE-film, *date of censorship:* December 1936

footage: original 65 m, surviving 50.2 m

screenplay, set design, directed by: Irena Dodalová, Karel Dodal, *animation:* Hermína Týrlová, *music:* Bedřich Kerten

sound, black-and-white

A commercial promoting Telefunken radio lamps.

The Wizard of Tones / Čaroděj tónů

production: IRE-film, *date of censorship:* December 1936

footage: original 60 m, surviving 50.7 m (Czech version), 48.4 m (German version)

screenplay, set design, directed by: Irena Dodalová, Karel Dodal, *animation:* Hermína Týrlová, *music:* Bedřich Kerten

sound, colour

A commercial promoting the Telefunken radio receiver. The film was also made in a German version entitled *Der Tonzauberer.*

1937

Slattern and Glossie / Šmudlík a Leskulinka

production: IRE-film, *date of censorship:* April 1937

footage: original 60 m, surviving 41 m (black-and-white version), 50.2 m (colour version)

set design, directed by: Irena Dodalová, Karel Dodal, *screenplay:* Leo Heilbrunn, *animation:* Hermína Týrlová, *music:* Bedřich Kerten

sound, black-and-white – virage, colour

A commercial promoting Obé polish.

Fantaisie érotique

production: IRE-film, *date of censorship:* not submitted

footage: original unknown, surviving 54.9 m

screenplay, set design, directed by: Irena Dodalová, Karel Dodal, *animation:* Hermína Týrlová, *music:* Bedřich Kerten

sound, colour

Abstract geometric patterns result in a symphony of motion and colour in the rhythm of music.

The Play of Bubbles / Hra bublinek

production: IRE-film, *date of censorship:* June 1937

footage: original 60 m, surviving 56.6 m

screenplay, set design, directed by: Irena Dodalová, Karel Dodal, *animation:* Hermína Týrlová, *music:* Bedřich Kerten

sound, colour

A colour abstract film instantly turns into a commercial promoting Saponia soap.

Everything for a Scrambled Pancake! / Všechno pro trhanec

production: IRE-film, *date of censorship:* June 1937

footage: original 130 m, surviving 123.6 m (Czech version), 125 m (Slovak and German versions)

screenplay, set design, directed by: Irena Dodalová, Karel Dodal, *animation:* Hermína Týrlová, *music:* Bedřich Kerten

sound, black-and-white, colour

A commercial promoting Vitello milk margarine. The film was also made in a Slovak version entitled *Všetko pro drobenec* and in a German version, entitled *Alles um einen Schmarren.*

An Autumn Song / Píseň podzimu

production: IRE-film, *date of censorship:* October 1937

footage: original 55 m, surviving 55.5 m

screenplay, set design, directed by: Irena Dodalová, Karel Dodal, *animation:* Hermína Týrlová, *music:* Bedřich Kerten

sound, black-and-white

A commercial promoting fabrics and haberdashery produced by the Czech company Prokop and Čáp.

The Unforgettable Poster / Nezapomenutelný plakát

production: IRE-film, *date of censorship:* October 1937

footage: original 110 m, surviving 96.3 m

screenplay, set design, directed by: Irena Dodalová, Karel Dodal, *animation:* Hermína Týrlová, *music:* Bedřich Kerten

sound, colour

A commercial promoting Sana margarine.

1938

The Prophecy of Ms Antonie / Věštba paní Antonie

production: IRE-film, *date of censorship:* March 1938

footage: original 500 m, the film material is believed lost

screenplay, directed by: Karel Dodal

sound, black-and-white

A commercial promoting the Three Men washing powder.

Spring Is Here / Jaro je tady

production: IRE-film, *date of censorship:* March 1938

footage: original 90 m, surviving 39.9 m (fragments)

screenplay, set design, directed by: Irena Dodalová, Karel Dodal, *animation:* Hermína Týrlová, *music:* Bedřich Kerten

sound, black-and-white

A commercial promoting various fabrics produced by the Czech company Prokop and Čáp.

The Protest / Protest

production: IRE-film, *date of censorship:* June 1938

footage: original 80 m, surviving 41.4 m

screenplay, set design, directed by: Irena Dodalová, Karel Dodal, *animation:* Hermína Týrlová, *music:* Bedřich Kerten

sound, black-and-white, colour

A commercial promoting Mogul motor oil.

Ideas in Search of Light / Myšlenka hledající světlo

production: IRE-film, *date of censorship:* not submitted

footage: original unknown, surviving 271.5 m

screenplay, set design, directed by: Irena Dodalová, Karel Dodal, *animation:* Hermína Týrlová, *music:* Bedřich Kerten

sound, black-and-white

An abstract trick film bringing an anti-war message on the motifs of Beethoven's *Ninth Symphony.*

Karel Dodal and Irena Dodalová – films produced by other companies / 1934–1938

Elephant the Rescuer / Slon zachráncem

production: Baťa, *date of censorship:* June 1934

footage: original 175 m, surviving 174 m (Czech version), 175.3 m (German version)

directed by: J. Ros-Aga, *director of photography:* Josef Bulánek, *set design:* Karel Dodal

sound, black-and-white

A commercial promoting Baťa's rubber toys. The film was also made in a German version entitled *Der Elefant.*

White Magic / Bílé kouzlo

production: Crayon Film, Justin Karpner and Son, IRE-film, *date of censorship:* October 1934
footage: original 155 m, the film material is believed lost
directed by: unknown, *screenplay:* Karel Müller, *set design:* Karel Dodal, *animation:* Hermína Týrlová, *music:* Bedřich Kerten, *collaboration:* Irena Dodalová
sound, black-and-white
A cartoon comedy promoting Hellada soap.

A Lady-Killer / Dobyvatel srdcí

production: Justin Karpner and Son, IRE-film, *date of censorship:* November 1934
footage: original 115 m, the film material is believed lost
directed by: unknown, *screenplay:* Karel Müller, *set design:* Karel Dodal, *animation:* Hermína Týrlová, *music:* Bedřich Kerten, *collaboration:* Irena Dodalová
sound, black-and-white
A commercial promoting footwear by the Prague brand Papež.

Six Women in Search of Africa / Šest žen hledá Afrika

production: Leo Marten, Accord-Film, *date of censorship:* November 1934
footage: original 510 m, surviving 482 m
directed by: Leo Marten, *director of photography:* V. Kavalier, *set design:* Irena Dodalová, Karel Dodal
sound, black-and-white
A promotional film about six ladies driving to Africa and back in Aero automobiles, narrated by Josef Laufer and František Alexander Elstner. The cartoon passages capture the travel plan and link the documentyry sequences.

The Magic of the Sun / Kouzlo slunce

production: AB Praha, IRE-film, *date of censorship:* June 1938
footage: original 80 m, surviving fragments
screenplay, set design, directed by: Irena Dodalová, Karel Dodal, *animation:* Hermína Týrlová
sound, black-and-white
A commercial promoting Cinzano vermouth.

Acknowledgements

I would like to express my sincere gratitude to all who participated in this not too extensive, but, from the point of editing and publishing, very demanding book. I am mainly indebted to the National Film Archive and its former director, Vladimír Opěla, who incorporated the subject of the Dodals into the institution's program in 2004, as well as its current director, Michal Bregant, who kindly approved the publication of my manuscript in 2011. I thank the curator of the Collection of Animated Film at the National Film Archive, Michaela Mertová, for all the intense years of collaboration, and other colleagues from the Archive without whose fervour this publication would have been impossible. I am also grateful to many other colleagues for patiently commenting on the subsequent versions of my manuscript – mainly Vladimír Opěla, Ivan Klimeš, Petr Szczepanik and Jan Lukeš.

For their invaluable assistance, I am indebted to my Czech and foreign colleagues – archive keepers and historians – who helped me trace the Dodals in countless state and regional archives and museums in Prague, Brno, Plzeň, Tábor, Jablonec nad Nisou, Kroměříž, Zlín, Příbram, Bratislava, Berlin, Jerusalem, Budapest, New York and elsewhere. My thanks also go to my colleagues from the Czech Radio Archives.

I am extremely grateful for all the support in exploring the fate of Irena Dodalová in Theresienstadt, provided by many eyewitnesses and historians specializing in Shoah, such as Jaroslava Milotová (the Terezín Initiative), Tomáš Fedorovič (the Terezín Memorial), Jana Šplíchalová (the Jewish Museum in Prague), Anna Hájková (today based in Canada), Ronny Loewy (the German Film Institute, the Federal Republic of Germany), Efrat Komisar, Yelena Makarov and Ruth Bondy (Israel), Karel Margry (the Netherlands), Lisa Peschl (USA), Sofia Pantouvaki (Greece) and many others. Lubor M. Dohnal from the Film and TV School of Academy of Performing Arts in Prague, who donated the outtakes from the 1942 Theresienstadt filming to the National Film Archive, deserves a special mention. I am also indebted to the theatrologist Eva Šormová for her precious consultation and advice.

The work required reconstructing the Dodals' sojourn to Argentina. I thus thank the Czech native Helena Voldánová, an expert in Comenius studies; Irena Dodalová's students Oscar Sandoval Martínez, Nilio Omar Armas and Martin Barreiro; film historian Pablo de Vita; author Mado Reznik, and gallery keeper Enrique Martínez Glera. Prime thanks must moreover be expressed to Oscar Sandoval Martínez who donated a valuable collection of written and photographic documents on the artistic and lecturing activities of his female mentor in Argentina to the National Film Archive. In this context, I am indebted to my translator from Spanish, Zuzana Hejnicová.

My sincere thanks also go to the son of the Dodals' erstwhile friend, Evžen Popp; Karel Dodal's remote relative, the cartoonist Jaroslav Dodal; the great-niece of Hermína Týrlová, Ms Irena Suchelová; Irena Dodalová's remote relatives, the Cerhas couple from Záryby, and Jan Fára from the Society of the Citizens and Friends of Březové Hory. At the same time, my acknowledgements cannot omit the director Hana Pinkavová, Květa Krčilová, Růžena Vodičková, Hana Anděrová, Renée Lavecká and Josef Rippel who provided a lot of crucial information and archive documents. My gratitude also goes to the Zlín archive keeper, Jiří Novotný, the cameraman Svatopluk Malý, and Petr Štembera from the Prague Museum of Arts and Crafts. The consultations related to the world of advertising were kindly provided by Pavla Vošahlíková, Ivan Tomek and Róbert Török from the Magyar Kereskedelmi és Vendéglátóipari Múzeum.

I moreover thank my countless colleagues from abroad who I often merely know via e-mail – especially Gunnar Strøm from Norway, who helped me immensely in the search for the Prague production of Dezider Gross, and Marina Feodoroff from Paris, who provided valuable information about Berthold Bartosch.

And there are more names which cannot be forgotten in relation to this book. They include Márton Orosz, curator of photography and media art with the Budapest Museum of Fine Arts (Szépművészeti Muzeum) who, among other things, specializes in the history of inter-war Hungarian animation and the oeuvre of György Pál. It was he who helped me towards the end of my research to establish contact with the architect Richard J. Pavlicek in the United States, i.e. the person who, as a young university student, accompanied Karel Dodal at Minnesota University. And I also must thank the lady ceaselessly tending to this almost 100-year old architect, Ms Nancy DeMars, who effectively prompted our contact.

I sincerely regret that many of those who had once introduced me to the world of animation – Marie Benešová, Alena Munková, Čeněk Duba, Břetislav Pojar, František Vystrčil and many, many others – are not still with us to see this book coming to life. I also very much miss the entrepreneur Petr Dodal and the colleagues from the National Film Archive, mainly Karel Čáslavský and Milan Večeřa, whose wisdom helped me clarify many issues during our consultations.

And in closing, let me thank the Publishing House of the Academy of Performing Arts in Prague, which considerably contributed to the publication of this book. Last but not least, my deep recognition goes to all who participated in realizing the project about the Dodals and gave it such a unique style – the editor of the book, Václav Kofroň, and the designer of the artistic concept, Markéta Jelenová.

E. S.

Index

Eva Strusková

The Dodals

Pioneers of Czech Animated Film

Published by the National Film Archive
and the Academy of Performing Arts in Prague
(AMU Press)

Chief editor Václav Kofroň
English translation Lucie Vidmar
Editor of English translation Nick Stuart
Cover and layout Markéta Jelenová
Typesetting Robert Konopásek
Print PBtisk Příbram
1st edition
Prague 2013

ISBN 978-80-7004-155-0 (National Film Archive, Prague)
ISBN 978-80-7331-271-8 (Akademie múzických umění v Praze)

www.nfa.cz
www.namu.cz, www.amu.cz